BURT FRANKLIN: RESEARCH & SOURCE WORKS SERIES
Philosophy & Religious History Monographs 135

PLATO, AND THE OTHER COMPANIONS OF SOKRATES.

PLATO,

AND THE

OTHER COMPANIONS OF SOKRATES.

By GEORGE GROTE,
AUTHOR OF THE 'HISTORY OF GREECE'.

A NEW EDITION.

IN FOUR VOLUMES—Vol. II.

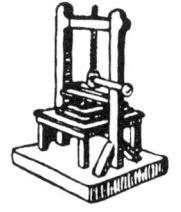

BURT FRANKLIN REPRINTS
New York, N. Y.

Published by LENOX HILL Pub. & Dist. Co. (Burt Franklin)
235 East 44th St., New York, N.Y. 10017
Reprinted: 1973
Printed in the U.S.A.

Burt Franklin: Research and Source Works Series
Philosophy and Religious History Monographs 135

Reprinted from the original edition in the Barnard College Library.

Library of Congress Cataloging in Publication Data

Grote, George, 1794-1871.
  Plato, and the other companions of Sokrates.
    Reprint of the 1888 ed. published by J. Murray, London.
    1. Plato. 2. Socrates. 3. Philosophy, Ancient. I. Title.
  B395.G6 1974   184   72-82021
  ISBN 0-8337-1476-7

CONTENTS.

CHAPTER XII.

ALKIBIADES I. AND II.

Situation supposed in the dialogue. Persons—Sokrates and Alkibiades 1
Exorbitant hopes and political ambition of Alkibiades 2
Questions put by Sokrates, in reference to Alkibiades in his intended function as adviser of the Athenians. What does he intend to advise them upon? What has he learnt, and what does he know? .. .. ib.
Alkibiades intends to advise the Athenians on questions of war and peace. Questions of Sokrates thereupon. We must fight those whom it is better to fight—to what standard does better refer? To just and unjust 3
How, or from whom, has Alkibiades learnt to discern or distinguish Just and Unjust? He never learnt it from any one; he always knew it, even as a boy .. 4
Answer amended. Alkibiades learnt it from the multitude, as he learnt to speak Greek.—The multitude cannot teach just and unjust, for they are at variance among themselves about it. Alkibiades is going to advise the Athenians about what he does not know himself 5
Answer farther amended. The Athenians do not generally debate about just or unjust—which they consider just in point to every one—but about expedient and inexpedient, which are not coincident with just and unjust. But neither does Alkibiades know the expedient. He asks Sokrates to explain. Sokrates declines: he can do nothing but question 6
Comment on the preceding — Sokratic method — the respondent makes the discoveries for himself .. .. ib.
Alkibiades is brought to admit that whatever is just, is good, honourable, expedient: and that whoever acts honourably, both does well, and procures for himself happiness thereby. Equivocal reasoning of Sokrates .. 7
Humiliation of Alkibiades. Other Athenian statesmen are equally ignorant. But the real opponents, against whom Alkibiades is to measure himself, are, the kings of Sparta and Persia. Eulogistic description of those kings. To match them, Alkibiades must make himself as good as possible 8
But good—for what end, and under what circumstances? Abundant illustrative examples 9
Alkibiades, puzzled and humiliated, confesses his ignorance. Encouragement given by Sokrates. It is an advantage to make such discovery in youth .. 10
Platonic Dialectic—its actual effect —its anticipated effect—applicable to the season of youth .. 11
Know Thyself—Delphian maxim —its urgent importance—What is myself? My mind is myself ib.
I cannot know myself, except by

CONTENTS OF VOLUME II.

	PAGE
looking into another mind. Self-knowledge is temperance. Temperance and Justice are the conditions both of happiness and of freedom	11
Alkibiades feels himself unworthy to be free, and declares that he will never quit Sokrates	12
Second Alkibiades—situation supposed	ib.
Danger of mistake in praying to the Gods for gifts which may prove mischievous. Most men are unwise. Unwise is the generic word: madmen, a particular variety under it	ib.
Relation between a generic term, and the specific terms comprehended under it, was not then familiar	13
Frequent cases, in which men pray for supposed benefits, and find that when obtained, they are misfortunes. Every one fancies that he knows what is beneficial: mischiefs of ignorance	14
Mistake in predications about ignorance generally. We must discriminate. Ignorance of *what?* Ignorance of good, is always mischievous: ignorance of other things, not always	ib.
Wise public counsellors are few. Upon what ground do we call these few wise? Not because they possess merely special arts or accomplishments, but because they know besides, upon what occasions and under what limits each of these accomplishments ought to be used	15
Special accomplishments, without the knowledge of the good or profitable, are oftener hurtful than beneficial	16
It is unsafe for Alkibiades to proceed with his sacrifice, until he has learnt what is the proper language to address to the Gods. He renounces his sacrifice, and throws himself upon the counsel of Sokrates	ib.
Different critical opinions respecting these two dialogues	17
Grounds for disallowing them—less strong against the Second than against the First	18
The supposed grounds for disallowance are in reality only marks of inferiority	19

	PAGE
The two dialogues may probably be among Plato's earlier compositions	20
Analogy with various dialogues in the Xenophontic Memorabilia—Purpose of Sokrates to humble presumptuous young men	21
Fitness of the name and character of Alkibiades for idealising this feature in Sokrates	ib.
Plato's manner of replying to the accusers of Sokrates. Magical influence ascribed to the conversation of Sokrates	22
The purpose proclaimed by Sokrates in the Apology is followed out in Alkibiadês I. Warfare against the false persuasion of knowledge	24
Difficulties multiplied for the purpose of bringing Alkibiades to a conviction of his own ignorance	25
Sokrates furnishes no means of solving these difficulties. He exhorts to Justice and Virtue—but these are acknowledged Incognita	26
Prolixity of Alkibiadês I.—Extreme multiplication of illustrative examples—How explained	ib.
Alkibiadês II. leaves its problem avowedly undetermined	27
Sokrates commends the practice of praying to the Gods for favours undefined—his views about the semi-regular, semi-irregular agency of the Gods—he prays to them for premonitory warnings	28
Comparison of Alkibiadês II. with the Xenophontic Memorabilia, especially the conversation of Sokrates with Euthydemus. Sokrates not always consistent with himself	29
Remarkable doctrine of Alkibiadês II.—that knowledge is not always Good. The knowledge of Good itself is indispensable: without that, the knowledge of other things is more hurtful than beneficial	ib.
Knowledge of Good—appears postulated and divined, in many of the Platonic dialogues, under different titles	31
The Good—the Profitable—what is it?—How are we to know it? Plato leaves this undetermined	ib.

CHAPTER XIII.

HIPPIAS MAJOR—HIPPIAS MINOR.

	PAGE
Hippias Major—situation supposed—character of the dialogue. Sarcasm and mockery against Hippias	33
Real debate between the historical Sokrates and Hippias in the Xenophontic Memorabilia—subject of that debate	34
Opening of the Hippias Minor—Hippias describes the successful circuit which he had made through Greece, and the renown as well as the gain acquired by his lectures	35
Hippias had met with no success at Sparta. Why the Spartans did not admit his instructions—their law forbids	ib.
Question, What is law? The lawmakers always aim at the Profitable, but sometimes fail to attain it. When they fail, they fail to attain law. The lawful is the Profitable: the Unprofitable is also unlawful	36
Comparison of the argument of the Platonic Sokrates with that of the Xenophontic Sokrates	37
The Just or Good is the beneficial or profitable. This is the only explanation which Plato ever gives—and to this he does not always adhere	38
Lectures of Hippias at Sparta—not upon geometry, or astronomy, &c., but upon the question—What pursuits are beautiful, fine, and honourable for youth?	39
Question put by Sokrates, in the name of a friend in the background, who has just been puzzling him with it—What is the Beautiful?	ib.
Hippias thinks the question easy to answer	40
Justice, Wisdom, Beauty must each be something. What is Beauty, or the Beautiful?	ib.
Hippias does not understand the question. He answers by indicating one particularly beautiful object	ib.
Cross-questioning by Sokrates—Other things also are beautiful; but each thing is beautiful only by comparison, or under some particular circumstances — it is sometimes beautiful, sometimes not beautiful	41
Second answer of Hippias—*Gold*, is that by the presence of which all things become beautiful—scrutiny applied to the answer. Complaint by Hippias about vulgar analogies	ib.
Third answer of Hippias—questions upon it—proof given that it fails of universal application	42
Farther answers, suggested by Sokrates himself—1. The Suitable or Becoming—objections thereunto—it is rejected	43
2. The useful or profitable—objections—it will not hold	44
3. The Beautiful is a variety of the Pleasurable—that which is received through the eye and the ear	45
Objections to this last—What property is there common to both sight and hearing, which confers upon the pleasures of these two senses the exclusive privilege of being beautiful?	ib.
Answer — There is, belonging to each and to both in common, the property of being innocuous and profitable pleasures — upon this ground they are called beautiful	46
This will not hold—the Profitable is the cause of Good, and is therefore different from Good—to say that the beautiful is the Profitable, is to say that it is different from Good — but this has been already declared inadmissible	ib.
Remarks upon the Dialogue—the explanations ascribed to Hippias are special conspicuous examples: those ascribed to Sokrates are attempts to assign some general concept	47
Analogy between the explanations here ascribed to Sokrates, and those given by the Xenophontic Sokrates in the Memorabilia	49
Concluding thrust exchanged between Hippias and Sokrates	51
Rhetoric against Dialectic	52
Men who dealt with real life, contrasted with the speculative and analytical philosophers	ib.

CONTENTS OF VOLUME II.

	PAGE
Concrete Aggregates—abstract or logical Aggregates. Distinct aptitudes required by Aristotle for the Dialectician	53
Antithesis of Absolute and Relative, here brought into debate by Plato, in regard to the Idea of Beauty	54
Hippias Minor — characters and situation supposed	55
Hippias has just delivered a lecture, in which he extols Achilles as better than Odysseus — the veracious and straightforward hero better than the mendacious and crafty	56
This is contested by Sokrates. The veracious man and the mendacious man are one and the same —the only man who can answer truly if he chooses, is he who can also answer falsely if he chooses, *i. e.*, the knowing man —the ignorant man cannot make sure of doing either the one or the other	57
Analogy of special arts—it is only the arithmetician who can speak falsely on a question of arithmetic when he chooses	ib.
View of Sokrates respecting Achilles in the Iliad. He thinks that Achilles speaks falsehood cleverly. Hippias maintains that if Achilles ever speaks falsehood, it is with an innocent purpose, whereas Odysseus does the like with fraudulent purpose	58
Issue here taken — Sokrates contends that those who hurt, or cheat, or lie wilfully, are better than those who do the like unwillingly—he entreats Hippias to enlighten him and answer his questions	ib.
Questions of Sokrates—multiplied analogies of the special arts. The unskilful artist, who runs, wrestles, or sings badly, whether he will or not, is worse than the skilful, who can sing well when he chooses, but can also sing badly when he chooses	59
It is better to have the mind of a bowman who misses his mark only by design, than that of one who misses even when he intends to hit	60
Dissent and repugnance of Hippias	ib.
Conclusion — That none but the good man can do evil wilfully: the bad man does evil unwillingly. Hippias cannot resist the reasoning, but will not accept the conclusion — Sokrates confesses his perplexity	61
Remarks on the dialogue. If the parts had been inverted, the dialogue would have been cited by critics as a specimen of the sophistry and corruption of the Sophists	62
Polemical purpose of the dialogue — Hippias humiliated by Sokrates	63
Philosophical purpose of the dialogue—theory of the Dialogues of Search generally, and of Knowledge as understood by Plato	ib.
The Hippias is an exemplification of this theory—Sokrates sets forth a case of confusion, and avows his inability to clear it up. Confusion — shown up in the Lesser Hippias—Error in the Greater	64
The thesis maintained here by Sokrates, is also affirmed by the historical Sokrates in the Xenophontic Memorabilia	66
Aristotle combats the thesis. Arguments against it	67
Mistake of Sokrates and Plato in dwelling too exclusively on the intellectual conditions of human conduct	ib.
They rely too much on the analogy of the special arts—they take no note of the tacit assumptions underlying the epithets of praise and blame	68
Value of a Dialogue of Search, that it shall be suggestive, and that it shall bring before us different aspects of the question under review	69
Antithesis between Rhetoric and Dialectic	70

CHAPTER XIV.

HIPPARCHUS—MINOS.

Hipparchus— Question — What is the definition of Lover of Gain? He is one who thinks it right to gain from things worth nothing. Sokrates cross-examines upon this explanation. No man ex-

CONTENTS OF VOLUME II. ix

pects to gain from things which he knows to be worth nothing: in this sense, no man is a lover of gain.. 71
Gain is good. Every man loves good: therefore all men are lovers of gain 72
Apparent contradiction. Sokrates accuses the companion of trying to deceive him — accusation is retorted upon Sokrates.. 73
Precept inscribed formerly by Hipparchus the Peisistratid—never deceive a friend. Eulogy of Hipparchus by Sokrates .. .. .. *ib.*
Sokrates allows the companion to retract some of his answers. The companion affirms that some gain is good, other gain is evil .. 74
Questions by Sokrates—bad gain is *gain*, as much as good gain. What is the common property, in virtue of which both are called Gain? Every acquisition, made with no outlay, or with a smaller outlay, is gain. Objections—the acquisition may be evil—embarrassment confessed .. .. *ib.*
It is essential to gain, that the acquisition made shall be greater not merely in quantity, but also in value, than the outlay. The valuable is the profitable—the profitable is the good. Conclusion comes back. That Gain is Good 75
Recapitulation. The debate has shown that all gain is good, and that there is no evil gain — all men are lovers of gain — no man ought to be reproached for being so—the companion is compelled to admit this, though he declares that he is not persuaded *ib.*
Minos. Question put by Sokrates to the companion, What is Law, or The Law? All law is the same, *quatenus* law: what is the common constituent attribute?.. 76
Answer—Law is, 1. The consecrated and binding customs. 2. The decree of the city. 3. Social or civic opinion .. .. .. *ib.*
Cross-examination by Sokrates— just and lawfully-behaving men are so through law; unjust and lawless men are so through the absence of law. Law is highly honourable and useful: lawlessness is ruinous. Accordingly, bad decrees of the city—or bad social opinion—cannot be law .. 77

Suggestion by Sokrates—Law is the *good* opinion of the city—but good opinion is true opinion, or the finding out of reality. Law therefore wishes (tends) to be the finding out of reality, though it does not always succeed in doing so 77
Objection taken by the Companion —That there is great discordance of laws in different places —he specifies several cases of such discordance at some length. Sokrates reproves his prolixity, and requests him to confine himself to question or answer .. 78
Farther questions by Sokrates— Things heavy and light, just and unjust, honourable and dishonourable, &c., are so, and are accounted so everywhere. Real things are always accounted real. Whoever fails in attaining the real, fails in attaining the lawful .. .. *ib.*
There are laws of health and of cure, composed by the few physicians wise upon those subjects, and unanimously declared by them. So also there are laws of farming, gardening, cookery, declared by the few wise in those respective pursuits. In like manner, the laws of a city are the judgments declared by the few wise men who know how to rule 79
That which is right is the regal law, the only true and real law —that which is not right, is not law, but only seems to be law in the eyes of the ignorant 80
Minos, King of Krete—his laws were divine and excellent, and have remained unchanged from time immemorial .. .. *ib.*
Question about the character of Minos—Homer and Hesiod declare him to have been admirable, the Attic tragedians defame him as a tyrant, because he was an enemy of Athens 81
That Minos was really admirable —and that he has found out truth and reality respecting the administration of the city—we may be sure from the fact that his laws have remained so long unaltered .. .. *ib.*
The question is made more determinate — What is it that the good lawgiver prescribes and measures out for the health of

CONTENTS OF VOLUME II.

	PAGE
the mind, as the physician measures out food and exercise for the body? Sokrates cannot tell. Close	81
The Hipparchus and Minos are analogous to each other, and both of them inferior works of Plato, perhaps unfinished	82
Hipparchus — double meaning of φιλοκερδής and κέρδος	ib.
State of mind of the agent, as to knowledge, frequent inquiry in Plato. No tenable definition found	83
Admitting that there is bad gain, as well as good gain, what is the meaning of the word *pain*? None is found	ib.
Purpose of Plato in the dialogue—to lay bare the confusion, and to force the mind of the respondent into efforts for clearing it up	84
Historical narrative and comments given in the dialogue respecting Hipparchus — afford no ground for declaring the dialogue to be spurious	ib.
Minos. Question — What is the characteristic property connoted by the word Νόμος or law?.. ..	86
This question was discussed by the historical Sokrates, Memorabilia of Xenophon	ib.
Definitions of law—suggested and refuted. Law includes, as a portion of its meaning, justice, goodness, usefulness, &c. Bad decrees are not laws	86
Sokrates affirms that law is everywhere the same—it is the declared judgment and command of the Wise man upon the subject to which it refers—it is truth and reality, found out and certified by him	87
Reasoning of Sokrates in the Minos is unsound, but Platonic. The Good, True, and Real, coalesce in the mind of Plato—he acknowledges nothing to *be* Law, except what he thinks ought to be Law	88
Plato worships the Ideal of his own mind — the work of systematic constructive theory by the Wise Man	89
Different applications of this general Platonic view, in the Minos, Politikus, Kratylus, &c. *Natural Rectitude* of Law, Government, Names, &c.	ib.
Eulogy on Minos, as having established laws on this divine type or natural rectitude	90
The Minos was arranged by Aristophanes at first in a Trilogy along with the Leges	91
Explanations of the word Law—confusion in its meaning	ib.

CHAPTER XV.

THEAGES.

Theagês—has been declared spurious by some modern critics—grounds for such opinion not sufficient	98
Persons of the dialogue—Sokrates, with Demodokus and Theagês, father and son. Theagês (the son), eager to acquire knowledge, desires to be placed under the teaching of a Sophist	99
Sokrates questions Theagês, inviting him to specify what he wants	ib.
Theagês desires to acquire that wisdom by which he can govern freemen with their own consent	100
Incompetence of the best practical statesmen to teach any one else. Theagês requests that Sokrates will himself teach him	ib.
Sokrates declares that he is not competent to teach — that he knows nothing except about matters of love. Theagês maintains that many of his young friends have profited largely by the conversation of Sokrates ..	101
Sokrates explains how this has sometimes happened—he recites his experience of the divine sign or Dæmon	ib.
The Dæmon is favourable to some persons, adverse to others. Upon this circumstance it depends how far any companion profits by the society of Sokrates, Aristeides has not learnt anything from Sokrates, yet has improved much by being near to him	102
Theagês expresses his anxiety to be received as the companion of Sokrates	103

Remarks on the Theagês—analogy with the Lachês 104
Chief peculiarity of the Theagês—stress laid upon the divine sign or Dæmon .. .. ib.
Plato employs this divine sign here to render some explanation of the singularity and eccentricity of Sokrates, and of his unequal influence upon different companions .. .. ib.
Sokrates, while continually finding fault with other teachers, refused to teach himself—difficulty of finding an excuse for his refusal. The Theagês furnishes an excuse 106
Plato does not always, nor in other dialogues, allude to the divine sign in the same way. Its character and working essentially impenetrable. Sokrates a privileged person .. .. ib.

CHAPTER XVI.
ERASTÆ OR ANTERASTÆ—RIVALES.

Erastæ—subject and persons of the dialogue—dramatic introduction—interesting youths in the palæstra 111
Two rival Erastæ—one of them literary, devoted to philosophy—the other gymnastic, hating philosophy.. .. .. ib.
Question put by Sokrates—What is philosophy? It is the perpetual accumulation of knowledge, so as to make the largest sum total 112
In the case of the body, it is not the maximum of exercise which does good, but the proper, measured quantity. For the mind also, it is not the maximum of knowledge, but the measured quantity which is good. Who is the judge to determine this measure? .. .. ib.
No answer given. What is the best conjecture? Answer of the literary Erastes. A man must learn that which will yield to him the greatest reputation as a philosopher — as much as will enable him to talk like an intelligent critic, though not to practise 113
The philosopher is one who is second-best in several different arts—a Pentathlus—who talks well upon each.. .. .. ib.
On what occasions can such second-best men be useful? There are always regular practitioners at hand, and no one will call in the second-best man when he can have the regular practitioner .. 114
Philosophy cannot consist in multiplication of learned acquirements .. .. ib.
Sokrates changes his course of examination—questions put to show that there is one special art, regal and political, of administering and discriminating the bad from the good 115
In this art the philosopher must not only be second-best, competent to talk—but he must be a fully qualified practitioner, competent to act .. .. ib.
Close of the dialogue—humiliation of the literary Erastes 116
Remarks—animated manner of the dialogue .. .. ib.
Definition of philosophy — here sought for the first time—Platonic conception of measure—referee not discovered 117
View taken of the second-best critical talking man, as compared with the special proficient and practitioner 118
Plato's view—that the philosopher has a province special to himself, distinct from other specialties—dimly indicated—regal or political art 119
Philosopher—the supreme artist controlling other artists 120

CHAPTER XVII.
ION.

Ion. Persons of the dialogue. Difference of opinion among modern critics as to its genuineness 124
Rhapsodes as a class in Greece. They competed for prizes at the festivals. Ion has been triumphant 124

xii   CONTENTS OF VOLUME II.

	PAGE		PAGE
Functions of the Rhapsodes. Recitation—exposition of the poets—arbitrary exposition of the poets was then frequent	125	inspired by the Gods. Varieties of madness, good and bad..	129
The popularity of the Rhapsodes was chiefly derived from their recitation—powerful effect which they produced	ib.	Special inspiration from the Gods was a familiar fact in Grecian life—privileged communications from the Gods to Sokrates—his firm belief in them..	130
Ion both reciter and expositor—Homer was considered more as an instructor than as a poet	126	Condition of the inspired person—his reason is for the time withdrawn	131
Plato disregards and disapproves the poetic or emotional working	ib.	Ion does not admit himself to be inspired and out of his mind	132
Ion devoted himself to Homer exclusively. Questions of Sokrates to him—How happens it that you cannot talk equally upon other poets? The poetic art is one	127	Homer talks upon all subjects—Is Ion competent to explain what Homer says upon all of them? Rhapsodic art. What is its province?	ib.
Explanation given by Sokrates—both the Rhapsode and the Poet work, not by art and system, but by divine inspiration—fine poets are bereft of their reason, and possessed by inspiration from some God	ib.	The Rhapsode does not know special matters, such as the craft of the pilot, physician, farmer, &c., but he knows the business of the general, and is competent to command soldiers, having learnt it from Homer	133
Analogy of the Magnet, which holds up by attraction successive stages of iron rings. The Gods first inspire Homer, then act through him and through Ion upon the auditors	128	Conclusion. Ion expounds Homer, not with any knowledge of what he says, but by divine inspiration	134
This comparison forms the central point of the dialogue. It is an expansion of a judgment delivered by Sokrates in the Apology	129	The generals in Greece usually possessed no professional experience — Homer and the poets were talked of as the great teachers—Plato's view of the poet, as pretending to know everything, but really knowing nothing	ib.
Platonic Antithesis: systematic procedure distinguished from unsystematic: which latter was either blind routine, or madness		Knowledge, opposed to divine inspiration without knowledge	136
		Illustration of Plato's opinion respecting the uselessness of written geometrical treatises	ib.

CHAPTER XVIII.

LACHES.

Lachês. Subject and persons of the dialogue—whether it is useful that two young men should receive lessons from a master of arms. Nikias and Lachês differ in opinion	138	Both of them give opinions offhand, according to their feelings on the special case—Sokrates requires that the question shall be generalised, and examined as a branch of education	141
Sokrates is invited to declare his opinion — he replies that the point cannot be decided without a competent professional judge..	139	Appeal of Sokrates to the judgment of the One Wise Man—this man is never seen or identified	142
Those who deliver an opinion must begin by proving their competence to judge—Sokrates avows his own incompetence	140	We must know what virtue is, before we give an opinion on education—virtue, as a whole, is too large a question—we will enquire about one branch of virtue—courage	ib.
Nikias and Lachês submit to be cross-examined by Sokrates	141	Question — what is courage?	

PAGE	PAGE
Laches answers by citing one particularly manifest case of courage—mistake of not giving a general explanation 143	therefore as a definition of courage 146
Second answer. Courage is a sort of endurance of the mind—Sokrates points out that the answer is vague and incorrect—endurance is not always courage: even intelligent endurance is not always courage.. .. .. *ib.*	Remarks. Warfare of Sokrates against the false persuasion of knowledge. Brave generals deliver opinions confidently about courage without knowing what it is .. .. *ib.*
Confusion. New answer given by Nikias. Courage is a sort of Intelligence—the intelligence of things terrible and not terrible. Objections of Lachês 144	No solution given by Plato—apparent tendency of his mind, in looking for a solution. Intelligence — cannot be understood without reference to some object or end 147
Questions of Sokrates to Nikias. It is only future events, not past or present, which are terrible; but intelligence of future events cannot be had without intelligence of past or present 145	Object—is supplied in the answer of Nikias. Intelligence — of things terrible and not terrible. Such intelligence is not possessed by professional artists .. 148
Courage therefore must be intelligence of good and evil generally. But this definition would include the whole of virtue, and we declared that courage was only a part thereof—it will not hold	Postulate of a Science of Ends, or Teleology, dimly indicated by Plato. The Unknown Wise Man —correlates with the undiscovered Science of Ends .. .. .. *ib.*
	Perfect condition of the intelligence—is the one sufficient condition of virtue 149
	Dramatic contrast between Lachês and Sokrates, as cross-examiners 150

CHAPTER XIX

CHARMIDES.

Scene and personages of the dialogue. Crowded palæstra. Emotions of Sokrates 153	What good does self-knowledge procure for us? What is the object known, in this case? Answer: There is no object of knowledge, distinct from the knowledge itself 155
Question, What is Temperance? addressed by Sokrates to the temperate Charmides. Answer, It is a kind of sedateness or slowness 154	Sokrates doubts the possibility of any knowledge, without a given *cognitum* as its object. Analogies to prove that knowledge of knowledge is impossible.. 156
But Temperance is a fine or honourable thing, and slowness is, in many or most cases, not fine or honourable, but the contrary. Temperance cannot be slowness .. .. *ib.*	All knowledge must be relative to some object 157
Second answer. Temperance is a variety of the feeling of shame. Refuted by Sokrates .. .. *ib.*	All properties are relative—everything in nature has its characteristic property with reference to something else .. .. *ib.*
Third answer. Temperance consists in doing one's own business. Defended by Kritias. Sokrates pronounces it a riddle, and refutes it. Distinction between making and doing 155	Even if cognition of cognition were possible, cognition of non-cognition would be impossible. A man may know what he knows, but he cannot know what he is ignorant of. He knows the fact *that* he knows: but he does not know how much he knows, and how much he does not know .. 158
Fourth answer, by Kritias. Temperance consists in self-knowledge .. .. *ib.*	
Questions of Sokrates thereupon.	Temperance, therefore, as thus de-

xiv   CONTENTS OF VOLUME II.

	PAGE		PAGE
fined, would be of little or no value	159	tives, all ultimately disallowed..	163
But even granting the possibility of that which has just been denied, still Temperance would be of little value. Suppose that all separate work were well performed, by special practitioners, we should not attain our end—Happiness	ib.	Trial and Error, the natural process of the human mind. Plato stands alone in bringing to view and dramatising this part of the mental process. Sokrates accepts for himself the condition of conscious ignorance	164
Which of the varieties of knowledge contributes most to well-doing or happiness? That by which we know good and evil	160	Familiar words—constantly used, with much earnest feeling, but never understood nor defined—ordinary phenomenon in human society	165
Without the science of good and evil, the other special science will be of little or of no service. Temperance is not the science of good and evil, and is of little service	161	Different ethical points of view in different Platonic dialogues	167
		Self-knowledge is here declared to be impossible	ib.
Sokrates confesses to entire failure in his research. He cannot find out what temperance is: although several concessions have been made which cannot be justified..	ib.	In other dialogues, Sokrates declares self-knowledge to be essential and inestimable. Necessity for the student to have presented to him dissentient points of view	ib.
Temperance is and must be a good thing: but Charmides cannot tell whether he is temperate or not; since what temperance is remains unknown	162	Courage and Temperance are shown to have no distinct meaning, except as founded on the general cognizance of good and evil	168
Expressions both from Charmides and Kritias of praise and devotion to Sokrates, at the close of the dialogue. Dramatic ornament throughout	ib.	Distinction made between the special sciences and the science of Good and Evil. Without this last, the special sciences are of no use	ib.
The Charmides is an excellent specimen of Dialogues of Search. Abundance of guesses and tenta-		Knowledge, always relative to some object known. Postulate or divination of a Science of Teleology	169
		Courage and Temperance, handled both by Plato and by Aristotle. Comparison between the two	170

CHAPTER XX.

Lysis.

Analogy between Lysis and Charmides. Richness of dramatic incident in both. Youthful beauty	172	illustration of the Platonico-Sokratic manner	177
Scenery and personages of the Lysis	ib.	Sokrates begins to examine Menexenus respecting friendship. Who is to be called a friend? Halt in the dialogue	178
Origin of the conversation. Sokrates promises to give an example of the proper way of talking to a youth, for his benefit	173	Questions addressed to Lysis. Appeal to the maxims of the poets. Like is the friend of like. Canvassed and rejected	ib.
Conversation of Sokrates with Lysis	ib.	Other poets declare that likeness is a cause of aversion; unlikeness, of friendship. Reasons pro and con. Rejected	179
Lysis is humiliated. Distress of Hippothalês	177		
Lysis entreats Sokrates to talk in the like strain to Menexenus	ib.	Confusion of Sokrates. He suggests, That the Indifferent (neither good nor evil) is friend to the Good	180
Value of the first conversation between Sokrates and Lysis, as an			

CONTENTS OF VOLUME II. xv

Suggestion canvassed. If the Indifferent is friend to the Good, it is determined to become so by the contact of felt evil, from which it is anxious to escape .. 180
Principle illustrated by the philosopher. His intermediate condition—not wise, yet painfully feeling his own ignorance 181
Sokrates dissatisfied. He originates a new suggestion. The Primum Amabile, or object originally dear to us, *per se:* by relation or resemblance to which other objects become dear .. .. *ib.*
The cause of love is desire. We desire that which is akin to us —or our own 182
Good is of a nature akin to every one, evil is alien to every one. Inconsistency with what has been previously laid down 183
Failure of the enquiry. Close of the dialogue 184
Remarks. No positive result. Sokratic purpose in analysing the familiar words—to expose the false persuasion of knowledge .. *ib.*
Subject of Lysis. Suited for a Dialogue of Search. Manner of Sokrates, multiplying defective explanations, and showing reasons why each is defective 185
The process of trial and error is better illustrated by a search without result than with result. Usefulness of the dialogue for self-working minds 186
Subject of friendship, handled both by the Xenophontic Sokrates, and by Aristotle .. .. *ib.*
Debate in the Lysis partly verbal, partly real. Assumptions made by the Platonic Sokrates, questionable, such as the real Sokrates would have found reason for challenging.. .. : 188
Peculiar theory about friendship broached by Sokrates. Persons neither good nor evil by nature, yet having a superficial tinge of evil, and desiring good to escape from it 189
This general theory illustrated by the case of the philosopher or lover of wisdom. Painful consciousness of ignorance the attribute of the philosopher. Value set by Sokrates and Plato upon this attribute 190
Another theory of Sokrates. The Primum Amabile, or original and primary object of Love. Particular objects are loved through association with this. The object is Good 191
Statement by Plato of the general law of mental association .. .. *ib.*
Theory of the Primum Amabile, here introduced by Sokrates, with numerous derivative objects of love. Platonic Idea. Generic communion of Aristotle, distinguished by him from the feebler analogical communion 192
Primum Amabile of Plato, compared with the Prima Amicitia of Aristotle. Each of them is head of an analogical aggregate, not member of a generic family 194
The Good and Beautiful, considered as objects of attachment.. *ib.*

CHAPTER XXI.

EUTHYDEMUS.

Dramatic and comic exuberance of the Euthydêmus. Judgments of various critics 195
Scenery and personages .. .. *ib.*
The two Sophists, Euthydemus and Dionysodorus: manner in which they are here presented 196
Conversation carried on with Kleinias, first by Sokrates, next by the two Sophists .. .. *ib.*
Contrast between the two different modes of interrogation.. 197
Wherein this contrast does not consist.. 198
Wherein it does consist 199
Abuse of fallacies by the Sophists —their bidding for the applause of the by-standers .. .. .. *ib.*
Comparison of the Enthydêmus with the Parmenidês 200
Necessity of settling accounts with the negative, before we venture upon the affirmative, is common to both: in the one the process is solitary and serious; in the other, it is vulgarised and ludicrous 201
Opinion of Stallbaum and other

critics about the Euthydêmus, that Euthydêmus and Dionysodorus represent the way in which Protagoras and Gorgias talked to their auditors 202
That opinion is unfounded. Sokrates was much more Eristic than Protagoras, who generally manifested himself by continuous speech or lecture .. .. .. ib.
Sokrates in the Euthydêmus is drawn suitably to the purpose of that dialogue 203
The two Sophists in the Euthydêmus are not to be taken as real persons, or representatives of real persons.. 204
Colloquy of Sokrates with Kleinias —possession of good things is useless, unless we also have intelligence how to use them.. .. ib.
But intelligence— of what? It must be such intelligence, or such an art, as will include both the making of what we want, and the right use of it when made .. 205
Where is such an art to be found? The regal or political art looks like it; but what does this art do for us? No answer can be found. Ends in puzzle 206
Review of the cross-examination just pursued by Sokrates. It is very suggestive—puts the mind upon what to look for 207
Comparison with other dialogues— Republic, Philêbus, Protagoras. The only distinct answer is found in the Protagoras 208
The talk of the two Sophists, though ironically admired while it is going on, is shown at the end to produce no real admiration, but the contrary .. .. .. ib.
Mistaken representations about the Sophists—Aristotle's definition —no distinguishable line can be drawn between the Sophist and the Dialectician 210
Philosophical purpose of the Euthydêmus— exposure of fallacies, in Plato's dramatic manner, by multiplication of particular examples 211
Aristotle (Soph. Elench.) attempts a classification of fallacies: Plato enumerates them without classification 212
Fallacies of equivocation propounded by the two Sophists in the Euthydêmus .. .. ib.
Fallacies—*à dicto secundum quid, ad dictum simpliciter*—in the Euthydêmus 213

Obstinacy shown by the two Sophists in their replies—determination not to contradict themselves 214
Farther verbal equivocations.. .. ib.
Fallacies involving deeper logical principles—contradiction is impossible.—To speak falsely is impossible.. 215
Plato's Euthydêmus is the earliest known attempt to set out and expose fallacies—the only way of exposing fallacies is to exemplify the fallacy by particular cases, in which the conclusion proved is known *aliunde* to be false and absurd 216
Mistake of supposing fallacies to have been invented and propagated by Athenian Sophists— they are inherent inadvertencies and liabilities to error, in the ordinary process of thinking. Formal debate affords the best means of correcting them 217
Wide-spread prevalence of erroneous belief, misguided by one or other of these fallacies, attested by Sokrates, Plato, Bacon, &c.,—complete enumeration of heads of fallacies by Mill 218
Value of formal debate as a means for testing and confuting fallacies 221
Without the habit of formal debate, Plato could not have composed his Euthydêmus, nor Aristotle the treatise De Sophisticis Elenchis .. .. ib.
Probable popularity of the Euthydêmus at Athens—welcomed by all the enemies of Dialectic.. .. 222
Epilogue of Plato to the Dialogue, trying to obviate this inference by opponents—Conversation between Sokrates and Kriton .. 223
Altered tone in speaking of Euthydêmus—Disparagement of persons half-philosophers, half-politicians.. 224
Kriton asks Sokrates for advice about the education of his sons —Sokrates cannot recommend a teacher—tells him to search for himself 225
Euthydêmus is here cited as representative of Dialectic and philosophy 226
Who is the person here intended by Plato, half-philosopher, half-politician? Is it Isokrates? .. 227
Variable feeling at different times, between Plato and Isokrates .. 228

CONTENTS OF VOLUME II. xvii

CHAPTER XXVI.—*continued.*

the doctrines of Homer, Herakleitus, Empedoklês, &c., all except Parmenides 323
Plato here blends together three distinct theories, for the purpose of confuting them: yet he also professes to urge what can be said in favour of them. Difficulty of following his exposition 324
The doctrine of Protagoras is completely distinct from the other doctrines. The identification of them as one and the same is only constructive—the interpretation of Plato himself .. .. *ib.*
Explanation of the doctrine of Protagoras—*Homo Mensura* 325
Perpetual implication of Subject with Object — Relate and Correlate 327
Such relativity is no less true in regard to the ratiocinative combinations of each individual, than in regard to his percipient capacities 328
Evidence from Plato proving implication of Subject and Object, in regard to the intelligible world 330
The Protagorean measure is even more easily shown in reference to the intelligible world than in reference to sense 331
Object always relative to Subject —Either without the other, impossible. Plato admits this in Sophistes 335
Plato's representation of the Protagorean doctrine in intimate conjunction with the Herakleitean .. .. *ib.*
Relativity of sensible facts, as described by him 336
Relations are nothing in the object purely and simply, without a comparing subject 337
Relativity twofold — to the comparing Subject — to another Object, besides the one directly described .. .. *ib.*
Statement of the doctrine of Herakleitus—yet so as to implicate it with that of Protagoras 338
Agent and Patient — No absolute Ens 339
Arguments derived from dreams, fevers, &c., may be answered .. 340
Exposition of the Protagorean

doctrine, as given here by Sokrates is to a great degree just. You cannot explain the facts of consciousness by independent Subject and Object 340
Plato's attempt to get behind the phenomena. Reference to a double potentiality— Subjective and Objective 343
Arguments advanced by the Platonic Sokrates against the Protagorean doctrine. He says that it puts the wise and foolish on a par — that it contradicts the common consciousness. Not every one, but the wise man only, is a measure 345
In matters of present sentiment every man can judge for himself. Where future consequences are involved special knowledge is required 346
Plato, when he impugns the doctrine of Protagoras, states that doctrine without the qualification properly belonging to it. All belief relative to the condition of the believing mind .. 347
All exposition and discussion is an assemblage of individual judgments and affirmations. This fact is disguised by elliptical forms of language 349
Argument—That the Protagorean doctrine equalises all men and animals. How far true. Not true in the sense requisite to sustain Plato's objection 350
Belief on authority is true to the believer himself—The efficacy of authority resides in the believer's own mind 352
Protagorean formula—is false, to those who dissent from it.. .. 352
Plato's argument—That the wise man alone is a measure—Reply to it 353
Plato's argument as to the distinction between present sensation and anticipation of the future .. 355
The formula of Relativity does not imply that every man believes himself to be infallible .. *ib.*
Plato's argument is untenable— That if the Protagorean formula be admitted, dialectic discussion would be annulled—The reverse is true—Dialectic recog-

VOL. II. *b*

xviii CONTENTS OF VOLUME II.

CHAPTER XXVI.—continued.

nises the autonomy of the individual mind 356
Contrast with the Treatise De Legibus—Plato assumes infallible authority — sets aside Dialectic 358
Plato in denying the Protagorean formula, constitutes himself the measure for all. Counter-proposition to the formula .. .. ib.
Import of the Protagorean formula is best seen when we state explicitly the counter-proposition 360
Unpopularity of the Protagorean formula — Most believers insist upon making themselves a measure for others, as well as for themselves. Appeal to Abstractions .. .. ib.
Aristotle failed in his attempts to refute the Protagorean formula —Every reader of Aristotle will claim the right of examining for himself Aristotle's canons of truth 363
Plato's examination of the other doctrine — That knowledge is Sensible Perception. He adverts to sensible facts which are different with different Percipients 364
Such is not the case with all the facts of sense. The conditions of unanimity are best found among select facts of sense—weighing, measuring, &c. .. .. ib.
Arguments of Sokrates in examining this question. Divergence between one man and another arises, not merely from different sensual impressibility, but from mental and associative difference 365
Argument—That sensible Perception does not include memory—Probability that those who held the doctrine meant to include memory 367
Argument from the analogy of seeing and not seeing at the same time 368
Sokrates maintains that we do not see *with* our eyes, but that the mind sees *through* the eyes: that the mind often conceives and judges by itself, without the aid of any bodily organ 370
Indication of several judgments which the mind makes by itself —It perceives Existence, Difference, &c. 371
Sokrates maintains that knowledge is to be found, not in the Sensible Perceptions themselves, but in the comparisons and computations of the mind respecting them .. .. ib.
Examination of this view—Distinction from the views of modern philosophers 372
Different views given by Plato in other dialogues 373
Plato's discussion of this question here exhibits a remarkable advance in analytical psychology. The mind rises from Sensation, first to Opinion, then to Cognition 374
Plato did not recognise Verification from experience, or from facts of sense, as either necessary or possible 378
Second definition given by Theætêtus—That Cognition consists in right or true opinion 379
Objection by Sokrates—This definition assumes that there are false opinions. But how can false opinions be possible? How can we conceive Non-Ens; or confound together two distinct realities? .. .. ib.
Waxen memorial tablet in the mind, on which past impressions are engraved. False opinion consists in wrongly identifying present sensations with past impressions 380
Sokrates refutes this assumption. Dilemma. Either false opinion is impossible, or else a man may know what he does not know 381
He draws distinction between possessing knowledge, and having it actually in hand. Simile of the pigeon-cage with caught pigeons turned into it and flying about .. .. ib.
Sokrates refutes this. Suggestion of Theætêtus—That there may be non-cognitions in the mind as well as cognitions, and that false opinion may consist in confounding one with the other. Sokrates rejects this 382

CHAPTER XXVI.—continued.

He brings another argument to prove that Cognition is not the same as true opinion. Rhetors persuade or communicate true opinion; but they do not teach or communicate knowledge .. 383
New answer of Theætêtus—Cognition is true opinion, coupled with rational explanation.. .. 384
Criticism on the answer by Sokrates. Analogy of letters and words, primordial elements and compounds. Elements cannot be explained: compounds alone can be explained .. .. .. ib.
Sokrates refutes this criticism. If the elements are unknowable, the compound must be unknowable also 385
Rational explanation may have one of three different meanings. 1. Description in appropriate language. 2. Enumeration of all the component elements in the compound. In neither of these meanings will the definition of Cognition hold .. .. ib.
Third meaning. To assign some mark, whereby the thing to be explained differs from everything else. The definition will not hold. For rational explanation, in this sense, is already included in true opinion 386
Conclusion of the dialogue—Summing up by Sokrates—Value of the result, although purely negative 387
Remarks on the dialogue. View of Plato. False persuasion of knowledge removed. Importance of such removal.. .. .. ib.
Formation of the testing or verifying power in men's minds. Value of the Theætêtus, as it exhibits Sokrates demolishing his own suggestions 388
Comparison of the Philosopher with the Rhetor. The Rhetor is enslaved to the opinions of auditors 389
The Philosopher is master of his own debates 390
Purpose of Dialogue to qualify for a life of philosophical Search .. 391
Difficulties of the Theætêtus are not solved in any other Dialogue ib.
Plato considered that the search for Truth was the noblest occupation of life 393
Contrast between the philosopher and the practical statesman — between Knowledge and Opinion 394

CHAPTER XXVII.

Sophistes—Politikus.

Persons and circumstances of the two dialogues 396
Relation of the two dialogues to the Theætêtus 398
Plato declares that his first purpose is to administer a lesson in logical method: the special question chosen, being subordinate to that purpose 399
Method of logical Definition and Division 400
Sokrates tries the application of this method, first, upon a vulgar subject. To find the logical place and deduction of the Angler. Superior classes above him. Bisecting division .. .. ib.
Such a lesson in logical classification was at that time both novel and instructive. No logical manuals then existed 402
Plato describes the Sophist as analogous to an angler. He traces the Sophist by descending subdivision from the acquisitive genus of art.. 403
The Sophist traced down from the same, by a second and different descending subdivision 404
Also, by a third .. .. ib.
The Sophist is traced down, from the genus of separating or discriminating art 405
In a logical classification, low and vulgar items deserve as much attention as grand ones. Conflict between emotional and scientific classification 406

CHAPTER XXVII.—*continued.*

The purifier—a species under the genus discriminator — separates good from evil. Evil is of two sorts; the worst sort is, Ignorance, mistaking itself for knowledge 408
Exhortation is useless against this worst mode of evil. Cross-examination, the shock of the Elenchus, must be brought to bear upon it. This is the sovereign purifier 409
The application of this Elenchus is the work of the Sophist, looked at on its best side. But looked at as he really is, he is a juggler who teaches pupils to dispute about every thing—who palms off falsehood for truth .. .. *ib.*
Doubt started by the Eleate. How can it be possible either to think or to speak falsely? 410
He pursues the investigation of this problem by a series of questions 411
The Sophist will reject our definition and escape, by affirming that to speak falsely is impossible. He will require us to make out a rational theory, explaining Non-Ens .. .. .. *ib.*
The Eleate turns from Non-Ens to Ens. Theories of various philosophers about Ens 412
Difficulties about Ens are as great as those about Non-Ens 413
Whether Ens is Many or One? If Many, how Many? Difficulties about One and the Whole. Theorists about Ens cannot solve them .. .. *ib.*
Theories of those who do not recognise a definite number of Entia or elements. Two classes thereof.. 414
1. The Materialist Philosophers. 2. The Friends of Forms or Idealists, who recognise such Forms as the only real Entia .. *ib.*
Argument against the Materialists —Justice must be something, since it may be either present or absent, making sensible difference — But Justice is not a body 415
At least many of them will concede this point, though not all.

Ens is common to the corporeal and the incorporeal. Ens is equivalent to potentiality 416
Argument against the Idealists — who distinguish Ens from the generated, and say that we hold communion with the former through our minds, with the latter through our bodies and senses .. .. *ib.*
Holding communion—What? Implies Relativity. Ens is known by the mind. It therefore suffers—or undergoes change. Ens includes both the unchangeable and the changeable 417
Motion and Rest are both of them Entia or Realities. Both agree in Ens. Ens is a *tertium quid*—distinct from both. But how can anything be distinct from both? 418
Here the Eleate breaks off without solution. He declares his purpose to show, That Ens is as full of puzzle as Non-Ens.. .. *ib.*
Argument against those who admit no predication to be legitimate, except identical. How far Forms admit of intercommunion with each other .. .. *ib.*
No intercommunion between any distinct forms. Refuted. Common speech is inconsistent with this hypothesis 419
Reciprocal intercommunion of all Forms—inadmissible.. .. .. *ib.*
Some Forms admit of intercommunion, others not. This is the only admissible doctrine. Analogy of letters and syllables .. *ib.*
Art and skill are required to distinguish what Forms admit of intercommunion, and what Forms do not. This is the special intelligence of the Philosopher, who lives in the bright region of Ens: the Sophist lives in the darkness of Non-Ens.. 420
The Eleate comes to enquire what Non-Ens is. He takes for examination five principal Forms—Motion — Rest — Ens — Same—Different .. .. *ib.*
Form of Diversum pervades all the others 421
Motion is different from Diversum,

CONTENTS OF VOLUME II. xxi

himself. Polus takes up the debate with Sokrates 321
Polemical tone of Sokrates. At the instance of Polus he gives his own definition of rhetoric. It is no art, but an empirical knack of catering for the immediate pleasure of hearers, analogous to cookery. It is a branch under the general head flattery ib.
Distinction between the true arts which aim at the good of the body and mind—and the counterfeit arts, which pretend to the same, but in reality aim at immediate pleasure 322
Questions of Polus. Sokrates denies that the Rhetors have any real power, because they do nothing which they really wish .. 323
All men wish for what is good for them. Despots and Rhetors, when they kill any one, do so because they think it good for them. If it be really not good, they do not do what they will, and therefore have no real power 324
Comparison of Archelaus, usurping despot of Macedonia—Polus affirms that Archelaus is happy, and that every one thinks so—Sokrates admits that every one thinks so, but nevertheless denies it 325
Sokrates maintains—1. That it is a greater evil to do wrong, than to suffer wrong. 2. That if a man has done wrong, it is better for him to be punished than to remain unpunished 326
Sokrates offers proof—Definition of Pulchrum and Turpe—Proof of the first point 327
Proof of the second point .. .. ib.
The criminal labours under a mental distemper, which though not painful, is a capital evil. Punishment is the only cure for him. To be punished is best for him 328
Misery of the Despot who is never punished. If our friend has done wrong, we ought to get him punished: if our enemy, we ought to keep him unpunished 329
Argument of Sokrates paradoxical —Doubt expressed by Kalliklês whether he means it seriously .. 330
Principle laid down by Sokrates —That every one acts with a view to the attainment of happiness and avoidance of misery ib.

Peculiar view taken by Plato of Good—Evil—Happiness 331
Contrast of the usual meaning of these words, with the Platonic meaning .. .. ib.
Examination of the proof given by Sokrates—Inconsistency between the general answer of Polus and his previous declarations—Law and Nature 332
The definition of Pulchrum and Turpe, given by Sokrates, will not hold 334
Worse or better—for whom? The argument of Sokrates does not specify. If understood in the sense necessary for his inference, the definition would be inadmissible .. .. ib.
Plato applies to every one a standard of happiness and misery peculiar to himself. His view about the conduct of Archelaus is just, but he does not give the true reasons for it 335
If the reasoning of Plato were true, the point of view in which punishment is considered would be reversed 336
Plato pushes too far the analogy between mental distemper and bodily distemper—Material difference between the two—Distemper must be felt by the distempered persons 337
Kalliklês begins to argue against Sokrates—he takes a distinction between Just by Law and Just by nature—Reply of Sokrates, that there is no variance between the two, properly understood 338
What Kalliklês says is not to be taken as a sample of the teachings of Athenian sophists. Kalliklês—rhetor and politician .. 339
Uncertainty of referring to Nature as an authority. It may be pleaded in favour of opposite theories. The theory of Kalliklês is made to appear repulsive by the language in which he expresses it 340
Sokrates maintains that self-command and moderation is requisite for the strong man as well as for others. Kalliklês defends the negative 343
Whether the largest measure of desires is good for a man, provided he has the means of satisfying them? Whether all varieties of desire are good?

	PAGE
Whether the pleasurable and the good are identical?	344
Kalliklês maintains that pleasurable and good are identical. Sokrates refutes him. Some pleasures are good, others bad. A scientific adviser is required to discriminate them	345
Contradiction between Sokrates in the Gorgias, and Sokrates in the Protagoras	ib.
Views of critics about this contradiction	346
Comparison and appreciation of the reasoning of Sokrates in both dialogues	ib.
Distinct statement in the Protagoras. What are good and evil, and upon what principles the scientific adviser is to proceed in discriminating them. No such distinct statement in the Gorgias	347
Modern ethical theories. Intuition. Moral sense—not recognised by Plato in either of the dialogues	348
In both dialogues the doctrine of Sokrates is self-regarding as respects the agent: not considering the pleasures and pains of other persons, so far as affected by the agent	349
Points wherein the doctrine of the two dialogues is in substance the same, but differing in classification	ib.
Kalliklês, whom Sokrates refutes in the Gorgias, maintains a different argument from that which Sokrates combats in the Protagoras	350
The refutation of Kalliklês by Sokrates in the Gorgias, is unsuccessful—it is only so far successful as he adopts unintentionally the doctrine of Sokrates in the Protagoras	351
Permanent elements—and transient elements—of human agency—how each of them is appreciated in the two dialogues	353
In the Protagoras	ib.
In the Gorgias	354
Character of the Gorgias generally—discrediting all the actualities of life	355
Argument of Sokrates resumed—multifarious arts of flattery, aiming at immediate pleasure	357
The Rhetors aim at only flattering the public—even the best past Rhetors have done nothing else	

	PAGE
—citation of the four great Rhetors by Kalliklês	357
Necessity for temperance, regulation, order. This is the condition of virtue and happiness	358
Impossible to succeed in public life, unless a man be thoroughly akin to and in harmony with the ruling force	359
Danger of one who dissents from the public, either for better or for worse	ib.
Sokrates resolves upon a scheme of life for himself—to study permanent good, and not immediate satisfaction	360
Sokrates announces himself as almost the only man at Athens, who follows out the true political art. Danger of doing this	361
Mythe respecting Hades, and the treatment of deceased persons therein, according to their merits during life — the philosopher who stood aloof from public affairs, will then be rewarded	ib.
Peculiar ethical views of Sokrates—Rhetorical or dogmatical character of the Gorgias	362
He merges politics in Ethics—he conceives the rulers as spiritual teachers and trainers of the community	ib.
Idéal of Plato—a despotic lawgiver or man-trainer, on scientific principles, fashioning all characters pursuant to certain types of his own	363
Platonic analogy between mental goodness and bodily health — incomplete analogy — circumstances of difference	ib.
Sokrates in the Gorgias speaks like a dissenter among a community of fixed opinions and habits. Impossible that a dissenter, on important points, should acquire any public influence	364
Sokrates feels his own isolation from his countrymen. He is thrown upon individual speculation and dialectic	365
Antithesis between philosophy and rhetoric	ib.
Position of one who dissents, upon material points, from the fixed opinions and creed of his countrymen	366
Probable feelings of Plato on this subject. Claim put forward in the Gorgias of an independent locus standi for philosophy, but	

without the indiscriminate cross-examination pursued by Sokrates 367
Importance of maintaining the utmost liberty of discussion. Tendency of all ruling orthodoxy towards intolerance 368
Issue between philosophy and rhetoric—not satisfactorily handled by Plato. Injustice done to rhetoric. Ignoble manner in which it is presented by Polus and Kalliklês 369
Perikles would have accepted the defence of rhetoric, as Plato has put it into the mouth of Gorgias 370
The Athenian people recognise a distinction between the pleasurable and the good: but not the same as that which Plato conceived 371
Rhetoric was employed at Athens in appealing to all the various established sentiments and opinions. Erroneous inferences raised by the Kalliklês of Plato 373
The Platonic Idéal exacts, as good, some order, system, discipline. But order may be directed to bad ends as well as to good. Divergent ideas about virtue .. 374
How to discriminate the right order from the wrong. Plato does not advise us 375
The Gorgias upholds the independence and dignity of the dissenting philosopher.. .. .. ib.

CHAPTER XXV.

PHÆDON.

The Phædon is affirmative and expository 377
Situation and circumstances assumed in the Phædon. Pathetic interest which they inspire .. ib.
Simmias and Kebês, the two collocutors with Sokrates. Their feelings and those of Sokrates .. 378
Emphasis of Sokrates in insisting on freedom of debate, active exercise of reason, and independent judgment for each reasoner 379
Anxiety of Sokrates that his friends shall be on their guard against being influenced by his authority —that they shall follow only the convictions of their own reason 380
Remarkable manifestation of earnest interest for reasoned truth and the liberty of individual dissent 381
Phædon and Symposion—points of analogy and contrast 382
Phædon—compared with Republic and Timæus. No recognition of the triple or lower souls. Antithesis between soul and body .. 383
Different doctrines of Plato about the soul. Whether all the three souls are immortal, or the rational soul alone 385
The life and character of a philosopher is a constant struggle to emancipate his soul from his body. Death alone enables him to do this completely 386
Souls of the ordinary or unphilosophical men pass after death into the bodies of different animals. The philosopher alone is relieved from all communion with body.. 387
Special privilege claimed for philosophers in the Phædon apart from the virtuous men who are not philosophers 388
Simmias and Kebês do not admit readily the immortality of the soul, but are unwilling to trouble Sokrates by asking for proof. Unabated interest of Sokrates in rational debate 390
Simmias and Kebês believe fully in the pre-existence of the soul, but not in its post-existence. Doctrine—That the soul is a sort of harmony—refuted by Sokrates .. ib.
Sokrates unfolds the intellectual changes or wanderings through which his mind had passed.. .. 391
First doctrine of Sokrates as to cause. Reasons why he rejected it .. .. ib.
Second doctrine. Hopes raised by the treatise of Anaxagoras.. .. 393
Disappointment because Anaxagoras did not follow out the optimistic principle into detail. Distinction between causes efficient and causes co-efficient .. 394
Sokrates could neither trace out the optimistic principle for himself, nor find any teacher thereof. He renounced it, and embraced a third doctrine about cause .. 395
He now assumes the separate existence of ideas. These ideas are

xxiv   CONTENTS OF VOLUME II.

	PAGE		PAGE

the causes why particular objects manifest certain attributes 396
Procedure of Sokrates if his hypothesis were impugned. He insists upon keeping apart the discussion of the hypothesis and the discussion of its consequences . 397
Exposition of Sokrates welcomed by the hearers. Remarks upon it 398
The philosophical changes in Sokrates all turned upon different views as to a true cause .. .. ib.
Problems and difficulties of which Sokrates first sought solution .. 399
Expectations entertained by Sokrates from the treatise of Anaxagoras. His disappointment. His distinction between causes and co-efficients 400
Sokrates imputes to Anaxagoras the mistake of substituting physical agencies in place of mental. This is the same which Aristophanes and others imputed to Sokrates 401
The supposed theory of Anaxagoras cannot be carried out, either by Sokrates himself or any one else. Sokrates turns to general words, and adopts the theory of ideas 403
Vague and dissentient meanings attached to the word Cause. That is a cause, to each man, which gives satisfaction to his inquisitive feelings 404
Dissension and perplexity on the question.—What is a cause? revealed by the picture of Sokrates —no intuition to guide him .. 407
Different notions of Plato and Aristotle about causation, causes regular and irregular. Inductive theory of causation, elaborated in modern times .. .. ib.
Last transition of the mind of Sokrates from things to words—to the adoption of the theory of ideas. Great multitude of ideas assumed, each fitting a certain number of particulars 410
Ultimate appeal to hypothesis of extreme generality 411
Plato's demonstration of the immortality of the soul rests upon the assumption of the Platonic ideas. Reasoning to prove this 412
The soul always brings life, and is essentially living. It cannot receive death: in other words, it is immortal 413
The proof of immortality includes pre-existence as well as post-existence—animals as well as man—also the metempsychosis or translation of the soul from one body to another 414
After finishing his proof that the soul is immortal, Sokrates enters into a description, what will become of it after the death of the body. He describes a Νεκυία .. 415
Sokrates expects that his soul is going to the islands of the blest. Reply to Kriton about burying his body 416
Preparations for administering the hemlock. Sympathy of the gaoler. Equanimity of Sokrates ib.
Sokrates swallows the poison. Conversation with the gaoler 417
Ungovernable sorrow of the friends present. Self-command of Sokrates. Last words to Kriton, and death .. .. ib.
Extreme pathos, and probable trustworthiness of these personal details 419
Contrast between the Platonic Apology and the Phædon .. .. ib.
Abundant dogmatic and poetical invention of the Phædon compared with the profession of ignorance which we read in the Apology 421
Total renunciation and discredit of the body in the Phædon. Different feeling about the body in other Platonic dialogues .. 422
Plato's argument does not prove the immortality of the soul. Even if it did prove that, yet the mode of pre-existence and the mode of post-existence, of the soul, would be quite undetermined 423
The philosopher will enjoy an existence of pure soul unattached to any body 425
Plato's demonstration of the immortality of the soul did not appear satisfactory to subsequent philosophers. The question remained debated and problematical 426

PLATO.

CHAPTER XII.

ALKIBIADES I. AND II.

ALKIBIADES I.—ON THE NATURE OF MAN.

THIS dialogue is carried on between Sokrates and Alkibiades. It introduces Alkibiades as about twenty years of age, having just passed through the period of youth, and about to enter on the privileges and duties of a citizen. The real dispositions and circumstances of the historical Alkibiades (magnificent personal beauty, stature, and strength, high family and connections,— *[margin: Situation supposed in the dialogue. Persons— Sokrates and Alkibiades.]* great wealth already possessed, since his father had died when he was a child,—a full measure of education and accomplishments— together with exorbitant ambition and insolence, derived from such accumulated advantages) are brought to view in the opening address of Sokrates. Alkibiades, during the years of youth which he had just passed, had been surrounded by admirers who tried to render themselves acceptable to him, but whom he repelled with indifference, and even with scorn. Sokrates had been among them, constantly present and near to Alkibiades, but without ever addressing a word to him. The youthful beauty being now exchanged for manhood, all these admirers had retired, and Sokrates alone remains. His attachment is to Alkibiades himself :—to promise of mind rather than to attractions of person. Sokrates has been always hitherto restrained, by his divine sign or Dæmon, from speaking to Alkibiades. But this prohibition has now been removed; and he accosts him for the first time, in the full belief that he shall be able to give improving counsel, essential to the success of that political career upon which the youth is about to enter.[1]

Exorbitant hopes and political ambition of Alkibiades. You are about to enter on public life (says Sokrates to Alkibiades) with the most inordinate aspirations for glory and aggrandisement. You not only thirst for the acquisition of ascendancy such as Perikles possesses at Athens, but your ambition will not be satisfied unless you fill Asia with your renown, and put yourself upon a level with Cyrus and Xerxes. Now such aspirations cannot be gratified except through my assistance. I do not deal in long discourses such as you have been accustomed to hear from others: I shall put to you only some short interrogatories, requiring nothing more than answers to my questions.[2]

Questions put by Sokrates, in reference to Alkibiades in his intended function as adviser of the Athenians. What does he intend to advise them upon? Sokr.—You are about to step forward as adviser of the public assembly. Upon what points do you intend to advise them? Upon points which you know better than they? Alk.—Of course. Sokr.—All that you know, has been either learnt from others or found out by yourself. Alk. —Certainly. Sokr.—But you would neither have learnt any thing, nor found out any thing, without the desire to learn or find out: and you would have felt no such desire, in respect to that which you believed yourself to know already. That which you now know, therefore, there was a time when you believed yourself not

---

[1] Plato, Alkib. i. 103, 104, 105. Perikles is supposed to be still alive and political leader of Athens—104 B.
I have briefly sketched the imaginary situation to which this dialogue is made to apply. The circumstances of it belong to Athenian manners of the Platonic age.
Some of the critics, considering that the relation supposed between Sokrates and Alkibiades is absurd and unnatural, allege this among their reasons for denying the authenticity of the dialogue. But if any one reads the concluding part of the Symposion—the authenticity of which has never yet been denied by any critic—he will find something a great deal more abnormal in what is *there* recounted about Sokrates and Alkibiades.
In a dialogue composed by Æschines Socraticus (cited by the rhetor Aristeides—Περὶ Ῥητορικῆς, Or. xlv. p. 23-24), expressions of intense love for Alkibiades are put into the mouth of Sokrates. Æschines was γνήσιος ἑταῖρος Σωκράτους, not less than Plato. The different companions of Sokrates thus agreed in their picture of the relation between him and Alkibiades.

[2] Plato, Alkib. i. 106 B. *Ἆρα ἐρωτᾷς εἴ τινα ἔχω εἰπεῖν λόγον μακρόν, οἵους δὴ ἀκούειν εἴθισαι; οὐ γάρ ἐστι τοιοῦτον τὸ ἐμόν.* I give here, as elsewhere, not an exact translation, but an abstract.

CHAP. XII.   WHAT CAN HE ADVISE UPON?   3

to know? *Alk.*—Necessarily so. *Sokr.*—Now all that you have learnt, as I am well aware, consists of three things—letters, the harp, gymnastics. Do you intend to advise the Athenians when they are debating about letters, or about harp-playing, or about gymnastics? *Alk.*— Neither of the three. *Sokr.*—Upon what occasions, then, do you propose to give advice? Surely, not when the Athenians are debating about architecture, or prophetic warnings, or the public health: for to deliver opinions on each of these matters, belongs not to you but to professional men—architects, prophets, physicians; whether they be poor or rich, high-born or low-born? If not *then*, upon what other occasions will you tender your counsel? *Alk.*—When they are debating about affairs of their own. {he learnt, and what does he know?}

Sokr.—But about what affairs of their own? Not about affairs of shipbuilding: for of that you know nothing. *Alk.* —When they are discussing war and peace, or any other business concerning the city. *Sokr.*—You mean when they are discussing the question with whom they shall make war or peace, and in what manner? But it is certain that we must fight those whom it is best to fight—also *when* it is best—and *as long as* it is best. *Alk.*—Certainly. *Sokr.*—Now, if the Athenians wished to know whom it was best to wrestle with, and when or how long it was best—which of the two would be most competent to advise them, you or the professional trainer? *Alk.*—The trainer, undoubtedly. *Sokr.*—So, too, about playing the harp or singing. But when you talk about *better*, in wrestling or singing, what standard do you refer to? Is it not to the gymnastic or musical art? *Alk.*—Yes. *Sokr.*—Answer me in like manner about war or peace, the subjects on which you are going to advise your countrymen, whom, and at what periods, it is *better* to fight, and *better* not to fight? What in this last case do you mean by *better*? To what standard, or to what end, do you refer?[1] *Alk.*—I cannot say. *Sokr.*—But is it not a disgrace, {Alkibiades intends to advise the Athenians on questions of war and peace. Questions of Sokrates thereupon. We must fight those whom it is better to fight—to what standard does better refer? To just and unjust.}

---

[1] Plato, Alkib. i. 108 E—109 A.
ἴθι δή, καὶ τὸ ἐν τῷ πολεμεῖν βέλ- τιον καὶ τὸ ἐν τῷ εἰρήνην ἄγειν, τοῦτο   τὸ βέλτιον τί ὀνομάζεις; ὥσπερ ἐκεῖ ἐφ᾽ ἑκάστῳ ἔλεγες τὸ ἄμεινον, ὅτι μουσικώτερον, καὶ ἐπὶ τῷ ἑτέρῳ, ὅτι

since you profess to advise your countrymen when and against whom it is better for them to war,—not to be able to say to what end your *better* refers? Do not you know what are the usual grounds and complaints urged when war is undertaken? *Alk.*— Yes: complaints of having been cheated, or robbed, or injured. *Sokr.*—Under what circumstances? *Alk.*—You mean, whether justly or unjustly? That makes all the difference. *Sokr.*—Do you mean to advise the Athenians to fight those who behave justly, or those who behave unjustly? *Alk.*—The question is monstrous. Certainly not those who behave justly. It would be neither lawful nor honourable. *Sokr.*—Then when you spoke about *better*, in reference to war or peace, what you meant was *juster*—you had in view justice and injustice? *Alk.*—It seems so. *Sokr.*—How is this? How do you know, or where have you learnt, to distinguish just from unjust? Have you frequented some master, without my knowledge, to teach you this? If you have, pray introduce me to him, that I also may learn it from him. *Alk.*—You are jesting. *Sokr.*—Not at all: I love you too well to jest. *Alk.*—But what if I had no master? Cannot I know about justice and injustice, without a master? *Sokr.*—Certainly: you might find out for yourself, if you made search and investigated. But this you would not do, unless you were under the persuasion that you did not already know. *Alk.*— Was there not a time when I really believed myself not to know it? *Sokr.*—Perhaps there may have been: tell me *when* that time was. Was it last year? *Alk.*—No: last year I thought that I knew. *Sokr.*—Well, then—two years, three years, &c., ago? *Alk.*—No: the case was the same—then, also, I thought that I knew. *Sokr.*—But before that, you were a mere boy; and during your boyhood you certainly believed yourself to know what was just and unjust; for I well recollect hearing you then complain confidently of other boys, for acting unjustly towards you. *Alk.*—Certainly: I was not then ignorant on the point: I knew distinctly that they were acting unjustly towards me.

How, or from whom, has Alkibiades learnt to discern or distinguish Just and Unjust? He never learnt it from any one: he always knew it, even as a boy.

γυμναστικώτερον· πειρῶ δὴ καὶ ἐνταῦ- ἄμεινον καὶ τὸ ἐν τῷ πολεμεῖν οἷς δεῖ;
θα λέγειν τὸ βέλτιον . . . . . πρὸς *Alkib.* Ἀλλὰ σκοπῶν οὐ δύναμαι ἐν-
τί τείνει τὸ ἐν τῷ εἰρήνην τε ἄγειν νοῆσαι.

Sokr.—You knew, then, even in your boyhood, what was just and what was unjust? *Alk.*—Certainly: I knew even then. *Sokr.*—At what moment did you first find it out? Not when you already believed yourself to know: and what time was there when you did not believe yourself to know? *Alk.*—Upon my word, I cannot say.

Sokr.—Since, accordingly, you neither found it out for yourself, nor learnt it from others, how come you to know justice or injustice at all, or from what quarter? *Alk.*—I was mistaken in saying that I had not learnt it. I learnt it, as others do, from the multitude.[1] *Sokr.*—Your teachers are none of the best: no one can learn from them even such small matters as playing at draughts: much less, what is just and unjust. *Alk.*—I learnt it from them as I learnt to speak Greek, in which, too, I never had any special teacher. *Sokr.*—Of that the multitude are competent teachers, for they are all of one mind. Ask which is a tree or a stone,—a horse or a man,—you get the same answer from every one. But when you ask not simply which are *horses*, but also which horses are fit to run well in a race—when you ask not merely which are *men*, but which men are healthy or unhealthy—are the multitude all of one mind, or all competent to answer? *Alk.*—Assuredly not. *Sokr.*—When you see the multitude differing among themselves, that is a clear proof that they are not competent to teach others. *Alk.*—It is so. *Sokr.*—Now, about the question, What is just and unjust— are the multitude all of one mind, or do they differ among themselves? *Alk.*—They differ prodigiously: they not only dispute, but quarrel and destroy each other, respecting justice and injustice, far more than about health and sickness.[2] *Sokr.*—How, then, can we say that the multitude know what is just and unjust, when they thus fiercely dispute about it among themselves? *Alk.*—I now perceive that we cannot say so. *Sokr.*—

Answer amended. Alkibiades learnt it from the multitude, as he learnt to speak Greek.—The multitude cannot teach just and unjust, for they are at variance among themselves about it. Alkibiades is going to advise the Athenians about what he does not know himself.

---

[1] Plato, Alkib. i. 110 D-E. ἔμαθον, οἶμαι, καὶ ἐγὼ ὥσπερ καὶ οἱ ἄλλοι .... παρὰ τῶν πολλῶν.

[2] Plato, Alkib. i. 112 A. Sokr. Τί δὲ δή; νῦν περὶ τῶν δικαίων καὶ ἀδίκων ἀνθρώπων καὶ πραγμάτων, οἱ πολλοὶ δοκοῦσί σοι ὁμολογεῖν αὑτοὶ ἑαυτοῖς ἢ ἀλλήλοις; Alkib. Ἥκιστα, νὴ Δί', ὦ Σώκρατες. Sokr. Τί δέ; μάλιστα περὶ αὐτῶν διαφέρεσθαι; Alkib. πολύ γε.

How can we say, therefore, that they are fit to teach others: and how can you pretend to know, who have learnt from no other teachers? *Alk.*—From what you say, it is impossible. *Sokr.*—No: not from what *I* say, but from what *you* say yourself. I merely ask questions: it is you who give all the answers.[1] And what you have said amounts to this—that Alkibiades knows nothing about what is just and unjust, but believes himself to know, and is going to advise the Athenians about what he does not know himself?

Alk.—But, Sokrates, the Athenians do not often debate about what is just and unjust. They think that question self-evident: they debate generally about what is expedient or not expedient. Justice and expediency do not always coincide. Many persons commit great crimes, and are great gainers by doing so: others again behave justly, and suffer from it.[2] *Sokr.*—Do you then profess to know what is expedient or inexpedient? From whom have you learnt—or when did you find out for yourself? I might ask you the same round of questions, and you would be compelled to answer in the same manner. But we will pass to a different point. You say that justice and expediency are not coincident. Persuade *me* of this, by interrogating me as I interrogated you. *Alk.*—That is beyond my power. *Sokr.*—But when you rise to address the assembly, you will have to persuade *them*. If you can persuade them, you can persuade me. Assume *me* to be the assembly, and practise upon me.[3] *Alk.*—You are too hard upon me, Sokrates. It is for you to speak, and prove the point. *Sokr.*—No: I can only question: you must answer. You will be most surely persuaded when the point is determined by your own answers.[4]

Answer farther amended. The Athenians do not generally debate about just or unjust—which they consider plain to every one—but about expedient and inexpedient, which are not coincident with just and unjust. But neither does Alkibiades know the expedient. He asks Sokrates to explain. Sokrates declines: he can do nothing but question.

Such is the commencing portion (abbreviated or abstracted)

---

[1] Plato, Alkib. i. 112-113.
[2] Plato, Alkib. i. 113 D. Οἶμαι μὲν ὀλιγάκις Ἀθηναίους βουλεύεσθαι πότερα δικαιότερα ἢ ἀδικώτερα· τὰ μὲν γὰρ τοιαῦτα ἡγοῦνται δῆλα εἶναι, &c.
[3] Plato, Alkib. i. 114 B-C. This same argument is addressed by Sokrates to Glaukon, in Xenoph. Memor. iii. 6, 14-15.
[4] Plato, Alkib. i. 114 E. Οὐκοῦν εἰ λέγεις ὅτι ταῦθ᾽ οὕτως ἔχει, μάλιστ᾽ ἂν εἴης πεπεισμένος;

of Plato's First Alkibiadês. It exhibits a very characteristic specimen of the Sokratico-Platonic method: both in its negative and positive aspect. By the negative, false persuasion of knowledge is exposed. Alkibiades believes himself competent to advise about just and unjust, which he has neither learnt from any teacher nor investigated for himself—which he has picked up from the multitude, and supposes to be clear to every one, but about which nevertheless there is so much difference of appreciation among the multitude, that fierce and perpetual quarrels are going on. On the positive side, Sokrates restricts himself to the function of questioning: he neither affirms nor denies any thing. It is Alkibiades who affirms or denies every thing, and who makes all the discoveries for himself out of his own mind, instigated indeed, but not taught, by the questions of his companion.

Comment on the preceding. Sokratic method—the respondent makes the discoveries for himself.

By a farther series of questions, Sokrates next brings Alkibiades to the admission that what is just, is also honourable, good, expedient—what is unjust, is dishonourable, evil, inexpedient: and that whoever acts justly, and honourably, thereby acquires happiness. Admitting, first, that an act which is good, honourable, just, expedient, &c., considered in one aspect or in reference to some of its conditions—may be at the same time bad, dishonourable, unjust, inexpedient, &c., considered in another aspect or in reference to other conditions; Sokrates nevertheless brings his respondent to admit, that every act, *in so far as it is just and honourable*, is also good and expedient.[1] And he contends farther, that whoever acts honourably, does well: now every man who does well, becomes happy, or secures good things thereby: there-

Alkibiades is brought to admit that whatever is just, is good, honourable, expedient: and that whoever acts honourably, both does well, and procures for himself happiness thereby. Equivocal reasoning of Sokrates.

---
[1] Plato, Alkib. i. 115 B—116 A.
Οὐκοῦν τὴν τοιαύτην βοηθείαν καλὴν μὲν λέγεις κατὰ τὴν ἐπιχείρησιν τοῦ σῶσαι οὓς ἔδει· τοῦτο δ' ἐστὶν ἀνδρία·
.... κακὴν δέ γε κατὰ τοὺς θανάτους τε καὶ τὰ ἕλκη. ...
Οὐκοῦν ὧδε δίκαιον προσαγορεύειν ἑκάστην τῶν πράξεων· εἴπερ ᾗ κακὸν ἀπεργάζεται κακὴν καλεῖς, καὶ ᾗ ἀγαθὸν ἀγαθὴν κλητέον.

Ἀρ' οὖν καὶ ᾗ ἀγαθὸν καλόν,—ᾗ δὲ κακὸν αἰσχρόν; Ναί.
Compare Plato, Republic, v. p. 479, where he maintains that in every particular case, what is just, honourable, virtuous, &c., is also unjust, dishonourable, vicious, &c. Nothing remains unchanged, nor excludes the contrary, except the pure, self-existent, Idea or general Concept.—αὐτὸ-δικαιοσύνη, &c.

fore the just, the honourable, and the good or expedient, coincide.[1] The argument, whereby this conclusion is here established, is pointed out by Heindorf, Stallbaum, and Steinhart, as not merely inconclusive, but as mere verbal equivocation and sophistry—the like of which, however, we find elsewhere in Plato.[2]

Humiliation of Alkibiades. Other Athenian statesmen are equally ignorant. But the real opponents, against whom Alkibiades is to measure himself, are, the kings of Sparta and Persia. Eulogistic description of those kings. To match them, Alkibiades must make himself as good as possible.

Alkibiades is thus reduced to a state of humiliating embarrassment, and stands convicted, by his own contradictions and confession, of ignorance in its worst form: that is, of being ignorant, and yet confidently believing himself to know.[3] But other Athenian statesmen are no wiser. Even Perikles is proved to be equally deficient—by the fact that he has never been able to teach or improve any one else, not even his own sons and those whom he loved best.[4] "At any rate" (contends Alkibiades) "I am as good as my competitors, and can hold my ground against them." But Sokrates reminds him that the real competitors with whom he ought to compare himself, are, foreigners, liable to become the enemies of Athens, and against whom he, if he pretends to lead Athens, must be able to contend. In an harangue of unusual length, Sokrates shows that the kings of Sparta and Persia are of nobler breed, as well as more highly and carefully trained, than the Athenian statesmen.[5] Alkibiades must be rescued from his present ignorance, and exalted, so as to be capable of competing with these kings: which object cannot be attained except through the auxiliary interposition of Sokrates. Not that Sokrates professes to be himself already on this elevation, and to stand in need of no farther improvement. But he can, nevertheless, help others to attain it for themselves, through the discipline and stimulus of his interrogatories.[6]

---

[1] Plato, Alkib. i. 116 E.
[2] The words εὖ πράττειν—εὐπραγία have a double sense, like our "doing well". Stallbaum, Proleg. p. 175; Steinhart, Einl. p. 149.
We have, p. 116 B, the equivocation between καλῶς πράττειν and εὖ πράττειν, also with κακῶς πράττειν, p. 134 A, 135 A; compare Heindorf ad Platon. Charmid. p. 172 A, p. 174 B; also Platon. Gorgias, p. 507 C, where similar equivocal meanings occur.
[3] Plato, Alkib. i. p. 118.
[4] Plato, Alkib. i. p. 118-119.
[5] Plato, Alkib. i. p. 120-124.
[6] Plato, Alkib. i. p. 124.

CHAP. XII. EXAMPLES OF "GOOD". 9

The dialogue then continues. *Sokr.*—We wish to become as good as possible. But in what sort of virtue? *Alk.*— In that virtue which belongs to good men. *Sokr.*— Yes, but *good*, in what matters? *Alk.*—Evidently, to men who are good in transacting business. *Sokr.*— Ay, but what kind of business? business relating to horses, or to navigation? If that be meant, we must go and consult horse-trainers or mariners? *Alk.*— {But good—for what end, and under what circumstances? Abundant illustrative examples.} No, I mean such business as is transacted by the most esteemed leaders in Athens. *Sokr.*—You mean the intelligent men. Every man is good, in reference to that which he understands : every man is bad, in reference to that which he does not understand. *Alk.*—Of course. *Sokr.*—The cobbler understands shoemaking, and is therefore good at *that* : he does not understand weaving, and is therefore bad at that. The same man thus, in your view, will be both good and bad?[1] *Alk.*—No : that cannot be. *Sokr.*—Whom then do you mean, when you talk of *the good?* *Alk.*—I mean those who are competent to command in the city. *Sokr.*—But to command whom or what—horses or men? *Alk.*— To command men. *Sokr.*—But what men, and under what circumstances? sick men, or men on shipboard, or labourers engaged in harvesting, or in what occupations? *Alk.*—I mean, men living in social and commercial relation with each other, as we live here ; men who live in common possession of the same laws and government. *Sokr.*—When men are in communion of a sea voyage and of the same ship, how do we name the art of commanding them, and to what purpose does it tend? *Alk.*—It is the art of the pilot ; and the purpose towards which it tends, is, bringing them safely through the dangers of the sea. *Sokr.*— When men are in social and political communion, to what purpose does the art of commanding them tend? *Alk.*—Towards the better preservation and administration of the city.[2] *Sokr.*— But what do you mean by *better* ? What is that, the presence or absence of which makes *better* or *worse* ? If in regard to the

---

[1] Plato, Alkib. i. p. 125 B.
'Ο αὐτὸς ἄρα τούτῳ γε τῷ λόγῳ κακός τε καὶ ἀγαθός.
Plato slides unconsciously here, as in other parts of his reasonings, *à dicto secundum quid, ad dictum simpliciter.*

[2] Plato, Alkib. i. p. 126 A. τί δέ; ἦν σὺ καλεῖς εὐβουλίαν, εἰς τί ἐστιν; *Alk.* Εἰς τὸ ἄμεινον τὴν πόλιν διοικεῖν καὶ σώζεσθαι. *Sokr.* Ἄμεινον δὲ διοικεῖται καὶ σώζεται τίνος παραγιγνομένου ἢ ἀπογιγνομένου;

management of the body, you put to me the same question, I should reply, that it is the presence of health, and the absence of disease. What reply will you make, in the case of the city? *Alk.*—I should say, when friendship and unanimity among the citizens are present, and when discord and antipathy are absent. *Sokr.*—This unanimity, of what nature is it? Respecting what subject? What is the art or science for realising it? If I ask you what brings about unanimity respecting numbers and measures, you will say the arithmetical and the metrêtic art. *Alk.*—I mean that friendship and unanimity which prevails between near relatives, father and son, husband and wife. *Sokr.*—But how can there be unanimity between any two persons, respecting subjects which one of them knows, and the other does not know? For example, about spinning and weaving, which the husband does not know,—or about military duties, which the wife does not know,—how can there be unanimity between the two? *Alk.* —No : there cannot be. *Sokr.*—Nor friendship, if unanimity and friendship go together? *Alk.*—Apparently there cannot. *Sokr.*—Then when men and women each perform their own special duties, there can be no friendship between them. Nor can a city be well administered, when each citizen performs his own special duties? or (which is the same thing) when each citizen acts justly? *Alk.*—Not so : I think there may be friendship, when each person performs his or her own business. *Sokr.* —Just now you said the reverse. What is this friendship or unanimity which we must understand and realise, in order to become good men?

Alk.—In truth, I am puzzled myself to say. I find myself in a state of disgraceful ignorance, of which I had no previous suspicion. *Sokr.*—Do not be discouraged. If you had made this discovery when you were fifty years old, it would have been too late for taking care of yourself and applying a remedy : but at your age, it is the right time for making the discovery. *Alk.*—What am I to do, now that I have made it? *Sokr.*—You must answer my questions. If my auguries are just, we shall soon be both of us better for the process.[1]

Alkibiades, puzzled and humiliated, confesses his ignorance. Encouragement given by Sokrates.—It is an advantage to make such discovery in youth.

[1] Plato, Alkib. i. 127 D-E. *Alk.* τι λέγω, κινδυνεύω δὲ καὶ πάλαι λεληθέναι ἐμαυτὸν αἴσχιστ' ἔχων. Ἀλλὰ μὰ τοὺς θεούς, οὐδ' αὐτὸς οἶδα ὅ

Here we have again, brought into prominent relief, the dialectic method of Plato, under two distinct aspects:
1. Its actual effects, in exposing the false supposition of knowledge, in forcing upon the respondent the humiliating conviction, that he does not know familiar topics which he supposed to be clear both to himself and to others. 2. Its anticipated effects, if continued, in remedying such defect: and in generating out of the mind of the respondent, real and living knowledge. *Platonic Dialectic—its actual effect—its anticipated effect—applicable to the season of youth.* Lastly, it is plainly intimated that this shock of humiliation and mistrust, painful but inevitable, must be undergone in youth.

The dialogue continues, in short questions and answers, of which the following is an abstract. *Sokr.*—What is meant by a man *taking care of himself?* Before I can take care of myself, I must know what *myself* is: I must *know myself*, according to the Delphian motto. I cannot make myself better, without knowing what *myself* is.[1] That which belongs to me is not *myself*: my body is not myself, but an instrument governed by myself.[2] My mind or soul only, is myself. To take care of myself is, to take care of my mind. At any rate, if this be not strictly true,[3] my mind is the most important and dominant element within me. The physician who knows his own body, does not for that reason know himself: much less do the husbandman or the tradesman, who know their own properties or crafts, know themselves, or perform what is truly their own business. *Know Thyself—Delphian maxim—its urgent importance—What is myself? My mind is myself.*

Since temperance consists in self-knowledge, neither of these professional men, as such, is temperate: their professions are of a vulgar cast, and do not belong to the *I cannot know my-*

Sokr. Ἀλλὰ χρὴ θαρρεῖν· εἰ μὲν γὰρ αὐτὸ ᾖσθου πεπονθὼς πεντηκονταέτης, χαλεπὸν ἂν ἦν σοι ἐπιμεληθῆναι σαυτοῦ· νῦν δὲ ἣν ἔχεις ἡλικίαν, αὕτη ἐστίν, ἐν ᾗ δεῖ αὐτὸ αἰσθέσθαι.
Alk. Τί οὖν τὸν αἰσθόμενον χρὴ ποιεῖν;
Sokr. Ἀποκρίνεσθαι τὰ ἐρωτώμενα· καὶ ἐὰν τοῦτο ποιῇς, ἂν θεὸς ἐθέλῃ, εἴ τι δεῖ καὶ τῇ ἐμῇ μαντείᾳ πιστεύειν, σύ τε κἀγὼ βελτιόνως σχήσομεν.

[1] Plato, Alkib. i. 129 B. τίν' ἂν τρόπον εὑρεθείη αὐτὸ τὸ αὐτό;
[2] Plato, Alkib. i. 128-130. All this is greatly expanded in the dialogue— p. 128 D: Οὐκ ἄρα ὅταν τῶν σαυτοῦ ἐπιμελῇ, σαυτοῦ ἐπιμέλει; This same antithesis is employed by Isokrates, De Permutatione, sect. 309, p. 492, Bekker. He recommends αὐτοῦ πρότερον ἢ τῶν αὐτοῦ ποιεῖσθαι τὴν ἐπιμέλειαν.
[3] Plato considers this point to be not clearly made out. Alkib. i. 130.

self, except by looking into another mind. Self-knowledge is temperance. Temperance and Justice are the conditions both of happiness and of freedom.

virtuous life.[1] How are we to know our own minds? We know it by looking into another mind, and into the most rational and divine portion thereof: just as the eye can only know itself by looking into another eye, and seeing itself therein reflected.[2] It is only in this way that we can come to know ourselves, or become temperate: and if we do not know ourselves, we cannot even know what belongs to ourselves, or what belongs to others: all these are branches of one and the same cognition. We can have no knowledge of affairs, either public or private: we shall go wrong, and shall be unable to secure happiness either for ourselves or for others. It is not wealth or power which are the conditions of happiness, but justice and temperance. Both for ourselves individually, and for the public collectively, we ought to aim at justice and temperance, not at wealth and power. The evil and unjust man ought to have no power, but to be the slave of those who are better than himself.[3] He is fit for nothing but to be a slave: none deserve freedom except the virtuous.

Alkibiades feels himself unworthy to be free, and declares that he will never quit Sokrates.

Sokr.—How do you feel your own condition now, Alkibiades. Are you worthy of freedom? Alk.—I feel but too keenly that I am not. I cannot emerge from this degradation except by your society and help. From this time forward I shall never leave you.[4]

ALKIBIADES II.

The other Platonic dialogue, termed the Second Alkibiades, introduces Alkibiades as about to offer prayer and sacrifice to the Gods.

Second Alkibiadès— situation supposed.

Sokr.—You seem absorbed in thought, Alkibiades, and not unreasonably. In supplicating the Gods, caution is required not to pray for gifts which are really mischievous. The Gods sometimes grant men's prayers, even when ruinously destructive; as they

Danger of mistake in praying to the Gods for gifts

---

[1] Plato, Alkib. i. 131 B.
[2] Plato, Alkib. i. 133.
[3] Plato, Alkib. i. 134-135 B-C.
Πρὶν δέ γε ἀρετὴν ἔχειν, τὸ ἄρχεσθαι

ἄμεινον ὑπὸ τοῦ βελτίονος ἢ τὸ ἄρχειν ἀνδρὶ, οὐ μόνον παιδί. . . . Πρέπει ἄρα τῷ κακῷ δουλεύειν· ἄμεινον γάρ.
[4] Plato, Alkib. i. 135.

granted the prayers of Œdipus, to the destruction of his own sons. *Alk.*—Œdipus was mad: what man in his senses would put up such a prayer? *Sokr.*— You think that madness is the opposite of good sense or wisdom. You recognise men wise and unwise: and you farther admit that every man must be one or other of the two,—just as every man must be either healthy or sick: there is no third alternative possible? *Alk.*—I think so. *Sokr.*—But each thing can have but one opposite:[1] to be unwise, and to be mad, are therefore identical? *Alk.*—They are. *Sokr.*—Wise men are only few, the majority of our citizens are unwise: but do you really think them mad? How could any of us live safely in the society of so many madmen? *Alk.*—No: it cannot be so: I was mistaken. *Sokr.*— Here is the illustration of your mistake. All men who have gout, or fever, or ophthalmia are sick; but all sick men have not gout, or fever, or ophthalmia. So, too, all carpenters, or shoemakers, or sculptors, are craftsmen; but all craftsmen are not carpenters, or shoemakers, or sculptors. In like manner, all mad men are unwise; but all unwise men are not mad. *Unwise* comprises many varieties and gradations—of which the extreme is, being mad: but these varieties are different among themselves, as one disease differs from another, though all agree in being disease—and one art differs from another, though all agree in being art.[2]

which may prove mischievous.
Most men are unwise. Unwise is the generic word: mad-men, a particular variety under it.

(We may remark that Plato here, as in the Euthyphron, brings under especial notice one of the most important distinctions in formal logic—that between a generic term and the various specific terms comprehended under it. Possessing as yet no technical language for characterising this distinction, he makes it understood by an induction of several separate but analogous cases. Because the distinction is familiar now to instructed men, we must not suppose that it was familiar then.)

Relation between a generic term, and the specific terms comprehended under it, was not then familiar.

---

[1] Plato, Alkib. ii. p. 139 B.
Καὶ μὴν δύο γε ὑπεναντία ἑνὶ πράγματι πῶς ἂν εἴη;
That each thing has one opposite,

and no more, is asserted in the Protagoras also, p. 192-193.
[2] Plato, Alkib. ii. p. 139-140 A-B.
Καὶ γὰρ οἱ πυρέττοντες πάντες νοσοῦ-

Sokr.—Whom do you call wise and unwise? Is not the wise man, he who knows what it is proper to say and do—and the unwise man, he who does not know? *Alk.*—Yes. *Sokr.*—The unwise man will thus often unconsciously say or do what ought not to be said or done? Though not mad like Œdipus, he will nevertheless pray to the Gods for gifts, which will be hurtful to him if obtained. You, for example, would be overjoyed if the Gods were to promise that you should become despot not only over Athens, but also over Greece. *Alk.*—Doubtless I should: and every one else would feel as I do. *Sokr.*—But what if you were to purchase it with your life, or to damage yourself by the employment of it? *Alk.*—Not on those conditions.[1] *Sokr.*—But you are aware that many ambitious aspirants, both at Athens and elsewhere (among them, the man who just now killed the Macedonian King Archelaus, and usurped his throne), have acquired power and aggrandisement, so as to be envied by every one: yet have presently found themselves brought to ruin and death by the acquisition. So, also, many persons pray that they may become fathers; but discover presently that their children are the source of so much grief to them, that they wish themselves again childless. Nevertheless, though such reverses are perpetually happening, every one is still not only eager to obtain these supposed benefits, but importunate with the Gods in asking for them. You see that it is not safe even to accept without reflection boons offered to you, much less to pray for boons to be conferred.[2] *Alk.*—I see now how much mischief ignorance produces. Every one thinks himself competent to pray for what is beneficial to himself; but ignorance makes him unconsciously imprecate mischief on his own head.

Sokr.—You ought not to denounce ignorance in this unqualified manner. You must distinguish and specify—Ignorance of what? and under what modifications of persons and circumstances? *Alk.*—How? Are there

<small>Frequent cases, in which men pray for supposed benefits, and find that, when obtained, they are misfortunes. Every one fancies that he knows what is beneficial: michiefs of ignorance.</small>

<small>Mistake in predications about ignorance</small>

σιν, οὐ μέντοι οἱ νοσοῦντες πάντες πυρέττουσιν οὐδὲ ποδαγρῶσιν οὐδέ γε ὀφθαλμιῶσιν· ἀλλὰ νόσος μὲν πᾶν τὸ τοιοῦτόν ἐστι, διαφέρειν δέ φασιν οὓς δὴ καλοῦμεν ἰατροὺς τὴν ἀπεργασίαν αὐτῶν·
οὐ γὰρ πᾶσαι οὔτε ὅμοιαι οὔτε ὁμοίως διαπράττονται, ἀλλὰ κατὰ τὴν αὑτῆς δύναμιν ἑκάστη.
[1] Plato, Alkib. ii. p. 141.
[2] Plato, Alkib. ii. p. 141-142.

any matters or circumstances in which it is better for a man to be ignorant, than to know? *Sokr.*—You will see that there are such. Ignorance of good, or ignorance of what is best, is always mischievous: moreover, assuming that a man knows what is best, then all other knowledge will be profitable to him. In his special case, ignorance on any subject cannot be otherwise than hurtful. But if a man be ignorant of good, or of what is best, in his case knowledge on other subjects will be more often hurtful than profitable. To a man like Orestes, so misguided on the question, "What is good?" as to resolve to kill his mother,—it would be a real benefit, if for the time he did not know his mother. Ignorance on that point, in his state of mind, would be better for him than knowledge.[1] *Alk.*—It appears so.

Sokr.—Follow the argument farther. When we come forward to say or do any thing, we either know what we are about to say and do, or at least believe ourselves to know it. Every statesman who gives counsel to the public, does so in the faith of such knowledge. Most citizens are unwise, and ignorant of good as well as of other things. The wise are but few, and by their advice the city is conducted. Now upon what ground do we call these few, wise and useful public counsellors? If a statesman knows war, but does not know whether it is best to go to war, or at what juncture it is best—should we call him wise? If he knows how to kill men, or dispossess them, or drive them into exile,—but does not know upon whom, or on what occasions, it is good to inflict this treatment—is he a useful counsellor? If he can ride, or shoot, or wrestle, well,—we give him an epithet derived from this special accomplishment: we do not call him wise. What would be the condition of a community composed of bowmen, horsemen, wrestlers, rhetors, &c., accomplished and excellent each in his own particular craft, yet none of them knowing what is good, nor when, nor on what occasions, it is good to employ

---

[1] Plato, Alkib. ii. p. 144.

their craft? When each man pushes forward his own art and speciality, without any knowledge whether it is good on the whole either for himself or for the city, will not affairs thus conducted be reckless and disastrous?[1] *Alk.*—They will be very bad indeed.

Sokr.—If, then, a man has no knowledge of good or of the
Special ac- better—if upon this cardinal point he obeys fancy
complish- without reason—the possession of knowledge upon
ments, with-
out the special subjects will be oftener hurtful than profitable
knowledge
of the good to him; because it will make him more forward in
or profit- action, without any good result. Possessing many
able, are
oftener arts and accomplishments,—and prosecuting one after
hurtful another, but without the knowledge of good,—he will
than bene-
ficial. only fall into greater trouble, like a ship sailing
without a pilot. Knowledge of good is, in other words, knowledge of what is useful and profitable. In conjunction with this, all other knowledge is valuable, and goes to increase a man's competence as a counsellor: apart from this, all other knowledge will not render a man competent as a counsellor, but will be more frequently hurtful than beneficial.[2] Towards right living, what we need is, the knowledge of good: just as the sick stand in need of a physician, and the ship's crew of a pilot. *Alk.*—I admit your reasoning. My opinion is changed. I no longer believe myself competent to determine what I ought to accept from the Gods, or what I ought to pray for. I incur serious danger of erring, and of asking for mischiefs, under the belief that they are benefits.

Sokr.—The Lacedæmonians, when they offer sacrifice, pray
It is unsafe simply that they may obtain what is honourable and
for Alki-
biades to good, without farther specification. This language is

---

[1] Plato, Alkib. ii. p. 145.
[2] Plato, Alkib. ii. 145 C:
Ὅστις ἄρα τι τῶν τοιούτων οἶδεν, ἐὰν μὲν παρέπηται αὐτῷ ἡ τοῦ βελτίστου ἐπιστήμη—αὕτη δ' ἦν ἡ αὐτὴ δήπου ἥπερ καὶ ἡ τοῦ ὠφελίμου —φρόνιμόν γε αὐτὸν φήσομεν καὶ ἀποχρῶντα ξύμβουλον καὶ τῇ πόλει καὶ αὐτὸν αὑτῷ· τὸν δὲ μὴ τοιοῦτον, τἀναντία τούτων. (Τοιοῦτον is Schneider's emendation for ποιοῦντα.) Ibid. 146 C: Οὐκοῦν φαμὲν πάλιν τοὺς πολλοὺς διημαρτηκέναι τοῦ βελτίστου, ὡς τὰ πολλά γε,

οἶμαι, ἄνευ νοῦ δόξῃ πεπιστευκότας; Ibid. 146 E: Ὁρᾷς οὖν, ὅτε γ' ἔφην κινδυνεύειν τό γε τῶν ἄλλων ἐπιστημῶν κτῆμα, ἐάν τις ἄνευ τῆς τοῦ βελτίστου ἐπιστήμης κεκτημένος ᾖ, ὀλιγάκις μὲν ὠφελεῖν, βλάπτειν δὲ τὰ πλείω τὸν ἔχοντ' αὐτό. Ibid. 147 A: Ὁ δὲ δὴ τὴν καλουμένην πολυμάθειάν τε καὶ πολυτεχνίαν κεκτημένος, ὀρφανὸς δὲ ὢν ταύτης τῆς ἐπιστήμης, ἀγόμενος δὲ ὑπὸ μιᾶς ἑκάστης τῶν ἄλλων, ἆρ' οὐχὶ τῷ ὄντι δικαίως πολλῷ χειμῶνι χρήσεται, ἄτ', οἶμαι, ἄνευ κυβερνήτου διατελῶν ἐν πελάγει, &c.

CHAP. XII. KNOWLEDGE OF GOOD IS REQUIRED.

acceptable to the Gods, more acceptable than the costly festivals of Athens. It has procured for the Spartans more continued prosperity than the Athenians have enjoyed.[1] The Gods honour wise and just men,—that is, men who know what they ought to say and do both towards Gods and towards men— more than numerous and splendid offerings.[2] You see, therefore, that it is not safe for you to proceed with your sacrifice, until you have learnt what is the proper language to be used, and what are the really good gifts to be prayed for. Otherwise your sacrifice will not prove acceptable, and you may even bring upon yourself positive mischief.[3] *Alk.*—When shall I be able to learn this, and who is there to teach me? I shall be delighted to meet him. *Sokr.*—There is a person at hand most anxious for your improvement. What he must do is, first to disperse the darkness from your mind,—next, to impart that which will teach you to discriminate evil from good, which at present you are unable to do. *Alk.*—I shall shrink from no labour to accomplish this object. Until then, I postpone my intended sacrifice: and I tender my sacrificial wreath to you, in gratitude for your counsel.[4] *Sokr.*—I accept the wreath as a welcome augury of future friendship and conversation between us, to help us out of the present embarrassment.

proceed with his sacrifice, until he has learnt what is the proper language to address to the Gods. He renounces his sacrifice, and throws himself upon the counsel of Sokrates.

The two dialogues, called First and Second Alkibiadês, of which I have just given some account, resemble each other more than most of the Platonic dialogues, not merely in the personages introduced, but in general spirit, in subject, and even in illustrations. The First Alkibiadês was recognised as authentic by all critics without exception, until the days of Schleiermacher. Nay, it was not only recognised, but extolled as one of the most valuable and important of all the Platonic compositions; proper to be studied first, as a key to all the rest. Such was the view of

Different critical opinions respecting these two dialogues.

---

[1] Plato, Alkib. ii. p. 148.
[2] Plato, Alkib. ii. p. 150.
[3] Plato, Alkib. ii. p. 150.
[4] Plato, Alkib. ii. p. 151.

Jamblichus and Proklus, transmitted to modern times; until it received a harsh contradiction from Schleiermacher, who declared the dialogue to be both worthless and spurious. The Second Alkibiadês was also admitted both by Thrasyllus, and by the general body of critics in ancient times: but there were some persons (as we learn from Athenæus)[1] who considered it to be a work of Xenophon; perceiving probably (what is the fact) that it bears much analogy to several conversations which Xenophon has set down. But those who held this opinion are not to be considered as of one mind with critics who reject the dialogue as a forgery or imitation of Plato. Compositions emanating from Xenophon are just as much Sokratic, probably even more Sokratic, than the most unquestioned Platonic dialogues, besides that they must of necessity be contemporary also. Schleiermacher has gone much farther: declaring the Second as well as the First to be an unworthy imitation of Plato.[2]

Grounds for disallowing them—less strong against the Second than against the First.

Here Ast agrees with Schleiermacher fully, including both the First and Second Alkibiadês in his large list of the spurious. Most of the subsequent critics go with Schleiermacher only half-way: Socher, Hermann, Stallbaum, Steinhart, Susemihl, recognise the First Alkibiadês, but disallow the Second.[3] In my judgment, Schleiermacher and Ast are more consistently right, or more consistently wrong, in rejecting both, than the other critics who find or make so capital a distinction between the two. The similarity of tone and topics between the two is obvious, and is indeed admitted by all. Moreover, if I were compelled to make a choice, I should say that the grounds for suspicion are rather less strong against the Second than against the First; and that Schleiermacher, reasoning upon the objections admitted by his opponents as conclusive against the Second, would have no difficulty in showing that his own objections against the First were still more forcible. The long speech

---

[1] Athenæus, xi. p. 506.
[2] See the Einleitung of Schleiermacher to Alkib. i. part ii. vol. iii. p. 293 seq. Einleitung to Alkib. ii. part i. vol. ii. p. 365 seq. His notes on the two dialogues contain various additional reasons, besides what is urged in his Introduction.

[3] Socher, Ueber Platon's Schriften, p. 112. Stallbaum, Prolegg. to Alkib. i. and ii. vol. v. pp. 171-304. K. F. Hermann, Gesch. und Syst. der Platon. Philos. p. 420-439. Steinhart, Einleitungen to Alkib. i. and ii. in Hieronymus Müller's Uebersetzung des Platon's Werke, vol. i. pp. 135-509.

GENUINENESS OF THE DIALOGUES.

assigned in the First Alkibiadês to Sokrates, about the privileges of the Spartan and Persian kings,[1] including the mention of Zoroaster, son of Oromazes, and the Magian religion, appears to me more unusual with Plato than anything which I find in the Second Alkibiadês. It is more Xenophontic[2] than Platonic.

But I must here repeat, that because I find, in this or any other dialogue, some peculiarities not usual with Plato, I do not feel warranted thereby in declaring the dialogue spurious. In my judgment, we must look for a large measure of diversity in the various dialogues; and I think it an injudicious novelty, introduced by Schleiermacher, to set up a canonical type of Platonism, all deviations from which are to be rejected as forgeries. Both the First and the Second Alkibiadês appear to me genuine, even upon the showing of those very critics who disallow them. Schleiermacher, Stallbaum, and Steinhart, all admit that there is in both the dialogues a considerable proportion of Sokratic and Platonic ideas: but they maintain that there are also other ideas which are not Sokratic or Platonic, and that the texture, style, and prolixity of the Second Alkibiadês (Schleiermacher maintains this about the First also) are unworthy of Plato. But if we grant these premises, the reasonable inference would be, not to disallow it altogether, but to admit it as a work by Plato, of inferior merit; perhaps of earlier days, before his powers of composition had attained their maturity. To presume that because Plato composed many excellent dialogues, therefore all that he composed must have been excellent, —is a pretension formally disclaimed by many critics, and asserted by none.[3] Steinhart himself allows that the Second Alkibiadês, though not composed by Plato, is the work of some other author contemporary, an untrained Sokratic disciple attempting to imitate Plato.[4] But we do not know that there

The supposed grounds for disallowance are in reality only marks of inferiority.

---

[1] Plato, Alkib. i. p. 121-124.
Whoever reads the objections in Steinhart's Einleitung (p. 148-150) against the First Alkibiadês, will see that they are quite as forcible as what he urges against the Second; only, that in the case of the First, he gives to these objections their legitimate bearing, allowing them to tell against the merit of the dialogue, but not against its authenticity.

[2] See Xenoph. Œkonom. c. 4; Cyropæd. vii. 5, 58-64, viii. 1, 5-8-45; Laced. Repub. c. 15.

[3] Stallbaum (Prolegg. ad Alcib. i. p. 186) makes this general statement very justly, but he as well as other critics are apt to forget it in particular cases.

[4] Steinhart, Einleitung, p. 516-519. Stallbaum and Boeckh indeed assign the dialogue to a later period. Hein-

were any contemporaries who tried to imitate Plato: though Theopompus accused him of imitating others, and called most of his dialogues useless as well as false: while Plato himself, in his inferior works, will naturally appear like an imitator of his better self.

I agree with Schleiermacher and the other recent critics in considering the First and Second Alkibiadês to be inferior in merit to Plato's best dialogues; and I contend that their own premisses justify no more. They may probably be among his earlier productions, though I do not believe that the First Alkibiadês was composed during the lifetime of Sokrates, as Socher, Steinhart, and Stallbaum endeavour to show.[1] I have already given my

The two dialogues may probably be among Plato's earlier compositions.

---

[1] Stallbaum refers the composition of Alkib. i. to a time not long before the accusation of Sokrates, when the enemies of Sokrates were calumniating him in consequence of his past intimacy with Alkibiades (who had before that time been killed in 404 B.C.) and when Plato was anxious to defend his master (Prolegg. p. 186). Socher and Steinhart (p. 210) remark that such writings would do little good to Sokrates under his accusation. They place the composition of the dialogue earlier, in 406 B.C. (Steinhart, p. 151-

derf (ad Lysin, p. 211) thinks it the work "antiqui auctoris, sed non Platonis".

Steinhart and others who disallow the authenticity of the Second Alkibiadês, insist much (p. 518) upon the enormity of the chronological blunder, whereby Sokrates and Alkibiadês are introduced as talking about the death of Archelaus king of Macedonia, who was killed in 399 B.C., in the same year as Sokrates, and four years after Alkibiades. Such an anachronism (Steinhart urges) Plato could never allow himself to commit. But when we read the Symposion, we find Aristophanes in a company of which Sokrates, Alkibiades, and Agathon form a part, alluding to the διοίκισις of Mantineia, which took place in 386 B.C. No one has ever made this glaring anachronism a ground for disallowing the Symposion. Steinhart says that the style of the Second Alkibiadês copies Plato too closely (die ängstlich platonisirende Sprache des Dialogs, p. 515), yet he agrees with Stallbaum that in several places it departs too widely from Plato.

152), and they consider it the first exercise of Plato in the strict dialectic method. Both Steinhart and Hermann (Gesch. Plat. Phil. p. 440) think that the dialogue has not only a speculative but a political purpose; to warn and amend Alkibiades, and to prevent him from surrendering himself blindly to the democracy.

I cannot admit the hypothesis that the dialogue was written in 406 B.C. (when Plato was twenty-one years of age, at most twenty-two), nor that it had any intended bearing upon the real historical Alkibiades, who left Athens in 415 B.C. at the head of the armament against Syracuse, was banished three months afterwards, and never came back to Athens until May 407 B.C. (Xenoph. Hellen. i. 4, 13; i. 5, 17). He then enjoyed four months of great ascendancy at Athens, left it at the head of the fleet to Asia in Oct. 407 B.C., remained in command of the fleet for about three months or so, then fell into disgrace and retired to Chersonese, never revisiting Athens. In 406 B.C. Alkibiades was again in banishment, out of the reach of all such warnings as Hermann and Steinhart suppose that Plato intended to address to him in Alkib. i.

Steinhart says (p. 152), "In dieser Zeit also, *wenige Jahre nach seiner triumphirenden Rückkehr*, wo Alkibiades," &c. Now Alkibiades left the Athenian service, irrevocably, within less *than one year* after his triumphant return.

Steinhart has not realised in his mind the historical and chronological conditions of the period.

reasons, in a previous chapter, for believing that Plato composed no dialogues at all during the lifetime of Sokrates; still less in that of Alkibiadês, who died four years earlier. There is certainly nothing in either Alkibiadês I. or II. to shake this belief.

If we compare various colloquies of Sokrates in the Xenophontic Memorabilia, we shall find Alkibiadês I. and II. very analogous to them both in purpose and spirit. In Alkibiadês I. the situation conceived is the same as that of Sokrates and Glaukon, in the third book of the Memorabilia. Xenophon recounts how the presumptuous Glaukon, hardly twenty years of age, fancied himself already fit to play a conspicuous part in public affairs, and tried to force himself, in spite of rebuffs and humiliations, upon the notice of the assembly.[1] {*margin:* Analogy with various dialogues in the Xenophontic Memorabilia—Purpose of Sokrates to humble presumptuous young men.}
No remonstrances of friends could deter him, nor could anything, except the ingenious dialectic of Sokrates, convince him of his own impertinent forwardness and exaggerated self-estimation. Probably Plato (Glaukon's elder brother) had heard of this conversation, but whether the fact be so or not, we see the same situation idealised by him in Alkibiadês I., and worked out in a way of his own. Again, we find in the Xenophontic Memorabilia another colloquy, wherein Sokrates cross-questions, perplexes, and humiliates, the studious youth Euthydemus,[2] whom he regards as over-confident in his persuasions and too well satisfied with himself. It was among the specialties of Sokrates to humiliate confident young men, with a view to their future improvement. He made his conversation "an instrument of chastisement," in the language of Xenophon: or (to use a phrase of Plato himself in the Lysis) he conceived "that the proper way of talking to youth whom you love, was, not to exalt and puff them up, but to subdue and humiliate them".[3]

If Plato wished to idealise this feature in the character of

---

[1] Xenoph. Memor. iii. 6.
[2] Xenoph. Mem. iv. 2.
[3] Xenoph. Mem. i. 4, 1. σκεψάμενοι μὴ μόνον ἃ ἐκεῖνος (Sokrates) κολαστηρίου ἕνεκα τοὺς πάντ' οἰομένους εἰδέναι ἐρωτῶν ἤλεγχεν, ἀλλὰ καὶ ἃ λέγων συνημέρευε τοῖς συνδιατρίβουσιν, &c. So in the Platonic Lysis, the youthful Lysis says to Sokrates, "Talk to Menexenus, ἵν' αὐτὸν κολάσῃς" (Plat. Lysis, 211 B). And Sokrates himself says, a few lines before (210 E), Οὕτω χρὴ τοῖς παιδικοῖς διαλέγεσθαι, ταπεινοῦντα καὶ συστέλλοντα, καὶ μὴ ὥσπερ σὺ χαυνοῦντα καὶ διαθρύπτοντα.

Fitness of the name and character of Alkibiades for idealising this feature in Sokrates. Sokrates, no name could be more suitable to his purpose than that of Alkibiadês: who, having possessed as a youth the greatest personal beauty (to which Sokrates was exquisitely sensible) had become in his mature life distinguished not less for unprincipled ambition and insolence, than for energy and ability. We know the real Alkibiadês both from Thucydides and Xenophon, and we also know that Alkibiades had in his youth so far frequented the society of Sokrates as to catch some of that dialectic ingenuity, which the latter was expected and believed to impart.[1] The contrast, as well as the companionship, between Sokrates and Alkibiades was eminently suggestive to the writers of Sokratic dialogues, and nearly all of them made use of it, composing dialogues in which Alkibiades was the principal name and figure.[2] It would be surprising indeed if Plato had never done the same: which is what we must suppose, if we adopt Schleiermacher's view, that both Alkibiadês I. and II. are spurious. In the Protagoras as well as in the Symposion, Alkibiades figures; but in neither of them is he the principal person, or titular hero, of the piece. In Alkibiadês I. and II., he is introduced as the solitary respondent to the questions of Sokrates —κολαστηρίου ἕνεκα: to receive from Sokrates a lesson of humiliation such as the Xenophontic Sokrates administers to Glaukon and Euthydemus, taking care to address the latter when alone.[3]

Plato's manner of I conceive Alkibiadês I. and II. as composed by Plato among his earlier writings (perhaps between 399-390 B.C.)[4] giving an imaginary picture of the way in which

---

[1] The sensibility of Sokrates to youthful beauty is as strongly declared in the Xenophontic Memorabilia (i. 3, 8-14), as in the Platonic Lysis, Charmidês, or Symposion.
The conversation reported by Xenophon between Alkibiades, when not yet twenty years of age, and his guardian Periklês, the first man in Athens—wherein Alkibiades puzzles Periklês by a Sokratic cross-examination—is likely enough to be real, and was probably the fruit of his society with Sokrates (Xen. Memor. i. 2, 40).
[2] Stallbaum observes (Prolegg. ad Alcib. i. p. 215, 2nd ed.), "Ceterum etiam Æschines, Euclides, Phædon, et Antisthenes, dialogos *Alcibiadis* nomine inscriptos composuisse narrantur".
Respecting the dialogues composed by Æschines, see the first note to this chapter.
[3] Xenoph. Mem. iv. 2, 8.
[4] The date which I here suppose for the composition of Alkib. i. (*i.e.* after the death of Sokrates, but early in the literary career of Plato), is farther sustained (against those critics who place it in 406 B.C. or 402 B.C. before the death of Sokrates) by the long discourse (p. 121-124) of Sokrates about

CHAP. XII.   FITNESS OF THE NAME.

Sokrates handled every respondent just as he chose" (to use the literal phrase of Xenophon[1]): taming even that most overbearing youth, whom Aristophanes characterises as the lion's whelp.[2] In selecting Alkibiades as the sufferer under such a chastising process, Plato rebuts in his own ideal style that charge which Xenophon answers with prosaic directness— the charge made against Sokrates by his enemies, that he taught political craft without teaching ethical sobriety; and that he had encouraged by his training the lawless propensities of Alkibiades.[3] When Schleiermacher, and others who disallow the dialogue, argue that the inordinate insolence ascribed to Alkibiades, and the submissive deference towards Sokrates also ascribed to him, are incongruous and incompatible attributes,— I reply that such a conjunction is very improbable in any real character. But this does not hinder Plato from combining them in one and the same ideal character, as we shall farther see when we come to the manifestation of Alkibiades in the Symposion:

replying to the accusers of Sokrates. Magical influence ascribed to the conversation of Sokrates.

the Persian and Spartan kings. In reference to the Persian monarchy Sokrates says (p. 122 B), ἐπεί ποτ' ἐγὼ ἤκουσα ἀνδρὸς ἀξιοπίστου τῶν ἀναβεβηκότων παρὰ βασιλέα, ὃς ἔφη παρελθεῖν χώραν πάνυ πολλὴν καὶ ἀγαθήν— ἣν καλεῖν τοὺς ἐπιχωρίους ζώνην τῆς βασιλέως γυναικός, &c. Olympiodorus and the Scholiast both suppose that Plato here refers to Xenophon and the Anabasis, in which a statement very like this is found (i. 4, 9). It is plain, therefore, that *they* did not consider the dialogue to have been composed before the death of Sokrates. I think it very probable that Plato had in his mind Xenophon (either his Anabasis, or personal communications with him); but at any rate visits of Greeks to the Persian court became very numerous between 399-390 B.C., whereas Plato can hardly have seen any such visitors at Athens in 406 B.C. (before the close of the war), nor probably in 402 B.C., when Athens, though relieved from the oligarchy, was still in a state of great public prostration. Between 399 B.C. and the peace of Antalkidas (387 B.C.), visitors from Greece to the interior of Persia became more and more frequent, the Persian kings interfering very actively in Grecian politics. Plato may easily have seen during these years intelligent Greeks who had been up to the Persian court on military or political business. Both the Persian kings and the Spartan kings were then in the maximum of power and ascendancy—it is no wonder therefore that Sokrates should here be made to dwell upon their prodigious dignity in his discourse with Alkibiades. Steinhart (Einl. p. 150) feels the difficulty of reconciling this part of the dialogue with his hypothesis that it was composed in 406 B.C.: yet he and Stallbaum both insist that it *must* have been composed before the death of Sokrates, for which they really produce no grounds at all.

[1] Xen. Mem. i. 2, 14. τοῖς δὲ διαλεγομένοις αὐτῷ πᾶσι χρώμενον ἐν τοῖς λόγοις ὅπως βούλοιτο.

[2] Aristoph. Ran. 1431. οὐ χρὴ λέοντος σκύμνον ἐν πόλει τρέφειν. Thucyd. vi. 15. φοβηθέντες γὰρ αὐτοῦ (Alkib.) οἱ πολλοὶ τὸ μέγεθος τῆς τε κατὰ τὸ ἑαυτοῦ σῶμα παρανομίας ἐς τὴν δίαιταν, καὶ τῆς διανοίας ὧν καθ' ἓν ἕκαστον, ἐν ὅτῳ γίγνοιτο, ἔπρασσεν, ὡς τυραννίδος ἐπιθυμοῦντι πολέμιοι καθέστασαν, &c.

[3] Xenoph. Memorab. i. 2, 17.

in which dialogue we find a combination of the same elements, still more extravagant and high-coloured. Both here and there we are made to see that Sokrates, far from encouraging Alkibiades, is the only person who ever succeeded in humbling him. Plato attributes to the personality and conversation of Sokrates an influence magical and almost superhuman: which Cicero and Plutarch, proceeding probably upon the evidence of the Platonic dialogues, describe as if it were historical fact. They represent Alkibiades as shedding tears of sorrow and shame, and entreating Sokrates to rescue him from a sense of degradation insupportably painful.[1] Now Xenophon mentions Euthydemus and other young men as having really experienced these profound and distressing emotions.[2] But he does not at all certify the same about Alkibiades, whose historical career is altogether adverse to the hypothesis. The Platonic picture is an *idéal*, drawn from what may have been actually true about other interlocutors of Sokrates, and calculated to reply to Melêtus and his allies.

Looking at Alkibiadês I. and II. in this point of view, we shall find both of them perfectly Sokratic both in topics and in manner—whatever may be said about unnecessary prolixity and common-place here and there. The leading ideas of Alkibiadês I. may be found, nearly all, in the Platonic Apology. That warfare, which Sokrates proclaims in the Apology as having been the mission of his life, against the false persuasion of knowledge, or against beliefs ethical and æsthetical, firmly entertained without having been preceded by conscious study or subjected to serious examination—is exemplified in Alkibiadês I. and II. as emphatically as in any Platonic composition. In both these dialogues, indeed (especially in the first), we find an excessive repetition of specialising illustrations, often needless and sometimes tiresome: a defect easily intelligible if we assume them to have been written when Plato was still a novice in the art of dialogic composition. But both dialogues are fully impregnated with the spirit of the Sokratic process, exposing, though with exuberant prolixity, the

The purpose proclaimed by Sokrates in the Apology is followed out in Alkib. I. Warfare against the false persuasion of knowledge.

---

[1] Cicero, Tusc. Disp. iii. 32, 77; Plutarch, Alkib. c. 4-6. Compare Plato, Alkib. i. p. 127 D, 135 C; Symposion, p. 215-216.
[2] Xenoph. Memor. iv. 2, 39-40.

CHAP. XII.   PURPOSE OF THE DIALOGUE.   25

firm and universal belief, held and affirmed by every one even at the age of boyhood, without any assignable grounds or modes of acquisition, and amidst angry discordance between the affirmation of one man and another. The emphasis too with which Sokrates insists upon his own single function of merely questioning, and upon the fact that Alkibiades gives all the answers and pronounces all the self-condemnation with his own mouth[1]—is remarkable in this dialogue: as well as the confidence with which he proclaims the dialogue as affording the only, but effective, cure.[2] The ignorance of which Alkibiades stands unexpectedly convicted, is expressly declared to be common to him with the other Athenian politicians: an exception being half allowed to pass in favour of the semi-philosophical Perikles, whom Plato judges here with less severity than elsewhere[3]— and a decided superiority being claimed for the Spartan and Persian kings, who are extolled as systematically trained from childhood.

The main purpose of Sokrates is to drive Alkibiades into self-contradictions, and to force upon him a painful consciousness of ignorance and mental defect, upon grave and important subjects, while he is yet young enough to amend it. Towards this purpose he is made to lay claim to a divine mission similar to that which the real Sokrates announces in the Apology.[4] A number of perplexing questions and difficulties are accumulated: it is not meant that these difficulties are insoluble, but that they cannot be solved by one who has never seriously reflected on them—by one who (as the Xenophontic Sokrates says to Euthydemus),[5] is so confident of knowing the subject that he has never meditated upon it at all. The disheartened Alkibiades feels the necessity of improving himself and supplicates the assistance of Sokrates: who reminds him that he must first determine what "Himself" is. Here again we find ourselves upon the track of Sokrates in the Platonic Apology, and under the influence of the memorable inscription at Delphi—*Nosce teipsum*. Your mind is yourself: your body is a mere instrument of your

Difficulties multiplied for the purpose of bringing Alkibiades to a conviction of his own ignorance.

[1] Plato, Alkib. i. p. 112-113.
[2] Plato, Alkib. i. p. 127 E.
[3] Plato, Alkib. i. p. 118-120.
[4] Plato, Alkib. i. p. 124 C—127 E.
[5] Xenoph. Mem. iv. 2, 36. Ἀλλὰ ταῦτα μέν, ἔφη ὁ Σωκράτης, ἴσως, διὰ τὸ σφόδρα πιστεύειν εἰδέναι, οὐδ' ἔσκεψαι.
[6] Plato, Alkib. i. p. 128-132 A.

mind: your wealth and power are simple appurtenances or adjuncts. To know yourself, which is genuine Sophrosynê or temperance, is to know your mind: but this can only be done by looking into another mind, and into its most intelligent compartment: just as the eye can only see itself by looking into the centre of vision of another eye.[1]

At the same time, when, after having convicted Alkibiades of deplorable ignorance, Sokrates is called upon to prescribe remedies—all distinctness of indication disappears. It is exacted only when the purpose is to bring difficulties and contradictions to view: it is dispensed with, when the purpose is to solve them. The conclusion is, that assuming happiness as the acknowledged ultimate end,[2] Alkibiades cannot secure this either for himself or for his city, by striving for wealth and power, private or public: he can only secure it by acquiring for himself, and implanting in his countrymen, justice, temperance, and virtue. This is perfectly Sokratic, and conformable to what is said by the real Sokrates in the Platonic Apology. But coming at the close of Alkibiadês I., it presents no meaning and imparts no instruction: because Sokrates had shown in the earlier part of the dialogue, that neither he himself, nor Alkibiades, nor the general public, knew what justice and virtue were. The positive solution which Sokrates professes to give, is therefore illusory. He throws us back upon those old, familiar, emotional, associations, unconscious products and unexamined transmissions from mind to mind— which he had already shown to represent the fancy of knowledge without the reality—deep-seated belief without any assignable intellectual basis, or outward standard of rectitude.

Sokrates furnishes no means of solving these difficulties. He exhorts to Justice and Virtue—but these are acknowledged Incognita.

Throughout the various Platonic dialogues, we find alternately two distinct and opposite methods of handling—the generalising of the special, and the specialising of the general. In Alkibiadês I., the specialising of the general preponderates—as it does in most of the conversations of the Xenophontic Memorabilia: the

Prolixity of Alkibiadês I.—Extreme multiplication of illustrative examples—

---

[1] Plato, Alkib. i. p. 133. A Platonic metaphor, illustrating the necessity for two separate minds co-operating in dialectic colloquy.
[2] Plat. Alkibiad. i. p. 134.

number of exemplifying particulars is unusually great. Sokrates does not accept as an answer a general term, without illustrating it by several of the specific terms comprehended under it: and this several times on occasions when an instructed reader thinks it superfluous and tiresome: hence, partly, the inclination of some modern critics to disallow the dialogue. But we must recollect that though a modern reader practised in the use of general terms may seize the meaning at once, an Athenian youth of the Platonic age would not be sure of doing the same. No conscious analysis had yet been applied to general terms: no grammar or logic then entered into education. Confident affirmation, without fully knowing the meaning of what is affirmed, is the besetting sin against which Plato here makes war: and his precautions for exposing it are pushed to extreme minuteness. So, too, in the Sophistês and Politikus, when he wishes to illustrate the process of logical division and subdivision, he applies it to cases so trifling and so multiplied, that Socher is revolted and rejects the dialogues altogether. But Plato himself foresees and replies to the objection; declaring expressly that his main purpose is, not to expound the particular subject chosen, but to make manifest and familiar the steps and conditions of the general classifying process—and that prolixity cannot be avoided.[1] We must reckon upon a similar purpose in Alkibiadês I. The dialogue is a specimen of that which Aristotle calls Inductive Dialectic, as distinguished from Syllogistic: the Inductive he considers to be plainer and easier, suitable when you have an ordinary collocutor—the Syllogistic is the more cogent, when you are dealing with a practised disputant.[2]

How explained.

It has been seen that Alkibiadês I., though professing to give something like a solution, gives what is really no solution at all. Alkibiadês II., similar in many respects, is here different, inasmuch as it does not even profess to solve the difficulty which had been raised. The general mental defect—false persuasion of know-

Alkibiadês II. leaves its problem avowedly undetermined.

---

[1] Plato, Politikus, 285-286.
Aristotel. Topic. i. 104, a. 16. Πόσα τῶν λόγων εἴδη τῶν διαλεκτικῶν —ἔστι δὲ τὸ μὲν ἐπαγωγή, τὸ δὲ συλλογισμός .... ἔστι δ' ἡ μὲν ἐπα- γωγὴ πιθανώτερον καὶ σαφέστερον καὶ κατὰ τὴν αἴσθησιν γνωριμώτερον καὶ τοῖς πολλοῖς κοινόν· ὁ δὲ συλλογισμὸς βιαστικώτερον καὶ πρὸς τοὺς ἀντιλογικοὺς ἐνεργέστερον.

ledge without the reality—is presented in its application to a particular case. Alkibiades is obliged to admit that he does not know what he ought to pray to the Gods for: neither what is *good*, to be granted, nor what is *evil*, to be averted. He relies upon Sokrates for dispelling this mist from his mind: which Sokrates promises to do, but adjourns for another occasion.

Sokrates here ascribes to the Spartans, and to various philo-sophers, the practice of putting up prayers in unde-fined language, for good and honourable things gene-rally. He commends that practice. Xenophon tells us that the historical Sokrates observed it:[1] but he tells us also that the historical Sokrates, though not praying for any special presents from the Gods, yet prayed for and believed himself to receive special revelations and advice as to what was good to be done or avoided in particular cases. He held that these special revelations were essential to any tolerable life: that the dispensations of the Gods, though administered upon regular principles on certain sub-jects and up to a certain point, were kept by them designedly inscrutable beyond that point: but that the Gods would, if properly solicited, afford premonitory warnings to any favoured person, such as would enable him to keep out of the way of evil, and put himself in the way of good. He declared that to consult and obey oracles and prophets was not less a maxim of prudence than a duty of piety: for himself, he was farther privileged through his divine sign or monitor, which he implicitly fol-lowed.[2] Such premonitory warnings were the only special favour which he thought it suitable to pray for—besides good things generally. For special presents he did not pray, because he professed not to know whether any of the ordinary objects of desire were good or bad. He proves in his conversation with Euthydêmus, that all those acquisitions which are usually accounted means of happiness—beauty, strength, wealth, reputa-

Sokrates commends the practice of praying to the Gods for favours undefined— His views about the semi-regu-lar, semi-irregular agency of the Gods— He prays to them for premonitory warnings.

---

[1] Xenoph. Mem. i. 3, 2; Plat. Alk. ii. p. 143-148.
[2] These opinions of Sokrates are announced in various passages of the Xenophontic Memorabilia, i. 1, 1-10— ἔφη δὲ δεῖν, ἃ μὲν μαθόντας ποιεῖν ἔδωκαν οἱ θεοί, μανθάνειν· ἃ δὲ μὴ δῆλα τοῖς ἀνθρώποις ἐστί, πειρᾶσθαι διὰ μαν-τικῆς παρὰ τῶν θεῶν πυνθάνεσθαι· τοὺς θεοὺς γάρ, οἷς ἂν ὦσιν ἵλεῳ, σημαίνειν —i. 3, 4; i. 4, 2-15; iv. 3, 12; iv. 7, 10 iv. 8, 5-11.

CHAP. XII.   PRAYER AND SACRIFICE.   29

tion, nay, even good health and wisdom—are sometimes good or causes of happiness, sometimes evil or causes of misery; and therefore cannot be considered either as absolutely the one or absolutely the other.[1]

This impossibility of determining what is good and what is evil, in consequence of the uncertainty in the dispensations of the Gods and in human affairs—is a doctrine forcibly insisted on by the Xenophontic Sokrates in his discourse with Euthydêmus, and much akin to the Platonic Alkibiadês II., being applied to the special case of prayer. But we must not suppose that Sokrates adheres to this doctrine throughout all the colloquies of the Xenophontic Memorabilia: on the contrary, we find him, in other places, reasoning upon such matters, as health, strength, and wisdom, as if they were decidedly good.[2] The fact is, that the arguments of Sokrates, in the Xenophontic Memorabilia, vary materially according to the occasion and the person with whom he is discoursing: and the case is similar with the Platonic dialogues: illustrating farther the questionable evidence on which Schleiermacher and other critics proceed, when they declare one dialogue to be spurious, because it contains reasoning inconsistent with another. *Comparison of Alkibiadês II. with the Xenophontic Memorabilia, especially the conversation of Sokrates with Euthydemus. Sokrates not always consistent with himself.*

We find in Alkibiadês II. another doctrine which is also proclaimed by Sokrates in the Xenophontic Memorabilia: that the Gods are not moved by costly sacrifice more than by humble sacrifice, according to the circumstances of the offerer:[3] they attend only to the mind of the offerer, whether he be just and wise: that is, "whether he knows what ought to be done both towards Gods and towards men".[4]

But we find also in Alkibiadês II. another doctrine, more remarkable. Sokrates will not proclaim absolutely that knowledge is good, and that ignorance is evil. In some cases, he contends, ignorance is good; and he discriminates which the cases are. That which we *Remarkable doctrine of Alkibiadês II.—That knowledge*

---

[1] Xenoph. Memor. iv. 2, 31-32-36. Ταῦτα οὖν ποτὲ μὲν ὠφελοῦντα ποτὲ δὲ βλάπτοντα, τί μᾶλλον ἀγαθὰ ἢ κακά ἐστιν;
[2] For example, Xen. Mem. iv. 5, 6
—σοφίαν τὸ μέγιστον ἀγαθόν, &c.
[3] Plato, Alkib. ii. p. 149-150; Xen. Mem. i. 3. Compare Plato, Legg. x. p. 885; Isokrat. ad Nikok.
[4] Plato, Alkib. ii. p. 149 E, 150 B.

is not always Good. The knowledge of Good itself is indispensable; without that, the knowledge of other things is more hurtful than beneficial.

are principally interested in knowing, is *Good*, or The *Best*—The *Profitable*:[1] phrases used as equivalent. The knowledge of this is good, and the ignorance of it mischievous, under all supposable circumstances. And if a man knows good, the more he knows of everything else, the better; since he will be sure to make a good use of his knowledge. But if he does not know good, the knowledge of other things will be hurtful rather than beneficial to him. To be skilful in particular arts and accomplishments, under the capital mental deficiency supposed, will render him an instrument of evil and not of good. The more he knows—and the more he believes himself to know—the more forward will he be in acting, and therefore the greater amount of harm will he do. It is better that he should act as little as possible. Such a man is not fit to direct his own conduct, like a freeman: he must be directed and controlled by others, like a slave. The greater number of mankind are fools of this description— ignorant of good: the wise men who know good, and are fit to direct, are very few. The wise man alone, knowing good, follows reason: the rest trust to opinion, without reason.[2] He alone is competent to direct both his own conduct and that of the society.

The stress which is laid here upon the knowledge of good, as distinguished from all other varieties of knowledge—the identification of the good with the profitable, and of the knowledge of good with reason (νοῦς), while other varieties of knowledge are ranked with opinion (δόξα)—these are points which, under one phraseology or another, pervade many of the Platonic dialogues. The old phrase of Herakleitus—Πολυμαθίη νόον οὐ διδάσκει— "much learning does not teach reason"—seems to have been present to the mind of Plato in composing this dialogue. The man of much learning and art, without the knowledge of good, and surrendering himself to the guidance of one or other among

---

[1] Plato, Alkib. ii. p. 145 C. Ὅστις ἄρα τι τῶν τοιούτων οἶδεν, ἐὰν μὲν παρέπηται αὐτῷ ἡ τοῦ βελτίστου ἐπιστήμη—αὕτη δ᾽ ἦν ἡ αὐτὴ δήπου ἥπερ καὶ ἡ τοῦ ὠφελίμου—also 146 B.

[2] Plato, Alk. ii. p. 146 A-D. ἄνευ νοῦ δόξῃ πεπιστευκότας.

"GOOD" EXTOLLED BUT NOT DEFINED.

his accomplishments, is like a vessel tossed about at sea without a pilot.[1]

What Plato here calls the knowledge of Good, or Reason— the just discrimination and comparative appreciation of Ends and Means—appears in the Politikus and Euthydêmus, under the title of the Regal or Political Art, of employing or directing[2] the results of all other arts, which are considered as subordinate: in the Protagoras, under the title of art of calculation or mensuration: in the Philêbus, as measure and proportion: in the Phædrus (in regard to rhetoric) as the art of turning to account, for the main purpose of persuasion, all the special processes, stratagems, decorations, &c., imparted by professional masters. In the Republic, it is personified in the few venerable Elders who constitute the Reason of the society, and whose directions all the rest (Guardians and Producers) are bound implicitly to follow: the virtue of the subordinates consisting in this implicit obedience. In the Leges, it is defined as the complete subjection in the mind, of pleasures and pains to right Reason,[3] without which, no special aptitudes are worth having. In the Xenophontic Memorabilia, it stands as a Sokratic authority under the title of Sophrosynê or Temperance:[4] and the Profitable is declared identical with the Good, as the directing and limiting principle for all human pursuits and proceedings.[5]

Knowledge of Good— appears postulated and divined, in many of the Platonic dialogues, under different titles.

But what are we to understand by the *Good*, about which there are so many disputes, according to the acknowledgment of Plato as well as of Sokrates? And what are we to understand by the Profitable? In what relation does it stand to the Pleasurable and the Painful?

The Good— The Profitable—What is it? How are we to know it? Plato leaves this undetermined.

These are points which Plato here leaves undetermined. We shall find him again touching them, and trying different ways of determining them, in the Protagoras, the Gorgias, the Republic,

---

[1] Plato, Alkib. ii. p. 147 A. ὁ δὲ δὴ τὴν καλουμένην πολυμάθειάν τε καὶ πολυτεχνίαν κεκτημένος, ὀρφανὸς δὲ ὢν ταύτης τῆς ἐπιστήμης, ἀγόμενος δὲ ὑπὸ μιᾶς ἑκάστης τῶν ἄλλων, &c.
[2] Plato, Politikus, 292 B, 304 B,
305 A; Euthydêmus, 291 B, 292 B. Compare Xenophon, Œkonomicus, i. 8, 13.
[3] Leges, iii. 689 A-D, 691 A.
[4] Xenoph. Memor. i. 2, 17; iv. 3, 1.
[5] Xenoph. Memor. iv. 6, 8; iv. 7, 7.

and elsewhere. We have here the title and the postulate, but nothing more, of a comprehensive Teleology, or right comparative estimate of ends and means one against another, so as to decide when, how far, under what circumstances, &c., each ought to be pursued. We shall see what Plato does in other dialogues to connect this title and postulate with a more definite meaning.

CHAPTER XIII.

HIPPIAS MAJOR—HIPPIAS MINOR.

BOTH these two dialogues are carried on between Sokrates and the Eleian Sophist Hippias. The general conception of Hippias—described as accomplished, eloquent, and successful, yet made to say vain and silly things—is the same in both dialogues: in both also the polemics of Sokrates against him are conducted in a like spirit, of affected deference mingled with insulting sarcasm. Indeed the figure assigned to Hippias is so contemptible, that even an admiring critic like Stallbaum cannot avoid noticing the "petulans pene et proterva in Hippiam oratio," and intimating that Plato has handled Hippias more coarsely than any one else. Such petulance Stallbaum attempts to excuse by saying that the dialogue is a youthful composition of Plato:[1] while Schleiermacher numbers it among the

Hippias Major— Situation supposed— Character of the dialogue. Sarcasm and mockery against Hippias.

---

[1] Stallbaum, Prolegg. in Hipp. Maj. p. 149-150; also Steinhart (Einleitung, p. 42-43), who says, after an outpouring of his usual invective against the Sophist:—" Nevertheless the coarse jesting of the dialogue seems almost to exceed the admissible limit of comic effect," &c. Again, p. 50, Steinhart talks of the banter which Sokrates carries on with Hippias, in a way not less cruel (grausam) than purposeless, tormenting him with a string of successive new propositions about the definition of the Beautiful, which propositions, as fast as Hippias catches at them, he again withdraws of his own accord, and thus at last dismisses him (as he had dismissed Ion) uninstructed and unimproved, without even leaving behind in him the sting of anger, &c.

It requires a powerful hatred against the persons called Sophists, to make a critic take pleasure in a comedy wherein silly and ridiculous speeches are fastened upon the name of one of them, in his own day not merely honoured but acknowledged as deserving honour by remarkable and varied accomplishments—and to make the critic describe the historical Hippias (whom we only know from Plato and Xenophon—see Steinhart, note 7. p. 89; Socher, p. 221) as if he had really delivered these speeches, or something equally absurd.

How this comedy may be appreciated is doubtless a matter of individual taste. For my part, I agree with Ast in thinking it misplaced and unbecoming: and I am not surprised that he wishes to remove the dialogue from the Platonic canon, though I do not concur either in this inference, or in the general principle on which it proceeds,

reasons for suspecting the dialogue, and Ast, among the reasons for declaring positively that Plato is not the author.[1] This last conclusion I do not at all accept: nor even the hypothesis of Stallbaum, if it be tendered as an excuse for improprieties of tone: for I believe that the earliest of Plato's dialogues was composed after he was twenty-eight years of age—that is, after the death of Sokrates. It is however noway improbable, that both the Greater and Lesser Hippias may have been among Plato's earlier compositions. We see by the Memorabilia of Xenophon that there was repeated and acrimonious controversy between Sokrates and Hippias: so that we may probably suppose feelings of special dislike, determining Plato to compose two distinct dialogues, in which an imaginary Hippias is mocked and scourged by an imaginary Sokrates.

One considerable point in the Hippias Major appears to have a bearing on the debate between Sokrates and Hippias in the Xenophontic Memorabilia: in which debate, Hippias taunts Sokrates with always combating and deriding the opinions of others, while evading to give opinions of his own. It appears that some antecedent debates between the two had turned upon the definition of the Just, and that on these occasions Hippias had been the respondent, Sokrates the objector.

Real debate between the historical Sokrates and Hippias in the Xenophontic Memorabilia—Subject of that debate.

Hippias professes to have reflected upon these debates, and to be now prepared with a definition which neither Sokrates nor any one else can successfully assail, but he will not say what the definition is, until Sokrates has laid down one of his own. In reply to this challenge, Sokrates declares the Just to be equivalent to the Lawful or Customary: he defends this against various

viz., that all objections against the composition of a dialogue are to be held as being also objections against its genuineness as a work of Plato. The Nubes of Aristophanes, greatly superior as a comedy to the Hippias of Plato, is turned to an abusive purpose when critics put it into court as evidence about the character of the real Sokrates.

K. F. Hermann, in my judgment, takes a more rational view of the Hippias Major (Gesch. und Syst. der Plat. Phil. p. 487-647). Instead of expatiating on the glory of Plato in deriding an accomplished contemporary, he dwells upon the logical mistakes and confusion which the dialogue brings to view; and he reminds us justly of the intellectual condition of the age, when even elementary distinctions in logic and grammar had been scarcely attended to.

Both K. F. Hermann and Socher consider the Hippias to be not a juvenile production of Plato, but to belong to his middle age.

[1] Schleierm. Einleitung. p. 401; Ast, Platon's Leben und Schriften, p. 457-459.

objections of Hippias, who concludes by admitting it.[1] Probably this debate, as reported by Xenophon, or something very like it, really took place. If so, we remark with surprise the feebleness of the objections of Hippias, in a case where Sokrates, if he had been the objector, would have found such strong ones—and the feeble replies given by Sokrates, whose talent lay in starting and enforcing difficulties, not in solving them.[2] Among the remarks which Sokrates makes in illustration to Hippias, one is—that Lykurgus had ensured superiority to Sparta by creating in the Spartans a habit of implicit obedience to the laws.[3] Such is the character of the Xenophontic debate.

Here, in the beginning of the Hippias Major, the Platonic Sokrates remarks that Hippias has been long absent from Athens: which absence, the latter explains, by saying that he has visited many cities in Greece, giving lectures with great success, and receiving high pay: and that especially he has often visited Sparta, partly to give lectures, but partly also to transact diplomatic business for his countrymen the Eleians, who trusted him more than any one else for such duties. His lectures (he says) were eminently instructive and valuable for the training of youth: moreover they were so generally approved, that even from a small Sicilian town called Inykus, he obtained a considerable sum in fees. *Opening of the Hippias Major— Hippias describes the successful circuit which he had made through Greece, and the renown as well as the gain acquired by his lectures.*

Upon this Sokrates asks—In which of the cities were your gains the largest: probably at Sparta? *Hip.*—No; I received nothing at all at Sparta. *Sokr.*—How? You amaze me! Were not your lectures calculated to improve the Spartan youth? or did not the Spartans desire to have their youth improved? or had they no money? *Hip.*—Neither one nor the other. The Spartans, like others, desire the improvement of their youth: they also have plenty of money: more- *Hippias had met with no success at Sparta. Why the Spartans did not admit his instructions. Their law forbids.*

---

[1] Xenoph. Mem. iv. 4, 12-25.
[2] Compare the puzzling questions which Alkibiades when a youth is reported to have addressed to Perikles, and which he must unquestionably have heard from Sokrates himself, respecting the meaning of the word Νόμος (Xen. Mem. i. 2, 42). All the difficulties in determining the definition of Νόμος, occur also in determining that of Νόμιμον, which includes both Jus Scriptum and Jus Moribus Receptum.
[3] Xen. Mem. iv. 4, 15.

over my lectures were very beneficial to them as well as to the rest.[1] *Sokr.*—How could it happen then, that at Sparta, a city great and eminent for its good laws, your valuable instructions were left unrewarded ; while you received so much at the inconsiderable town of Inykus ? *Hip.*—It is not the custom of the country, Sokrates, for the Spartans to change their laws, or to educate their sons in a way different from their ordinary routine. *Sokr.*—How say you ? It is not the custom of the country for the Spartans to do right, but to do wrong ? *Hip.*—I shall not say *that*, Sokrates. *Sokr.*—But surely they would do right, in educating their children better and not worse ? *Hip.*—Yes, they would do right : but it is not lawful for them to admit a foreign mode of education. If any one could have obtained payment there for education, I should have obtained a great deal ; for they listen to me with delight and applaud me : but, as I told you, their law forbids.

Sokr.—Do you call law a hurt or benefit to the city ? *Hip.*—

<small>Question, What is law ? The lawmakers always aim at the Profitable, but sometimes fail to attain it. When they fail, they fail to attain law. The lawful is the Profitable : the Unprofitable is also unlawful.</small> Law is enacted with a view to benefit : but it sometimes hurts, if it be badly enacted.[2] *Sokr.*—But what ? Do not the enactors enact it as the maximum of good, without which the citizens cannot live a regulated life ? *Hip.*—Certainly : they do so. *Sokr.* —Therefore, when those who try to enact laws miss the attainment of good, they also miss the lawful and law itself. How say you ? *Hip.*—They do so, if you speak with strict propriety : but such is not the language which men commonly use. *Sokr.*—What men ? the knowing ? or the ignorant ? *Hip.*—The Many. *Sokr.*—The Many ; is it *they* who know what truth is ? *Hip.*—Assuredly not. *Sokr.*—But surely those who do know, account the profitable to be in truth more lawful than the unprofitable, to all men. Don't you admit this ? *Hip.*—Yes, I admit they account it so in truth. *Sokr.*—Well, and it is so, too : the truth *is* as the knowing men account it. *Hip.*—Most certainly. *Sokr.*—Now you affirm, that it is more profitable to the Spartans to be educated according to your scheme, foreign as it is, than according to their own native scheme. *Hip.*—I affirm it,

---

[1] Plato, Hipp. Maj. 283-284. [2] Plato, Hipp. Maj. 284 C-D.

and with truth too. *Sokr.*—You affirm besides, that things more profitable are at the same time more lawful? *Hip.*—I said so. *Sokr.*—According to your reasoning, then, it is more lawful for the Spartan children to be educated by Hippias, and more unlawful for them to be educated by their fathers—if in reality they will be more benefited by you? *Hip.*—But they *will* be more benefited by me. *Sokr.*—The Spartans therefore act unlawfully, when they refuse to give you money and to confide to you their sons? *Hip.*—I admit that they do: indeed your reasoning seems to make in my favour, so that I am noway called upon to resist it. *Sokr.*—We find then, after·all, that the Spartans are enemies of law, and that too in the most important matters—though they are esteemed the most exemplary followers of law.[1]

Perhaps Plato intended the above argument as a derisory taunt against the Sophist Hippias, for being vain enough to think his own tuition better than that of the Spartan community. If such was his intention, the argument might have been retorted against Plato himself, for his propositions in the Republic and Leges: and we know that the enemies of Plato did taunt him with his inability to get these schemes adopted in any actual community. {Comparison of the argument of the Platonic Sokrates, with that of the Xenophontic Sokrates.} But the argument becomes interesting when we compare it with the debate before referred to in the Xenophontic Memorabilia, where Sokrates maintains against Hippias that the Just is equivalent to the Lawful. In that Xenophontic dialogue, all the difficulties which embarrass this explanation are kept out of sight, and Sokrates is represented as gaining an easy victory over Hippias. In this Platonic dialogue, the equivocal use of the word νόμιμον is expressly adverted to, and Sokrates reduces Hippias to a supposed absurdity, by making him pronounce the Spartans to be enemies of law:—παρανόμους bearing a double sense, and the proposition being true in one sense, false in the other. In the argument of the Platonic Sokrates, a law which does not attain its intended purpose of benefiting the

[1] Plato, Hipp. Maj. 285.

community, is no law at all,—not lawful :[1] so that we are driven back again upon the objections of Alkibiades against Perikles (in the Xenophontic Memorabilia) in regard to what constitutes a law. In the argument of the Xenophontic Sokrates, law means a law actually established, by official authority or custom—and the Spartans are produced as eminent examples of a lawfully minded community. As far as we can assign positive opinion to the Platonic Sokrates in the Hippias Major, he declares that the profitable or useful (being that which men always aim at in making law) is The Lawful, whether actually established or not : and that the unprofitable or hurtful (being that which men always intend to escape) is The Unlawful, whether prescribed by any living authority or not. This (he says) is the opinion of the wise men who know : though the ignorant vulgar hold the contrary opinion. The explanation of τὸ δίκαιον given by the Xenophontic Sokrates (τὸ δίκαιον = τὸ νόμιμον), would be equivalent, if we construe τὸ νόμιμον in the sense of the Platonic Sokrates (in Hippias Major) as an affirmation that The Just was the generally useful—Τὸ δίκαιον = τὸ κοινῇ σύμφερον.

There exists however in all this, a prevalent confusion between Law (or the Lawful) as actually established, and Law (or the Lawful) as it ought to be established, in the judgment of the critic, or of those whom he follows : that is (to use the phrase of Mr. Austin in his 'Province of Jurisprudence') Law as it would be, if it conformed to its assumed measure or test. In the first of these senses, τὸ νόμιμον is not one and the same, but variable according to place and time—one thing at Sparta, another thing elsewhere: accordingly it would not satisfy the demand of Plato's mind, when he asks for an explanation of τὸ δίκαιον. It is an explanation in the second of the two senses which Plato seeks—a common measure or test applicable universally, at all times and places. In so far as he ever finds one, it is that which I have mentioned above as delivered by the Platonic Sokrates in this dialogue : viz., the Just or Good, that which ought to be the measure or test of Law and Positive

The Just or Good is the beneficial or profitable. This is the only explanation which Plato ever gives— and to this he does not always adhere.

---

[1] Compare a similar argument of Sokrates against Thrasymachus—Republic, i. 339.

Morality, is, the beneficial or profitable. This (I repeat) is the only approach to a solution which we ever find in Plato. But this is seldom clearly enunciated, never systematically followed out, and sometimes, in appearance, even denied.

I resume the thread of the Hippias Major. Sokrates asks Hippias what sort of lectures they were that he delivered with so much success at Sparta? The Spartans (Hippias replies) knew nothing and cared nothing about letters, geometry, arithmetic, astronomy: but they took delight in hearing tales about heroes, early ancestors, foundation-legends of cities, &c., which his mnemonic artifice enabled him to deliver.[1] The Spartans delight in you (observes Sokrates) as children delight in old women's tales. Yes (replies Hippias), but that is not all: I discoursed to them also, recently, about fine and honourable pursuits, much to their admiration: I supposed a conversation between Nestor and Neoptolemus, after the capture of Troy, in which the veteran, answering a question put by his youthful companion, enlarged upon those pursuits which it was fine, honourable, beautiful for a young man to engage in. My discourse is excellent, and obtained from the Spartans great applause. I am going to deliver it again here at Athens, in the school-room of Pheidostratus, and I invite you, Sokrates, to come and hear it, with as many friends as you can bring.[2]

Lectures of Hippias at Sparta—not upon geometry, or astronomy, &c., but upon the question— What pursuits are beautiful, fine, and honourable for youth.

I shall come willingly (replied Sokrates). But first answer me one small question, which will rescue me from a present embarrassment. Just now, I was shamefully puzzled in conversation with a friend, to whom I had been praising some things as honourable and beautiful,—blaming other things as mean and ugly. He surprised me by the interrogation—How do you know, Sokrates, what things are beautiful, and what are ugly? Come now, can you tell me, What is the Beautiful? I, in my stupidity, was altogether puzzled, and could not answer the question. But after I had parted from

Question put by Sokrates, in the name of a friend in the background, who has just been puzzling him with it— What is the Beautiful?

[1] Plat. Hipp. Maj. 285 E.   [2] Plat. Hipp. Maj. 286 A-B.

him, I became mortified and angry with myself; and I vowed that the next time I met any wise man, like you, I would put the question to him, and learn how to answer it; so that I might be able to renew the conversation with my friend. Your coming here is most opportune. I entreat you to answer and explain to me clearly what the Beautiful is; in order that I may not again incur the like mortification. You can easily answer: it is a small matter for you, with your numerous attainments.

Oh—yes—a small matter (replies Hippias); the question is easy to answer. I could teach you to answer many questions harder than that; so that no man shall be able to convict you in dialogue.[1]

Hippias thinks the question easy to answer.

Sokrates then proceeds to interrogate Hippias, in the name of the absentee, starting one difficulty after another as if suggested by this unknown prompter, and pretending to be himself under awe of so impracticable a disputant.

All persons are just, through Justice—wise, through Wisdom —good, through Goodness or the Good—beautiful, through Beauty or the Beautiful. Now Justice, Wisdom, Goodness, Beauty or the Beautiful, must each be *something*. Tell me what the Beautiful is?

Justice, Wisdom, Beauty must each be something. What is Beauty, or the Beautiful?

Hippias does not conceive the question. Does the man want to know what is a beautiful thing? *Sokr.* —No; he wants to know what is *The Beautiful*. *Hip.*—I do not see the difference. I answer that a beautiful maiden is a beautiful thing. No one can deny that.[2]

Sokr.—My disputatious friend will not accept your answer. He wants you to tell him, What is the Self-Beautiful? —that Something through which all beautiful things become beautiful. Am I to tell him, it is because a beautiful maiden is a beautiful thing? He will say —Is not a beautiful mare a beautiful thing also? and a beautiful lyre as well? *Hip.*—Yes; both of them are so. *Sokr.*—Ay, and a beautiful pot, my friend will add, well moulded and rounded by a skilful potter, is a beautiful thing too. *Hip.*—How, Sokrates? Who can your

Hippias does not understand the question. He answers by indicating one particularly beautiful object.

---

[1] Plat. Hipp. Maj. 286 C-D.   [2] Plat. Hipp. Maj. 287 A.

disputatious friend be? Some ill-taught man, surely; since he introduces such trivial names into a dignified debate. *Sokr.*— Yes; that is his character: not polite, but vulgar, anxious for nothing else but the truth. *Hip.*—A pot, if it be beautifully made, must certainly be called beautiful; yet still, all such objects are unworthy to be counted as beautiful, if compared with a maiden, a mare, or a lyre.

Sokr.—I understand. You follow the analogy suggested by Herakleitus in his dictum—That the most beautiful ape is ugly, if compared with the human race. So you say, the most beautiful pot is ugly, when compared with the race of maidens. *Hip.*—Yes. That is my meaning. *Sokr.*—Then my friend will ask you in return, whether the race of maidens is not as much inferior to the race of Gods, as the pot to the maiden? whether the most beautiful maiden will not appear ugly, when compared to a Goddess? whether the wisest of men will not appear an ape, when compared to the Gods, either in beauty or in wisdom.[1] *Hip.*— No one can dispute it. *Sokr.*—My friend will smile and say—You forget what was the question put. I asked you, What is the Beautiful?—the Self-Beautiful: and your answer gives me, as the Self-Beautiful, something which you yourself acknowledge to be no more beautiful than ugly? If I had asked you, from the first, what it was that was both beautiful and ugly, your answer would have been pertinent to the question. Can you still think that the Self-Beautiful,—that Something, by the presence of which all other things become beautiful,—is a maiden, or a mare, or a lyre? *Cross-questioning by Sokrates—Other things also are beautiful, but each thing is beautiful only by comparison, or under some particular circumstances: it is sometimes beautiful, sometimes not beautiful.*

Hip.—I have another answer to which your friend can take no exception. That, by the presence of which all things become beautiful, is Gold. What was before ugly, will (we all know), when ornamented with gold, appear beautiful. *Sokr.*—You little know what sort of man my friend is. He will laugh at your answer, and ask you—Do you think, then, that Pheidias did not know his profession as a sculptor? How came *Second answer of Hippias—Gold, is that by the presence of which all things become beautiful. Scrutiny applied to the answer.*

[1] Plat. Hipp. Maj. 289.

<small>Complaint by Hippias about vulgar analogies.</small> he not to make the statue of Athênê all gold, instead of making (as he has done) the face, hands, and feet of ivory, and the pupils of the eyes of a particular stone? Is not ivory also beautiful, and particular kinds of stone? *Hip.*—Yes, each is beautiful, where it is becoming. *Sokr.*—And ugly, where it is not becoming.[1] *Hip.*—Doubtless. I admit that what is becoming or suitable, makes that to which it is applied appear beautiful: that which is not becoming or suitable, makes it appear ugly. *Sokr.*—My friend will next ask you, when you are boiling the beautiful pot of which we spoke just now, full of beautiful soup, what sort of ladle will be suitable and becoming— one made of gold, or of fig-tree wood? Will not the golden ladle spoil the soup, and the wooden ladle turn it out good? Is not the wooden ladle, therefore, better than the golden? *Hip.*—By Hêraklês, Sokrates! what a coarse and stupid fellow your friend is! I cannot continue to converse with a man who talks of such matters. *Sokr.*—I am not surprised that you, with your fine attire and lofty reputation, are offended with these low allusions. But I have nothing to spoil by intercourse with this man; and I entreat you to persevere, as a favour to me. He will ask you whether a wooden soup-ladle is not more beautiful than a ladle of gold,—since it is more suitable and becoming? So that though you said—The Self-Beautiful is Gold—you are now obliged to acknowledge that gold is not more beautiful than fig-tree wood?

Hip.—I acknowledge that it is so. But I have another answer ready which will silence your friend. I presume you wish me to indicate as The Beautiful, something which will never appear ugly to any one, at any time, or at any place.[2] *Sokr.*—That is exactly what I desire. *Hip.*— Well, I affirm, then, that to every man, always, and everywhere, the following is most beautiful. A man being healthy, rich, honoured by the Greeks, having come to old age and buried his own parents well, to be himself buried by his own sons well and magnificently. *Sokr.* —Your answer sounds imposing; but my friend will laugh it to scorn, and will remind me again, that his question pointed to the

<small>Third answer of Hippias—questions upon it—proof given that it fails of universal application.</small>

---

[1] Plat. Hipp. Maj. 290.   [2] Plato, Hipp. Maj. 291 C-D.

Beautiful *itself*[1]—something which, being present as attribute in any subject, will make that subject (whether stone, wood, man, God, action, study, &c.) beautiful. Now that which you have asserted to be beautiful to every one everywhere, was not beautiful to Achilles, who accepted by preference the lot of dying before his father—nor is it so to the heroes, or to the sons of Gods, who do not survive or bury their fathers. To some, therefore, what you specify is beautiful—to others it is not beautiful but ugly: that is, it is both beautiful and ugly, like the maiden, the lyre, the pot, on which we have already remarked. *Hip.*—I did not speak about the Gods or Heroes. Your friend is intolerable, for touching on such profanities.[2] *Sokr.*—However, you cannot deny that what you have indicated is beautiful only for the sons of men, and not for the sons of Gods. My friend will thus make good his reproach against your answer. He will tell me, that all the answers, which we have as yet given, are too absurd. And he may perhaps at the same time himself suggest another, as he sometimes does in pity for my embarrassment.

Sokrates then mentions, as coming from hints of the absent friend, three or four different explanations of the Self-Beautiful: each of which, when first introduced, he approves, and Hippias approves also: but each of which he proceeds successively to test and condemn. It is to be remarked that all of them are general explanations: not consisting in conspicuous particular instances, like those which had come from Hippias. His explanations are the following:— *Farther answers, suggested by Sokrates himself— 1. The Suitable or Becoming— Objections thereunto— it is rejected.*

1. The suitable or becoming (which had before been glanced at). It is the suitable or becoming which constitutes the Beautiful.[3]

To this Sokrates objects: The suitable, or becoming, is what causes objects to *appear* beautiful—not what causes them to *be really* beautiful. Now the latter is that which we are seeking. The two conditions do not always go together. Those objects, institutions, and pursuits which *are really* beautiful (fine, honourable) very often do not appear so, either to individuals or to

---

[1] Plato, Hipp. Maj. 292 D. [2] Plato, Hipp. Maj. 293 B.
[3] Plato, Hipp. Maj. 293 E.

cities collectively; so that there is perpetual dispute and fighting on the subject. The suitable or becoming, therefore, as it is certainly what makes objects appear beautiful, so it cannot be what makes them really beautiful.[1]

2. The useful or profitable.—We call objects beautiful, looking to the purpose which they are calculated or intended to serve: the human body, with a view to running, wrestling, and other exercises—a horse, an ox, a cock, looking to the service required from them—implements, vehicles on land and ships at sea, instruments for music and other arts all upon the same principle, looking to the end which they accomplish or help to accomplish. Laws and pursuits are characterised in the same way. In each of these, we give the name Beautiful to the useful, in so far as it is useful, when it is useful, and for the purpose to which it is useful. To that which is useless or hurtful, in the same manner, we give the name Ugly.[2]

2. The useful or profitable—Objections—It will not hold.

Now that which is capable of accomplishing each end, is useful for such end: that which is incapable, is useless. It is therefore capacity, or power, which is beautiful: incapacity, or impotence, is ugly.[3]

Most certainly (replies Hippias): this is especially true in our cities and communities, wherein political power is the finest thing possible, political impotence, the meanest.

Yet, on closer inspection (continues Sokrates), such a theory will not hold. Power is employed by all men, though unwillingly, for bad purposes: and each man, through such employment of his power, does much more harm than good, beginning with his childhood. Now power, which is useful for the doing of evil, can never be called beautiful.[4]

You cannot therefore say that Power, taken absolutely, is beautiful. You must add the qualification—Power used for the production of some good, is beautiful. This, then, would be the profitable—the cause or generator of good.[5] But the cause is different from its effect:—the generator or father is different

---

[1] Plato, Hipp. Maj. 294 B-E.
[2] Plat. Hipp. Maj. 295 C-D.
[3] Plat. Hipp. Maj. 295 E. Οὐκοῦν τὸ δυνατὸν ἕκαστον ἀπεργάζεσθαι, εἰς ὅπερ δυνατόν, εἰς τοῦτο καὶ χρήσιμον· τὸ δὲ ἀδύνατον ἄχρηστον; . . . . Δύναμις μὲν ἄρα καλόν—ἀδυναμία δὲ αἰσχρόν;
[4] Plat. Hipp. Maj. 296 C-D.
[5] Plat. Hipp. Maj. 297 B.

CHAP. XIII. THE USEFUL—THE PLEASURABLE.

from the generated or son. The beautiful would, upon this view, be the cause of the good. But then the beautiful would be different from the good, and the good different from the beautiful? Who can admit this? It is obviously wrong: it is the most ridiculous theory which we have yet hit upon.[1]

3. The Beautiful is a particular variety of the agreeable or pleasurable: that which characterises those things which cause pleasure to us through sight and hearing. Thus the men, the ornaments, the works of painting or sculpture, upon which we look with admiration,[2] are called beautiful: also songs, music, poetry, fable, discourse, in like manner; nay even laws, customs, pursuits, which we consider beautiful, might be brought under the same head.[3]

3. The Beautiful is a variety of the Pleasurable—that which is received through the eye and the ear.

The objector, however, must now be dealt with. He will ask us—Upon what ground do you make so marked a distinction between the pleasures of sight and hearing, and other pleasures? Do you deny that these others (those of taste, smell, eating, drinking, sex) are really pleasures? No, surely (we shall reply); we admit them to be pleasures,—but no one will tolerate us in calling them beautiful: especially the pleasures of sex, which as pleasures are the greatest of all, but which are ugly and disgraceful to behold. He will answer—I understand you: you are ashamed to call these pleasures beautiful, because they do not seem so to the multitude: but I did not ask you, what *seems* beautiful to the multitude—I asked you, what *is* beautiful.[4] You mean to affirm, that all pleasures which do not belong to sight and hearing, are not beautiful: Do you mean, all which do

Objections to this last—What property is there common to both sight and hearing, which confers upon the pleasures of these two senses the exclusive privilege of being beautiful?

---

[1] Plat. Hipp. Maj. 297 D-E. εἰ οἷόν τ᾽ ἐστίν, ἐκείνων εἶναι (κινδυνεύει) γελοιότερος τῶν πρώτων.
[2] Plat. Hipp. Maj. 298 A-B.
[3] Plat. Hipp. Maj. 298 D.
Professor Bain observes:—"The eye and the ear are the great avenues to the mind for the æsthetic class of influences; the other senses are more or less in the monopolist interest. The blue sky, the green woods, and all the beauties of the landscape, can fill the vision of a countless throng of admirers. So with the pleasing sounds, &c." 'The Emotions and the Will,' ch. xiv. (The Æsthetic Emotions), sect. 2, p. 226, 3rd ed.
[4] Plato, Hipp. Maj. 298 E, 299 A.
Μανθάνω, ἄν ἴσως φαίη, καὶ ἐγώ, ὅτι πάλαι αἰσχύνεσθε ταύτας τὰς ἡδονὰς φάναι καλὰς εἶναι, ὅτι οὐ δοκεῖ τοῖς ἀνθρώποις· ἀλλ᾽ ἐγὼ οὐ τοῦτο ἠρώτων, ὃ δοκεῖ τοῖς πολλοῖς καλὸν εἶναι, ἀλλ᾽ ὅ, τι ἔστιν.

not belong to both? or all which do not belong to one or the other? We shall reply—To either one of the two—or to both the two. Well! but, why (he will ask) do you single out these pleasures of sight and hearing, as beautiful exclusively? What is there peculiar in them, which gives them a title to such distinction? All pleasures are alike, so far forth as pleasures, differing only in the more or less. Next, the pleasures of sight cannot be considered as beautiful by reason of their coming through sight—for that reason would not apply to the pleasures of hearing : nor again can the pleasures of hearing be considered as beautiful by reason of their coming through hearing.[1] We must find something possessed as well by sight as by hearing, common to both, and peculiar to them,—which confers beauty upon the pleasures of both and of each. Any attribute of one, which does not also belong to the other, will not be sufficient for our purpose.[2] Beauty must depend upon some essential characteristic which both have in common.[3] We must therefore look out for some such characteristic, which belongs to both as well as to each separately.

Now there is one characteristic which may perhaps serve.

Answer— There is, belonging to each and to both in common, the property of being innocuous and profitable pleasures— Upon this ground they

The pleasures of sight and hearing, both and each, are distinguished from other pleasures by being the most innocuous and the best.[4] It is for this reason that we call them beautiful. The Beautiful, then, is profitable pleasure—or pleasure producing good—for the profitable is, that which produces good.[5]

Nevertheless the objector will not be satisfied even with this. He will tell us—You declare the Beautiful to be Pleasure producing good. But we before

---

[1] Plato, Hipp. Maj. 299 D-E.
[2] Plato, Hipp. Maj. 300 B. A separate argument between Sokrates and Hippias is here as it were interpolated; Hippias affirms that he does not see how any predicate can be true of both which is not true of either separately. Sokrates points out that two men are Both, even in number, while each is One, an odd number. You cannot say of the two that they are one, nor can you say of either that he is Both. There are two classes of predicates; some which are true of either but not true of the two together, or vice versâ; some again which are true of the two and true also of each one—such as just, wise, handsome, &c. p. 301-303 B.
[3] Plat. Hipp. Maj. 302 C. τῇ οὐσίᾳ τῇ ἐπ' ἀμφότερα ἑπομένῃ ᾤμην, εἴπερ ἀμφότερά ἐστι καλά, ταύτῃ δεῖν αὐτὰ καλὰ εἶναι, τῇ δὲ κατὰ τὰ ἕτερα ἀπολειπομένῃ μή. καὶ ἔτι νῦν οἴομαι.
[4] Plat. Hipp. Maj. 303 E. ὅτι ἀσινέστεραι αὗται τῶν ἡδονῶν εἰσι καὶ βέλτισται, καὶ ἀμφότεραι καὶ ἑκατέρα.
[5] Plat. Hipp. Maj. 303 E. λέγετε δὴ τὸ καλὸν εἶναι, ἡ δ ο ν ὴ ν ὠ φ έ λ ι μ ο ν.

agreed, that the producing agent or cause is different from what is produced or the effect. Accordingly, the Beautiful is different from the good : or, in other words, the Beautiful is not good, nor is the Good beautiful—if each of them is a different thing.[1] Now these propositions we have already pronounced to be inadmissible, so that your present explanation will not stand better than the preceding.

are called beautiful. This will not hold— The Profitable is the cause of Good, and is therefore different from Good —To say that the Beautiful is the Profitable, is to say that it is different from Good —But this has been already declared inadmissible.

Thus finish the three distinct explanations of Τὸ καλὸν, which Plato in this dialogue causes to be first suggested by Sokrates, successively accepted by Hippias, and successively refuted by Sokrates. In comparing them with the three explanations which he puts into the mouth of Hippias, we note this distinction : That the explanations proposed by Hippias are conspicuous particular exemplifications of the Beautiful, substituted in place of the general concept: as we remarked, in the Dialogue Euthyphron, that the explanations of the Holy given by Euthyphron in reply to Sokrates, were of the same exemplifying character. On the contrary, those suggested by Sokrates keep in the region of abstractions, and seek to discover some more general concept, of which the Beautiful is only a derivative or a modification, so as to render a definition of it practicable. To illustrate this difference by the language of Dr. Whewell respecting many of the classifications in Natural History, we may say—That ac-

Remarks upon the Dialogue— The explanations ascribed to Hippias are special conspicuous examples : those ascribed to Sokrates are attempts to assign some general concept.

---

[1] Plat. Hipp. Maj. 303 E—304 A. Οὔκουν ὠφέλιμον, φήσει, τὸ ποιοῦν τἀγαθόν, τὸ δὲ ποιοῦν καὶ τὸ ποιούμενον, ἕτερον νῦν δὴ ἐφάνη, καὶ εἰς τὸν πρότερον λόγον ἥκει ὑμῖν ὁ λόγος; οὔτε γὰρ τὸ ἀγαθὸν ἂν εἴη καλὸν οὔτε τὸ καλὸν ἀγαθόν, εἴπερ ἄλλο αὐτῶν ἑκάτερόν ἐστιν.

These last words deserve attention, because they coincide with the doctrine ascribed to Antisthenes, which has caused so many hard words to be applied to him (as well as to Stilpon) by critics, from Kolôtes downwards. The general principle here laid down by Plato is—A is something different from B, therefore A is not B and B is not A. In other words, A cannot be predicated of B nor B of A. Antisthenes said in like manner—Ἄνθρωπος and Ἀγαθὸς are different from each other, therefore you cannot say Ἄνθρωπός ἐστιν ἀγαθός. You can only say Ἄνθρωπός ἐστιν Ἄνθρωπος—Ἀγαθός ἐστιν ἀγαθός.

I have touched farther upon this point in my chapter upon Antisthenes and the other Viri Sokratici.

cording to the views here represented by Hippias, the group of objects called beautiful is given by Type, not by Definition :[1] while Sokrates proceeds like one convinced that some common characteristic attribute may be found, on which to rest a Definition. To search for Definitions of general words, was (as Aristotle remarks) a novelty, and a valuable novelty, introduced by Sokrates. His contemporaries, the Sophists among them, were not accustomed to it: and here the Sophist Hippias (according to Plato's frequent manner) is derided as talking nonsense,[2] because, when asked for an explanation of The Self-Beautiful, he answers by citing special instances of beautiful objects. But we must remember, first, that Sokrates, who is introduced as trying several general explanations of the Self-Beautiful, does not find one which will stand: next, that even if one such could be found, particular instances can never be dispensed with, in the way of illustration; lastly, that there are many general terms (the Beautiful being one of them) of which no definitions can be provided, and which can only be imperfectly explained, by enumerating a variety of objects to which the term in question is applied.[3] Plato

[1] See Dr. Whewell's 'History of the Inductive Sciences,' ii. 120 seq.; and Mr. John Stuart Mill's 'System of Logic,' iv. 8, 3.
I shall illustrate this subject farther when I come to the dialogue called Lysis.
[2] Stallbaum, in his notes, bursts into exclamations of wonder at the incredible stupidity of Hippias—" En hominis stuporem prorsus admirabilem," p. 289 E.
[3] Mr. John Stuart Mill observes in his System of Logic, i. 1, 5: "One of the chief sources of lax habits of thought is the custom of using connotative terms without a distinctly ascertained connotation, and with no more precise notion of their meaning than can be loosely collected from observing what objects they are used to denote. It is in this manner that we all acquire, and inevitably so, our first knowledge of our vernacular language. A child learns the meaning of Man, White, &c., by hearing them applied to a number of individual objects, and finding out, by a process of generalisation of which he is but imperfectly conscious, what those different objects have in common. In many cases objects bear a general resemblance to each other, which leads to their being familiarly classed together under a common name, while it is not immediately apparent what are the particular attributes upon the possession of which in common by them all their general resemblance depends. In this manner names creep on from subject to subject until all traces of a common meaning sometimes disappear, and the word comes to denote a number of things not only independently of any common attribute, but which have actually no attribute in common, or none but what is shared by other things to which the name is capriciously refused. It would be well if this degeneracy of language took place only in the hands of the untaught vulgar; but some of the most remarkable instances are to be found in terms of art, and among technically educated persons, such as English lawyers. *Felony*, e.g., is a law-term with the sound of which all are familiar: *but there is no lawyer who would undertake to tell what a felony is, otherwise than by enumerating the various offences so called.* Originally the word *felony* had a meaning; it denoted all offences, the

thought himself entitled to objectivise every general term, or to assume a substantive Ens, called a Form or Idea, corresponding to it. This was a logical mistake quite as serious as any which we know to have been committed by Hippias or any other Sophist. The assumption that wherever there is a general term, there must also be a generic attribute corresponding to it—is one which Aristotle takes much pains to negative : he recognises terms of transitional analogy, as well as terms equivocal: while he also especially numbers the Beautiful among equivocal terms.[1]

We read in the Xenophontic Memorabilia a dialogue between Sokrates and Aristippus, on this same subject—What is the Beautiful, which affords a sort of contrast between the Dialogues of Search and those of Exposition. In the Hippias Major, we have the problem approached on several different sides, various suggestions being proposed, and each successively disallowed, on reasons shown, as failures: while in the Xenophontic dialogue, Sokrates declares an affirmative doctrine, and stands to it—but no pains are taken to bring out the' objections against it and rebut them. The doctrine is, that the Beautiful is coincident with the Good, and that both of them are resolvable into the Useful : thus all beautiful objects, unlike as they may be to the eye or touch, bear that name because they have in common the attribute of conducing to one and the same purpose—the security, advantage, or gratification, of man, in some form or other. This is one of the three explanations broached by the Platonic Sokrates, and afterwards refuted by him, in the Hippias : while his declaration (which Hippias puts aside as unseemly)—that a pot and a wooden soup-ladle conveniently made are beautiful—is perfectly in harmony with that of the Xenophontic Sokrates, that a basket for carrying dung is beautiful, if it performs its work well.[2] We must moreover

Analogy between the explanations here ascribed to Sokrates, and those given by the Xenophontic Sokrates in the Memorabilia.

penalty of which included forfeiture of lands or goods, but subsequent Acts of Parliament have declared various offences to be felonies without enjoining that penalty, and have taken away that penalty from others which continue nevertheless to be called felonies, insomuch that the acts so called have now no property whatever in common save that of being unlawful and punishable."

[1] Aristot. Topic. i. 106, a. 21. Τὰ πολλαχῶς λεγόμενα—τὰ πλεοναχῶς λεγόμενα—are perpetually noted and distinguished by Aristotle.
[2] Xen. Mem. iii. 6, 2, 7 ; iv. 6, 8. Plato, Hipp. Maj. 288 D, 290 D.
I am obliged to translate the words τὸ Καλόν by the Beautiful or beauty, to avoid a tiresome periphrasis. But in reality the Greek words include

remark, that the objections whereby the Platonic Sokrates, after proposing the doctrine and saying much in its favour, finds himself compelled at last to disallow it—these objections are not produced and refuted, but passed over without notice, in the Xenophontic dialogue, wherein Sokrates affirms it decidedly.[1] The

more besides: they mean also the *fine*, the *honourable or that which is worthy of honour*, the *exalted*, &c. If we have difficulty in finding any common property connoted by the English word, the difficulty in the case of the Greek word is still greater.

[1] In regard to the question, Wherein consists Το Καλόν? and objections against the theory of the Xenophontic Sokrates, it is worth while to compare the views of modern philosophers. Dugald Stewart says (on the Beautiful, 'Philosophical Essays,' p. 214 seq.), "It has long been a favourite problem with philosophers to ascertain the common quality or qualities which entitle a thing to the denomination of Beautiful. But the success of their speculations has been so inconsiderable, that little can be inferred from them except the impossibility of the problem to which they have been directed. The speculations which have given occasion to these remarks have evidently originated in a prejudice which has descended to modern times from the scholastic ages. That when a word admits of a variety of significations, these different significations must all be species of the same genus, and must consequently include some essential idea common to every individual to which the generic term can be applied. Of this principle, which has been an abundant source of obscurity and mystery in the different sciences, it would be easy to expose the unsoundness and futility. Socrates, whose plain good sense appears, on this as on other occasions, to have fortified his understanding to a wonderful degree against the metaphysical subtleties which misled his successors, was evidently apprised fully of the justice of the foregoing remarks, if any reliance can be placed on the account given by Xenophon of his conversation with Aristippus about the Good and the Beautiful," &c.

Stewart then proceeds to translate a portion of the Xenophontic dialogue (Memorab. iii. 8). But unfortunately he does not translate the whole of it. If he had he would have seen that he has misconceived the opinion of Sokrates, who maintains the very doctrine here disallowed by Stewart, viz., That there is an essential idea common to all beautiful objects, the fact of being conducive to human security, comfort, or enjoyment. This is unquestionably an important common property, though the multifarious objects which possess it may be unlike in all other respects.

As to the general theory I think that Stewart is right: it is his complimentment to Sokrates, on this occasion, which I consider misplaced. He certainly would not have agreed with Sokrates (nor should I agree with him) in calling by the epithet *beautiful* a basket for carrying dung when well made for its own purpose, or a convenient boiling-pot, or a soup-ladle made of fig-tree wood, as the Platonic Sokrates affirms in the Hippias (288 D, 290 D). The Beautiful and the Useful sometimes coincide; more often, or at least very often, they do not. Hippias is made to protest, in this dialogue, against the mention of such vulgar objects as the pot and the ladle; and this is apparently intended by Plato as a defective point in his character, denoting silly affectation and conceit, like his fine apparel. But Dugald Stewart would have agreed in the sentiment ascribed to Hippias—that vulgar and mean objects have no place in an inquiry into the Beautiful; and that they belong, when well-formed for their respective purposes, to the category of the Useful.

The Xenophontic Sokrates in the Memorabilia is mistaken in confounding the Beautiful with the Good and the Useful. But his remarks are valuable in another point of view, as they insist most forcibly on the essential relativity both of the Beautiful and the Good.

The doctrine of Dugald Stewart is supported by Mr. John Stuart Mill ('System of Logic,' iv. 4, 5; and Professor Bain has expounded the whole subject still more fully in a chapter (xiv. p. 225 seq., on the Æsthetic Emotions) of his work on the Emotions and the Will.

affirming Sokrates, and the objecting Sokrates, are not on the stage at once.

The concluding observations of this dialogue, interchanged between Hippias and Sokrates, are interesting as bringing out the antithesis between rhetoric and dialectic—between the concrete and exemplifying, as contrasted with the abstract and analytical. Immediately after Sokrates has brought his own third suggestion to an inextricable embarrassment, Hippias remarks—

"Well, Sokrates, what do you think now of all these reasonings of yours? They are what I declared them to be just now,—scrapings and parings of discourse, divided into minute fragments. But the really beautiful and precious acquirement is, to be able to set out well and finely a regular discourse before the Dikastery or the public assembly, to persuade your auditors, and to depart carrying with you not the least but the greatest of all prizes—safety for yourself, your property, and your friends. These are the real objects to strive for. Leave off your petty cavils, that you may not look like an extreme simpleton, handling silly trifles as you do at present."[1] *Concluding thrust exchanged between Hippias and Sokrates.*

"My dear Hippias," (replies Sokrates) "you are a happy man, since you know what pursuits a man ought to follow, and have yourself followed them, as you say, with good success. But I, as it seems, am under the grasp of an unaccountable fortune: for I am always fluctuating and puzzling myself, and when I lay my puzzle before you wise men, I am requited by you with hard words. I am told just what you have now been telling me, that I busy myself about matters silly, petty, and worthless. When on the contrary, overborne by your authority, I declare as you do, that it is the finest thing possible to be able to set out well and beautifully a regular discourse before the public assembly, and bring it to successful conclusion—then there are other men at hand who heap upon me bitter reproaches: especially that one man, my nearest kinsman and inmate, who never omits to convict me. When on my return home he hears me repeat what you have told me, he asks, if I am not ashamed of my impudence in talking about beautiful (honourable) pursuits, when I am so

[1] Plat. Hipp. Maj. 304 A.

manifestly convicted upon this subject, of not even knowing what the Beautiful (Honourable) is. How can you (he says), being ignorant what the Beautiful is, know *who* has set out a discourse beautifully and *who* has not—*who* has performed a beautiful exploit and *who* has not? Since you are in a condition so disgraceful, can you think life better for you than death? Such then is my fate—to hear disparagement and reproaches from you on the one side, and from him on the other. Necessity however perhaps requires that I should endure all these discomforts : for it will be nothing strange if I profit by them. Indeed I think that I have already profited both by your society, Hippias, and by his : for I now think that I know what the proverb means—Beautiful (Honourable) things are difficult."[1]

Here is a suitable termination for one of the Dialogues of
Rhetoric against Dialectic. Search : "My mind has been embarrassed by contradictions as yet unreconciled, but this is a stage indispensable to future improvement". We have moreover an interesting passage of arms between Rhetoric and Dialectic : two contemporaneous and contending agencies, among the stirring minds of Athens, in the time of Plato and Isokrates. The Rhetor accuses the Dialectician of departing from the conditions of reality—of breaking up the integrity of those concretes, which occur in nature each as continuous and indivisible wholes. Each of the analogous particular cases forms a continuum or concrete by itself, which may be compared with the others, but cannot be taken to pieces, and studied in separate fragments.[2] The Dialectician on his side treats the Abstract (τὸ καλὸν) as the real Integer, and the highest abstraction as the first of all integers, containing in itself and capable of evolving all the subordinate integers : the various accompaniments, which go along with each Abstract to make up a concrete, he disregards as shadowy and transient disguises.

Hippias accuses Sokrates of never taking into his view Wholes,

---

[1] Plat. Hipp. Maj. 304 D-E.
[2] Plat. Hipp. Maj. 301 B. 'Αλλὰ γὰρ δὴ σύ, ὦ Σώκρατες, τὰ μὲν ὅλα τῶν πραγμάτων οὐ σκοπεῖς, οὐδ' ἐκεῖνοι, οἷς σὺ εἴωθας διαλέγεσθαι, κρούετε δὲ ἀπολαμβάνοντες τὸ καλὸν καὶ ἕκαστον τῶν ὄντων ἐν τοῖς λόγοις κατατέμνοντες· διὰ ταῦτα οὕτω μεγάλα ὑμᾶς λανθάνει

καὶ διανεκῆ σώματα τῆς οὐσίας πεφυκότα. Compare 301 E.
The words διανεκῆ σώματα τῆς οὐσίας πεφυκότα, correspond as nearly as can be to the logical term *Concrete*, opposed to *Abstract*. Nature furnishes only Concreta, not Abstracta.

CHAP. XIII.   AGGREGATES.   53

and of confining his attention to separate parts and fragments, obtained by logical analysis and subdivision. Aristophanes, when he attacks the Dialectic of Sokrates, takes the same ground, employing numerous comic metaphors to illustrate the small and impalpable fragments handled, and the subtle transpositions which they underwent in the reasoning. Isokrates again deprecates the over-subtlety of dialectic debate, contrasting it with discussions (in his opinion) more useful ; wherein entire situations, each with its full clothing and assemblage of circumstances, were reviewed and estimated.[1] All these are protests, by persons accustomed to deal with real life, and to talk to auditors both numerous and commonplace, against that conscious analysis and close attention to general and abstract terms, which Sokrates first insisted on and transmitted to his disciples. On the other side, we have the emphatic declaration made by the Platonic Sokrates (and made still earlier by the Xenophontic[2] or historical Sokrates)—That a man was not fit to talk about beautiful things in the concrete—that he had no right to affirm or deny that attribute, with respect to any given subject—that he was even fit to live unless he could explain what was meant by The Beautiful, or Beauty in the abstract. Here are two distinct and conflicting intellectual habits, the antithesis between which, indicated in this dialogue, is described at large and forcibly in the Theætêtus.[3]

Men who dealt with real life, contrasted with the speculative and analytical philosophers.

When Hippias accuses Sokrates of neglecting to notice Wholes or Aggregates, this is true in the sense of Concrete Wholes—the phenomenal sequences and co-existences, perceived by sense or imagined. But the Universal (as Aristotle says)[4] is one kind of Whole : a Logical

Concrete Aggregates —Abstract or logical Aggregates. Distinct ap-

---

[1] Aristophan. Nubes, 130. λόγων ἀκριβῶν σχινδαλάμους—παιπάλη. Nub. 261, Aves, 430. λεπτοτάτων λήρων ἱερεῦ, Nub. 359. γνώμαις λεπταῖς, Nub. 1404. σκαριφισμοῖσι λήρων, Ran. 1497. σμιλεύματα—id. 819. Isokrates, Πρὸς Νικοκλέα, s. 69, an'ithesis of the λόγοι πολιτικοὶ and λόγοι ἐριστικοί—μάλιστα μὲν καὶ ἀπὸ τῶν καιρῶν θεωρεῖν συμβουλεύοντας, εἰ δὲ μὴ, καθ᾽ ὅλων τῶν πραγμάτων λέγοντας—which is almost exactly the phrase ascribed to Hippias by Plato in this Hippias Major. Also Isokrates, Contra Sophistas, s. 24-25, where he contrasts the useless λογίδια, debated by the contentious dialecticians (Sokrates and Plato being probably included in this designation), with his own λόγοι πολιτικοί. Compare also Isokrates, Or. xv. De Permutatione, s. 211-213-285-287.
[2] Xen. Mem. i. 1, 16.
[3] Plato, Theætêt. pp. 173-174-175.
[4] Aristot. Physic. i. 1. τὸ γὰρ ὅλον κατὰ τὴν αἴσθησιν γνωριμώτερον, τὸ

titudes required by Aristotle for the Dialectician.	Whole, having logical parts. In the minds of Sokrates and Plato, the Logical Whole separable into its logical parts and into them only, were preponderant.

One other point deserves peculiar notice, in the dialogue under
Antithesis of Absolute and Relative, here brought into debate by Plato, in regard to the Idea of Beauty.	our review. The problem started is, What is the Beautiful—the Self-Beautiful, or Beauty *per se*: and it is assumed that this must be Something,[1] that from the accession of which, each particular beautiful thing becomes beautiful. But Sokrates presently comes to make a distinction between that which is really beautiful and that which appears to be beautiful.

Some things (he says) appear beautiful, but are not so in reality : some are beautiful, but do not appear so. The problem, as he states it, is, to find, not what that is which makes objects appear beautiful, but what it is that makes them really beautiful. This distinction, as we find it in the language of Hippias, is one of degree only :[2] that *is* beautiful which appears so to every one and at all times. But in the language of Sokrates, the distinction is radical : to *be* beautiful is one thing, to *appear* beautiful is another ; whatever makes a thing appear beautiful without being so in reality, is a mere engine of deceit, and not what Sokrates is enquiring for.[3] The Self-Beautiful or real Beauty is so, whether any one perceives it to be beautiful or not : it is an Absolute, which exists *per se*, having no relation to any sentient or percipient subject.[4] At any rate, such is the manner in which Plato

---

δὲ καθόλου ὅλον τί ἐστι· πολλὰ γὰρ περιλαμβάνει ὡς μέρη τὸ καθόλου. Compare Simplikius, Schol. Brandis ad loc. p. 324, a. 10-26.

[1] Plato, Hipp. Maj. 286 E. αὐτὸ τὸ καλὸν ὅ, τί ἐστιν. Also 287 D, 289 D.

[2] Plato, Hipp. Maj. 291 D, 292 E.

[3] Plato, Hipp. Maj. 294 A-B, 299 A.

[4] Dr. Hutcheson, in his inquiry into the Original of our Ideas of Beauty and Virtue, observes (sect. i. and ii. p. 14-16) :—

"Beauty is either original or comparative, or, if any like the terms better, absolute or relative ; only let it be observed, that by *absolute* or *original*, is not understood any quality supposed to be in the object, which should of itself be beautiful, without relation to any mind which perceives it. For Beauty, like other names of sensible ideas, properly denotes the perception of some mind. . . . . Our inquiry is only about the qualities which are beautiful to men, or about the foundation of their sense of beauty, for (as above hinted) Beauty has always relation to the sense of some mind ; and when we afterwards show how generally the objects that occur to us are beautiful, we mean that such objects are agreeable to the sense of men, &c."

The same is repeated, sect. iv. p. 40; sect. vi. p. 72.

conceives it, when he starts here as a problem to enquire, What it is.

Herein we note one of the material points of disagreement between Plato and his master: for Sokrates (in the Xenophontic Memorabilia) affirms distinctly that Beauty is altogether relative to human wants and appreciations. The Real and Absolute, on the one hand, wherein alone resides truth and beauty—as against the phenomenal and relative, on the other hand, the world of illusion and meanness—this is an antithesis which we shall find often reproduced in Plato. I shall take it up more at large, when I come to discuss his argument against Protagoras in the Theætetus.

I now come to the Lesser Hippias: in which (as we have already seen in the Greater) that Sophist is described by epithets, affirming varied and extensive accomplishments, as master of arithmetic, geometry, astronomy, poetry (especially that of Homer), legendary lore, music, metrical and rhythmical diversities, &c. His memory was prodigious, and he had even invented for himself a technical scheme for assisting memory. He had composed poems, epic, lyric, and tragic, as well as many works in prose: he was, besides, a splendid lecturer on ethical and political subjects, and professed to answer any question which might be asked. Furthermore, he was skilful in many kinds of manual dexterity: having woven his own garments, plaited his own girdle, made his own shoes, engraved his own seal-ring, and fabricated for himself a curry-comb and oil-flask.[1] Lastly, he is described as wearing fine and showy apparel. What he is made to say is rather in harmony with this last point of character, than with the preceding. He talks with silliness and presumption, so as to invite and excuse the derisory sting of Sokrates. There is a third interlocutor, Eudikus: but he says very little, and other auditors are alluded to generally, who say nothing.[2]

Hippias Minor—Characters and situation supposed.

---

[1] Plato, Hipp. Minor, 368.
[2] Plato, Hipp. Minor, 369 D, 373 B.
Ast rejects both the dialogues called by the name of Hippias, as not composed by Plato. Schleiermacher doubts about both, and rejects the Hippias Minor (which he considers as perhaps worked up by a Platonic scholar from

Hippias has just delivered a lecture, in which he extols Achilles as better than Odysseus— the veracious and straightforward hero, better than the mendacious and crafty.

In the Hippias Minor, that Sophist appears as having just concluded a lecture upon Homer, in which he had extolled Achilles as better than Odysseus: Achilles being depicted as veracious and straightforward, Odysseus as mendacious and full of tricks. Sokrates, who had been among the auditors, cross-examines Hippias upon the subject of this affirmation.

Homer (says Hippias) considers veracious men, and mendacious men, to be not merely different, but opposite: and I agree with him. Permit me (Sokrates remarks) to ask some questions about the meaning of this from you, since I cannot ask any from Homer himself. You will answer both for yourself and him.[1]

---

a genuine sketch by Plato himself) but will not pass the same sentence upon the Hippias Major (Schleierm. Einleit. vol. ii. pp. 293-296; vol. v. 399-403. Ast, Platon's Leben und Schriften, pp. 457-464).

Stallbaum defends both the dialogues as genuine works of Plato, and in my judgment with good reason (Prolegg. ad Hipp. Maj. vol. iv. pp. 145-150; ad Hipp. Minor. pp. 227-235). Steinhart (Einleit. p. 99) and Socher (Ueber Platon, p. 144 seq., 215 seq.) maintain the same opinion on these dialogues as Stallbaum. It is to be remarked that Schleiermacher states the reasons both for and against the genuineness of the dialogues; and I think that even in his own statement the reasons *for* preponderate. The reasons which both Schleiermacher and Ast produce as proving the spuriousness, are in my view quite insufficient to sustain their conclusion. There is bad taste, sophistry, an overdose of banter and derision (they say very truly), in the part assigned to Sokrates: there are also differences of view, as compared with Sokrates in other dialogues; various other affirmations (they tell us) are *not* Platonic. I admit much of this, but I still do not accept their conclusion. These critics cannot bear to admit any Platonic work as genuine unless it affords to them ground for superlative admiration and glorification of the author. This postulate I altogether contest; and I think that differences of view, as between Sokrates in one dialogue and Sokrates in another, are both naturally to be expected and actually manifested (witness the Protagoras and Gorgias). Moreover Ast designates (p. 404) a doctrine as " durchaus unsokratisch" which Stallbaum justly remarks (p. 233) to have been actually affirmed by Sokrates in the Xenophontic Memorabilia. Stallbaum thinks that both the two dialogues (Socher, that the Hippias Minor only) were composed by Plato among his earlier works, and this may probably be true. The citation and refutation of the Hippias Minor by Aristotle (Metaphys. Δ. 1025, a. 6) counts with me as a strong corroborative proof that the dialogue is Plato's work. Schleiermacher and Ast set this evidence aside because Aristotle does not name Plato as the author. But if the dialogue had been composed by any one less celebrated than Plato, Aristotle would have named the author. Mention by Aristotle, though without Plato's name, is of greater value to support the genuineness than the purely internal grounds stated by Ast and Schleiermacher against it.

[1] Plat. Hipp. Minor, 365 C-D.

The remark here made by Sokrates —" The poet is not here to answer for himself, so that you cannot put any questions to him "—is a point of view familiar to Plato: insisted upon forcibly in the Protagoras (347 E), and farther generalised in the Phædrus, so as to apply to all written matter compared with personal converse (Phædrus, p. 275 D).

This ought to count, so far as it

CHAP. XIII   ANALOGY OF SPECIAL ARTS.   57

Mendacious men (answers Hippias, to a string of questions, somewhat prolix) are capable, intelligent, wise: they are not incapable or ignorant. If a man be incapable of speaking falsely, or ignorant, he is not mendacious. Now the capable man is one who can make sure of doing what he wishes to do, at the time and occasion when he does wish it, without let or hindrance.[1]

You, Hippias (says Sokrates), are expert on matters of arithmetic: you can make sure of answering truly any question put to you on the subject. You are *better* on the subject than the ignorant man, who cannot make sure of doing the same. But as you can make sure of answering truly, so likewise you can make sure of answering falsely, whenever you choose to do so. Now the ignorant man cannot make sure of answering falsely. He may, by reason of his ignorance, when he wishes to answer falsely, answer truly without intending it. You, therefore, the intelligent man and the good in arithmetic, are better than the ignorant and the bad for both purposes—for speaking falsely, and for speaking truly.[2] {This is contested by Sokrates. The veracious man and the mendacious man are one and the same. The only man who can answer truly if he chooses, is he who can also answer falsely if he chooses— i.e., the knowing man. The ignorant man cannot make sure of doing either one or the other.}

What is true about arithmetic, is true in other departments also. The only man who can speak falsely whenever he chooses is the man who can speak truly whenever he chooses. Now, the mendacious man, as we agreed, is the man who can speak falsely whenever he chooses. Accordingly, the mendacious man, and the veracious man, are the same. They are not different, still less opposite:—nay, the two epithets belong only to one and the same person. The veracious man is not better than the mendacious —seeing that he is one and the same.[3] {Analogy of special arts —It is only the arithmetician who can speak falsely on a question}

goes, as a fragment of proof that the Hippias Minor is a genuine work of Plato, instead of which Schleiermacher treats it (p. 295) as evincing a poor copy, made by some imitator of Plato, from the Protagoras.
[1] Plat. Hipp Minor, 366 B-C.
[2] Plato, Hippias Minor, 366 E. Πότερον σὺ ἂν μάλιστα ψεύδοιο καὶ ἀεὶ κατὰ ταὐτὰ ψευδῆ λέγοις περὶ τούτων, βουλόμενος ψεύδεσθαι καὶ μηδέποτε ἀληθῆ ἀποκρίνεσθαι; ἢ ὁ ἀμαθὴς εἰς λογισμοὺς δύναιτ᾽ ἂν σοῦ μᾶλλον ψεύδεσθαι βουλομένου; ἢ ὁ μὲν ἀμαθὴς πολλάκις ἂν βουλόμενος ψευδῆ λέγειν τἀληθῆ ἂν εἴποι ἄκων, εἰ τύχοι, διὰ τὸ μὴ εἰδέναι—σὺ δὲ ὁ σοφός, εἴπερ βούλοιο ψεύδεσθαι, ἀεὶ ἂν κατὰ τὰ αὐτὰ ψεύδοιο;
[3] Plato, Hipp. Minor, 367 C, 368 E, 369 A-B.

You see, therefore, Hippias, that the distinction which you drew and which you said that Homer drew, between Achilles and Odysseus, will not hold. You called Achilles veracious, and Odysseus, mendacious: but if one of the two epithets belongs to either of them, the other must belong to him also.[1]

View of Sokrates respecting Achilles in the Iliad. He thinks that Achilles speaks falsehood cleverly. Hippias maintains that if Achilles ever speaks falsehood, it is with an innocent purpose, whereas Odysseus does the like with fraudulent purpose.

Issue here taken. Sokrates contends that those who hurt, or cheat, or lie wilfully, are better than those who do the like unwillingly. He entreats Hippias to enlighten him and answer his questions.

Sokrates then tries to make out that Achilles speaks falsehood in the Iliad, and speaks it very cleverly, because he does so in a way to escape detection from Odysseus himself. To this Hippias replies, that if Achilles ever speaks falsehood, he does it innocently, without any purpose of cheating or injuring any one; whereas the falsehoods of Odysseus are delivered with fraudulent and wicked intent.[2] It is impossible (he contends) that men who deceive and do wrong wilfully and intentionally, should be better than those who do so unwillingly and without design. The laws deal much more severely with the former than with the latter.[3]

Upon this point, Hippias (says Sokrates), I dissent from you entirely. I am, unhappily, a stupid person, who cannot find out the reality of things: and this appears plainly enough when I come to talk with wise men like you, for I always find myself differing from you. My only salvation consists in my earnest anxiety to put questions and learn from you, and in my gratitude for your answers and teaching. I think that those who hurt mankind, or cheat, or lie, or do wrong, *wilfully*—are better than those who do the same *unwillingly*. Sometimes, indeed, from my stupidity, the opposite view presents itself to me, and I become confused: but now, after talking with you, the fit of confidence has come round upon me again, to pronounce and characterise the persons who do wrong *unwillingly*, as worse than those who do wrong *wilfully*. I entreat you to heal this disorder of my

---

[1] Plat. Hipp. Minor, 369 B. [2] Plat. Hipp. Minor, 370 E.
[3] Plat. Hipp. Minor, 372 A.

mind. You will do me much more good than if you cured my body of a distemper. But it will be useless for you to give me one of your long discourses : for I warn you that I cannot follow it. The only way to confer upon me real service, will be to answer my questions again, as you have hitherto done. Assist me, Eudikus, in persuading Hippias to do so.

Assistance from me (says Eudikus) will hardly be needed, for Hippias professed himself ready to answer any man's questions.

Yes—I did so (replies Hippias)—but Sokrates always brings trouble into the debate, and proceeds like one disposed to do mischief.

Eudikus repeats his request, and Hippias, in deference to him, consents to resume the task of answering.[1]

Sokrates then produces a string of questions, with a view to show that those who do wrong wilfully, are better than those who do wrong unwillingly. He appeals to various analogies. In running, the good runner is he who runs quickly, the bad runner is he who runs slowly. What is evil and base in running, is, to run slowly. It is the good runner who does this evil wilfully : it is the bad runner who does it unwillingly.[2] The like is true about wrestling and other bodily exercises. He that is good in the body, can work either strongly or feebly,—can do either what is honourable or what is base ; so that when he does what is base, he does it wilfully. But he that is bad in the body does what is base unwillingly, not being able to help it.[3]

Questions of Sokrates —multiplied analogies of the special arts. The unskilful artist, who runs, wrestles, or sings badly, whether he will or not, is worse than the skilful, who can sing well when he chooses, but can also sing badly when he chooses.

What is true about the bodily movements depending upon strength, is not less true about those depending on grace and elegance. To be wilfully ungraceful, belongs only to the well-constituted body : none but the badly-constituted body is ungraceful without wishing it. The same, also, about the feet, voice, eyes, ears, nose : of these organs, those which act badly through will and intention, are preferable to those which act badly without will or intention. Lameness of feet is a mis-

---

[1] Plat. Hipp. Min. 373 B. [2] Plat. Hipp. Min. 373 D-E.
[3] Plat. Hipp. Min. 374 B.

fortune and disgrace: feet which go lame only by intention are much to be preferred.[1]

Again, in the instruments which we use, a rudder or a bow,—or the animals about us, horses or dogs,—those are better with which we work badly when we choose; those are worse, with which we work badly without design, and contrary to our own wishes.

It is better to have the mind of a bowman who misses his mark only by design, than that of one who misses even when he intends to hit.

It is better to have the mind of a bowman who misses his mark by design, than that of one who misses when he tries to hit. The like about all other arts—the physician, the harper, the flute-player. In each of these artists, *that* mind is better, which goes wrong wilfully—*that* mind is worse, which goes wrong unwillingly, while wishing to go right. In regard to the minds of our slaves, we should all prefer those which go wrong only when they choose, to those which go wrong without their own choice.[2]

Having carried his examination through this string of analogous particulars, and having obtained from Hippias successive answers—"Yes—true in that particular case," Sokrates proceeds to sum up the result :—

Sokr.—Well! should we not wish to have our own minds as good as possible? *Hip.*—Yes. *Sokr.*—We have seen that they will be better if they do mischief and go wrong wilfully, than if they do so unwillingly? *Hip.*—But it will be dreadful, Sokrates, if the willing wrong-doers are to pass for better men than the unwilling.

Sokr.—Nevertheless—it seems so :—from what we have said.

Dissent and repugnance of Hippias.

Hip.—It does not seem so to me. *Sokr.*—I thought that it would have seemed so to you, as it does to me. However, answer me once more—Is not justice either a certain mental capacity? or else knowledge? or both together?[3] *Hip.*—Yes! it is. *Sokr.*—If justice be a capacity of the mind, the more capable mind will also be the juster: and we have already seen that the more capable soul is the better. *Hip.*—We have. *Sokr.*—If it be knowledge, the more knowing or wiser

---

[1] Plat. Hipp. Min. 374 C-D.
[2] Plat. Hipp. Min. 375 B-D.
[3] Plat. Hipp. Min. 375 D. ἡ δικαιοσύνη οὐχὶ ἢ δύναμίς τίς ἐστιν, ἢ ἐπιστήμη, ἢ ἀμφότερα;

mind will of course be the juster: if it be a combination of both capacity and knowledge, that mind which is more capable as well as more knowing, will be the juster—that which is less capable and less knowing, will be the more unjust. *Hip.*—So it appears. *Sokr.*—Now we have shown that the more capable and knowing mind is at once the better mind, and more competent to exert itself both ways—to do what is honourable as well as what is base—in every employment. *Hip.*—Yes. *Sokr.*—When, therefore, such a mind does what is base, it does so wilfully, through its capacity or intelligence, which we have seen to be of the nature of justice? *Hip.*—It seems so. *Sokr.*—Doing base things, is acting unjustly: doing honourable things, is acting justly. Accordingly, when this more capable and better mind acts unjustly, it will do so wilfully; while the less capable and worse mind will do so without willing it? *Hip.*—Apparently.

Sokr.—Now the good man is he that has the good mind: the bad man is he that has the bad mind. It belongs therefore to the good man to do wrong wilfully, to the bad man, to do wrong without wishing it—that is, if the good man be he that has the good mind? *Hip.*—But that is unquestionable—that he has it. *Sokr.*—Accordingly, he that goes wrong and does base and unjust things wilfully, if there be any such character—can be no other than the good man. *Hip.*—I do not know how to concede *that* to you, Sokrates.[1] *Sokr.*—Nor I, how to concede it to myself, Hippias: yet so it must appear to us, now at least, from the past debate. As I told you long ago, I waver hither and thither upon this matter; my conclusions never remain the same. No wonder indeed that I and other vulgar men waver: but if you wise men waver also, that becomes a fearful mischief even to us, since we cannot even by coming to you escape from our embarrassment.[2]

Conclusion—that none but the good man can do evil wilfully: the bad man does evil unwillingly. Hippias cannot resist the reasoning, but will not accept the conclusion. Sokrates confesses his perplexity.

I will here again remind the reader, that in this, as in the other dialogues, the real speaker is Plato throughout: and that

[1] Plat. Hipp. Min. 375 E, 376 B.   [2] Plato, Hipp. Min. 376 C.

it is he alone who prefixes the different names to words determined by himself.

Remarks on the dialogue. If the parts had been inverted, the dialogue would have been cited by critics as a specimen of the sophistry and corruption of the Sophists. Now, if the dialogue just concluded had come down to us with the parts inverted, and with the reasoning of Sokrates assigned to Hippias, most critics would probably have produced it as a tissue of sophistry justifying the harsh epithets which they bestow upon the Athenian Sophists—as persons who considered truth and falsehood to be on a par—subverters of morality—and corruptors of the youth of Athens.[1] But as we read it, all that, which in the mouth of Hippias would have passed for sophistry, is here put forward by Sokrates; while Hippias not only resists his conclusions, and adheres to the received ethical sentiment tenaciously, even when he is unable to defend it, but hates the propositions forced upon him, protests against the perverse captiousness of Sokrates, and requires much pressing to induce him to continue the debate. Upon the views adopted by the critics, Hippias ought to receive credit for this conduct, as a friend of virtue and morality. To me, such reluctance to debate appears a defect rather than a merit; but I cite the dialogue as illustrating what I have already said in another place—that

---

[1] Accordingly one of the Platonic critics, Schwalbe (Œuvres de Platon, p. 116), explains Plato's purpose in the Hippias Minor by saying, that Sokrates here serves out to the Sophists a specimen of their own procedure, and gives them an example of sophistical dialectic, by defending a sophistical thesis in a sophistical manner: That he chooses and demonstrates at length the thesis—the liar is not different from the truth-teller—as an exposure of the sophistical art of proving the contrary of any given proposition, and for the purpose of deriding and unmasking the false morality of Hippias, who in this dialogue talks reasonably enough.

Schwalbe, while he affirms that this is the purpose of Plato, admits that the part here assigned to Sokrates is unworthy of him; and Steinhart maintains that Plato never could have had any such purpose, "however frequently" (Steinhart says), "sophistical artifices may occur in this conversation of Sokrates, which artifices Sokrates no more disdained to employ than any other philosopher or rhetorician of that day" ("so häufig auch in seinen Erörterungen sophistische Kunstgriffe vorkommen mögen, die Sokrates eben so wenig verschmäht hat, als irgend ein Philosoph oder Redekünstler dieser Zeit"). Steinhart, Einleitung zum Hipp. Minor, p. 109.

I do not admit the purpose here ascribed to Plato by Schwalbe, but I refer to the passage as illustrating what Platonic critics think of the reasoning assigned to Sokrates in the Hippias Minor, and the hypotheses which they introduce to colour it.

The passage cited from Steinhart also—that Sokrates no more disdained to employ sophistical artifices than any other philosopher or rhetorician of the age—is worthy of note, as coming from one who is so very bitter in his invectives against the sophistry of the persons called Sophists, of which we have no specimens left.

Sokrates and Plato threw out more startling novelties in ethical doctrine, than either Hippias or Protagoras, or any of the other persons denounced as Sophists.

That Plato intended to represent this accomplished Sophist as humiliated by Sokrates, is evident enough : and the words put into his mouth are suited to this purpose. The eloquent lecturer, so soon as his admiring crowd of auditors has retired, proves unable to parry the questions of a single expert dialectician who remains behind, upon a matter which appears to him almost self-evident, and upon which every one (from Homer downward) agrees with him. Besides this, however, Plato is not satisfied without making him say very simple and absurd things. All this is the personal, polemical, comic scope of the dialogue. It lends (whether well-placed or not) a certain animation and variety, which the author naturally looked out for, in an aggregate of dialogues all handling analogous matters about man and society. *{Polemical purpose of the dialogue—Hippias humiliated by Sokrates.}*

But though the polemical purpose of the dialogue is thus plain, its philosophical purpose perplexes the critics considerably. They do not like to see Sokrates employing sophistry against the Sophists : that is, as they think, casting out devils by the help of Beelzebub. And certainly, upon the theory which they adopt, respecting the relation between Plato and Sokrates on one side, and the Sophists on the other, I think this dialogue is very difficult to explain. But I do not think it is difficult, upon a true theory of the Platonic writings.

In a former chapter, I tried to elucidate the general character and purpose of those Dialogues of Search, which occupy more than half the Thrasyllean Canon, and of which we have already reviewed two or three specimens—Euthyphron, Alkibiadês, &c. We have seen that they are distinguished by the absence of any affirmative conclusion : that they prove nothing, but only, at the most, disprove one or more supposable solutions : that they are not processes in which one man who knows communicates his knowledge to ignorant hearers, but in which all are alike ignorant, and all are employed, either in groping, or guessing, or testing the guesses of the rest. We have farther seen that the value of these *{Philosophical purpose of the dialogue—theory of the Dialogues of Search generally, and of Knowledge as understood by Plato.}*

Dialogues depends upon the Platonic theory about knowledge; that Plato did not consider any one to know, who could not explain to others all that he knew, reply to the cross-examination of a Sokratic Elenchus, and cross-examine others to test their knowledge: that knowledge in this sense could not be attained by hearing, or reading, or committing to memory a theorem, together with the steps of reasoning which directly conducted to it:—but that there was required, besides, an acquaintance with many counter-theorems, each having more or less appearance of truth; as well as with various embarrassing aspects and plausible delusions on the subject, which an expert cross-examiner would not fail to urge. Unless you are practised in meeting all the difficulties which he can devise, you cannot be said *to know*. Moreover, it is in this last portion of the conditions of knowledge, that most aspirants are found wanting.

Now the Greater and Lesser Hippias are peculiar specimens of these Dialogues of Search, and each serves the purpose above indicated. The Greater Hippias enumerates a string of tentatives, each one of which ends in acknowledged failure: the Lesser Hippias enunciates a thesis, which Sokrates proceeds to demonstrate, by plausible arguments such as Hippias is forced to admit. But though Hippias admits each successive step, he still mistrusts the conclusion, and suspects that he has been misled—a feeling which Plato[1] describes elsewhere as being frequent among the respondents of Sokrates. Nay, Sokrates himself shares in the mistrust—presents himself as an unwilling propounder of arguments which force themselves upon him,[2] and complains of his own mental embarrassment. Now you may call this sophistry, if you please; and you may silence

The Hippias is an exemplification of this theory—Sokrates sets forth a case of confusion, and avows his inability to clear it up. Confusion—shown up in the Lesser Hippias—Error in the Greater.

---

[1] Plato, Republ. vi. 487 B.
Καὶ ὁ Ἀδείμαντος, Ὦ Σώκρατες, ἔφη, πρὸς μὲν ταῦτά σοι οὐδεὶς ἂν οἷός τ' εἴη ἀντειπεῖν· ἀλλὰ γὰρ τοιόνδε τι πάσχουσιν οἱ ἀκούοντες ἑκάστοτε ἃ νῦν λέγεις· ἡγοῦνται δι' ἀπειρίαν τοῦ ἐρωτᾶν καὶ ἀποκρίνεσθαι, ὑπὸ τοῦ λόγου παρ' ἕκαστον τὸ ἐρώτημα σμικρὸν παραγόμενοι, ἀθροισθέντων τῶν σμικρῶν ἐπὶ τελευτῆς τῶν λόγων, μέγα τὸ σφάλμα καὶ ἐναντίον τοῖς πρώτοις ἀναφαίνεσθαι . . . ἐπεὶ τό γε ἀληθὲς οὐδέν τι μᾶλλον ταύτῃ ἔχειν.

This passage, attesting the effect of the Sokratic examination upon the minds of auditors, ought to be laid to heart by those Platonic critics who denounce the Sophists for generating scepticism and uncertainty.

[2] Plato, Hipp. Minor, 373 B; also the last sentence of the dialogue.

its propounders by calling them hard names. But such ethical prudery—hiding all the uncomfortable logical puzzles which start up when you begin to analyse an established sentiment, and treating them as non-existent because you refuse to look at them—is not the way to attain what Plato calls knowledge. If there be any argument, the process of which seems indisputable, while yet its conclusion contradicts, or seems to contradict, what is known upon other evidence—the full and patient analysis of that argument is indispensable, before you can become master of the truth and able to defend it. Until you have gone through such analysis, your mind must remain in that state of confusion which is indicated by Sokrates at the end of the Lesser Hippias. As it is a part of the process of Search, to travel in the path of the Greater Hippias—that is, to go through a string of erroneous solutions, each of which can be proved, by reasons shown, to *be* erroneous : so it is an equally important part of the same process, to travel in the path of the Lesser Hippias—that is, to acquaint ourselves with all those arguments, bearing on the case, in which two contrary conclusions appear to be both of them plausibly demonstrated, and in which therefore we cannot as yet determine which of them is erroneous—or whether both are not erroneous. The Greater Hippias exhibits errors,—the Lesser Hippias puts before us confusion. With both these enemies the Searcher for truth must contend : and Bacon tells us, that confusion is the worst enemy of the two—" Citius emergit veritas ex errore, quam ex confusione". Plato, in the Lesser Hippias, having in hand a genuine Sokratic thesis, does not disdain to invest Sokrates with the task (sophistical, as some call it, yet not the less useful and instructive) of setting forth at large this case of confusion, and avowing his inability to clear it up. It is enough for Sokrates that he brings home the painful sense of confusion to the feelings of his hearer as well as to his own. In that painful sentiment lies the stimulus provocative of farther intellectual effort.[1] The dialogue ends ; but the process of search, far from ending along with it, is emphatically declared to be unfinished, and to be

---

[1] See the passage in Republic, vii. ἐγερτικὸν τῆς νοήσεως is declared to arise 523-524, where the τὸ παρακλητικὸν καὶ from the pain of a felt contradiction.

in a condition not merely unsatisfactory but intolerable, not to be relieved except by farther investigation, which thus becomes a necessary sequel.

There are two circumstances which lend particular interest to this dialogue—Hippias Minor. 1. That the thesis out of which the confusion arises, is one which we know to have been laid down by the historical Sokrates himself. 2. That Aristotle expressly notices this thesis, as well as the dialogue in which it is contained, and combats it.

Sokrates in his conversation with the youthful Euthydemus (in the Xenophontic Memorabilia) maintains, that of two persons, each of whom deceives his friends in a manner to produce mischief, the one who does so wilfully is not so unjust as the one who does so unwillingly.[1] Euthydemus (like Hippias in this dialogue) maintains the opposite, but is refuted by Sokrates; who argues that justice is a matter to be learnt and known like letters; that the lettered man, who has learnt and knows letters, can write wrongly when he chooses, but never writes wrongly unless he chooses--while it is only the unlettered man who writes wrongly unwillingly and without intending it: that in like manner the just man, he that has learnt and knows justice, never commits injustice unless when he intends it—while the unjust man, who has not learnt and does not know justice, commits injustice whether he will or not. It is the just man therefore, and none but the just man (Sokrates maintains), who commits injustice knowingly and wilfully: it is the unjust man who commits injustice without wishing or intending it.[2]

The thesis maintained here by Sokrates, is also affirmed by the historical Sokrates in the Xenophontic Memorabilia.

This is the same view which is worked out by the Platonic Sokrates in the Hippias Minor: beginning with the antithesis between the veracious and mendacious man (as Sokrates begins in Xenophon); and concluding with the general result—that it

---

[1] Xen. Mem. iv. 2, 19. τῶν δὲ δὴ τοὺς φίλους ἐξαπατώντων ἐπὶ βλαβῇ (ἵνα μηδὲ τοῦτο παραλείπωμεν ἄσκεπτον) πότερος ἀδικώτερός ἐστιν, ὁ ἑκὼν ἢ ὁ ἄκων;

The natural meaning of ἐπὶ βλαβῇ would be, "for the purpose of mis- chief"; and Schneider, in his Index, gives "nocendi causâ". But in that meaning the question would involve an impossibility, for the words ὁ ἄκων exclude any such purpose.

[2] Xen. Mem. iv. 2, 19-22.

belongs to the good man to do wrong wilfully, to the bad man to do wrong unwillingly.

Aristotle,[1] in commenting upon this doctrine of the Hippias Minor, remarks justly, that Plato understands the epithets *veracious* and *mendacious* in a sense different from that which they usually bear. Plato understands the words as designating one who *can* tell the truth if he chooses—one who *can* speak falsely if he chooses: and in this sense he argues plausibly that the two epithets go together, and that no man can be mendacious unless he be also veracious. Aristotle points out that the epithets in their received meaning are applied, not to the power itself, but to the habitual and intentional use of that power. The power itself is doubtless presupposed or implied as one condition to the applicability of the epithets, and is one common condition to the applicability of both epithets: but the distinction, which they are intended to draw, regards the intentions and dispositions with which the power is employed. So also Aristotle observes that Plato's conclusion—" He that does wrong wilfully is a better man than he that does wrong unwillingly," is falsely collected from induction or analogy. The analogy of the special arts and accomplishments, upon which the argument is built, is not applicable. *Better* has reference, not to the amount of intelligence but to the dispositions and habitual intentions; though it presupposes a certain state and amount of intelligence as indispensable.

Aristotle combats the thesis. Arguments against it.

Both Sokrates and Plato (in many of his dialogues) commit the error of which the above is one particular manifestation—that of dwelling exclusively on the intellectual conditions of human conduct,[2] and omitting to give proper attention to the emotional and volitional, as essentially co-operating or preponderating in the complex meaning of ethical attributes. The reasoning ascribed to the Platonic Sokrates in the Hippias

Mistake of Sokrates and Plato in dwelling too exclusively on the intellectual conditions of human conduct.

---

[1] Aristotel. Metaphys. Δ. p. 1025, a. 8; compare Ethic. Nikomach. iv. p. 1127, b. 16.
[2] Aristotle has very just observations on these views of Sokrates, and on the incompleteness of his views when he resolved all virtue into knowledge, all vice into ignorance. See, among other passages, Aristot. Ethica Magna, i. 1182, a. 16; 1183, b. 9; 1190, b. 28; Ethic. Eudem. i. 1216, b. 4. The remarks of Aristotle upon Sokrates and Plato evince a real progress in ethical theory.

Minor exemplifies this one-sided view. What he says is true, but it is only a part of the truth. When he speaks of a person "who does wrong unwillingly," he seems to have in view one who does wrong without knowing that he does so: one whose intelligence is so defective that he does not know when he speaks truth and when he speaks falsehood. Now a person thus unhappily circumstanced must be regarded as half-witted or imbecile, coming under the head which the Xenophontic Sokrates called *madness*:[1] unfit to perform any part in society, and requiring to be placed under tutelage. Compared with such a person, the opinion of the Platonic Sokrates may be defended—that the mendacious person, who *can* tell truth when he chooses, is the better of the two in the sense of less mischievous or dangerous. But he is the object of a very different sentiment; moreover, this is not the comparison present to our minds when we call one man veracious, another man mendacious. We always assume, in every one, a measure of intelligence equal or superior to the admissible minimum; under such assumption, we compare two persons, one of whom speaks to the best of his knowledge and belief, the other, contrary to his knowledge and belief. We approve the former and disapprove the latter, according to the different intention and purpose of each (as Aristotle observes); that is, looking at them under the point of view of emotion and volition—which is logically distinguishable from the intelligence, though always acting in conjunction with it.

They rely too much on the analogy of the special arts—They take no note of the tacit assumptions underlying the epithets of praise and blame.

Again, the analogy of the special arts, upon which the Platonic Sokrates dwells in the Hippias Minor, fails in sustaining his inference. By a good runner, wrestler, harper, singer, speaker, &c., we undoubtedly mean one who can, if he pleases, perform some one of these operations well; although he can also, if he pleases, perform them badly. But the epithets *good* or *bad*, in this case, consider exclusively that element which was left out, and leave out that element which was exclusively considered, in the former case. The good singer is declared to stand distinguished from the bad

---

[1] Xen. Mem. iii. 9, 7. τοὺς διημαρτηκότας, ὧν οἱ πολλοὶ γιγνώσκουσι, μαινομένους καλεῖν, &c.

singer, or from the ἰδιώτης, who, if he sings at all, will certainly sing badly, by an attribute belonging to his intelligence and vocal organs. To sing well is a special accomplishment, which is possessed only by a few, and which no man is blamed for not possessing. The distinction between such special accomplishments, and justice or rectitude of behaviour, is well brought out in the speech which Plato puts into the mouth of the Sophist Protagoras.[1] " The special artists (he says) are few in number: one of them is sufficient for many private citizens. But every citizen, without exception, must possess justice and a sense of shame: if he does not, he must be put away as a nuisance—otherwise, society could not be maintained." The special artist is a citizen also; and as such, must be subject to the obligations binding on all citizens universally. In predicating of him that he is *good* or *bad* as a citizen, we merely assume him to possess the average intelligence of the community; and the epithet declares whether his emotional and volitional attributes exceed, or fall short of, the minimum required in the application of that intelligence to his social obligations. It is thus that the words *good* or *bad* when applied to him as a citizen, have a totally different bearing from that which the same words have when applied to him in his character of special artist.

The value of these debates in the Platonic dialogues consists in their raising questions like the preceding, for the reflection of the reader—whether the Platonic Sokrates may or may not be represented as taking what we think the right view of the question. For a Dialogue of Search, the great merit is, that it should be suggestive; that it should bring before our attention the conditions requisite for a right and proper use of these common ethical epithets, and the state of circumstances which is tacitly implied whenever any one uses them. No man ever learns to reflect upon the meaning of such familiar epithets, which he has been using all his life— unless the process be forced upon his attention by some special conversation which brings home to him an uncomfortable sentiment of perplexity and contradiction. If a man intends to

Value of a Dialogue of Search, that it shall be suggestive, and that it shall bring before us different aspects of the question under review.

[1] Plato, Protagoras, 322.

acquire any grasp of ethical or political theory, he must render himself master, not only of the sound arguments and the guiding analogies but also of the unsound arguments and the misleading analogies, which bear upon each portion of it.

There is one other point of similitude deserving notice, between the Greater and Lesser Hippias. In both of them, Hippias makes special complaint of Sokrates, for breaking the question in pieces and picking out the minute puzzling fragments—instead of keeping it together as a whole, and applying to it the predicates which it merits when so considered.[1] Here is the standing antithesis between Rhetoric and Dialectic : between those unconsciously acquired mental combinations which are poured out in eloquent, impressive, unconditional, and undistinguishing generalities— and the logical analysis which resolves the generality into its specialities, bringing to view inconsistencies, contradictions, limits, qualifications, &c. I have already touched upon this at the close of the Greater Hippias.

Antithesis between Rhetoric and Dialectic.

---

[1] Plato, Hipp. Min. 369 B-C. Ὦ Σώκρατες, ἀεὶ σύ τινας τοιούτους πλέκεις λόγους, καὶ ἀπολαμβάνων ὃ ἂν ᾖ δυσχερέστατον τοῦ λόγου, τούτου ἔχει κατὰ σμικρὸν ἐφαπτόμενος, καὶ οὐχ ὅλῳ ἀγωνίζει τῷ πράγματι, περὶ ὅτου ἂν ὁ λόγος ᾖ, &c.

A remark of Aristotle (Topica, viii. 164, b. 2) illustrates this dissecting function of the Dialectician.

ἔστι γάρ, ὡς ἁπλῶς εἰπεῖν, διαλεκτικὸς ὁ προτατικὸς καὶ ἐνστατικός· ἔστι δὲ τὸ μὲν προτείνεσθαι, ἓν ποιεῖν τὰ πλείω (δεῖ γὰρ ἐν ὅλῳ ληφθῆναι πρὸς ὃ ὁ λόγος), τὸ δ' ἐνίστασθαι, τὸ ἓν πολλά· ἢ γὰρ διαιρεῖ, ἢ ἀναιρεῖ, τὸ μὲν διδούς, τὸ δὲ οὔ, τῶν προτεινομένων.

CHAPTER XIV.

HIPPARCHUS—MINOS.

IN these two dialogues, Plato sets before us two farther specimens of that error and confusion which beset the enquirer during his search after "reasoned truth". Sokrates forces upon the attention of a companion two of the most familiar words of the market-place, to see whether a clear explanation of their meaning can be obtained.

In the dialogue called Hipparchus, the debate turns on the definition of τὸ φιλοκερδές or ὁ φιλοκερδής—the love of gain or the lover of gain. Sokrates asks his Companion to define the word. The Companion replies —He is one who thinks it right to gain from things worth nothing.[1] Does he do this (asks Sokrates) knowing that the things are worth nothing? or not knowing? If the latter, he is simply ignorant. He knows it perfectly well (is the reply). He is cunning and wicked; and it is because he cannot resist the temptation of gain, that he has the impudence to make profit by such things, though well aware that they are worth nothing. *Sokr.*—Suppose a husbandman, knowing that the plant which he is tending is worthless—and yet thinking that he ought to gain by it: does not that correspond to your description of the lover of gain? *Comp.*—The lover of gain, Sokrates, thinks that he ought to gain from every thing. *Sokr.*—Do not answer in that reckless manner,[2] as if you had been wronged by any one; but answer with

Hipparchus —Question —What is the definition of Lover of Gain? He is one who thinks it right to gain from things worth nothing. Sokrates cross-examines upon this explanation. No man expects to gain from things which he knows to be worth nothing: in this sense, no man is a lover of gain.

---
[1] Plato, Hipparch. 225 A. οἳ ἂν κερδαίνειν ἀξιῶσιν ἀπὸ τῶν μηδενὸς ἀξίων.
[2] Plato, Hipparch. 225 C.

attention. You agree that the lover of gain knows the value of that from which he intends to derive profit; and that the husbandman is the person cognizant of the value of plants. *Comp.*—Yes: I agree. *Sokr.*—Do not therefore attempt, you are so young, to deceive an old man like me, by giving answers not in conformity with your own admissions; but tell me plainly, Do you believe that the experienced husbandman, when he knows that he is planting a tree worth nothing, thinks that he shall gain by it? *Comp.*—No, certainly: I do not believe it.

Sokrates then proceeds to multiply illustrations to the same general point. The good horseman does not expect to gain by worthless food given to his horse: the good pilot, by worthless tackle put into his ship: the good commander, by worthless arms delivered to his soldiers: the good fifer, harper, bowman, by employing worthless instruments of their respective arts, if they know them to be worthless.

None of these persons (concludes Sokrates) correspond to your description of the lover of gain. Where then can you find a lover of gain? On your explanation, no man is so.[1] *Comp.*—I mean, Sokrates, that the lovers of gain are those, who, through greediness, long eagerly for things altogether petty and worthless; and thus display a love of gain.[2] *Sokr.*—Not surely knowing them to be worthless—for this we have shown to be impossible—but ignorant that they are worthless, and believing them to be valuable. *Comp.*—It appears so. *Sokr.*—Now gain is the opposite of loss: and loss is evil and hurt to every one: therefore gain (as the opposite of loss) is good. *Comp.*—Yes. *Sokr.*—It appears then that the lovers of good are those whom you call lovers of gain? *Comp.*—Yes: it appears so. *Sokr.*—Do not you yourself love good—all good things? *Comp.*—Certainly. *Sokr.*—And I too, and every one else. All men love good things, and hate evil. Now we agreed that gain was a good: so that by this reasoning, it appears that all men are lovers of gain—while by the former reasoning, we made out that none were so.[3] Which of the two

Gain is good. Every man loves good: therefore all men are lovers of gain.

---

[1] Plat. Hipparch. 226 D.
[2] Plat. Hipparch. 226 D. 'Ἀλλ' ἐγώ, ὦ Σώκρατες, βούλομαι λέγειν τούτους φιλοκερδεῖς εἶναι, οἳ ἑκάστοτε ὑπὸ ἀπληστίας καὶ πάνυ σμικρὰ καὶ ὀλίγου ἄξια καὶ οὐδενὸς γλίχονται ὑπερφυῶς καὶ φιλοκερδοῦσιν.
[3] Plat. Hipparch. 227 C.

CHAP. XIV. APPARENT CONTRADICTION. 73

shall we adopt, to avoid error. *Comp.*—We shall commit no error, Sokrates, if we rightly conceive the lover of gain. He is one who busies himself upon, and seeks to gain from, things from which good men do not venture to gain. *Sokr.*—But, my friend, we agreed just now, that gain was a good, and that all men always love good. It follows therefore, that good men as well as others love all gains, if gains are good things. *Comp.*—Not, certainly, those gains by which they will afterwards be hurt. *Sokr.*—Be hurt: you mean, by which they will become losers. *Comp.*—I mean that and nothing else. *Sokr.*—Do they become losers by gain, or by loss? *Comp.*—By both: by loss, and by evil gain. *Sokr.*—Does it appear to you that any useful and good thing is evil? *Comp.*—No. *Sokr.*—Well! we agreed just now that gain was the opposite of loss, which was evil; and that, being the opposite of evil, gain was good. *Comp.*—That was what we agreed. *Sokr.*—You see how it is: you are trying to deceive me: you purposely contradict what we just now agreed upon. *Comp.*—Not at all, by Zeus: on the contrary, it is you, Sokrates, who deceive me, wriggling up and down in your talk, I cannot tell how.[1] *Sokr.*—Be careful what you say: I should be very culpable, if I disobeyed a good and wise monitor. *Comp.*— Whom do you mean: and what do you mean? *Sokr.*—Hipparchus, son of Peisistratus. *Apparent contradiction. Sokrates accuses the companion of trying to deceive him. Accusation is retorted upon Sokrates.*

Sokrates then describes at some length the excellent character of Hipparchus: his beneficent rule, his wisdom, his anxiety for the moral improvement of the Athenians: the causes, different from what was commonly believed, which led to his death; and the wholesome precepts which he during his life had caused to be inscribed on various busts of Hermes throughout Attica. One of these busts or Hermæ bore the words —Do not deceive a friend.[2] *Precept inscribed formerly by Hipparchus the Peisistratid— "Never deceive a friend". Eulogy of Hipparchus by Sokrates.*

---

[1] Plat. Hipparch. 228 A. *Sokr.* Ὁρᾷς οὖν; ἐπιχειρεῖς με ἐξαπατᾶν, ἐπίτηδες ἐναντία λέγων οἷς ἄρτι ὡμολογήσαμεν. *Comp.* Οὐ μὰ Δί', ὦ Σώκρατες· ἀλλὰ τοὐναντίον σὺ ἐμὲ ἐξαπατᾷς, καὶ οὐκ οἶδα ὅπῃ ἐν τοῖς λόγοις ἄνω καὶ κάτω στρέφεις.

[2] Plat. Hipparch. 228 B—229 D. The picture here given of Hipparchus deserves notice. We are informed that he was older than his brother Hippias, which was the general belief at Athens, as Thucydides (i. 20, vi. 58) affirms, though himself contra-

The Companion resumes :—Apparently, Sokrates, either you do not account me your friend, or you do not obey Hipparchus: for you are certainly deceiving me in some unaccountable way in your talk. You cannot persuade me to the contrary.

Sokr.—Well then! in order that you may not think yourself deceived, you may take back any move that you choose, as if we were playing at draughts. Which of your admissions do you wish to retract—That all men desire good things? That loss (to be a loser) is evil? That gain is the opposite of loss: that to gain is the opposite of to lose? That to gain, as being the opposite of evil, is a good thing? *Comp.*—No. I do not retract any one of these. *Sokr.*—You think then, it appears, that some gain is good, other gain evil? *Comp.*—Yes, that is what I do think.[1] *Sokr.*—Well, I give you back that move: let it stand as you say. Some gain is good: other gain is bad. But surely the good gain is no more *gain*, than the bad gain: both are *gain*, alike and equally. *Comp.*—How do you mean?

Sokrates allows the companion to retract some of his answers. The companion affirms that some gain is good, other gain is evil.

Sokrates then illustrates his question by two or three analogies. Bad food is just as much *food*, as good food: bad drink, as much *drink* as good drink: a good man is no more *man* than a bad man.[2]

Sokr.—In like manner, bad gain, and good gain, are (both of them) *gain* alike—neither of them more or less than the other. Such being the case, what is that common quality possessed by both, which induces

Questions by Sokrates —Bad gain is *gain*, as much as good gain. What is the common property, in virtue of which both

dicting it, and affirming that Hippias was the elder brother. Plato however agrees with Thucydides in this point, that the three years after the assassination of Hipparchus, during which Hippias ruled alone, were years of oppression and tyranny; and that the hateful recollection of the Peisistratidæ, which always survived in the minds of the Athenians, was derived from these three last years.

The picture which Plato here gives of Hipparchus is such as we might expect from a philosopher. He dwells upon the pains which Hipparchus took to have the recitation of the Homeric poems made frequent and complete: also upon his intimacy with the poets Anakreon and Simonides. The colouring which Plato gives to the intimacy between Aristogeiton and Harmodius is also peculiar. The ἐραστής is represented by Plato as eager for the education and improvement of the ἐρώμενος; and the jealousy felt towards Hipparchus is described as arising from the distinguished knowledge and abilities of Hipparchus, which rendered him so much superior and more effective as an educator.

[1] Plat. Hipparch. 229 E, 230 A.
[2] Plat. Hipparch. 230 C.

CHAP. XIV.   GENERAL CONCEPTION OF GAIN.   75

you to call them by the same name *Gain?*[1] Would you call *Gain* any acquisition which one makes either with a smaller outlay or with no outlay at all?[2] *Comp.* —Yes. I should call that gain. *Sokr.*—For example, if after being at a banquet, not only without any outlay, but receiving an excellent dinner, you acquire an illness? *Comp.*—Not at all : that is no gain. *Sokr.* —But if from the banquet you acquire health, would that be gain or loss? *Comp.*—It would be gain. *Sokr.* —Not every acquisition therefore is gain, but only such acquisitions as are good and not evil : if the acquisition be evil, it is loss. *Comp.*—Exactly so. *Sokr.*—Well, now, you see, you are come round again to the very same point : Gain is good. Loss is evil. *Comp.*—I am puzzled what to say.[3] *Sokr.*—You have good reason to be puzzled. are called Gain? Every acquisition, made with no outlay, or with a smaller outlay, is gain. Objections —the acquisition may be evil. Embarrassment confessed.

But tell me : you say that if a man lays out little and acquires much, that is gain? *Comp.*—Yes : but not if it be evil : it is gain, if it be good, like gold or silver. *Sokr.*— I will ask you about gold and silver. Suppose a man by laying out one pound of gold acquires two pounds of silver, is it gain or loss ? *Comp.*—It is loss, decidedly, Sokrates : gold is twelve times the value of silver. *Sokr.*—Nevertheless he has acquired more : double is more than half. *Comp.*—Not in value : double silver is not more than half gold. *Sokr.*—It appears then that we must include value as essential to gain, not merely quantity. The valuable is gain : the valueless is no gain. The valuable is that which is valuable to possess : is that the profitable, or the unprofitable ? *Comp.*—It is the profitable. *Sokr.*— But the profitable is good ? *Comp.*—Yes : it is. *Sokr.*—Why then, here, the same conclusion comes back to us as agreed, for the third or fourth time. The gainful is good. *Comp.*—It appears so.[4] It is essential to gain, that the acquisition made shall be greater not merely in quantity, but also in value, than the outlay. The valuable is the profitable— the profitable is the good. Conclusion comes back, That Gain is Good.

Sokr.—Let me remind you of what has passed. You contended

---

[1] Plat. Hipparch. 230 E. διὰ τί ποτε ἀμφότερα αὐτὰ κέρδος καλεῖς; τί ταὐτὸν ἐν ἀμφοτέροις ὁρῶν;
[2] Plat. Hipparch. 231 A.
[3] Plat. Hipparch. 231 C. *Sokr.* Ὁρᾷς
οὖν, ὡς πάλιν αὖ περιτρέχεις εἰς τὸ αὐτὸ —τὸ μὲν κέρδος ἀγαθὸν φαίνεται, ἡ δὲ ζημία κακόν; *Comp.* Ἀπορῶ ἔγωγε ὅ, τι εἴπω. *Sokr.* Οὐκ ἀδίκως γε σὺ ἀπορῶν.
[4] Plato, Hipparch. 231 D-E, 232 A.

Recapitulation. The debate has shown that all gain is good, and that there is no evil gain. All men are lovers of Gain. No man ought to be reproached for being so. The Companion is compelled to admit this, though he declares that he is not persuaded.

that good men did not wish to acquire all sorts of gain, but only such as were good, and not such as were evil. But now, the debate has compelled us to acknowledge that all gains are good, whether small or great. *Comp.*—As for me, Sokrates, the debate has compelled me rather than persuaded me.[1] *Sokr.*— Presently, perhaps, it may even persuade you. But now, whether you have been persuaded or not, you at least concur with me in affirming that all gains, whether small or great, are good. That all good men wish for all good things. *Comp.*—I do concur. *Sokr.* —But you yourself stated that evil men love all gains, small and great? *Comp.*—I said so. *Sokr.*—According to your doctrine then, all men are lovers of gain, the good men as well as the evil? *Comp.*—Apparently so. *Sokr.*—It is therefore wrong to reproach any man as a lover of gain: for the person who reproaches is himself a lover of gain, just as much.

The Minos, like the Hipparchus, is a dialogue carried on between Sokrates and a companion not named. It relates to Law, or The Law—

Minos. Question put by Sokrates to the Companion, What is Law, or The Law? All Law is the same, quatenus law: What is the common constituent attribute?

Sokr.—What is Law (asks Sokrates)? *Comp.*— Respecting what sort of Law do you enquire (replies the Companion)? *Sokr.*—What! is there any difference between one law and another law, as to that identical circumstance, of being Law? Gold does not differ from gold, so far as the being gold is concerned —nor stone from stone, so far as being stone is concerned. In like manner, one law does not differ from another, all are the same, in so far as each is Law alike:—not, one of them more, and another less. It is about this as a whole that I ask you—What is Law?

Comp.—What should Law be, Sokrates, other than the various assemblage of consecrated and binding customs and beliefs?[2] *Sokr.*—Do you think, then, that discourse

Answer— Law is,

---

[1] Plat. Hipparch. 232 A-B. *Sokr.* Οὐκοῦν νῦν πάντα τὰ κέρδη ὁ λόγος ἡμᾶς ἠνάγκακε καὶ σμικρὰ καὶ μεγάλα ὁμολογεῖν ἀγαθὰ εἶναι; *Comp.* Ἠνάγκακε γάρ, ὦ Σώκρατες, μᾶλλον ἐμέ γε ἢ πέπεικεν. *Sokr.* Ἀλλ' ἴσως μετὰ τοῦτο καὶ πείσειεν ἄν.

[2] Plato, Minos, 313 B. Τί οὖν ἄλλο νόμος εἴη ἂν ἀλλ' ἢ τὰ νομιζόμενα;

is, the things spoken: that sight is, the things seen? that hearing is, the things heard? Or are they not distinct, in each of the three cases—and is not Law also one thing, the various customs and beliefs another? *Comp.*—Yes! I now think that they are distinct.[1] *Sokr.*—Law is that whereby these binding customs become binding. What is it? *Comp.*—Law can be nothing else than the public resolutions and decrees promulgated among us. Law is the decree of the city.[2] *Sokr.*—You mean, that Law is social opinion. *Comp.*—Yes—I do.

Sokr.—Perhaps you are right: but let us examine. some persons wise :—they are wise through wisdom. You call some just :—they are just through justice. In like manner, the lawfully-behaving men are so through law: the lawless men are so through lawlessness. Now the lawfully-behaving men are just: the lawless men are unjust. *Comp.*—It is so. *Sokr.*— Justice and Law, are highly honourable: injustice and lawlessness, highly dishonourable: the former preserves cities, the latter ruins them. *Comp.*—Yes— it does. *Sokr.*—Well, then! we must consider law as something honourable; and seek after it, under the assumption that it is a good thing. You defined law to be the decree of the city: Are not some decrees good, others evil? *Comp.*—Unquestionably. *Sokr.* —But we have already said that law is not evil. *Comp.*—I admit it. *Sokr.*—It is incorrect therefore to answer, as you did broadly, that law is the decree of the city. An evil decree cannot be law. *Comp.*— I see that it is incorrect.[3]

Sokr.—Still—I think, myself, that law is opinion of some sort; and since it is not evil opinion, it must be good opinion. Now good opinion is true opinion: and true opinion is, the finding out of reality. *Comp.*— I admit it. *Sokr.*—Law therefore wishes or tends to

1. The consecrated and binding customs. 2. The decree of the city. 3. Social or civic opinion.

Cross-examination by Sokrates— Just and lawfully-behaving men are so through law: unjust and lawless men are so through the absence of law. Law is highly honourable and useful: lawlessness is ruinous. Accordingly, bad decrees of the city— or bad social opinion— cannot be law.

Suggestion by Sokrates —Law is the *good* opinion of the city—

---

[1] Plato, Minos, 313 B-C.
I pass over here an analogy started by Sokrates in his next question ;—as ὄψις to τὰ ὁρώμενα, so νόμος to τὰ νομιζόμενα, &c.

[2] Plato, Minos, 314 A. ἐπειδὴ νόμῳ τὰ νομιζόμενα νομίζεται, τίνι ὄντι τῷ νόμῳ νομίζεται;

[3] Plato, Minos. 314 B-C-D.

But good opinion is true opinion, or the finding out of reality. Law therefore wishes (tends) to be the finding out of reality, though it does not always succeed in doing so.

ne, the finding out of reality.¹ *Comp.*—But, Sokrates, if law is the finding out of reality—if we have therein already found out realities—how comes it that all communities of men do not use the same laws respecting the same matters? *Sokr.*—The law does not the less wish or tend to find out realities; but it is unable to do so. That is, if the fact be true as you state—that we change our laws, and do not all of us use the same. *Comp.*—Surely, the fact as a fact is obvious enough.²

Objection taken by the Companion—That there is great discordance of laws in different places. He specifies several cases of such discordance, at some length. Sokrates reproves his prolixity, and requests him to confine himself to question or answer.

(The Companion here enumerates some remarkable local rites, venerable in one place, abhorrent in another, such as the human sacrifices at Carthage, &c., thus lengthening his answer much beyond what it had been before. Sokrates then continues):—

Sokr.—Perhaps you are right, and these matters have escaped me. But if you and I go on making long speeches each for ourselves, we shall never come to an agreement. If we are to carry on our research together, we must do so by question and answer. Question me, if you prefer:—if not, answer me. *Comp.*—I am quite ready, Sokrates, to answer whatever you ask.

Farther questions by Sokrates—Things heavy and light, just and unjust, honourable and dishonourable, &c., are so

Sokr.—Well, then! do you think that just things are just, and that unjust things are unjust? *Comp.*— I think they are. *Sokr.*—Do not all men in all communities, among the Persians as well as here, now as well as formerly, think so too? *Comp.*— Unquestionably they do. *Sokr.*—Are not things which weigh more, accounted heavier; and things which weigh less, accounted lighter, here, at Carthage, and everywhere else?³ *Comp.*—Certainly. *Sokr.*—It seems, then, that honourable things are accounted honourable everywhere, and dishonourable

---

[1] Plato, Minos, 315 A. Οὐκοῦν ἡ ἀληθὴς δόξα τοῦ ὄντος ἐστὶν ἐξεύρεσις; . . . ὁ νόμος ἄρα βούλεται τοῦ ὄντος εἶναι ἐξεύρεσις;

[2] Plato, Minos, 315 A-B.

[3] Plato Minos, 316 A. Πότερον δὲ τὰ πλείον ἕλκοντα βαρύτερα νομίζεται ἐνθάδε, τὰ δὲ ἔλαττον, κουφότερα, ἢ τοὐναντίον;

The verb νομίζεται deserves attention here, being the same word as has been employed in regard to law, and derived from νόμος.

CHAP. XIV.   LAWFUL INCLUDED IN REAL.   79

things dishonourable? not the reverse. *Comp.*—Yes, it is so. *Sokr.*—Then, speaking universally, existent things or realities (not non-existents) are accounted existent and real, among us as well as among all other men? *Comp.*—I think they are. *Sokr.*—Whoever therefore fails in attaining the real fails in attaining the lawful.[1] *Comp.*—As you now put it, Sokrates, it would seem that the same things are accounted lawful both by us at all times, and by all the rest of mankind besides. But when I reflect that we are perpetually changing our laws, I cannot persuade myself of what you affirm.

and are accounted so everywhere. Real things are always accounted real. Whoever fails in attaining the real, fails in attaining the lawful.

Sokr.—Perhaps you do not reflect that pieces on the draughtboard, when their position is changed, still remain the same. You know medical treatises: you know that physicians are the really knowing about matters of health: and that they agree with each other in writing about them. *Comp.*—Yes—I know that. *Sokr.*—The case is the same whether they be Greeks or not Greeks: Those who know, must of necessity hold the same opinion with each other, on matters which they know: always and everywhere. *Comp.*—Yes—always and everywhere. *Sokr.*—Physicians write respecting matters of health what they account to be true, and these writings of theirs are the medical laws? *Comp.*—Certainly they are. *Sokr.*—The like is true respecting the laws of farming—the laws of gardening—the laws of cookery. All these are the writings of persons, knowing in each of the respective pursuits? *Comp.*—Yes.[2] *Sokr.*—In like manner, what are the laws respecting the government of a city? Are they not the writings of those who know how to govern—kings, statesmen, and men of superior excellence? *Comp.*—Truly so. *Sokr.*—Knowing men like these will not write differently from each other about the same things, nor change what they

There are laws of health and of cure, composed by the few physicians wise upon those subjects, and unanimously declared by them. So also there are laws of farming, gardening, cookery, declared by the few wise in those respective pursuits. In like manner, the laws of a city are the judgments declared by the few wise men who know how to rule.

---

[1] Plat. Min. 316 B. οὐκοῦν, ὡς κατὰ τοῖς ἄλλοις ἅπασιν. *Comp.* Ἔμοιγε δοκεῖ. πάντων εἰπεῖν, τὰ ὄντα νομίζεται εἶναι, *Sokr.* Ὃς ἂν ἄρα τοῦ ὄντος ἁμαρτάνῃ, οὐ τὰ μὴ ὄντα, καὶ παρ᾽ ἡμῖν καὶ παρὰ τοῦ νομίμου ἁμαρτάνει.
[2] Plato, Minos, 316 D-E.

have once written. If, then, we see some doing this, are we to declare them knowing or ignorant? *Comp.*—Ignorant—undoubtedly.

Sokr.—Whatever is right, therefore, we may pronounce to be lawful; in medicine, gardening, or cookery: whatever is not right, not to be lawful but lawless. And the like in treatises respecting just and unjust, prescribing how the city is to be administered: That which is right, is the regal law—that which is not right, is not so, but only seems to be law in the eyes of the ignorant—being in truth lawless. *Comp.*—Yes. *Sokr.*—We were correct therefore in declaring Law to be the finding out of reality. *Comp.*—It appears so.[1] *Sokr.*—It is the skilful husbandman who gives right laws on the sowing of land: the skilful musician on the touching of instruments: the skilful trainer, respecting exercise of the body: the skilful king or governor, respecting the minds of the citizens. *Comp.*—Yes—it is.[2]

Marginal notes: That which is right is the regal law, the only true and real law. That which is not right, is not law, but only seems to be law in the eyes of the ignorant.

Sokr.—Can you tell me which of the ancient kings has the glory of having been a good lawgiver, so that his laws still remain in force as divine institutions? *Comp.*—I cannot tell. *Sokr.*—But can you not say which among the Greeks have the most ancient laws? *Comp.*—Perhaps you mean the Lacedæmonians and Lykurgus? *Sokr.*—Why, the Lacedæmonian laws are hardly more than three hundred years old: besides, whence is it that the best of them come? *Comp.*—From Krete, they say. *Sokr.*—Then it is the Kretans who have the most ancient laws in Greece? *Comp.*—Yes. *Sokr.*—Do you know those good kings of Krete, from whom these laws are derived—Minos and Rhadamanthus, sons of Zeus and Europa? *Comp.*—Rhadamanthus certainly is said to have been a just man, Sokrates; but Minos quite the reverse—savage, ill-tempered, unjust. *Sokr.*—What you affirm, my friend, is a fiction of the Attic tragedians. It is not stated either by Homer or Hesiod; who are far more worthy of credit than all the tragedians put

Marginal notes: Minos, King of Krete—his laws were divine and excellent, and have remained unchanged from time immemorial.

---

[1] Plato, Minos, 317 C. τὸ μὲν ὀρθὸν νόμος ἐστὶ βασιλικός· τὸ δὲ μὴ ὀρθόν οὔ, ὃ δοκεῖ νόμος εἶναι τοῖς οὐκ εἰδόσιν· ἔστι γὰρ ἄνομον.
[2] Plato, Minos, 318 A.

together. *Comp.*—What is it that Homer and Hesiod say about Minos?[1]

Sokrates replies by citing, and commenting upon, the statements of Homer and Hesiod respecting Minos, as the cherished son, companion, and pupil, of Zeus; who bestowed upon him an admirable training, teaching him wisdom and justice, and thus rendering him consummate as a lawgiver and ruler of men. It was through these laws, divine as emanating from the teaching of Zeus, that Krete (and Sparta as the imitator of Krete) had been for so long a period happy and virtuous. As ruler of Krete, Minos had made war upon Athens, and compelled the Athenians to pay tribute. Hence he had become odious to the Athenians, and especially odious to the tragic poets who were the great teachers and charmers of the crowd. These poets, whom every one ought to be cautious of offending, had calumniated Minos as the old enemy of Athens.[2]

Question about the character of Minos—Homer and Hesiod declare him to have been admirable; the Attic tragedians defame him as a tyrant, because he was the enemy of Athens.

But that these tales are mere calumny (continues Sokrates), and that Minos was truly a good lawgiver, and a good shepherd (νομεὺς ἀγαθός) of his people—we have proof through the fact, that his laws still remain unchanged: which shows that he has really found out truth and reality respecting the administration of a city.[3] *Comp.*—Your view seems plausible, Sokrates. *Sokr.*— If I am right, then, you think that the Kretans have more ancient laws than any other Greeks? and that Minos and Rhadamanthus are the best of all ancient lawgivers, rulers, and shepherds of mankind? *Comp.* —I think they are.

That Minos was really admirable— and that he has found out truth and reality respecting the administration of the city— we may be sure from the fact that his laws have remained so long unaltered.

Sokr.—Now take the case of the good lawgiver and good shepherd for the body—If we were asked, what it is that he prescribes for the body, so as to render it better? we should answer, at once, briefly, and well, by saying—food and labour: the former to sustain the body, the latter to exercise and consolidate it.

The question is made more determinate. What is it that the good law-

---

[1] Plato, Minos, 318 E.
[2] Plato, Minos, 319-320.
[3] Plato, Minos, 321 B. τοῦτο μέ- γιστον σημεῖον, ὅτι ἀκίνητοι αὐτοῦ οἱ νόμοι εἰσίν, ἅτε τοῦ ὄντος περὶ πόλεως οἰκήσεως ἐξευρόντος εὖ τὴν ἀλήθειαν.

Comp.—Quite correct. *Sokr.*—And if after that we were asked, What are those things which the good lawgiver prescribes for the mind to make it better, what should we say, so as to avoid discrediting ourselves? *Comp.*—I really cannot tell. *Sokr.*—But surely it is discreditable enough both for your mind and mine—to confess, that we do not know upon what it is that good and evil for our minds depends, while we can define upon what it is that the good or evil of our bodies depends?[1]

<small>giver prescribes and measures out for the health of the mind—as the physician measures out food and exercise for the body? Sokrates cannot tell. Close.</small>

I have put together the two dialogues Hipparchus and Minos, partly because of the analogy which really exists between them, partly because that analogy is much insisted on by Boeckh, Schleiermacher, Stallbaum, and other recent critics; who not only strike them both out of the list of Platonic works, but speak of them with contempt as compositions. On the first point, I dissent from them altogether: on the second, I agree with them thus far—that I consider the two dialogues inferior works of Plato:—much inferior to his greatest and best compositions,—certainly displaying both less genius and less careful elaboration—probably among his early performances—perhaps even unfinished projects, destined for a farther elaboration, which they never received, and not published until after his decease. Yet in Hipparchus as well as in Minos, the subjects debated are important as regards ethical theory. Several questions are raised and partially canvassed: no conclusion is finally attained. These characteristics they have in common with several of the best Platonic dialogues.

<small>The Hipparchus and Minos are analogous to each other, and both of them inferior works of Plato, perhaps unfinished.</small>

In Hipparchus, the question put by Sokrates is, about the definition of ὁ φιλοκερδὴς (the lover of gain), and of κέρδος itself—gain. The first of these two words (like many in Greek as well as in English) is used in two senses. In its plain, etymological sense, it means an attribute belonging to all men: all men love gain, hate loss.

<small>Hipparchus—Double meaning of φιλοκερδὴς and κέρδος.</small>

[1] Plato, Minos, 321 C-D.

CHAP. XIV.   NO TENABLE DEFINITION.   83

But since this is predicable of all, there is seldom any necessity for predicating it of any one man or knot of men in particular. Accordingly, when you employ the epithet as a predicate of A or B, what you generally mean is, to assert something more than its strict etymological meaning : to declare that he has the attribute in unusual measure ; or that he has shown himself, on various occasions, wanting in other attributes, which on those occasions ought, in your judgment, to have countervailed it. The epithet thus comes to connote a sentiment of blame or reproach, in the mind of the speaker.[1]

The Companion or Collocutor, being called upon by Sokrates to explain τὸ φιλοκερδές, defines it in this last sense, as conveying or connoting a reproach. He gives three different explanations of it (always in this sense), loosely worded, each of which Sokrates shows to be untenable. A variety of parallel cases are compared, and the question is put (so constantly recurring in Plato's writings), what is the state of the agent's mind as to knowledge? The cross-examination makes out, that if the agent be supposed to know,—then there is no man corresponding to the definition of a φιλοκερδής : if the agent be supposed not to know —then, on the contrary, every man will come under the definition. The Companion is persuaded that there is such a thing as "love of gain" in the blamable sense. Yet he cannot find any tenable definition, to discriminate it from "love of gain" in the ordinary or innocent sense. *(State of mind of the agent, as to knowledge, frequent inquiry in Plato. No tenable definition found.)*

The same question comes back in another form, after Sokrates has given the liberty of retractation. The Collocutor maintains that there is *bad* gain, as well as *good* gain. But what is that common, generic, quality, designated by the word *gain*, apart from these two distinctive epithets? He cannot find it out or describe it. He gives two definitions, each of which is torn up by Sokrates. To deserve the name of *gain*, that which a man acquires must be good ; and it must surpass, in value as well *(Admitting that there is bad gain, as well as good gain, what is the meaning of the word gain? None is found.)*

---

[1] Aristotle adverts to this class of ethical epithets, connoting both an attribute in the person designated and an unfavourable sentiment in the speaker (Ethic. Nikom. ii. 6, p. 1107 a. 9).   Οὐ πᾶσα δ' ἐπιδέχεται πρᾶξις, οὐδὲ πᾶν πάθος, τὴν μεσότητα· ἔνια γὰρ εὐθὺς ὠνόμασται συνειλημμένα μετὰ τῆς φαυλότητος, οἷον, &c.

as in quantity, the loss or outlay which he incurs in order to acquire it. But when thus understood, all gains are good. There is no meaning in the distinction between good and bad gains: all men are lovers of gain.

With this confusion, the dialogue closes. The Sokratic notion of *good*, as what every one loves—*evil* as what every one hates—also of evil-doing, as performed by every evil-doer only through ignorance or mistake—is brought out and applied to test the ethical phraseology of a common-place respondent. But it only serves to lay bare a state of confusion and perplexity, without clearing up any thing. Herein, so far as I can see, lies Plato's purpose in the dialogue. The respondent is made aware of the confusion, which he did not know before; and this, in Plato's view, is a progress. The respondent cannot avoid giving contradictory answers, under an acute cross-examination: but he does not adopt any new belief. He says to Sokrates at the close—"The debate has constrained rather than persuaded me".[1] This is a simple but instructive declaration of the force put by Sokrates upon his collocutors; and of the reactionary effort likely to be provoked in their minds, with a view to extricate themselves from a painful sense of contradiction. If such effort be provoked, Plato's purpose is attained.

Purpose of Plato in the dialogue— To lay bare the confusion, and to force the mind of the respondent into efforts for clearing it up.

One peculiarity there is, analogous to what we have already seen in the Hippias Major. It is not merely the Collocutor who charges Sokrates, but also Sokrates who accuses the Collocutor—each charging the other with attempts to deceive a friend.[2] This seems intended by Plato to create an occasion for introducing what he had to say about Hipparchus—*apropos* of the motto on the Hipparchean Hermes—μὴ φίλον ἐξαπάτα.

The modern critics, who proclaim the Hipparchus not to be the work of Plato, allege as one of the proofs of spuriousness, the occurrence of this long narrative and comment upon the historical Hipparchus and his behaviour; which narrative (the critics maintain) Plato would never have introduced, seeing that it

Historical narrative and comments given in the dialogue respecting Hipparchus

---

[1] Plato, Hipparch. 232 B. ἠνάγκακε γὰρ (ὁ λόγος) μᾶλλον ἐμέ γε ἢ πέπεικεν.
[2] Plato, Hipparch. 225 E, 228 A.

contributes nothing to the settlement of the question —afford no ground for debated. But to this we may reply, first, That there declaring are other dialogues[1] (not to mention the Minos) in the dialogue to be spurious. which Plato introduces recitals of considerable length, historical or quasi-historical recitals; bearing remotely, or hardly bearing at all, upon the precise question under discussion; next, —That even if no such analogies could be cited, and if the case stood single, no modern critic could fairly pretend to be so thoroughly acquainted with Plato's views and the surrounding circumstances, as to put a limit on the means which Plato might choose to take, for rendering his dialogues acceptable and interesting. Plato's political views made him disinclined to popular government generally, and to the democracy of Athens in particular. Conformably with such sentiment, he is disposed to surround the rule of the Peisistratidæ with an ethical and philosophical colouring: to depict Hipparchus as a wise man busied in instructing and elevating the citizens; and to discredit the renown of Harmodius and Aristogeiton, by affirming them to have been envious of Hipparchus, as a philosopher who surpassed themselves by his own mental worth. All this lay perfectly in the vein of Plato's sentiment; and we may say the same about the narrative in the Minos, respecting the divine parentage and teaching of Minos, giving rise to his superhuman efficacy as a lawgiver and ruler. It is surely very conceivable, that Plato, as a composer of ethical dialogues or dramas, might think that such recitals lent a charm or interest to some of them. Moreover, something like variety, or distinctive features as between one dialogue and another, was a point of no inconsiderable moment. I am of opinion that Plato did so conceive these narratives. But at any rate, what I here contend is, that no modern critics have a right to assume as certain that he did not.

[1] See Alkibiad. ii. pp. 142-149-150; Alkibiad. i. pp. 121-122: Protagoras, 342-344; Politikus, 268 D., σχεδὸν παιδιὰν ἐγκερασαμένους, and the two or three pages which follow.
F. A. Wolf, and various critics after him, contend that the genuineness of the Hipparchus was doubted in antiquity, on the authority of Ælian, V. H. viii. 2. But I maintain that this is not the meaning of the passage, unless upon the supposition that the word μαθητὴς is struck out of the text conjecturally. The passage may be perfectly well construed, leaving μαθητὴς in the text: we must undoubtedly suppose the author to have made an assertion historically erroneous: but this is nowise impossible in the case of Ælian. If you construe the passage as it stands, without such conjectural alteration, it does not justify Wolf's inference.

I now come to the Minos. The subject of this dialogue is, the explanation or definition of Law. Sokrates says to his Companion or Collocutor,—Tell me what is the generic constituent of Law: All Laws are alike *quatenus* Law. Take no note of the difference between one law and another, but explain to me what characteristic property it is, which is common to all Law, and is implied in or connoted by the name Law.

Minos— Question— What is the characteristic property connoted by the word Νόμος or law?

This question is logically the same as that which Sokrates asks in the Hipparchus with reference to κέρδος or gain.

That the definition of Νόμος or Law was discussed by Sokrates, we know, not only from the general description of his debates given in Xenophon, but also from the interesting description (in that author) of the conversation between the youthful Alkibiades and Perikles.[1] The interrogations employed by Alkibiades on that occasion are Sokratic, and must have been derived, directly or indirectly, from Sokrates. They are partially analogous to the questions of Sokrates in the dialogue Minos, and they end by driving Perikles into a confusion, left unexplained, between Law and Lawlessness.

This question was discussed by the historical Sokrates, Memorabilia of Xenophon.

Definitions of Νόμος are here given by the Companion, who undergoes a cross-examination upon them. First, he says, that Νόμος = τὰ νομιζόμενα. But this is rejected by Sokrates, who intimates that Law is not the aggregate of laws enacted or of customs held binding: but that which lies behind these laws and customs, imparting to them their binding force.[2] We are to enquire what this is. The Companion declares that it is the public decree of the city: political or social opinion. But this again Sokrates contests: putting questions to show that Law includes, as a portion of its meaning, justice, goodness, beauty, and preservation of the city with its possessions; while lawlessness includes injustice, evil, ugliness, and destruction. There can be no such hing as bad or wicked law.[3] But among decrees of the city,

Definitions of law—suggested and refuted. Law includes, as a portion of its meaning, justice, goodness, usefulness, &c. Bad decrees are not laws.

[1] Xen. Mem. i. 1, 16; i. 2, 42-46.
[2] Plato, Minos, 314 A. ἐπειδὴ νόμῳ τὰ νομιζόμενα νομίζεται, τίνι ὄντι τῷ νόμῳ νομίζεται;
[3] Plato, Minos, 314 E. καὶ μὴν νόμος γε οὐκ ἦν πονηρός.

CHAP. XIV. DEFINITIONS OF LAW. 87

some are bad, some are good. Therefore to define Law as a decree of the city, thus generally, is incorrect. It is only the good decree, not the bad decree, which is Law. Now the good decree or opinion, is the true opinion: that is, it is the finding out of reality. Law therefore wishes or aims to be the finding out of reality: and if there are differences between different nations, this is because the power to find out does not always accompany the wish to find out.

As to the assertion—that Law is one thing here, another thing there, one thing at one time, another thing at another—Sokrates contests it. Just things are just (he says) everywhere and at all times; unjust things are unjust also. Heavy things are heavy, light things light, at one time, as well as at another. So also honourable things are everywhere honourable, base things everywhere base. In general phrase, existent things are everywhere existent,[1] non-existent things are not existent. Whoever therefore fails to attain the existent and real, fails to attain the lawful and just. It is only the man of art and knowledge, in this or that department, who attains the existent, the real, the right, true, lawful, just. Thus the authoritative rescripts or laws in matters of medicine, are those laid down by practitioners who know that subject, all of whom agree in what they lay down: the laws of cookery, the laws of agriculture and of gardening—are rescripts delivered by artists who know respectively each of those subjects. So also about Just and Unjust, about the political and social arrangements of the city— the authoritative rescripts or laws are, those laid down by the artists or men of knowledge in that department, all of whom agree in laying down the same: that is, all the men of art called kings or lawgivers. It is only the right, the true, the real—that which these artists attain—which is properly a law and is entitled to be so called. That which is not right is not a law,— ought not to be so called—and is only supposed to be a law by the error of ignorant men.[2]

Sokrates affirms that law is everywhere the same—It is the declared judgment and command of the Wise man, upon the subject to which it refers—It is truth and reality, found out and certified by him.

[1] M. Boeckh remarks justly in his note on this passage—"neque enim illud demonstratum est, eadem omnibus legitima esse — sed tantum, *notionem*" (rather the sentiment or emotion) "*legitimi* omnibus eandem esse. Sed omnia scriptor hic confundit."

[2] Plato, Minos, 317 C.

That the reasoning of Sokrates in this dialogue is confused and unsound (as M. Boeckh and other critics have remarked), I perfectly agree. But it is not the less completely Platonic; resting upon views and doctrines much cherished and often reproduced by Plato. The dialogue Minos presents, in a rude and awkward manner, without explanation or amplification, that worship of the Abstract and the Ideal, which Plato, in other and longer dialogues, seeks to diversify as well as to elaborate. The definitions of Law here combated and given by Sokrates, illustrate this. The good, the true, the right, the beautiful, the real—all coalesce in the mind of Plato. There is nothing (in his view) real, except *The* Good, *The* Just, &c. (τὸ αὐτο-ἀγαθὸν; αὐτο-δίκαιον—Absolute Goodness and Justice): particular good and just things have no reality, they are no more good and just than bad and unjust—they are one or the other, according to circumstances—they are ever variable, floating midway between the real and unreal.[1] The real alone is knowable, correlating with knowledge or with the knowing Intelligence Νοῦς. As Sokrates distinguishes elsewhere τὸ δίκαιον or αὐτο-δίκαιον from τὰ δίκαια—so here he distinguishes (νόμος from τὰ νομιζόμενα) *Law*, from the assemblage of actual commands or customs received as *laws* among mankind. These latter are variable according to time and place; but Law is always one and the same. Plato will acknowledge nothing to *be* Law, except that which (he thinks) *ought to be* Law: that which emanates from a lawgiver of consummate knowledge, who aims at the accomplishment of the good and the real, and knows how to discover and realise that end. So far as "the decree of the city" coincides with what would have been enacted by this lawgiver (*i. e.* so far as it is good and right), Sokrates admits it as a valid explanation of Law; but no farther. He considers the phrase *bad law* to express a logical impossibility, involving a contradiction *in adjecto*.[2] What others call a bad law, he regards as being

---

[1] See the remarkable passage in the fifth book of the Republic, pp. 479-480; compare vii. 538 E.
[2] Plato, Minos, 314 D. The same argument is brought to bear by the Platonic Sokrates against Hippias in the Hippias Major, 284-285. If the laws are not really profitable, which is the only real purpose for which they were established, they

CHAP. XIV.   LAW ACTUAL—LAW IDEAL.   89

no real law, but only a fallacious image, mistaken for such by the ignorant. He does not consider such ignorant persons as qualified to judge: he recognises only the judgment of the knowing one or few, among whom he affirms that there can be no difference of opinion. Every one admits just things to be just,—unjust things to be unjust,—heavy things to be heavy,— the existent and the real, to be the existent and the real. If then the lawgiver in any of his laws fails to attain this reality, he fails in the very purpose essential to the conception of law :[1] *i. e.* his pretended law is no law at all.

By *Law*, then, Plato means—not the assemblage of actual positive rules, nor any general property common to and characteristic of them, nor the free determination of an assembled Demos as distinguished from the mandates of a despot—but the Type of Law as it ought to be, and as it would be, if prescribed by a perfectly wise ruler, aiming at good and knowing how to realise it. This, which is the ideal of his own mind, Plato worships and reasons upon as if it were the only reality; as Law by nature, or natural Law, distinguished from actual positive laws : which last have either been set by some ill-qualified historical ruler, or have grown up insensibly. Knowledge, art, philosophy, systematic and constructive, applied by some one or few exalted individuals, is (in his view) the only cause capable of producing that typical result which is true, good, real, permanent, and worthy of the generic name. {*Plato worships the Ideal of his own mind—the work of systematic constructive theory by the Wise Man.*}

In the Minos, this general Platonic view is applied to Law: in the Politikus, to government and social administration : in the Kratylus, to naming or language. In the Politikus, we find the received classification of governments (monarchy, aristocracy, and democracy) discarded as improper ; and the assertion advanced, That there is only one government right, true, genuine, really existing—government by the uncontrolled authority and superintendence of the man of exalted intelligence : he who is master in the {*Different applications of this general Platonic view, in the Minos, Politikus, Kratylus, &c. Natural Rectitude of Law, Government, Names, &c.*}

---

are no laws at all. The Spartans are παράνομοι. Some of the answers assigned to Hippias (284 D) are pertinent enough; but he is overborne.

[1] Plato, Minos, 316 B. Ὅς ἂν ἄρα τοῦ ὄντος ἁμαρτάνῃ, τοῦ νομίμου ἁμαρτάνει.

art of governing, whether such man do in fact hold power anywhere or not. All other governments are degenerate substitutes for this type, some receding from it less, some more.[1] Again, in the Kratylus, where names and name-giving are discussed, Sokrates[2] maintains that things can only be named according to their true and real nature—that there is, belonging to each thing, one special and appropriate Name-Form, discernible only by the sagacity of the intelligent Lawgiver: who alone is competent to bestow upon each thing its right, true, genuine, real name, possessing rectitude by nature (ὀρθότης φύσει).[3] This Name-Form (according to Sokrates) is the same in all languages in so far as they are constructed by different intelligent Lawgivers, although the letters and syllables in which they may clothe the Form are very different.[4] If names be not thus apportioned by the systematic purpose of an intelligent Lawgiver, but raised up by insensible and unsystematic growth—they will be unworthy substitutes for the genuine type, though they are the best which actual societies possess; according to the opinion announced by Kratylus in that same dialogue, they will not be names at all.[5]

The Kretan Minos (we here find it affirmed), son, companion,

Eulogy on Minos, as having established

and pupil of Zeus, has learnt to establish laws of this divine type or natural rectitude: the proof of which is, that the ancient Kretan laws have for imme-

---

[1] Plato, Politikus, 293 C-E. ταύτην ὀρθὴν διαφερόντως εἶναι καὶ μόνην πολιτείαν, ἐν ᾗ τις ἂν εὑρίσκοι τοὺς ἄρχοντας ἀληθῶς ἐπιστήμονας καὶ οὐ δοκοῦντας μόνον . . . τότε καὶ κατὰ τοὺς τοιούτους ὅρους ἡμῖν μόνην ὀρθὴν πολιτείαν εἶναι ῥητέον. ὅσας δὲ ἄλλας λέγομεν, οὐ γνησίας οὐδ' ὄντως οὔσας λεκτέον, ἀλλὰ μεμιμημένας ταύτην, ἃς μὲν εὐνόμους λέγομεν, ἐπὶ τὰ καλλίω, τὰς δὲ ἄλλας ἐπὶ τὰ αἰσχίονα μεμιμῆσθαι.

The historical (Xenophontic) Sokrates asserts this same position in Xenophon's Memorabilia (iii. 9, 10). "Sokrates said that Kings and Rulers were those who knew how to command, not those who held the sceptre or were chosen by election or lot, or had acquired power by force or fraud," &c. The Kings of Sparta and Macedonia, the Βουλὴ and Δῆμος of Athens, the Despot of Syracuse or Pheræ, are here declared to be not real rulers at all.

[2] Plato, Kratylus, 387 D.

[3] Plato, Kratyl. 388 A-E.

[4] Plato, Kratyl. 389 E, 390 A, 432 E. Οὐκοῦν οὕτως ἀξιώσεις καὶ τὸν νομοθέτην τόν τε ἐνθάδε καὶ τὸν ἐν τοῖς βαρβάροις, ἕως ἂν τὸ τοῦ ὀνόματος εἶδος ἀποδιδῷ τὸ προσῆκον ἑκάστῳ ἐν ὁποιαισοῦν συλλαβαῖς, οὐδὲν χείρω νομοθέτην εἶναι τὸν ἐνθάδε ἢ τὸν ὁπουοῦν ἄλλοθι; Compare this with the Minos, 315 E, 316 D, where Sokrates evades, by an hypothesis very similar, the objection made by the collocutor, that the laws in one country are very different from those in another—ἴσως γὰρ οὐκ ἐννοεῖς ταῦτα μεταπεττευόμενα ὅτι ταὐτά ἐστιν.

[5] Plato, Kratyl. 430 A, 432 A, 433 D, 435 C.

Kratylus says that a name badly given is no name at all; just as Sokrates says in the Minos that a bad law is no law at all.

morial ages remained, and still do remain,[1] unchanged. But when Sokrates tries to determine, Wherein consists this Law-Type? What is it that the wise Lawgiver prescribes for the minds of the citizens—as the wise gymnastic trainer prescribes proper measure of nourishment and exercise for their bodies?—the question is left unanswered. Sokrates confesses with shame that he cannot answer it: and the dialogue ends in a blank. The reader—according to Plato's manner—is to be piqued and shamed into the effort of meditating the question for himself. *laws on this divine type or natural rectitude.*

An attempt to answer this question will be found in Plato's Treatise De Legibus—in the projected Kretan colony, of which he there sketches the fundamental laws. Aristophanes of Byzantium very naturally placed this treatise as sequel to the Minos; second in the Trilogy of which the Minos was first.[2] *The Minos was arranged by Aristophanes at first in a Trilogy along with the Leges.*

Whoever has followed the abstract of the Minos, which I have just given, will remark the different explanations of the word Law—both those which are disallowed, and that which is preferred, though left incomplete, by Sokrates. On this same subject, there are in many writers, modern as well as ancient, two distinct modes of confusion traceable—pointed out by eminent recent jurists, such as Mr. Bentham, Mr. Austin, and Mr. Maine. 1. Between Law as it is, and Law as it ought to be. 2. Between Laws Imperative, set by intelligent rulers, and enforced by penal sanction—and Laws signifying uniformities of fact expressed in general terms, such as the Law of Gravitation, Crystallisation, &c.—We can hardly say that in the dialogue Minos, Plato falls into the first of these two modes of confusion: for he expressly says that he only recognises the Ideal of Law, or Law as it ought to be (actual Laws everywhere being disallowed, except in so far as they conform thereunto). But he does fall into the second, when he identifies the Lawful with the Real or Existent. His Ideal stands in place of generalisations of fact. *Explanations of the word Law—Confusion in its meaning.*

There is also much confusion, if we compare the Minos with other dialogues: wherein Plato frequently talks of Laws as the

---

[1] Plato, Minos, 319 B, 321 A.
[2] I reserve for an Appendix some further remarks upon the genuineness of Hipparchus and Minos.

laws and customs actually existing or imperative in any given state—Athens, Sparta, or elsewhere (Νόμος = τὰ νομιζόμενα, according to the first words in the Minos). For example, in the harangue which he supposes to be addressed to Sokrates in the Kriton, and which he invests with so impressive a character—the Laws of Athens are introduced as speakers : but according to the principles laid down in the Minos, three-fourths of the Laws of Athens could not be regarded as laws at all. If therefore we take Plato's writings throughout, we shall not find that he is constant to one uniform sense of the word Law, or that he escapes the frequent confusion between Law as it actually exists and Law as it ought to be.[1]

[1] The first explanation of Νόμος advanced by the Companion in reply to Sokrates (viz. Νόμος = τὰ νομιζόμενα), coincides substantially with the meaning of Νόμος βασιλεύς in Pindar and Herodotus (see above, chap. viii.), who is an imaginary ruler, occupying a given region, and enforcing τὰ νομιζόμενα. It coincides also with the precept Νόμῳ πόλεως, as prescribed by the Pythian priestess to applicants who asked advice about the proper forms of religious worship (Xen. Mem. i. 3, 1); though this precept, when Cicero comes to report it (Legg. ii. 16, 40), appears divested of its simplicity, and overclouded with the very confusion touched upon in my text. Aristotle does not keep clear of the confusion (compare Ethic. Nikom. i. 1, 1094, b. 16, and v. 5, 1130, b. 24). I shall revert again to the distinction between νόμος and φύσις, in touching on other Platonic dialogues. Cicero expressly declares (Legg. ii. 5, 11), conformably to what is said by the Platonic Sokrates in the Minos, that a bad law, however passed in regular form, is no law at all ; and this might be well if he adhered consistently to the same phraseology, but he perpetually uses, in other places, the words *Lex* and *Leges* to signify laws actually in force at Rome, good or bad.

Mr. Bentham gives an explanation of Law or The Law, which coincides with Νόμος = τὰ νομιζόμενα. He says (Principles of Morals and Legislation, vol. ii. ch. 17, p. 257, ed. 1823), "Now Law, or The Law, taken indefinitely, is an abstract and collective term, which, when it means anything, can mean neither more nor less than the sum total of a number of individual laws taken together".

Mr. Austin in his Lectures, 'The Province of Jurisprudence Determined, has explained more clearly and copiously than any antecedent author, the confused meanings of the word Law adverted to in my text. See especially his first lecture and his fifth, pp. 88 seq. and 171 seq., 4th ed.

APPENDIX.

In continuing to recognise Hipparchus and Minos as Platonic works, contrary to the opinion of many modern critics, I have to remind the reader, not only that both are included in the Canon of Thrasyllus, but that the Minos was expressly acknowledged by Aristophanes of Byzantium, and included by him among the Trilogies : showing that it existed then (220 B.C.) in the Alexandrine Museum as a Platonic work. The similarity between the Hipparchus and Minos is recognised by all the Platonic critics, most of whom declare that both of them are spurious. Schleiermacher affirms and vindicates this opinion in his Einleitung and notes : but it will be convenient to take the arguments advanced to prove the spuriousness, as they are set forth by M. Boeckh, in his "Comment. in Platonis qui vulgo fertur Minoem " : in which treatise, though among his early works, the case is argued with all that copious learning and critical ability, which usually adorn his many admirable contributions to the improvement of philology.

M. Boeckh not only rejects the pretensions of Hipparchus and Minos to be considered as works of Plato, but advances an affirmative hypothesis to show what they are. He considers these two dialogues, together with those De Justo, and De Virtute (two short dialogues in the pseudo-Platonic list, not recognised by Thrasyllus) as among the dialogues published by Simon ; an Athenian citizen and a shoemaker by trade, in whose shop Sokrates is said to have held many of his conversations. Simon is reported to have made many notes of these conversations, and to have composed and published, from them, a volume of thirty-three dialogues (Diog. L. ii. 122), among the titles of which there are two—Περὶ Φιλοκερδοῦς and Περὶ Νόμου. Simon was, of course, contemporary with Plato ; but somewhat older in years. With this part of M. Boeckh's treatise, respecting the supposed authorship of Simon, I have nothing to do. I only notice the arguments by which he proposes to show that Hipparchus and Minos are not works of Plato.

In the first place, I notice that M. Boeckh explicitly recognises them as works of an author contemporary with Plato, not later than 380 B.C. (p. 46). Hereby many of the tests, whereby we usually detect spurious works, become inapplicable.

In the second place, he admits that the dialogues are composed in good Attic Greek, suitable to the Platonic age both in character and manners—"At veteris esse et Attici scriptoris, probus sermo, antiqui mores, totus denique character, spondeat," p. 32.

The reasons urged by M. Boeckh to prove the spuriousness of the Minos, are first, that it is unlike Plato—next, that it is too much like Plato. "Dupliciter dialogus a Platonis ingenio discrepat: partim quod parum, partim quod nimium, similis ceteris ejusdem scriptis sit. Parum similis est in rebus permultis. Nam cum Plato adhuc vivos ac videntes aut nuper defunctos notosque homines, ut scenicus poeta actores, moribus ingeniisque accurate descriptis, nominatim producat in medium—in isto opusculo cum Socrate colloquens persona plané incerta est ac nomine carens: quippe cum imperitus scriptor esset artis illius colloquiis suis *dulcissimas veneres* illas inferendi, quæ ex peculiaribus personarum moribus pingendis redundant, atque à Platone ut flores per amplos dialogorum hortos sunt disseminatæ" (pp. 7-8): again, p. 9, it is complained that there is an "infinitus secundarius collocutor" in the Hipparchus.

Now the sentence, just transcribed from M. Boeckh, shows that he had in his mind as standard of comparison, a certain number of the Platonic works, but that he did not take account of all of them. The Platonic Protagoras begins with a dialogue between Sokrates and an unknown, nameless person; to whom Sokrates, after a page of conversation with him, recounts what has just passed between himself, Protagoras, and others. Next, if we turn to the Sophistês and Politikus, we find that in both of them, not simply the secundarius collocutor, but even the principal speaker, is an unknown and nameless person, described only as a Stranger from Elea, and never before seen by Sokrates. Again, in the Leges, the principal speaker is only an Ἀθηναῖος ξένος, without a name. In the face of such analogies, it is unsafe to lay down a peremptory rule, that no dialogue can be the work of Plato, which acknowledges as *collocutor* an unnamed person.

Then again—when M. Boeckh complains that the Hipparchus and Minos are destitute of those "*flores et dulcissimæ Veneres*" which Plato is accustomed to spread through his dialogues—I ask, Where are the "dulcissimæ Veneres" in the Parmenidês, Sophistês, Politikus, Leges, Timæus, Kritias? I find none. The presence of "dulcissimæ **Veneres**" is not a condition *sine quâ non*, in every composition which pretends to Plato as its author : nor can the absence of them be admitted as a reason for disallowing Hipparchus and Minos.

The analogy of the Sophistês and Politikus (besides Symposium, Republic, and Leges) farther shows, that there is nothing wonderful in finding the titles of Hipparchus and Minos derived from the subjects (Περί Φιλοκερδοῦς and Περὶ Νόμου), not from the name of one of the collocutors :—whether we suppose the titles to have been bestowed by Plato himself, or by some subsequent editor (Boeckh, p. 10).

To illustrate his first ground of objection—Dissimilarity between the Minos and the true Platonic writings—M. Boeckh enumerates (pp. 12-23) several passages of the dialogue which he considers unplatonic. Moreover, he includes among them (p. 12) examples of confused and illogical reasoning. I confess that to me this evidence is noway sufficient to prove that Plato is not the author. That certain passages may be picked out which are obscure, confused, inelegant—is certainly no sufficient evidence. If I thought so, I should go along with Ast in rejecting the Euthydêmus, Menon, Lachês, Charmidês, Lysis, &c., against all which Ast argues as spurious, upon evidence of the same kind. It is not too much to say, that against almost every one of the dialogues, taken severally, a case of the same kind, more or less plausible, might be made out. You might in each of them find passages peculiar, careless, awkwardly expressed. The expression τὴν ἀνθρωπείαν ἀγέλην τοῦ σώματος, which M. Boeckh insists upon so much as improper, would probably have been considered as a mere case of faulty text, if it had occurred in any other dialogue : and so it may fairly be considered in the Minos.

Moreover as to faults of logic and consistency in the reasoning, most certainly these cannot be held as proving the Minos not to be Plato's work. I would engage to produce, from most of his dialogues, defects of reasoning quite as grave as any which the Minos exhibits. On the principle assumed by M. Boeckh, every one who agreed with Panætius in considering the elaborate proof given in the Phædon, of the immortality of the soul, as illogical and delusive—would also agree with Panætius in declaring that the Phædon was not the work of Plato. It is one question, whether the reasoning in any dialogue be good or bad : it is another question, whether the dialogue be written by Plato or not. Unfortunately, the Platonic critics often treat the first question as if it determined the second.

M. Boeckh himself considers that the evidence arising from dissimilarity (upon which I have just dwelt) is not the strongest part of his case. He relies more upon the evidence arising from *too much simi-*

larity, as proving still more clearly the spuriousness of the Minos. "Jam pergamus ad alteram partem nostræ argumentationis, *eamque etiam firmiorem*, de *nimia similitudine* Platonicorum aliquot locorum, quæ imitationem doceat subesse. Nam de hoc quidem conveniet inter omnes doctos et indoctos, Platonem se ipsum haud posse imitari : nisi si quis dubitet de sanâ ejus mente" (p. 23). Again, p. 26, "Jam vero in nostro colloquio Symposium, Politicum, Euthyphronem, Protagoram, Gorgiam, Cratylum, Philêbum, dialogos expressos ac tantum non compilatos reperies ". And M. Boeckh goes on to specify various passages of the Minos, which he considers to have been imitated, and badly imitated, from one or other of these dialogues.

I cannot agree with M. Boeckh in regarding this *nimia similitudo* as the strongest part of his case. On the contrary, I consider it as the weakest : because his own premisses (in my judgment) not only do not prove his conclusion, but go far to prove the opposite. When we find him insisting, in such strong language, upon the great analogy which subsists between the Minos and seven of the incontestable Platonic dialogues, this is surely a fair proof that its author is the same as their author. To me it appears as conclusive as internal evidence ever can be ; unless there be some disproof *aliunde* to overthrow it. But M. Boeckh produces no such disproof. He converts these analogies into testimony in his own favour, simply by bestowing upon them the name *imitatio,—stulta imitatio* (p. 27). This word involves an hypothesis, whereby the point to be proved is assumed—viz. : difference of authorship. "Plato cannot have imitated himself" (M. Boeckh observes). I cannot admit such impossibility, even if you describe the fact in that phrase : but if you say "Plato in one dialogue thought and wrote like Plato in another"—you describe the same fact in a different phrase, and it then appears not merely possible but natural and probable. Those very real analogies, to which M. Boeckh points in the word *imitatio*, are in my judgment cases of the Platonic thought in one dialogue being like the Platonic thought in another. The *similitudo*, between Minos and these other dialogues, can hardly be called *nimia*, for M. Boeckh himself points out that it is accompanied with much difference. It is a similitude, such as we should expect between one Platonic dialogue and another : with this difference, that whereas, in the Minos, Plato gives the same general views in a manner more brief, crude, abrupt—in the other dialogues he works them out with greater fulness of explanation and illustration, and some degree of change not unimportant. That there should be this amount of difference between one dialogue of Plato and another appears to me perfectly natural. On the óther hand—that there should have been a contemporary *falsarius* (scriptor miser, insulsus, vilissimus, to use phrases of M. Boeckh), who studied and pillaged the best dialogues of Plato, for the purpose of putting together a short and perverted abbreviation of them—and who contrived to get his miserable abbreviation recognised by the Byzantine Aristophanes among the genuine dialogues notwithstanding the existence of the Platonic school—this, I think highly improbable.

I cannot therefore agree with M. Boeckh in thinking, that "ubique se prodens Platonis imitatio" (p. 31) is an irresistible proof of spuriousness: nor can I think that his hypothesis shows itself to advantage, when he says, p. 10—" Ipse autem dialogus (Minos) quum post Politicum compositus sit, quod quædam in eo dicta rebus ibi expositis manifesté nitantur, ut paullo post ostendemus—quis est qui artificiosissimum philosophum, postquam ibi (in Politico) accuratius de naturâ legis egisset, de eâ iterum putet negligenter egisse?"—I do not think it so impossible as it appears to M. Boeckh, that a philosopher, after having *written* upon a given subject *accuratius*, should subsequently write upon it *negligenter*. But if I granted this ever so fully, I should still contend that there remains another alternative. The negligent workmanship may have preceded the accurate: an alternative which I think is probably the truth, and which has nothing to exclude it except M. Boeckh's pure hypothesis, that the Minos must have been copied from the Politikus.

While I admit then that the Hipparchus and Minos are among the inferior and earlier compositions of Plato, I still contend that there is no ground for excluding them from the list of his works. Though the Platonic critics of this century are for the most part of an adverse opinion, I have with me the general authority of the critics anterior to this century—from Aristophanes of Byzantium down to Bentley and Ruhnken—see Boeckh, pp. 7-32.

Yxem defends the genuineness of the Hipparchus—(Ueber Platon's Kleitophon, p. 8. Berlin, 1846).

CHAPTER XV.

THEAGES.

Theagês— has been declared spurious by some modern critics— grounds for such opinion not sufficient.

THIS is among the dialogues declared by Schleiermacher, Ast, Stallbaum, and various other modern critics, to be spurious and unworthy of Plato: the production of one who was not merely an imitator, but a bad and silly imitator.[1] Socher on the other hand defends the dialogue against them, reckoning it as a juvenile production of Plato.[2] The arguments which are adduced to prove its spuriousness appear to me altogether insufficient. It has some features of dissimilarity with that which we read in other dialogues—these the above-mentioned critics call un-Platonic: it has other features of similarity—these they call bad imitation by a *falsarius*: lastly, it is inferior, as a performance, to the best of the Platonic dialogues. But I am prepared to expect (and have even the authority of Schleiermacher for expecting) that some dialogues will be inferior to others. I also reckon with certainty, that between two dialogues, both genuine, there will be points of similarity as well as points of dissimilarity. Lastly, the critics find marks of a bad, recent, un-Platonic style: but Dionysius of Halikarnassus —a judge at least equally competent upon such a matter—found no such marks. He expressly cites the dialogue as the work of

---

[1] Stallbaum, Proleg. pp. 220-225, "ineptus tenebrio," &c. Schleiermacher, Einleitung, part ii. v. iii. pp. 247-252. Ast, Platon's Leben und Schriften, pp. 495-497.
Ast speaks with respect (differing in this respect from the other two) of the Theagês as a composition, though he does not believe it to be the work of Plato. Schleiermacher also admits (see the end of his Einleitung) that the style in general has a good Platonic colouring, though he considers some particular phrases as un-Platonic.

[2] Socher, Ueber Platon, pp. 92-102. M. Cobet also speaks of it as a work of Plato (Novæ Lectiones, &c., p. 624. Lugd. Bat. 1858).

Plato,[1] and explains the peculiar phraseology assigned to Demodokus by remarking, that the latter is presented as a person of rural habits and occupations.

Demodokus, an elderly man (of rank and landed property), and his youthful son Theagês, have come from their Deme to Athens, and enter into conversation with Sokrates: to whom the father explains, that Theagês has contracted, from the conversation of youthful companions, an extraordinary ardour for the acquisition of wisdom. The son has importuned his father to put him under the tuition of one of the Sophists, who profess to teach wisdom. The father, though not unwilling to comply with the request, is deterred by the difficulty of finding a good teacher and avoiding a bad one. He entreats the advice of Sokrates, who invites the young man to explain what it is that he wants, over and above the usual education of an Athenian youth of good family (letters, the harp, wrestling, &c.), which he has already gone through.[2] *Persons of the dialogue—Sokrates, with Demodokus and Theagês, father and son. Theagês (the son), eager to acquire knowledge, desires to be placed under the teaching of a Sophist.*

Sokr.—You desire wisdom: but what kind of wisdom? That by which men manage chariots? or govern horses? or pilot ships? *Theag.*—No: that by which men are governed. *Sokr.*—But what men? those in a state of sickness—or those who are singing in a chorus—or those who are under gymnastic training? Each of *Sokrates questions Theagês, inviting him to specify what he wants.*

---

[1] Dionys. Hal. Ars Rhetor. p. 405, Reiske. Compare Theagês, 121 D. εἰς τὸ ἄστυ καταβαίνοντες.

In general, in discussions on the genuineness of any of the Platonic dialogues, I can do nothing but reply to the arguments of those critics who consider them spurious. But in the case of the Theagês there is one argument which tends to mark Plato positively as the author.

In the Theagês, p. 125, the senarius σοφοὶ τύραννοι τῶν σοφῶν συνουσίᾳ is cited as a verse of *Euripides*. Now it appears that this is an error of memory, and that the verse really belongs to *Sophokles*, ἐν Αἴαντι Λοκρῷ. If the error had only appeared in this dialogue, Stallbaum would probably have cited it as one more instance of stupidity on the part of the *ineptus tenebrio* whom he supposes to have written the dialogue. But unfortunately the error does not belong to the Theagês alone. It is found also in the Republic (viii. 568 B), the most unquestionable of all the Platonic compositions. Accordingly, Schleiermacher tells us in his note that the *falsarius* of the Theagês has copied this error out of the abovenamed passage of the Republic of Plato (notes, p. 500).

This last supposition of Schleiermacher appears to me highly improbable. Since we know that the mistake is one made by Plato himself, surely we ought rather to believe that he made it in two distinct compositions. In other words, the occurrence of the same exact mistake in the Republic and the Theagês affords strong presumption that both are by the same author—Plato.

[2] Plato, Theagês, 122.

these classes has its own governor, who bears a special title, and belongs to a special art by itself—the medical, musical, gymnastic, &c. *Theag.*—No: I mean that wisdom by which we govern, not these classes alone, but all the other residents in the city along with them—professional as well as private—men as well as women.[1]

Sokrates now proves to Theagês, that this function and power which he is desirous of obtaining, is, the function and power of a despot: and that no one can aid him in so culpable a project. I might yearn (says Theagês) for such despotic power over all: so probably would you and every other man. But it is not *that* to which I now aspire. I aspire to govern freemen, with their own consent; as was done by Themistokles, Perikles, Kimon, and other illustrious statesmen,[2] who have been accomplished in the political art.

Theagês desires to acquire that wisdom by which he can govern freemen with their own consent.

Sokr.—Well, if you wished to become accomplished in the art of horsemanship, you would put yourself under able horsemen: if in the art of darting the javelin, under able darters. By parity of reasoning, since you seek to learn the art of statesmanship, you must frequent able statesmen.[3]

Theag.—No, Sokrates. I have heard of the language which you are in the habit of using to others. You pointed out to them that these eminent statesmen cannot train their own sons to be at all better than curriers: of course therefore they cannot do *me* any good.[4]

Incompetence of the best practical statesmen to teach any

---

[1] Plato, Theagês, 124 A-B. Schleiermacher (Einleit. p. 250) censures the prolixity of the inductive process in this dialogue, and the multitude of examples here accumulated to prove a general proposition obvious enough without proof. Let us grant this to be true; we cannot infer from it that the dialogue is not the work of Plato. By very similar arguments Socher endeavours to show that the Sophistès and the Politikus are not works of Plato, because in both these dialogues logical division and differentiation is accumulated with tiresome prolixity, and applied to most trivial subjects. But Plato himself (in Politikus, pp. 285-286) explains why he does so, and tells us that he wishes to familiarise his readers with logical subdivision and classification as a process. In like manner I maintain that prolixity in the λόγοι ἐπακτικοί is not to be held as proof of spurious authorship, any more than prolixity in the process of logical subdivision and classification.

I noticed the same objection in the case of the First Alkibiadês.
[2] Plato, Theagês, 126 A.
[3] Plato, Theagês, 126 C.
[4] Plato, Theagês, 126 D. Here again Stallbaum (p. 222) urges, among his reasons for believing the dialogue to be spurious—How absurd to represent the youthful Theagês as knowing what arguments Sokrates had addressed to others! But the youthful Theætêtus is also represented as having heard from others the cross-examinations made by Sokrates (Theætêt. 148 E). So like-

Sokr.—But what can your father do for you better than this, Theagês? What ground have you for complaining of him? He is prepared to place you under any one of the best and most excellent men of Athens, whichever of them you prefer. *Theag.*—Why will not you take me yourself, Sokrates? I look upon you as one of these men, and I desire nothing better.[1]

one else. Theagês requests that Sokrates will himself teach him.

Demodokus joins his entreaties with those of Theagês to prevail upon Sokrates to undertake this function. But Sokrates in reply says that he is less fit for it than Demodokus himself, who has exercised high political duties, with the esteem of every one : and that if practical statesmen are considered unfit, there are the professional Sophists, Prodikus, Gorgias, Polus, who teach many pupils, and earn not merely good pay, but also the admiration and gratitude of every one—of the pupils as well as their senior relatives.[2]

Sokr.—I know nothing of the fine things which these Sophists teach : I wish I did know. I declare everywhere, that I know nothing whatever except one small matter—what belongs to love. In that, I surpass every one else, past as well as present.[3] *Theag.*— Sokrates is only mocking us. I know youths (of my own age and somewhat older), who were altogether worthless and inferior to every one, before they went to him; but who, after they had frequented his society, became in a short time superior to all their former rivals. The like will happen with me, if he will only consent to receive me.[4]

Sokrates declares that he is not competent to teach—that he knows nothing except about matters of love. Theagês maintains that many of his young friends have profited largely by the conversation of Sokrates.

Sokr.—You do not know how this happens; I will explain it to you. From my childhood, I have had a peculiar superhuman something attached to me by divine appointment : a voice, which, whenever it occurs, warns me to abstain from that which I am

Sokrates explains how this

---

wise the youthful sons of Lysimachus —(Lachês, 181 A); compare also Lysis, 211 A.

[1] Plato, Theagês, 127 A.
[2] Plato, Theagês, 127 D-E, 128 A.
[3] Plato, Theagês, 128 B. ἀλλὰ καὶ

λέγω δήπου ἀεί, ὅτι ἐγὼ τυγχάνω, ὡς ἔπος εἰπεῖν, οὐδὲν ἐπιστάμενος πλήν γε σμικροῦ τινὸς μαθήματος, τῶν ἐρωτικῶν, τοῦτο μέντοι τὸ μάθημα παρ' ὁντινοῦν ποιοῦμαι δεινὸς εἶναι, καὶ τῶν προγεγονότων ἀνθρώπων καὶ τῶν νῦν.
[4] Plato, Theagês, 128 C.

102 THEAGES. CHAP. XV.

has sometimes happened— He recites his experience of the divine sign or Dæmon. about to do, but never impels me.[1] Moreover, when any one of my friends mentions to me what he is about to do, if the voice shall then occur to me it is a warning for him to abstain. The examples of Charmides and Timarchus (here detailed by Sokrates) prove what I say: and many persons will tell you how truly I forewarned them of the ruin of the Athenian armament at Syracuse.[2] My young friend Sannion is now absent, serving on the expedition under Thrasyllus to Ionia: on his departure, the divine sign manifested itself to me, and I am persuaded that some grave calamity will befall him.

These facts I mention to you (Sokrates continues) because it is *The Dæmon is favourable to some persons, adverse to others. Upon this circumstance it depends how far any companion profits by the society of Sokrates. Aristeides has not learnt anything from Sokrates, yet has improved much by being near to him.* that same divine power which exercises paramount influence over my intercourse with companions.[3] Towards many, it is positively adverse; so that I cannot even enter into companionship with them. Towards others, it does not forbid, yet neither does it co-operate: so that they derive no benefit from me. There are others again in whose case it co-operates; these are the persons to whom you allude, who make rapid progress.[4] With some, such improvement is lasting: others, though they improve wonderfully while in my society, yet relapse into commonplace men when they leave me. Aristeides, for example (grandson of Aristeides the Just), was one of those who made rapid progress while he was with me. But he was forced to absent himself on military service; and on returning, he found as my companion Thucydides (son of Melesias), who however had quarrelled with me for some debate of the day before. I understand (said Aristeides to me) that Thucydides has taken offence and gives himself airs; he forgets what a poor creature he was, before he came to you.[5] I

[1] Plato, Theagês, 128 D. ἔστι γάρ τι θείᾳ μοίρᾳ παρεπόμενον ἐμοὶ ἐκ παιδὸς ἀρξάμενον δαιμόνιον· ἔστι δὲ τοῦτο φωνή, ἣ ὅταν γένηται, ἀεί μοι σημαίνει, ὃ ἂν μέλλω πράττειν, τούτου ἀποτροπήν, προτρέπει δὲ οὐδέποτε.
[2] Plato, Theag. 129.
[3] Plato, Theagês, 129 E. ταῦτα δὴ πάντα εἴρηκά σοι, ὅτι ἡ δύναμις αὕτη τοῦ δαιμονίου τούτου καὶ εἰς τὰς συνουσίας τῶν μετ' ἐμοῦ συνδιατριβόντων τὸ ἅπαν δύναται. πολλοῖς μὲν γὰρ ἐναντιοῦται, καὶ οὐκ ἔστι τούτοις ὠφεληθῆναι μετ' ἐμοῦ διατρίβουσιν.
[4] Plato, Theag. 129 E. οἷς δ' ἂν συλλάβηται τῆς συνουσίας ἡ τοῦ δαιμονίου δύναμις, οὗτοί εἰσιν ὧν καὶ σὺ ᾔσθησαι· ταχὺ γὰρ παραχρῆμα ἐπιδιδόασιν.
[5] Plato, Theag. 130 A-B. Τί δαί; οὐκ οἶδεν, ἔφη, πρὶν σοὶ συγγενέσθαι, οἷον ἦν τὸ ἀνδράποδον;

myself, too, have fallen into a despicable condition. When I left you, I was competent to discuss with any one and make a good figure, so that I courted debate with the most accomplished men. Now, on the contrary, I avoid them altogether—so thoroughly am I ashamed of my own incapacity. Did the capacity (I, *Sokrates*, asked Aristeides) forsake you all at once, or little by little? Little by little, he replied. And when you possessed it (I asked), did you get it by learning from me? or in what other way? I will tell you, Sokrates (he answered), what seems incredible, yet is nevertheless true.[1] I never learnt from you any thing at all. You yourself well know this. But I always made progress, whenever I was along with you, even if I were only in the same house without being in the same room; but I made greater progress, if I was in the same room—greater still, if I looked in your face, instead of turning my eyes elsewhere—and the greatest of all, by far, if I sat close and touching you. But now (continued Aristeides) all that I then acquired has dribbled out of me.[2]

Sokr.—I have now explained to you, Theagês, what it is to become my companion. If it be the pleasure of the God, you will make great and rapid progress: if not, not. Consider, therefore, whether it is not safer for you to seek instruction from some of those who are themselves masters of the benefits which they impart, rather than to take your chance of the result with me.[3] *Theag.*— I shall be glad, Sokrates, to become your companion, and to make trial of this divine coadjutor. If he shows himself propitious, that will be the best of all: if not, we can then take counsel, whether I shall try to propitiate him by prayer, sacrifice, or any other means which the prophets may recommend—or whether I shall go to some other teacher.[4]

Theagês expresses his anxiety to be received as the companion of Sokrates.

---

[1] Plato, Theag. 130 D. Ἡνίκα δέ σοι παρεγένετο (ἡ δύναμις), πότερον μαθόντι παρ' ἐμοῦ τι παρεγένετο, ἢ τινι ἄλλῳ τρόπῳ; Ἐγώ σοι, ἔφη, ἐρῶ, ὦ Σώκρατες, ἄπιστον μὲν νὴ τοὺς θεούς, ἀληθὲς δέ. ἐγὼ γὰρ ἔμαθον μὲν παρὰ σοῦ οὐδὲν πώποτε, ὡς αὐτὸς οἶσθα· ἐπεδίδουν δὲ ὁπότε σοι συνείην, κἂν εἰ ἐν τῇ αὐτῇ μόνον οἰκίᾳ εἴην, μὴ ἐν τῷ αὐτῷ δὲ οἰκήματι, &c.

[2] Plato, Theag. 130 E. πολὺ δὲ μάλιστα καὶ πλεῖστον ἐπεδίδουν, ὁπότε παρ' αὐτόν σε καθοίμην ἐχόμενός σου καὶ ἁπτόμενος. νῦν δέ, ἦ δ' ὅς, πᾶσα ἐκείνη ἡ ἕξις ἐξερρύηκεν.

[3] Plato, Theag. 130 E. ὅρα οὖν μή σοι ἀσφαλέστερον ᾖ παρ' ἐκείνων τινὶ παιδεύεσθαι, οἳ ἐγκρατεῖς αὐτοί εἰσι τῆς ὠφελείας, ἣν ὠφελοῦσι τοὺς ἀνθρώπους, μᾶλλον ἢ παρ' ἐμοῦ ὅ, τι ἂν τύχῃ, τοῦτο πρᾶξαι.

[4] Plato, Theag. 131 A.

The Theagês figured in the list of Thrasyllus as first in the fifth Tetralogy : the other three members of the same Tetralogy being Charmidês, Lachês, Lysis. Some persons considered it suitable to read as first dialogue of all.[1] There are several points of analogy between the Theagês and the Lachês, though with a different turn given to them. Aristeides and Thucydides are mentioned in both of them : Sokrates also is solicited to undertake the duty of teacher. The ardour of the young Theagês to acquire wisdom reminds us of Hippokrates at the beginning of the Protagoras. The string of questions put by Sokrates to Theagês, requiring that what is called wisdom shall be clearly defined and specialised, has its parallel in many of the Platonic dialogues. Moreover the declaration of Sokrates, that he knows nothing except about matters of love, but that in them he is a consummate master—is the same as what he explicitly declares both in the Symposion and other dialogues.[2]

Remarks on the Theagês—Analogy with the Lachês.

But the chief peculiarity of the Theagês consists in the stress which is laid upon the Dæmon, the divine voice, the inspiration of Sokrates. This divine auxiliary is here described, not only as giving a timely check or warning to Sokrates, when either he or his friends contemplated any inauspicious project—but also as intervening, in the case of those youthful companions with whom he conversed, to promote the improvement of one, to obstruct that of others; so that whether Sokrates will produce any effect or not in improving any one, depends neither upon his own efforts nor upon those of the recipient, but upon the unpredictable concurrence of a divine agency.[3]

Chief peculiarity of the Theagês— Stress laid upon the divine sign or Dæmon.

Plato employs the Sokratic Dæmon, in the Theagês, for a philosophical purpose, which, I think, admits of reasonable explanation. During the eight (perhaps ten) years of his personal communion with Sokrates,

Plato employs this divine sign here to

---

[1] Diog. L. iii. 59-61.
[2] Symposion, 177 E. οὔτε γὰρ ἂν πού ἐγὼ ἀποφήσαιμι, ὃς οὐδέν φημι ἄλλο ἐπίστασθαι ἢ τὰ ἐρωτικά. Compare the same dialogue, p. 212 B, 216 C. Phædrus, 227 E, 257 A; Lysis, 204 B. Compare also Xenoph. Memor. ii. 6, 28; Xenoph. Sympos. iv. 27.

It is not reasonable to treat this declaration of Sokrates, in the Theagês, as an evidence that the dialogue is the work of a *falsarius*, when a declaration quite similar is ascribed to Sokrates in other Platonic dialogues.
[3] See some remarks on this point in Appendix.

CHAP. XV.   THE DÆMON AS VIEWED BY PLATO.   105

he had had large experience of the variable and un- *render some*
accountable effect produced by the Sokratic conver- *explanation of the sin-*
sation upon different hearers: a fact which is also *gularity and eccentricity*
attested by the Xenophontic Memorabilia. This differ- *of Sokrates,*
ence of effect was in no way commensurate to the *and of his unequal in-*
intelligence of the hearers. Chærephon, Apollodôrus, *fluence upon different*
Kriton, seem to have been ordinary men:—[1] while *companions.*
Kritias and Alkibiades, who brought so much discredit both upon
Sokrates and his teaching, profited little by him, though they
were among the ablest pupils that he ever addressed: moreover
Antisthenes, and Aristippus, probably did not appear to Plato
(since he greatly dissented from their philosophical views) to have
profited much by the common companionship with Sokrates.
Other companions there must have been also personally known
to Plato, though not to us: for we must remember that Sokrates
passed his whole day in talking with all listeners. Now when
Plato in after life came to cast the ministry of Sokrates into
dramatic scenes, and to make each scene subservient to the illustration of some philosophical point of view, at least a negative—
he was naturally led to advert to the Dæmon or divine inspiration, which formed so marked a feature in the character of his
master. The concurrence or prohibition of this divine auxiliary
served to explain why it was that the seed, sown broadcast by
Sokrates, sometimes fructified, and sometimes did not fructify,
or speedily perished afterwards—when no sufficient explanatory
peculiarity could be pointed out in the ground on which it fell.
It gave an apparent reason for the perfect singularity of the
course pursued by Sokrates: for his preternatural acuteness in
one direction, and his avowed incapacity in another: for his
mastery of the Elenchus, convicting men of ignorance, and his
inability to supply them with knowledge: for his refusal to
undertake the duties of a teacher. All these are mysterious
features of the Sokratic character. The intervention of the
Dæmon appears to afford an explanation, by converting them
into religious mysteries: which, though it be no explanation at
all, yet is equally efficacious by stopping the mouth of the questioner, and by making him believe that it is guilt and impiety to

[1] Xenophon, Apol. Sokr. 28. 'Απολ- ἄλλως δ' εὐήθης.—Plat. Phædon, 117
λόδωρος—ἐπιθυμήτης μὲν ἰσχυρῶς αὐτοῦ, D.

ask for explanation—as Sokrates himself declared in regard to astronomical phenomena, and as Herodotus feels, when his narrative is crossed by strange religious legends.[1]

In this manner, the Theagês is made by Plato to exhibit one way of parrying the difficulty frequently addressed to Sokrates by various hearers: "You tell us that the leading citizens cannot even teach their own sons, and that the Sophists teach nothing worth having: you perpetually call upon us to seek for better teachers, without telling us where such are to be found. We entreat you to teach us yourself, conformably to your own views."

Sokrates, while continually finding fault with other teachers, refused to teach himself. Difficulty of finding an excuse for his refusal. The Theagês furnishes an excuse.

If a leader of political opposition, after years employed in denouncing successive administrators as ignorant and iniquitous, refuses, when invited, to take upon himself the business of administration—an intelligent admirer must find some decent pretence to colour the refusal. Such a pretence is found for Sokrates in the Theagês: "I am not my own master on this point. I am the instrument of a divine ally, without whose active working I can accomplish nothing: who forbids altogether my teaching of one man—tolerates, without assisting, my unavailing lessons to another—assists efficaciously in my teaching of a third, in which case alone the pupil receives any real benefit. The assistance of this divine ally is given or withheld according to motives of his own, which I cannot even foretell, much less influence. I should deceive you therefore if I undertook to teach, when I cannot tell whether I shall do good or harm."

The reply of Theagês meets this scruple. He asks permission to make the experiment, and promises to propitiate the divine auxiliary by prayer and sacrifice: under which reserve Sokrates gives consent.

It is in this way that the Dæmon or divine auxiliary serves the purpose of reconciling what would otherwise be an inconsistency in the proceedings of Sokrates. I mean, that such is the purpose served in *this* dialogue: I know perfectly that Plato deals with the

Plato does not always, nor in other dialogues, allude to the divine sign

[1] Xen. Mem. iv. 7, 5-6; Herodot. ii. 3, 45-46.

case differently elsewhere: but I am not bound (as I have said more than once) to force upon all the dialogues one and the same point of view. That the agency of the Gods was often and in the most important cases, essentially undiscoverable and unpredictable, and that in such cases they might sometimes be prevailed on to give special warnings to favoured persons—were doctrines which the historical Sokrates in Xenophon asserts with emphasis.[1] The Dæmon of Sokrates was believed, both by himself and his friends, to be a special privilege and an extreme case of divine favour and communication to him.[2] It was perfectly applicable to the scope of the Theagês, though Plato might not choose always to make the same employment of it. It is used in the same general way in the Theætêtus;[3] doubtless with less expansion, and blended with another analogy (that of the midwife) which introduces a considerable difference.[4]

In the same way. Its character and working essentially impenetrable. Sokrates a privileged person.

[1] Xenoph, Memor. i. 1, 8-9-19. Euripid. Hecub. 944.

φύρουσι δ' αὐτὰ θεοὶ πάλιν τε καὶ πρόσω, ταραγμὸν ἐντιθέντες, ὡς ἀγνωσίᾳ σέβωμεν αὐτούς.

[2] Xenoph. Mem. iv. 3, 12.
[3] Plato, Theætêt. 150 D-E.
[4] Plato, Apolog. Sokr. 33 C. ἐμοὶ δὲ τοῦτο, ὡς ἐγὼ φημι, προστέτακται ὑπὸ τοῦ θεοῦ πράττειν καὶ ἐκ μαντειῶν καὶ ἐξ ἐνυπνίων καὶ παντὶ τρόπῳ, ᾧπέρ τίς ποτε καὶ ἄλλη θεία μοίρα ἀνθρώπῳ καὶ ὁτιοῦν προσέταξε πράττειν. 40 A. ἡ γὰρ εἰωθυιά μοι μαντικὴ ἡ τοῦ δαιμονίου ἐν μὲν τῷ πρόσθεν χρόνῳ παντὶ πάνυ πυκνὴ ἀεὶ ἦν καὶ πάνυ ἐπὶ σμικροῖς ἐναντιουμένη, εἴ τι μέλλοιμι μὴ ὀρθῶς πράξειν. Compare Xenophon, Memor. iv. 8, 5; Apol. Sokr. c. 13.

APPENDIX.

Τὸ δαιμόνιον σημεῖον.

Here is one of the points most insisted on by Schleiermacher and Stallbaum, as proving that the Theagês is not the work of Plato. These critics affirm (to use the language of Stallbaum, Proleg. p. 220) "Quam Plato alias de Socratis dæmonio prodidit sententiam, ea longissimè recedit ab illâ ratione, quæ in hoc sermone exposita est". He says that the representation of the Dæmon of Sokrates, given in the Theagês, has been copied from a passage in the Theætêtus, by an imitator who has not understood the passage, p. 150, D, E. But Socher (p. 97) appears to me to have shown satisfactorily, that there is no such material difference as these critics affirm between this passage of the Theætêtus and the Theagês. In the Theætêtus, Sokrates declares, that none of his companions learnt any thing from him, but that all of them οἷσπερ ἂν ὁ θεὸς παρείκῃ (the very same term is used at the close of the Theagês—131 A, ἐὰν μὲν παρείκῃ ἡμῖν —τὸ δαιμόνιον) made astonishing progress and improvement in his company. Stallbaum says, "Itaque ὁ θεὸς, qui ibi memoratur, non est Socratis dæmonium, sed potius deus *i.e.* sors divina. Quod non perspiciens *noster tenebrio* protenus illud dæmonium, quod Socrates sibi semper adesse dictitabat, ad eum dignitatis et potentiæ gradum evexit, ut, &c." I agree with Socher in thinking that the phrase ὁ θεὸς in the Theætêtus has substantially the same meaning as τὸ δαιμόνιον in the Theagês. Both Schleiermacher (Notes on the Apology, p. 432) and Ast (p. 482), have notes on the phrase τὸ δαιμόνιον—and I think the note of Ast is the more instructive of the two. In Plato and Xenophon, the words τὸ δαιμόνιον, τὸ θεῖον, are in many cases undistinguishable in meaning from ὁ δαίμων, ὁ θεός. Compare the Phædrus, 242 E, about θεὸς and θεῖόν τι. Sokrates, in his argument against Meletus in the Apology (p. 27) emphatically argues that no man could believe in any thing δαιμόνιον, without also believing in δαίμονες. The special θεῖόν τι καὶ

APPENDIX.

δαιμόνιον (Apol. p. 31 C), which presented itself in regard to him and his proceedings, was only one of the many modes in which (as he believed) ὁ θεός commanded and stimulated him to work upon the minds of the Athenians:—ἐμοὶ δὲ τοῦτο, ὡς ἐγώ φημι, προστέτακται ὑπὸ τοῦ θεοῦ πράττειν καὶ ἐκ μαντειῶν καὶ ἐξ ἐνυπνίων καὶ παντὶ τρόπῳ, ᾧπέρ τίς ποτε καὶ ἄλλη θεία μοῖρα ἀνθρώπῳ καὶ ὁτιοῦν προσέταξε πράττειν (Apol. p. 33 C). So again in Apol. p. 40 A, B, ἡ εἰωθυῖά μοι μαντικὴ ἡ τοῦ δαιμονίου—and four lines afterwards we read the very same fact intimated in the words, τὸ τοῦ θεοῦ σημεῖον, where Sokratis dæmonium—and Deus—are identified: thus refuting the argument above cited from Stallbaum. There is therefore no such discrepancy, in reference to τὸ δαιμόνιον, as Stallbaum and Schleiermacher contend for. We perceive indeed this difference between them —that in the Theætêtus, the simile of the obstetric art is largely employed, while it is not noticed in the Theagês. But we should impose an unwarrantable restriction upon Plato's fancy, if we hindered him from working out his variety and exuberance of metaphors, and from accommodating each dialogue to the metaphor predominant with him at the time.

Moreover, in respect to what is called the Dæmon of Sokrates, we ought hardly to expect that either Plato or Xenophon would always be consistent even with themselves. It is unsafe for a modern critic to determine beforehand, by reason or feelings of his own, in what manner either of them would speak upon this mysterious subject. The belief and feeling of a divine intervention was very real on the part of both, but their manner of conceiving it might naturally fluctuate: and there was, throughout all the proceedings of Sokrates, a mixture of the serious and the playful, of the sublime and the eccentric, of ratiocinative acuteness with impulsive superstition—which it is difficult to bring into harmonious interpretation. Such heterogeneous mixture is forcibly described in the Platonic Symposium, pp. 215-222. When we consider how undefined, and undefinable, the idea of this δαιμόνιον was, we cannot wonder if Plato ascribes to it different workings and manifestations at different times. Stallbaum affirms that it is made ridiculous in the Theagês: and Kühner declares that Plutarch makes it ridiculous, in his treatise De Genio Sokratis (Comm. ad. Xenoph. Memor. p. 23). But this is because its agency is described more in detail. You can easily present it in a ridiculous aspect, by introducing it as intervening on petty and insignificant matters. Now it is remarkable, that in the Apology, we are expressly told that it actually did intervene on the most trifling occasions—πάνυ ἐπὶ σμικροῖς ἐναντιουμένη. The business of an historian of philosophy is, to describe it as it was really felt and believed by Sokrates and Plato—whether a modern critic may consider the description ridiculous or not. When Schleiermacher says (Einleitung, p. 248), respecting the *falsarius* whom he supposes to have written the Theagês—"Damit ist ihm begegnet, auf eine höchst verkehrte Art wunderbar zusammenzurühren diese göttliche Schickung, und jenes persönliche Vorgefühl welches dem Sokrates zur göttlichen Stimme ward".—I contend that the mistake is chargeable to Schleiermacher himself, for bisecting into two phenomena that which appears in the Apology as the same phenomenon under two different names—τὸ δαιμόνιον—τὸ τοῦ θεοῦ σημεῖον. Besides, to treat the Dæmon as a mere "personal presentiment" of Sokrates, may be a true view:—but it is the view of one who does not inhale the same religious atmosphere as Sokrates, Plato, and Xenophon. It cannot therefore be properly applied in explaining their sayings or doings. Kühner, who treats the Theagês as not composed by Plato, grounds this belief partly on the assertion, that the δαιμόνιον of Sokrates is described therein as something peculiar to Sokrates; which, according to Kühner, was the fiction of a subsequent time. By Sokrates and his contemporaries (Kühner says) it was considered "non sibi soli tanquam proprium quoddam beneficium a Diis tributum, sed commune sibi esse cum cæteris hominibus" (pp. 20-21). I dissent entirely from this view, which is contradicted by most of the passages noticed even by Kühner himself. It is at variance with the Platonic Apology, as well as with the Theætêtus (150 D), and Republic (vi. 496 C). Xenophon does indeed try, in the first Chapter of the Memorabilia, as the defender of Sokrates, to soften the *invidia* against Sokrates, by intimating that other persons had communications from the Gods as well as he. But we see plainly, even from other passages of the Memorabilia, that this was not the persuasion of Sokrates himself, nor of his friends, nor of his enemies. They all considered it (as it is depicted in the Theagês also) to be a special privilege and revelation.

CHAPTER XVI.

ERASTÆ OR ANTERASTÆ—RIVALES.

THE main subject of this short dialogue is—What is philosophy? ἡ φιλοσοφία—τὸ φιλοσοφεῖν. How are we to explain or define it? What is its province and purport? Instead of the simple, naked, self-introducing, conversation, which we read in the Menon, Hipparchus, Minos, &c., Sokrates recounts a scene and colloquy, which occurred when he went into the house of Dionysius the grammatist or school-master,[1] frequented by many elegant and high-born youths as pupils. Two of these youths were engaged in animated debate upon some geometrical or astronomical problem, in the presence of various spectators; and especially of two young men, rivals for the affection of one of them. Of these rivals, the one is a person devoted to music, letters, discourse, philosophy:—the other hates and despises these pursuits, devoting himself to gymnastic exercise, and bent on acquiring the maximum of athletic force.[2] It is much the same contrast as that between the brothers Amphion and Zethus in the Antiopê of Euripides—which is beautifully employed as an illustration by Plato in the Gorgias.[3] *Erastæ— Subject and persons of the dialogue —Dramatic introduction—interesting youths in the palæstra.*

As soon as Sokrates begins his interrogatories, the two youths relinquish[4] their geometrical talk, and turn to him as attentive listeners. Their approach affects his emotions hardly less than those of the Erastes. He first *Two rival Erastæ— one of them literary, de-*

---

[1] Plato, Erastæ, 132. εἰς Διονυσίου τοῦ γραμματιστοῦ εἰσῆλθον, καὶ εἶδον αὐτόθι τῶν τε νέων τοὺς ἐπιεικεστάτους δοκοῦντας εἶναι τὴν ἰδέαν καὶ πατέρων εὐδοκίμων καὶ τούτων ἐραστάς.
[2] Plato, Erast. 132 E.
[3] Plato, Gorgias, 485-486. Compare

Cicero De Oratore, ii. 37, 156.
[4] The powerful sentiment of admiration ascribed to Sokrates in the presence of these beautiful youths deserves notice as a point in his character. Compare the beginning of the Charmidês and the Lysis.

<small>voted to philosophy—the other gymnastic, hating philosophy.</small> enquires from the athletic Erastes, What is it that these two youths are so intently engaged upon? It must surely be something very fine, to judge by the eagerness which they display? How do you mean *fine* (replies the athlete)? They are only prosing about astronomical matters—talking nonsense—philosophising! The literary rival, on the contrary, treats this athlete as unworthy of attention, speaks with enthusiastic admiration of philosophy, and declares that all those to whom it is repugnant are degraded specimens of humanity.

Sokr.—You think philosophy a fine thing? But you cannot tell whether it is fine or not, unless you know what it is?[1] Pray explain to me what philosophy is. *Erast.* <small>Question put by Sokrates, What is philosophy? It is the perpetual accumulation of knowledge, so as to make the largest sum total.</small> —I will do so readily. Philosophy consists in the perpetual growth of a man's knowledge—in his going on perpetually acquiring something new, both in youth and old age, so that he may learn as much as possible during life. Philosophy is polymathy.[2] *Sokr.*—You think philosophy not only a fine thing, but good? *Erast.*—Yes—very good. *Sokr.*—But is the case similar in regard to gymnastic? Is a man's bodily condition benefited by taking as much exercise, or as much nourishment, as possible? Is such very great quantity good for the body?[3]

It appears after some debate (in which the other or athletic Erastes sides with Sokrates[4]) that in regard to exercise and food, it is not the great quantity, or the small quantity, which is good for the body—but the moderate or measured quantity.[5] For the mind, the case is admitted to be similar. Not the *much*, nor the *little*, of learning is good for it—but the right or measured amount. *Sokr.*—And who is the competent judge, <small>In the case of the body, it is not the maximum of exercise which does good, but the proper, measured, quantity. For the mind</small>

<small>[1] Plat. Erast. 133 A-B.
[2] Plato, Erast. 133 D. τὴν φιλοσοφίαν—πολυμάθειαν.
[3] Plat. Erast. 133 E.
[4] Plat. Erast. 134 B-C. The literary Erastes says to Sokrates, "To *you* I have no objection to concede this point, and to admit that my previous answer must be modified. But if I were to debate the point only with *him* (the athletic rival), I could perfectly well have defended my answer, and even a worse answer still, for *he* is quite worthless (οὐδὲν γάρ ἐστι)."
This is a curious passage, illustrating the dialectic habits of the day, and the pride felt in maintaining an answer once given.
[5] Plato, Erastæ, 134 B-D. τὰ μέτρια μάλιστα ὠφελεῖν, ἀλλὰ μὴ τὰ πολλὰ μηδὲ τὰ ὀλίγα.</small>

how much of either is right measure for the body? *also, it is not the maximum of knowledge, but the measured quantity which is good. Who is the judge to determine this measure?*
Erast.—The physician and the gymnastic trainer.
Sokr.—Who is the competent judge, how much seed is right measure for sowing a field? *Erast.*—The farmer.
Sokr.—Who is the competent judge, in reference to the sowing and planting of knowledge in the mind, which varieties are good, and how much of each is right measure?

The question is one which none of the persons present can answer.[1] None of them can tell who is the special referee, about training of mind; corresponding to the physician or the farmer in the analogous cases. Sokrates then puts a question somewhat different: *Sokr.* —Since we have agreed, that the man who prosecutes philosophy ought not to learn many things, still less all things—what is the best conjecture that we can make, respecting the matters which he ought to learn? *Erast.*—The finest and most suitable acquirements for him to aim at, are those which will yield to him the greatest reputation as a philosopher. He ought to appear accomplished in every variety of science, or at least in all the more important; and with that view, to learn as much of each as becomes a freeman to know:—that is, what belongs to the intelligent critic, as distinguished from the manual operative: to the planning and superintending architect, as distinguished from the working carpenter.[2] *No answer given. What is the best conjecture? Answer of the literary Erastes. A man must learn that which will yield to him the greatest reputation as a philosopher—as much as will enable him to talk like an intelligent critic, though not to practise.*

Sokr.—But you cannot learn even two different arts to this extent —much less several considerable arts. *Erast.*—I do not of course mean that the philosopher can be supposed to know each of them accurately, like the artist himself—but only as much as may be expected from the free and cultivated citizen. That is, he shall be able to appreciate, better than other hearers, the observations made by the artist: and farther to deliver a reasonable opinion of his own, so as to be accounted, by all the hearers, more accomplished in the affairs of the art than themselves.[3]

Sokr.—You mean that the philosopher is to be second-best in

[1] Plato, Erast. 134 E, 135 A. ἔχεται, μὴ ὅσα χειρουργίας.
[2] Plat. Erast. 135 B. ὅσα ξυνέσεως [3] Plat. Erast. 135 D.

The philosopher is one who is second-best in several different arts—a Pentathlus—who talks well upon each.

several distinct pursuits : like the Pentathlus, who is not expected to equal either the runner or the wrestler in their own separate departments, but only to surpass competitors in the five matches taken together.[1] *Erast.*—Yes—I mean what you say. He is one who does not enslave himself to any one matter, nor works out any one with such strictness as to neglect all others : he attends to all of them in reasonable measure.[2]

Upon this answer Sokrates proceeds to cross-examine :—*Sokr.*

On what occasions can such second-best men be useful? There are always regular practitioners at hand, and no one will call in the second-best man when he can have the regular practitioner.

Do you think that good men are useful, bad men useless? *Erast.*—Yes—I do. *Sokr.*—You think that philosophers, as you describe them, are useful? *Erast.*—Certainly: extremely useful. *Sokr.*—But tell me on what occasions such second-best men are useful : for obviously they are inferior to each separate artist. If you fall sick will you send for one of *them*, or for a professional physician? *Erast.*— I should send for both. *Sokr.*—That is no answer : I wish to know, which of the two you will send for, first and by preference? *Erast.*—No doubt—I shall send for the professional physician. *Sokr.*—The like also, if you are in danger on shipboard, you will entrust your life to the pilot rather than to the philosopher : and so as to all other matters, as long as a professional man is to be found, the philosopher is of no use? *Erast.*—So it appears. *Sokr.*—Our philosopher then is one of the useless persons : for we assuredly have professional men at hand. Now we agreed before, that good men were useful, bad men useless.[3] *Erast.*—Yes ; that was agreed.

Sokr.—If then you have correctly defined a philosopher to be one who has a second-rate knowledge on many subjects, he is useless so long as there exist professional artists on each subject. Your definition cannot therefore be correct. Philosophy must be something quite apart from this multifarious and busy meddling with

Philosophy cannot consist in multiplication of learned acquirements.

---

[1] Plat. Erast. 135 E, 136 A. καὶ οὕτως γίγνεσθαι περὶ πάντα ὕπακρόν τινα ἄνδρα τὸν πεφιλοσοφηκότα. The five matches were leaping, running, throw- ing the quoit and the javelin, wrestling.
[2] Plat. Erast. 136 B. ἀλλὰ πάντων μετρίως ἐφῆφθαι.
[3] Plat. Erast. 136 C-D.

different professional subjects, or this multiplication of learned acquirements. Indeed I fancied, that to be absorbed in professional subjects and in variety of studies, was vulgar and discreditable rather than otherwise.[1]

Let us now, however (continues Sokrates), take up the matter in another way. In regard to horses and dogs, those who punish rightly are also those who know how to make them better, and to discriminate with most exactness the good from the bad? *Erast.*—Yes: such is the fact.

Sokr.—Is not the case similar with men? Is it not the same art, which punishes men rightly, makes them better, and best distinguishes the good from the bad? whether applied to one, few, or many? *Erast.*—It is so.[2] *Sokr.*—The art or science, whereby men punish evil-doers rightly, is the judicial or justice: and it is by the same that they know the good apart from the bad, either one or many. If any man be a stranger to this art, so as not to know good men apart from bad, is he not also ignorant of himself, whether he be a good or a bad man? *Erast.*—Yes: he is. *Sokr.*—To be ignorant of yourself, is to be wanting in sobriety or temperance; to know yourself is to be sober or temperate. But this is the same art as that by which we punish rightly—or justice. Therefore justice and temperance are the same: and the Delphian rescript, *Know thyself*, does in fact enjoin the practice both of justice and of sobriety.[3] *Erast.*—So it appears. *Sokr.*—Now it is by this same art, when practised by a king, rightly punishing evil-doers, that cities are well governed; it is by the same art practised by a private citizen or house-master, that the house is well-governed: so that this art, justice or sobriety, is at the same time political, regal, economical; and the just and sober man is at once the true king, statesman, house-master.[4] *Erast.*—I admit it.

Sokr.—Now let me ask you. You said that it was discreditable for the philosopher, when in company with a physician or any other craftsman talking about matters of his own craft, not to be able to follow what he said

Sokrates changes his course of examination. Questions put to show that there is one special art, regal and political, of administering and discriminating the bad from the good.

In this art the philosopher must not only be

---

[1] Plato, Erast. 137 B.
[2] Plato, Erast. 137 C-D.
[3] Plato, Erast. 138 A.
[4] Plato, Erast. 138 C.

<small>second-best, competent to talk—but he must be a fully qualified practitioner, competent to act.</small> and comment upon it. Would it not also be discreditable to the philosopher, when listening to any king, judge, or house-master, about professional affairs, not to be able to understand and comment? *Erast.*—Assuredly it would be most discreditable upon matters of such grave moment. *Sokr.*—Shall we say then, that upon these matters also, as well as all others, the philosopher ought to be a Pentathlus or second-rate performer, useless so long as the special craftsman is at hand? or shall we not rather affirm, that he must not confide his own house to any one else, nor be the second-best within it, but must himself judge and punish rightly, if his house is to be well administered? *Erast.*—That too I admit.[1] *Sokr.*—Farther, if his friends shall entrust to him the arbitration of their disputes, —if the city shall command him to act as Dikast or to settle any difficulty,—in those cases also it will be disgraceful for him to stand second or third, and not to be first-rate? *Erast.*—I think it will be. *Sokr.*—You see then, my friend, philosophy is something very different from much learning and acquaintance with multifarious arts or sciences.[2]

Upon my saying this (so Sokrates concludes his recital of the conversation) the literary one of the two rivals was ashamed and held his peace; while the gymnastic rival declared that 1 was in the right, and the other hearers also commended what I had said.

<small>Close of the dialogue— Humiliation of the literary Erastes.</small>

<small>Remarks— Animated manner of the dialogue.</small> The antithesis between the philo-gymnast, hater of philosophy, —and the enthusiastic admirer of philosophy, who nevertheless cannot explain what it is—gives much point and vivacity to this short dialogue. This last person is exhibited as somewhat presumptuous and confident; thus affording a sort of excuse for the humiliating

---

[1] Plato, Erast. 138 E. Πότερον οὖν καὶ περὶ ταῦτα λέγωμεν, πένταθλον αὐτὸν δεῖν εἶναι καὶ ὕπακρον, τὰ δευτερεῖα ἔχοντα πάντων, τὸν φιλόσοφον, καὶ ἀχρεῖον εἶναι, ἕως ἂν τούτων τις ᾖ; ἢ πρῶτον μὲν τὴν αὑτοῦ οἰκίαν οὐκ ἄλλῳ ἐπιτρεπτέον οὐδὲ τὰ δευτερεῖα ἐν τούτῳ ἑκτέον, ἀλλ' αὐτὸν κολαστέον δικάζοντα ὀρθῶς, εἰ μέλλει εὖ οἰκεῖσθαι αὐτοῦ ἡ οἰκία;

[2] Plato, Erast. 139 A. Πολλοῦ ἄρα δεῖ ἡμῖν, ὦ βέλτιστε, τὸ φιλοσοφεῖν πολυμάθειά τε εἶναι καὶ ἡ περὶ τὰς τέχνας πραγματεία.

ART OF GOVERNMENT ESSENTIAL.

cross-examination put upon him by Sokrates to the satisfaction of his stupid rival. Moreover, the dramatic introduction is full of animation, like that of the Charmidês and Lysis.

Besides the animated style of the dialogue, the points raised for discussion in it are of much interest. The word philosophy has at all times been vague and ambiguous. Certainly no one before Sokrates—probably no one before Plato—ever sought a definition of it. In no other Platonic dialogue than this, is the definition of it made a special topic of research.

It is here handled in Plato's negative, elenchtic, tentative, manner. By some of his contemporaries, philosophy was really considered as equivalent to polymathy, or to much and varied knowledge : so at least Plato represents it as being considered by Hippias the Sophist, contrary to the opinion of Protagoras.[1] The exception taken by Sokrates to a definition founded on simple quantity, without any standard point of sufficiency by which much or little is to be measured, introduces that governing idea of τὸ μέτριον (the moderate, that which conforms to a standard measure) upon which Plato insists so much in other more elaborate dialogues. The conception of a measure, of a standard of measurement—and of conformity thereunto, as the main constituent of what is good and desirable —stands prominent in his mind,[2] though it is not always handled in the same way. We have seen it, in the Second Alkibiadês, indicated under another name as knowledge of Good or of the Best : without which, knowledge on special matters was declared to be hurtful rather than useful.[3] Plato considers that this Measure is neither discernible nor applicable except by a specially trained intelligence. In the Erastæ as elsewhere, such an intelligence is called for in general terms : but when it is asked, Where is the person possessing such intelligence, available in the case of mental training—neither Sokrates nor any one else can point him out. To suggest a question, and direct

Definition of philosophy— here sought for the first time—Platonic conception of measure— referee not discovered.

---

[1] Plato, Protag. 318 E. Compare, too, the Platonic dialogues, Hippias Major and Minor.
[2] See about ἡ τοῦ μετρίου φύσις, as οὐσία—as ὄντως γιγνόμενον.—Plato, Politikus, 283-284. Compare also the Philêbus, p. 64 D, and the Protagoras, pp. 356-357, where ἡ μετρητικὴ τέχνη is declared to be the principal saviour of life and happiness.
[3] Plato, Alkib. ii. 145-146 ; supra, ch. xii. p. 16.

attention to it, yet still to leave it unanswered—is a practice familiar with Plato. In this respect the Erastæ is like other dialogues. The answer, if any, intended to be understood or divined, is, that such an intelligence is the philosopher himself.

The second explanation of philosophy here given—that the philosopher is one who is second-best in many departments, and a good talker upon all, but inferior to the special master in each—was supposed by Thrasyllus in ancient times to be pointed at Demokritus. By many Platonic critics, it is referred to those persons whom they single out to be called Sophists. I conceive it to be applicable (whether intended or not) to the literary men generally of that age, the persons called Sophists included. That which Perikles expressed by the word, when he claimed the love of wisdom and the love of beauty as characteristic features of the Athenian citizen—referred chiefly to the free and abundant discussion, the necessity felt by every one for talking over every thing before it was done, yet accompanied with full energy in action as soon as the resolution was taken to act.[1] Speech, ready and pertinent, free conflict of opinion on many different topics—was the manifestation and the measure of knowledge acquired. Sokrates passed his life in talking, with every one indiscriminately, and upon each man's particular subject; often perplexing the artist himself. Xenophon recounts conversations with various professional men—a painter, a sculptor, an armourer—and informs us that it was instructive to all of them, though Sokrates was no practitioner in any craft.[2] It was not merely Demokritus, but Plato and Aristotle also, who talked or wrote upon almost every subject included in contemporary observation. The voluminous works of Aristotle,—the Timæus, Republic, and Leges, of Plato,— embrace a large variety of subjects, on each of which, severally taken, these two great men were second-best or inferior to some special proficient. Yet both of them had judgments to give,

View taken of the second-best critical talking man, as compared with the special proficient and practitioner.

---

[1] Thucyd. ii. 39 fin.—40. καὶ ἕν τε τούτοις τὴν πόλιν ἀξίαν εἶναι θαυμάζεσθαι, καὶ ἔτι ἐν ἄλλοις. φιλοκαλοῦμέν γὰρ μετ᾽ εὐτελείας καὶ φιλοσοφοῦμεν ἄνευ μαλακίας, &c., and the remarkable sequel of the same chapter about the intimate conjunction of abundant speech with energetic action in the Athenian character.

[2] Xen. Mem. iii. 10; iii. 11; iii. 12.

CHAP. XVI. PHILOSOPHY HAS A PROVINCE OF HER OWN. 119

which it was important to hear, upon all subjects :[1] and both of them could probably talk better upon each than the special proficient himself. Aristotle, for example, would write better upon rhetoric than Demosthenes—upon tragedy, than Sophokles. Undoubtedly, if an oration or a tragedy were to be composed—if resolution or action were required on any real state of particular circumstances—the special proficient would be called upon to act : but it would be a mistake to infer from hence, as the Platonic Sokrates intimates in the Erastæ, that the second-best, or theorizing reasoner, was a useless man. The theoretical and critical point of view, with the command of language apt for explaining and defending it, has a value of its own ; distinct from, yet ultimately modifying and improving, the practical. And such comprehensive survey and comparison of numerous objects, without having the attention exclusively fastened or enslaved to any one of them, deserves to rank high as a variety of intelligence—whether it be adopted as the definition of a philosopher, or not.

Plato undoubtedly did not conceive the definition of the philosopher in the same way as Sokrates. The close of the Erastæ is employed in opening a distant and dim view of the Platonic conception. We are given to understand, that the philosopher has a province of his own, wherein he is not second-best, but a first-rate actor and adviser. To indicate, in many different ways, that there is or must be such a peculiar, appertaining to philosophy—distinct from, though analogous to, the peculiar of each several art—is one leading purpose in many Platonic dialogues. But what is the peculiar of the philosopher? Here, as elsewhere, it is marked out in a sort of misty outline, not as by one who already knows and is familiar with it, but as one who is trying to find it without being sure that he has succeeded. Here, we have it described as the art of discriminating good from evil, governing, and applying penal sanctions rightly. This is the supreme art or

Plato's view—that the philosopher has a province special to himself, distinct from other specialties — dimly indicated— regal or political art.

[1] The πένταθλος or ὕπακρος, whom Plato criticises in this dialogue, coincides with what Aristotle calls "the man of universal education or culture".—Ethic. Nikom. I. i. 1095, a. 1.
ἕκαστος δὲ κρίνει καλῶς ἃ γιγνώσκει, καὶ τούτων ἐστὶν ἀγαθὸς κριτής· καθ' ἕκαστον ἄρα, ὁ πεπαιδευμένος· ἁπλῶς δέ, ὁ περὶ πᾶν πεπαιδευμένος.

science, of which the philosopher is the professor ; and in which, far from requiring advice from others, he is the only person competent both to advise and to act : the art which exercises control over all other special arts, directing how far, and on what occasions, each of them comes into appliance. It is philosophy, looked at in one of its two aspects : not as a body of speculative truth, to be debated, proved, and discriminated from what cannot be proved or can be disproved—but as a critical judgment bearing on actual life, prescribing rules or giving directions in particular cases, with a view to the attainment of foreknown ends, recognised as *expetenda*.[1] This is what Plato understands by the measuring or calculating art, the regal or political art, according as we use the language of the Protagoras, Politikus, Euthydêmus, Republic. Both justice and sobriety are branches of this art ; and the distinction between the two loses its importance when the art is considered as a whole—as we find both in the Erastæ and in the Republic.[2]

Philosopher —the supreme artist, controlling other artists.

Here, in the Erastæ, this conception of the philosopher as the supreme artist controlling all other artists, is darkly indicated and crudely sketched. We shall find the same conception more elaborately illustrated in other dialogues ; yet never passing out of that state of dreamy grandeur which characterises Plato as an expositor.

[1] The difference between the second explanation of philosophy and the third explanation, suggested in the Erastæ, will be found to coincide pretty nearly with the distinction which Aristotle takes much pains to draw between σοφία and φρόνησις.—Ethic. Nikomach. vi. 5, pp. 1140-1141; also Ethic. Magn. i. pp. 1197-1198.

[2] See Republic, iv. 433 A ; Gorgias, 526 C ; Charmidês, 164 B ; and Heindorf's note on the passage in the Charmidês.

APPENDIX.

This is one of the dialogues declared to be spurious by Schleiermacher, Ast, Socher, and Stallbaum,—all of them critics of the present century. In my judgment, their grounds for such declaration are altogether inconclusive. They think the dialogue an inferior composition, unworthy of Plato; and they accordingly find reasons, more or less ingenious, for relieving Plato from the discredit of it. I do not think so meanly of the dialogue as they do; but even if I did, I should not pronounce it to be spurious, without some evidence bearing upon that special question. No such evidence, of any value, is produced.

It is indeed contended, on the authority of a passage in Diogenes (ix. 37), that Thrasyllus himself doubted of the authenticity of the Erastæ. The passage is as follows, in his life of Demokritus—εἴπερ οἱ 'Αντερασταὶ Πλάτωνός εἰσι, φησὶ Θράσυλλος, οὗτος ἂν εἴη ὁ παραγενόμενος ἀνώνυμος, τῶν περὶ Οἰνοπίδην καὶ 'Αναξαγόραν ἕτερος, ἐν τῇ πρὸς Σωκράτην ὁμιλίᾳ διαλεγόμενος περὶ φιλοσοφίας· ᾧ, φησίν, ὡς πεντάθλῳ ἔοικεν ὁ φιλόσοφος· καὶ ἦν ὡς ἀληθῶς ἐν φιλοσοφίᾳ πένταθλος (Demokritus).

Now in the first place, Schleiermacher and Stallbaum both declare that Thrasyllus can never have said that which Diogenes here makes him say (Schleierm. p. 510; Stallbaum, Prolegg. ad. Erast. p. 266, and not. p. 273).

Next, it is certain that Thrasyllus did consider it the undoubted work of Plato, for he enrolled it in his classification, as the third dialogue in the fourth tetralogy (Diog. L. iii. 59).

Yxem, who defends the genuineness of the Erastæ (Ueber Platon's Kleitophon, pp. 6-7, Berlin, 1846), insists very properly on this point; not merely as an important fact in itself, but as determining the sense of the words εἴπερ οἱ 'Αντερασταὶ Πλάτωνός εἰσι, and as showing that the words rather affirm, than deny, the authenticity of the dialogue. "If the Anterastæ are the work of Plato, *as they are universally admitted to be.*" You must supply the parenthesis in this way, in order to make Thrasyllus consistent with himself. Yxem cites a passage from Galen, in which εἴπερ is used, and in which the parenthesis must be supplied in the way indicated : no doubt at all being meant to be hinted. And I will produce another passage out of Diogenes himself, where εἴπερ is used in the same way ; not as intended to convey the smallest doubt, but merely introducing the premiss for a conclusion immediately following. Diogenes says, respecting the Platonic Ideas, εἴπερ ἐστὶ μνήμη, τὰς ἰδέας ἐν τοῖς οὖσιν ὑπάρχειν (iii. 15). He does not intend to suggest any doubt whether there be such a fact as memory. Εἴπερ is sometimes the equivalent of ἐπειδήπερ : as we learn from Hermann ad Viger. VIII. 6, p. 512.

There is therefore no fair ground for supposing that Thrasyllus doubted the genuineness of the Erastæ. And when I read what modern critics say in support of their verdict of condemnation, I feel the more authorised in dissenting from it. I will cite a passage or two from Stallbaum.

Stallbaum begins his Prolegomena as follows, pp. 205-206 : "Quanquam hic libellus genus dicendi habet purum, castum, elegans, nihil ut inveniri queat quod à Platonis aut Xenophontis elegantiâ abhorreat —tamen quin à Boeckhio, Schleiermachero, Astio, Sochero, Knebelio, aliis jure meritoque pro suppositicio habitus sit, haudquaquam dubitamus. Est enim materia operis adeo non ad Platonis mentem rationemque elaborata, ut potius cuivis alii Socraticorum quam huic rectè adscribi posse videatur."

After stating that the Erastæ may be divided into two principal sections, Stallbaum proceeds :—"Neutra harum partium ita tractata est, ut nihil desideretur, quod ad justam argumenti explicationem merito requiras—nihil inculcatum reperiatur, quod vel alio modo illustratum vel omnino omissum esse cupias".

I call attention to this sentence as a fair specimen of the grounds upon which the Platonic critics proceed when they strike dialogues out of the Platonic Canon. If there be anything wanting in it which is required for what they consider a proper setting forth of the argument —if there be anything which they would desire to see omitted or otherwise illustrated—this is with them a reason for deciding that it is not Plato's work. That is, if there be any defects in it of any kind, it cannot be admitted as Plato's work ;—*his genuine works have no defects.* I protest altogether against this *ratio decidendi.* If I acknowledged it and applied it consistently I should strike out every dialogue in the Canon. Certainly, the presumption in favour of the Catalogue of Thrasyllus must be counted as *nil*, if it will not outweigh such feeble counter-arguments as these.

One reason given by Stallbaum for considering the Erastæ as spurious is, that the Sophists are not derided in it. "Quis est igitur, qui Platonem sibi persuadeat illos non fuisse castigaturum, et omnino non significaturum, quinam illi essent, adversus quos hanc disputationem instituisset?" It is strange to be called on by learned men to strike out all dialogues from the Canon in which there is no derision of the Sophists. Such derision exists already in excess: we hear until we are tired how mean it is to receive money for lecturing. Again, Stallbaum says that the persons whose opinions are here attacked are not specified by name. But who are the εἰδῶν φίλοι attacked in the Sophistês? They are not specified by name, and critics differ as to the persons intended.

CHAPTER XVII.

ION.

Ion. Persons of the dialogue. Difference of opinion among modern critics as to its genuineness.
The dialogue called Ion is carried on between Sokrates and the Ephesian rhapsode Ion. It is among those disallowed by Ast, first faintly defended, afterwards disallowed, by Schleiermacher,[1] and treated contemptuously by both. Subsequent critics, Hermann,[2] Stallbaum, Steinhart, consider it as genuine, yet as an inferior production, of little worth, and belonging to Plato's earliest years.

Rhapsodes as a class in Greece. They competed for prizes at the festivals. Ion has been triumphant.
I hold it to be genuine, and it may be comparatively early; but I see no ground for the disparaging criticism which has often been applied to it. The personage whom it introduces to us as subjected to the cross-examination of Sokrates is a rhapsode of celebrity; one among a class of artists at that time both useful and esteemed. They recited or sang,[3] with appropriate accent and gesture, the compositions of Homer and of other epic poets: thus serving to the Grecian epic, the same purpose as the actors served to the dramatic, and the harp-singers (κιθαρῳδοὶ) to the lyric. There were various solemn festivals such as that of Æsculapius at Epidaurus, and (most especially) the Panathenæa at Athens, where prizes were awarded for the competition of the rhapsodes. Ion is described as having competed triumphantly in the festival at Epidaurus, and carried off the first prize. He appeared there in a splendid costume, crowned

---

[1] Schleiermacher, Einleit. zum Ion, pp. 261-266; Ast, Leben und Schriften des Platon, p. 466.

[2] K. F. Hermann, Gesch. und Syst. der Plat. Phil. pp. 437-438; Steinhart, Einleitung, p. 15.

[3] The word ᾄδειν is in this very dialogue (532 D, 535 A) applied to the rhapsodizing of Ion.

THE RHAPSODES.

with a golden wreath, amidst a crowd which is described as containing more than 20,000 persons.[1]

Much of the acquaintance of cultivated Greeks with Homer and the other epic poets was both acquired and maintained through such rhapsodes; the best of whom contended at the festivals, while others, less highly gifted as to vocal power and gesticulation, gave separate declamations and lectures of their own, and even private lessons to individuals.[2] Euthydêmus, in one of the Xenophontic conversations with Sokrates, and Antisthenes in the Xenophontic Symposion, are made to declare that the rhapsodes as a class were extremely silly. This, if true at all, can apply only to the expositions and comments with which they accompanied their recital of Homer and other poets. Moreover we cannot reasonably set it down (though some modern critics do so) as so much incontestable truth: we must consider it as an opinion delivered by one of the speakers in the conversation, but not necessarily well founded.[3] Unquestionably, the comments made upon Homer (both in that age and afterwards) were often fanciful and misleading. Metrodorus, Anaxagoras, and others, resolved the Homeric narrative into various allegories, physical, ethical, and theological: and most men who had an opinion to defend, rejoiced to be able to support or enforce it by some passages of Homer, well or ill-explained—just as texts of the Bible are quoted in modern times. In this manner, Homer was pressed into the service of every disputant; and the Homeric poems were presented as containing, or at least as implying, doctrines quite foreign to the age in which they were composed.[4]

The Rhapsodes, in so far as they interpreted Homer, were

Functions of the Rhapsodes. Recitation— Exposition of the poets. Arbitrary exposition of the poets was then frequent.

[1] Plato, Ion, 535 D.

[2] Xen. Sympos. iii. 6. Nikêratus says that he heard the rhapsodes nearly every day. He professes to be able to repeat both the Iliad and the Odyssey from memory.

[3] Xen. Mem. iv. 2, 10; Sympos. iii. 6; Plato, Ion, 530 E.
Steinhart cites this judgment about the rhapsodes as if it had been pronounced by the Xenophontic Sokrates himself, which is not the fact (Steinhart, Einleitung, p. 3).

[4] Diogenes Laert. ii. 11; Nitzsch, Die Heldensage der Griechen, pp. 74-78; Lobeck, Aglaophamus, p. 157.
Seneca, Epistol. 88: "modo Stoicum Homerum faciunt—modo Epicureum . . . modo Peripateticum, tria genera bonorum inducentem: modo Academicum, incerta omnia dicentem. Apparet nihil horum esse in illo, cui omnia insunt: ista enim inter se dissident."

The popularity of the Rhapsodes was chiefly derived from their recitation. Powerful effect which they produced.

probably not less disposed than others to discover in him their own fancies. But the character in which they acquired most popularity, was, not as expositors, but as reciters, of the poems. The powerful emotion which, in the process of reciting, they both felt themselves, and communicated to their auditors, is declared in this dialogue: "When that which I recite is pathetic (says Ion), my eyes are filled with tears: when it is awful or terrible, my hair stands on end, and my heart leaps. Moreover I see the spectators also weeping, sympathising with my emotions, and looking aghast at what they hear."[1] This assertion of the vehement emotional effect produced by the words of the poet as declaimed or sung by the rhapsode, deserves all the more credit—because Plato himself, far from looking upon it favourably, either derides or disapproves it. Accepting it as a matter of fact, we see that the influence of rhapsodes, among auditors generally, must have been derived more from their efficacy as actors than from their ability as expositors.

Ion however is described in this dialogue as combining the two functions of reciter and expositor: a partnership like that of Garrick and Johnson, in regard to Shakspeare. It is in the last of the two functions, that Sokrates here examines him: considering Homer, not as a poet appealing to the emotions of hearers, but as a teacher administering lessons and imparting instruction. Such was the view of Homer entertained by a large proportion of the Hellenic world. In that capacity, his poems served as a theme for rhapsodes, as well as for various philosophers and Sophists who were not rhapsodes, nor accomplished reciters.

Ion both reciter and expositor— Homer was considered more as an instructor than as a poet.

The reader must keep in mind, in following the questions put by Sokrates, that this pædagogic and edifying view of Homer is the only one present to the men of the Sokratic school—and especially to Plato. Of the genuine functions of the gifted poet, who touches the chords of strong and diversified emotion — "qui

Plato disregards and disapproves the poetic or emotional working.

---

[1] Plato, Ion, 535 C-E. The description here given is the more interesting because it is the only intimation remaining of the strong effect produced by these rhapsodic representations.

pectus inaniter angit, Irritat, mulcet, falsis terroribus implet" (Horat. Epist. II. 1, 212)—Plato takes no account: or rather, he declares open war against them, either as childish delusions[1], or as mischievous stimulants, tending to exalt the unruly elements of the mind, and to overthrow the sovereign authority of reason. We shall find farther manifestations on this point in the Republic and Leges.

Ion professes to have devoted himself to the study of Homer exclusively, neglecting other poets: so that he can interpret the thoughts, and furnish reflections upon them, better than any other expositor.[2] How does it happen (asked Sokrates) that you have so much to say about Homer, and nothing at all about other poets? Homer may be the best of all poets: but he is still only one of those who exercise the poetic art, and he must necessarily talk about the same subjects as other poets. Now the art of poetry is *One* altogether—like that of painting, sculpture, playing on the flute, playing on the harp, rhapsodizing, &c.[3] Whoever is competent to judge and explain one artist,—what he has done well and what he has done ill,—is competent also to judge any other artist in the same profession.

Ion devoted himself to Homer exclusively. Questions of Sokrates to him—How happens it that you cannot talk equally upon other poets? The poetic art is one.

I cannot explain to you how it happens (replies Ion): I only know the fact incontestably—that when I talk about Homer, my thoughts flow abundantly, and every one tells me that my discourse is excellent. Quite the reverse, when I talk of any other poet.[4]

I can explain it (says Sokrates). Your talent in expounding Homer is not an art, acquired by system and method —otherwise it would have been applicable to other poets besides. It is a special gift, imparted to you by divine power and inspiration. The like is true of the poet whom you expound. His genius does not spring from art, system, or method: it is a special gift ema-

Explanation given by Sokrates. Both the Rhapsode and the Poet work, not by art and

---

[1] The question of Sokrates (Ion, 535 D), about the emotion produced in the hearers by the recital of Homer's poetry, bears out what is here asserted.
[2] Plato, Ion, 536 E.
[3] Plato, Ion, 531 A, 532 C-D. ποιη- τικὴ γάρ πού ἐστι τὸ ὅλον. . . . Οὐκοῦν ἐπειδὰν λάβῃ τις καὶ ἄλλην τέχνην ἡντινοῦν ὅλην, ὁ αὐτὸς τρόπος τῆς σκέψεώς ἐστι περὶ ἁπασῶν τῶν τεχνῶν; 533 A.
[4] Plato, Ion, 533 C.

system, but by divine inspiration. Fine poets are bereft of their reason, and possessed by inspiration from some God.
nating from the inspiration of the Muses.[1] A poet is a light, airy, holy, person, who cannot compose verses at all, so long as his reason remains within him.[2] The Muses take away his reason, substituting in place of it their own divine inspiration and special impulse, either towards epic, dithyramb, encomiastic hymns, hyporchemata, &c., one or other of these. Each poet receives one of these special gifts, but is incompetent for any of the others: whereas, if their ability had been methodical or artistic, it would have displayed itself in all of them alike. Like prophets, and deliverers of oracles, these poets have their reason taken away, and become servants of the Gods.[3] It is not *they* who, bereft of their reason, speak in such sublime strains: it is the God who speaks to us, and speaks through them. You may see this by Tynnichus of Chalkis; who composed his Pæan, the finest of all Pæans, which is in every one's mouth, telling us himself, that it was the invention of the Muses—but who never composed anything else worth hearing. It is through this worthless poet that the God has sung the most sublime hymn:[4] for the express purpose of showing us that these fine compositions are not human performances at all, but divine: and that the poet is only an interpreter of the Gods, possessed by one or other of them, as the case may be.

Homer is thus (continues Sokrates) not a man of art or reason, but the interpreter of the Gods; deprived of his reason, but possessed, inspired, by them. You, Ion, are the interpreter of Homer: and the divine inspiration, carrying away your reason, is exercised over you through him. It is in this way that the influence of

Analogy of the Magnet, which holds up by attraction successive stages of

---

[1] Plato, Ion, 533 E—534 A. πάντες γὰρ οἵ τε τῶν ἐπῶν ποιηταὶ οἱ ἀγαθοὶ οὐκ ἐκ τέχνης ἀλλ' ἔνθεοι ὄντες καὶ κατεχόμενοι πάντα ταῦτα τὰ καλὰ λέγουσι ποιήματα, καὶ οἱ μελοποιοὶ οἱ ἀγαθοὶ ὡσαύτως· ὥσπερ οἱ κορυβαντιῶντες οὐκ ἔμφρονες ὄντες ὀρχοῦνται, οὕτω καὶ οἱ μελοποιοὶ οὐκ ἔμφρονες ὄντες τὰ καλὰ μέλη ταῦτα ποιοῦσιν, &c.

[2] Plato, Ion, 534 B. κοῦφον γὰρ χρῆμα ποιητής ἐστι καὶ πτηνὸν καὶ ἱερόν, καὶ οὐ πρότερον οἷός τε ποιεῖν πρὶν ἂν ἔνθεός τε γένηται καὶ ἔκφρων καὶ ὁ νοῦς μηκέτι ἐν αὐτῷ ἐνῇ· ἕως δ' ἂν τουτὶ ἔχῃ τὸ κτῆμα, ἀδύνατος πᾶς ποιεῖν ἐστιν ἄνθρωπος καὶ χρησμῳδεῖν.

[3] Plato, Ion, 534 C-D. διὰ ταῦτα δὲ ὁ θεὸς ἐξαιρούμενος τούτων τὸν νοῦν τούτοις χρῆται ὑπηρέταις καὶ τοῖς χρησμῳδοῖς καὶ τοῖς μάντεσι τοῖς θείοις, ἵνα ἡμεῖς οἱ ἀκούοντες εἰδῶμεν, ὅτι οὐχ οὗτοί εἰσιν οἱ ταῦτα λέγοντες οὕτω πολλοῦ ἄξια, ἀλλ' ὁ θεὸς αὐτός ἐστιν ὁ λέγων, διὰ τούτων δὲ φθέγγεται πρὸς ἡμᾶς.

[4] Plato, Ion, 534 E. ταῦτα ἐνδεικνύμενος ὁ θεὸς ἐξεπίτηδες διὰ τοῦ φαυλοτάτου ποιητοῦ τὸ κάλλιστον μέλος ᾖσεν.

CHAP. XVII.   THE MAGNET.   129

the Magnet is shown, attracting and holding up succes- *iron rings.*
sive stages of iron rings.[1] The first ring is in contact *The Gods*
                                                            first inspire
with the Magnet itself: the second is suspended to   *Homer, then*
                                                            act through
the first, the third to the second, and so on. The   *him and*
                                                            through Ion
attractive influence of the Magnet is thus transmitted   *upon the*
through a succession of different rings, so as to keep   *auditors.*
suspended several which are a good way removed from itself.
So the influence of the Gods is exerted directly and immediately
upon Homer: through him, it passes by a second stage to you:
through him and you, it passes by a third stage to those auditors
whom you so powerfully affect and delight, becoming however
comparatively enfeebled at each stage of transition.

The passage and comparison here given by Sokrates—remarkable as an early description of the working of the
Magnet—forms the central point or kernel of the   *This compa-*
                                                  rison forms
dialogue called Ion. It is an expansion of a judg- *the central*
                                                   point of the
ment delivered by Sokrates himself in his Apology to *dialogue. It*
                                                     is an expan-
the Dikasts, and it is repeated in more than one place *sion of a*
                                                       judgment
by Plato.[2] Sokrates declares in his Apology that he *delivered by*
had applied his testing cross-examination to several   *Sokrates in*
                                                       the Apology.
excellent poets; and that finding them unable to give
any rational account of their own compositions, he concluded
that they composed without any wisdom of their own, under the
same inspiration as prophets and declarers of oracles. In the
dialogue before us, this thought is strikingly illustrated and
amplified.

The contrast between systematic, professional, procedure, de-
liberately taught and consciously acquired, capable *Platonic an-*
                                                     tithesis:
of being defended at every step by appeal to intel- *Systematic*
                                                     procedure
ligible rules founded upon scientific theory, and   *distinguish-*
enabling the person so qualified to impart his quali- *ed from un-*
                                                      systematic:
fication to others—and a different procedure purely   *which latter*
impulsive and unthinking, whereby the agent, having   *was either*
                                                      blind rou-
in his mind a conception of the end aimed at, proceeds *tine, or*
                                                       madness
from one intermediate step to another, without know-   *inspired by*
ing why he does so or how he has come to do so, and   *the Gods.*

---

[1] Plato, Ion, 533 D-E.
[2] Plato, Apol. Sokr. p. 22 D; Plato, Menon, p. 99 D.

Varieties of madness, good and bad. without being able to explain his practice if questioned or to impart it to others—this contrast is a favourite one with Plato. The last-mentioned procedure—the unphilosophical or irrational—he conceives under different aspects: sometimes as a blind routine or insensibly acquired habit,[1] sometimes as a stimulus applied from without by some God, superseding the reason of the individual. Such a condition Plato calls *madness*, and he considers those under it as persons out of their senses. But he recognises different varieties of madness, according to the God from whom it came: the bad madness was a disastrous visitation and distemper—the good madness was a privilege and blessing, an inspiration superior to human reason. Among these privileged madmen he reckoned prophets and poets; another variety under the same genus, is, that mental love, between a well-trained adult, and a beautiful, intelligent, youth, which he regards as the most exalted of all human emotions.[2] In the Ion, this idea of a privileged madness —inspiration from the Gods superseding reason—is applied not only to the poet, but also to the rhapsode who recites the poem, and even to the auditors whom he addresses. The poet receives the inspiration directly from the Gods: he inoculates the rhapsode with it, who again inoculates the auditors—the fervour is, at each successive communication, diminished. The auditor represents the last of the rings; held in suspension, through the intermediate agency of other rings, by the inherent force of the magnet.[3]

We must remember, that privileged communications from the **Special inspiration from the Gods was a familiar fact in Grecian life. Privileged communications from the Gods to Sokrates—** Gods to men, and special persons recipient thereof, were acknowledged and witnessed everywhere as a constant phenomenon of Grecian life. There were not only numerous oracular temples, which every one could visit to ask questions in matters of doubt—but also favoured persons who had received from the Gods the gift of predicting the future, of interpreting omens, of determining the good or bad indications

---

[1] Plato, Phædon, 82 A; Gorgias, 463 A, 465 A.
[2] This doctrine is set forth at length by Sokrates in the Platonic Phædrus, in the second discourse of Sokrates about Eros, pp. 244-245-249 D.
[3] Plato, Ion, 535 E. οὗτός ἐστιν ὁ θεατὴς τῶν δακτυλίων ὁ ἔσχατος . . . . ὁ δὲ μέσος σὺ ὁ ῥαψῳδὸς καὶ ὑποκριτής, ὁ δὲ πρῶτος, αὐτὸς ὁ ποιητής.

CHAP. XVII.   SPECIAL INSPIRATION.   131

furnished by animals sacrificed.[1] In every town or his firm belief in them.
village—or wherever any body of men were assembled
—there were always persons who prophesied or delivered oracles, and to whom special revelations were believed to be vouchsafed, during periods of anxiety. No one was more familiar with this fact than the Sokratic disciples: for Sokrates himself had perhaps a greater number of special communications from the Gods than any man of his age : his divine sign having begun when he was a child, and continuing to move him frequently, even upon small matters, until his death : though the revelations were for the most part negative, not affirmative—telling him often what was not to be done—seldom what was to be done—resembling in this respect his own dialogues with other persons. Moreover Sokrates inculcated upon his friends emphatically, that they ought to have constant recourse to prophecy : that none but impious men neglected to do so : that the benevolence of the Gods was nowhere more conspicuous than in their furnishing such special revelations and warnings, to persons whom they favoured : that the Gods administered the affairs of the world partly upon principles of regular sequence, so that men by diligent study might learn what they were to expect,—but partly also, and by design, in a manner irregular and undecypherable, such that it could not be fathomed by any human study, and could not be understood except through direct and special revelation from themselves.[2]

Here, as well as elsewhere, Plato places inspiration, both of the prophet and the poet, in marked contrast with reason Condition of the inspired person—his reason is for
and intelligence. Reason is supposed to be for the
time withdrawn or abolished, and inspiration is intro-

---

[1] Not only the χρησμολόγοι, μάντεις, oracular temples, &c., are often mentioned in Herodotus, Thucydides, Xenophon, &c., but Aristotle also recognises οἱ νυμφόληπτοι καὶ θεόληπτοι τῶν ἀνθρώπων, ἐπιπνοίᾳ δαιμονίου τινὸς ὥσπερ ἐνθουσιάζοντες, as a real and known class of persons. See Ethic. Eudem. i. p. 1214, a. 23; Ethic. Magna, ii. p. 1207, b. 8.
The μάντις is a recognised profession, the gift of Apollo, not merely according to Homer, but according to Solon (Frag. xi. 52, Schn.):

Ἄλλον μάντιν ἔθηκεν ἄναξ ἑκάεργος
Ἀπόλλων,
ἔγνω δ' ἀνδρὶ κακὸν τηλόθεν ἐρχόμενον, &c.

[2] These views of Sokrates are declared in the Memorabilia of Xenophon, i. 1, 6-10 ; i. 4, 2-18 ; iv. 3, 12.
It is plain from Xenophon (Mem. i. 1, 3) that many persons were offended with Sokrates because they believed— or at least because he affirmed—that he received more numerous and special revelations from the Gods than any one else.

the time withdrawn. duced by the Gods into its place. "When Monarch Reason sleeps, this mimic wakes." The person inspired (prophet or poet) becomes for the time the organ of an extraneous agency, speaking what he neither originates nor understands. The genuine gift of prophecy[1] (Plato says) attaches only to a disabled, enfeebled, distempered, condition of the intelligence; the gift of poetry is conferred by the Gods upon the most inferior men, as we see by the case of Tynnichus—whose sublime pæan shows us, that it is the Gods alone who utter fine poetry through the organs of a person himself thoroughly incompetent.

It is thus that Plato, setting before himself a process of systematised reason,—originating in a superior intellect, laying down universal principles and deducing consequences from them—capable of being consistently applied, designedly taught, and defended against objections—enumerates the various mental conditions opposed to it, and ranks inspiration as one of them. In this dialogue, Sokrates seeks to prove that the success of Ion as a rhapsode depends upon his being out of his mind or inspired. But Ion does not accept the compliment: *Ion.*—You speak well, Sokrates; but I should be surprised if you spoke well enough to create in me the new conviction, that I am possessed and mad when I eulogize Homer. I do not think that you would even yourself say so, if you heard me discourse on the subject.[2]

Ion does not admit himself to be inspired and out of his mind.

Sokr.—But Homer talks upon all subjects. Upon which of them can you discourse? *Ion.*—Upon all. *Sokr.*— Not surely upon such as belong to special arts, professions. Each portion of the matter of knowledge is included under some special art, and is known through that art by those who possess it. Thus, you and I, both of us, know the number of our fingers; we know it through the same art, which both of us possess— the arithmetical. But Homer talks of matters be-

Homer talks upon all subjects—Is Ion competent to explain what Homer says upon all of them? Rhapsodic art. What is its province?

---

[1] Plato, Timæus, 71 E. ἱκανὸν δὲ σημεῖον ὡς μαντικὴν ἀφροσύνῃ θεὸς ἀνθρωπίνῃ δέδωκεν· οὐδεὶς γὰρ ἔννους ἐφάπτεται μαντικῆς ἐνθέου καὶ ἀληθοῦς, ἀλλ' ἢ καθ' ὕπνον τὴν τῆς φρονήσεως πεδηθεὶς δύναμιν, ἢ διὰ νόσον ἤ τινα ἐνθουσιασμὸν παραλλάξας.

Compare Plato, Menon, pp. 99-100. οἱ χρησμῳδοί τε καὶ οἱ θεομάντεις .... λέγουσι μὲν ἀληθῆ καὶ πολλὰ ἴσασι δὲ οὐδὲν ὧν λέγουσι. Compare Plato, Legg. iv. 719.

[2] Plato, Ion, 536 E.

longing to many different arts or occupations, that of the physician, the charioteer, the fisherman, &c. You cannot know these; since you do not belong to any of these professions, but are a rhapsode. Describe to me what are the matters included in the rhapsodic art. The rhapsodic art is one art by itself, distinct from the medical and others : it cannot know every thing ; tell me what matters come under its special province.[1] *Ion.*— The rhapsodic art does not know what belongs to any one of the other special arts : but that of which it takes cognizance, and that which I know, is, what is becoming and suitable to each variety of character described by Homer : to a man or woman— to a freeman or slave—to the commander who gives orders or to the subordinate who obeys them, &c. This is what belongs to the peculiar province of the rhapsode to appreciate and understand.[2] *Sokr.*—Will the rhapsode know what is suitable for the commander of a ship to say to his seamen, during a dangerous storm, better than the pilot ? Will the rhapsode know what is suitable for one who gives directions about the treatment of a sick man, better than the physician ? Will the rhapsode know what is suitable to be said by the herdsman when the cattle are savage and distracted, or to the female slaves when busy in spinning ? *Ion.*—No: the rhapsode will not know these things so well as the pilot, the physician, the grazier, the mistress, &c.[3] *Sokr.* —Will the rhapsode know what is suitable for the military commander to say, when he is exhorting his soldiers ? *Ion.*—Yes : the rhapsode will know this well : at least I know it well.

Sokr.—Perhaps, Ion, you are not merely a rhapsode, but possess also the competence for being a general. If you know matters belonging to military command, do you know them in your capacity of general, or in your capacity of rhapsode ? *Ion.*—I think there is no difference. *Sokr.*—How say you ? Do you affirm that the rhapsodic art, and the strategic art, are one ? *Ion.*—I think they are one. *Sokr.*—Then whosoever is a good rhapsode, is also a good general ? *Ion.*—Unquestionably. *Sokr.*—And of course, whoever is a good general,

The rhapsode does not know special matters, such as the craft of the pilot, physician, farmer, &c., but he knows the business of the general, and is com-

---

[1] Plato, Ion, 538-539.
[2] Plato, Ion, 540 A. ἃ τῷ ῥαψῳδῷ προσήκει καὶ σκοπεῖσθαι καὶ διακρίνειν παρὰ τοὺς ἄλλους ἀνθρώπους, 539 E.
[3] Plato, Ion, 540 B-C.

petent to command soldiers, having learnt it from Homer.

is also a good rhapsode? *Ion.*—No: I do not think that. *Sokr.*—But you do maintain, that whosoever is a good rhapsode, is also a good general? *Ion.*—Decidedly. *Sokr.*—You are yourself the best rhapsode in Greece? *Ion.*—By far. *Sokr.*—Are you then also the best general in Greece? *Ion.*—Certainly I am, Sokrates: and that too, by having learnt it from Homer.[1]

After putting a question or two, not very forcible, to ask how it happens that Ion, being an excellent general, does not obtain a military appointment from Athens, Sparta, or some other city, Sokrates winds up the dialogue as follows :—

Conclusion. Ion expounds Homer, not with any knowledge of what he says, but by divine inspiration.

Well, Ion, if it be really true that you possess a rational and intelligent competence to illustrate the beauties of Homer, you wrong and deceive me, because after promising to deliver to me a fine discourse about Homer, you will not even comply with my preliminary entreaty—that you will first tell me what those matters are, on which your superiority bears. You twist every way like Proteus, until at last you slip through my fingers and appear as a general. If your powers of expounding Homer depend on art and intelligence, you are a wrong-doer and deceiver, for not fulfiling your promise to me. But you are not chargeable with wrong, if the fact be as I say ; that is, if you know nothing about Homer, but are only able to discourse upon him finely and abundantly, through a divine inspiration with which you are possessed by him. Choose whether you wish me to regard you as a promise-breaker, or as a divine man. *Ion.*—I choose the last : it is much better to be regarded as a divine man.[2]

The generals in Greece usually pos-

It seems strange to read such language put into Ion's mouth (we are not warranted in regarding it as what any rhapsode ever did say), as the affirmation—that every good rhapsode was also a good general, and that he

1 Plato, Ion, 540 D—541 B.
2 Plato, Ion, 541 E—542 A. εἰ μὲν ἀληθῆ λέγεις, ὡς τέχνῃ καὶ ἐπιστήμῃ οἷός τε εἶ Ὅμηρον ἐπαινεῖν, ἀδικεῖς . . . εἰ δὲ μὴ τεχνικὸς εἶ, ἀλλὰ θείᾳ μοίρᾳ κατεχόμενος ἐξ Ὁμήρου μηδὲν εἰδὼς πολλὰ καὶ καλὰ λέγεις περὶ τοῦ ποιητοῦ, ὥσπερ ἐγὼ εἶπον περὶ σοῦ, οὐδὲν ἀδικεῖς· ἑλοῦ οὖν, πότερα βούλει νομίζεσθαι ὑφ᾽ ἡμῶν ἄδικος ἀνὴρ εἶναι ἢ θεῖος.

had become the best of generals simply through complete acquaintance with Homer. But this is only a caricature of a sentiment largely prevalent at Athens, according to which the works of the poets, especially the Homeric poems, were supposed to be a mine of varied instruction, and were taught as such to youth.[1] In Greece, the general was not often required (except at Sparta, and not always even there) to possess professional experience.[2] Sokrates, in one of the Xenophontic conversations, tries to persuade Nikomachides, a practised soldier (who had failed in getting himself elected general, because a successful Chorêgus had been preferred to him), how much the qualities of an effective Chorêgus coincided with those of an effective general.[3] The poet Sophokles was named by the Athenians one of the generals of the very important armament for reconquering Samos: though Perikles, one of his colleagues, as well as his contemporary Ion of Chios, declared that he was an excellent poet, but knew nothing of generalship.[4] Plato frequently seeks to make it evident how little the qualities required for governing numbers, either civil or military, were made matter of professional study or special teaching. The picture of Homer conveyed in the tenth book of the Platonic Republic is, that of a man who pretends to know

sessed no professional experience—Homer and the poets were talked of as the great teachers—Plato's view of the poet, as pretending to know everything, but really knowing nothing.

---

[1] Aristophan. Ranæ, 1032.

'Ορφεὺς μὲν γὰρ τελετάς θ' ἡμῖν κατέδειξε φόνων τ' ἀπέχεσθαι
Μουσαῖος δ' ἐξακέσεις τε νόσων καὶ χρησμούς, Ἡσίοδος δὲ
Γῆς ἐργασίας, καρπῶν ὥρας, ἀρότους· ὁ δὲ θεῖος Ὅμηρος
'Απὸ τοῦ τιμὴν καὶ κλέος ἔσχεν, πλὴν τοῦδ', ὅτι χρήστ' ἐδίδαξε,
Τάξεις, ἀρετάς, ὁπλίσεις ἀνδρῶν; . . . .
'Ἀλλ' ἄλλους τοι πολλοὺς ἀγαθοὺς (ἐδίδαξεν), ὧν ἦν καὶ Λάμαχος ἥρως.

See these views combated by Plato, Republ. x. 599-600-606 E.
The exaggerated pretension here ascribed to Ion makes him look contemptible—like the sentiment ascribed to him, 535 E, "If I make the auditors weep, I myself shall laugh and pocket money," &c.

[2] Xenoph. Memor. iii. 5, 21, in the conversation between the younger Perikles and Sokrates—τῶν δὲ στρατηγῶν οἱ πλεῖστοι αὐτοσχεδιάζουσιν. Also iii. 5, 24.

Compare, respecting the generals, the striking lines of Euripides, Androm. 698, and the encomium of Cicero (Academ. Prior. 2, 1) respecting the quickness and facility with which Lucullus made himself an excellent general.

[3] Xen. Mem. iii. 4, especially iii. 4, 6, where Nikomachides asks with surprise, λέγεις σύ, ὦ Σώκρατες, ὡς τοῦ αὐτοῦ ἀνδρός ἐστι χορηγεῖν τε καλῶς καὶ στρατηγεῖν;

[4] See the very curious extract from the contemporary Ion of Chios, in Athenæus, xiii. 604. Aristophanes of Byzantium says that the appointment of Sophokles to this military function (about B.C. 440) arose from the extraordinary popularity of his tragedy Antigonê, exhibited a little time before. See Boeckh's valuable 'Dissertation on the Antigonê,' appended to his edition thereof, pp. 121-124.

everything, but really knows nothing: an imitative artist, removed by two stages from truth and reality,—who gives the shadows of shadows, resembling only enough to satisfy an ignorant crowd. This is the picture there presented of poets generally, and of Homer as the best among them. The rhapsode Ion is here brought under the same category as the poet Homer, whom he has by heart and recites. The whole field of knowledge is assumed to be distributed among various specialties, not one of which either of the two can claim. Accordingly, both of them under the mask of universal knowledge, conceal the reality of universal ignorance.

Knowledge, opposed to divine inspiration without knowledge. Ion is willing enough (as he promises) to exhibit before Sokrates one of his eloquent discourses upon Homer. But Sokrates never permits him to arrive at it: arresting him always by preliminary questions, and requiring him to furnish an intelligible description of the matter which his discourse is intended to embrace, and thus to distinguish it from other matters left untouched. A man who cannot comply with this requisition,—who cannot (to repeat what I said in a previous chapter) stand a Sokratic cross-examination on the subject—possesses no rational intelligence of his own proceedings: no art, science, knowledge, system, or method. If as a practitioner he executes well what he promises (which is often the case), and attains success—he does so either by blind imitation of some master, or else under the stimulus and guidance of some agency foreign to himself—of the Gods or Fortune.

This is the Platonic point of view; developed in several different ways and different dialogues, but hardly anywhere more conspicuously than in the Ion.

Illustration of Plato's opinion respecting the uselessness of written geometrical treatises. I have observed that in this dialogue, Ion is anxious to embark on his eloquent expository discourse, but Sokrates will not allow him to begin: requiring as a preliminary stage that certain preliminary difficulties shall be first cleared up. Here we have an illustration of Plato's doctrine, to which I adverted in a former chapter,[1]—that no written geometrical treatise

---

[1] Chap. viii. p. 353.

could impart a knowledge of geometry to one ignorant thereof. The geometrical writer begins by laying down a string of definitions and axioms; and then strikes out boldly in demonstrating his theorems. But Plato would refuse him the liberty of striking out, until he should have cleared up the preliminary difficulties about the definitions and axioms themselves. This the geometrical treatise does not even attempt.[1]

---

[1] Compare Plato, Republic, vi. 510 C; vii. 533 C-D

CHAPTER XVIII.

LACHES.

THE main substance of this dialogue consists of a discussion, carried on by Sokrates with Nikias and Lachês, respecting Courage. Each of the two latter proposes an explanation of Courage : Sokratês criticises both of them, and reduces each to a confessed contradiction.

Lachês. Subject and persons of the dialogue. Whether it is useful that two young men should receive lessons from a master of arms. Nikias and Lachês differ in opinion.

The discussion is invited, or at least dramatically introduced, by two elderly men—Lysimachus, son of Aristeides the Just,—and Melêsias son of Thucydides the rival of Perikles. Lysimachus and Melêsias, confessing with shame that they are inferior to their fathers, because their education has been neglected, wish to guard against the same misfortune in the case of their own sons : respecting the education of whom, they ask the advice of Nikias and Lachês. The question turns especially upon the propriety of causing their sons to receive lessons from a master of arms just then in vogue. Nikias and Lachês, both of them not merely distinguished citizens but also commanders of Athenian armies, are assumed to be well qualified to give advice. Accordingly they deliver their opinions : Nikias approving such lessons as beneficial, in exalting the courage of a young man, and rendering him effective on the field of battle : while Lachês takes an opposite view, disparages the masters of arms as being no soldiers, and adds that they are despised by the Lacedæmonians, to whose authority on military matters general deference was paid in Greece.[1] Sokratês,—commended greatly by

[1] Plato, Lachês, 182-183.

Nikias for his acuteness and sagacity, by Lachês for his courage in the battle of Delium,—is invited to take part in the consultation. Being younger than both, he waits till they have delivered their opinions, and is then called upon to declare with which of the two his own judgment will concur.[1]

Sokr.—The question must not be determined by a plurality of votes, but by <u>superiority of knowledge</u>.[2] If we were debating about the proper gymnastic discipline for these young men, we should consult a known artist or professional trainer, or at least some one who had gone through a course of teaching and practice under the trainer. The first thing to be enquired therefore is, whether, in reference to the point now under discussion, there be any one of us professionally or technically competent, who has studied under good masters, and has proved his own competence as a master by producing well-trained pupils. The next thing is, to understand clearly what it is, with reference to which such competence is required.[3] *Nikias.*—Surely the point before us is, whether it be wise to put these young men under the lessons of the master of arms? That is what we want to know. *Sokr.*—Doubtless it is: but that is only one particular branch of a wider and more comprehensive enquiry. When you are considering whether a particular ointment is good for your eyes, it is your eyes, and their general benefit, which form the subject of investigation—not the ointment simply. The person to assist you will be, he who understands professionally the general treatment of the eyes. So in this case, you are enquiring whether lessons in arms will be improving for the minds and character of your sons. Look out therefore for some one who is professionally competent, from having studied under good masters, in regard to the general treatment of the mind.[4] *Lachês.*—But there are various persons who, without ever having studied under masters, possess greater technical com-

Sokrates is invited to declare his opinion. He replies that the point cannot be decided without a competent professional judge.

---

[1] Plato, Lachês, 184 D.
Nikias is made to say that Sokrates has recently recommended to him Damon, as a teacher of μουσική to his sons, and that Damon had proved an admirable teacher as well as companion (180 D). Damon is mentioned by Plato generally with much eulogy.

[2] Plato, Lachês, 184 E. ἐπιστήμῃ δεῖ κρίνεσθαι ἀλλ' οὐ πλήθει τὸ μέλλον καλῶς κριθήσεσθαι.
[3] Plato, Lachês, 185 C.
[4] Plato, Lachês, 185 E. εἴ τις ἡμῶν τεχνικὸς περὶ ψυχῆς θεραπείαν, καὶ οἷός τε καλῶς τοῦτο θεραπεῦσαι, καὶ ὅτῳ διδάσκαλοι ἀγαθοὶ γεγόνασι, τοῦτο σκεπτέον.

petence than others who have so studied. *Sokr.*—There are such persons: but you will never believe it upon their own assurance, unless they can show you some good special work actually performed by themselves.

Sokr.—Now then, Lysimachus, since you have invited Lachês and Nikias, as well as me, to advise you on the means of most effectively improving the mind of your son, it is for us to show you that we possess competent professional skill respecting the treatment of the youthful mind. We must declare to you who are the masters from whom we have learnt, and we must prove their qualifications. Or if we have had no masters, we must demonstrate to you our own competence by citing cases of individuals, whom we have successfully trained, and who have become incontestably good under our care. If we can fulfil neither of these two conditions, we ought to confess our incompetence and decline advising you. We must not begin to try our hands upon so precious a subject as the son of a friend, at the hazard of doing him more harm than good.[1]

Those who deliver an opinion must begin by proving their competence to judge— Sokrates avows his own incompetence.

As to myself, I frankly confess that I have neither had any master to impart to me such competence, nor have I been able to acquire it by my own efforts. I am not rich enough to pay the Sophists, who profess to teach it. But as to Nikias and Lachês, they are both older and richer than I am : so that they may well have learnt it from others, or acquired it for themselves. They must be thoroughly satisfied of their own knowledge on the work of education ; otherwise they would hardly have given such confident opinions, pronouncing what pursuits are good or bad for youth. For my part, I trust them implicitly: the only thing which surprises me, is, that they dissent from each other.[2] It is for you therefore, Lysimachus, to ask Nikias and Lachês,—Who have been their masters? Who have been their fellow-pupils? If they have been their own masters, what proof can they produce of previous success in teaching, and what examples can they cite of pupils whom they have converted from bad to good?[3]

---

[1] Plato, Lachês, 186 B.
[2] Plato, Lachês, 186 C-D. δοκοῦσι δή μοι δυνατοὶ εἶναι παιδεῦσαι ἄνθρωπον· οὐ γὰρ ἄν ποτε ἀδεῶς ἀπεφαίνοντο περὶ ἐπιτηδευμάτων νέῳ χρηστῶν τε καὶ πονη- ρῶν, εἰ μὴ αὐτοῖς ἐπίστευον ἱκανῶς εἰδέ- ναι. τὰ μὲν οὖν ἄλλα, ἔγωγε τούτοις πιστεύω, ὅτι δὲ διαφέρεσθον ἀλλήλοιν, ἐθαύμασα.
[3] Plato, Lachês, 186-187.

CHAP. XVIII. HOW TO FIND THE WISE MAN. 141

Nikias.—I knew from the beginning that we should both of us fall under the cross-examination of Sokrates, and be compelled to give account of our past lives. For my part, I have already gone through this scrutiny before, and am not averse to undergo it again. *Lachês.*—And I, though I have never experienced it before, shall willingly submit to learn from Sokrates, whom I know to be a man thoroughly courageous and honest in his actions. I hate men whose lives are inconsistent with their talk.[1]—Thus speak both of them.

Nikias and Lachês submit to be cross-examined by Sokrates.

This portion of the dialogue, which forms a sort of preamble to the main discussion, brings out forcibly some of the Platonic points of view. We have seen it laid down in the Kriton—That in questions about right and wrong, good and evil, &c., we ought not to trust the decision of the Many, but only that of the One Wise Man. Here we learn something about the criteria by which this One man may be known. He must be one who has gone through a regular training under some master approved in ethical or educational teaching: or, if he cannot produce such a certificate, he must at least cite sufficient examples of men whom he has taught well himself. This is the Sokratic comparison, assimilating the general art of living well to the requirements of a special profession, which a man must learn through express teaching, from a master who has proved his ability, and through conscious application of his own. Nikias and Lachês give their opinions offhand and confidently, upon the question whether lessons from the master of arms be profitable to youth or not. Plato, on the contrary, speaking through Sokrates, points out that this is only one branch of the more comprehensive question as to education generally—"What are the qualities and habits proper to be imparted to youth by training? What is the proper treatment of the mind? No one

Both of them give opinions offhand, according to their feelings on the special case—Sokrates requires that the question shall be generalised, and examined as a branch of education.

[1] Plato, Lachês, 188. "Ego odi homines ignavâ operâ et philosophâ sententiâ," is a line cited by Cicero out of one of the Latin comic writers.

is competent to decide the special question, except he who has professionally studied the treatment of the mind." To deal with the special question, without such preliminary general preparation, involves rash and unverified assumptions, which render any opinion so given dangerous to act upon. Such is the judgment of the Platonic Sokrates, insisting on the necessity of taking up ethical questions in their most comprehensive aspect.

Consequent upon this preamble, we should expect that Lachês and Nikias would be made to cite the names of those who had been their masters; or to produce some examples of persons effectively taught by themselves. This would bring us a step nearer to that One Wise Man—often darkly indicated, but nowhere named or brought into daylight—from whom alone we can receive a trustworthy judgment. But here, as in the Kriton and so many other Platonic dialogues, we get only a Pisgah view of our promised adviser—nothing more. The discussion takes a different turn.

Appeal of Sokrates to the judgment of the One Wise Man. This man is never seen or identified.

Sokr.—" We will pursue a line of enquiry which conducts to the same result, and which starts even more decidedly from the beginning.[1] We are called upon to advise by what means virtue can be imparted to these youths, so as to make them better men. Of course this implies that we know what virtue is: otherwise how can we give advice as to the means of acquiring it? *Lachês.*—We could give no advice at all. *Sokr.*—We affirm ourselves therefore to know what virtue is? *Lachês.*—We do. *Sokr.*—Since therefore we know, we can farther declare what it is.[2] *Lachês.*—Of course we can. *Sokr.*—Still, we will not at once enquire as to the whole of virtue, which might be an arduous task, but as to a part of it—Courage: that part to which the lessons of the master of arms are supposed to tend. We will

We must know what virtue is, before we give an opinion on education. Virtue, as a whole, is too large a question. We will enquire about one branch of virtue—courage.

---

[1] Plato, Lachês, 189 E. καὶ ἡ τοιάδε σκέψις εἰς ταὐτὸν φέρει, σχεδὸν δέ τι καὶ μᾶλλον ἐξ ἀρχῆς εἴη ἄν.
[2] Plato, Lachês, 190 C. φαμὲν ἄρα,
ὦ Λάχης, εἰδέναι αὐτὸ (τὴν ἀρετὴν) ὅ, τι ἔστι. Φαμὲν μέντοι. Οὐκοῦν ὅ γε ἴσμεν, κἂν εἴποιμεν δήπου, τί ἔστι. Πῶς γὰρ οὔ;

CHAP. XVIII. EXAMPLE NO SUBSTITUTE FOR DEFINITION. 143

first enquire what courage is: after that has been determined, we will then consider how it can best be imparted to these youths."

"Try then if you can tell me, Lachês, what courage is. *Lachês.* —There is no difficulty in telling you that. Whoever keeps his place in the rank, repels the enemy, and does not run away, is a courageous man."[1]

Here is the same error in replying, as was committed by Euthyphron when asked, What is the Holy? and by Hippias about the Beautiful. One particular case of courageous behaviour, among many, is indicated, as if it were an explanation of the whole: but the general feature common to all acts of courage is not declared. Sokrates points out that men are courageous, not merely among hoplites who keep their rank and fight, but also among the Scythian horsemen who fight while running away; others also are courageous against disease, poverty, political adversity, pain and fear of every sort; others moreover, against desires and pleasures. What is the common attribute which in all these cases constitutes Courage? If you asked me what is *quickness*—common to all those cases when a man runs, speaks, plays, learns, &c., quickly—I should tell you that it was that which accomplished much in a little time. Tell me in like manner, what is the common fact or attribute pervading all cases of courage? *Question, What is courage? Lachês answers by citing one particularly manifest case of courage. Mistake of not giving a general explanation.*

Lachês at first does not understand the question:[2] and Sokrates elucidates it by giving the parallel explanation of quickness. Here, as elsewhere, Plato takes great pains to impress the conception in its full generality, and he seems to have found difficulty in making others follow him.

Lachês then gives a general definition of courage. It is a sort of endurance of the mind.[3]

Surely not *all* endurance (rejoins Sokrates)? You admit that courage is a fine and honourable thing *Second answer. Courage is a sort of endurance*

---

[1] Plato, Lachês, 190 D-E.
[2] Plato, Lachês, 191-192.
πάλιν οὖν πειρῶ εἰπεῖν ἀνδρείαν πρῶτον, τί ὂν ἐν πᾶσι τούτοις ταὐτόν ἐστιν. ἢ οὔπω καταμανθάνεις ὃ λέγω; *Lachês.* Οὐ πάνυ τι. . . . *Sokr.* πειρῶ δὴ τὴν

ἀνδρείαν οὕτως εἰπεῖν, τίς οὖσα δύναμις ἡ αὐτὴ ἐν ἡδονῇ καὶ ἐν λύπῃ καὶ ἐν ἅπασιν οἷς νῦν δὴ ἐλέγομεν αὐτὴν εἶναι, ἔπειτ' ἀνδρεία κέκληται.
[3] Plato, Lachês, 192 B. καρτερία τις τῆς ψυχῆς.

of the mind.
Sokrates points out that the answer is vague and incorrect. Endurance is not always courage: even intelligent endurance is not always courage.

But endurance without intelligence is hurtful and dishonourable: it cannot therefore be courage. Only intelligent endurance, therefore, can be courage. And then what is meant by *intelligent?* Intelligent—of what—or to what end? A man, who endures the loss of money, understanding well that he will thereby gain a larger sum, is he courageous? No. He who endures fighting, knowing that he has superior skill, numbers, and all other advantages on his side, manifests more of intelligent endurance, than his adversary who knows that he has all these advantages against him, yet who nevertheless endures fighting. Nevertheless this latter is the most courageous of the two.[1] Unintelligent endurance is in this case courage: but unintelligent endurance was acknowledged to be bad and hurtful, and courage to be a fine thing. We have entangled ourselves in a contradiction. We must at least show our own courage, by enduring until we can get right. For my part (replies Lachês) I am quite prepared for such endurance. I am piqued and angry that I cannot express what I conceive. I seem to have in my mind clearly what courage is: but it escapes me somehow or other, when I try to put it in words.[2]

Sokrates now asks aid from Nikias. *Nikias.*—My explanation of courage is, that it is a sort of knowledge or intelligence. *Sokr.*—But what sort of intelligence? Not certainly intelligence of piping or playing the harp. Intelligence of what?

Nikias.—Courage is intelligence of things terrible, and things not terrible, both in war and in all other conjunctures. *Lachês.*—What nonsense! Courage is a thing totally apart from knowledge or intelligence.[3] The physician knows best what is terrible, and what is not terrible, in reference to disease: the husbandman, in reference to agriculture. But they are not for that reason courageous. *Nikias.*—They are not; but neither do they know what is terrible, or what is not terrible. Physicians can predict the result of a

Confusion. New answer given by Nikias. Courage is a sort of intelligence—the intelligence of things terrible and not terrible. Objections of Lachês.

---

[1] Plato, Lachês, 192 D-E. ἡ φρόνιμος καρτερία... ἴδωμεν δή, ἡ εἰς τί φρόνιμος· ἢ ἡ εἰς ἅπαντα καὶ τὰ μεγάλα καὶ τὰ σμικρά;

[2] Plato, Lachês, 193 C, 194 B.

[3] Plato, Lachês, 195 A. τὴν τῶν δεινῶν καὶ θαρραλέων ἐπιστήμην καὶ ἐν πολέμῳ καὶ ἐν τοῖς ἄλλοις ἅπασιν.

CHAP. XVIII. COURAGE RESOLVED INTO INTELLIGENCE. 145

patient's case : they can tell what may cure him, or what will kill him. But whether it be better for him to die or to recover —*that* they do not know, and cannot tell him. To some persons, death is a less evil than life :—defeat, than victory :—loss of wealth, than gain. None except the person who can discriminate these cases, knows what is really terrible and what is not so. He alone is really courageous.[1] *Lachês.*—Where is there any such man? It can be only some God. Nikias feels himself in a puzzle, and instead of confessing it frankly as I have done, he is trying to help himself out by evasions more fit for a pleader before the Dikastery.[2]

Sokr.—You do not admit, then, Nikias, that lions, tigers, boars, &c., and such animals, are courageous? *Nikias.*—No : they are without fear—simply from not knowing the danger—like children : but they are not courageous, though most people call them so. I may call them bold, but I reserve the epithet courageous for the intelligent. *Lachês.*—See how Nikias strips those, whom every one admits to be courageous, of this honourable appellation! *Nikias.*—Not altogether, Lachés : I admit you, and Lamachus, and many other Athenians, to be courageous, and of course therefore intelligent. *Lachês.*—I feel the compliment : but such subtle distinctions befit a Sophist rather than a general in high command.[3] *Sokr.*—The highest measure of intelligence befits one in the highest command. What you have said, Nikias, deserves careful examination. You remember that in taking up the investigation of courage, we reckoned it only as a portion of virtue : you are aware that there are other portions of virtue, such as justice, temperance, and the like. Now you define courage to be, intelligence of what is terrible or not terrible : of that which causes

Questions of Sokrates to Nikias. It is only future events, not past or present, which are terrible. But intelligence of future events cannot be had without intelligence of past or present.

Lachês—'Ὡς ἄτοπα λέγει!—χωρὶς δή που σοφία ἐστὶν ἀνδρείας.

It appears from two other passages (195 E, and 198 B) that θαρράλεος here is simply the negation of δεινὸς, and cannot be translated by any affirmative word.

[1] Plato, Lachês, 195-196.
[2] Plato, Lachês, 196 B.
[3] Plato, Lachês, 197. Καὶ γὰρ πρέπει, ὦ Σώκρατες, σοφιστῇ τὰ τοιαῦτα μᾶλλον

κομψεύεσθαι ἢ ἀνδρὶ ὃν ἡ πόλις ἀξιοῖ αὐτῆς προϊστάναι.

Assuredly the distinctions which Plato puts into the mouth of Nikias are nowise more subtle than those which he is perpetually putting into the mouth of Sokrates. He cannot here mean to distinguish the Sophists from Sokrates, but to distinguish the dialectic talkers, including both one and the other, from the active political leaders.

fear, or does not cause fear. But nothing causes fear, except future or apprehended evils: present or past evils cause no fear. Hence courage, as you define it, is intelligence respecting future evils, and future events not evil. But how can there be intelligence respecting the future, except in conjunction with intelligence respecting the present and the past? In every special department, such as medicine, military proceedings, agriculture, &c., does not the same man, who knows the phenomena of the future, know also the phenomena of present and past? Are they not all inseparable acquirements of one and the same intelligent mind?[1]

Courage therefore must be intelligence of good and evil generally.
But this definition would include the whole of virtue, and we declared that courage was only a part thereof. It will not hold therefore as a definition of courage.

Since therefore courage, according to your definition, is the knowledge of futurities evil and not evil, or future evil and good—and since such knowledge cannot exist without the knowledge of good and evil generally—it follows that courage is the knowledge of good and evil generally.[2] But a man who knows thus much, cannot be destitute of any part of virtue. He must possess temperance and justice as well as courage. Courage, therefore, according to your definition, is not a part of virtue, it is the whole. Now we began the enquiry by stating that it was only a part of virtue, and that there were other parts of virtue which it did not comprise. It is plain therefore that your definition of courage is not precise, and cannot be sustained. We have not yet discovered what courage is.[3]

Remarks. Warfare of Sokrates against the

Here ends the dialogue called Lachês, without any positive result. Nothing is proved except the ignorance of two brave and eminent generals respecting the moral attribute known by the name *Courage:* which never-

[1] Plato, Lachês, 198 D. περὶ ὅσων ἐστὶν ἐπιστήμη, οὐκ ἄλλη μὲν εἶναι περὶ γεγονότος, εἰδέναι ὅπῃ γέγονεν, ἄλλη δὲ περὶ γιγνομένων, ὅπῃ γίγνεται, ἄλλη δὲ ὅπῃ ἂν κάλλιστα γένοιτο καὶ γενήσεται τὸ μήπω γεγονός—ἀλλ' ἡ αὐτή. οἷον περὶ τὸ ὑγιεινὸν εἰς ἅπαντας τοὺς χρόνους οὐκ ἄλλη τις ἢ ἡ ἰατρική, μία οὖσα, ἐφορᾷ καὶ γιγνόμενα καὶ γεγονότα καὶ γενησόμενα, ὅπῃ γενήσεται.

199 B. ἡ δέ γ' αὐτὴ ἐπιστήμη τῶν αὐτῶν καὶ μελλόντων καὶ πάντως ἐχόντων εἶναι [ὡμολόγηται].

[2] Plato, Lachês, 199 C. κατὰ τὸν σὸν λόγον οὐ μόνον δεινῶν τε καὶ θαρραλέων ἡ ἐπιστήμη ἀνδρεία ἐστίν, ἀλλὰ σχεδόν τι ἡ περὶ πάντων ἀγαθῶν τε καὶ κακῶν καὶ πάντως ἐχόντων, &c.

[3] Plato, Lachês, 199 E. Οὐκ ἄρα εὑρήκαμεν, ἀνδρεία ὅ, τι ἔστιν.

theless they are known to possess, and have the full sentiment and persuasion of knowing perfectly; so that they give confident advice as to the means of imparting it. "I am unaccustomed to debates like these" (says Lachês): "but I am piqued and mortified —because I feel that I know well what Courage is, yet somehow or other I cannot state my own thoughts in words." Here is a description [1] of the intellectual deficiency which Sokrates seeks to render conspicuous to the consciousness, instead of suffering it to remain latent and unknown, as it is in the ordinary mind. Here, as elsewhere, he impugns the false persuasion of knowledge, and the unconscious presumption of estimable men in delivering opinions upon ethical and social subjects, which have become familiar and interwoven with deeply rooted associations, but have never been studied under a master, nor carefully analysed and discussed, nor looked at in their full generality. This is a mental defect which he pronounces to be universal: belonging not less to men of action like Nikias and Lachês, than to Sophists and Rhetors like Protagoras and Gorgias.

false persuasion of knowledge. Brave generals deliver opinions confidently about courage, without knowing what it is.

Here, as elsewhere, Plato (or the Platonic Sokrates) exposes the faulty solutions of others, but proposes no better solution of his own, and even disclaims all ability to do so. We may nevertheless trace, in the refutation which he gives of the two unsatisfactory explanations, hints guiding the mind into that direction in which Plato looks to supply the deficiency. Thus when Lachês, after having given as his first answer (to the question, What is Courage?) a definition not even formally sufficient, is put by Sokrates upon giving his second answer,—That Courage is intelligent endurance: Sokrates asks him [2]—" Yes, *intelligent:* but intelligent to

No solution given by Plato. Apparent tendency of his mind, in looking for a solution. Intelligence —cannot be understood without reference to some object or end.

---

[1] Plato, Lachês, 194. Καίτοι ἀήθης γ' εἰμὶ (Lachês) τῶν τοιούτων λόγων· ἀλλά τίς με καὶ φιλονεικία εἴληφε πρὸς τὰ εἰρημένα, καὶ ὡς ἀληθῶς ἀγανακτῶ, εἰ οὑτωσὶ ἃ νοῶ μὴ οἷός τ' εἰμὶ εἰπεῖν· νοεῖν μὲν γὰρ ἔμοιγε δοκῶ περὶ ἀνδρείας ὅ, τι ἔστιν, οὐκ οἶδα δ' ὅπη με ἄρτι διέφυγεν, ὥστε μὴ ξυλλαβεῖν τῷ λόγῳ αὐτὴν καὶ εἰπεῖν ὅ, τι ἔστιν.

Compare the Charmidês, p. 159 A, 160 D, where Sokrates professes to tell Charmides, If temperance is really in you, you can of course inform us what it is.

[2] Plato, Lachês, 192 D.

ἡ φρόνιμος καρτερία . . . ἴδωμεν δή, ἡ εἴς τι φρόνιμος· ἢ ἡ εἰς ἅπαντα καὶ τὰ μεγάλα καὶ τὰ σμικρά;

what end? Do you mean, to all things alike, great as well as little?" We are here reminded that *intelligence*, simply taken, is altogether undefined; that intelligence must relate to *something*—and when human conduct is in question, must relate to some end; and that the Something, and the End, to which it relates, must be set forth, before the proposition can be clearly understood.

Coming to the answer given by Nikias, we perceive that this deficiency is in a certain manner supplied. Courage is said to consist in knowledge: in knowledge of things terrible, and things not terrible. When Lachês applies his cross-examination to the answer, the manner in which Nikias defends it puts us upon a distinction often brought to view, though not always adhered to, in the Platonic writings. There can be no doubt that death, distemper, loss of wealth, defeat, &c., are terrible things (*i.e.* the prospect of them inspires fear) in the estimation of mankind generally. Correct foresight of such contingencies, and of the antecedents tending to produce or avert them, is possessed by the physician and other professional persons: who would therefore, it should seem, possess the knowledge of things terrible and not terrible. But Nikias denies this. He does not admit that the contingencies here enumerated are, always or necessarily, proper objects of fear. In some cases, he contends, they are the least of two evils. Before you can be said to possess the knowledge of things terrible and not terrible, you must be able to take correct measure not only of the intervening antecedents or means, but also of the end itself as compared with other alternative ends: whether, in each particular case, it be the end most to be feared, or the real evil under the given circumstances. The professional man can do the former, but he cannot do the latter. He advises as to means, and executes: but he assumes his own one end as an indisputable datum. The physician seeks to cure his patient, without ever enquiring whether it may not be a less evil for such patient to die than to survive.

Object—is supplied in the answer of Nikias. Intelligence —of things terrible and not terrible. Such intelligence is not possessed by professional artists.

The ulterior, yet not less important, estimate of the comparative worth of different ends, is reserved for that unknown master whom Nikias himself does not farther

Postulate of a Science of

specify, and whom Lachês sets aside as nowhere to be found, under the peculiar phrase of "some God". Subjectively considered, this is an appeal to the judgment of that One Wise Man, often alluded to by Plato as an absent Expert who might be called into court—yet never to be found at the exact moment, nor produced in visible presence: Objectively considered, it is a postulate or divination of some yet undiscovered Teleology or Science of Ends: that Science of the Good, which (as we have already noticed in Alkibiadês II.) Plato pronounces to be the crowning and capital science of all—and without which he there declared, that knowledge on all other topics was useless and even worse than useless.[1] The One Wise Man—the *Science of Good*—are the Subject and Object corresponding to each other, and postulated by Plato. None but the One Wise Man can measure things terrible and not terrible: none else can estimate the good or evil, or the comparative value of two alternative evils, in each individual case. The items here directed to be taken into the calculation, correspond with what is laid down by Sokrates in the Protagoras, not with that laid down in the Gorgias: we find here none of that marked antithesis between pleasure and good—between pain and evil—upon which Sokrates expatiates in the Gorgias.

Ends, or Teleology, dimly indicated by Plato. The Unknown Wise Man—correlates with the undiscovered Science of Ends.

This appears still farther when the cross-examination is taken up by Sokrates instead of by Lachês. We are then made to perceive, that the knowledge of things terrible and not terrible is a part, but an inseparable part, of the knowledge of good and evil generally: the lesser cannot be had without the greater—and the greater carries with it not merely courage, but all the other virtues besides. None can know good or evil generally except the perfectly Wise Man. The perfect condition of the Intelligence, is the sole and all-sufficient condition of virtue. None can possess one mode of virtue separately.

Perfect condition of the intelligence—is the one sufficient condition of virtue.

This is the doctrine to which the conclusion of the Lachês points, though the question debated is confessedly left without solution. It is a doctrine which seems to have been really main-

---

[1] Plato, Alkib. ii. 146-147. See above, ch. xii. p. 16.

tained by the historical Sokrates, and is often implied in the reasonings of the Platonic Sokrates, but not always nor consistently.

In reference to this dialogue, the dramatic contrast is very forcible, between the cross-examination carried on by Lachês, and that carried on by Sokrates. The former is pettish and impatient, bringing out no result, and accusing the respondent of cavil and disingenuousness: the latter takes up the same answer patiently, expands it into the full generality wrapped up in it, and renders palpable its inconsistency with previous admissions.

Dramatic contrast between Lachês and Sokrates, as cross-examiners.

APPENDIX.

Ast is the only critic who declares the Lachês not to be Plato's work (Platon's Leben und Schr. pp. 451-456). He indeed even finds it difficult to imagine how Schleiermacher can accept it as genuine (p. 454). He justifies this opinion by numerous reasons— pointing out what he thinks glaring defects, absurdity, and bad taste, both in the ratiocination and in the dramatic handling, also *dicta* alleged to be *un-Platonic*. Compare Schleiermacher's Einleitung zum Lachês, p. 324 seq.

I do not concur with Ast in the estimation of those passages which serve as premisses to his conclusion. But even if I admitted his premisses, I still should not admit his conclusion. I should conclude that the dialogue was an inferior work of Plato, but I should conclude nothing beyond. Stallbaum (Prolegg. ad Lachet. p. 29-30, 2nd ed.) and Socher discover "adolescentiæ vestigia" in it, which are not apparent to me.

Socher, Stallbaum, and K. F. Hermann pass lightly over the objections of Ast ; and Steinhart (Einleit. p. 355) declares them to be unworthy of a serious answer. For my part, I draw from these dissensions among the Platonic critics a conviction of the uncertain evidence upon which all of them proceed. Each has his own belief as to what Plato *must* say, *ought to* say, and *could not* have said ; and each adjudicates thereupon with a degree of confidence which surprises me. The grounds upon which Ast rejects Lachês, Charmidês, and Lysis, though inconclusive, appear to me not more inconclusive than those on which he and other critics reject the Erastæ, Theagês, Hippias Major, Alkibiadês II., &c.

The dates which Stallbaum, Schleiermacher, Socher, and Steinhart assign to the Lachês (about 406-404 B.C.) are in my judgment erroneous. I have already shown my reasons for believing that not one of the Platonic dialogues was composed until after the death of Sokrates. The hypotheses also of Steinhart (p. 357) as to the special purposes of Plato in composing the dialogue are unsupported by any evidence ;

and are all imagined so as to fit his supposition as to the date. So also Schleiermacher tells us that a portion of the Lachês is intended by Plato as a defence of himself against accusations which had been brought against him, a young man, for impertinence in having attacked Lysias in the Phædrus, and Protagoras in the Protagoras, both of them much older than Plato. But Steinhart justly remarks that this explanation can only be valid if we admit Schleiermacher's theory that the Phædrus and the Protagoras are earlier compositions than the Lachês, which theory Steinhart and most of the others deny. Steinhart himself adapts his hypotheses to his own idea of the date of the Lachês : and he is open to the same remark as he himself makes upon Schleiermacher.

CHAPTER XIX.

CHARMIDES.

As in Lachês, we have pursued an enquiry into the nature of Courage—so in Charmidês, we find an examination of Temperance, Sobriety, Moderation.[1] Both dialogues conclude without providing any tenable explanation. In both there is an abundant introduction—in Charmidês, there is even the bustle of a crowded palæstra, with much dramatic incident—preluding to the substantive discussion. I omit the notice of this dramatic incident, though it is highly interesting to read.

The two persons with whom Sokrates here carries on the discussion, are Charmides and Kritias; both of whom, as historical persons, were active movers in the oligarchical government of the Thirty, with its numerous enormities. In this dialogue, Charmides appears as a youth just rising into manhood, strikingly beautiful both in face and stature: Kritias his cousin is an accomplished literary man of mature age. The powerful emotion which Sokrates describes himself as experiencing,[2] from the sight and close neighbourhood of the beautiful Charmides, is remarkable, as a manifestation of Hellenic sentiment. The same exaltation of the feelings and imagination, which is now produced only by beautiful women, was then excited chiefly by fine youths. Charmides is described by Kritias as exhibiting dis-

Scene and personages of the dialogue. Crowded palæstra. Emotions of Sokrates.

---

[1] I translate σωφροσύνη Temperance, though it is very inadequate, but I know no single English word better suited.

[2] Plato, Charm. 154 C. Ficinus, in his Argumentum to this dialogue (p. 767), considers it as mainly allegorical, especially the warm expressions of erotic sentiment contained therein, which he compares to the Song of Solomon. "Etsi omnia in hoc dialogo mirificam habeant allegoriam, amatoria maxime, non aliter quam Cantica Salomonis—mutavi tamen nonnihil—nonnihil etiam prætermisi. Quæ enim consonabant castigatissimis auribus Atticorum, rudioribus fortè auribus minimé consonarent."

positions at once philosophical and poetical:[1] illustrating the affinity of these two intellectual veins, as Plato conceived them. He is also described as eminently temperate and modest:[2] from whence the questions of Sokrates take their departure.

Question, What is Temperance? addressed by Sokrates to the temperate Charmides. Answer, It is a kind of sedateness or slowness.

You are said to be temperate, Charmides (says Sokrates). If so, your temperance will surely manifest itself within you in some way, so as to enable you to form and deliver an opinion, What Temperance is. Tell us in plain language what you conceive it to be. Temperance, replies Charmides (after some hesitation),[3] consists in doing every thing in an orderly and sedate manner, when we walk in the highway, or talk, or perform other matters in the presence of others. It is, in short, a kind of sedateness or slowness.

But Temperance is a fine or honourable thing, and slowness is, in many or most cases, not fine or honourable, but the contrary. Temperance cannot be slowness.

Sokrates begins his cross-examination upon this answer, in the same manner as he had begun it with Laches in respect to courage. *Sokr.*—Is not temperance a fine and honourable thing? Does it not partake of the essence, and come under the definition, of what is fine and honourable?[4] *Char.*—Undoubtedly it does. *Sokr.*—But if we specify in detail our various operations, either of body or mind — such as writing, reading, playing on the harp, boxing, running, jumping, learning, teaching, recollecting, comprehending, deliberating, determining, &c.—we shall find that to do them quickly is more fine and honourable than to do them slowly. Slowness does not, except by accident, belong to the fine and honourable : therefore temperance, which does so belong to it, cannot be a kind of slowness.[5]

Second answer. Temperance is a variety of

Charmides next declares Temperance to be a variety of the feeling of shame or modesty. But this (observes Sokrates) will not hold, more than the former explanation : since Homer has pronounced shame not to be

---

[1] Plato, Charm. 155 A.
[2] Plato, Charm. 157 D. About the diffidence of Charmides in his younger years, see Xen. Mem. iii. 7, 1.
[3] Plato, Charm. 159 B. τὸ κοσμίως πάντα πράττειν καὶ ἡσυχῇ, ἔν τε ταῖς ὁδοῖς βαδίζειν καὶ διαλέγεσθαι. . . . συλλήβδην ἡσυχιότης τις.
[4] Plato, Charm. 159 C—160 D. οὐ τῶν καλῶν μέντοι ἡ σωφροσύνη ἐστίν; . . . ἐπειδὴ ἐν τῷ λόγῳ τῶν καλῶν τι ἡμῖν ἡ σωφροσύνη ὑπετέθη.
[5] Plato, Charm. 160 C.

good, for certain persons aud under certain circumstances.[1]

"Temperance consists in doing one's own business." Here we have a third explanation, proposed by Charmides and presently espoused by Kritias. Sokrates professes not to understand it, and pronounces it to be like a riddle.[2] Every tradesman or artisan does the business of others as well as his own. Are we to say for that reason that he is not temperate? I distinguish (says Kritias) between *making* and *doing*: the artisan *makes* for others, but he does not *do* for others, and often cannot be said to *do* at all. *To do*, implies honourable, profitable, good, occupation: this alone is a man's own business, and this I call temperance. When a man acts so as to harm himself, he does not do his own business.[3] The doing of good things, is temperance.[4]

Sokr.—Perhaps it is. But does the well-doer always and certainly know that he is doing well? Does the temperate man know his own temperance? *Krit.*—He certainly must. Indeed I think that the essence of temperance is, *Self-knowledge*. *Know thyself*—is the precept of the Delphian God, who means thereby the same as if he had said—Be temperate. I now put aside all that I have said before, and take up this new position, That temperance consists in a man's knowing himself. If you do not admit it, I challenge your cross-examination.[5]

Sokr.—I cannot tell you whether I admit it or not, until I have investigated. You address me as if I professed to know the subject: but it is because I do not know, that I examine, in conjunction with you, each successive answer.[6] If temperance

---

[1] Plato, Charm. 161 A.
[2] Plato, Charm. 161 C—162 B. σωφροσύνη—τὸ τὰ αὑτοῦ πράττειν . . . αἰνίγματί τινι ἔοικεν.
There is here a good deal of playful vivacity in the dialogue: Charmidès gives this last answer, which he has heard from Kritias, who is at first not forward to defend it, until Charmides forces him to come forward, by hints and side-insinuations. This is the dramatic art and variety of Plato, charming to read, but not bearing upon him as a philosopher.
[3] Plato, Charm. 163 C D. τὰ καλῶς καὶ ὠφελίμως ποιούμενα . . . οἰκεῖα μόνα τὰ τοιαῦτα ἡγεῖσθαι, τὰ δὲ βλαβερὰ πάντα ἀλλότρια . . . ὅτι τὰ οἰκεῖά τε καὶ τὰ αὑτοῦ ἀγαθὰ καλοίης, καὶ τὰς τῶν ἀγαθῶν ποιήσεις πράξεις.
[4] Plato, Charm. 163 E. τὴν τῶν ἀγαθῶν πρᾶξιν σωφροσύνην εἶναι σαφῶς σοι διορίζομαι.
[5] Plato, Charm. 164-165.
[6] Plato, Charm. 165 C.

Side notes: the feeling of shame. Refuted by Sokrates. Third answer. Temperance consists in doing one's own business. Defended by Kritias. Sokrates pronounces it a riddle, and refutes it. Distinction between making and doing. Fourth answer, by Kritias, Temperance consists in self-knowledge.

consists in knowing, it must be a knowledge of something. *Krit.*—It is so: it is knowledge of a man's self. *Sokr.*—What good does this knowledge procure for us? as medical knowledge procures for us health—architectural knowledge, buildings, &c.? *Krit.*—It has no positive result of analogous character: but neither have arithmetic nor geometry. *Sokr.*—True, but in arithmetic and geometry, we can at least indicate a something known, distinct from the knowledge. Number and proportion are distinct from arithmetic, the science which takes cognizance of them. Now what is that, of which temperance is the knowledge,—distinct from temperance itself? *Krit.*—It is on this very point that temperance differs from all the other cognitions. Each of the others is knowledge of something different from itself, but not knowledge of itself: while temperance is knowledge of all the other sciences and of itself also.[1] *Sokr.*—If this be so, it will of course be a knowledge of ignorance, as well as a knowledge of knowledge? *Krit.*—Certainly.

Sokr.—According to your explanation, then, it is only the temperate man who knows himself. He alone is able to examine himself, and thus to find out what he really knows and does not know: he alone is able to examine others, and thus to find out what each man knows, or what each man only believes himself to know without really knowing. Temperance, or self-knowledge, is the knowledge what a man knows, and what he does not know.[2] Now two questions arise upon this: First, is it possible for a man to know, that he knows what he does know, and that he does not know what he does not know? Next, granting it to be possible, in what way do we gain by it? The first of these two questions involves much difficulty. How can there be any cognition, which is not cognition of a given *cognitum*, but cognition merely of other cognitions and non-cognitions? There is no vision except of some colour, no audition except of some sound: there can be no vision of

---

[1] Plato, Charm. 166 C. αἱ μὲν ἄλλαι ἐπιστήμη ἐστὶ καὶ αὐτὴ ἑαυτῆς. So also πᾶσαι ἄλλου εἰσὶν ἐπιστῆμαι, ἑαυτῶν δ' 166 E.
οὔ· ἡ δὲ μόνη τῶν τε ἄλλων ἐπιστημῶν [2] Plato, Charm. 167 A.

CHAP. XIX.   COGNITION OF COGNITION.   157

visions, or audition of auditions. So likewise, all desire is desire of some pleasure ; there is no desire of desires. All volition is volition of some good ; there is no volition of volitions : all love applies to something beautiful—there is no love of other loves. The like is true of fear, opinion, &c. It would be singular therefore, if contrary to all these analogies, there were any cognition not of some *cognitum*, but of itself and other cognitions.[1]

It is of the essence of cognition to be cognition of something, and to have its characteristic property with reference to some correlate.[2] What is greater, has its property of being greater in relation to something else, which is less—not in relation to itself. It cannot be greater than itself, for then it would also be less than itself. It cannot include in itself the characteristic property of the *correlatum* as well as that of the *relatum*. So too about what is older, younger, heavier, lighter : there is always a something distinct, to which reference is made. Vision does not include in itself both the property of seeing, and that of being seen : the *videns* is distinct from the *visum*. A movement implies something else to be moved : a heater something else to be heated. All knowledge must be relative to some object.

In all these cases (concludes Sokrates) the characteristic property is essentially relative, implying something distinguishable from, yet correlating with, itself. May we generalise the proposition, and affirm, That all properties are relative, and that every thing in nature has its characteristic property with reference, not to itself, but to something else ? Or is this true only of some things and not of all—so that cognition may be in the latter category ? All properties are relative—everything in nature has its characteristic property with reference to something else.

This is an embarrassing question, which I do not feel qualified to decide : neither the general question, whether there be any cases of characteristic properties having no reference to any thing beyond themselves, and therefore not relative, but absolute—nor the particular question, whether cognition be one of those cases, implying no separate *cognitum*, but being itself both *relatum* and *correlatum*—cognition of cognition.[3]

---

[1] Plato, Charm. 167-168.
[2] Plato, Charm. 168 B. ἔστι μὲν αὐτὴ ἡ ἐπιστήμη τινὸς ἐπιστήμη, καὶ ἔχει τινὰ τοιαύτην δύναμιν ὥστε τινὸς εἶναι.

[3] Plato, Charm. 168-169. 169 A : μεγάλου δή τινος ἀνδρὸς δεῖ, ὅστις τοῦτο κατὰ πάντων ἱκανῶς διαιρήσεται, πότερον οὐδὲν τῶν ὄντων τὴν αὑτοῦ δύναμιν αὐτὸ

But even if cognition of cognition be possible, I shall not admit it as an explanation of what temperance is, until I have satisfied myself that it is beneficial. For I have a presentiment that temperance must be something beneficial and good.[1] Let us concede for the present discussion (continues Sokrates) that cognition of cognition is possible. Still how does this prove that there can be cognition of non-cognition? that a man can know both what he knows and what he does not know? For this is what we declared self-knowledge and temperance to be.[2] To have cognition of cognition is one thing : to have cognition of non-cognition is a different thing, not necessarily connected with it. If you have cognition of cognition, you will be enabled to distinguish that which is cognition from that which is not—but no more. Now the knowledge or ignorance of the matter of health is one thing, known by medical science : that of justice is a different thing, known by political science. The knowledge of knowledge simply—cognition of cognition—is different from both. The person who possesses this last only, without knowing either medicine or politics, will become aware that he knows something and possesses some sort of knowledge, and will be able to verify so much with regard to others. But *what* it is that he himself knows, or that others know, he will not thereby be enabled to find out : he will not distinguish whether that which is known belong to physiology or to politics ; to do this, special acquirements are needed. You, a temperate man therefore, as such, do not know *what* you know and *what* you do not know; you know the bare fact, *that* you know and *that* you do not know. You will not be competent to cross-examine any one who professes to know medicine or any other particular subject, so as to ascertain whether the man really possesses what he pretends to

Even if cognition of cognition were possible, cognition of non-cognition would be impossible. A man may know what he knows, but he cannot know what he is ignorant of. He knows the fact that he knows : but he does not know how much he knows, and how much he does not know.

πρὸς ἑαυτὸ πέφυκεν ἔχειν, ἀλλὰ πρὸς ἄλλο—ἢ τὰ μέν, τὰ δ' οὔ· καὶ εἰ ἔστιν αὖ ἅτινα αὐτὰ πρὸς ἑαυτὰ ἔχει, ἆρ' ἐν τούτοις ἐστὶν ἐπιστήμη, ἣν δὴ ἡμεῖς σωφροσύνην φαμὲν εἶναι. ἐγὼ μὲν οὐ πιστεύω ἐμαυτῷ ἱκανὸς εἶναι ταῦτα διελέσθαι.
[1] Plato, Charm. 169 B. ὠφέλιμόν τι

κἀγαθὸν μαντεύομαι εἶναι.
[2] Plato, Charm. 169 D. νῦν μὲν τοῦτο ξυγχωρήσωμεν, δυνατὸν εἶναι γενέσθαι ἐπιστήμην ἐπιστήμης—ἴθι δὴ οὖν, εἰ ὅ,τι μάλιστα δυνατὸν τοῦτο, τί μᾶλλον οἷόν τέ ἐστιν εἰδέναι ἅ τέ τις οἶδε καὶ ἃ μή; τοῦτο γὰρ δήπου ἔφαμεν εἶναι τὸ γιγνώσκειν αὐτὸν καὶ σωφρονεῖν.

HOW IS TEMPERANCE USEFUL?

possess. There will be no point in common between you and him. You, as a temperate man, possess cognition of cognition, but you do not know any special *cognitum:* the special man knows his own special *cognitum*, but is a stranger to cognition generally. You cannot question him, nor criticise what he says or performs, in his own specialty—for of that you are ignorant :—no one can do it except some fellow *expert*. You can ascertain that he possesses *some* knowledge : but whether he possesses that particular knowledge to which he lays claim, or whether he falsely pretends to it, you cannot ascertain :—since, as a temperate man, you know only cognition and non-cognition generally. To ascertain this point, you must be not only a temperate man, but a man of special cognition besides.[1] You can question and test no one, except another temperate man like yourself.

But if this be all that temperance can do, of what use is it to us (continues Sokrates)? It is indeed a great benefit to know how much we know, and how much we do not know : it is also a great benefit to know respecting others, how much *they* know, and how much they do not know. If thus instructed, we should make fewer mistakes : we should do by ourselves only what we knew how to do,—we should commit to others that which they knew how to do, and which we did not know. But temperance (meaning thereby cognition of cognition and of non-cognition generally) does not confer such instruction, nor have we found any science which does.[2] How temperance benefits us, does not yet appear. *Temperance therefore as thus defined would be of little or no value.*

But let us even concede—what has been just shown to be impossible—that through temperance we become aware of what we do know and what we do not know. Even upon this hypothesis, it will be of little service to us. We have been too hasty in conceding that it would be a great benefit if each of us did only what he knew, committing to others to do only what they *But even granting the possibility of that which has just been denied, still Temperance would be of*

---

[1] Plato, Charm. 170-171. 171 C : Παντὸς ἄρα μᾶλλον, εἰ ἡ σωφροσύνη ἐπιστήμης ἐπιστήμη μόνον ἐστὶ καὶ ἀνεπιστημοσύνης, οὔτε ἰατρὸν διακρῖναι οἷά τε ἔσται ἐπιστάμενον τὰ τῆς τέχνης, ἢ μὴ ἐπιστάμενον προσποιούμενον δὲ ἢ οἰόμενον, οὔτε ἄλλον οὐδένα τῶν ἐπισταμένων καὶ ὁτιοῦν, πλήν γε τὸν αὑτοῦ ὁμότεχνον, ὥσπερ οἱ ἄλλοι δημιουργοί.

[2] Plato, Charm. 172 A. ὁρᾷς, ὅτι οὐδαμοῦ ἐπιστήμη οὐδεμία τοιαύτη οὖσα πέφανται.

160   CHARMIDES.   CHAP. XIX.

little value. Suppose that all separate work were well performed, by special practitioners, we should not attain our end—Happiness. knew. I have an awkward suspicion (continues Sokrates) that after all, this would be no great benefit.[1] It is true that upon this hypothesis, all operations in society would be conducted scientifically and skilfully. We should have none but competent pilots, physicians, generals, &c., acting for us, each of them doing the work for which he was fit. The supervision exercised by temperance (in the sense above defined) would guard us against all pretenders. Let us even admit that as to prediction of the future, we should have none but competent and genuine prophets to advise us; charlatans being kept aloof by this same supervision. We should thus have every thing done scientifically and in a workmanlike manner. But should we for that reason do well and be happy? Can that be made out, Kritias?[2]

Krit.—You will hardly find the end of well-doing anywhere
Which of the varieties of knowledge contributes most to well-doing or happiness? That by which we know good and evil. else, if you deny that it follows on doing scientifically or according to knowledge.[3] *Sokr.*—But according to knowledge, of *what?* Of leather-cutting, brazen work, wool, wood, &c.? *Krit.*—No, none of these. *Sokr.*— Well then, you see, we do not follow out consistently your doctrine—That the happy man is he who lives scientifically, or according to knowledge. For all these men live according to knowledge, and still you do not admit them to be happy. Your definition of happiness applies only to some portion of those who live according to knowledge, but not to all. How are we to distinguish which of them? Suppose a man to know every thing past, present, and future; which among the fractions of such omniscience would contribute most to make him happy? Would they all contribute equally? *Krit.*—By no means. *Sokr.*—Which of them then would contribute most? Would it be that by which he knew the art of gaming? *Krit.*—Certainly not. *Sokr.*—Or that by which he knew the art of computing? *Krit.*—No. *Sokr.*—Or

[1] Plato, Charm. 172-173.
[2] Plato, Charm. 173 C-D. κατεσκευασμένον δὴ οὕτω τὸ ἀνθρώπινον γένος ὅτι μὲν ἐπιστημόνως ἂν πράττοι καὶ ζῴη, ἕπομαι—ὅτι δ' ἐπιστημόνως ἂν πράττοντες εὖ ἂν πράττοιμεν καὶ εὐδαιμονοῖμεν, τοῦτο δὲ οὔπω δυνάμεθα μαθεῖν, ὦ φίλε Κριτία.
[3] Plato, Charm. 173 D. Ἀλλὰ μέντοι, ἦ δ' ὅς, οὐ ῥᾳδίως εὑρήσεις ἄλλο τι τέλος τοῦ εὖ πράττειν ἐὰν τὸ ἐπιστημόνως ἀτιμάσῃς.

CHAP. XIX.   SCIENCE OF GOOD AND EVIL.   161

that by which he knew the conditions of health? *Krit.*—That will suit better. *Sokr.*- Jut which of them most of all? *Krit.* —That by which he knew good and evil.[1]

Sokr.—Here then, you have been long dragging me round in a circle, keeping back the fact, that well-doing and happiness does not arise from living according to science generally, not of all other matters taken together—but from living according to the science of this one single matter, good and evil. If you exclude this last, and leave only the other sciences, each of these others will work as before : the medical man will heal, the weaver will prepare clothes, the pilot will navigate his vessel, the general will conduct his army — each of them scientifically. Nevertheless, that each of these things shall conduce to our well- *Without the science of good and evil, the other special science will be of little or no service. Temperance is not the science of good and evil, and is of little service.*
being and profit, will be an impossibility, if the science of good and evil be wanting.[2] Now this science of good and evil, the special purpose of which is to benefit us,[3] is altogether different from temperance ; which you have defined as the science of cognition and non-cognition, and which appears not to benefit us at all. *Krit.*—Surely it does benefit us : for it presides over and regulates all the other sciences, and of course regulates this very science, of good and evil, among the rest. *Sokr.*—In what way can it benefit us ? It does not procure for us any special service, such as good health : *that* is the province of medicine : in like manner, each separate result arises from its own producing art. To confer benefit is, as we have just laid down, the special province of the science of good and evil.[4] Temperance, as the science of cognition and non-cognition, cannot work any benefit at all.

Thus then, concludes Sokrates, we are baffled in every way :

[1] Plato, Charm. 174.
[2] Plato, Charm. 174 C-D. ἐπεὶ εἰ θέλεις ἐξελεῖν ταύτην τὴν ἐπιστήμην (of good and evil) ἐκ τῶν ἄλλων ἐπιστημῶν, ἧττόν τι ἡ μὲν ἰατρικὴ ὑγιαίνειν ποιήσει, ἡ δὲ σκυτικὴ ὑποδεδέσθαι, ἡ δὲ ὑφαντικὴ ἠμφιέσθαι, ἡ δὲ κυβερνητικὴ κωλύσει ἐν τῇ θαλάττῃ ἀποθνήσκειν καὶ ἡ στρατηγικὴ ἐν πολέμῳ; Οὐδὲν ἧττον, ἔφη. Ἀλλὰ τὸ εὖ τε τούτων ἕκαστα γίγνεσθαι καὶ ὠφελίμως ἀπολελοιπὸς ἡμᾶς ἔσται ταύτης ἀπούσης.

[3] Plato, Charm. 174 D. ἧς ἔργον ἐστὶ τὸ ὠφελεῖν ἡμᾶς, &c.

[4] Plato, Charm. 175 A. Οὐκ ἄρα ὑγιείας ἔσται δημιουργός (ἡ σωφροσύνη). Οὐ δῆτα. Ἄλλης γὰρ ἦν τέχνης ὑγιεία, ἦ οὔ; Ἄλλης. Οὐδ' ἄρα ὠφελείας, ὦ ἑταῖρε· ἄλλῃ γὰρ αὖ ἀπέδομεν τοῦτο τὸ ἔργον τέχνῃ νῦν δή· ἦ γάρ; Πάνυ γε. Πῶς οὖν ὠφέλιμος ἔσται ἡ σωφροσύνη, οὐδεμιᾶς ὠφελείας οὖσα δημιουργός; Οὐδαμῶς, ὦ Σώκρατες, ἔοικέ γε.

162   CHARMIDES.   CHAP. XIX.

Sokrates confesses to entire failure in his research. He cannot find out what temperance is: although several concessions have been made which cannot be justified.

we cannot find out what temperance is, nor what that name has been intended to designate. All our tentatives have failed ; although, in our anxiety to secure some result, we have accepted more than one inadmissible hypothesis. Thus we have admitted that there might exist cognition of cognition, though our discussion tended to negative such a possibility. We have farther granted, that this cognition of cognition, or science of science, might know all the operations of each separate and special science : so that the temperate man (*i.e.* he who possesses cognition of cognition) might know both what he knows and what he does not know : might know, namely, that he knows the former and that he does not know the latter. We have granted this, though it is really an absurdity to say, that what a man does not know at all, he nevertheless does know after a certain fashion.[1] Yet after these multiplied concessions against strict truth, we have still been unable to establish our definition of temperance : for temperance as we defined it has, after all, turned out to be thoroughly unprofitable.

It is plain that we have taken the wrong road, and that I

Temperance is and must be a good thing : but Charmides cannot tell whether he is temperate or not; since what temperance is remains unknown.

(Sokrates) do not know how to conduct the enquiry. For temperance, whatever it may consist in, must assuredly be a great benefit : and you, Charmides, are happy if you possess it. How can I tell (rejoins Charmides) whether I possess it or not : since even men like you and Kritias cannot discover what it is?[2]

Expressions both from Charmides

Here ends the dialogue called Charmidês,[3] after the interchange of a few concluding compliments, forming

---

[1] Plato, Charm. 175 B. καὶ γὰρ ἐπιστήμην ἐπιστήμης εἶναι ξυνεχωρήσαμεν, οὐκ ἐῶντος τοῦ λόγου οὐδὲ φάσκοντος εἶναι· καὶ ταύτῃ αὖ τῇ ἐπιστήμῃ καὶ τὰ τῶν ἄλλων ἐπιστημῶν ἔργα γιγνώσκειν ξυνεχωρήσαμεν, οὐδὲ τοῦτ' ἐῶντος τοῦ λόγου, ἵνα δὴ ἡμῖν γένοιτο ὁ σώφρων ἐπιστήμων ὧν τε οἶδεν, ὅτι οἶδε, καὶ ὧν μὴ οἶδεν, ὅτι οὐκ οἶδε. τοῦτο μὲν δὴ καὶ παντάπασι μεγαλοπρεπῶς ξυνεχωρήσαμεν, οὐδ' 'πισκεψάμενοι τὸ ἀδύνατον εἶναι, ἅ τις μὴ οἶδε μηδαμῶς, ταῦτα εἰδέναι ἀμῶς γέ πως· ὅτι γὰρ οὐκ οἶδε, φησὶν αὐτὰ εἰδέναι ἡ ἡμετέρα ὁμολογία. καίτοι, ὡς ἐγᾦμαι, οὐδενὸς ὅτου οὐχὶ ἀλογώτερον τοῦτ' ἂν φανείη. This would not appear an absurdity to Aristotle. See Analyt. Priora, ii. p. 67, a. 21 ; Anal. Post. i. 71, a. 28.

[2] Plato, Charm. 176 A.

[3] See Appendix at end of chapter.

part of the great dramatic richness which characterises this dialogue from the beginning. I make no attempt to reproduce this latter attribute; though it is one of the peculiar merits of Plato in reference to ethical enquiry, imparting to the subject a charm which does not naturally belong to it. I confine myself to the philosophical bearing of the dialogue. According to the express declaration of Sokrates, it ends in nothing but disappointment. No positive result is attained. The problem— What is Temperance?—remains unsolved, after four or five different solutions have been successively tested and repudiated.

and Kritias of praise and devotion to Sokrates, at the close of the dialogue. Dramatic ornament throughout.

The Charmidês (like the Lachês) is a good illustrative specimen of those Dialogues of Search, the general character and purpose of which I have explained in my sixth chapter. It proves nothing: it disproves several hypotheses: but it exhibits (and therein consists its value) the anticipating, guessing, tentative, and eliminating process, without which no defensible conclusions can be obtained—without which, even if such be found, no advocate can be formed capable of defending them against an acute cross-examiner. In most cases, this tentative process is forgotten or ignored: even when recognised as a reality, it is set aside with indifference, often with ridicule. A writer who believes himself to have solved any problem, publishes his solution together with the proofs; and acquires deserved credit for it, if those proofs give satisfaction. But he does not care to preserve, nor do the public care to know, the steps by which such solution has been reached. Nevertheless in most cases, and in all cases involving much difficulty, there has been a process, more or less tedious, of tentative and groping —of guesses at first hailed as promising, then followed out to a certain extent, lastly discovered to be untenable. The history of science,[1] astronomical, physical, chemical, physiological, &c.,

The Charmidês is an excellent specimen of Dialogues of Search. Abundance of guesses and tentatives, all ultimately disallowed.

[1] It is not often that historians of science take much pains to preserve and bring together the mistaken guesses and tentatives which have preceded great physical discoveries. One instance in which this has been ably and carefully done is in the 'Biography of Cavendish,' the chemist and natural philosopher, by Dr. Geo. Wilson.

The great chemical discovery of the composition of water, accomplished during the last quarter of the eighteenth century, has been claimed as the privilege of three eminent scientific men

wherever it has been at all recorded, attests this constant antecedence of a period of ignorance, confusion, and dispute, even in cases where ultimately a solution has been found commanding the nearly unanimous adhesion of the scientific world. But on subjects connected with man and society, this period of dispute and confusion continues to the present moment. No unanimity has ever been approached, among nations at once active in intellect and enjoying tolerable liberty of dissent. Moreover— apart from the condition of different sciences among mature men —we must remember that the transitive process, above described, represents the successive stages by which every adult mind has been gradually built up from infancy. Trial and error—alternate guess and rejection, generation and destruction of sentiments and beliefs—is among the most widespread facts of human intelligence.[1] Even those ordinary minds, which in mature life harden with the most exemplary fidelity into the locally prevalent type of orthodoxy,—have all in their earlier years gone through that semi-fluid and indeterminate period, in which the type to come is yet a matter of doubt—in which the head might have been permanently lengthened or permanently flattened, according to the direction in which pressure was applied.

We shall follow Plato towards the close of his career (Treatise De Legibus), into an imperative and stationary ortho-

—Cavendish, Watt, and Lavoisier. The controversy on the subject, voluminous and bitter, has been the means of recording each successive scientific phase and point of view. It will be found admirably expounded in this biography. Wilson sets forth the misconceptions, confusion of ideas, approximations to truth seen but not followed out, &c., which prevailed upon the scientific men of that day, especially under the misleading influence of the "phlogiston theory," then universally received.

To Plato such a period of mental confusion would have been in itself an interesting object for contemplation and description. He might have dramatised it under the names of various disputants, with the cross-examining Elenchus, personified in Sokrates, introduced to stir up the debate, either by first advocating, then refuting, a string of successive guesses and dreams (Charmidês, 173 A) of his own, or by exposing similar suggestions emanating from others; especially in regard to the definition of *phlogiston*, an entity which then overspread and darkened all chemical speculation, but which every theorist thought himself obliged to define. The dialogues would have ended (as the Protagoras, Lysis, Charmidês, &c., now end) by Sokrates deriding the ill success which had attended them in the search for an explanation, and by his pointing out that while all the theorists talked familiarly about *phlogiston* as a powerful agent, none of them could agree what it was.

See Dr. Wilson's 'Biography of Cavendish,' pp. 36-198-320-325, and elsewhere.

[1] It is strikingly described by Plato in one of the most remarkable passages of the speech of Diotima in the Symposion, pp. 207-208.

doxy of his own: but in the dialogues which I have already reviewed, as well as in several others which I shall presently notice, no mention is made of any given affirmative doctrine as indispensable to arrive at ultimately. Plato here concentrates his attention upon the indeterminate period of the mind: looking upon the mind not as an empty vessel, requiring to be filled by ready-made matter from without—nor as a blank sheet, awaiting a foreign hand to write characters upon it—but as an assemblage of latent capacities, which must be called into action by stimulus and example, but which can only attain improvement through multiplied trials and multiplied failures. *Trial and Error, the natural process of the human mind. Plato stands alone in bringing to view and dramatising this part of the mental process. Sokrates accepts for himself the condition of conscious ignorance.* Whereas in most cases these failures are forgotten, the peculiarity of Plato consists in his bringing them to view with full detail, explaining the reasons of each. He illustrates abundantly, and dramatises with the greatest vivacity, the intellectual process whereby opinions are broached, at first adopted, then mistrusted, unmade, and re-made—or perhaps not re-made at all, but exchanged for a state of conscious ignorance. The great hero and operator in this process is the Platonic Sokrates, who accepts for himself this condition of conscious ignorance, and even makes it a matter of comparative pride, that he stands nearly alone in such confession.[1] His colloquial influence, working powerfully and almost preternaturally,[2] not only serves both to spur and to direct the activity of hearers still youthful and undecided, but also exposes those who have already made up their minds and confidently believe themselves to know. Sokrates brings back these latter from the false persuasion of knowledge to the state of conscious ignorance, and to the prior indeterminate condition of mind, in which their opinions have again to be put together by the tentative and guessing process. This tentative process, prosecuted under the drill of Sokrates, is in itself full of charm and interest for Plato, whether it ends by finding a good solution or only by discarding a bad one.

The Charmidês is one of the many Platonic dialogues wherein

[1] Plato, Apolog. Sokr. pp. 21-22-23.
[2] Plato, Symposion, 213 E, 215-216; Menon, 80 A-B.

Familiar words—constantly used, with much earnest feeling, but never understood nor defined—ordinary phenomenon in human society.

such intellectual experimentation appears depicted without any positive result: except as it adds fresh matter to illustrate that wide-spread mental fact,— (which has already come before the reader, in Euthyphron, Alkibiadês, Hippias, Erastæ, Lachês, &c., as to holiness, beauty, philosophy, courage, &c., and is now brought to view in the case of *temperance* also; all of them words in every one's mouth, and tacitly assumed by every one as known quantities)—the perpetual and confident judgments which mankind are in the habit of delivering—their apportionment of praise and blame, as well as of reward and punishment consequent on praise and blame—without any better basis than that of strong emotion imbibed they know not how, and without being able to render any rational explanation even of the familiar words round which such emotions are grouped. No philosopher has done so much as Plato to depict in detail this important fact—the habitual condition of human society, modern as well as ancient, and for that very reason generally unnoticed.[1] The emotional or subjective value of temperance is all that Sokrates determines, and which indeed he makes his point of departure. Temperance is essentially among the fine, beautiful, honourable, things:[2] but its rational or objective value (*i.e.*, what is the common object characterising all temperate acts or persons), he cannot determine. Here indeed Plato is not always consistent with himself: for we shall come to other dialogues wherein he professes himself incompetent to say whether a thing be beautiful or not, until it be determined what the thing is:[3] and we have already found

---

[1] "Whoever has reflected on the generation of ideas in his own mind, or has investigated the causes of misunderstandings among mankind, will be obliged to proclaim as a fact deeply seated in human nature—That most of the misunderstandings and contradictions among men, most of the controversies and errors both in science and in society, arise usually from our assuming (consciously or unconsciously) fundamental maxims and fundamental facts as if they were self-evident, and as if they must be assumed by every one else besides. Accordingly we never think of closely examining them, until at length experience has taught us that these *self-evident* matters are exactly what stand most in need of proof, and what form the special root of divergent opinions."—(L. O. Bröcker —Untersuchungen über die Glaubwürdigkeit der alt-Römischen Geschichte, p. 490.)

[2] Plato, Charm. 159 B, 160 D. ἡ σωφροσύνη—τῶν καλῶν τι—ἐν τῷ λόγῳ τῶν καλῶν τι. So also Sokrates, in the Lachès (192 C), assumes that courage is τῶν πάνυ καλῶν πραγμάτων, though he professes not to know nor to be able to discover what courage is.

[3] See Gorgias, 462 B, 448 E; Menon, 70 B.

Sokrates declaring (in the Hippias Major), that we cannot determine whether any particular object is beautiful or not, until we have first determined, What is Beauty in the Absolute, or the Self-Beautiful? a problem nowhere solved by Plato.

Among the various unsuccessful definitions of temperance propounded, there is more than one which affords farther example to show how differently Plato deals with the same subject in different dialogues. Here we have the phrase—"to do one's own business"—treated as an unmeaning puzzle, and exhibited as if it were analogous to various other phrases, with which the analogy is more verbal than real. But in the Republic, Plato admits this phrase as well understood, and sets it forth as the constituent element of justice; in the Gorgias, as the leading mark of philosophical life.[1] *Different ethical points of view in different Platonic dialogues.*

Again, another definition given by Kritias is, That temperance consists in knowing yourself, or in self-knowledge. In commenting upon this definition, Sokrates makes out—first, that self-knowledge is impossible: next, that if possible, it would be useless. You cannot know yourself, he argues: you cannot know what you know, and what you do not know: to say that you know what you know, is either tautological or untrue—to say that you know what you do not know, is a contradiction. All cognition must be cognition of something distinct from yourself: it is a relative term which must have some correlate, and cannot be its own correlate: you cannot have cognition of cognition, still less cognition of non-cognition. *Self-knowledge is here declared to be impossible.*

This is an important point of view, which I shall discuss more at length when I come to the Platonic Theætêtus. I bring it to view here only as contrasting with the different language held by the Platonic Sokrates in other dialogues; where he insists on the great value and indispensable necessity of self-knowledge, as a preliminary to all other knowledge—upon the duty of eradicating from men's minds that false persuasion of their own knowledge which they universally che- *In other dialogues, Sokrates declares self-knowledge to be essential and inestimable. Necessity for the student to have pre-*

[1] Plato, Republ. iv. 433, vi. 496 C, viii. 550 A; Gorgias, 526 C. Compare also Timæus, 72 A, Xen. Mem. ii. 9, 1.

sented to him dissentient points of view.

rished—and upon the importance of forcing them to know their own ignorance as well as their own knowledge. In the face of this last purpose, so frequently avowed by the Platonic Sokrates (indirectly even in this very dialogue),[1] we remark a material discrepancy, when he here proclaims self-knowledge to be impossible. We must judge every dialogue by itself, illustrating it when practicable by comparison with others, but not assuming consistence between them as a postulate *à priori*. It is a part of Plato's dramatic and tentative mode of philosophising to work out different ethical points of view, and to have present to his mind one or other of them, with peculiar force in each different dialogue. The subject is thus brought before us on all its sides, and the reader is familiarised with what a dialectician might say, whether capable of being refuted or not. Inconsistency between one dialogue and another is not a fault in the Platonic dialogues of Search; but is, on the contrary, a part of the training process, for any student who is destined to acquire that full mastery of question and answer which Plato regards as the characteristic test of knowledge. It is a puzzle and provocative to the internal meditation of the student.

In analyzing the Lachês, we observed that the definition of

Courage and Temperance are shown to have no distinct meaning, except as founded on the general cognizance of good and evil.

courage given by Nikias was shown by Sokrates to have no meaning, except in so far as it coincided with the general knowledge or cognition of good and evil. Here, too, in the Charmidês, we are brought in the last result to the same terminus—the general cognition of good and evil. But Temperance, as previously defined, is not comprehended under that cognition, and is therefore pronounced to be unprofitable.

This cognition of good and evil—the science of the profitable—

Distinction made between the special sciences and the science of Good and Evil. With-

is here (in the Charmidês) proclaimed by Sokrates to have a place of its own among the other sciences; and even to be first among them, essentially necessary to supervise and direct them, as it had been declared in Alkibiadês II. Now the same supervising place and directorship had been claimed by

---

[1] Plato, Charm. 166 D.

Kritias for Temperance as he defines it—that is, self-knowledge, or the cognition of our cognitions and non-cognitions. But Sokrates doubts even the reality of such self-knowledge: and granting for argument's sake that it exists, he still does not see how it can be profitable. For the utmost which its supervision can ensure would be, that each description of work shall be scientifically done, by the skilful man, and not by the unskilful. But it is not true, absolutely speaking (he argues), that acting scientifically or with knowledge is sufficient for well doing or for happiness: for the question must next be asked—Knowledge—of what? Not knowledge of leather-cutting, carpenter's or brazier's work, arithmetic, or even medicine: these, and many others, a man may possess, and may act according to them; but still he will not attain the end of being happy. All cognitions contribute in greater or less proportion towards that end: but what contributes most, and most essentially, is the cognition of good and evil, without which all the rest are insufficient. Of this last-mentioned cognition or science, it is the special object to ensure profit or benefit:[1] to take care that everything done by the other sciences shall be done well or in a manner conducing towards the end Happiness. After this, there is no province left for temperance—*i.e.*, self-knowledge, or the knowledge of cognitions and non-cognitions: no assignable way in which it can yield any benefit.[2]

out this last, the special sciences are of no use.

Two points are here to be noted, as contained and debated in the handling of this dialogue. 1. Knowledge absolutely, is a word without meaning: all knowledge is relative, and has a definite object or *cognitum*: there can be no *scientia scientiarum*. 2. Among the various objects of knowledge (*cognita* or *cognoscenda*), one is, *good and evil*. There is a science of good and evil, the function of which is, to watch over and compare the results of the other sciences, in order to promote results of happiness, and to prevent results of misery: without the supervision of this latter science, the other sciences might be all

Knowledge, always relative to some object known. Postulate or divination of a Science of Teleology.

---

[1] Plato, Charm. 174 D. Οὐχ αὕτη δέ γε, ὡς ἔοικεν, ἐστὶν ἡ σωφροσύνη, ἀλλ' ἧς ἔργον ἐστὶ τὸ ὠφελεῖν ἡμᾶς. Οὐ γὰρ ἐπιστημῶν γε καὶ ἀνεπιστημοσυνῶν ἡ ἐπιστήμη ἐστίν, ἀλλὰ ἀγαθοῦ τε καὶ κακοῦ.

[2] Plato, Charm. 174 E. Οὐκ ἄρα ὑγιείας ἔσται δημιουργός; Οὐ δῆτα.

Ἄλλης γὰρ ἦν τέχνης ὑγίεια; ἢ οὔ; Ἄλλης· Οὐδ' ἄρα ὠφελείας, ὦ ἑταῖρε· ἄλλῃ γὰρ αὖ ἀπέδομεν τοῦτο τὸ ἔργον τέχνῃ νῦν δή· ἦ γάρ; Πάνυ γε. Πῶς οὖν ὠφέλιμος ἔσται ἡ σωφροσύνη, οὐδεμιᾶς ὠφελείας οὖσα δημιουργός; Οὐία μῶς, ὦ Σώκρατες, ἔοικέ γε.

exactly followed out, but no rational comparison could be had between them.[1] In other words, there is a science of Ends, estimating the comparative worth of each End in relation to other Ends (Teleology): distinct from those other more special sciences, which study the means each towards a separate End of its own. Here we fall into the same track as we have already indicated in Lachês and Alkibiadês II.

Courage and Temperance, handled both by Plato and by Aristotle. Comparison between the two.

These matters I shall revert to in other dialogues, where we shall find them turned over and canvassed in many different ways. One farther observation remains to be made on the Lachês and Charmidês, discussing as they do Courage (which is also again discussed in the Protagoras) and Temperance. An interesting comparison may be made between them and the third book of the Nikomachean Ethics of Aristotle,[2] where the same two subjects are handled in the Aristotelian manner. The direct, didactic, systematising, brevity of Aristotle contrasts remarkably with the indirect and circuitous prolixity, the multiplied suggestive comparisons, the shifting points of view, which we find in Plato. Each has its advantages : and both together will be found not more than sufficient, for any one who is seriously bent on acquiring what Plato calls knowledge, with the cross-examining power included in it. Aristotle is greatly superior to Plato in one important attribute of a philosopher : in the care which he takes to discriminate the different significations of the same word : the univocal and the equivocal, the generically identical from the remotely analogical, the proper from the improper, the literal from the metaphorical. Of such precautions we discover little or no trace in Plato, who sometimes seems not merely to neglect, but even to deride them. Yet Aristotle, assisted as he was by all Plato's speculations before us, is not to be understood as having superseded the necessity for that negative Elenchus which animates the Platonic dialogues of Search : nor would his affirmative doctrines have held their grounds before a cross-examining Sokrates.

[1] Compare what has been said upon the same subject in my remarks on Alkib. i. and ii. p.
[2] Aristot. Ethic. Nikom. iii. p. 1115, 1119; also Ethic. Eudem. iii. 1229-1231.

The comments of Aristotle upon the doctrine of Sokrates respecting Courage seem to relate rather to the Protagoras than to the Lachês of Plato. See Eth. Nik. 1116, 6, 4; Eth. Eud. 1229, a. 15.

APPENDIX.

The dialogue Charmidês is declared to be spurious, not only by Ast, but also by Socher (Ast, Platon's Leb. pp. 419-428 ; Socher, Ueber Platon, pp. 130-137). Steinhart maintains the genuineness of the dialogue against them ; declaring (as in regard to the Lachês) that he can hardly conceive how critics can mistake the truly Platonic character of it, though here too, as in the Lachês, he detects "adolescentiæ vestigia" (Steinhart, Einleit. zum Charmidês, pp. 290-293).

Schleiermacher considers Charmidês as well as Lachês to be appendixes to the Protagoras, which opinion both Stallbaum (Proleg. ad Charm. p. 121 ; Proleg. ad Lachet. p. 30, 2nd ed.) and Steinhart controvert.

The views of Stallbaum respecting the Charmidês are declared by Steinhart (p. 290) to be "recht äusserlich und oberflächlich". To me they appear much nearer the truth than the profound and recondite meanings, the far-sighted indirect hints, which Steinhart himself perceives or supposes in the words of Plato.

These critics consider the dialogue as composed during the government of the Thirty at Athens, in which opinion I do not concur.

CHAPTER XX.

LYSIS.

THE Lysis, as well as the Charmidês, is a dialogue recounted by
Sokrates himself, describing both incidents and a conversation in a crowded Palæstra; wherein not merely bodily exercises were habitually practised, but debate was carried on and intellectual instruction given by a Sophist named Mikkus, companion and admirer of Sokrates. There is a lively dramatic commencement, introducing Sokrates into the Palæstra, and detailing the preparation and scenic arrangements, before the real discussion opens. It is the day of the Hermæa, or festival of Hermes, celebrated by sacrifice and its accompanying banquets among the frequenters of gymnasia.

Analogy between Lysis and Charmidês. Richness of dramatic incident in both. Youthful beauty.

Lysis, like Charmidês, is an Athenian youth, of conspicuous beauty, modesty, and promise. His father Demokrates represents an ancient family of the Æxonian Deme in Attica, and is said to be descended from Zeus and the daughter of the Archêgetês or Heroic Founder of that Deme. The family moreover are so wealthy, that they have gained many victories at the Pythian, Isthmian, and Nemean games, both with horses and with chariots and four. Menexenus, companion of Lysis, is somewhat older, and is his affectionate friend. The persons who invite Sokrates into the palæstra, and give occasion to the debate, are Ktesippus and Hippothalês: both of them adults, yet in the vigour of age. Hippothalês is the Erastes of Lysis, passionately attached to him. He is ridiculed by Ktesippus for perpetually talking about Lysis, as well as for addressing to him compositions both in prose and verse, full of praise and

Scenery and personages of the Lysis.

CHAP. XX.   MODE OF TALKING WITH YOUTH.   173

flattery; extolling not only his personal beauty, but also his splendid ancestry and position.[1]

In reference to these addresses, Sokrates remonstrates with Hippothalês on the imprudence and mischief of addressing to a youth flatteries calculated to turn his head. He is himself then invited by Hippothalês to exhibit a specimen of the proper mode of talking to youth; such as shall be at once acceptable to the person addressed, and unobjectionable. Sokrates agrees to do so, if an opportunity be afforded him of conversing with Lysis.[2] Accordingly after some well-imagined incidents, interesting as marks of Greek manners—Sokrates and Ktesippus with others seat themselves in the palæstra, amidst a crowd of listeners.[3] Lysis, too modest at first to approach, is emboldened to sit down by seeing Menexenus seated by the side of Sokrates: while Hippothalês, not daring to put himself where Lysis can see him, listens, but conceals himself behind some of the crowd. Sokrates begins the conversation with Menexenus and Lysis jointly: but presently Menexenus is called away for a moment, and he talks with Lysis singly.

Sokr.—Well—Lysis—your father and mother love you extremely. *Lysis.*—Assuredly they do. *Sokr.*—They would wish you therefore to be as happy as possible. *Lysis.*—Undoubtedly. *Sokr.*—Do you think any man happy, who is a slave, and who is not allowed to do any thing that he desires? *Lysis.*—I do not think him happy at all. *Sokr.*—Since therefore your father and mother are so anxious that you should be happy, they of course allow you to do the things which you desire, and never reprove nor forbid you. *Lysis.*—Not at all, by Zeus, Sokrates: there are a great many things that they forbid me. *Sokr.*—How say you! they wish you to be happy—and they hinder you from doing what you wish! Tell me, for example, when one of your father's chariots is going to run a race, if you wished to mount and take the reins, would not they allow you to do so? *Lysis.*—No—certainly: they would not allow me. *Sokr.*—But whom do they allow, then? *Lysis.*—My father employs a paid charioteer. *Sokr.*—What! do they per-

Marginalia: Origin of the conversation. Sokrates promises to give an example of the proper way of talking to a youth, for his benefit.

Marginalia: Conversation of Sokrates with Lysis.

---
[1] Plato, Lysis, 203-205.
[2] Plato, Lysis, 206.
[3] Plato, Lysis, 206-207.

mit a hireling, in preference to *you*, to do what he wishes with the horses? and do they give him pay besides for doing so? *Lysis.*—Why—to be sure. *Sokr.*—But doubtless, I imagine, they trust the team of mules to your direction; and if you chose to take the whip and flog, they would allow you? *Lysis.*—Allow me? not at all. *Sokr.*—What! is no one allowed to flog them? *Lysis.*—Yes—certainly—the mule-groom. *Sokr.*—Is he a slave or free? *Lysis.*—A slave. *Sokr.*—Then, it seems, they esteem a slave higher than you their son; trusting their property to him rather than to you, letting *him* do what he pleases, while they forbid you. But tell me farther: do they allow you to direct yourself—or do not they even trust you so far as that? *Lysis.*—How can you imagine that they trust me? *Sokr.*—But does any one else direct you? *Lysis.*—Yes—this tutor here. *Sokr.*—Is he a slave? *Lysis.*—To be sure: belonging to our family. *Sokr.*—That is shocking: one of free birth to be under the direction of a slave! But what is it that he does, as your director? *Lysis.*—He conducts me to my teacher's house. *Sokr.*—What! do *they* govern you also, these teachers? *Lysis.*—Undoubtedly they do. *Sokr.*—Then your father certainly is bent on putting over you plenty of directors and governors. But surely, when you come home to your mother, she at least, anxious that you should be happy as far as she is concerned, lets you do what you please about the wool or the web, when she is weaving: she does not forbid you to meddle with the bodkin or any of the other instruments of her work? *Lysis.*—Ridiculous! not only does she forbid me, but I should be beaten if I did meddle. *Sokr.*—How is this, by Heraklês? Have you done any wrong to your father and mother? *Lysis.*—Never at all, by Zeus. *Sokr.*—From what provocation is it, then, that they prevent you in this terrible way, from being happy and doing what you wish? keeping you the whole day in servitude to some one, and never your own master? so that you derive no benefit either from the great wealth of the family, which is managed by every one else rather than by you—or from your own body, noble as it is. Even *that* is consigned to the watch and direction of another: while you, Lysis, are master of nothing, nor can do any one thing of what you desire. *Lysis.*—The reason is, Sokrates, that I am not yet old enough. *Sokr.*—That can hardly be the reason; for to a certain extent your father and mother do trust you, without waiting for you to grow older. If they want any thing to be written or read for them, they employ you for that purpose in preference to any one in the house : and you are then allowed to write or read first, whichever of the letters you think proper. Again, when you take up the lyre, neither father nor mother hinder you from tightening or relaxing the strings, or striking them either with your finger or with the plectrum. *Lysis.*—They do not. *Sokr.*—Why is it, then, that they do not hinder you in this last case, as they did in the cases before mentioned? *Lysis.*—I suppose it is because I know this last, but did not know the others. *Sokr.*— Well, my good friend, you see that it is not your increase of years that your father waits for ; but on the very day that he becomes convinced that you know better than he, he will entrust both himself and his property to your management. *Lysis.*—I suppose that he will. *Sokr.*—Ay—and your neighbour too will judge in the same way as your father. As soon as he is satisfied that you understand house-management better than he does, which do you think he will rather do—confide his house to you, or continue to manage it himself? *Lysis.*—I think he will confide it to me. *Sokr.*—The Athenians too : do not you think that they also will put their affairs into your management, as soon as they perceive that you have intelligence adequate to the task? *Lysis.*—Yes : I do. *Sokr.*—What do you say about the Great King also, by Zeus ! When his meat is being boiled, would he permit his eldest son who is to succeed to the rule of Asia, to throw in any thing that he pleases into the sauce, rather than us, if we come and prove to him that we know better than his son the way of preparing sauce? *Lysis.*—Clearly, he will rather permit us. *Sokr.*—The Great King will not let his son throw in even a pinch of salt : while we, if we chose to take up an entire handful, should be allowed to throw it in. *Lysis.*—No doubt. *Sokr.*—What if his son has a complaint in his eyes ; would the Great King, knowing him to be ignorant of medicine, allow him even to touch his own eyes—or would he forbid him? *Lysis.*— He would forbid him. *Sokr.*—As to us, on the contrary, if he accounted us good physicians, and if we desired even to open the eyes and drop a powder into them, he would not hinder us, in the conviction that we understood what we were doing. *Lysis.*

—You speak truly. *Sokr.*—All other matters, in short, on which he believed us to be wiser than himself or his son, he would entrust to us rather than to himself or his son? *Lysis.*—Necessarily so, Sokrates. *Sokr.*—This is the state of the case, then, my dear Lysis: On those matters on which we shall have become intelligent, all persons will put trust in us—Greeks as well as barbarians, men as well as women. We shall do whatever we please respecting them: no one will be at all inclined to interfere with us on such matters; not only we shall be ourselves free, but we shall have command over others besides. These matters will be really ours, because we shall derive real good from them.[1] As to those subjects, on the contrary, on which we shall not have acquired intelligence, no one will trust us to do what we think right: every one,—not merely strangers, but father and mother and nearer relatives if there were any,—will obstruct us as much as they can: we shall be in servitude so far as these subjects are concerned; and they will be really alien to us, for we shall derive no real good from them. Do you admit that this is the case?[2] *Lysis.*—I do admit it. *Sokr.*— Shall we then be friends to any one, or will any one love us, on those matters on which we are unprofitable? *Lysis.*—Certainly not. *Sokr.*—You see that neither does your father love you, nor does any man love another, in so far as he is useless? *Lysis.*— Apparently not. *Sokr.*—If then you become intelligent, my boy, all persons will be your friends and all persons will be your kinsmen: for you will be useful and good: if you do not, no one will be your friend,—not even your father nor your mother nor your other relatives.

Is it possible then, Lysis, for a man to think highly of himself on those matters on which he does not yet think aright? *Lysis.* —How can it be possible? *Sokr.*—If you stand in need of a teacher, you do not yet think aright? *Lysis.*—True. *Sokr.*— Accordingly, you are not presumptuous on the score of intelligence, since you are still without intelligence. *Lysis.*—By Zeus, Sokrates, I think not.[3]

[1] Plato, Lysis, 210 B. καὶ οὐδεὶς ἡμᾶς ἑκὼν εἶναι ἐμποδιεῖ, ἀλλ' αὐτοί τε ἐλεύθεροι ἐσόμεθα ἐν αὑτοῖς καὶ ἄλλων ἄρχοντες, ἡμέτερά τε ταῦτα ἔσται· ὀνησόμεθα γὰρ ἀπ' αὐτῶν.
[2] Plato, Lysis, 210 C. αὐτοί τε ἐν αὑτοῖς ἐσόμεθα ἄλλων ὑπήκοοι, καὶ ἡμῖν ἔσται ἀλλότρια· οὐδὲν γὰρ ἀπ' αὐτῶν ὀνησόμεθα. Συγχωρεῖς οὕτως ἔχειν; Συγχωρῶ.
[3] Plato, Lysis, 210 D. Οἷόν τε οὖν ἐπὶ τούτοις, ὦ Λύσι, μέγα φρονεῖν, ἐν οἷς

When I heard Lysis speak thus (continues Sokrates, who is here the narrator), I looked towards Hippothalês and I was on the point of committing a blunder: for it occurred to me to say, That is the way, Hippothalês, to address a youth whom you love: you ought to check and humble him, not puff him up and spoil him, as you have hitherto done. But when I saw him agitated and distressed by what had been said, I called to mind that, though standing close by, he wished not to be seen by Lysis. Accordingly, I restrained myself and said nothing of the kind.[1] *Lysis is humiliated. Distress of Hippothalês.*

Lysis accepts this as a friendly lesson, inculcating humility: and seeing Menexenus just then coming back, he says aside to Sokrates, Talk to Menexenus, as you have been talking to me. You can tell him yourself (replies Sokrates) what you have heard from me: you listened very attentively. Most certainly I shall tell him (says Lysis): but meanwhile pray address to him yourself some other questions, for me to hear. You must engage to help me if I require it (answers Sokrates): for Menexenus is a formidable disputant, scholar of our friend Ktesippus, who is here ready to assist him. I know he is (rejoined Lysis), and it is for that very reason that I want you to talk to him—that you may chasten and punish him.[2] *Lysis entreats Sokrates to talk in the like strain to Menexenus.*

I have given at length, and almost literally (with some few abbreviations), this first conversation between Sokrates and Lysis, because it is a very characteristic passage, exhibiting conspicuously several peculiar features of the Platonico-Sokratic interrogation. Facts common and familiar are placed in a novel point of view, ingeniously contrasted, and introduced as steppingstones to a very wide generality. Wisdom or knowledge is exalted into the ruling force with liberty of *Value of the first conversation between Sokrates and Lysis, as an illustration of the Platonico-Sokratic manner.*

τις μήπω φρονεῖ; Καὶ πῶς ἄν; ἔφη. Εἰ δ' ἄρα σὺ διδασκάλου δέει, οὔπω φρονεῖς. Ἀληθῆ.
Οὐδ' ἄρα μεγαλόφρων εἶ, εἴπερ ἄφρων ἔτι. Μὰ Δί', ἔφη, ὦ Σώκρατες, οὔ μοι δοκεῖ.
There is here a double sense of μέγα φρονεῖν, μεγαλόφρων, which cannot easily be made to pass into any other language.

[1] Plato, Lysis, 210 E.
[2] Plato, Lysis, 211 B-C. ἀλλ' ὅρα ὅπως ἐπικουρήσεις μοι, ἐάν με ἐλέγχειν ἐπιχειρῇ ὁ Μενέξενος. ἢ οὐκ οἶσθα ὅτι ἐριστικός ἐστι; Ναὶ μὰ Δία, ἔφη, σφόδρα γε. διὰ ταῦτά τοι καὶ βούλομαί σε αὐτῷ διαλέγεσθαι—ἵν' αὐτὸν κολάσῃς.
Compare Xenophon, Memor. i. 4, 1, where he speaks of the chastising purpose often contemplated by Sokrates in

action not admissible except under its guidance: the questions are put in an inverted half-ironical tone (not uncommon with the historical Sokrates[1]), as if an affirmative answer were expected as a matter of course, while in truth the answer is sure to be negative: lastly, the purpose of checking undue self-esteem is proclaimed. The rest of the dialogue, which contains the main substantive question investigated, I can report only in brief abridgment, with a few remarks following.

Sokrates begins, as Lysis requests, to interrogate Menexenus—first premising—Different men have different tastes: some love horses and dogs, others wealth or honours. For my part, I care little about all such acquisitions: but I ardently desire to possess friends, and I would rather have a good friend than all the treasures of Persia. You two, Menexenus and Lysis, are much to be envied, because at your early age, each of you has made an attached friend of the other. But I am so far from any such good fortune, that I do not even know how any man becomes the friend of another. This is what I want to ask from you, Menexenus, as one who must know,[2] having acquired such a friend already.

Sokrates begins to examine Menexenus respecting friendship. Who is to be called a friend? Halt in the dialogue.

When one man loves another, which becomes the friend of which? Does he who loves, become the friend of him whom he loves, whether the latter returns the affection or not? Or is the person loved, whatever be his own dispositions, the friend of the person who loves him? Or is reciprocity of affection necessary, in order that either shall be the friend of the other?

The speakers cannot satisfy themselves that the title of *friend* fits either of the three cases;[3] so that this line of interrogating comes to a dead lock. Menexenus avows his embarrassment, while Lysis expresses himself more hopefully.

Sokrates now takes up a different aspect of the question, and

his conversation—ἃ ἐκεῖνος κολαστηρίου ἕνεκα τοὺς πάντ' οἰομένους εἰδέναι ἐρωτῶν ἤλεγχεν.
[1] See the conversation of Sokrates with Glaukon in Xenophon, Memor. iii. 6; also the conversation with Perikles, iii. 5, 23-24.
[2] Plato, Lysis, 211-212.
[3] Plato, Lysis, 212-213. 213 C:—

εἰ μήτε οἱ φιλοῦντες (1) φίλοι ἔσονται, μήθ' οἱ φιλούμενοι (2), μήθ' οἱ φιλοῦντές τε καὶ φιλούμενοι (3), &c. Sokrates here professes to have shown grounds for rejecting all these three suppositions. But if we follow the preceding argument, we shall see that he has shown grounds only against the first two, not against the third.

turns to Lysis, inviting him to consider what has been laid down by the poets, "our fathers and guides in respect of wisdom".[1] Homer says that the Gods originate friendship, by bringing the like man to his like: Empedokles and other physical philosophers have also asserted, that like must always and of necessity be the friend of like. These wise teachers cannot mean (continues Sokrates) that bad men are friends of each other. The bad man can be no one's friend. He is not even like himself, but ever wayward and insane:—much less can he be like to any one else, even to another bad man. They mean that the good alone are like to each other, and friends to each other.[2] But is this true? What good, or what harm, can like do to like, which it does not also do to itself? How can there be reciprocal love between parties who render to each other no reciprocal aid? Is not the good man, so far forth as good, sufficient to himself,—standing in need of no one—and therefore loving no one? How can good men care much for each other, seeing that they thus neither regret each other when absent, nor have need of each other when present?

Questions addressed to Lysis. Appeal to the maxims of the poets. Like is the friend of like. Canvassed and rejected.

It appears, therefore, Lysis (continues Sokrates), that we are travelling in the wrong road, and must try another direction. I now remember to have recently heard some one affirming—contrary to what we have just said—that likeness is a cause of aversion, aud unlikeness a cause of friendship. He too produced evidence from the poets: for Hesiod tells us, that "potter is jealous of potter, and bard of bard". Things most alike are most full of envy, jealousy and hatred to each other: things most unlike, are most full of friendship. Thus the poor man is of necessity a friend to the rich, the weak man to the strong, for the sake of protection: the sick man, for similar reason, to the physician. In general, every ignorant man loves, and is a friend to, the man of knowledge. Nay, there are

Other poets declare that likeness is a cause of aversion; unlikeness, of friendship. Reasons pro and con. Rejected.

---

[1] Plato, Lysis, 213 E: σκοποῦντα κατὰ τοὺς ποιητάς· οὗτοι γὰρ ἡμῖν ὥσπερ πατέρες τῆς σοφίας εἰσὶ καὶ ἡγεμόνες.
[2] Plato, Lysis, 214.
[3] Plato, Lysis, 215 B: Ὁ δὲ μή του δεόμενος, οὐδέ τι ἀγαπῴη ἄν. . . . Ὁ δὲ μὴ ἀγαπῴη, οὐδ' ἂν φιλοῖ. . . . Πῶς οὖν οἱ ἀγαθοὶ τοῖς ἀγαθοῖς ἡμῖν φίλοι ἔσονται τὴν ἀρχήν, οἳ μήτε ἀπόντες ποθεινοὶ ἀλλήλοις—ἱκανοὶ γὰρ ἑαυτοῖς καὶ χωρὶς ὄντες—μήτε παρόντες χρείαν αὐτῶν ἔχουσι; τοὺς δὴ τοιούτους τίς μηχανὴ περὶ πολλοῦ ποιεῖσθαι ἀλλήλους;

also physical philosophers, who assert that this principle pervades all nature; that dry is the friend of moist, cold of hot, and so forth: that all contraries serve as nourishment to their contraries. These are ingenious teachers: but if we follow them, we shall have the cleverest disputants attacking us immediately, and asking—What! is the opposite essentially a friend to its opposite? Do you mean that unjust is essentially the friend of just —temperate of intemperate—good of evil? Impossible: the doctrine cannot be maintained.[1]

Confusion of Sokrates. He suggests, That the Indifferent (neither good nor evil) is friend to the Good.

My head turns (continues Sokrates) with this confusion and puzzle—since neither like is the friend of like, nor contrary of contrary. But I will now hazard a different guess of my own.[2] There are three genera in all: the good—the evil—and that which is neither good nor evil, the indifferent. Now we have found that good is not a friend to good—nor evil to evil— nor good to evil—nor evil to good. If therefore there exist any friendship at all, it must be the indifferent that is friend, either to its like, or to the good: for nothing whatever can be a friend to evil. But if the indifferent be a friend at all, it cannot be a friend to its own like; since we have already shown that like generally is not friend to like. It remains therefore, that the indifferent, in itself neither good nor evil, is friend to the good.[3]

Suggestion canvassed. If the Indifferent is friend to the Good, it is determined to become so by the contact of felt evil, from which it is anxious to escape.

Yet hold! Are we on the right scent? What reason is there to determine, on the part of the indifferent, attachment to the good? It will only have such attachment under certain given circumstances: when, though neither good nor evil in itself, it has nevertheless evil associated with it, of which it desires to be rid. Thus the body in itself is neither good nor evil: but when diseased, it has evil clinging to it, and becomes in consequence of this evil, friendly to the medical art as a remedy. But this is true only so long as the evil is only apparent, and not real: so long as it is a mere superficial appendage, and has not become incorporated with the

---
[1] Plato, Lysis, 215-216.   τὸς ἰλιγγιῶ ὑπὸ τῆς τοῦ λόγου ἀπορίας.
[2] Plato, Lysis, 216 C-D : τῷ ὄντι αὖ- —Λέγω τοίνυν ἀπομαντευόμενος, &c.
[3] Plato, Lysis, 216 D.

essential nature of the body. When evil has become engrained, the body ceases to be indifferent (*i.e.*, neither good nor evil), and loses all its attachment to good. Thus that which determines the indifferent to become friend of the good, is, the contact and pressure of accessory evil not in harmony with its own nature, accompanied by a desire for the cure of such evil.[1]

Under this head comes the explanation of the philosopher— the friend or lover of wisdom. The man already wise is not a lover of wisdom : nor the man thoroughly bad and stupid, with whose nature ignorance is engrained. Like does not love like, nor does contrary love contrary. The philosopher is intermediate between the two : he is not wise, but neither has he yet become radically stupid and unteachable. He has ignorance cleaving to him as an evil, but he knows his own ignorance, and yearns for wisdom as a cure for it.[2] *Principle illustrated by the philosopher. His intermediate condition— not wise, yet painfully feeling his own ignorance.*

The two young collocutors with Sokrates welcome this explanation heartily, and Sokrates himself appears for the moment satisfied with it. But he presently bethinks himself, and exclaims, Ah ! Lysis and Menexenus, our wealth is all a dream ! we have been yielding again to delusions ! Let us once more examine. You will admit that all friendship is on account of something and for the sake of something : it is relative both to some producing cause, and to some prospective end. Thus the body, which is in itself neither good nor evil, becomes when sick a friend to the medical art : on account of sickness, which is an evil—and for the sake of health, which is a good. The medical art is dear to us, because health is dear : but is there any thing behind, for *Sokrates dissatisfied. He originates a new suggestion. The Primum Amabile, or Object originally dear to us, per se: by relation or resemblance to which other objects become dear.*

---

[1] Plato, Lysis, 217 E : Τὸ μήτε κακὸν ἄρα μήτ᾽ ἀγαθὸν ἐνίοτε κακοῦ παρόντος οὔπω κακόν ἐστιν, ἔστι δ᾽ ὅτε ἤδη τὸ τοιοῦτον γέγονεν. Πάνυ γε. Οὐκοῦν ὅταν μήπω κακὸν ᾖ κακοῦ παρόντος, αὐτὴ μὲν ἡ παρουσία ἀγαθοῦ αὐτὸ ποιεῖ ἐπιθυμεῖν, ἡ δὲ κακὸν ποιοῦσα ἀποστερεῖ αὐτὸ τῆς τ᾽ ἐπιθυμίας ἅμα καὶ τῆς φιλίας τἀγαθοῦ. Οὐ γὰρ ἔτι ἐστὶν οὔτε κακὸν οὔτ᾽ ἀγαθόν, ἀλλὰ κακόν· φίλον δὲ ἀγαθῷ κακὸν οὐκ ἦν.

[2] Plato, Lysis, 218 A. διὰ ταῦτα δὴ φαῖμεν ἂν καὶ τοὺς ἤδη σοφοὺς μηκέτι φιλοσοφεῖν, εἴτε θεοὶ εἴτε ἄνθρωποί εἰσιν οὗτοι· οὐδ᾽ αὖ ἐκείνους φιλοσοφεῖν τοὺς οὕτως ἄγνοιαν ἔχοντας ὥστε κακοὺς εἶναι· κακὸν γὰρ καὶ ἀμαθῆ οὐδένα φιλοσοφεῖν. λείπονται δὴ οἱ ἔχοντες μὲν τὸ κακὸν τοῦτο, τὴν ἄγνοιαν, μήπω δὲ ὑπ᾽ αὐτοῦ ὄντες ἀγνώμονες μηδ᾽ ἀμαθεῖς, ἀλλ᾽ ἔτι ἡγούμενοι μὴ εἰδέναι ἃ μὴ ἴσασιν. διὸ δὴ φιλοσοφοῦσιν οἱ οὔτε ἀγαθοὶ οὔτε κακοί πω ὄντες. ὅσοι δὲ κακοί, οὐ φιλοσοφοῦσιν, οὐδὲ οἱ ἀγαθοί.

Compare Plato, Symposion, 204.

the sake of which health also is dear? It is plain that we cannot push the series of references onward for ever, and that we must come ultimately to something which is dear *per se*, not from reference to any ulterior *aliud*. We must come to some *primum amabile*, dear by its own nature, to which all other dear things refer, and from which they are derivatives.[1] It is this *primum amabile* which is the primitive, essential, and constant, object of our affections: we love other things only from their being associated with it. Thus suppose a father tenderly attached to his son, and that the son has drunk hemlock, for which wine is an antidote; the father will come by association to prize highly, not merely the wine which saves his son's life, but even the cup in which the wine is contained. Yet it would be wrong to say that he prizes the wine or the cup as much as his son: for the truth is, that all his solicitude is really on behalf of his son, and extends only in a derivative and secondary way to the wine and the cup. So about gold and silver: we talk of prizing highly gold and silver—but this is incorrect, for what we really prize is, not gold, but the ulterior something, whatever it be, for the attainment of which gold and other instrumental means are accumulated. In general terms—when we say that B is dear on account of A, we are really speaking of A under the name of B. What is really dear, is that primitive object of love, *primum amabile*, towards which all the affections which we bear to other things, refer and tend.[2]

Is it then true (continues Sokrates) that good is our *primum amabile*, and dear to us in itself? If so, is it dear to us on account of evil? that is, only as a remedy for evil; so that if evil were totally banished, good would cease to be prized? Is it true that evil is the cause why any thing is dear to us?[3] This cannot be: be-

The cause of love is desire. We desire that which is akin to us or our own.

---

[1] Plato, Lysis, 219 C-D. Ἆρ' οὖν οὐκ ἀνάγκη ἀπειπεῖν ἡμᾶς οὕτως ἰόντας, καὶ ἀφικέσθαι ἐπί τινα ἀρχὴν, ἢ οὐκέτ' ἐπανοίσει ἐπ' ἄλλο φίλον, ἀλλ' ἥξει ἐπ' ἐκεῖνο ὅ ἐστι πρῶτον φίλον, οὗ ἕνεκα καὶ τἆλλα φαμὲν πάντα φίλα εἶναι;

[2] Plato, Lysis, c. 37, p. 220 B. Ὅσα γάρ φαμεν φίλα εἶναι ἡμῖν ἕνεκα φίλου τινός, ἑτέρῳ ῥήματι φαινόμεθα λέγοντες αὐτό· φίλον δὲ τῷ ὄντι κινδυνεύει ἐκεῖνο αὐτὸ εἶναι, εἰς ὃ πᾶσαι αὗται αἱ λεγόμεναι φιλίαι τελευτῶσιν.

[3] Plato, Lysis, 220 D. We may see that in this chapter Plato runs into a confusion between τὸ διά τι and τὸ ἕνεκά του, which two he began by carefully distinguishing. Thus in 218 D he says, ὁ φίλος ἐστὶ τῷ φίλος—ἕνεκά του καὶ διά τι. Again 219 A, he says—τὸ σῶμα τῆς ἰατρικῆς φίλον ἐστίν, διὰ τὴν νόσον, ἕνεκα τῆς ὑγιείας. This is a very clear and important distinction.

It is continued in 220 D—ὅτι διὰ τὸ κακὸν τἀγαθὸν ἠγαπῶμεν καὶ ἐφιλοῦμεν,

cause even if all evil were banished, the appetites and desires, such of them as were neither good nor evil, would still remain : and the things which gratify those appetites will be dear to us. It is not therefore true that evil is the cause of things being dear to us. We have just found out another cause for loving and being loved—desire. He who desires, loves what he desires and as long as he desires : he desires moreover that of which he is in want, and he is in want of that which has been taken away from him—of his own.[1] It is therefore this *own* which is the appropriate object of desire, friendship, and love. If you two, Lysis and Menexenus, love each other, it is because you are somehow of kindred nature with each other. The lover would not become a lover, unless there were, between him and his beloved, a certain kinship or affinity in mind, disposition, tastes, or form. We love, by necessary law, that which has a natural affinity to us ; so that the real and genuine lover may be certain of a return of affection from his beloved.[2]

But is there any real difference between what is akin and what is like ? We must assume that there is : for we showed before, that like was useless to like, and therefore not dear to like. Shall we say that good

Good is of a nature akin to every one, evil is alien

ὡς φάρμακον ὂν τοῦ κακοῦ τὸ ἀγαθόν, τὸ δὲ κακόν νόσημα. But in 220 E—τὸ δὲ τῷ ὄντι φίλον πᾶν τοὐναντίον τούτου φαίνεται πεφυκός· φ ί λ ο ν γ ὰ ρ ἡ μ ῖ ν ἀ ν ε φ ά ν η ὂ ν ἐ χ θ ρ ο ῦ ἕ ν ε κ α. To make the reasoning consistent with what had gone before, these two last words ought to be exchanged for διὰ τὸ ἐχθρόν. Plato had laid down the doctrine that good is loved—διὰ τὸ κακόν, not ἕνεκα τοῦ κακοῦ. Good is loved on *account of evil*, but for *the sake of obtaining* a remedy to or cessation of the evil.

Steinhart (in his note on Hieron. Müller's translation of Plato, p. 268) calls this a "sophistisches Räthselspiel" ; and he notes other portions of the dialogue which "remind us of the deceptive tricks of the Sophists" (die Trugspiele der Sophisten, see pp. 222-224-227-230). He praises Plato here for his "fine pleasantry on the deceptive arts of the Sophists". Admitting that Plato puts forward sophistical quibbles with the word φίλος, he tells us that this is suitable for the purpose

of puzzling the contentious young man Menexenus. The confusion between ἕνεκά του and διά τι (noticed above) appears to be numbered by Steinhart among the fine jests against Protagoras, Prodikus, or some of the Sophists. I can see nothing in it except an unconscious inaccuracy in Plato's reasoning.

[1] Plato, Lysis, 221 E. Τὸ ἐπιθυμοῦν, οὗ ἂν ἐνδεὲς ᾖ, τούτου ἐπιθυμεῖ—ἐνδεὲς δὲ γίγνεται οὗ ἄν τις ἀφαιρῆται—τοῦ οἰκείου δή, ὡς ἔοικεν, ὅ τε ἔρως καὶ ἡ φιλία καὶ ἡ ἐπιθυμία τυγχάνει οὖσα. This is the same doctrine as that which we read, expanded and cast into a myth with comic turn, in the speech of Aristophanes in the Symposion, pp. 191-192-193. ἕκαστος οὖν ἡμῶν ἔστιν ἀνθρώπου σύμβολον, ἅτε τετμημένος ὥσπερ αἱ ψῆτται ἐξ ἑνὸς δύο. ζητεῖ δὴ ἀεὶ τὸ αὑτοῦ ἕκαστος ξύμβολον (191 D)—δικαίως ἂν ὑμνοῖμεν Ἔρωτα, ὃς ἔν τε τῷ παρόντι πλεῖστα ἡμᾶς ὀνίνησιν εἰς τὸ οἰκεῖον ἄγων, &c. (193 D).

[2] Plato, Lysis, 221-222.

to every one. is of a nature akin to every one, and evil of a nature foreign to every one? If so, then there can be no friendship except between one good man and another good man. But this too has been proved to be impossible. All our tentatives have been alike unsuccessful.

Inconsistency with what has been previously laid down.

In this dilemma (continues Sokrates, the narrator) I was about to ask assistance from some of the older men around. But the tutors of Menexenus and Lysis came up to us and insisted on conveying their pupils home—the hour being late. As the youths were departing I said to them— Well, we must close our dialogue with the confession, that we have all three made a ridiculous figure in it: I, an old man, as well as you two youths. Our hearers will go away declaring, that we fancy ourselves to be friends each to the other two; but that we have not yet been able to find out what a friend is.[1]

Failure of the enquiry. Close of the dialogue.

Thus ends the main discussion of the Lysis: not only without any positive result, but with speakers and hearers more puzzled than they were at the beginning: having been made to feel a great many difficulties which they never felt before. Nor can I perceive any general purpose running through the dialogue, except that truly Sokratic and Platonic purpose—To show, by cross-examination on the commonest words and ideas, that what every one appears to know, and talks about most confidently, no one really knows or can distinctly explain.[2] This is the meaning of the final declaration

Remarks. No positive result. Sokratic purpose in analysing the familiar words—to expose the false persuasion of knowledge.

---

[1] Plato, Lysis, 223 B. Νῦν μὲν καταγέλαστοι γεγόναμεν ἐγώ τε, γερὼν ἀνήρ, καὶ ὑμεῖς, &c.

[2] Among the many points of analogy between the Lysis and the Charmidês, one is, That both of them are declared to be spurious and unworthy of Plato, by Socher as well as by Ast (Ast, Platon's Leben, pp. 429-434; Socher, Ueber Platon, pp. 137-144).

Schleiermacher ranks the Lysis as second in his Platonic series of dialogues, an appendix to the Phædrus (Einl. p. 174 seq.); K. F. Hermann, Stallbaum, and nearly all the other critics dissent from this view: they place the Lysis as an early dialogue, along with Charmidês and Lachês, anterior to the Protagoras (K. F. Hermann, Gesch. und Syst. Plat. Phil. pp. 447-448; Stallbaum, Proleg. ad Lys. p. 90 (110 2nd ed.); Steinhart, Einl. p. 221) near to or during the government of the Thirty. All of them profess to discover in the Lysis "adolescentiæ vestigia".

Ast and Socher characterise the dialogue as a tissue of subtle sophistry and eristic contradiction, such as (in

put into the mouth of Sokrates. "We believe ourselves to be each other's friends, yet we none of us know what a friend is." The question is one, which no one had ever troubled himself to investigate, or thought it requisite to ask from others. Every one supposed himself to know, and every one had in his memory an aggregate of conceptions and beliefs which he accounted tantamount to knowledge: an aggregate generated by the unconscious addition of a thousand facts and associations, each separately unimportant and often inconsistent with the remainder: while no rational analysis had ever been applied to verify the consistency of this spontaneous product, or to define the familiar words in which it is expressed. The reader is here involved in a cloud of confusion respecting Friendship. No way out of it is shown, and how is he to find one? He must take the matter into his own active and studious meditation: which he has never yet done, though the word is always in his mouth, and though the topic is among the most common and familiar, upon which "the swain treads daily with his clouted shoon".

This was a proper subject for a dialogue of Search. In the dialogue Lysis, Plato describes Sokrates as engaged in one of these searches, handling, testing, and dropping, one point of view after another, respecting the idea and foundation of friendship. He speaks, professedly, as a diviner or guesser; following out obscure promptings which he does not yet understand himself.[1] In this character, he suggests several different explanations, not only distinct but inconsistent with each other; each of them true to a certain extent, under certain conditions and circumstances: but each of

Subject of Lysis suited for a Dialogue of Search. Manner of Sokrates, multiplying defective explanations, and showing reasons why each is defective.

their opinion) Plato cannot have composed. Stallbaum concedes the sophistry, but contends that it is put by Plato intentionally, for the purpose of deriding, exposing, disgracing, the Sophists and their dialectical tricks: "ludibrii causâ" (p. 88); "ut illustri aliquo exemplo demonstretur dialecticam istam, quam adolescentes magno quodam studio sectabantur, nihil esse aliud, nisi inanem quandam argutiarum captatricem," &c. (p. 87). Nevertheless he contends that along with this derisory matter there is intermingled serious reasoning which may be easily distinguished (p. 87), but which certainly he does not clearly point out. (Compare pp. 108-9-14-15, 2nd ed.) Schleiermacher and Steinhart also (pp. 222-224-227) admit the sophistry in which Sokrates is here made to indulge. But Steinhart maintains that there is an assignable philosophical purpose in the dialogue, which Plato purposely wrapped up in enigmatical language, but of which he (Steinhart) professes to give the solution (p. 228).

[1] Plato, Lysis, 216 D. λέγω τοίνυν ἀπομαντευόμενος, &c.

them untrue, when we travel beyond those limits: other contradictory considerations then interfering. To multiply defective explanations, and to indicate why each is defective, is the whole business of the dialogue.

The process of trial and error is better illustrated by a search without result than with result. Usefulness of the dialogue for self-working minds.

Schleiermacher discovers in this dialogue indications of a positive result not plainly enunciated: but he admits that Aristotle did not discover them—nor can I believe them to have been intended by the author.[1] But most critics speak slightingly of it, as alike sceptical and sophistical: and some even deny its authenticity on these grounds. Plato might have replied by saying that he intended it as a specimen illustrating the process of search for an unknown *quæsitum;* and as an exposition of what can be said for, as well as against, many different points of view. The process of trial and error, the most general fact of human intelligence, is even better illustrated when the search is unsuccessful: because when a result is once obtained, most persons care for nothing else and forget the antecedent blunders. To those indeed, who ask only to hear the result as soon as it is found, and who wait for others to look for it—such a dialogue as the Lysis will appear of little value. But to any one who intends to search for it himself, or to study the same problem for himself, the report thus presented of a previous unsuccessful search, is useful both as guidance and warning. Every one of the tentative solutions indicated in the Lysis has something in its favour, yet is nevertheless inadmissible. To learn the grounds which ultimately compel us to reject what at first appears admissible, is instruction not to be despised; at the very least, it helps to preserve us from mistake, and to state the problem in the manner most suitable for obtaining a solution.

In truth, no one general solution is attainable, such as Plato here professes to search for.[2] In one of the three Xenophontic dialogues wherein the subject of friend-

Subject of friendship, handled

---

[1] Schleiermacher, Einleitung zum Lysis, i. p. 177.

[2] Turgot has some excellent remarks on the hopelessness of such problems as that which Plato propounds, here as well as in other dialogues, to find definitions of common and vague terms.

We read in his article Etymologie, in the Encyclopédie (vol. iii. pp. 70-72 of his Œuvres Complets):

"Qu'on se représente la foule des acceptions du mot *esprit*, depuis son sens primitif *spiritus, haleine,* jusqu' à ceux qu'on lui donne dans la chimie,

ship is discussed we find the real Sokrates presenting both by it with a juster view of its real complications.[1] The phontic same remark may be made upon Aristotle's manner of Sokrates, handling friendship in the Ethics. He seems plainly Aristotle. to allude to the Lysis (though not mentioning it by name); and to profit by it at least in what he puts out of consideration, if not in what he brings forward.[2] He discards the physical and cosmical analogies, which Plato borrows from Empedokles and Herakleitus, as too remote and inapplicable: he considers that the question must be determined by facts and principles relating to human dispositions and conduct. In other ways, he circumscribes the problem, by setting aside (what Plato includes) all objects of attachment which are not capable of reciprocating attachment.[3] The problem, as set forth here by Plato, is conceived in great generality. In what manner does one man become the friend of another?[4] How does a man become the object

dans la littérature, dans la jurisprudence, *esprit acide*, esprit de Montaigne, *esprit des loix*, &c.—qu'on essaie d'extraire de toutes ces acceptions une idée qui soit commune à toutes—on verra s'évanouir tous les caractères qui distinguent *l'esprit* de toute autre chose, dans quelque sens qu'on le prenne. . . La multitude et l'incompatibilité des acceptions du mot *esprit*, sont telles, que personne n'a été tenté de les comprendre toutes dans une seule *définition*, et de définir l'esprit en général. Mais le vice de cette méthode n'est pas moins réel lorsqu'il n'est pas assez sensible pour empêcher qu'on ne la suive.

"A mesure que le nombre et la diversité des acceptions diminue, l'absurdité s'affoiblit: et quand elle disparoit, il reste encore l'erreur. J'ose dire, que presque toutes les *définitions* où l'on annonce qu'on va définir les choses *dans le sens le plus général*, ont ce défaut, et ne définissent véritablement rien : parceque leurs auteurs, en voulant renfermer toutes les acceptions d'un mot, ont entrepris une chose impossible : je veux dire, de rassembler sous une seule idée générale des idées très différentes entre elles, et qu'un même nom n'a jamais pu désigner que successivement, en cessant en quelque sorte d'être le même mot."

See also the remarks of Mr. John Stuart Mill on the same subject. System of Logic, Book IV. chap. 4, s. 5.

[1] See Xenophon, Memor. ii. 4-5-6. In the last of these three conversations (s. 21-22), Sokrates says to Kritobulus 'Ἀλλ' ἔχει μὲν ποικίλως πως ταῦτα, ὦ Κριτόβουλε· φύσει γὰρ ἔχουσιν οἱ ἄνθρωποι τὰ μὲν φιλικά· δέονται τε γὰρ ἀλλήλων, καὶ ἐλεοῦσι, καὶ συνεργοῦντες ὠφελοῦσι, καὶ τοῦτο συνιέντες χάριν ἔχουσιν ἀλλήλοις, τὰ δὲ πολεμικά· τά τε γὰρ αὐτὰ καλὰ καὶ ἡδέα νομίζοντες ὑπὲρ τούτων μάχονται, καὶ διχογνωμονοῦντες ἐναντιοῦνται· πολεμικὸν δὲ καὶ ἔρις καὶ ὀργή· καὶ δυσμενὲς μὲν ὁ τοῦ πλεονεκτεῖν ἔρως, μισητὸν δὲ ὁ φθόνος.

This observation of Sokrates is very true and valuable—that the causes of friendship and the causes of enmity are both of them equally natural, *i.e.* equally interwoven with the constant conditions of individual and social life. This is very different from the vague, partial, and encomiastic predicates with which τὸ φύσει is often decorated elsewhere by Sokrates himself, as well as by Plato and Aristotle.

[2] Aristot. Eth. Nikom. viii. i. p. 1155 b. Compare Plato, Lysis, 214 A—215 E.

[3] Aristot. Ethic. Nik. viii. 2, p. 1155, b. 28 ; Plato, Lysis, 212 D.

[4] Plato, Lysis, 212 A : ὄντινα τρόπον γίγνεται φίλος ἕτερος ἑτέρου. 223 ad fin. : ὃ, τί ἐστὶν ὁ φίλος.

of friendship or love from another? What is that object towards which our love or friendship is determined? These terms are so large, that they include everything belonging to the Tender Emotion generally.[1]

The debate in the Lysis is partly verbal : *i.e.*, respecting the word φίλος, whether it means the person loving, or the person loved, or whether it shall be confined to those cases in which the love is reciprocal, and then applied to both. Herein the question is about the meaning of words—a word and nothing more. The following portions of the dialogue enter upon questions not verbal but real—"Whether we are disposed to love what is like to ourselves, or what is unlike or opposite to ourselves?" Though both these are occasionally true, it is shown that as general explanations neither of them will hold. But this is shown by means of the following assumptions, which not only those whom Plato here calls the "very clever Disputants,"[2] but Sokrates himself at other times, would have called in question, viz. : "That bad men cannot be friends to each other—that men like to each

Debate in the Lysis partly verbal, partly real. Assumptions made by the Platonic Sokrates, questionable, such as the real Sokrates would have found reason for challenging.

---

[1] See the chapter on Tender Emotion in Mr. Bain's elaborate classification and description of the Emotions. 'The Emotions and the Will,' ch. vii. p. 94 seq. (3rd ed., p. 124).

In the Lysis, 216 C-D, we read, among the suppositions thrown out by Sokrates, about τὸ φίλον—κινδυνεύει κατὰ τὴν ἀρχαίαν παροιμίαν τὸ καλὸν φίλον εἶναι. ἔοικε γοῦν μαλακῷ τινι καὶ λείῳ καὶ λιπαρῷ· διὸ καὶ ἴσως ῥᾳδίως διολισθαίνει καὶ διαδύεται ἡμᾶς, ἅτε τοιοῦτον ὄν· λέγω γὰρ τἀγαθὸν καλὸν εἶναι. This allusion to the soft and the smooth is not very clear; a passage in Mr. Bain's chapter serves to illustrate it.

"Among the sensations of the senses we find some that have the power of awakening tender emotion. The sensations that incline to tenderness are, in the first place, the effects of very gentle or soft stimulants, such as soft touches, gentle sounds, slow movements, temperate warmth, mild sunshine. These sensations must be felt in order to produce the effect, which is mental and not simply organic. We have seen that an acute sensation raises a vigorous muscular expression, as in wonder; a contrast to this is exhibited by gentle pressure or mild radiance. Hence tenderness is passive emotion by pre-eminence: we see it flourishing best in the quiescence of the moving members. Remotely there may be a large amount of action stimulated by it, but the proper outgoing accompaniment of it is organic not muscular."

That the sensations of the soft and the smooth dispose to the Tender Emotion is here pointed out as a fact in human nature, agreeably to the comparison of Plato. Mr. Bain's treatise has the rare merit of describing fully the physical as well as the mental characteristics of each separate emotion.

[2] Plato, Lysis, 216 A.: οἱ πάνσοφοι ἄνδρες οἱ ἀντιλογικοί, &c. Yet Plato, in the Phædrus and Symposion, indicates colloquial debate as the great generating cause of the most intense and durable friendship. Aristeides the Rhetor says, Orat. xlvii. (Πρὸς Καπίτωνα), p. 418, Dindorf, ἐπεὶ καὶ Πλάτων τὸ ἀληθὲς ἁπανταχοῦ τιμᾷ, καὶ τὰς ἐν τοῖς λόγοις συνουσίας ἀφορμὴν φιλίας ἀληθινῆς ὑπολαμβάνει.

other (therefore good men as well as bad) can be of no use to each other, and therefore there can be no basis of friendship between them—that the good man is self-sufficing, stands in need of no one, and therefore will not love any one."[1] All these assumptions Sokrates would have found sufficient reason for challenging, if they had been advanced by Protagoras or any other opponents. They stand here as affirmed by him; but here, as elsewhere in Plato, the reader must apply his own critical intellect, and test what he reads for himself.

It is thus shown, or supposed to be shown, that the persons who love are neither the Good, nor the Bad: and that the objects loved, are neither things or persons similar, nor opposite, to the persons loving. Sokrates now adverts to the existence of a third category—Persons who are neither good, nor bad, but intermediate between the two—Objects which are intermediate between likeness and opposition. He announces as his own conjecture,[2] that the Subject of friendly or loving feeling, is, that which is neither good nor evil: the Object of the feeling, Good: and the cause of the feeling, the superficial presence of evil, which the subject desires to see removed.[3] The evil must be present in a superficial and removable manner—like whiteness in the hair caused by white paint, not by the grey colour of old age. Sokrates applies this to the state of mind of the philosopher, or lover of knowledge: who is not yet either thoroughly good or thoroughly bad,—either thoroughly wise or thoroughly unwise— but in a state intermediate between the two: ignorant, yet conscious of his own ignorance, and feeling it as a misfortune which he was anxious to shake off.[4]

Peculiar theory about friendship broached by Sokrates. Persons neither good nor evil by nature, yet having a superficial tinge of evil, and desiring good, to escape from it.

---

[1] Plato, Lysis, 214-215. The discourse of Cicero, De Amicitiâ, is composed in a style of pleasing rhetoric; suitable to Lælius, an ancient Roman senator and active politician, who expressly renounces the accurate subtlety of Grecian philosophers (v. 18). There is little in it which we can compare with the Platonic Lysis; but I observe that he too, giving expression to his own feelings, maintains that there can be no friendship except between the good and virtuous: a position which is refuted by the "nefaria vox," cited by himself as spoken by C. Blossius, xi. 37.

[2] Plato, Lysis, 216 D. λέγω τοίνυν ἀπομαντευόμενος, &c.

[3] Plato, Lysis, 216-217.

[4] Plato, Lysis, 218 C. λείπονται δὴ οἱ ἔχοντες μὲν τὸ κακὸν τοῦτο, τὴν ἄγνοιαν, μήπω δὲ ὑπ' αὐτοῦ ὄντες ἀγνώμονες μηδ' ἀμαθεῖς, ἀλλ' ἔτι ἡγούμενοι μὴ εἰδέναι ἃ μὴ ἴσασι· διὸ δὴ φιλοσοφοῦσιν οἱ οὔτε ἀγαθοὶ οὔτε κακοί πω ὄντες· ὅσοι δὲ κακοί,

This meaning of philosophy, though it is not always and consistently maintained throughout the Platonic writings, is important as expanding and bringing into system the position laid down by Sokrates in the Apology. He there disclaimed all pretensions to wisdom, but he announced himself as a philosopher, in the above literal sense: that is, as ignorant, yet as painfully conscious of his own ignorance, and anxiously searching for wisdom as a corrective to it: while most men were equally ignorant, but were unconscious of their own ignorance, believed themselves to be already wise, and delivered confident opinions without ever having analysed the matters on which they spoke.

This general theory illustrated by the case of the philosopher or lover of wisdom. Painful consciousness of ignorance the attribute of the philosopher. Value set by Sokrates and Plato upon this attribute.

The conversation of Sokrates (as I have before remarked) was intended, not to teach wisdom, but to raise men out of this false persuasion of wisdom, which he believed to be the natural state of the human mind, into that mental condition which he called philosophy. His Elenchus made them conscious of their ignorance, anxious to escape from it, and prepared for mental efforts in search of knowledge: in which search Sokrates assisted them, but without declaring, and even professing inability to declare, where that truth lay in which the search was to end. He considered that this change was in itself a great and serious improvement, converting what was evil, radical, and engrained—into evil superficial and removable; which was a preliminary condition to any positive acquirement. The first thing to be done was to create searchers after truth, men who would look at the subject for themselves with earnest attention, and make up their own individual convictions. Even if nothing ulterior were achieved, that alone would be a great deal. Such was the scope of the Sokratic conversation; and such the conception of philosophy (the capital peculiarity which Plato borrowed from Sokrates), which is briefly noted in this passage of the Lysis, and developed in other Platonic dialogues, especially in the Symposion,[1] which we shall reach presently.

Still, however, Sokrates is not fully satisfied with this hypo-

οὐ φιλοσοφοῦσιν, οὐδὲ οἱ ἀγαθοί. Compare the phrase of Seneca, Epist. 59, p. 211, Gronov.: " Elui difficile est: non enim inquinati sumus, sed infecti ". [1] Plato. Sympos. 202-203-204. Phædrus, 278 D.

thesis, but passes on to another. If we love anything, we must love it (he says) for the sake of something. This implies that there must exist, in the background, a something which is the primitive and real object of affection. The various things which we actually love, are not loved for their own sake, but for the sake of this *primum amabile*, and as shadows projected by it: just as a man who loves his son, comes to love by association what is salutary or comforting to his son—or as he loves money for the sake of what money will purchase. The *primum amabile*, in the view of Sokrates, is *Good;* particular things loved, are loved as shadows of good.

Another theory of Sokrates. The Primum Amabile, or original and primary object of Love. Particular objects are loved through association with this. The object is, Good.

This is a doctrine which we shall find reproduced in other dialogues. We note with interest here, that it appears illustrated, by a statement of the general law of mental association—the calling up of one idea by other ideas or by sensations, and the transference of affections from one object to others which have been apprehended in conjunction with it, either as antecedents or consequents. Plato states this law clearly in the Phædon and elsewhere:[1] but he here conceives it imperfectly: for he seems to believe that, if an affection be transferred by association from a primitive object A, to other objects, B, C, D, &c., A always continues to be the only real object of affection, while B, C, D, &c., operate upon the mind merely by carrying it back to A. The affection towards B, C, D, &c., therefore is, in the view of Plato, only the affection for A under other denominations and disguises.[2] Now this is doubtless often the case; but often also, perhaps even more generally, it is not the case. After a certain length of repetition and habit, all conscious reference to the primitive object of affection will commonly be left out, and the affection towards the secondary object will become a feeling both substantive and immediate. What was originally loved as means, for the sake of an ulterior end, will in time come to be loved as

Statement by Plato of the general law of mental association.

---

[1] Plato, Phædon, 73-74.
It is declared differently, and more clearly, by Aristotle in the treatise Περὶ Μνήμης καὶ Ἀναμνήσεως, pp. 451-452.
[2] Plato, Lysis, 220 B. ὅσα γάρ φαμεν φίλα εἶναι ἡμῖν ἕνεκα φίλου τινός, ἑτέρῳ ῥήματι φαινόμεθα λέγοντες αὐτό· φίλον δὲ τῷ ὄντι κινδυνεύει ἐκεῖνο αὐτὸ εἶναι, εἰς ὃ πᾶσαι αὗται αἱ λεγόμεναι φιλίαι τελευτῶσιν.

an end for itself; and to constitute a new centre of force, from whence derivatives may branch out. It may even come to be loved more vehemently than any primitive object of affection, if it chance to accumulate in itself derivative influences from many of those objects.[1] This remark naturally presents itself, when we meet here for the first time, distinctly stated by Plato, the important psychological doctrine of the transference of affections by association from one object to others.

Theory of the Primum Amabile, here introduced by Sokrates, with numerous derivative objects of love. Platonic Idea. Generic communion of Aristotle, distinguished by him from the feebler analogical communion.

The *primum amabile*, here introduced by Sokrates, is described in restricted terms, as valuable merely to correct evil, and as having no value *per se*, if evil were assumed not to exist. In consequence chiefly of this restriction, Sokrates discards it as unsatisfactory. Such restriction, however, is noway essential to the doctrine: which approaches to, but is not coincident with, the Ideal Good or Idea of Good, described in other dialogues as what every one yearns after and aspires to, though without ever attaining it and without even knowing what it is.[2] The Platonic Idea was conceived as a substantive, intelligible, Ens, distinct in its nature from all the particulars bearing the same name, and separated from them all by a gulf which admitted no gradations of nearer and farther— yet communicating itself to, or partaken by, all of them, in some inexplicable way. Aristotle combated this doctrine, denying the separate reality of the Idea, and admitting only a common generic essence, dwelling in and pervading the particulars, but pervading them all equally. The general word connoting this generic unity was said by Aristotle (retaining the Platonic phraseology) to be λεγόμενον κατὰ μίαν ἰδέαν or καθ' ἕν.

But apart from and beyond such generic unity, which implied a common essence belonging to all, Aristotle recognised a looser, more imperfect, yet more extensive, communion, founded upon

---

[1] There is no stronger illustration of this than the love of money, which is the very example that Plato himself here cites.

The important point to which I here call attention, in respect to the law of Mental Association, is forcibly illustrated by Mr. James Mill in his 'Analysis of the Human Mind,' chapters xxi. and xxii., and by Professor Bain in his works on the Senses and the Intellect,—Intellect, chap. i. sect. 47-48, p. 404 seq. ed. 3; and on the Emotions and the Will, chap. iv. sect. 4-5, p. 428 seq. (3rd ed. p. 363 seq.).

[2] Plato, Republ. vi. pp. 505-506.

CHAP. XX. GENERIC AND ANALOGICAL AGGREGATES. 193

common relationship towards some 'Ἀρχή—First Principle—or First Object. Such relationship was not always the same in kind : it might be either resemblance, concomitance, antecedence or consequence, &c. : it might also be different in degree, closer or more remote, direct or indirect. Here, then, there was room for graduation, or ordination of objects as former and latter, first, second, third, &c., according as, when compared with each other, they were more or less related to the common root.

This imperfect communion was designated by Aristotle under the title κατ' ἀναλογίαν, as contrasted with κατὰ γένος : the predicate which affirmed it was said to be applied, not κατὰ μίαν ἰδέαν or καθ' ἕν, but πρὸς μίαν φύσιν or πρὸς ἕν :[1] it was affirmed neither entirely συνωνύμως (which would imply generic communion), nor entirely ὁμωνύμως (which would be casual and imply no communion at all), but midway between the two, so as to admit of a graduated communion, and an arrangement as former and later, first cousin, or second, third cousin. Members

---

[1] Arist. Metaphys. Λ. 1072, a. 26-29 ; Bonitz, Comm. p. 497 id. Πρῶτον ὀρεκτόν—Πρῶτον νοητόν (πρῶτον ὀρεκτὸν —"quod per se appetibile est et concupiscitur"). "Quod autem primum est in aliquâ serie, id præcipue etiam habet qualitatem, quæ in reliquâ cernitur serie, c. a. 993, b. 24 : ergo prima illa substantia est τὸ ἄριστον"—also Γ. 1004, a. 25-26, 1005, a. 7, about the πρῶτον ἕν—πρῶτον ὄν. These were τὰ πολλαχῶς λεγόμενα—τὰ πλεοναχῶς λεγόμενα—which were something less than συνώνυμα and more than ὁμώνυμα; intermediate between the two, having no common λόγος or generical unity, and yet not entirely equivocal, but designating a κοινὸν κατ' ἀναλογίαν : not κατὰ μίαν ἰδέαν λεγόμενα, but πρὸς ἕν or πρὸς μίαν φύσιν ; having a certain relation to one common φύσις called τὸ πρῶτον. See the Metaphys. Γ. 1003, a. 33—τό δὲ ὂν λέγεται μὲν πολλαχῶς, ἀλλὰ πρὸς ἓν καὶ μίαν τινὰ φύσιν, καὶ οὐχ ὁμωνύμως, ἀλλ' ὥσπερ τὸ ὑγιεινὸν ἅπαν πρὸς ὑγιείαν, τὸ μὲν τῷ φυλάττειν, τὸ δὲ τῷ ποιεῖν, τὸ δὲ τῷ σημεῖον εἶναι τῆς ὑγιείας, τὸ δ' ὅτι δεκτικὸν αὐτῆς— καὶ τὸ ἰατρικὸν πρὸς ἰατρικήν, &c. The Scholion of Alexander upon this passage is instructive (p. 638, a. Brandis) ; and a very copious explanation of the whole doctrine is given by M. Brentano, in his valuable treatise, 'Von der mannigfachen Bedeutung des Seienden' nach Aristoteles,' Freiburg, 1862, pp. 85-108- 147. Compare Aristotel. Politic. III. i. 9, p. 1275, a. 35.

The distinction drawn by Aristotle between τὸ κοινὸν κατ' ἰδέαν and τὸ κοινὸν κατ' ἀναλογίαν— between τὰ κατὰ μίαν ἰδέαν λεγόμενα, and τὰ πρὸς ἓν or πρὸς μίαν φύσιν λεγόμενα—this distinction corresponds in part to that which is drawn by Dr. Whewell between classes which are given by Definition, and natural groups which are given by Type. "Such a natural group" (says Dr. Whewell) "is steadily fixed, though not precisely limited ; it is given, though not circumscribed ; it is determined, not by a boundary without but by a central point within, &c." The coincidence between this doctrine and the Aristotelian is real, though only partial : τὸ πρῶτον φίλον, τὸ πρῶτον ὀρεκτόν, may be considered as types of objects loveable, objects desirable, &c., but ἡ ὑγιεία cannot be considered as a type of τὰ ὑγιεινὰ nor ἡ ἰατρικὴ as a type of τὰ ἰατρικά, though it is "the central point" to which all things so called are referred. See Dr. Whewell's doctrine stated in the Philosophy of the Inductive Sciences, i. 476-477 ; and the comments of Mr. John Stuart Mill on the doctrine—'System of Logic,' Book iv. ch. 7. I have adverted to this same doctrine in remarking on the Hippias Major, supra, p. 47 ; also

of the same Genus were considered to be brothers, all on a par: but wherever there was this graduated cousinship or communion (signified by the words Former and Later, more or less in degree of relationship), Aristotle did not admit a common Genus, nor did Plato admit a Substantive Idea.[1]

Now the Πρῶτον φίλον or Primum Amabile which we find in the Lysis, is described as the principium or initial root of one of these imperfectly united aggregates; ramifying into many branches more or less distant, in obedience to one or other of the different laws of association. Aristotle expresses the same idea in another form of words: instead of a Primum Amabile, he gives us a Prima Amicitia—affirming that the diversities of friendship are not species comprehended under the same genus, but gradations or degeneracies departing in one direction or other from the First or pure Friendship. The Primum Amabile, in Plato's view, appears to be the Good, though he does not explicitly declare it: the Prima Amicitia, with Aristotle, is friendship subsisting between two good persons, who have had sufficient experience to know, esteem, and trust, each other.[2]

Primum Amabile of Plato, compared with the Prima Amicitia of Aristotle. Each of them is head of an analogical aggregate, not member of a generic family.

In regard to the Platonic Lysis, I have already observed that no positive result can be found in it, and that all the hypotheses broached are successively negatived. What is kept before the reader's mind, however, more than anything else, though not embodied in any distinct formula, is—The Good and the Beautiful considered as objects of love or attachment.

The Good and Beautiful, considered as objects of attachment.

---

on the Philêbus, infra, chap. 32, vol. III.

[1] This is attested by Aristotle, Eth. Nik. i. 64, p. 1096, a. 16. Οἱ δὲ κομίσαντες τὴν δόξαν ταύτην, οὐκ ἐποίουν ἰδέας ἐν οἷς τὸ πρότερον καὶ τὸ ὕστερον ἔλεγον· διόπερ οὐδὲ τῶν ἀριθμῶν ἰδέαν κατεσκεύαζον: compare Ethic. Eudem. i. 8, 1218, a. 2. He goes on to object that Plato, having laid this down as a general principle, departed from it in recognizing an ἰδέαν ἀγαθοῦ, because τἀγαθὸν was predicated in all the categories, in that of οὐσία as well as in that of πρός τι—τὸ δὲ καθ' αὑτὸ καὶ ἡ οὐσία πρότερον τῇ φύσει τοῦ πρός τι—ὥστε οὐκ ἂν εἴη κοινή τις ἐπὶ τούτων ἰδέα.

[2] Aristotel. Eth. Nikom. viii. 2, 1155, b. 12, viii. 5, 1157, a. 30, viii. 4; Eth. Eudem. vii. 2, 1236, a. 15. The statement is more full in the Eudemian Ethics than in the Nikomachean; he begins the seventh book by saying that φιλία is not said μοναχῶς but πλεοναχῶς; and in p. 1236 he says Ἀνάγκη ἄρα τρία φιλίας εἴδη εἶναι, καὶ μήτε καθ' ἓν ἁπάσας μηθ' ὡς εἴδη ἑνὸς γένους, μήτε πάμπαν λέγεσθαι ὁμωνύμως· πρὸς μίαν γάρ τινα λέγονται καὶ πρώτην, ὥσπερ τὸ ἰατρικόν, &c. The whole passage is instructive, but is too long to cite.

Bonitz gives some good explanations of these passages. Observationes Criticæ in Aristotelis quæ feruntur *Magna Moralia* et *Eudemia*, pp. 55-57.

CHAPTER XXI.

EUTHYDEMUS.

DRAMATIC vivacity, and comic force, holding up various persons to ridicule or contempt, are attributes which Plato manifests often and abundantly. But the dialogue in which these qualities reach their maximum, is, the Euthydêmus. Some portions of it approach to the Nubes of Aristophanes: so that Schleiermacher, Stallbaum, and other admiring critics have some difficulty in explaining, to their own satisfaction,[1] how Plato, the sublime moralist and lawgiver, can here have admitted so much trifling and buffoonery. Ast even rejects the dialogue as spurious; declaring it to be unworthy of Plato and insisting on various peculiarities, defects, and even absurdities, which offend his critical taste. His conclusion in this case has found no favour: yet I think it is based on reasons quite as forcible as those upon which other dialogues have been condemned:[2] upon reasons, which, even if admitted, might prove that the dialogue was an inferior performance, but would not prove that Plato was not the author. *Dramatic and comic exuberance of the Euthydêmus. Judgments of various critics.*

Sokrates recounts (to Kriton) a conversation in which he has just been engaged with two Sophists, Euthydêmus and Dionysodorus, in the undressing-room belonging to the gymnasium of the Lykeium. There were present, besides, Kleinias, a youth of remarkable beauty and intelligence, cousin of the great Alkibiades—Ktesippus, an adult man, yet still young, friend of Sokrates and devotedly attached to Kleinias *Scenery and personages.*

---

[1] Schleiermacher, Einleitung zum Euthydemos, vol. iii. pp. 400-403-407: Stallbaum, Proleg. in Euthydem. p. 14.
[2] Ast, Platon's Leben und Schriften, pp. 408-418.

—and a crowd of unnamed persons, partly friends of Kleinias, partly admirers and supporters of the two Sophists.

This couple are described and treated throughout by Sokrates, with the utmost admiration and respect: that is, in terms designating such feelings, but intended as the extreme of irony or caricature. They are masters of the art of Contention, in its three varieties [1]—1. Arms, and the command of soldiers. 2. Judicial and political rhetoric, fighting an opponent before the assembled Dikasts or people. 3. Contentious Dialectic— they can reduce every respondent to a contradiction, if he will only continue to answer their questions—whether what he says be true or false.[2] All or each of these accomplishments they are prepared to teach to any pupil who will pay the required fee: the standing sarcasm of Plato against the paid teacher, occurring here as in so many other places. Lastly, they are brothers, old and almost toothless—natives of Chios, colonists from thence to Thurii, and exiles from Thurii and resident at Athens, yet visiting other cities for the purpose of giving lessons.[3] Their dialectic skill is described as a recent acquisition,—made during their old age, only in the preceding year,—and completing their excellence as professors of the tripartite Eristic. But they now devote themselves to it more than to the other two parts. Moreover they advertise themselves as teachers of virtue.

Conversation carried on with Kleinias, first by Sokrates, next by the two Sophists.

The two Sophists, having announced themselves as competent to teach virtue and stimulate pupils to a virtuous life, are entreated by Sokrates to exercise their beneficent influence upon the youth Kleinias, in whose improvement he as well as Ktesippus feels the warmest interest. Sokrates gives a specimen of what he wishes by putting a series of questions himself. Euthydêmus follows, and begins questioning Kleinias; who, after answering

---

[1] Plato, Euthyd. pp. 271-272.
[2] Plat. Euthyd. p. 272 B. ἐξελέγχειν τὸ ἀεὶ λεγόμενον, ὁμοίως ἐάν τε ψεῦδος ἐάν τ' ἀληθὲς ᾖ: p. 275 C. οὐδὲν διαφέρει, ἐὰν μόνον ἐθέλῃ ἀποκρίνεσθαι ὁ νεανίσκος.
[3] Plat. Euthyd. p. 273 B-C. "quamvis essent ætate grandiores et *edentuli*," says Stallbaum in his Proleg. p. 10. He seems to infer this from page 294 C;

the inference, though not very certain, is plausible.
Steinhart, in his Einleitung zum Euthydemos (vol. ii. p. 2 of Hieronym. Müller's translation of Plato) repeats these antecedents of Euthydemus and Dionysodorus, as recited in the dialogue before us, as if they were matter of real history, exemplifications of the character of the class called Sophists. He

three or four successive questions, is forced to contradict himself. Dionysodorus then takes up the last answer of Kleinias, puts him through another series of interrogations, and makes him contradict himself again. In this manner the two Sophists toss the youthful respondent backwards and forwards to each other, each contriving to entangle him in some puzzle and contradiction. They even apply the same process to Sokrates, who cannot avoid being entangled in the net ; and to Ktesippus, who becomes exasperated, and retorts upon them with contemptuous asperity. The alternate interference of the two Sophists is described with great smartness and animation ; which is promoted by the use of the dual number, peculiar to the Greek language, employed by Plato in speaking of them.

This mode of dialectic, conducted by the two Sophists, is interrupted on two several occasions by a counter-exhibition of dialectic on the part of Sokrates : who, under colour of again showing to the couple a specimen of that which he wishes them to do, puts two successive batches of questions to Kleinias in his own manner.[1] The contrast between Sokrates and the two Sophists, in the same work, carried on respectively by him and by them, of interrogating Kleinias, is evidently meant as one of the special matters to arrest attention in the dialogue. The questions put by the couple are made to turn chiefly on verbal quibbles and ambiguities: they are purposely designed to make the respondent contradict himself, and are proclaimed to be certain of bringing about this result, provided the respondent will conform to the laws of dialectic—by confining his answer to the special point of the question, without adding any qualification of his own, or asking for farther explanation from the questioner, or reverting to any antecedent answer lying apart from the actual question of the moment. Sokrates, on the contrary, addresses interrogations, each of which has a clear and substantive meaning, and most of which Kleinias is able to answer without embarrassment : he professes no other design except that of encouraging Kleinias to

Contrast between the two different modes of interrogation.

---

might just as well produce what is said by the comic poets Eupolis and Aristophanes—the proceedings as recounted by the Sokratic disciple in the φροντιστήριον (Nubes)—as evidence about the character of Sokrates.

[1] Plat. Euthydèm. pp. 279-288.
[2] Plat. Euthyd. pp. 275 E—276 E. Πάντα τοιαῦτα ἡμεῖς ἐρωτῶμεν ἄφυκτα, pp. 287 B—295 B—296 A, &c.

virtue, and assisting him to determine in what virtue consists: he resorts to no known quibbles or words of equivocal import. The effect of the interrogations is represented as being, not to confound and silence the youth, but to quicken and stimulate his mind and to call forth an unexpected amount of latent knowledge: insomuch that he makes one or two answers very much beyond his years, exciting the greatest astonishment and admiration, in Sokrates as well as in Kriton.[1] In this respect, the youth Kleinias serves the same illustrative purpose as the youthful slave in the Menon:[2] each is supposed to be quickened by the interrogatory of Sokrates, into a manifestation of knowledge noway expected, nor traceable to any teaching. But in the Menon, this magical evocation of knowledge from an untaught youth is explained by the theory of reminiscence, pre-existence, and omniscience, of the soul: while in the Euthydêmus, no allusion is made to any such theory, nor to any other cause except the stimulus of the Sokratic cross-questioning.

In the dialogue *Euthydêmus*, then, one main purpose of Plato is to exhibit in contrast two distinct modes of questioning: one practised by Euthydemus and Dionysodorus; the other, by Sokrates. Of these two, it is the first which is shown up in the most copious and elaborate manner: the second is made subordinate, serving mainly as a standard of comparison with the first. We must take care however to understand in what the contrast between the two consists, and in what it does not consist.

Wherein this contrast does not consist.

The contrast does not consist in this—that Sokrates so contrives his string of questions as to bring out some established and positive conclusion, while Euthydemus and his brother leave everything in perplexity. Such is not the fact. Sokrates ends without any result, and with a confession of his inability to find any. Professing earnest anxiety to stimulate Kleinias in the path of virtue, he is at the same time unable to define what the

---

[1] Plat. Euthydêm. pp. 290-291. The unexpected wisdom, exhibited by the youth Kleinias in his concluding answer, can be understood only as illustrating the obstetric efficacy of Sokratic interrogations. See Winckelmann, Proleg. ad Euthyd. pp. xxxiii. xxxiv. The words τῶν κρειττόνων must have the usual signification, as recognised by Routh and Heindorf, though Schleiermacher treats it as absurd, p. 552, notes.

[2] Plato, Menon, pp. 82-85.

capital condition of virtue is.[1] On this point, then, there is no contrast between Sokrates and his competitors: if they land their pupil in embarrassment, so does he. Nor, again, does Sokrates stand distinguished from them by affirming (or rather implying in his questions) nothing but what is true and indisputable.[2]

The real contrast between the competitors, consists, first in the pretensions—next in the method. The two Sophists are described as persons of exorbitant arrogance, professing to teach virtue,[3] and claiming a fee as if they did teach it: Sokrates disdains the fee, doubts whether such teaching is possible, and professes only to encourage or help forward on the road a willing pupil. The pupil in this case is a given subject, Kleinias, a modest and intelligent youth: and the whole scene passes in public before an indiscriminate audience. To such a pupil, what is needed is, encouragement and guidance. Both of these are really administered by the questions of Sokrates, which are all suggestive and pertinent to the matter in hand, though failing to reach a satisfactory result: moreover, Sokrates attends only to Kleinias, and is indifferent to the effect on the audience around. The two Sophists, on the contrary, do not say a word pertinent to the object desired. Far from seeking (as they promised) to encourage Kleinias,[4] they confuse and humiliate him from the beginning: all their implements for teaching consist only of logical puzzles; lastly, their main purpose is to elicit applause from the by-standers, by reducing both the modest Kleinias and every other respondent to contradiction and standstill.

Wherein it does consist.

Such is the real contrast between Sokrates and the two Sophists, and such is the real scene which we read in the dialogue. The presence, as well as the loud manifestations of an indiscriminate crowd in the Lykeium, are essential features of the drama.[5] The

Abuse of fallacies by the Sophists—their bidding for the applause of

---

[1] Plat. Euthydêm. pp. 291 A—293 A; Plat. Kleitophon, pp. 409-410.

[2] See Plat. Euthydêm. p. 281 C-D, where undoubtedly the positions laid down by Sokrates would not have passed without contradiction by an opponent.

[3] Plat. Euthydêm. pp. 273 D, 275 A, 304 B.

[4] Plat. Euthyd. p. 278 C. ἐφάτην γὰρ ἐπιδείξασθαι τὴν προτρεπτικὴν σοφίαν.

[5] The ὄχλος (surrounding multitude) is especially insisted on in the first sentence of the dialogue, and is perpetually adverted to throughout all the recital of Sokrates to Kriton, pp. 276 B-D, 303 B.

the bystanders.   point of view which Plato is working out, is, the abusive employment, the excess, and the misplacement, of logical puzzles : which he brings before us as administered for the humiliation of a youth who requires opposite treatment,—in the prosecution of an object which they do not really promote—and before undiscerning auditors, for whose applause the two Sophists are bidding.[1] The whole debate upon these fallacies is rendered ridiculous ; and when conducted with Ktesippus, degenerates into wrangling and ribaldry.

The bearing of the Euthydêmus, as I here state it, will be better understood if we contrast it with the Parmenidês. In this last-mentioned dialogue, the amount of negative dialectic and contradiction is greater and more serious than that which we read in the Euthydêmus. One single case of it is elaborately built up in the long Antinomies at the close of the Parmenidês (which occupy as much space, and contain nearly as much sophistry, as the speeches assigned to the two Sophists in Euthydêmus), while we are given to understand that many more remain behind.[2] These perplexing Antinomies (addressed by the veteran Parmenidês to Sokrates as his junior), after a variety of other objections against the Platonic theory of Ideas, which theory Sokrates has been introduced as affirming,—are drawn up for the avowed purpose of checking premature affirmation, and of illustrating the difficult exercises and problems which must be solved, before affirmation can become justifiable. This task, though long and laborious, cannot be evaded (we are here told) by aspirants in philosophy. But it is a task which ought only to be undertaken in conjunction with a few select companions. "Before any large audience, it would be unseemly and inadmissible : for the public are not aware that without such roundabout and devious journey in all directions, no man can hit upon truth or acquire intelligence."[3]

Comparison of the Euthydêmus with the Parmenidês.

---

[1] Plat. Euthydêm. p. 303 B.

[2] Plato, Parmenid. p. 136 B. I shall revert to this point when I notice the Parmenidês.

[3] Plat. Parmen. pp. 135-136. ἕλκυσον δὲ σαυτὸν καὶ γύμνασαι μᾶλλον διὰ τῆς δοκούσης ἀχρήστου εἶναι καὶ καλουμένης ὑπὸ τῶν πολλῶν ἀδολεσχίας, ἕως ἔτι νέος εἶ—εἰ μὲν οὖν πλείους ἦμεν, οὐκ ἂν ἄξιον ἦν δεῖσθαι, (to request Parmenides to give a specimen of dialectic) ἀπρεπῆ γὰρ τὰ τοιαῦτα πολλῶν ἐναντίον λέγειν, ἄλλως τε καὶ τηλικούτῳ· ἀγνοοῦσι γὰρ οἱ πολλοὶ ὅτι ἄνευ ταύτης τῆς διὰ πάντων διεξόδου τε καὶ πλάνης, ἀδύνατον ἐντυχόντα τῷ ἀληθεῖ νοῦν σχεῖν.

COMPARISON WITH THE PARMENIDES. 201

This important proposition—That before a man can be entitled to lay down with confidence any affirmative theory, in the domain of philosophy or "reasoned truth," he must have had before him the various knots tied by negative dialectic, and must find out the way of untying them—is a postulate which lies at the bottom of Plato's Dialogues of Search, as I have remarked in the eighth chapter of this work. But there is much difference in the time, manner, and circumstances, under which such knots are brought before the student for solution. In the Parmenidês, the process is presented as one both serious and indispensable, yet requiring some precautions: the public must be excluded, for they do not understand the purpose: and the student under examination must be one who is competent or more than competent to bear the heavy burthen put upon him, as Sokrates is represented to be in the Parmenidês.[1] In the Euthydêmus, on the contrary, the process is intended to be made ridiculous; accordingly these precautions are disregarded. The crowd of indiscriminate auditors are not only present, but are the persons whose feelings the two Sophists address—and who either admire what is said as dexterous legerdemain, or laugh at the interchange of thrusts, as the duel becomes warmer: in fact, the debate ends with general mirth, in which the couple themselves are among the loudest. Lastly, Kleinias, the youth under interrogation, is a modest novice; not represented, like Lysis in the dialogue just reviewed, as in danger of corruption from the exorbitant flatteries of an Erastes, nor as requiring a lowering medicine to be administered by a judicious friend. When the Xenophontic (historical) Sokrates cross-examines and humiliates Euthydêmus (a youth, but nevertheless more advanced than Kleinias in the Platonic Euthydêmus is represented to be), we shall see that he not only lays a train for the process by antecedent suggestions, but takes especial care to attack Euthydêmus when alone.[3] The cross-examination

Necessity of settling accounts with the negative, before we venture upon the affirmative, is common to both: in the one the process is solitary and serious; in the other, it is vulgarised and ludicrous.

---

[1] See the compliments to Sokrates, on his strenuous ardour and vocation for philosophy, addressed by Parmenidês, p. 135 D.
[2] Plat. Euthyd. p. 303 B. Ἐνταῦθα μέντοι, ὦ φίλε Κρίτων, οὐδεὶς ὅστις οὐ τῶν παρόντων ὑπερεπῄνεσε τὸν λόγον, καὶ τὼ ἄνδρε (Euthydêmus and Dionysodorus) γελῶντε καὶ κροτοῦντε καὶ χαίροντε ὀλίγου παρετάθησαν.
[3] Xenophon. Memor. iv. 2, 5-8. ὡς δ' ᾔσθετο (Sokrates) αὐτὸν ἑτοιμότερον

pursued by Sokrates inflicts upon this accomplished young man the severest distress and humiliation, and would have been utterly intolerable, if there had been by-standers clapping their hands (as we read in the Platonic Euthydêmus) whenever the respondent was driven into a corner. We see that it was hardly tolerable even when the respondent was alone with Sokrates; for though Euthydêmus bore up against the temporary suffering, cultivated the society of Sokrates, and was handled by him more gently afterwards; yet there were many other youths whom Sokrates cross-examined in the same way, and who suffered so much humiliation from the first solitary colloquy, that they never again came near him (so Xenophon expressly tells us)[1] for a second. This is quite enough to show us how important is the injunction delivered in the Platonic Parmenidês—to carry on these testing colloquies apart from indiscriminate auditors, in the presence, at most, of a few select companions.

Opinion of Stallbaum and other critics about the Euthydêmus, that Euthydêmus and Dionysodorus represent the way in which Protagoras and Gorgias talked to their auditors.

Stallbaum, Steinhart, and other commentators denounce in severe terms the Eristics or controversial Sophists of Athens, as disciples of Protagoras and Gorgias, infected with the mania of questioning and disputing every thing, and thereby corrupting the minds of youth. They tell us that Sokrates was the constant enemy of this school, but that nevertheless he was unjustly confounded with them by the comic poets, and others; from which confusion alone his unpopularity with the Athenian people arose.[2] In the Platonic dialogue of Euthydêmus the two Sophists (according to these commentators) represent the way in which Protagoras and Gorgias with their disciples reasoned: and the purpose of the dialogue is to contrast this with the way in which Sokrates reasoned.

That opinion is unfounded.

Now, in this opinion, I think that there is much of unfounded assumption, as well as a misconception of the real contrast intended in the Platonic Euthydêmus. Compar-

---

ὑπομένοντα, ὅτε διαλέγοιτο, καὶ προθυμότερον ἀκούοντα, μόνος ἦλθεν εἰς τὸ ἡνιοποιεῖον· παρακαθεζομένου δ' αὐτῷ τοῦ Εὐθυδήμου, Εἰπέ μοι, ἔφη, &c.
[1] Xen. Mem. iv. 2, 39-40. Compare the remarks of Sokrates in Plato, Theætêtus, p. 151 C.
[2] Stallbaum, Prolegg. ad Plat. Euthydêm. pp. 9-11-13; Winckelmann, Proleg. ad eundem, pp. xxxiii.-xxxiv.

CHAP. XXI. SOKRATES AN ERISTIC. 203

ing Protagoras with Sokrates, I maintain that Sokrates was decidedly the more Eristic of the two, and left behind him a greater number of active disciples. In so far as we can trust the picture given by Plato in the dialogue called Protagoras, we learn that the Sophist of that name chiefly manifested himself in long continuous speeches or rhetoric; and though he also professed, if required, to enter into dialectic colloquy, in this art he was no match for Sokrates.[1] Moreover, we know by the evidence of Sokrates himself, that *he* was an Eristic not only by taste, but on principle, and by a sense of duty. He tells us, in the Platonic Apology, that he felt himself under a divine mission to go about convicting men of ignorance, and that he had prosecuted this vocation throughout many years of a long life. Every one of these convictions must have been brought about by one or more disputes of his own seeking: every such dispute, with occasional exceptions, made him unpopular, in the outset at least, with the person convicted: the rather, as his ability in the process is known, upon the testimony of Xenophon[2] as well as of Plato, to have been consummate. It is therefore a mistake to decry Protagoras and the Protagoreans (if there were any) as the special Eristics, and to represent Sokrates as a tutelary genius, the opponent of such habits. If the commentators are right (which I do not think they are) in declaring the Athenian mind to have been perverted by Eristic, Sokrates is much more chargeable with the mischief than Protagoras. And the comic poets, when they treated Sokrates as a specimen and teacher of Eristic, proceeded very naturally upon what they actually saw or heard of him.[3]

Sokrates was much more Eristic than Protagoras, who generally manifested himself by continuous speech or lecture.

The fact is, that the Platonic Sokrates when he talks with the two Sophists in the dialogue Euthydêmus, is a character drawn by Plato for the purpose of that dialogue, and is very different from the real historical Sokrates,

Sokrates in the Euthydêmus is drawn suit-

---

[1] See Plat. Protag., especially pp. 329 and 336. About the eristic disposition of Sokrates, see the striking passage in Plato, Theætêt. 169 B-C; also Lachês, 187, 188.
[2] Xen. Mem. i. 2.
[3] Stallbaum, Proleg. in Platon.

Euthydêm. pp. 50-51. "Sed hoc utcunque se habet, illud quidem ex Aristophane pariter atque ex ipso Platone evidenter apparet, Socratem non tantum ab orationum scriptoribus, sed etiam ab aliis, in vanissimorum sophistarum loco habitum fuisse."

ably to the purpose of that dialogue. whom the public of Athens saw and heard in the market-place or gymnasia. He is depicted as a gentle, soothing, encouraging talker, with his claws drawn in, and affecting inability even to hold his own against the two Sophists: such indeed as he sometimes may have been in conversing with particular persons (so Xenophon [1] takes pains to remind his readers in the Memorabilia), but with entire elimination of that characteristic aggressive Elenchus for which he himself (in the Platonic Apology) takes credit, and which the auditors usually heard him exhibit.

This picture, accurate or not, suited the dramatic scheme of the Euthydêmus. Such, in my judgment, is the value and meaning of the Euthydêmus, as far as regards personal contrasts. One style of reasoning is represented by Sokrates, the other by the two Sophists: both are the creatures of Plato, having the same dramatic reality as Sokrates and Strepsiades, or the Δίκαιος Λόγος and Ἄδικος Λόγος, of Aristophanes, but no more.

The two Sophists in the Euthydêmus are not to be taken as real persons, or representatives of real persons.

That they correspond to any actual persons at Athens, is neither proved nor probable. The comic poets introduce Sokrates as talking what was either nonsensical, or offensive to the feelings of the Athenians: and Sokrates (in the Platonic Apology) complains that the Dikasts judged him, not according to what he had really said or done, but according to the impression made on them by this dramatic picture. The Athenian Sophists would have equal right to complain of those critics, who not only speak of Euthydêmus and Dionysodorus with a degree of acrimony applicable only to historical persons, but also describe them as representative types of Protagoras, Gorgias, and their disciples.[2]

The conversation of Sokrates with the youth Kleinias is

---

[1] Xen. Mem. i. 4, 1; iv. 2, 40.

[2] The language of Schleiermacher is more moderate than that of Stallbaum, Steinhart, and others. He thinks moreover, that the polemical purpose of this dialogue is directed not against Protagoras or Gorgias, but against the Megarics and against Antisthenes, who (so Schleiermacher supposes) had brought the attack upon themselves by attacking Plato first (Einleitung zum Euthyd. p. 404 seq.). Schleiermacher cannot make out who the two Sophists were personally, but he conceives them as obscure persons, deserving no notice.

This is a conjecture which admits of no proof; but if any real victim is here intended by Plato, we may just as reasonably suppose Antisthenes as Protagoras.

remarkable for its plainness and simplicity. His purpose is to implant or inflame in the youth the aspiration and effort towards wisdom or knowledge (φιλοσοφία, in its etymological sense). "You, like every one else, wish to do well or to be happy. The way to be happy is, to have many good things. Every one knows this: every one knows too, that among these good things, wealth is an indisputable item:[1] likewise health, beauty, bodily activity, good birth, power over others, honour in our city, temperance, justice, courage, wisdom, &c. Good fortune does not count as a distinct item, because it resolves itself into wisdom.[2]—But it is not enough to have all these good things: we must not only have them but use them: moreover, we must use them not wrongly, but rightly. If we use them wrongly, they will not produce their appropriate consequences. They will even make us more miserable than if we had them not, because the possession of them will prompt us to be active and meddlesome: whereas, if we have them not, we shall keep in the back-ground and do little.[3] But to use these good things rightly, depends upon wisdom, knowledge, intelligence. It thus appears that the enumerated items are not really good, except on the assumption that they are under the guidance of intelligence: if they are under the guidance of ignorance, they are not good; nay, they even produce more harm than good, since they are active instruments in the service of a foolish master.[4]

Colloquy of Sokrates with Kleinias—possession of good things is useless, unless we also have intelligence how to use them.

"But what intelligence do we want for the purpose? Is it *all* intelligence? Or is there any one single variety of intelligence, by the possession of which we shall become good and happy?[5] Obviously, it must be such as will be profitable to us.[6] We have seen that

But intelligence—of what? It must be such intelligence, or

---

[1] Plato, Euthydêm. p. 279 A. ἀγαθὰ δὲ ποῖα ἄρα τῶν ὄντων τυγχάνει ἡμῖν ὄντα; ἢ οὐ χαλεπὸν οὐδὲ σεμνοῦ ἀνδρὸς πάνυ τι οὐδὲ τοῦτο ἔοικεν εἶναι εὑρεῖν; πᾶς γὰρ ἂν ἡμῖν εἴποι ὅτι τὸ πλουτεῖν ἀγαθόν;
[2] Plato, Euthydêm. pp. 279-280.
[3] Plato, Euthydêm. p. 281 C. ἧττον δὲ κακῶς πράττων, ἄθλιος ἧττον ἂν εἴη.
[4] Plato, Euthyd. p. 282 E. If we compare this with p. 279 C-D we shall

see that the argument of Sokrates is open to the exception which he himself takes in the case of εὐτυχία—δὶς ταὐτὰ λέγειν. Wisdom is counted twice over.
[5] Plato, Euthydêm. p. 282 E. Sokrates here breaks off the string of questions to Kleinias, but resumes them, p. 288 D.
[6] Plato, Euthydêm. p. 288 D. τίνα ποτ᾽ οὖν ἂν κτησάμενοι ἐπιστήμην ὀρθῶς

such an art, as will include both the making of what we want, and the right use of it when made. there is no good in possessing wealth—that we should gain nothing by knowing how to acquire wealth or even to turn stones into gold, unless we at the same time knew how to use it rightly. Nor should we gain any thing by knowing how to make ourselves healthy, or even immortal, unless we knew how to employ rightly our health or immortality. We want knowledge or intelligence, of such a nature, as to include both acting, making, or construction—and rightly using what we have done, made, or constructed.[1] The makers of lyres and flutes may be men of skill, but they cannot play upon the instruments which they have made: the logographers compose fine discourses, but hand them over for others to deliver. Even masters in the most distinguished arts—such as military commanders, geometers, arithmeticians, astronomers, &c., do not come up to our requirement. They are all of them varieties under the general class *hunters:* they find and seize, but hand over what they have seized for others to use. The hunter, when he has caught or killed game, hands it over to the cook; the general, when he has taken a town, delivers it to the political leader or minister: the geometer makes over his theorems to be employed by the dialectician or comprehensive philosopher.[2]

"Where then can we find such an art—such a variety of knowledge or intelligence—as we are seeking? The regal or political art looks like it: that art which regulates and enforces all the arrangements of the city. But what is the work which this art performs? What product does it yield, as the medical art supplies good health, and the farmer's art, provision? What good does it effect? You may say that it makes the citizens wealthy, free, harmonious in their intercourse. But we have already seen that these acquisitions are not good, unless they be under the guidance of intelligence: that nothing is really good, except some variety of intelligence.[3] Does the regal art then confer knowledge? If

Where is such an art to be found? The regal or political art looks like it; but what does this art do for us? No answer can be found. Ends in puzzle.

κτησαίμεθα; ἆρ' οὐ τοῦτο μὲν ἁπλοῦν, ὅτι ταύτην ἥτις ἡμᾶς ὀνήσει;
[1] Plato, Euthyd. p. 289 B. τοιαύτης τινὸς ἆρ' ἡμῖν ἐπιστήμης δεῖ, ἐν ᾗ συμπέπτωκεν ἅμα τό τε ποιεῖν καὶ τὸ ἐπίστασθαι χρῆσθαι ᾧ ἂν ποιῇ.
[2] Plato, Euthyd. p.290 C-D.
[3] Plato, Euthyd. p. 292 B. Ἀγαθὸν

so, does it confer every variety of knowledge—that of the carpenter, currier, &c., as well as others? Not certainly any of these, for we have already settled that they are in themselves neither good nor bad. The regal art can thus impart no knowledge except itself; and what is *itself*? how are we to use it? If we say, that we shall render other men *good*—the question again recurs, *Good*—in what respect? *useful*—for what purpose?[1]

"Here then" (concludes Sokrates), "we come to a dead lock : we can find no issue.[2] We cannot discover what the regal art does for us or gives us : yet this is the art which is to make us happy." In this difficulty, Sokrates turns to the two Sophists, and implores their help. The contrast between him and them is thus brought out.

The argument of Sokrates, which I have thus abridged from the Euthydêmus, arrives at no solution : but it is nevertheless eminently suggestive, and puts the question in a way to receive solution. What is the regal or political art which directs or regulates all others? A man has many different impulses, dispositions, qualities, aptitudes, advantages, possessions, &c., which we describe by saying that he is an artist, a general, a tradesman, clever, just, temperate, brave, strong, rich, powerful, &c. But in the course of life, each particular situation has its different exigencies, while the prospective future has its exigencies also. The whole man is one, with all these distinct and sometimes conflicting attributes : in following one impulse, he must resist others—in turning his aptitudes to one object, he must turn them away from others—he must, as Plato says, distinguish the right use of his force from the wrong, by virtue of knowledge, intelligence, reason. Such discriminating intelligence, which in this dialogue is called the Regal or political art,—what is the object of it? It is intelligence or knowledge,— But *of what*? Not certainly of the way how each particular act is to be performed—how each particular end is to be attained.

Review of the cross-examination just pursued by Sokrates. It is very suggestive —puts the mind upon what to look for.

δέ γέ που ὡμολογήσαμεν ἀλλήλοις— οὐδὲν εἶναι ἄλλο ἢ ἐπιστήμην τινά.
[1] Plat. Euthydêm. p. 292 D. Ἀλλὰ τίνα δὴ ἐπιστήμην; ἦ τί χρησόμεθα; τῶν μὲν γὰρ ἔργων οὐδενὸς δεῖ αὐτὴν δημιουργὸν εἶναι τῶν μήτε κακῶν μήτε ἀγαθῶν, ἐπιστήμην δὲ παραδιδόναι μηδεμίαν ἄλλην ἢ αὐτὴν ἑαυτήν · λέγωμεν δὴ οὖν, τίς ποτέ ἐστιν αὕτη ᾗ τί χρησόμεθα;
[2] Plat. Euthyd. p. 292 E.

Each of these separately is the object of some special knowledge. But the whole of a man's life is passed in a series of such particular acts, each of which is the object of some special knowledge: what then remains as the object of Regal or political intelligence, upon which our happiness is said to depend? Or how can it have any object at all?

Comparison with other dialogues— Republic, Philêbus, Protagoras. The only distinct answer is found in the Protagoras. The question here raised is present to Plato's mind in other dialogues, and occurs under other words, as for example, What is good? Good is the object of the Regal or political intelligence; but what is Good? In the Republic he raises this question, but declines to answer it, confessing that he could not make it intelligible to his hearers :[1] in the Gorgias, he takes pains to tell us what it *is not:* in the Philêbus, he does indeed tell us what it is, but in terms which need explanation quite as much as the term which they are brought to explain. There is only one dialogue in which the question is answered affirmatively, in clear and unmistakable language, and with considerable development—and that is, the Protagoras: where Sokrates asserts and proves at length, that Good is at the bottom identical with pleasure, and Evil with pain: that the measuring or calculating intelligence is the truly regal art of life, upon which the attainment of Good depends: and that the object of that intelligence—the items which we are to measure, calculate, and compare—is pleasures and pains, so as to secure to ourselves as much as possible of the former, and escape as much as possible of the latter.

In my remarks on the Protagoras, I shall state the view which I take of the doctrine laid down in that dialogue by Sokrates. Persons may think the answer insufficient: most of the Platonic critics declare it to be absolutely wrong. But at any rate it is the only distinct answer which Plato ever gives, to the question raised by Sokrates in the Euthydêmus and elsewhere.

From the abstract just given of the argument of Sokrates in *The talk of the two Sophists, though* the Euthydêmus, it will be seen to be serious and pertinent, though ending with a confession of failure. The observations placed in contrast with it and

---

[1] Plato, Republic, vi. pp. 505-506.

ascribed to the two Sophists, are distinguished by being neither serious nor pertinent; but parodies of debate for the most part, put together for the express purpose of appearing obviously silly to the reader. Plato keeps up the dramatic or ironical appearance, that they are admired and welcomed not only by the hearers, but even by Sokrates himself. Nevertheless, it is made clear at the end that all this is nothing but irony, and that the talk which Plato ascribes to Euthydêmus and Dionysodorus produced, according to his own showing, no sentiment of esteem for their abilities among the by-standers, but quite the reverse. Whether there were individual Sophists at Athens who talked in that style, we can neither affirm nor deny: but that there were an established class of persons who did so, and made both money and reputation by it, we can securely deny. It is the more surprising that the Platonic commentators should desire us to regard Euthydêmus and Dionysodorus as representative samples of a special class named Sophists, since one of the most eminent of those commentators (Stallbaum),[1] both admits that Sokrates himself was generally numbered in the class and called by the name—and affirms also (incorrectly, in my opinion) that the interrogations of Sokrates, which in this dialogue stand contrasted with those of the two Sophists, do not enunciate the opinions either of Sokrates or of Plato himself, but the opinions of these very Sophists, which Plato adopts and utters for the occasion.[2]

ironically admired while it is going on, is shown at the end to produce no real admiration, but the contrary.

---

[1] Stallbaum, Proleg. in Platon. Euthydem. p. 50. "Illud quidem ex Aristophane pariter atque ipso Platone evidenter apparet, Socratem non tantum ab orationum scriptoribus, sed etiam ab aliis in vanissimorum sophistarum numero habitum fuisse." Ib. p. 49 (cited in a previous note). "Videtur pervulgata fuisse hominum opinio, quâ Socratem inter vanos sophistas numerandum esse existimabant." Again p. 44, where Stallbaum tells us that Sokrates was considered by many to belong "misellorum Sophistarum gregi".

[2] Stallbaum, Proleg. ad Plat. Euthydem. p. 30. "Cavendum est magnopere, ne quæ hic à Socrate disputantur, pro ipsius decretis habeamus: *sunt enim omnia ad mentem Sophistarum disputata*, quos ille, reprehensis eorum opinionibus, sperat eo adductum iri, ut gravem prudentemque earum defensionem suscipiant." Compare p. 66. Stallbaum says that Plato often reasons, adopting for the occasion the doctrine of the Sophists. See his Prolegg. to the Lachês and Charmidês, and still more his Proleg. to the Protagoras, where he tells us that Plato introduces his spokesman Sokrates not only as arguing *ex mente Sophistarum*, but also as employing captious and delusive artifice, such as in this dialogue is ascribed to Euthydemus and Dionysodorus.—pp. 23-24. "Itaque Socrates, missâ hujus rei disputatione, repentè ad alia progreditur,

EUTHYDEMUS.

Mistaken representations about the Sophists —Aristotle's definition— no distinguishable line can be drawn between the Sophist and the Dialectician.

The received supposition that there were at Athens a class of men called Sophists who made money and reputation by obvious fallacies employed to bring about contradictions in dialogue—appears to me to pervert the representations given of ancient philosophy. Aristotle defines a Sophist to be "one who seeks to make money by apparent wisdom which is not real wisdom":—the Sophist (he says) is an Eristic who, besides money-making, seeks for nothing but victory in debate and humiliation of his opponent:—Distinguishing the Dialectician from the Sophist (he says), the Dialectician impugns or defends, by probable arguments, probable tenets—that is, tenets which are believed by a numerous public or by a few wise and eminent individuals :—while the Sophist deals with tenets which are probable only in appearance and not in reality—that is to say, tenets which almost every one by the slightest attention recognises as false.[1] This definition is founded, partly on the personal character and purpose ascribed to the Sophist: partly upon the distinction between apparent and real wisdom, assumed to be known and permanent.

Now such pseudo-wisdom was declared by Sokrates to be the natural state of all mankind, even the most eminent, which it was his mission to expose : moreover, the determination, what is to be comprised in this description, must depend upon the

scilicet *similibus laqueis* hominem denuo irretiturus. Nemini facilé obscurum erit, hoc quoque loco Protagoram *argutis conclusiunculis deludi*" (*i.e.* by Sokrates) "atque *callidé eo permoveri*," &c. "Quanquam nemo erit, quin videat, *callidé deludi Protagoram*, ubi ex eo, quod qui injusté faciat, is neutiquam agat σωφρόνως, protinus colligitur justitiam et σωφροσύνην unum idemque esse."—p. 25. "Disputat enim Socrates pleraque omnia ad mentem ipsius Protagoræ."— p. 30. " Platonem ipsum hæc non probâsse, sed e vulgi opinione et mente explicasse, vel illud non obscuré significat," &c.—p. 33.
[1] Aristotel. Topic. i. 1, p. 100, b. 21. ἔνδοξα δὲ τὰ δοκοῦντα πᾶσιν ἢ τοῖς πλείστοις ἢ τοῖς σοφοῖς, καὶ τούτοις ἢ πᾶσιν ἢ τοῖς πλείστοις ἢ τοῖς μάλιστα γνωρίμοις καὶ ἐνδόξοις. Ἐριστικὸς δὲ ἔστι συλλογισμὸς ὁ ἐκ φαινομένων ἐνδόξων, μὴ ὄντων δὲ—καὶ ὁ ἐξ ἐνδόξων ἢ φαινομένων ἐνδόξων φαινόμενος. Οὐθὲν γὰρ τῶν λεγομένων ἐνδόξων ἐπιπόλαιον ἔχει παντελῶς τὴν φαντασίαν, καθάπερ περὶ τὰς τῶν ἐριστικῶν λόγων ἀρχὰς συμβέβηκεν ἔχειν. Παραχρῆμα γὰρ καὶ ὡς ἐπὶ τὸ πολὺ τοῖς καὶ μικρὰ συνορᾶν δυναμένοις, κατάδηλος ἐν αὐτοῖς ἡ τοῦ ψεύδους ἔστι φύσις.
De Sophisticis Elenchis, i. p. 165, a. 21. ἔστι γὰρ ἡ σοφιστικὴ φαινομένη σοφία, οὖσα δ᾽ οὔ· καὶ ὁ σοφιστὴς χρηματιστὴς ἀπὸ φαινομένης σοφίας, ἀλλ᾽ οὐκ οὔσης, p. 165, b. 10, p. 171, b. 8-27. Οἱ φιλέριδες, ἐριστικοὶ, ἀγωνιστικοὶ, are persons who break the rules of dialectic (ἀδικομαχία) for the purpose of gaining victory ; οἱ σοφισταί are those who do the same thing for the purpose of getting money. See also Metaphys. iii. 1004, b. 17.

judges to whom it is submitted, since much of the works of Aristotle and Plato would come under the category, in the judgment of modern readers both vulgar and instructed. But apart from this relative and variable character of the definition, when applied to philosophy generally—we may confidently assert, that there never was any real class of intellectual men, in a given time or place, to whom it could possibly apply. Of individuals, the varieties are innumerable: but no professional body of men ever acquired gain or celebrity by maintaining theses, and employing arguments, which every one could easily detect as false. Every man employs sophisms more or less; every man does so inadvertently, some do it by design also; moreover, almost every reasoner does it largely, in the estimation of his opponents. No distinct line can be drawn between the Sophist and the Dialectician: the definition given by Aristotle applies to an ideal in his own mind, but to no reality without: Protagoras and Prodikus no more correspond to it than Sokrates and Plato. Aristotle observes, with great truth, that all men are dialecticians and testers of reasoning, up to a certain point: he might have added that they are all Sophists also, up to a certain point.[1] Moreover, when he attempts to found a scientific classification of intellectual processes upon a difference in the purposes of different practitioners—whether they employ the same process for money or display, or beneficence, or mental satisfaction to themselves—this is altogether unphilosophical. The medical art is the same, whether employed to advise gratis, or in exchange for a fee.[2]

Though I maintain that no class of professional Sophists (in the meaning given to that term by the Platonic critics after Plato and Aristotle) ever existed—and though the distinction between the paid and the gratuitous discourser is altogether unworthy to enter into the history of philosophy—yet I am not the less persuaded that the Platonic dialogue Euthydêmus, and the treatise of Aristotle De Sophisticis Elenchis, are very striking and useful compositions. This last- *Philosophical purpose of the Euthydêmus—exposure of fallacies, in Plato's dramatic manner, by multiplication of particular examples.*

---

[1] Aristot. Sophist. Elench. p. 172, a. 30.
[2] Aristot. Rhetor. i. 1, 1355, b. 18. He here admits that the only difference between the Dialectician and the Sophist lies in their purposes—that the

mentioned treatise was composed by Aristotle very much under the stimulus of the Platonic dialogue Euthydêmus, to which it refers several times—and for the purpose of distributing the variety of possible fallacies under a limited number of general heads, each described by its appropriate characteristic, and represented by its illustrative type. Such attempt at arrangement— one of the many valuable contributions of Aristotle to the theory of reasoning—is expressly claimed by him as his own. He takes a just pride in having been the first to introduce system where none had introduced it before.[1] No such system was known to Plato, who (in the Euthydêmus) enumerates a string of fallacies one after another without any project of classifying them, and who presents them as it were in concrete, as applied by certain disputants in an imaginary dialogue. The purpose is, to make these fallacies appear conspicuously in their character of fallacies: a purpose which is assisted by presenting the propounders of them as ridiculous and contemptible. The lively fancy of Plato attaches suitable accessories to Euthydêmus and Dionysodorus. They are old men, who have been all their lives engaged in teaching rhetoric and tactics, but have recently taken to dialectic, and acquired perfect mastery thereof without any trouble—who make extravagant promises—and who as talkers play into each other's hands, making a shuttlecock of the respondent, a modest novice every way unsuitable for such treatment.

Aristotle (Soph. Elench.) attempts a classification of fallacies: Plato enumerates them without classification.

Thus different is the Platonic manner, from the Aristotelian manner, of exposing fallacies. But those exhibited in the former appear as members of one or more among the classes framed by the latter. The fallacies which we read in the Euthydêmus are chiefly verbal: but some are verbal, and something beyond.

Thus, for example, if we take the first sophism introduced by the two exhibitors, upon which they bring the youth Kleinias, by suitable questions, to declare successively both sides of the alternative— "Which of the two is it that learns, the wise or the

Fallacies of equivoca-

---

mental activity employed by both is the same. ὁ γὰρ σοφιστικὸς οὐκ ἐν τῇ δυνάμει ἀλλ' ἐν τῇ προαιρέσει· πλὴν ἐνταῦθα μὲν (in Rhetoric) ἔσται ὁ μὲν κατὰ τὴν ἐπιστήμην ὁ δὲ κατὰ τὴν προαίρεσιν, ῥήτωρ, ἐκεῖ δὲ (in Dialectic)

σοφιστὴς μὲν κατὰ τὴν προαίρεσιν, δια- λεκτικὸς δὲ οὐ κατὰ τὴν προαίρεσιν, ἀλλὰ κατὰ τὴν δύναμιν.

[1] See the last chapter of the treatise De Sophisticis Elenchis.

ignorant?"—Sokrates himself elucidates it by pointing out that the terms used are equivocal:[1] You might answer it by using the language ascribed to Dionysodorus in another part of this dialogue — "Neither and Both".[2] The like may be said about the fallacy in page 284 D—" Are there persons who speak of things as they are? Good men speak of things as they are: they speak of good men well, of bad men badly: therefore, of course, they speak of stout men stoutly, and of hot men hotly. Ay! rejoins the respondent Ktesippus, angrily—they speak of cold men coldly, and say that they talk coldly."[3] These are fallacies of double meaning of words—or double construction of phrases: as we read also in page 287 D, where the same Greek verb (νοεῖν) may be construed either to *think* or to *mean*: so that when Sokrates talks about what a predication *means*—the Sophists ask him—"Does anything *think*, except things having a soul? Did you ever know any predication that had a soul?"

tion propounded by the two Sophists in the Euthydêmus.

Again, the two Sophists undertake to prove that Sokrates, as well as the youth Kleinias and indeed every one else, knows everything. "Can any existing thing *be* that which it is, and at the same time *not be* that which it is?—No.—You know some things?—Yes.— Then if you know, *you are knowing*?—Certainly. I am knowing of those particular things.—That makes no difference: if you are knowing, you necessarily know everything.—Oh! no: for there are many things which I do not know.—Then if there be anything which you do not know, *you are not knowing*? —Yes, doubtless—of that particular thing.—Still you are *not knowing*: and just now you said that you were *knowing*: and thus, at one and the same time, you are what you are, and you are not what you are.[4]

Fallacies—à dicto secundum quid, ad dictum simpliciter—in the Euthydêmus.

"But *you* also" (retorts Sokrates upon the couple), "do not

---

[1] Plato, Euthydêm. pp. 275 D—278 D. Aristotle also adverts to this fallacy, but without naming the Euthydêmus. See Soph. El. 4, 165, b. 30.

[2] Plato, Euthydêm. p. 300 D. Οὐδέτερα καὶ ἀμφότερα.

[3] Plato, Euthydêm. p. 284 E. τοὺς γοῦν ψυχροὺς ψυχρῶς λέγουσί τε καὶ φασὶ διαλέγεσθαι. The metaphorical sense of ψυχρὸς in criticism is *pointless, stupid, out of taste, out of place, &c.*

[4] Plato, Euthydêm. p. 293 C. Aristotle considers *know* to be an equivocal word; he admits that in certain senses you may both *know* and *not know* the same thing. Anal. Prior. ii. 67, b. 8. Anal. Post. i. 71, a. 25.

you also know some things, not know others?—By no means.—What! do you know nothing?—Far from it.—Then you know all things?—Certainly we do,—and you too : if you know one thing, you know all things.—What! do you know the art of the carpenter, the currier, the cobbler—the number of stars in the heaven, and of grains of sand in the desert, &c.?—Yes : we know all these things."

The two Sophists maintain their consistency by making reply in the affirmative to each of these successive questions: though Ktesippus pushes them hard by enquiries as to a string of mean and diverse specialties.[1] This is one of the purposes of the dialogue : to represent the two Sophists as willing to answer any thing, however obviously wrong and false, for the purpose of avoiding defeat in the dispute—as using their best efforts to preserve themselves in the position of questioners, and to evade the position of respondents—and as exacting a categorical answer —Yes or No—to every question which they put without any qualifying words, and without any assurance that the meaning of the question was understood.[2]

Obstinacy shown by the two Sophists in their replies—determination not to contradict themselves.

The base of these fallacious inferences is, That respecting the same subject, you cannot both affirm and deny the same predicate : you cannot say, A is knowing—A is not knowing ($\dot{\epsilon}\pi\iota\sigma\tau\dot{\eta}\mu\omega\nu$). This is a fallacy more than verbal : it is recognised by Aristotle (and by all subsequent logicians) under the name—*à dicto secundum quid, ad dictum simpliciter.*

It is very certain that this fallacy is often inadvertently committed by very competent reasoners, including both Plato and Aristotle.

Again—Sophroniskus was my father—Chæredemus was the father of Patrokles.—Then Sophroniskus was different from a father: therefore he was not a father. You are different from a stone, therefore you are not a stone : you are different from gold, therefore you are not gold. By parity of reasoning, Sophroniskus is different from a father— therefore he is not a father. Accordingly, you, Sokrates, have no father.[3]

Farther verbal equivocations.

---

[1] Plato, Euthydêm. pp. 293-294.   [2] Plato, Euthydêm. pp. 295-296.
[3] Plato, Euthydêm. pp. 297-298.

But (retorts Ktesippus upon the couple) your father is different from my father.—Not at all.—How can that be?—What! is your father, then, the father of all men and of all animals?— Certainly he is. A man cannot be at the same time a father, and not a father. He cannot be at the same time a man, and not a man—gold, and not gold.[1] You have got a dog (Euthydêmus says to Ktesippus).—Yes.— The dog is the father of puppies?—Yes.—The dog, being a father, is yours?—Certainly.—Then your father is a dog, and you are brother of the puppies.

You beat your dog sometimes? Then you beat your father.[2]

Those animals, and those alone are *yours* (sheep, oxen, &c.), which you can give away, or sell, or sacrifice at pleasure. But Zeus, Apollo, and Athênê are *your* Gods. The Gods have a soul and are animals. Therefore your Gods are your animals. Now you told us that those alone were your animals, which you could give away, or sell, or sacrifice at pleasure. Therefore you can give away, or sell, or sacrifice at pleasure, Zeus, Apollo, and Athênê.[3]

This fallacy depends upon the double and equivocal meaning of *yours*—one of its different explanations being treated as if it were the only one.

Other puzzles cited in this dialogue go deeper:—Contradiction is impossible—To speak falsely is impossible.[4] These paradoxes were maintained by Antisthenes and others, and appear to have been matters of dialectic debate throughout the fourth and third centuries. I shall say more of them when I speak about the Megarics and Antisthenes. Here I only note, that in this dialogue, Ktesippus is represented as put to silence by them, and Sokrates as making an answer which is no answer at all.[5] We see how much trouble these paradoxes gave

Fallacies involving deeper logical principles— contradiction is impossible. —To speak falsely is impossible.

---

[1] Plato, Euthydêm. p. 298. Some of the fallacies in the dialogue (Πότερον ὁρῶσιν οἱ ἄνθρωποι τὰ δυνατὰ ὁρᾷν ἢ τὰ ἀδύνατα; . . . Ἢ οὐχ οἷόν τε σιγῶντα λέγειν; p. 300 A) are hardly translatable into English, since they depend upon equivocal constructions peculiar to the Greek language. Aristotle refers them to the general head παρ' ἀμφιβολίαν. The same about προσήκει τὸν μάγειρον κατακόπτειν, p. 301 D.

[2] Plat. Euthyd. p. 298.

[3] Plat. Euthydêm. p. 302. This same fallacy, in substance, is given by Aristotle, De Sophist. El. 17, 176 a. 3, 179, a. 5, but with different exemplifying names and persons.

[4] Plato, Euthydêm. pp. 285-286.

[5] Plato, Euthydêm. pp. 286 B—287 A.

to Plato, when we read the Sophistês, in which he handles the last of the two in a manner elaborate, but (to my judgment) unsatisfactory.

The Euthydêmus of Plato is memorable in the history of philosophy as the earliest known attempt to set out, and exhibit to attention, a string of fallacious modes of reasoning. Plato makes them all absurd and ridiculous. He gives a caricature of a dialectic debate, not unworthy of his namesake Plato Comicus—or of Aristophanes, Swift, or Voltaire. The sophisms appear for the most part so silly, as he puts them, that the reader asks himself how any one could have been ever imposed upon by such a palpable delusion? Yet such confidence is by no means justified. A sophism, perfectly analogous in character to those which Plato here exposes to ridicule, may, in another case, easily escape detection from the hearer, and even from the reasoner himself. People are constantly misled by fallacies arising from the same word bearing two senses, from double construction of the same phrase, from unconscious application of a *dictum secundum quid*, as if it were a *dictum simpliciter;* from Petitio Principii, &c., Ignoratio Elenchi, &c. Neither Plato himself, nor Aristotle, can boast of escaping them.[1] If these fallacies appear, in the examples chosen by Plato for the Euthydêmus, so obviously inconclusive that they can deceive no one— the reason lies not in the premisses themselves, but in the particular conclusions to which they lead : which conclusions are known on other grounds to be false, and never to be seriously maintainable by any person. Such conclusions as—" Sokrates had no father : Sophroniskus, if father of Sokrates, was father of all men and all animals : In beating your dog, you beat your father : If you know one thing, you know everything," &c., being known *aliunde* to be false, prove that there has been some fallacy in the premisses whereby they have been established. Such cases serve as a *reductio ad absurdum* of the antecedent pro-

---

[1] See a passage in Plato's Charmidês, where Heindorf remarks with propriety upon his equivocal use of the words εὖ ζῆν and εὖ πράττειν—also the Gorgias, p. 507 D, with the notes of Routh and Heindorf. I have noticed both passages in discussing these two dialogues.

cess. They make us aware of one mode of liability to error, and put us on our guard against it in analogous cases. This is a valuable service, and all the more valuable, because the liability to error is real and widespread, even from fallacies perfectly analogous to those which seem so silly under the particular exemplifications which Plato selects and exposes. Many of the illustrations of the Platonic Euthydêmus are reproduced by Aristotle in the Treatise de Sophisticis Elenchis, together with other fallacies, discriminated with a certain method and system.[1]

The true character of these fallacies is very generally overlooked by the Platonic critics, in their appreciation of the Euthydêmus ; when they point our attention to the supposed tricks and frauds of the persons whom they called Sophists, as well as to mischievous corruptions alleged to arise from Eristic or formal contentious debate. These critics speak as if they thought that such fallacies were the special inventions of Athenian Sophists for the purposes of Athenian Eristic : as if such causes of error were inoperative on persons of ordinary honesty or intelligence, who never consulted or heard the Sophists. It has been the practice of writers on logic, from Aristotle down to Whately, to represent logical fallacies as frauds devised and maintained by dishonest practitioners, whose art Whately assimilates to that of jugglers. *Mistake of supposing fallacies to have been invented and propagated by Athenian Sophists— they are inherent inadvertencies and liabilities to error, in the ordinary process of thinking. Formal debate affords the best means of correcting them.*

This view of the case appears to me incomplete and misleading. It substitutes the rare and accidental in place of the constant and essential. The various sophisms, of which Plato in the Euthydêmus gives the *reductio ad absurdum*, are not the inventions of Sophists. They are erroneous tendencies of the reasoning process, frequently incident to human thought and speech : specimens of those ever-renewed "inadvertencies of ordinary thinking" (to recur to a phrase cited in my preface), which it is the peculiar mission of philosophy or "reasoned truth" to rectify. Moreover the practice of formal debate, which is usually denounced with so much asperity—if it affords on some occasions opportunity to produce such fallacies, presents not merely equal opportunity, but the only effective means, for exposing and con-

[1] Aristotle, De Sophist. Elench. ; also Arist. Rhet. ii. p. 1401, a-b.

futing them. Whately in his Logic,[1] like Plato in the Euthydêmus, when bringing these fallacies into open daylight in order that every one may detect them, may enliven the theme by presenting them as the deliberate tricks of a Sophist. Doubtless they are so by accident : yet their essential character is that of infirmities incident to the *intellectus sibi permissus* : operative at Athens before Athenian Sophists existed, and in other regions also, where these persons never penetrated.

Widespread prevalence of erroneous belief, misguided by one or other of these fallacies, attested by Sokrates, Plato, Bacon, &c., —complete enumeration of heads of fallacies by Mill.

The wide diffusion and constant prevalence of such infirmities is attested not less by Sokrates in his last speech, wherein he declares real want of knowledge and false persuasion of knowledge, to be universal, the mission of his life being to expose them, though he could not correct them—than by Bacon in his reformatory projects, where he enumerates the various Idola worshipped by the human intellect, and the false tendencies acquired "*in primâ digestione mentis*". The psychological analysis of the sentiment of belief with its different sources, given in Mr. Alexander Bain's work on the Emotions and the Will, shows how this takes place; and exhibits true or sound belief, in so far as it ever is acquired, as an acquisition only attained after expulsion of earlier antecedent error.[2] Of such error, and

---

[1] Whately's Logic, ch. v. sect. 5. Though Whately, like other logicians, keeps the Sophists in the foreground, as the fraudulent enemy who sow tares among that which would otherwise come up as a clean crop of wheat—yet he intimates also incidentally how widespread and frequent such fallacies are, quite apart from dishonest design. He says—" It seems by most persons to be taken for granted, that a Fallacy is to be dreaded merely as a weapon fashioned and wielded by a skilful Sophist: or, if they allow that a man may with honest intentions slide into one, unconsciously, in the heat of *argument*—still they seem to suppose, that where there is no *dispute*, there is no cause to dread Fallacy. Whereas there is much danger, even in what may be called *solitary reasoning*, of sliding unawares into some Fallacy, by which one may be so far deceived as even to act upon the conclusion so obtained. By *solitary reasoning*, is meant the case in which we are not seeking for arguments to prove a given question, but labouring to elicit from our previous stock of knowledge some useful inference."

"To speak of all the Fallacies that have ever been enumerated, as too glaring and obvious to need even being mentioned—because the simple instances given in books, and there stated in the plainest and consequently most easily detected form, are such as (in that form) would deceive no one—this, surely, shows either extreme weakness or extreme unfairness."—Aristotle himself makes the same remark as Whately —That the man who is easily taken in by a Fallacy advanced by another, will be easily misled by the like Fallacy in his own solitary reasoning. Sophist. Elench. 16, 175, a. 10.

[2] See the instructive and original chapter on the generation, sources, and growth of Belief, in Mr. Bain's work, 'Emotions and Will,' p. 568 seq. After laying down the fundamental

of the different ways in which apparent evidence is mistaken for real evidence, a comprehensive philosophical exposition is farther given by Mr. John Stuart Mill, in the fifth book of his System of Logic, devoted to the subject of Fallacies. Every variety of erroneous procedure is referable to some one or more of the general heads of Fallacy there enumerated. It is the Fallacies of Ratiocination, of which the two Sophists, in the Platonic Euthydêmus, are made to exhibit specimens: and when we regard such Fallacies, as one branch among several in a complete logical scheme, we shall see at once that they are not inventions of the Athenian Sophists—still less inventions for the purpose of Eristic or formal debate. For every one of these Fallacies is of a nature to ensnare men, and even to ensnare them more easily, in the common, informal, conversation of life—or in their separate thoughts. Besides mistakes on matters of fact, the two main

characteristic of Belief, as referable altogether to intended action, either certain to come, or contingent under supposed circumstances, and after enumerating the different Sources of Belief.—1. Intuitive or Instinctive. 2. Experience. 3. The Influence of the Emotions (sect. x. p. 579)—Mr. Bain says: "Having in our constitution primordial fountains of activity in the spontaneous and voluntary impulses, we follow the first clue that experience gives us, and accept the indication with the whole force of these natural promptings. Being under the strongest impulses to act somehow, an animal accepts any lead that is presented, and if successful, abides by that lead with unshaken confidence. This is that instinct of credulity so commonly attributed to the infant mind. It is not the single instance, or the repetition of two or three, that makes up the strong tone of confidence; it is the mind's own active determination, finding some definite vent in the gratification of its ends, and abiding by the discovery with the whole energy of the character, until the occurrence of some check, failure, or contradiction. The force of belief, therefore, is not one rising from zero to a full development by slow degrees, according to the length of the experience. We must treat it rather as a strong primitive manifestation, derived from the natural activity of the system, and taking its direction and rectification from experience (p. 583). The anticipation of nature, so strenuously repudiated by Bacon, is the offspring of this characteristic of the mental system. With the active tendency at its maximum, and the exercise of intelligence and acquired knowledge at the minimum, there can issue nothing but a quantity of rash enterprises. The respectable name *generalisation*, implying the best products of enlightened scientific research, has also a different meaning, expressing one of the most erroneous impulses and crudest determinations of untutored human nature. To extend some familiar and narrow experience, so as to comprehend cases the most distant, is a piece of mere reckless instinct, demanding severe discipline for its correction. I have mentioned the case of our supposing all other minds constituted like our own. The veriest infant has got this length in the career of fallacy. Sound belief, instead of being a pacific and gentle growth, is in reality the battering of a series of strongholds, the conquering of a country in hostile occupation. This is a fact common both to the individual and to the race. Observation is unanimous on the point. It will probably be long ere the last of the delusions attributable to this method of believing first and proving afterwards can be eradicated from humanity." [3rd ed., p. 505 seq.]

causes which promote the success and encourage the multiplication of Fallacies generally, are first, the emotional bias towards particular conclusions, which disposes persons to accept any apparent evidence, favourable to such conclusion, as if it were real evidence: next, the careless and elliptical character of common speech, in which some parts of the evidence are merely insinuated, and other parts altogether left out. It is this last circumstance which gives occasion to the very extensive class of Fallacies called by Mr. Mill Fallacies of Confusion: a class so large, that the greater number of Fallacies might plausibly be brought under it.[1]

[1] Mill, 'System of Logic,' Book V., to which is prefixed the following citation from Hobbes's 'Logica'. "Errare non modo affirmando et negando, sed etiam in sentiendo, et in tacitâ hominum cogitatione, contingit."

Mr. Mill points out forcibly both the operation of moral or emotional bias in perverting the intellect, and causing sophisms or fallacies to produce conviction; and the increased chance afforded for the success of a sophism by the suppression of part of the premisses, which is unavoidable in informal discussions.

"Bias is not a direct source of wrong conclusions (v. 1-3). We cannot believe a proposition only by wishing, or only by dreading, to believe it. Bias acts indirectly by placing the intellectual grounds of belief in an incomplete or distorted shape before a man's eyes. It makes him shrink from the irksome labour of a rigorous induction. It operates too by making him look out eagerly for reasons, or apparent reasons, to support opinions which are conformable, or resist those which are repugnant, to his interests or feelings; and when the interests or feelings are common to great numbers of persons, reasons are accepted or pass current which would not for a moment be listened to in that character, if the conclusion had nothing more powerful than its reasons to speak in its behalf. The natural or acquired prejudices of mankind are perpetually throwing up philosophical theories, the sole recommendation of which consists in the premisses which they afford for proving cherished doctrines, or justifying favourite feelings; and when any one of these theories has become so thoroughly discredited as no longer to serve the purpose, another is always ready to take its place."—"Though the opinions of the generality of mankind, when not dependent upon mere habit and inculcation, have their root much more in the inclinations than in the intellect, it is a necessary condition to the triumph of the moral bias that it should first pervert the understanding."

Again in v. 2, 3. "It is not in the nature of bad reasoning to express itself unambiguously. When a sophist, whether he is imposing upon himself or attempting to impose upon others, can be constrained to throw his argument into so distinct a form, it needs, in a large number of cases, no farther exposure. In all arguments, everywhere but in the schools, some of the links are suppressed: *à fortiori*, when the arguer either intends to deceive, or is a lame and inexpert thinker, little accustomed to bring his reasoning processes to any test; and it is in those steps of the reasoning which are made in this tacit and half-conscious, or even wholly unconscious, manner, that the error oftenest lurks. In order to detect the fallacy the proposition thus silently assumed must be supplied, but the reasoner, most likely, has never really asked himself what he was assuming; his confuter, unless permitted to extort it from him by the Socratic mode of interrogation, must himself judge what the suppressed premiss ought to be, in order to support the conclusion." Mr. Mill proceeds to illustrate this confusion by an excellent passage cited from Whately's 'Logic'. I may add, that Aristotle

VALUE OF FORMAL DEBATE.

We thus see not only that the fallacious agencies are self-operative, generating their own weeds in the common soil of human thought and speech, without being planted by Athenian Sophists or watered by Eristic — but that this very Eristic affords the best means of restraining their diffusion. It is only in formal debate that the disputant can be forced to make clear to himself and declare explicitly to others, without reserve or omission, all the premisses upon which his conclusion rests — that every part of these premisses becomes liable to immediate challenge by an opponent — that the question comes distinctly under consideration, what is or is not sufficient evidence — that the premisses of one argument can be compared with the premisses of another, so that if in the former you are tempted to acquiesce in them as sufficient because you have a bias favourable to the conclusion, in the latter you may be made to feel that they are *insufficient*, because the conclusion which they prove is one which you know to be untrue *(reductio ad absurdum)*. The habit of formal debate (called by those who do not like it, Eristic [1]) is thus an indispensable condition both for the exposure and confutation of fallacies, which exist quite independent of that habit — owing their rise and prevalence to deep-seated psychological causes.

Without the experience acquired by this habit of dialectic debate at Athens, Plato could not have composed his Euthydêmus, exhibiting a *reductio ad absurdum* of several verbal fallacies — nor could we have had the

Value of formal debate as a means for testing and confuting fallacies.

Without the habit of formal debate, Plato

himself makes a remark substantially the same — That the same fallacy may be referred to one general head or to another, according to circumstances. Sophist. Elench. 33, 182, b. 10.

[1] The Platonic critics talk about the Eristics (as they do about the Sophists) as if that name designated a known and definite class of persons. This is altogether misleading. The term is vituperative, and was applied by different persons according to their own tastes.

Ueberweg remarks with great justice, that Isokrates called all speculators on philosophy by the name of Eristics. " Als ob jener Rhetor nicht (wie ja doch Spengel selbst gut nachgewiesen hat) alle und jede Spekulation mit dem Nahmen der Eristik bezeichnete."

(Untersuchungen über die Zeitfolge der Plat. Schriften, p. 257.) In reference to the distinction which Aristotle attempts to draw between Dialectic and Eristic — the former legitimate, the latter illegitimate — we must remark that even in the legitimate Dialectic the purpose prominent in his mind is that of victory over an opponent. He enjoins that you are not only to guard against your opponent, lest he should out-manœuvre you, but you are to conceal and disguise the sequence of your questions so as to out-manœuvre him. Χρὴ δ' ὅπερ φυλάττεσθαι παραγγέλλομεν ἀποκρινομένους, αὐτοὺς ἐπιχειροῦντας πειρᾶσθαι λανθάνειν. Anal. Prior. ii. 66, a. 32. Compare Topic. 108, a. 25, 156, a. 23, 164, b. 35.

logical theories of Aristotle, embodied in the Analytica and Topica with its annexed treatise De Sophisticis Elenchis, in which various fallacies are discriminated and classified. These theories, and the corollaries connected with them, do infinite honour to the comprehensive intellect of Aristotle: but he could not have conceived them without previous study of the ratiocinative process. He, as the first theorizer, must have had before him abundant arguments explicitly laid out, and contested, or open to be contested, at every step by an opponent.[1] Towards such habit of formal argumentation, a strong repugnance was felt by many of the Athenian public, as there is among modern readers generally: but those who felt thus, had probably little interest in the speculations either of Plato or of Aristotle. That the Platonic critics should themselves feel this same repugnance, seems to me not consistent with their admiration for the great dialectician and logician of antiquity: nor can I at all subscribe to their view, when they present to us the inherent infirmities of the human intellect as factitious distempers generated by the habit of formal debate, and by the rapacity of Protagoras, Prodikus, and others.

I think it probable that the dialogue of Euthydêmus, as far as the point to which I have brought it (*i.e.*, where Sokrates finishes his recital to Kriton of the conversation which he had had with the two Sophists), was among the most popular of all the Platonic dialogues: not merely because of its dramatic vivacity and charm of expression, but because it would be heartily welcomed by the numerous enemies of Dialectic at Athens. We must remember that in the estimation of most persons at Athens, Dialectic included Sokrates and all the *viri Sokratici* (Plato among them), just as much as the persons called Sophists. The discreditable picture here given of Euthydêmus and Dionysodorus, would be considered as telling against Dialectic and the Sokratic Elenchus generally: while the rhetors, and others who dealt in long continuous discourse, would treat it as a blow

---

[1] Mill, 'System of Logic,' Book VI. 1, 1. "Principles of Evidence and Theories of Method, are not to be constructed *à priori*. The laws of our rational faculty, like those of every other natural agency, are only got by seeing the agent at work."

inflicted upon the rival art of dialogue, by the professor of the dialogue himself. In Plato's view, the dialogue was the special and appropriate manifestation of philosophy.

That the natural effect of the picture here drawn by Plato, was, to justify the antipathy of those who hated philosophy—we may see by the epilogue which Plato has thought fit to annex: an epilogue so little in harmony with what has preceded, that we might almost imagine it to be an afterthought—yet obviously intended to protect philosophy against imputations. Sokrates having concluded the recital, in his ironical way, by saying that he intended to become a pupil under the two Sophists, and by inviting Kriton to be a pupil along with him—Kriton replies by saying that he is anxious to obtain instruction from any one who can give it, but that he has no sympathy with Euthydêmus, and would rather be refuted by him, than learn from him to refute in such a manner. Kriton proceeds to report to Sokrates the remarks of a by-stander (an able writer of discourses for the Dikastery) who had heard all that passed; and who expressed his surprise that Sokrates could have remained so long listening to such nonsense, and manifesting so much deference for a couple of foolish men. Nevertheless (continued the by-stander) this couple are among the most powerful talkers of the day upon philosophy. This shows you how worthless a thing philosophy is: prodigious fuss, with contemptible result—men careless what they say, and carping at every word that they hear.[1]

Margin note: Epilogue of Plato to the Dialogue, trying to obviate this inference by opponents—Conversation between Sokrates and Kriton.

Now, Sokrates (concludes Kriton), this man is wrong for depreciating philosophy, and all others who depreciate it are wrong also. But he was right in blaming *you*, for disputing with such a couple before a large crowd.

Sokr.—What kind of person is this censor of philosophy? Is he a powerful speaker himself in the Dikastery? Or is he only a composer of discourses to be spoken by others? *Krit.*—The latter. I do not think that he has ever spoken in court: but every one says that he knows judicial practice well, and that he composes admirable speeches.[2]

[1] Plat. Euthyd. pp. 304-305. [2] Plat. Euthyd. p. 305.

Sokr.—I understand the man. He belongs to that class whom Prodikus describes as the border-men between philosophy and politics. Persons of this class account themselves the wisest of mankind, and think farther that besides being such in reality, they are also admired as such by many: insomuch that the admiration for them would be universal, if it were not for the professors of philosophy. Accordingly they fancy, that if they could once discredit these philosophers, the prize of glory would be awarded to themselves, without controversy, by every one : they being in truth the wisest men in society, though liable, if ever they are caught in dialectic debate, to be overpowered and humbled by men like Euthydêmus.[1] They have very plausible grounds for believing in their own wisdom, since they pursue both philosophy and politics to a moderate extent, as far as propriety enjoins ; and thus pluck the fruit of wisdom without encountering either dangers or contests. *Krit.*—What do you say to their reasoning, Sokrates? It seems to me specious. *Sokr.*—Yes, it is specious, but not well founded. You cannot easily persuade them, though nevertheless it is true, that men who take a line mid-way between two pursuits, are *better* than either, if both pursuits be bad—*worse* than either, if both pursuits be good, but tending to different ends—*better* than one and *worse* than the other, if one of the pursuits be bad and the other good—*better* than both, if both be bad, but tending to different ends. Such being the case, if the pursuit of philosophy and that of active politics be both of them good, but tending to different objects, these men are inferior to the pursuers of one as well as of the other : if one be good, the other bad, they are worse than the pursuers of the former, better than the pursuers of the latter : if both be bad, they are better than either. Now I am sure that these men themselves account both philosophy and politics to be good. Accordingly, they are inferior both to philosophers and politicians :[2] they occupy only the third rank, though they pretend to be in the first. While

---

[1] Plat. Euthyd. p. 305 D. εἶναι μὲν γὰρ τῇ ἀληθείᾳ σφᾶς σοφωτάτους, 'ν δὲ τοῖς ἰδίοις λόγοις ὅταν ἀποληφθῶσιν, ὑπὸ τῶν ἀμφὶ Εὐθύδημον κολούεσθαι.

Οἱ ἀμφὶ Εὐθύδημον may mean Euthydêmus himself and alone; yet I incline to think that it here means Euthydêmus and his like.

[2] Plat. Euthyd. p. 306 B.

we pardon such a pretension, and refrain from judging these men severely, we must nevertheless recognise them for such as they really are. We must be content with every one, who announces any scheme of life, whatever it be, coming within the limits of intelligence, and who pursues his work with persevering resolution.[1]

Krit.—I am always telling you, Sokrates, that I too am embarrassed where to seek instructors for my sons. Conversation with you has satisfied me, that it is madness to bestow so much care upon the fortune and position of sons, and so little upon their instruction. Yet when I turn my eyes to the men who make profession of instructing, I am really astonished. To tell you the truth, every one of them appears to me extravagantly absurd,[2] so that I know not how to help forward my son towards philosophy. *Sokr.*— Don't you know, Kriton, that in every different pursuit, most of the professors are foolish and worthless, and that a few only are excellent and above price? Is not this the case with gymnastic, commercial business, rhetoric, military command? Are not most of those who undertake these pursuits ridiculously silly?[3] *Krit.*—Unquestionably: nothing can be more true. *Sokr.*—Do you think *that* a sufficient reason for avoiding all these pursuits yourself, and keeping your son out of them also? *Krit.*—No: it would be wrong to do so. *Sokr.*—Well then, don't do so. Take no heed about the professors of philosophy, whether they are good or bad; but test philosophy itself, well and carefully. If it shall appear to you worthless, dissuade not merely your sons, but every one else also, from following it.[4] But if it shall appear to you as valuable as I consider it to be, then take courage to pursue and practise it, you and your children both, according to the proverb.—

_{Kriton asks Sokrates for advice about the education of his sons —Sokrates cannot recommend a teacher— tells him to search for himself.}

[1] Plat. Euthyd. p. 306 C. συγγιγνώσκειν μὲν οὖν αὐτοῖς χρὴ τῆς ἐπιθυμίας καὶ μὴ χαλεπαίνειν, ἡγεῖσθαι μέντοι τοιούτους εἶναι οἷοί εἰσι· πάντα γὰρ ἄνδρα χρὴ ἀγαπᾶν, ὅστις καὶ ὁτιοῦν λέγει ἐχόμενον φρονήσεως πρᾶγμα, καὶ ἀνδρείως ἐπεξιὼν διαπονεῖται.
[2] Plato, Euthyd. p. 306 E. καί μοι δοκεῖ εἷς ἕκαστος αὐτῶν σκοποῦντι πάνυ ἀλλόκοτος εἶναι, &c.
[3] Plato, Euthyd. p. 307 B. ἐν ἑκάστῃ τούτων τοὺς πολλοὺς πρὸς ἕκαστον τὸ ἔργον οὐ καταγελάστους ὁρᾷς;
[4] Plato, Euthyd. p. 307 B. ἐάσας χαίρειν τοὺς ἐπιτηδεύοντας φιλοσοφίαν, εἴτε χρηστοί εἰσιν εἴτε πονηροί, αὐτὸ τὸ πρᾶγμα βασανίσας καλῶς τε καὶ εὖ, ἐὰν μέν σοι φαίνηται φαυλὸν ὄν, &c.

2—15

Euthydêmus is here cited as representative of true Dialectic and philosophy.

The first part of this epilogue, which I have here given in abridgment, has a bearing very different from the rest of the dialogue, and different also from most of the other Platonic dialogues. In the epilogue, Euthydêmus is cited as the representative of true dialectic and philosophy: the opponents of philosophy are represented as afraid of being put down by Euthydêmus: whereas, previously, he had been depicted as contemptible,—as a man whose manner of refuting opponents was more discreditable to himself than to the opponent refuted; and who had no chance of success except among hearers like himself. We are not here told that Euthydêmus was a bad specimen of philosophers, and that there were others better, by the standard of whom philosophy ought to be judged. On the contrary, we find him here announced by Sokrates as among those dreaded by men adverse to philosophy,—and as not undeserving of that epithet which the semi-philosopher cited by Kritôn applies to "one of the most powerful champions of the day".

Plato, therefore, after having applied his great dramatic talent to make dialectic debate ridiculous, and thus said much to gratify its enemies—changes his battery, and says something against these enemies, without reflecting whether it is consistent or not with what had preceded. Before the close, however, he comes again into consistency with the tone of the earlier part, in the observation which he assigns to Kritôn, that most of the professors of philosophy are worthless; to which Sokrates rejoins that this is not less true of all other professions. The concluding inference is, that philosophy is to be judged, not by its professors, but by itself; and that Kritôn must examine it for himself, and either pursue it or leave it alone, according as his own convictions dictated.

This is a valuable admonition, and worthy of Sokrates, laying full stress as it does upon the conscientious conviction which the person examining may form for himself. But it is no answer to the question of Kritôn; who says that he had already heard from Sokrates, and was himself convinced, that philosophy was of first-rate importance—and that he only desired to learn where he could find teachers to forward the progress of his son in it. As in so many other dialogues, Plato leaves the problem started, but unsolved. The impulse towards philosophy being assured, those who feel it ask Plato in what direction they are to move towards it. He gives no answer. He can neither perform the service himself, nor recommend any one else, as competent. We shall find such silence made matter of pointed animadversion, in the fragment called Kleitophon.

The person, whom Kriton here brings forward as the censor of Sokrates and the enemy of philosophy, is peculiarly marked. In general, the persons whom Plato ranks as enemies of philosophy are the rhetors and politicians: but the example here chosen is not comprised in either of these classes: it is a semi-philosopher, yet a writer of discourses for others. Schleiermacher, Heindorf, and Spengel, suppose that Isokrates is the person intended: Winckelmann thinks it is Thrasymachus: others refer it to Lysias, or Theodorus of Byzantium:[1] Socher and Stallbaum doubt whether any special person is intended, or any thing beyond some supposed representative of a class described by attributes. I rather agree with those who refer the passage to Isokrates. He might naturally be described as one steering a middle course between philosophy and rhetoric: which in fact he himself proclaims in the Oration De Permutatione, and which agrees with the language of Plato in the dialogue Phædrus, where Isokrates is mentioned by name along with Lysias. In the Phædrus, moreover, Plato speaks of Isokrates with unusual esteem, especially as a favourable contrast with Lysias, and as a person who, though not yet a philosopher, may be expected to improve, so as in no long time to deserve that appellation.[2] We

Who is the person here intended by Plato, half-philosopher, half-politician? Is it Isokrates?

---

[1] Stallbaum, Proleg. ad Euthyd. p. 47; Winckelmann, Proleg. p. xxxv.
  Heindorf, in endeavouring to explain the difference between Plato's language in the Phædrus and in the Euthydêmus respecting Isokrates, assumes as a matter beyond question the theory of Schleiermacher, that the Phædrus was composed during Plato's early years. I have already intimated my dissent from this theory.

[2] Plato, Phædrus, p. 278 E.
  I have already observed that I do not agree with Schleiermacher and the other critics who rank the Phædrus as the earliest or even among the earliest compositions of Plato. That it is of much later composition I am persuaded, but of what particular date can only be conjectured. The opinion of K. F. Hermann, Stallbaum, and others, that it was composed about the time when Plato began his school at Athens (387-386 B.C.) is sufficiently probable.
  The Euthydêmus may be earlier or may be later than the Phædrus. I incline to think it later. The opinion of Stallbaum (resting upon the mention of Alkibiadês, p. 275 A), that it was composed in or before 404 B.C., appears to me untenable (Stallbaum, Proleg. p. 64). Plato would not be

must remember that Plato in the Phædrus attacks by name, and with considerable asperity, first Lysias, next Theodorus and Thrasymachus the rhetors—all three persons living and of note. Being sure to offend all these, Plato might well feel disposed to avoid making an enemy of Isokrates at the same time, and to except him honourably by name from the vulgar professors of rhetoric. In the Euthydêmus (where the satire is directed not against the rhetors, but against their competitors the dialecticians or pseudo-dialecticians) he had no similar motive to address compliments to Isokrates: respecting whom he speaks in a manner probably more conformable to his real sentiments, as the unnamed representative of a certain type of character—a semi-philosopher, fancying himself among the first men in Athens, and assuming unwarrantable superiority over the genuine philosopher; but entitled to nothing more than a decent measure of esteem, such as belonged to sincere mediocrity of intelligence.

Variable feeling at different times, between Plato and Isokrates. That there prevailed at different times different sentiments, more or less of reciprocal esteem or reciprocal jealousy, between Plato and Isokrates, ought not to be matter of surprise. Both of them were celebrated teachers of Athens, each in his own manner, during the last forty years of Plato's life: both of them enjoyed the favour of foreign princes, and received pupils from outlying, sometimes distant, cities—from Bosphorus and Cyprus in the East, and from Sicily in the West. We know moreover that during the years immediately preceding Plato's death (347 B.C.), his pupil Aristotle, then rising into importance as a teacher of rhetoric, was engaged in acrimonious literary warfare, seemingly

likely to introduce Sokrates speaking of Alkibiadês as a deceased person, at whatever time the dialogue was composed. Nor can I agree with Steinhart, who refers it to 402 B.C. (Einleitung, p. 26). Ueberweg (Untersuch. über die Zeitfolge der Plat. Schr. pp. 265-267) considers the Euthydêmus later (but not much later) than the Phædrus, subsequent to the establishment of the Platonic school at Athens (387-386 B.C.) This seems to me more probable than the contrary.

Schleiermacher, in arranging the Platonic dialogues, ranks the Euthydêmus as an immediate sequel to the Menon, and as presupposing both Gorgias and Theætêtus (Einl. pp. 400-401). Socher agrees in this opinion, but Steinhart rejects it (Einleit. p. 26), placing the Euthydêmus immediately after the Protagoras, and immediately before the Menon and the Gorgias; according to him, Euthydêmus, Menon, and Gorgias, form a well marked Trilogy.

Neither of these arrangements rests upon any sufficient reasons. The chronological order cannot be determined.

of his own seeking, with Isokrates (then advanced in years) and some of the Isokratean pupils. The little which we learn concerning the literary and philosophical world of Athens, represents it as much distracted by feuds and jealousies. Isokrates on his part has in his compositions various passages which appear to allude (no name being mentioned) to Plato among others, in a tone of depreciation.[1]

Isokrates seems, as far as we can make out, to have been in early life, like Lysias, a composer of speeches to be spoken by clients in the Dikastery. This lucrative profession was tempting, since his family had been nearly ruined during the misfortunes of Athens at the close of the Peloponnesian war. Having gained reputation by such means, Isokrates became in his mature age a teacher of Rhetoric, and a composer of discourses, not for private use by clients, but for the general reader, on political or educational topics. In this character, he corresponded to the description given by Plato in the Euthydêmus: being partly a public adviser, partly a philosopher. But the general principle under which Plato here attacks him, though conforming to the doctrine of the Platonic Republic, is contrary to that of Plato in other dialogues. " You must devote yourself either wholly to philosophy, or wholly to politics : a mixture of the two is worse than either" —this agrees with the Republic, wherein Plato enjoins upon each man one special and exclusive pursuit, as well as with the doctrine maintained against Kalliklês in the Gorgias—but it differs from the Phædrus, where he ascribes the excellence of Perikles as a statesmen and rhetor, to the fact of his having acquired a large tincture of philosophy.[2] Cicero quotes this last passage as applicable to his own distinguished career, a combination of philosophy with politics. He dissented altogether from the doctrine here laid down by Plato in the Euthydêmus, and many other eminent men would have dissented from it also.

As a doctrine of universal application, in fact, it cannot be

---

[1] Isokrates, ad Philipp. Or. v. s. 14, p. 84; contra Sophistas, Or. xiii.; Or. xiii. s. 2-24, pp. 291-295 ; Encom. Helenæ, Or. x. init. ; Panathenaic. Or. xii. s. 126, p. 257 ; Or. xv. De Permutatione, s. 90, p. 440, Bekk.

[2] See the facts about Isokrates in a good Dissertation by H. P. Schroder, Utrecht, 1859, Quæstiones Isocrateæ, p. 51, seq.
Plato, Phædrus, p. 270; Plutarch, Periklês, c. 23 ; Plato, Republic, iii. p. 397.

[3] Cicero, De Orator. iii. 34, 138 ; Orator. iv. 14 ; Brutus, 11, 44.

defended. The opposite scheme of life (which is maintained by Isokrates in De Permutatione and by Kalliklês in the Platonic Gorgias)[1]—that philosophy is to be attentively studied in the earlier years of life as an intellectual training, to arm the mind with knowledge and capacities which may afterwards be applied to the active duties of life—is at least equally defensible, and suits better for other minds of a very high order. Not only Xenophon and other distinguished Greeks, but also most of the best Roman citizens, held the opinion which Plato in the Gorgias ascribes to Kalliklês and reprobates through the organ of Sokrates—That philosophical study, if prolonged beyond what was necessary for this purpose of adequate intellectual training, and if made the permanent occupation of life, was more hurtful than beneficial.[2] Certainly, a man may often fail in the attempt to combine philosophy with active politics. No one failed in such a career more lamentably than Dion, the friend of Plato—and Plato himself, when he visited Sicily to second Dion. Moreover Alkibiadês and Kritias were cited by Anytus and the other accusers of Sokrates as examples of the like mischievous conjunction. But on the other hand, Archytas at Tarentum (another friend of Plato and philosopher) administered his native city with success, as long (seemingly) as Periklês administered Athens. Such men as these two are nowise inferior either to the special

---

[1] Isokrates, De Permutatione, Or. xv. sect. 278-288, pp. 485-486, Bekk.; Plato, Gorgias, pp. 484-485.

[2] The half-philosophers and half-politicians to whom Sokrates here alludes, are characterised by one of the Platonic critics as "jene oberflächlichen und schwächlichen Naturen die sich zwischen beiden Richtungen stellen, und zur Erreichung selbstsüchtiger und beschränkter Zwecke von beiden aufnehmen was sie verstehen und was ihnen gefällt" (Steinhart, Einleit. p. 25). On the other hand we find in Tacitus a striking passage respecting the studies of Agricola in his youth at Massilia. "Memoriâ teneo, solitum ipsum narrare, se in primâ juventâ studium philosophiæ acrius, ultra quam concessum Romano ac senatori, hausisse —ni prudentia matris incensum ac flagrantem animum exercuisset: Scilicet sublime et erectum ingenium, pulchritudinem ac speciem excelsæ magnæque gloriæ vehementius quam lauté appetebat: retinuitque, quod est difficillimum, ex sapientiâ modum" (Vit. Agr. c. 4). Tacitus expresses himself in the same manner about the purpose with which Helvidius Priscus applied himself to philosophy (Hist. iv. 6): "non, ut plerique, ut nomine magnifico segne otium velaret, sed quo constantior adversus fortuita rempublicam capesseret".

Compare also the memorable passage in the Funeral Oration pronounced by Periklês (Thuc. ii. 40)—φιλοσοφοῦμεν ἄνευ μαλακίας, &c., which exhibits the like views.

Aulus Gellius (x. 22), who cites the doctrine which Plato ascribes to Kalliklês in the Gorgias (about the propriety of confining philosophy to the function of training and preparation for active pursuits), tries to make out that this was Plato's own opinion.

philosopher or to the special politician. Plato has laid down an untenable generality, in this passage of the Euthydêmus, in order to suit a particular point which he wished to make against Isokrates, or against the semi-philosopher indicated, whoever else he may have been.

CHAPTER XXII.

MENON.

THIS dialogue is carried on between Sokrates and Menon, a man of noble family, wealth, and political influence, in the Thessalian city of Larissa. He is supposed to have previously frequented, in his native city, the lectures and society of the rhetor Gorgias.[1] The name and general features of Menon are probably borrowed from the Thessalian military officer, who commanded a division of the Ten Thousand Greeks, and whose character Xenophon depicts in the Anabasis: but there is nothing in the Platonic dialogue to mark that meanness and perfidy which the Xenophontic picture indicates. The conversation between Sokrates and Menon is interrupted by two episodes: in the first of these, Sokrates questions an unlettered youth, the slave of Menon: in the second, he is brought into conflict with Anytus, the historical accuser of the historical Sokrates.

Persons of the Dialogue.

The dialogue is begun by Menon, in a manner quite as abrupt as the Hipparchus and Minos:

Menon.—Can you tell me, Sokrates, whether virtue is teachable—or acquirable by exercise—or whether it comes by nature—or in what other manner it comes? *Sokr.* —I cannot answer your question. I am ashamed to say that I do not even know what virtue is: and when I do not know what a thing is, how can I know any thing about its attributes or accessories? A man who does not know, Menon, cannot tell whether he is handsome, rich, &c., or the contrary. *Menon.*—Cer-

Question put by Menon— Is virtue teachable? Sokrates confesses that he does not know what virtue is. Surprise of Menon.

---

[1] Cicero notices Isokrates as having heard Gorgias in Thessaly (Orator. 53, 176).

CHAP. XXII.   IS VIRTUE TEACHABLE ?   233

tainly not. But is it really true, Sokrates, that you do not know what virtue is? Am I to proclaim this respecting you, when I go home?[1] *Sokr.*—Yes—undoubtedly : and proclaim besides that I have never yet met with any one who *did* know. *Menon.* —What! have you not seen Gorgias at Athens, and did not he appear to you to know? *Sokr.*—I have met him, but I do not quite recollect what he said. We need not consider what he said, since he is not here to answer for himself.[2] But you doubtless recollect, and can tell me, both from yourself, and from him, what virtue is? *Menon.*—There is *no difficulty* in telling you.[3]

Many commentators here speak as if such disclaimer on the part of Sokrates had reference merely to certain im- Sokrates stands alone in this confession. Unpopularity entailed by it. pudent pretensions to universal knowledge on the part of the Sophists. But this (as I have before remarked) is a misconception of the Sokratic or Platonic point of view. The matter which Sokrates proclaims that *he* does not know, is, what, not Sophists alone, but every one else also, professes to know well. Sokrates stands alone in avowing that he does not know it, and that he can find no one else who knows. Menon treats the question as one of no difficulty — one on which confessed ignorance was discreditable. "What!" says Menon, "am I really to state respecting you, that you do not know what virtue is?" The man who makes such a confession will be looked upon by his neighbours with surprise and displeasure—not to speak of probable consequences yet worse. He is one whom the multifarious agencies employed by King Nomos (which we shall find described more at length in the Protagoras) have failed to mould into perfect and uninquiring conformity, and he is still in process of examination to form a judgment for himself.

Menon proceeds to answer that there are many virtues : the virtue of a man—competence to transact the business Answer of Menon— plurality of of the city, and in such business to benefit his friends

---

[1] Plato, Menon, p. 71 B-C. Ἀλλὰ σύ, ὦ Σώκρατες, οὐδ᾽ ὅ τι ἀρετή ἐστιν οἶσθα, ἀλλὰ ταῦτα περὶ σοῦ καὶ οἴκαδε ἀπαγγέλλωμεν;

[2] Plato, Menon, p. 71 D. ἐκεῖνον μέντοι νῦν ἐῶμεν, ἐπειδὴ καὶ ἄπεστιν. Sokrates sets little value upon opinions unless where the person giving them is present to explain and defend : compare what he says about the uselessness of citation from poets, from whom you can ask no questions, Plato, Protagor. p. 347 E.

[3] Plato, Menon, p. 71 E. Ἀλλ᾽ οὐ χαλεπόν, ὦ Σώκρατες, εἰπεῖν, &c.

virtues, one belonging to each different class and condition. Sokrates enquires for the property common to all of them. and injure his enemies: the virtue of a woman—to administer the house well, preserving every thing within it, and obeying her husband: the virtue of a child, of an old man, a slave, &c. There is in short a virtue—and its contrary, a vice—belonging to each of us in every work, profession, and age.[1] But (replies Sokrates) are they not all the same, *quatenus* virtue? Health, *quatenus* Health, is the same in a man or a woman: is not the case similar with virtue? *Menon.*—Not exactly similar. *Sokr.*—How so? Though there are many diverse virtues, have not all of them one and the same form in common, through the communion of which they *are* virtues? In answer to my question, you ought to declare what this common form is. Thus, both the man who administers the city, and the woman who administers the house, must act both of them with justice and moderation. Through the same qualities, both the one and the other are good. There is thus some common constituent: tell me what it is, according to you and Gorgias? *Menon.*—It is to be competent to exercise command over men. *Sokr.*—But that will not suit for the virtue of a child or a slave. Moreover, must we not superadd the condition, to command justly, and not unjustly? *Menon.*—I think so: justice is virtue. *Sokr.*—Is it virtue—or is it one particular variety of virtue?[3] *Menon.*—How do you mean? *Sokr.*—Just as if I were to say about roundness, that it is not figure, but a particular variety of figure: because there are other figures besides roundness. *Menon.* —Very true: I say too, that there are other virtues besides justice —namely, courage, moderation, wisdom, magnanimity, and several others also. *Sokr.*—We are thus still in the same predicament. In looking for one virtue, we have found many; but we cannot find that one form which runs through them all. *Menon.*—I cannot at present tell what that one is.[4]

---

[1] Plato, Menon, p. 72 A. καθ' ἑκάστην γὰρ τῶν πράξεων καὶ τῶν ἡλικιῶν πρὸς ἕκαστον ἔργον ἑκάστῳ ἡμῶν ἡ ἀρετή ἐστιν. ὡσαύτως δὲ καὶ ἡ κακία.

Though Sokrates disapproves this method of answering—τὸ ἐξαριθμεῖν τὰς ἀρετάς (to use the expression of Aristotle)—yet Aristotle seems to think it better than searching for one general definition. See Politica, i. 13, p. 1260, a. 15-30, where he has the Platonic Menon in his mind.

[2] Plato, Menon, p. 73 D.
[3] Plato, Menon, p. 73 E. Πότερον ἀρετή, ὦ Μένων, ἡ ἀρετή τις;
[4] Plato, Menon, p. 74 A. οὐ γὰρ δύναμαί πω, ὦ Σώκρατες, ὡς σὺ ζητεῖς, μίαν ἀρετὴν λαβεῖν κατὰ πάντων.

Sokrates proceeds to illustrate his meaning by the analogies of figure and colour. You call *round* a figure, and *square* a figure: you call *white* and *black* both colour, the one as much as the other, though they are unlike and even opposite.[1] Tell me, What is this same common property in both, which makes you call both of them figure — both of them colour? Take this as a preliminary exercise, in order to help you in answering my enquiry about virtue.[2] Menon cannot answer, and Sokrates answers his own question. He gives a general definition, first of figure, next of colour. He first defines figure in a way which implies colour to be known. This is pointed out; and he then admits that in a good definition, suitable to genuine dialectical investigation, nothing should be implied as known, except what the respondent admits himself to know. Figure and colour are both defined suitably to this condition.[3]

Analogous cases cited — definitions of figure and colour.

All this preliminary matter seems to be intended for the purpose of getting the question clearly conceived as a general question—of exhibiting and eliminating the narrow and partial conceptions which often unconsciously substitute themselves in the mind, in place of that which ought to be conceived as a generic whole—and of clearing up what is required in a good definition. A generic whole, including various specific portions distinguishable from each other, was at that time little understood by any one. There existed no grammar, nor any rules of logic founded on analysis of the intellectual processes. To predicate of the genus what was true only of the species—to predicate as distinctively characterizing the species, what is true of the whole genus in which it is contained—to lose the integrity of the genus in its separate parcels or fragments [4]—these were errors which men had never yet been expressly taught to avoid. To assign the one common meaning, constituent of or connoted by a generic term,

Importance at that time of bringing into conscious view, logical subordination and distinctions — Neither logic nor grammar had then been cast into system.

---

[1] Plato, Menon, p. 74 D.
[2] Plato, Menon, c. 7, pp. 74-75.
Πειρῶ εἰπεῖν, ἵνα καὶ γένηταί σοι μελέτη πρὸς τὴν περὶ τῆς ἀρετῆς ἀπόκρισιν (75 A).
The purpose of practising the respondent is here distinctly announced.
[3] Plato, Menon, p. 75 C-E.
[4] Plato, Menon, p. 79 A. ἐμοῦ δεηθέντος σου μὴ καταγνύναι μηδὲ κερματίζειν τὴν ἀρετήν, &c. 79 B: ἐμοῦ δεηθέντος ὅλην εἰπεῖν τὴν ἀρετήν, &c.

had never yet been put before them as a problem. Such preliminary clearing of the ground is instructive even now, when formal and systematic logic has become more or less familiar: but in the time of Plato, it must have been indispensably required, to arrive at a full conception of any general question.[1]

Definition of virtue given by Menon; Sokrates pulls it to pieces. Menon having been thus made to understand the formal requisites for a definition, gives as his definition of virtue the phrase of some lyric poet—" To delight in, or desire, things beautiful, fine, honourable—and to have the power of getting them ". But Sokrates remarks that honourable things are good things, and that every one without exception desires good. No one desires evil except when he mistakes it for good. On this point all men are alike; the distinctive feature of virtue must then consist in the second half of the definition—in the power of acquiring good things, such as health, wealth, money, power, dignities, &c.[2] But the acquisition of these things is not virtuous, unless it be made consistently with justice and moderation: moreover the man who acts justly is virtuous, even though he does not acquire them. It appears then that every agent who acts with justice

[1] These examples of trial, error, and exposure, have great value and reflect high credit on Plato, when we regard them as an intellectual or propædeutic discipline, forcing upon hearers an attention to useful logical distinctions at a time when there existed no systematic grammar or logic. But surely they must appear degraded, as they are presented in the Prolegomena of Stallbaum, and by some other critics. We are there told that Plato's main purpose in this dialogue was to mock and jeer the Sophists and their pupil, and that for this purpose Sokrates is made to employ not his own arguments but arguments borrowed from the Sophists themselves—"ut callidé suam ipsius rationem occultare existimandus sit, quo magis illudat Sophistarum alumnum" (p. 15). "Quæ quidem argumentatio" (that of Sokrates) "admodum cavendum est ne pro Socraticâ vel Platonicâ accipiatur. Est enim prorsus ad mentem Sophistarum aliorumque id genus hominum comparata," &c. (p. 16). Compare pp. 12-13 seq.
The Sophists undoubtedly had no distinct consciousness, any more than other persons, of these logical distinctions, which were then for the first time pressed forcibly upon attention.

[2] Plato, Menon, p. 77 B. δοκεῖ τοίνυν μοι ἀρετὴ εἶναι, καθάπερ ὁ ποιητὴς λέγει, χαίρειν τε καλοῖσι καὶ δύνασθαι. καὶ ἐγὼ τοῦτο λέγω ἀρετὴν ἐπιθυμοῦντα τῶν καλῶν δυνατὸν εἶναι πορίζεσθαι.
Whoever this lyric poet was, his real meaning is somewhat twisted by Sokrates in order to furnish a basis for ethical criticism, as the song of Simonides is in the Protagoras. A person having power, and taking delight in honourable or beautiful things—is a very intelligible Hellenic idéal, as an object of envy and admiration. Compare Protagoras, p. 351 C: εἴπερ τοῖς καλοῖς ζώη ἡδόμενος. A poor man may be φιλόκαλος as well as a rich man: φιλοκαλοῦμεν μετ' εὐτελείας, is the boast of Periklês in the name of the Athenians, Thucyd. ii. 40.
Plato, Menon, p. 78 C. *Sokr.* Ἀγαθὰ δὲ καλεῖς οὐχὶ οἷον ὑγίειάν τε καὶ πλοῦτον; καὶ χρυσίον λέγω καὶ ἀργύριον κτᾶσθαι καὶ τιμὰς ἐν πόλει καὶ ἀρχάς; μὴ ἄλλ' ἄττα λέγεις τἀγαθὰ ἢ τὰ τοιαῦτα; *Menon.* Οὐκ· ἀλλὰ πάντα λέγω τὰ τοιαῦτα.

and moderation is virtuous. But this is nugatory as a definition of virtue: for justice and moderation are only known as parts of virtue, and require to be themselves defined. No man can know what a part of virtue is, unless he knows what virtue itself is.[1] Menon must look for a better definition, including nothing but what is already known or admitted.

Menon.—Your conversation, Sokrates, produces the effect of the shock of the torpedo: you stun and confound me: you throw me into inextricable perplexity, so that I can make no answer. I have often discoursed copiously—and, as I thought, effectively—upon virtue; but now you have shown that I do not even know what virtue is. *Sokr.*—If I throw you into perplexity, it is only because I am myself in the like perplexity and ignorance. I do not know what virtue is, any more than you: and I shall be glad to continue the search for finding it, if you will assist me.

Menon.—But how are you to search for that of which you are altogether ignorant? Even if you do find it, how can you ever know that you have found it? *Sokr.*—You are now introducing a troublesome doctrine, laid down by those who are averse to the labour of thought. They tell us that a man cannot search either for what he knows, or for what he does not know. For the former, research is superfluous: for the latter it is unprofitable and purposeless, since the searcher does not know what he is looking for.

I do not believe this doctrine (continues Sokrates). Priests, priestesses, and poets (Pindar among them) tell us, that the mind of man is immortal and has existed throughout all past time, in conjunction with successive bodies; alternately abandoning one body, or dying—and taking up new life or reviving in another body. In this perpetual succession of existences, it has seen every thing,—both here and in Hades and everywhere else—and has learnt every thing. But though thus omniscient, it has forgotten the larger portion of its knowledge. Yet what has

Menon complains that the conversation of Sokrates confounds him like an electric shock—Sokrates replies that he is himself in the same state of confusion and ignorance. He urges continuance of search by both.

But how is the process of search available to any purpose? No man searches for what he already knows; and for what he does not know, it is useless to search, for he cannot tell when he has found it.

Theory of reminiscence propounded by Sokrates—anterior immortality of the soul—

[1] Plato, Menon, p. 79.

what is called teaching is the revival and recognition of knowledge acquired in a former life, but forgotten.

been thus forgotten may again be revived. What we call learning, is such revival. It is reminiscence of something which the mind had seen in a former state of existence, and knew, but had forgotten. Since then all the parts of nature are analogous, or cognate —and since the mind has gone through and learnt them all—we cannot wonder that the revival of any one part should put it upon the track of recovering for itself all the rest, both about virtue and about every thing else, if a man will only persevere in intent meditation. All research and all learning is thus nothing but reminiscence. In our researches, we are not looking for what we do not know : we are looking for what we do know, but have forgotten. There is therefore ample motive, and ample remuneration, for prosecuting enquiries : and your doctrine which pronounces them to be unprofitable, is incorrect.[1]

Illustration of this theory— knowledge may be revived by skilful questions in the mind of a man thoroughly untaught. Sokrates questions the slave of Menon.

Sokrates proceeds to illustrate the position, just laid down, by cross-examining Menon's youthful slave, who, though wholly untaught and having never heard any mention of geometry, is brought by a proper series of questions to give answers out of his own mind, furnishing the solution of a geometrical problem. The first part of the examination brings him to a perception of the difficulty, and makes him feel a painful perplexity, from which he desires to obtain relief :[2] the second part guides his mind in the efforts necessary for fishing up a solution out of its own pre-existing, but forgotten, stores. True opinions, which he had long had within him without knowing it, are awakened by interrogation, and become cognitions. From the fact that the mind thus

---

[1] Plato, Menon, pp. 81 C-D. Ἅτε οὖν ἡ ψυχὴ ἀθάνατός τε οὖσα καὶ πολλάκις γεγονυῖα, καὶ ἑωρακυῖα καὶ τὰ ἐνθάδε καὶ τὰ ἐν Ἅιδου καὶ πάντα χρήματα, οὐκ ἔστιν ὅ τι οὐ μεμάθηκεν· ὥστε οὐδὲν θαυμαστὸν καὶ περὶ ἀρετῆς καὶ περὶ ἄλλων οἷόν τε εἶναι αὐτὴν ἀναμνησθῆναι ἅ γε καὶ πρότερον ἠπίστατο. Ἅτε γὰρ τῆς φύσεως ἁπάσης συγγενοῦς οὔσης καὶ μεμαθηκυίας τῆς ψυχῆς ἅπαντα, οὐδὲν κωλύει ἓν μόνον ἀναμνησθέντα, ὃ δὴ μάθησιν καλοῦσιν ἄνθρωποι, τἆλλα πάντα αὐτὸν ἀνευρεῖν, ἐάν τις ἀνδρεῖος ᾖ καὶ μὴ ἀποκάμνῃ ζητῶν. Τὸ γὰρ ζητεῖν ἄρα καὶ τὸ μανθάνειν ἀνάμνησις ὅλον ἐστίν.

[2] Plato, Menon, p. 84 C. Οἴει οὖν ἂν αὐτὸν πρότερον ἐπιχειρῆσαι ζητεῖν ἢ μανθάνειν τοῦτο ὃ ᾤετο εἰδέναι οὐκ εἰδώς, πρὶν εἰς ἀπορίαν κατέπεσεν ἡγησάμενος μὴ εἰδέναι, καὶ ἐπόθησε τὸ εἰδέναι; Οὔ μοι δοκεῖ. Ὤνητο ἄρα ναρκήσας;

possesses the truth of things which it has not acquired in this life, Sokrates infers that it must have gone through a pre-existence of indefinite duration, or must be immortal.[1]

The former topic of enquiry is now resumed : but at the instance of Menon, the question taken up, is not— "What is virtue?" but—"Is virtue teachable or not?" Sokrates, after renewing his objection against the inversion of philosophical order by discussing the second question without having determined the first, enters upon the discussion hypothetically, assuming as a postulate, that nothing can be taught except knowledge. The question then stands thus—"Is virtue knowledge?" If it be, it can be taught : if not, it cannot be taught.[2] *Enquiry taken up— Whether virtue is teachable? without determining what virtue is.*

Sokrates proceeds to prove that virtue is knowledge, or a mode of knowledge. Virtue is good : all good things are profitable. But none of the things accounted good are profitable, unless they be rightly employed ; that is, employed with knowledge or intelligence. This is true not only of health, wealth, beauty, strength, power, &c., but also of the mental attributes justice, moderation, courage, quick apprehension, &c. All of these are profitable, and therefore good, if brought into action under knowledge or right intelligence ; none of them are profitable or good, without this condition— which is therefore the distinctive constituent of virtue.[3] *Virtue is knowledge —no possessions, no attributes, either of mind or body, are good or profitable, except under the guidance of knowledge.*

Virtue, therefore, being knowledge or a mode of knowledge, cannot come by nature, but must be teachable.

Yet again there are other contrary reasons (he proceeds) which prove that it cannot be teachable. For if it were so, there would be distinct and assignable teachers and learners of it, and the times and places could be pointed out where it is taught and learnt. We see that this is the case with all arts and professions. But in regard to virtue, there are neither recognised teachers, nor learners, nor years of learning. The Sophists pretend to be teachers of it, but are not :[4] *Virtue, as being knowledge, must be teachable. Yet there are opposing reasons, showing that it cannot be teachable.* No

[1] Plato, Menon, p. 86. Οὐκοῦν εἰ ἀεὶ ἡ ἀλήθεια ἡμῖν τῶν ὄντων ἐστὶν ἐν τῇ ψυχῇ, ἀθάνατος ἂν ἡ ψυχὴ εἴη;
[2] Plato, Menon, p. 87.
[3] Plato, Menon, p. 89.
[4] Plato, Menon, p. 92.

240   MENON.   CHAP. XXII.

teachers of it can be found. the leading and esteemed citizens of the community do not pretend to be teachers of it, and are indeed incompetent to teach it even to their own sons—as the character of those sons sufficiently proves.[1]

Conversation of Sokrates with Anytus, who detests the Sophists, and affirms that any one of the leading politicians can teach virtue. Here, a new speaker is introduced into the dialogue—Anytus, one of the accusers of Sokrates before the Dikastery. The conversation is carried on for some time between Sokrates and him. Anytus denies altogether that the Sophists are teachers of virtue, and even denounces them with bitter contempt and wrath. But he maintains that the leading and esteemed citizens of the state do really teach it. Anytus however presently breaks off in a tone of displeasure and menace towards Sokrates himself.[2] The conversation is then renewed with Menon, and it is shown that the leading politicians cannot be considered as teachers of virtue, any more than the Sophists. There exist no teachers of it; and therefore we must conclude that it is not teachable.

The state of the discussion as it stands now, is represented by two hypothetical syllogisms, as follows:—

Confused state of the discussion. No way of acquiring virtue is shown.
1. If virtue is knowledge, it is teachable :
   But virtue is knowledge :
   Therefore virtue is teachable.
2. If virtue is knowledge, it is teachable :
   But virtue is not teachable :
   Therefore virtue is not knowledge.

The premisses of each of these two syllogisms contradict the conclusion of the other. Both cannot be true. If virtue is not acquired by teaching, and does not come by nature, how are there any virtuous men?

Sokrates modifies his Sokrates continues his argument: The second premiss of the first syllogism—that virtue is knowledge—is true, but not the whole truth. In proving it we assumed that

---

[1] Plato, Menon, p. 97. Isokrates (adv. Sophistas, s. 25, p. 401) expressly declares that he does not believe ὡς ἔστι δικαιοσύνη διδακτόν. There is no τέχνη which can teach it, if a man be κακῶς πεφυκώς. But if a man be well-disposed, then education in λόγοι πολι- τικοί will serve συμπαρακελεύσασθαί γε καὶ συνασκῆσαι. For a man to announce himself as a teacher of justice or virtue, was an unpopular and invidious pretension. Isokrates is anxious to guard himself against such unpopularity.
[2] Plato, Menon, p. 94 E.

CHAP. XXII. KNOWLEDGE AND RIGHT OPINION. 241

there was nothing except knowledge which guided us *premisses—knowledge is not the only thing which guides to good results—right opinion will do the same.*
to useful and profitable consequences. But this assumption will not hold. There is something else besides knowledge, which also guides us to the same useful results. That something is *right opinion*, which is quite different from knowledge. The man who holds right opinions is just as profitable to us, and guides us quite as well to right actions, as if he knew. Right opinions, so long as they stay in the mind, are as good as knowledge, for the purpose of guidance in practice. But the difference is, that they are evanescent and will not stay in the mind: while knowledge is permanent and ineffaceable. They are exalted into knowledge, when bound in the mind by a chain of causal reasoning :[1] that is, by the process of reminiscence, before described.

Virtue then (continues Sokrates)—that which constitutes the virtuous character and the permanent, trustworthy, useful guide—consists in knowledge. But there is also right opinion, a sort of *quasi-knowledge*, which produces in practice effects as good as knowledge, only that it is not deeply or permanently fixed in the mind.[2] It is this right opinion, or *quasi-knowledge*, which esteemed and distinguished citizens possess, and by means of which they render useful service to the city. That they do not possess knowledge, is certain; for if they did, they would be able to teach it to others, and especially to their own sons: and this it has been shown that they cannot do.[3] They deliver *Right opinion cannot be relied on for staying in the mind, and can never give rational explanations, nor teach others—good practical statesmen receive right opinion by inspiration from the Gods.* true opinions and predictions, and excellent advice, like prophets and oracular ministers, by divine inspiration and possession, without knowledge or wisdom of their own. They are divine and inspired persons, but not wise or knowing.[4]

---

[1] Plato, Menon, pp. 97 E—98 A. καὶ γὰρ αἱ δόξαι αἱ ἀληθεῖς, ὅσον μὲν ἂν χρόνον παραμένωσιν, καλόν τι χρῆμα καὶ πάντα τἀγαθὰ ἐργάζονται· πολὺν δὲ χρόνον οὐκ ἐθέλουσι παραμένειν, ἀλλὰ δραπετεύουσιν ἐκ τῆς ψυχῆς τοῦ ἀνθρώπου. ὥστε οὐ πολλοῦ ἄξιαί εἰσιν, ἕως ἄν τις αὐτὰς δήσῃ αἰτίας λογισμῷ· τοῦτο δ' ἐστὶν ἀνάμνησις, ὡς ἐν τοῖς πρόσθεν ἡμῖν ὡμολόγηται.

[2] Plato, Menon, p. 99 A. ᾧ δὲ ἄνθρω- πος ἡγεμών ἐστιν ἐπὶ τὸ ὀρθόν, δύο ταῦτα, δόξα ἀληθὴς καὶ ἐπιστήμη.

[3] Plato, Menon, p. 99 B. Οὐκ ἄρα σοφίᾳ τινὶ οὐδὲ σοφοὶ ὄντες οἱ τοιοῦτοι ἄνδρες ἡγοῦντο ταῖς πόλεσιν, οἱ ἀμφὶ Θεμιστοκλέα. . . . διὸ καὶ οὐχ οἷοί τε ἄλλους ποιεῖν τοιούτους οἷοι αὐτοί εἰσιν, ἅτε οὐ δι' ἐπιστήμην ὄντες τοιοῦτοι.

[4] Plato, Menon, p. 99 D. καὶ τοὺς πολιτικοὺς οὐχ ἥκιστα τούτων φαῖμεν, ἂν θείους τε εἶναι καὶ ἐνθουσιάζειν, ἐπίπνους

And thus (concludes Sokrates) the answer to the question originally started by Menon—"Whether virtue is teachable?"—is as follows. Virtue in its highest sense, in which it is equivalent to or coincident with knowledge, is teachable: but no such virtue exists. That which exists in the most distinguished citizens under the name of virtue,—or at least producing the results of virtue in practice—is not teachable. Nor does it come by nature, but by special inspiration from the Gods. The best statesmen now existing cannot make any other person like themselves: if any one of them could do this, he would be, in comparison with the rest, like a real thing compared with a shadow.[1]

All the real virtue that there is, is communicated by special inspiration from the Gods.

Nevertheless the question which we have just discussed—"How virtue arises or is generated?"—must be regarded as secondary and dependent, not capable of being clearly understood until the primary and principal question—"What is virtue?"—has been investigated and brought to a solution.

But what virtue itself is, remains unknown.

This last observation is repeated by Sokrates at the end—as it had been stated at the beginning, and in more than one place during the continuance—of the dialogue. In fact, Sokrates seems at first resolved to enforce the natural and necessary priority of the latter question: but is induced by the solicitation of Menon to invert the order.[3]

Remarks on the dialogue. Proper order for examining the different topics is pointed out by Sokrates.

The propriety of the order marked out, but not pursued, by Sokrates is indisputable. Before you can enquire how virtue is generated or communicated, you must be satisfied that you know what virtue is. You must know the essence of the subject—or those predicates which the word connotes (= the meaning of the term) before you investigate its accidents and antecedents.[4] Menon begins by being satisfied that he knows what

Mischief of debating ulterior and secondary questions, when the fundamental notions and word are unsettled.

---

[1] Plato, Menon, p. 100.
ὄντας καὶ κατεχομένους ἐκ τοῦ θεοῦ, ὅταν κατορθῶσι λέγοντες πολλὰ καὶ μεγάλα πράγματα, μηδὲν εἰδότες ὧν λέγουσιν.

[2] Plato, Menon, p. 100 B.
[3] Plato, Menon, p. 86.
[4] To use the phrase of Plato himself in the Euthyphron, p. 11 A, the

virtue is: so satisfied, that he accounts it discreditable for a man not to know: although he is made to answer like one who has never thought upon the subject, and does not even understand the question. Sokrates, on the other hand, not only confesses that he does not himself know, but asserts that he never yet met with a man who did know. One of the most important lessons in this, as in so many other Platonic dialogues, is the mischief of proceeding to debate ulterior and secondary questions, without having settled the fundamental words and notions: the false persuasion of knowledge, common to almost every one, respecting these familiar ethical and social ideas. Menon represents the common state of mind. He begins with the false persuasion that he as well as every one else knows what virtue is: and even when he is proved to be ignorant, he still feels no interest in the fundamental enquiry, but turns aside to his original object of curiosity —"Whether virtue is teachable". Nothing can be more repugnant to an ordinary mind than the thorough sifting of deep-seated, long familiarised, notions — τὸ γὰρ ὀρθοῦσθαι γνώμαν, ὀδυνᾷ.

The confession of Sokrates that neither he nor any other person in his experience knows what virtue is—that it must be made a subject of special and deliberate investigation—and that no man can know what justice, or any other part of virtue is, unless he first knows what virtue as a whole is [1]—are matters to be kept in mind also, as contrasting with other portions of the Platonic dialogues, wherein virtue, justice, &c., are tacitly assumed (according to the received habit) as matters known and understood. The contributions which we obtain from the Menon towards finding out the Platonic notion of virtue, are negative rather than positive. The comments of Sokrates upon Menon's first definition include the doctrine often announced in Plato—That no man by nature desires suffering or evil; every man desires good: if

Doctrine of Sokrates in the Menon —desire of good alleged to be universally felt— in what sense this is true.

οὐσία must be known before the πάθη are sought—κινδυνεύεις, ὦ Εὐθύφρον, ἐρωτώμενος τὸ ὅσιον, ὅ, τί ποτ᾽ ἐστι, τὴν μὲν οὐσίαν μοι αὐτοῦ οὐ βούλεσθαι δηλῶσαι, πάθος δέ τι περὶ αὐτοῦ λέγειν, ὅ, τι πέπονθε τοῦτο τὸ ὅσιον, φιλεῖσθαι ὑπὸ πάντων θεῶν· ὅ τι δὲ ὄν, οὔπω εἶπες.

Compare Lachês, p. 190 B, and Gorgias, pp. 448 E, 462 C.

[1] Plato, Menon, p. 79 B-C. τὴν γὰρ δικαιοσύνην μόριον φῂς ἀρετῆς εἶναι καὶ ἕκαστα τούτων. . . . οἴει τινα εἰδέναι μόριον ἀρετῆς ὅ τι ἔστιν, αὐτὴν μὴ εἰδότα; Οὐκ ἔμοιγε δοκεῖ.

he seeks or pursues suffering or evil, he does so merely from error or ignorance, mistaking it for good.[1] This is true, undoubtedly, if we mean what is good or evil for himself: and if by good or evil we mean (according to the doctrine enforced by Sokrates in the Protagoras) the result of items of pleasure and pain, rightly estimated and compared by the Measuring Reason. Every man naturally desires pleasure, and the means of acquiring pleasure, for himself: every man naturally shrinks from pain, or the causes of pain, to himself: every one compares and measures the items of each with more or less wisdom and impartiality. But the proposition is not true, if we mean what is good or evil for others: and if by good we mean (as Sokrates is made to declare in the Gorgias) something apart from pleasure, and by evil something apart from pain (understanding pleasure and pain in their largest sense). A man sometimes desires what is good for others, sometimes what is evil for others, as the case may be. Plato's observation therefore cannot be admitted—That as to the wish or desire, all men are alike: one man is no better than another.[2]

The second portion of Plato's theory, advanced to explain what virtue is, presents nothing more satisfactory. Virtue is useful or profitable: but neither health, strength, beauty, wealth, power, &c., are profitable, unless rightly used: nor are justice, moderation, courage, quick apprehension, good memory, &c., profitable, unless they are accompanied and guided by knowledge or prudence.[3] Now if by *profitable* we have reference not to the individual agent alone, but to other persons concerned also, the proposition is true, but not instructive or distinct. For what is meant by *right use*? To what ends are the gifts here enumerated to be turned, in order to constitute right use? What again is meant by *knowledge*? knowledge of what?[4] This is a question put by Sokrates in many other dialogues, and necessary to be put here also. Moreover, knowledge is a term which requires to be determined, not merely to some assignable object, but also in its general import,

Sokrates requires knowledge as the principal condition of virtue, but does not determine— knowledge, of what.

---

[1] Plato, Menon, p. 77.
[2] Plato, Menon, p. 78 B. τὸ μὲν βούλεσθαι πᾶσιν ὑπάρχει, καὶ ταύτῃ γε οὐδὲν ὁ ἕτερος τοῦ ἑτέρου βελτίων.
[3] Plato, Menon, pp. 87-88.
[4] See Republic, vi. p. 505 B, where this question is put, but not answered, respecting φρόνησις.

no less than virtue. We shall come presently to an elaborate dialogue (Theætêtus) in which Plato makes many attempts to determine knowledge generally, but ends in a confessed failure. Knowledge must be knowledge *possessed by some one*, and must be knowledge of *something*. What is it, that a man must know, in order that his justice or courage may become profitable? Is it pleasures and pains, with their causes, and the comparative magnitude of each (as Sokrates declares in the Protagoras), in order that he may contribute to diminish the sum of pains, increase that of pleasures, to himself or to the society? If this be what he is required to know, Plato should have said so—or if not, what else—in order that the requirement of knowledge might be made an intelligible condition.

Though the subject of direct debate in the Menon is the same as that in the Protagoras (whether virtue be teachable?) yet the manner of treating this subject is very different in the two. One point of difference between the two has been just noticed. Another difference is, that whereas in Menon the teachability of virtue is assumed to be disproved, because there are no recognised teachers or learners of it—in the Protagoras this argument is produced by Sokrates, but is combated at length (as we shall presently see) by a counter-argument on the part of the Sophists, without any rejoinder from Sokrates. Of this counter-argument no notice is taken in the Menon: although, if it be well-founded, it would have served Anytus no less than Protagoras, as a solution of the difficulties raised by Sokrates. Such diversity of handling and argumentative fertility, are characteristic of the Platonic procedure. I have already remarked, that the establishment of positive conclusions, capable of being severed from their premisses, registered in the memory, and used as principles for deduction—is foreign to the spirit of these Dialogues of Search. To settle a question and finish with it—to get rid of the debate, as if it were a troublesome temporary necessity—is not what Plato desires. His purpose is, to provoke the spirit of enquiry—to stimulate responsive efforts of the mind by a painful shock of exposed ignorance—and to open before it a multiplicity of new roads with varied points of view.

Subject of Menon, same as that of the Protagoras—diversity of handling—Plato is not anxious to settle a question and get rid of it.

Nowhere in the Platonic writings is this provocative shock more vividly illustrated than in the Menon, by the simile of the electrical fish: a simile as striking as that of the magnet in Ion.[1] Nowhere, again, is the true character of the Sokratic intellect more clearly enunciated. "You complain, Menon, that I plunge your mind into nothing but doubt, and puzzle, and conscious ignorance. If I do this, it is only because my own mind is already in that same condition.[2] The only way out of it is, through joint dialectical colloquy and search; in which I invite you to accompany me, though I do not know when or where it will end." And then, for the purpose of justifying as well as encouraging such prolonged search, Sokrates proceeds to unfold his remarkable hypothesis—eternal pre-existence, boundless past experience, and omniscience, of the mind—identity of cognition with recognition, dependent on reminiscence. "Research or enquiry (said some) is fruitless. You must search either for that which you know, or for that which you do not know. The first is superfluous—the second impossible: for if you do not know what a thing is, how are you to be satisfied that the answer which you find is that which you are looking for? How can you distinguish a true solution from another which is untrue, but plausible?"

Anxiety of Plato to keep up and enforce the spirit of research.

Here we find explicitly raised, for the first time, that difficulty which embarrassed the different philosophical schools in Greece for the subsequent three centuries—What is the criterion of truth? Wherein consists the process called verification and proof, of that which is first presented as an hypothesis? This was one of the great problems debated between the Academics, the Stoics, and the Sceptics, until the extinction of the schools of philosophy.[3]

Great question discussed among the Grecian philosophers—criterion of truth—Wherein consists the process of verification?

[1] Plato, Menon, p. 80 A. νάρκη θαλασσία. Compare what I have said above about the Ion, ch. XVII., p. 128.
[2] Plato, Menon, p. 80 D.
[3] Sokrates here calls this problem an ἐριστικὸς λόγος. Stallbaum (in his Prolegom. to the Menon, p. 14) describes it as a "quæstiunculam, haud dubie e sophistarum disciplinâ arreptam" If the Sophists were the first to raise this question, I think that by doing so they rendered service to the interests of philosophy. The question is among the first which ought to be thoroughly debated and sifted, if we are to have a body of "reasoned truth" called philosophy.

I dissent from the opinion of Stallbaum (p. 20), though it is adopted both by Socher (Ueber Platon, p. 185) and

Not one of these schools was satisfied with the very peculiar answer which the Platonic Sokrates here gives to the question. When truth is presented to us (he intimates), we recognise it as an old friend after a long absence. We know it by reason of its conformity to our antecedent, pre-natal, experience (in the Phædon, such pre-natal experience is restricted to commerce with the substantial, intelligible, Ideas, which are not mentioned in the Menon): the soul or mind is immortal, has gone through an indefinite succession of temporary lives prior to the present, and will go through an indefinite succession of temporary lives posterior to the present— "longæ, canitis si cognita, vitæ Mors media est". The mind has thus become omniscient, having seen, heard, and learnt every thing, both on earth and in Hades: but such knowledge exists as a confused and unavailable mass, having been buried and forgotten on the commencement of its actual life.

None of the philosophers were satisfied with the answer here made by Plato—that verification consists in appeal to pre-natal experience.

Since all nature is in universal kindred, communion, or interdependence, that which we hear or see here, recalls to the memory, by association, portions of our prior forgotten omni-

by Steinhart (Einleitung zum Menon, p. 123), that the Menon was composed by Plato during the lifetime of Sokrates. Schleiermacher (Einleitung zum Gorgias, p. 22 ; Einleitung zum Menon, pp. 329-330), Ueberweg (Aechth. Plat. Schr. p. 226), and K. F. Hermann, on the other hand, regard the Menon as composed after the death of Sokrates, and on this point I agree with them, though whether it was composed not long after that event (as K. F. Hermann thinks) or thirteen years after it (as Schleiermacher thinks), I see no sufficient grounds for deciding. I incline to the belief that its composition is considerably later than Hermann supposes ; the mention of the Theban Ismenias is one among the reasons rendering such later origin probable. Plato probably borrowed from the Xenophontic Anabasis the name, country, and social position of Menon, who may have received teaching from Gorgias, as we know that Proxenus did, Xen. Anab. ii. 6, 16. The reader can compare the Einleitung of Schleiermacher (in which he professes to prove that the Menon is a corollary to the Theætêtus and Gorgias, and an immediate antecedent to the Euthydêmus, —that it solves the riddle of the Protagoras—and that it presupposes and refers back to the Phædrus) with the Einleitung of Steinhart (p. 120 seq.), who contests all these propositions, saying that the Menon is decidedly later than the Euthydêmus, and decidedly earlier than the Theætêtus, Gorgias, and Phædrus ; with the opinions of Stallbaum and Hermann, who recognise an order different from that either of Steinhart or Schleiermacher ; and with that of Ast, who rejects the Menon altogether as unworthy of Plato. Every one of these dissentient critics has *something* to say for his opinion, while none of them (in my judgment) can make out anything like a conclusive case. The mistake consists in assuming that there must have been a peremptory order and intentional interdependence among the Platonic Dialogues, and next in trying to show by internal evidence what that order was.

science.[1] It is in this recall or reminiscence that search, learning, acquisition of knowledge, consists. Teaching and learning are words without meaning: the only process really instructive is that of dialectic debate, which, if indefatigably prosecuted, will dig out the omniscience buried within.[2] So vast is the theory generated in Plato's mind, by his worship of dialectic,

---

[1] The doctrine of communion or interdependence pervading all Nature, with one continuous cosmical soul penetrating everywhere, will be found set forth in the kosmology of the Timæus, pp. 37-42-43. It was held, with various modifications, both by the Pythagoreans and the Stoics. Compare Cicero, Divinat. ii. 14-15; Virgil, Æneid vi. 715 seqq.; Georgic. iv. 220; Sextus Empir. adv. Mathem. ix. 127; Ekphantus Pythagoreus ap. Stobæum, Tit. 48, vol. ii. p. 320, Gaisford.

The view here taken by Plato, that all nature is cognate and interdependent—ἅτε γὰρ τῆς φύσεως ἁπάσης συγγενοῦς οὔσης—is very similar to the theory of Leibnitz:—"Ubique per materiam disseminata statuo principia vitalia seu percipientia. Omnia in naturâ sunt analogica." (Leibnitz, Epist. ad Wagnerum, p. 466; Leibn. Opp. Erdmann). Farther, that the human mind by virtue of its interdependence or kindred with all nature, includes a confused omniscience, is also a Leibnitzian view. "Car comme tout est plein (ce qui rend toute la matière liée) et comme dans le plein tout mouvement fait quelqu' effet sur les corps distans à mesure de la distance, de sorte que chaque corps est affecté non seulement par ceux qui le touchent, et se ressent en quelque façon de tout ce qui leur arrive—mais aussi par leur moyen se ressent de ceux qui touchent les premiers dont il est touché immédiatement. Il s'ensuit que cette communication va à quelque distance que ce soit. Et par consequent tout corps se ressent de tout ce qui se fait dans l'Univers: tellement que celui, qui voit tout, pourroit lire dans chacun ce qui se fait partout et même ce qui s'est fait et se fera, en remarquant dans le présent ce qui est éloigné tant selon les temps que selon les lieux: σύμπνοια πάντα, disoit Hippocrate. Mais une âme ne peut lire en elle même que ce qui y est représenté distinctement: elle ne sauroit developper tout d'un coup ses régles, car elles vont à l'infini. Ainsi quoique chaque monade créée représente tout l'Univers, elle représente plus distinctement le corps qui lui est particulièrement affecté, et dont elle fait l'Entéléchie. Et comme ce corps exprime tout l'Univers par la connexion de toute la matière dans le plein, l'âme représente aussi tout l'Univers en représentant ce corps qui lui appartient d'une manière particulière" (Leibnitz, Monadologie, sect. 61-62, No. 88, p. 710; Opp. Leibn. ed. Erdmann).

Again, Leibnitz, in another Dissertation:—"Comme à cause de la plénitude du monde tout est lié, et chaque corps agit sur chaque autre corps, plus ou moins, selon la distance, et en est affecté par la réaction—il s'ensuit que chaque monade est un miroir vivant, ou doué d'action interne, représentatif de l'Univers, suivant son point de vue, et aussi réglé que l'Univers même" (Principes de la Nature et de la Grace, p. 714; ed. Erdmann; also Système Nouveau, p. 128, a. 36).

Leibnitz expresses more than once how much his own metaphysical views agreed with those of Plato. Lettre à M. Bourguet, pp. 723-725. He expresses his belief in the pre-existence of the soul: "Tout ce que je crois pouvoir assurer, est, que l'âme de tout animal a préexisté, et a été dans un corps organique: qui enfin, par beaucoup de changemens, involutions, et évolutions, est devenu l'animal présent" (Lettre à M. Bourguet, p. 731). And in the Platonic doctrine of reminiscence to a certain point: "Il y a quelque chose de solide dans ce que dit Platon de la réminiscence" (p. 137, b. 10). Also Leibnitz's Nouveaux Essais sur l'Entendement Humain, p. 196, b. 28; and Epistol. ad Hanschium, p. 446, a. 12.

See the elaborate account of the philosophy of Leibnitz by Dr. Kuno Fischer—Geschichte der neueren Philosophie, vol. ii. pp. 226-232.

[2] Plato, Menon, p. 81 D. ἐάν τις ἀνδρεῖος ᾖ, καὶ μὴ ἀποκάμνῃ ζητῶν. Compare also p. 86 B.

CHAP. XXII.   LEARNING—REMINISCENCE.   249

respecting that process of search to which more than half of his dialogues are devoted.

In various other dialogues of Plato, the same hypothesis is found repeated. His conception of the immortality of the soul or mind, includes pre-existence as well as post-existence: a perpetual succession of temporary lives, each in a distinct body, each terminated by death, and each followed by renewed life for a time in another body. In fact, the pre-existence of the mind formed the most important part of Plato's theory about immortality: for he employed it as the means of explaining how the mind became possessed of general notions. As the doctrine is stated in the Menon, it is made applicable to all minds (instead of being confined, as in Phædrus, Phædon, and elsewhere, to a few highly gifted minds, and to commerce with the intelligible substances called Ideas). This appears from the person chosen to illustrate the alleged possibility of stimulating artificial reminiscence: that person is an unlettered youth, taken at hazard from among the numerous slaves of Menon.[1]

Plato's view of the immortality of the soul—difference between the Menon, Phædrus, and Phædon.

It is true, indeed (as Schleiermacher observes), that the questions put by Sokrates to this youth are in great proportion leading questions, suggesting their own answers. They would not have served their purpose unless they had been such. The illustration here furnished, of the Sokratic interrogatory process, is highly interesting, and his theory is in a great degree true.[2] Not all learning, but an important part of learning, consists in reminiscence — not indeed of

Doctrine of Plato, that new truth may be elicited by skilful examination out of the unlettered mind—how far correct?

---

[1] Plato, Menon, pp. 82 A, 85 E. προσκάλεσον τῶν πολλῶν ἀκολούθων τουτωνὶ τῶν σαυτοῦ ἕνα, ὅντινα βούλει, ἵνα ἐν τούτῳ σοι ἐπιδείξωμαι. Stallbaum says that this allusion to the numerous slaves in attendance is intended to illustrate conspicuously the wealth and nobility of Menon. In my judgment, it is rather intended to illustrate the operation of pure accident—the perfectly ordinary character of the mind worked upon—"one among many, which you please".

[2] Plutarch (Fragment. Περὶ ψυχῆς). Εἰ ἀφ' ἑτέρου ἕτερον ἐννοοῦμεν; οὐκ ἄν, εἰ μὴ προέγνωστο. Τὸ ἐπιχείρημα Πλατωνικόν. Εἰ προστίθεμεν τὸ ἔλλειπον τοῖς αἰσθητοῖς;—καὶ αὐτὸ Πλατωνικόν.

Plutarch, in the same fragment, indicates some of the objections made by Bion and Straton against the doctrine of ἀνάμνησις. How (they asked) does it happen that this reminiscence brings up often what is false or absurd? (asked Bion). If such reminiscence exists (asked Straton) how comes it that we require demonstrations to conduct us to knowledge? and how is it that no man can play on the flute or the harp without practice?

Ὅτι Βίων ἠπόρει περὶ τοῦ ψεύδους, εἰ καὶ αὐτὸ κατ' ἀνάμνησιν, ὡς τὸ ἐναντίον

acquisitions made in an antecedent life, but of past experience and judgments in this life. Of such experience and judgments every one has travelled through a large course; which has disappeared from his memory, yet not irrevocably. Portions of it may be revived, if new matter be presented to the mind, fitted to excite the recollection of them by the laws of association. By suitable interrogations, a teacher may thus recall to the memory of his pupils many facts and judgments which have been hitherto forgotten: he may bring into juxtaposition those which have never before been put together in the mind: and he may thus make them elicit instructive comparisons and inferences. He may provoke the pupils to strike out new results for themselves, or to follow, by means of their own stock of knowledge, in the path suggested by the questions. He may farther lead them to perceive the fallacy of erroneous analogies which at first presented themselves as plausible; and to become painfully sensible of embarrassment and perplexing ignorance, before he puts those questions which indicate the way of escape from it. Upon the necessity of producing such painful consciousness of ignorance Plato insists emphatically, as is his custom.[1]

γε, ἢ οὔ; καὶ τί ἡ ἀλογία; Ὅτι Στράτων ἠπόρει, εἰ ἔστιν ἀνάμνησις, πῶς ἄνευ ἀποδείξεων οὐ γιγνόμεθα ἐπιστήμονες; πῶς δὲ οὐδεὶς αὐλητὴς ἢ κιθαριστὴς γέγονεν ἄνευ μελέτης;

[1] Plato, Menon, p. 84. The sixteenth Dissertation of Maximus Tyrius presents a rhetorical amplification of this doctrine—πᾶσα μάθησις, ἀνάμνησις—in which he enters fully into the spirit of the Menon and the Phædon—αὐτοδίδακτόν τι χρῆμα ἡ ψυχή—ἡ ψυχῆς εὕρεσις, αὐτογενής τις οὖσα, καὶ αὐτοφυής, καὶ ξύμφυτος, τί ἄλλο ἔστιν ἢ δόξαι ἀληθεῖς ἐγειρόμεναι, ὧν τῇ ἐπεγέρσει τε καὶ ξυντάξει ἐπιστήμη ὄνομα; (c. 6). Compare also Cicero, Tusc. D. i. 24. The doctrine has furnished a theme for very elegant poetry: both in the Consolatio Philosophiæ of Boethius—the piece which ends with

" Ac si Platonis Musa personat verum,
   Quod quisque discit, immemor recordatur"—

and in Wordsworth—" Our birth is but a sleep and a forgetting," &c.

On the other hand Aristotle alludes also to the same doctrine and criticises it; but he does not seem (so far as I can understand this brief allusion) to seize exactly Plato's meaning. This is the remark of the Scholiast on Aristotle; and I think it just. It is curious to compare the way in which ἀνάμνησις is handled by Plato in the Menon and Phædon, and by Aristotle in the valuable little tract—Περὶ μνήμης καὶ ἀναμνήσεως (p. 451, b.). Aristotle has his own way of replying to the difficulty raised in the question of Menon, and tries to show that sometimes we *know* in one sense and *do not know* in another. See Aristotel. Anal. Prior., ii. p. 67, a. 22; Anal. Poster. i. p. 71, a. 27; and the Scholia on the former passage, p. 193, b. 21, ed. Brandis.

Sir William Hamilton, in one of the Appendixes to his edition of Reid's Works (Append. D. p. 890 seq.),. has given a learned and valuable translation and illustration of the treatise of Aristotle Περὶ Ἀναμνήσεως. I note, however, with some surprise, that while collecting many interesting comments from writers who lived *after* Aristotle, he has not adverted to what was said upon this same subject by Plato, *before*

Plato does not intend here to distinguish (as many modern writers distinguish) geometry from other sciences, as if geometry were known *à priori*, and other sciences known *à posteriori* or from experience. He does not suppose that geometrical truths are such that no man can possibly believe the contrary of them; or that they are different in this respect from the truths of any other science. He here maintains that all the sciences lie equally in the untaught mind,[1] but buried, forgotten, and confused: so as to require the skill of the questioner not merely to recall them into consciousness, but to disentangle truth from error. Far from supposing that the untaught mind has a natural tendency to answer correctly geometrical questions, he treats erroneous answers as springing up more naturally than true answers, and as requiring a process of painful exposure before the mind can be put upon the right track. The questioner, without possessing any knowledge himself, (so Plato thinks,) can nevertheless exercise an influence at once stimulating, corrective, and directive. He stimulates the action of the associative process, to call up facts, comparisons, and analogies, bearing on the question: he arrests the respondent on a wrong answer, creating within him a painful sense of ignorance and embarrassment: he directs him by his subsequent questions into the path of right answers. His obstetric aid (to use the simile in Plato's Theætêtus), though presupposing the pregnancy of the respondent mind, is indispensable both to forward the childbirth, and to throw away any offspring which may happen to be deformed. In the Theætêtus, the main stress is laid on that part of the dialogue which is performed by the questioner: in the Menon, upon the latent competence and large dead stock of an untaught respondent.

Plato's doctrine about à priori reasonings— Different from the modern doctrine.

The mind of the slave questioned by Sokrates is discovered to be pregnant. Though he has received no teaching from any professed geometer, he is nevertheless found competent, when subjected to a skilful interrogatory, to arrive at last, through a series of mistakes, at correct answers, determining certain simple pro-

Aristotle. It was the more to be expected that he would do this, since he insists so emphatically upon the complete originality of Aristotle.

[1] Plato, Menon, p. 85 E. οὗτος γὰρ (the untaught slave) ποιήσει περὶ πάσης γεωμετρίας ταὐτὰ ταῦτα, καὶ τῶν ἄλλων μαθημάτων ἁπάντων.

blems of geometry. He knows nothing about geometry: nevertheless there exist in his mind true opinions respecting that which he does not know. These opinions are "called up like a dream" by the interrogatories: which, if repeated and diversified, convert the opinions into knowledge, taken up by the respondent out of himself.[1] The opinions are inherited from an antecedent life and born with him, since they have never been taught to him during this life.

It is thus that Plato applies to philosophical theory the doctrine (borrowed from the Pythagoreans) of pre-natal experience and cognitions: which he considers, not as inherent appurtenances of the mind, but as acquisitions made by the mind during various antecedent lives. These ideas (Plato argues) cannot have been acquired during the present life, because the youth has received no special teaching in geometry. But Plato here takes no account of the multiplicity and diversity of experiences gone through, comparisons made, and acquirements lodged, in the mind of a youthful adult however unlettered. He recognises no acquisition of knowledge except through special teaching. So, too, in the Protagoras, we shall find him putting into the mouth of Sokrates the doctrine—That virtue is not taught and cannot be taught, because there were no special masters or times of teaching. But in that dialogue we shall also see Plato furnishing an elaborate reply to this doctrine in the speech of Protagoras; who indicates the multifarious and powerful influences which are perpetually operative, even without special professors, in creating and enforcing ethical sentiment. If Plato had taken pains to study the early life of the untaught slave, with its stock of facts, judgments, comparisons, and inferences suggested by analogy, &c., he might easily have found enough to explain the competence of the slave to answer the questions appearing in the dialogue. And even if enough could not have been found, to afford a direct and specific explanation—

Plato's theory about pre-natal experience. He took no pains to ascertain and measure the extent of post-natal experience.

---

[1] Plato, Menon, p. 85. τῷ οὐκ εἰδότι ἄρα περὶ ὧν ἂν μὴ εἰδῇ ἔνεισιν ἀληθεῖς δόξαι. . . . καὶ νῦν μέν γε αὐτῷ ὥσπερ ὄναρ ἄρτι ἀνακεκίνηνται αἱ δόξαι αὗται· εἰ δὲ αὐτόν τις ἀνερήσεται πολλάκις τὰ αὐτὰ ταῦτα καὶ πολλαχῇ, οἶσθ' ὅτι τελευτῶν οὐδενὸς ἧττον ἀκριβῶς ἐπιστήσεται περὶ αὐτῶν. . . . Οὐκοῦν οὐδενὸς διδάξαντος ἀλλ' ἐρωτήσαντος ἐπιστήσεται, ἀναλαβὼν αὐτὸς ἐξ αὑτοῦ τὴν ἐπιστήμην;

we must remember that only a very small proportion of the long series of mental phenomena realised in the infant, the child, the youth, ever comes to be remembered or recorded. To assume that the large unknown remainder would be insufficient, if known, to afford the explanation sought, is neither philosophical nor reasonable. This is assumed in every form of the doctrine of innate ideas: and assumed by Plato here without even trying any explanation to dispense with the hypothesis: simply because the youth interrogated had never received any special instruction in geometry.

I have already observed, that though great stress is laid in this dialogue upon the doctrine of opinions and knowledge inherited from an antecedent life — upon the distinction between true opinion and knowledge—and upon the identity of the process of learning with reminiscence—yet nothing is said about universal Ideas or Forms, so much dwelt upon in other dialogues. In the Phædrus and Phædon, it is with these universal Ideas that the mind is affirmed to have had communion during its prior existence, as contrasted with the particulars of sense apprehended during the present life: while in the Menon, the difference pointed out between true opinions and knowledge is something much less marked and decisive. Both the one and the other are said to be, not acquired during this life, but inherited from antecedent life: to be innate, yet unperceived— revived by way of reminiscence and interrogation. True opinions are affirmed to render as much service as knowledge, in reference to practice. There is only this distinction between them—that true opinions are transient, and will not remain in the mind until they are bound in it by causal reasoning, or become knowledge.

Little or nothing is said in the Menon about the Platonic Ideas or Forms.

What Plato meant by this "causal reasoning, or computation of cause," is not clearly explained. But he affirms very unequivocally, first, that the distinction between true opinion and knowledge is one of the few things of which he feels assured [1]—next, with somewhat less confidence, that the distinction consists only in

What Plato meant by Causal Reasoning—his distinction between knowledge

---

[1] Plato, Menon, p. 98 B. ὅτι δέ εἴπερ τι ἄλλο φαίην ἂν εἰδέναι, ὀλίγα ἐστί τι ἀλλοῖον ὀρθὴ δόξα καὶ ἐπιστήμη, δ' ἂν φαίην, ἓν δ' οὖν καὶ τοῦτο οὐ πάνυ μοι δοκῶ τοῦτο εἰκάζειν· ἀλλ' ἐκείνων θείην ἂν ὧν οἶδα.

and right opinion. the greater security which knowledge affords for permanent in-dwelling in the mind. This appears substantially the same distinction as what is laid down in other words towards the close of the dialogue—That those, who have only true opinions and not knowledge, judge rightly without knowing how or why; by an aptitude not their own but supplied to them from without for the occasion, in the nature of inspiration or prophetic *œstrus*. Hence they are unable to teach others, or to transfer this occasional inspiration to any one else. They cannot give account of what they affect to know, nor answer scrutinizing questions to test it. This power of answering and administering cross-examination, is Plato's characteristic test of real knowledge—as I have already observed in my sixth chapter.

To translate the views of Plato into analogous views of a modern philosopher, we may say—That right opinion, as contrasted with knowledge, is a discriminating and acute empirical judgment: inferring only from old particulars to new particulars (without the intermediate help and guarantee of general propositions distinctly enunciated and interpreted), but selecting for every new case the appropriate analogies out of the past, with which it ought to be compared. Many persons judge in this manner fairly well, and some with extreme success. But let them be ever so successful in practice, they proceed without any conscious method; they are unable to communicate the grounds of their inferences to others: and when they are right, it is only by haphazard—that is (to use Plato's language), through special inspiration vouchsafed to them by the Gods. But when they ascend to knowledge, and come to judge scientifically, they then distribute these particular facts into classes—note the constant sequences as distinguished from the occasional—and draw their inferences in every new case according to such general laws or uniformities of antecedent and consequent. Such uniform and unconditional antecedents are the only causes of which we have cognizance. They admit of being described in the language which Plato here uses ($αἰτίας\ λογισμῷ$), and they also serve as reasons for justifying or explaining our inferences to others.[1]

This distinction compared with modern philosophical views.

---

[1] We have seen that in the Menon Plato denies all $διδαχή$, and recognises nothing but $ἀνάμνησις$. The doctrine of the Timæus (p. 51 D-E) is very dif-

CHAP. XXII.   ANYTUS, HATER OF THE SOPHISTS.   255

The manner in which Anytus, the accuser of Sokrates before the Dikastery, is introduced into this dialogue, deserves notice. The questions are put to him by Sokrates—"Is virtue teachable? How is Menon to learn virtue, and from whom? Ought he not to do as he would do if he wished to learn medicine or music: to put himself under some paid professional man as teacher?" Anytus answers these questions in the affirmative: but asks, where such professional teachers of virtue are to be found. "There are the Sophists," replies Sokrates. Upon this Anytus breaks out into a burst of angry invective against the Sophists; denouncing them as corruptors of youth, whom none but a madman would consult, and who ought to be banished by public authority.

Manifestation of Anytus—intense antipathy to the Sophists and to philosophy generally.

ferent. He there lays especial stress on the distinction between διδαχή and πειθώ—the first belonging to ἐπιστήμη, the second to δόξα. Also in Gorgias, 454, and in Republic, v. pp. 477-479, about δόξα and ἐπιστήμη. In those dialogues the distinction between the two is presented as marked and fundamental, as if δόξα alone was fallible and ἐπιστήμη infallible. In the Menon the distinction appears as important, but not fundamental; the Platonic Ideas or Universals being *not* recognised as constituting a substantive world by themselves. In this respect the Menon is nearer to the truth in describing the difference between ὀρθὴ δόξα and ἐπιστήμη. Mr. John Stuart Mill (in the chapter of his System of Logic wherein the true theory of the Syllogism is for the first time expounded) has clearly explained what that difference amounts to. All our inferences are *from* particulars, sometimes *to* new particulars directly and at once (δόξα), sometimes *to* generals in the first instance, and through them *to* new particulars; which latter, or scientific process, is highly valuable as a security for correctness (ἐπιστήμη). "Not only" (says Mr. Mill) " *may* we reason from particulars to particulars without passing through generals, but we perpetually *do* so reason. All our earliest inferences are of this nature. From the first dawn of intelligence we draw inferences, but years elapse before we learn the use of general language. We are constantly reasoning from ourselves to other people, or from one person to another, without giving ourselves the trouble to erect our observations into general maxims of human or external nature. If we have an extensive experience and retain its impressions strongly, we may acquire in this manner a very considerable power of accurate judgment, which we may be utterly incapable of justifying or of communicating to others. Among the higher order of practical intellects, there have been many of whom it was remarked how admirably they suited their means to their ends, without being able to give any sufficient account of what they did; and applied, or seemed to apply, recondite principles which they were wholly unable to state. This is a natural consequence of having a mind stored with appropriate particulars, and having been accustomed to reason at once from these to fresh particulars, without practising the habit of stating to one's self or others the corresponding general propositions. The cases of men of talent performing wonderful things they know not how, are examples of the rudest and most spontaneous forms of the operations of superior minds. It is a defect in them, and often a source of errors, not to have generalised as they went on; but generalisation, though a help, the most important indeed of all helps, is not an essential" (Mill, Syst. of Logic, Book II. ch. iii.). Compare the first chapter of the Metaphysica of Aristotle, p. 980, a. 15, b. 7.

Why are you so bitter against the Sophists? asks Sokrates. Have any of them ever injured you? *Anyt.*—No; never: I have never been in the company of any one of them, nor would I ever suffer any of my family to be so. *Sokr.*—Then you have no experience whatever about the Sophists? *Anyt.*—None: and I hope that I never may have. *Sokr.*—How then can you know about this matter, how far it is good or bad, if you have no experience whatever about it? *Anyt.*—Easily. I know what sort of men the Sophists are, whether I have experience of them or not. *Sokr.*—Perhaps you are a prophet, Anytus: for how else you can know about them, I do not understand, even on your own statement.[1]

Anytus then declares, that the persons from whom Menon ought to learn virtue are the leading practical politicians; and that any one of them can teach it. But Sokrates puts a series of questions, showing that the leading Athenian politicians, Themistoklês, Periklês, &c., have not been able to teach virtue even to their own sons: *à fortiori*, therefore, they cannot teach it to any one else. Anytus treats this series of questions as disparaging and calumnious towards the great men of Athens. He breaks off the conversation abruptly, with an angry warning to Sokrates to be cautious about his language, and to take care of his own safety.

The dialogue is then prosecuted and finished between Sokrates and Menon: and at the close of it, Sokrates says—"Talk to Anytus, and communicate to him that persuasion which you have yourself contracted,[2] in order that he may be more mildly disposed: for, if you persuade him, you will do some good to the Athenians as well as to himself."

The enemy and accuser of Sokrates is here depicted as the bitter enemy of the Sophists also. And Plato takes pains to exhibit the enmity of Anytus to the Sophists as founded on no facts or experience. Without having seen or ascertained anything about them, Anytus hates them as violently as if he had sustained from them some personal injury; a sentiment which many

<small>The enemy of Sokrates is also the enemy of the Sophists— Practical statesmen.</small>

---

[1] Plato, Menon, p. 92. τόνδε Ἄνυτον, ἵνα πραότερος ᾖ· ὡς ἐὰν
[2] Plato, Menon, ad fin. σὺ δὲ ταῦτα πείσῃς τοῦτον, ἔστιν ὅ, τι καὶ Ἀθηναίους ἅπερ αὐτὸς πέπεισαι, πεῖθε καὶ τὸν ξένον ὀνήσεις.

Platonic critics and many historians of philosophy have inherited from him.[1] Whether the corruption which these Sophists were accused of bringing about in the minds of youth, was intentional or not intentional on their part—how such corruption could have been perpetually continued, while at the same time the eminent Sophists enjoyed long and unabated esteem from the youth themselves and from their relatives—are difficulties which Anytus does not attempt to explain, though they are started here by Sokrates. Indeed we find the same topics employed by Sokrates himself, in his defence before the Dikasts against the same charge.[2] Anytus has confidence in no one except the practical statesmen: and when a question is raised about *their* power to impart their own excellence to others, he presently takes offence against Sokrates also. The same causes which have determined his furious antipathy against the Sophists, make him ready to transfer the like antipathy to Sokrates. He is a man of plain sense, practical habits, and conservative patriotism—who worships what he finds accredited as virtue, and dislikes the talkers and theorisers about virtue in general: whether they debated in subtle interrogation and dialectics, like Sokrates—or lectured in eloquent continuous discourse, like Protagoras. He accuses the Sophists, in this dialogue, of corrupting the youth; just as he and Melêtus, before the Dikastery, accused Sokrates of the same offence. He understands the use of words, to discuss actual business before the assembly or dikastery; but he hates discourse on the generalities of ethics or philosophy. He is essentially μισόλογος. The point which he condemns in the Sophists, is that which they have in common with Sokrates.

In many of the Platonic dialogues we have the antithesis between Sokrates and the Sophists brought out, as to the different point of view from which the one and

The Menon brings for-

---

[1] Upon the bitter antipathy here expressed by Anytus against the Sophists, whom nevertheless he admits that he does not at all know, Steinhart remarks as follows:—"Gerade so haben zu allen Zeiten Orthodoxe und Fanatiker aller Arten über ihre Gegner abgeurtheilt, ohne sie zu kennen oder auch nur kennen lernen zu wollen" (Einleit. zum Menon, not. 15, p. 173). Certainly orthodox and fanatical persons often do what is here imputed to them. But Steinhart might have found a still closer parallel with Anytus, in his own criticisms, and in those of many other Platonic critics on the Sophists; the same expressions of bitterness and severity, with the same slender knowledge of the persons upon whom they bear.

[2] Plato, Apol. Sokr. pp. 26 A, 33 D, 34 B.

ward the point of analogy between Sokrates and the Sophists, in which both were disliked by the practical statesmen.
the other approached ethical questions. But in this portion of the Menon, we find exhibited the feature of analogy between them, in which both one and the other stood upon ground obnoxious to the merely practical politicians. Far from regarding hatred against the Sophists as a mark of virtue in Anytus, Sokrates deprecates it as unwarranted and as menacing to philosophy in all her manifestations. The last declaration ascribed to Anytus, coupled with the last speech of Sokrates in the dialogue, show us that Plato conceives the anti-Sophistic antipathy as being anti-Sokratic also, in its natural consequences. That Sokrates was in common parlance a Sophist, disliked by a large portion of the general public, and ridiculed by Aristophanes, on the same grounds as those whom Plato calls Sophists—is a point which I have noticed elsewhere.

CHAPTER XXIII.

PROTAGORAS.

THE dialogue called Protagoras presents a larger assemblage of varied and celebrated characters, with more of dramatic winding, and more frequent breaks and resumptions in the conversation, than any dialogue of Plato—not excepting even Symposion and Republic. *Scenic arrangement and personages of the dialogue.*
It exhibits Sokrates in controversy with the celebrated Sophist Protagoras, in the presence of a distinguished society, most of whom take occasional part in the dialogue. This controversy is preceded by a striking conversation between Sokrates and Hippokrates—a youth of distinguished family, eager to profit by the instructions of Protagoras. The two Sophists Prodikus and Hippias, together with Kallias, Kritias, Alkibiades, Eryximachus, Phædrus, Pausanias, Agathon, the two sons of Periklês (Paralus and Xanthippus), Charmides, son of Glaukon, Antimœrus of Mende, a promising pupil of Protagoras, who is in training for the profession of a Sophist—these and others are all present at the meeting, which is held in the house of Kallias.[1] Sokrates himself recounts the whole—both his conversation with Hippokrates and that with Protagoras—to a nameless friend.

This dialogue enters upon a larger and more comprehensive ethical theory than anything in the others hitherto noticed. But it contains also a great deal in which we hardly recognise, or at least cannot verify, any distinct purpose, either of search or exposition. Much of it seems to be composed with a literary or poetical view, to enhance the charm or interest of the composition. The personal characteristics of each speaker—the intel-

[1] Plato, Protag. p. 315.

lectual peculiarities of Prodikus and Hippias—the ardent partisanship of Alkibiades—are brought out as in a real drama. But the great and marked antithesis is that between the Sophist Protagoras and Sokrates—the Hektor and Ajax of the piece: who stand forward in single combat, exchange some serious blows, yet ultimately part as friends.

Introduction. Eagerness of the youthful Hippokrates to become acquainted with Protagoras.

An introduction of some length impresses upon us forcibly the celebrity of the Great Sophist, and the earnest interest excited by his visit to Athens. Hippokrates, a young man of noble family and eager aspirations for improvement, having just learnt the arrival of Protagoras, comes to the house of Sokrates and awakens him before daylight, entreating that Sokrates will introduce him to the new-comer. He is ready to give all that he possesses in order that he may become wise like Protagoras.[1] While they are awaiting a suitable hour for such introduction, Sokrates puts a series of questions to test the force of Hippokrates.[2]

Sokrates questions Hippokrates as to his purpose and expectations from Protagoras.

Sokr.—You are now intending to visit Protagoras, and to pay him for something to be done for you—tell me what manner of man it is that you are going to visit—and what manner of man do you wish to become? If you were going in like manner to pay a fee for instruction to your namesake Hippokrates of Kos, you would tell me that you were going to him as to a physician—and that you wished to qualify yourself for becoming a physician. If you were addressing yourself with the like view to Pheidias or Polykleitus, you would go to them as to sculptors, and for the purpose of becoming yourself a sculptor. Now then that we are to go in all this hurry to Protagoras, tell me who he is and what title he bears, as we called Pheidias a sculptor? *Hipp.*—They call him a Sophist.[3] *Sokr.*—We are going to pay him then as a Sophist? *Hipp.*—Certainly. *Sokr.*—And what are you to become by going to him? *Hipp.*—Why, judging from the preceding analogies, I am to become a Sophist. *Sokr.*—But would not you be ashamed of presenting yourself to the Grecian public as a

---

[1] Plato, Protag. pp. 310-311 A.
[2] Plato, Protag. p. 311 B. καὶ ἐγὼ ποπειρώμενος τοῦ Ἱπποκράτους τῆς ῥώμης διεσκόπουν αὐτὸν καὶ ἠρώτων, &c.
[3] Plato, Protagoras, p. 311.

Sophist? *Hipp.*—Yes: if I am to tell you my real opinion.[1] *Sokr.*—Perhaps however you only propose to visit Protagoras, as you visited your schoolmaster and your musical or gymnastical teacher: not for the purpose of entering that career as a professional man, but to acquire such instruction as is suitable for a private citizen and a freeman? *Hipp.*—That is more the instruction which I seek from Protagoras. *Sokr.*—Do you know then what you are going to do? You are consigning your mind to be treated by one whom you call a Sophist: but I shall be surprised if you know what a Sophist is [2]—and if you do not know, neither do you know what it is—good or evil—to which you are consigning your mind. *Hipp.*—I think I *do* know. The Sophist is, as the name implies, one cognizant of matters wise and able.[3] *Sokr.*—That may be said also of painters and carpenters. If we were asked in what special department are painters cognizant of matters wise and able, we should specify that it was in the workmanship of portraits. Answer me the same question about the Sophist. What sort of workmanship does he direct? *Hipp.*—That of forming able speakers.[4] *Sokr.* —Your answer may be correct, but it is not specific enough: for we must still ask, About *what* is it that the Sophist forms able speakers? just as the harp-master makes a man an able speaker about harping, at the same time that he teaches him harping. About *what* is it that the Sophist forms able speakers:

---

[1] Plato, Protag. p. 312 A. σὺ δέ, ἦν δ' ἐγώ, πρὸς θεῶν, οὐκ ἂν αἰσχύνοιο εἰς τοὺς Ἕλληνας σαυτὸν σοφιστὴν παρέχων; Νὴ τὸν Δί', ὦ Σώκρατες, εἴπερ γε ἃ διανοοῦμαι χρὴ λέγειν. Ast (Platon's Leben, p. 78) and other Platonic critics treat this *Sophistomanie* (as they call it) of an Athenian youth as something ludicrous and contemptible: all the more ludicrous because (they say) none of them goes to qualify himself for becoming a Sophist, but would even be ashamed of the title. Yet if we suppose the same question addressed to a young Englishman of rank and fortune (as Hippokrates was at Athens), "Why do you put yourself under the teaching of Dr. —— at Eton or Professor —— at Oxford? Do you intend to qualify yourself for becoming a schoolmaster or a professor?" He will laugh at you for the question: if he answers it seriously, he will probably answer as Hippokrates does. But there is nothing at all in the question to imply that the schoolmaster or the professor is a worthless pretender—or the youth foolish, for being anxious to obtain instruction from him; which is the inference that Ast and other Platonic critics desire us to draw about the Athenian Sophists.

[2] Plato, Protag. p. 312 C. ὅ, τι δέ ποτε ὁ σοφιστής ἐστι, θαυμάζοιμ' ἂν εἰ οἶσθα, &c.

[3] Plato, Protag. p. 312 C. ὥς περ τοὔνομα λέγει, τὸν τῶν σοφῶν ἐπιστήμονα. (Quasi sophistes sit—ὁ τῶν σοφῶν ἴστης, Heindorf.) If this supposition of Heindorf be just, we may see in it an illustration of the etymological views of Plato, which I shall notice when I come to the Kratylus.

[4] Plato, Protag. p. 312 D. ποίας ἐργασίας ἐπιστάτης; ἐπιστάτην τοῦ ποιῆσαι δεινὸν λέγειν.

of course about that which he himself knows?[1] *Hipp.*—Probably. *Sokr.*—What then is that, about which the Sophist is himself cognizant, and makes his pupil cognizant? *Hipp.*—By Zeus, I cannot give you any farther answer.[2]

Sokr.—Do you see then to what danger you are going to submit your mind? If the question were about trusting your body to any one, with the risk whether it should become sound or unsound, you would have thought long, and taken much advice, before you decided. But now, when it is about your mind, which you value more than your body, and upon the good or evil of which all your affairs turn[3]—you are hastening without reflection and without advice, you are ready to pay all the money that you possess or can obtain, with a firm resolution already taken to put yourself at all hazard under Protagoras: whom you do not know—with whom you have never once talked—whom you call a Sophist, without knowing what a Sophist is? *Hipp.*—I must admit the case to be as you say.[4] *Sokr.*—Perhaps the Sophist is a man who brings for sale those transportable commodities, instruction or doctrine, which form the nourishment of the mind. Now the traders in food for the body praise indiscriminately all that they have to sell, though neither they nor their purchasers know whether it is good for the body; unless by chance any one of them be a gymnastic trainer or a physician.[5] So, too, these Sophists, who carry about food for the mind, praise all that they have to sell: but perhaps some of them are ignorant, and assuredly their purchasers are ignorant, whether it be good or bad for the mind: unless by accident any one possess medical knowledge about the mind. Now if you, Hippokrates, happen to possess such knowledge of what is good or bad for the mind, you may safely purchase doctrine from Protagoras or from any one else:[6] but if not, you are

Danger of going to imbibe the instruction of a Sophist without knowing beforehand what he is about to teach.

---

[1] Plato, Protag. p. 312 D-E. ἐρωτήσεως γὰρ ἔτι ἡ ἀπόκρισις ἡμῖν δεῖται, περὶ ὅτου ὁ σοφιστὴς δεινὸν ποιεῖ λέγειν· ὥσπερ ὁ κιθαριστὴς δεινὸν δήπου ποιεῖ λέγειν περὶ οὗπερ καὶ ἐπιστήμονα, περὶ κιθαρίσεως.
[2] Plato, Protag. p. 312 E.
[3] Plato, Protag. p. 313 A. ὃ δὲ περὶ πλείονος τοῦ σώματος ἡγεῖ, τὴν ψυχήν, καὶ ἐν ᾧ πάντ' ἐστὶ τὰ σὰ ἢ εὖ ἢ κακῶς πράττειν, χρηστοῦ ἢ πονηροῦ αὐτοῦ γενομένου, &c.
[4] Plato, Protag. p. 313 C.
[5] Plato, Protag. p. 313 D.
[6] Plato, Protag. p. 313 E. ἐὰν μή τις τύχῃ περὶ τὴν ψυχὴν αὖ ἰατρικὸς ὤν. εἰ μὲν οὖν σὺ τυγχάνεις ἐπιστήμων τούτων τί χρηστὸν καὶ πονηρόν, ἀσφαλές σοι ὠνεῖσθαι μαθήματα καὶ παρὰ Πρωταγόρου καὶ παρ' ἄλλου ὁτουοῦν· εἰ

hazarding and putting at stake your dearest interests. The purchase of doctrines is far more dangerous than that of eatables or drinkables. As to these latter, you may carry them away with you in separate vessels, and before you take them into your body you may invoke the *Expert*, to tell you what you may safely eat and drink, and when, and how much. But this cannot be done with doctrines. You cannot carry away *them* in a separate vessel to be tested; you learn them and take them into the mind itself; so that you go away, after having paid your money, actually damaged or actually benefited, as the case may be.[1] We will consider these matters in conjunction with our elders. But first let us go and talk with Protagoras—we can consult the others afterwards.

Such is the preliminary conversation of Sokrates with Hippokrates, before the interview with Protagoras. I have given it (like the introduction to the Lysis) at considerable length, because it is a very characteristic specimen of the Sokratico-Platonic point of view. It brings to light that false persuasion of knowledge, under which men unconsciously act, especially in what concerns the mind and its treatment. Common fame and celebrity suffice to determine the most vehement aspirations towards a lecturer, in one who has never stopped to reflect or enquire what the lecturer does. The pressure applied by Sokrates in his successive questions, to get beyond vague generalities into definite particulars—the insufficiency, thereby exposed, of the conceptions with which men usually rest satisfied—exhibit the working of his Elenchus in one of its most instructive ways. The parallel drawn between the body and the mind—the constant precaution taken in the case of the former to consult the professional man and to follow his advice in respect both to dis-

Remarks on the introduction. False persuasion of knowledge brought to light.

δὲ μή, ὅρα, ὦ φίλτατε, μὴ περὶ τοῖς φιλτάτοις κυβεύῃς τε καὶ κινδυνεύῃς.
[1] Plato, Protag. p. 314 A. σιτία μὲν γὰρ καὶ ποτὰ πριάμενον ἔξεστιν ἐν ἄλλοις ἀγγείοις ἀποφέρειν, καὶ πρὶν δέξασθαι αὐτὰ ἐς τὸ σῶμα πιόντα ἢ φαγόντα, καταθέμενον οἴκαδε ἔξεστι συμβουλεύσασθαι παρακαλέσαντα τὸν ἐπαΐοντα, ὅ, τι τε ἐδεστέον ἢ ποτέον καὶ ὅ, τι μή, καὶ ὁπόσον, καὶ ὁπότε · . . . . μαθήματα δὲ οὐκ ἔστιν ἐν ἄλλῳ ἀγγείῳ ἀπενεγκεῖν, ἀλλ' ἀνάγκη καταθέντα τὴν τιμὴν τὸ μάθημα ἐν αὐτῇ τῇ ψυχῇ λαβόντα καὶ μαθόντα ἀπιέναι ἢ βεβλαμμένον ἢ ὠφελημένον.

cipline and nourishment—are in the same vein of sentiment which we have already followed in other dialogues. Here too, as elsewhere, some similar *Expert*, in reference to the ethical and intellectual training of mind, is desiderated, as still more imperatively necessary. Yet where is he to be found? How is the business of mental training to be brought to a beneficial issue without him? Or is Protagoras the man to supply such a demand? We shall presently see.

Sokrates and Hippokrates proceed to the house of Kallias, and find him walking about in the fore-court with Protagoras, and some of the other company; all of whom are described as treating the Sophist with almost ostentatious respect. Prodikus and Hippias have each their separate hearers, in or adjoining to the court. Sokrates addresses Protagoras.

Sokr.—Protagoras, I and Hippokrates here are come to talk to you about something. *Prot.*—Do you wish to talk to me alone, or in presence of the rest? *Sokr.* —To us it is indifferent: but I will tell you what we come about, and you may then determine for yourself. This Hippokrates is a young man of noble family, and fully equal to his contemporaries in capacity. He wishes to become distinguished in the city; and he thinks he shall best attain that object through your society. Consider whether you would like better to talk with him alone, or in presence of the rest.[1]

Prot.—Your consideration on my behalf, Sokrates, is reasonable. A person of my profession must be cautious in his proceedings. I, a foreigner, visit large cities, persuading the youth of best family to frequent my society in preference to that of their kinsmen and all others; in the conviction that I shall do them good. I thus inevitably become exposed to much jealousy and even to

---

[1] Plat. Prot. p. 316. The motive assigned by Hippokrates, for putting himself under the teaching of Protagoras, is just the same as that which Xenophon assigns to his friend Proxenus for taking lessons and paying fees to the Leontine Gorgias (Xen. Anab. ii. 6, 16).

hostile conspiracies.[1] The sophistical art is an old one ;[2] but its older professors, being afraid of enmity if they proclaimed what they really were, have always disguised themselves under other titles. Some, like Homer, Hesiod, and Simonides, called themselves poets : others, Orpheus, Musæus, &c., professed to prescribe religious rites and mysteries : others announced themselves as gymnastic trainers or teachers of music. But I have departed altogether from this policy ; which indeed did not succeed in really deceiving any leading men—whom alone it was intended to deceive—and which, when found out, entailed upon its authors the additional disgrace of being considered deceivers. The true caution consists in open dealing ; and this is what I have always adopted. I avow myself a Sophist, educating men. I am now advanced in years, old enough to be the father of any of you, and have grown old in the profession : yet during all these years, thank God, I have suffered no harm either from my practice or my title.[3] If therefore you desire to converse with me, it will be far more agreeable to me to converse in presence of all who are now in the house.[4]

[1] The jealousy felt by fathers, mothers, and relatives against a teacher or converser who acquired great influence over their youthful relatives, is alluded to by Sokrates in the Platonic Apology (p. 37 E), and is illustrated by a tragical incident in the Cyropædia of Xenophon, iii. 1. 14-38. Compare also Xenophon, Memorab. i. 2, 52.

[2] Plat. Prot. p. 316 D. ἐγὼ δὲ τὴν σοφιστικὴν τέχνην φημὶ μὲν εἶναι παλαιάν.

[3] Plat. Prot. p. 317 C. ὥστε σὺν θεῷ εἰπεῖν μηδὲν δεινὸν πάσχειν διὰ τὸ ὁμολογεῖν σοφιστὴς εἶναι.

[4] Plat. Prot. p. 317 D. In the Menon, the Platonic Sokrates is made to say that Protagoras died at the age of seventy ; that he had practised forty years as a Sophist ; and that during all that long time he had enjoyed the highest esteem and reputation, even after his death, "down to the present day" (Menon, p. 91 E).

It must be remembered that the speech, of which I have just given an abstract, is delivered not by the historical, real, Protagoras, but by the character named *Protagoras*, depicted by Plato in this dialogue : i.e. the speech is composed by Plato himself. I read, therefore, with much surprise, a note of Heindorf (ad p. 316 D), wherein he says about Protagoras: "Callidé in postremis reticet, quod addere poterat, χρήματα διδόντας." "Protagoras cunningly keeps back, what he might have here added, that people gave him money for his teaching." Heindorf must surely have supposed that he was commenting upon a real speech, delivered by the historical person called Protagoras. Otherwise what can be meant by this charge of "cunning reticence or keeping back?" Protagoras here speaks what Plato puts into his mouth ; neither more nor less. What makes the remark of Heindorf the more preposterous is, that in page 328 B the very fact, which Protagoras is here said "cunningly to keep back," appears mentioned by Protagoras ; and mentioned in the same spirit of honourable frankness and fair-dealing as that which pervades the discourse which I have just (freely) translated. Indeed nothing can be more marked than the way in which Plato makes Protagoras dwell with emphasis on the frankness and openness of his dealing : nothing

On hearing this, Sokrates—under the suspicion (he tells us) that Protagoras wanted to show off in the presence of Prodikus and Hippias—proposes to convene all the dispersed guests, and to talk in their hearing. This is accordingly done, and the conversation recommences—Sokrates repeating the introductory request which he had preferred on behalf of Hippokrates.

Protagoras prefers to converse in presence of the assembled company.

Sokr.—Hippokrates is anxious to distinguish himself in the city, and thinks that he shall best attain this end by placing himself under your instruction. He would gladly learn, Protagoras, what will happen to him, if he comes into intercourse with you. *Prot.*—Young man, if you come to me, on the day of your first visit, you will go home better than you came, and on the next day the like : each successive day you will make progress for the better.[1] *Sokr.*—Of course he will ; there is nothing surprising in that : but towards *what*, and about *what*, will he make progress? *Prot.* —Your question is a reasonable one, and I am glad to reply to it. I shall not throw him back—as other Sophists do, with mischievous effect—into the special sciences, geometry, arithmetic, astronomy, music, &c., just after he has completed his course in them. I shall teach him what he really comes to learn : wisdom and good counsel, both respecting his domestic affairs, that he may manage his own family well—and respecting the affairs of the city, that he may address himself to them most efficaciously, both in speech and act. *Sokr.*—You speak of political or social science. You engage to make men good citizens. *Prot.*— Exactly so.[2]

Answers of Protagoras. He intends to train young men as virtuous citizens.

Sokr.—That is a fine talent indeed, which you possess, if you *do* possess it ; for (to speak frankly) I thought that the thing had not been teachable, nor intentionally communicable, by man to man.[3] I will tell you why

Sokrates doubts whether virtue is teach-

---

can be more at variance with the character which critics give us of the Sophists, as "cheats, who defrauded pupils of their money while teaching them nothing at all, or what they themselves knew to be false".

[1] Plato, Protag. p. 318 A. "Qui ad philosophorum scholas venit, quotidie secum aliquid boni ferat : aut sanior domum redeat, aut sanabilior." Seneca, Epistol. 108, p. 530.

[2] Plato, Protag. pp. 318-319. The declaration made by Protagoras —that he will not throw back his pupils into the special arts—is represented by Plato as intended to be an indirect censure on Hippias, then sitting by.

[3] Plato, Protag. p. 319 B. οὐ διδακτὸν εἶναι, μηδ᾽ ὑπ᾽ ἀνθρώπων παρασκευαστὸν ἀνθρώποις.

I think so. The Athenians are universally recognised as intelligent men. Now when our public assembly is convened, if the subject of debate be fortification, ship-building, or any other specialty which they regard as learnable and teachable, they will listen to no one except a professional artist or craftsman.[1] If any non-professional man presumes to advise them on the subject, they refuse to hear him, however rich and well-born he may be. It is thus that they act in matters of any special art;[2] but when the debate turns upon the general administration of the city, they hear every man alike—the brass-worker, leather-cutter, merchant, navigator, rich, poor, well-born, low-born, &c. Against none of them is any exception taken, as in the former case—that he comes to give advice on that which he has not learnt, and on which he has had no master.[3] It is plain that the public generally think it not teachable. Moreover our best and wisest citizens, those who possess civic virtue in the highest measure, cannot communicate to their own children this same virtue, though they cause them to be taught all those accomplishments which paid masters can impart. Periklês and others, excellent citizens themselves, have never been able to make any one else excellent, either in or out of their own family. These reasons make me conclude that social or political virtue is not teachable. I shall be glad if you can show me that it is so.[4]

Prot.—I will readily show you. But shall I, like an old man addressing his juniors, recount to you an illustrative mythe?[5] or shall I go through an expository discourse? The mythe perhaps will be the more acceptable of the two.

There was once a time when Gods existed, but neither men nor

able. Reasons for such doubt. Protagoras is asked to explain whether it is or not.

Explanation of Protagoras. He begins with a mythe.

---

[1] Plato, Protag. p. 319 C. καὶ τἆλλα πάντα οὕτως, ὅσα ἡγοῦνται μαθητά τε καὶ διδακτὰ εἶναι. ἐάν δέ τις ἄλλος ἐπιχειρῇ αὐτοῖς συμβουλεύειν ὃν ἐκεῖνοι μὴ οἴονται δημιουργὸν εἶναι, &c.

[2] Plato, Protag. p. 319 D. Περὶ μὲν οὖν ὧν οἴονται ἐν τέχνῃ εἶναι, οὕτω διαπράττονται.

[3] Plato, Protag. p. 319 D. καὶ τούτοις οὐδεὶς τοῦτο ἐπιπλήσσει ὥσπερ τοῖς πρότερον, ὅτι οὐδαμόθεν μαθών, οὐδὲ ὄντος διδασκάλου οὐδενὸς αὐτῷ, ἔπειτα συμβουλεύειν ἐπιχειρεῖ· δῆλον γὰρ ὅτι οὐχ ἡγοῦνται διδακτὸν εἶναι.

[4] Plato, Protag. pp. 319-320.

[5] Plato, Protag. p. 320 C. πότερον ὑμῖν, ὡς πρεσβύτερος νεωτέροις, μῦθον λέγων ἐπιδείξω, ἢ λόγῳ διεξελθών;

It is probable that the Sophists often delivered illustrative mythes or fables as a more interesting way of handling social matters before an audience. Such was the memorable fable called the choice of Hêraklês by Prodikus.

Mythe. First fabrication of men by the Gods. Prometheus and Epimetheus. Bad distribution of endowments to man by the latter. It is partly amended by Prometheus.

animals had yet come into existence. At the epoch prescribed by Fate, the Gods fabricated men and animals in the interior of the earth, out of earth, fire, and other ingredients: directing the brothers Prometheus and Epimetheus to fit them out with suitable endowments. Epimetheus, having been allowed by his brother to undertake the task of distributing these endowments, did his work very improvidently, wasted all his gifts upon the inferior animals, and left nothing for man. When Prometheus came to inspect what had been done, he found that other animals were adequately equipped, but that man had no natural provision for clothing, shoeing, bedding, or defence. The only way whereby Prometheus could supply the defect was, by breaking into the common workshop of Athênê and Hephæstus, and stealing from thence their artistic skill, together with fire.[1] Both of these he presented to man, who was thus enabled to construct for himself, by art, all that other animals received from nature and more besides.

Prometheus gave to mankind skill for the supply of individual wants, but could not give them the social art. Mankind are on the point of perishing when Zeus sends to them the dispositions essential for society.

Still however, mankind did not possess the political or social art; which Zeus kept in his own custody, where Prometheus could not reach it. Accordingly, though mankind could provide for themselves as individuals, yet when they attempted to form themselves into communities, they wronged each other so much, from being destitute of the political or social art, that they were presently forced again into dispersion.[2] The art of war, too, being a part of the political art, which mankind did not possess—they could not get up a common defence against hostile animals: so that the human race would have been presently destroyed, had not Zeus interposed to avert such a consummation. He sent Hermês to mankind, bearing with him

---

[1] Plato, Protag. pp. 321-322. ἀπορίᾳ οὖν ἐχόμενος ὁ Προμηθεὺς ἥντινα σωτηρίαν τῷ ἀνθρώπῳ εὕροι, κλέπτει Ἡφαίστου καὶ Ἀθηνᾶς τὴν ἔντεχνον σοφίαν σὺν πυρί. . . . Τὴν μὲν οὖν περὶ τὸν βίον σοφίαν ἄνθρωπος ταύτῃ ἔσχε, τὴν δὲ πολιτικὴν οὐκ εἶχεν· ἦν γὰρ παρὰ τῷ Διΐ, &c.

If the reader will compare this with the doctrine delivered in the Platonic Timæus—that the inferior animals spring from degenerate men—he will perceive the entire variance between the two (Timæus, pp. 91-92).

[2] Plato, Protag. p. 322 B. ἐζήτουν δὴ ἀθροίζεσθαι καὶ σώζεσθαι κτίζοντες πόλεις· ὅτ᾽ οὖν ἀθροισθεῖεν, ἠδίκουν ἀλλήλους, ἅτε οὐκ ἔχοντες τὴν πολιτικὴν τέχνην, ὥστε πάλιν σκεδαννύμενοι διεφθείροντο.

Justice and the sense of Shame (or Moderation), as the bonds and ornaments of civic society, coupling men in friendship.[1] Hermês asked Zeus—Upon what principle shall I distribute these gifts among mankind? Shall I distribute them in the same way as artistic skill is distributed, only to a small number—a few accomplished physicians, navigators, &c., being adequate to supply the wants of the entire community? Or are they to be apportioned in a certain dose to every man? Undoubtedly, to every man (was the command of Zeus). All without exception must be partakers in them. If they are confined exclusively to a few, like artistic or professional skill, no community can exist.[2] Ordain, by my authority, that every man, who cannot take a share of his own in justice and the sense of shame, shall be slain, as a nuisance to the community.

This fable will show you, therefore, Sokrates (continues Protagoras), that the Athenians have good reason for making the distinction to which you advert. When they are discussing matters of special art, they will hear only the few to whom such matters are known. But when they are taking counsel about social or political virtue, which consists altogether in justice and moderation, they naturally hear every one; since every one is presumed, as a condition of the existence of the commonwealth, to be a partaker therein.[3] Moreover, even though they know a man not to have these virtues in reality, they treat him as insane if he does not proclaim himself to have them, and make profession of virtue: whereas, in the case of the special arts, if a man makes

Protagoras follows up his mythe by a discourse. Justice and the sense of shame are not professional attributes, but are possessed by all citizens, and taught by all to all.

Compare Plato, Republic, i. p. 351 C, p. 352 B, where Sokrates sets forth a similar argument.

[1] Plato, Protagor. p. 322 C. Ἑρμῆν πέμπει ἄγοντα εἰς ἀνθρώπους αἰδῶ τε καὶ δίκην, ἵν' εἶεν πόλεων κόσμοι τε καὶ δεσμοὶ φιλίας συναγωγοί.

[2] Plato, Protag. p. 322 C-D. εἷς ἔχων ἰατρικὴν πολλοῖς ἱκανὸς ἰδιώταις, καὶ οἱ ἄλλοι δημιουργοί. καὶ δίκην δὴ καὶ αἰδῶ οὕτω θῶ ἐν τοῖς ἀνθρώποις, ἢ ἐπὶ πάντας νείμω; Ἐπὶ πάντας, ἔφη ὁ Ζεύς, καὶ πάντες μετεχόντων· οὐ γὰρ ἂν γένοιντο πόλεις, εἰ ὀλίγοι αὐτῶν μετέχοιεν ὥσπερ ἄλλων τεχνῶν. καὶ νόμον γε θὲς παρ' ἐμοῦ, τὸν μὴ δυνάμενον αἰδοῦς καὶ δίκης μετέχειν, κτείνειν ὡς νόσον πόλεως.

We see by p. 323 A that σωφροσύνη is employed as substitute or equivalent for αἰδώς: yet still αἰδὼς is the proper word to express Plato's meaning, as it denotes a distinct and positive regard to the feelings of others—a feeling of pain in each man's mind, when he discovers or believes that he is disapproved by his comrades. Hom. Il. O. 561—αἰδῶ θέσθ' ἐνὶ θυμῷ Ἀλλήλους τ' αἰδεῖσθε κατὰ κρατερὰς ὑσμίνας.

[3] Plat. Prot. pp. 322-323.

proclamation of his own skill as a physician or musician, they censure or ridicule him.[1]

Nevertheless, though they account this political or social virtue an universal endowment, they are far from thinking that it comes spontaneously or by nature. They conceive it to be generated by care and teaching. For in respect of all those qualities which come by nature or by accident, no one is ever angry with another or blames another for being found wanting. An ugly, dwarfish, or sickly man is looked upon simply with pity, because his defects are such as he cannot help. But when any one manifests injustice or other qualities the opposite of political virtue, then all his neighbours visit him with indignation, censure, and perhaps punishment: implying clearly their belief that this virtue is an acquirement obtained by care and learning.[2] Indeed the whole institution of punishment has no other meaning. It is in itself a proof that men think social virtue to be acquirable and acquired. For no rational man ever punishes malefactors because they *have* done wrong, or simply with a view to the past:—since what is already done cannot be undone. He punishes with a view to the future, in order that neither the same man, nor others who see him punished, may be again guilty of similar wrong. This opinion plainly implies the belief, that virtue is producible by training, since men punish for the purpose of prevention.[3]

Constant teaching of virtue. Theory of punishment.

---

[1] Plato, Protag. p. 323 C.
[2] Plato, Protag. pp. 323-324.
[3] Plato, Protag. p. 324 A-B. οὐδεὶς γὰρ κολάζει τοὺς ἀδικοῦντας πρὸς τούτῳ τὸν νοῦν ἔχων καὶ τούτου ἕνεκα ὅτι ἠδίκησεν, ὅστις μὴ ὥσπερ θηρίον ἀλογίστως τιμωρεῖται· ὁ δὲ μετὰ λόγου ἐπιχειρῶν κολάζειν οὐ τοῦ παρεληλυθότος ἕνεκα ἀδικήματος τιμωρεῖται—οὐ γὰρ ἂν τό γε πραχθὲν ἀγένητον θείη—ἀλλὰ τοῦ μέλλοντος χάριν, ἵνα μὴ αὖθις ἀδικήσῃ μήτε αὐτὸς οὗτος μήτε ἄλλος ὁ τοῦτον ἰδὼν κολασθέντα. καὶ τοιαύτην διάνοιαν ἔχων, διανοεῖται παιδευτὴν εἶναι ἀρετήν· ἀ π ο - τ ρ ο π ῆ ς γ ο ῦ ν ἕ ν ε κ α κ ο λ ά ζ ε ι.

This clear and striking exposition of the theory of punishment is one of the most memorable passages in Plato, or in any ancient author. And if we are to believe the words which immediately follow, it was the theory universally accepted at that time—ταύτην οὖν τὴν δόξαν πάντες ἔχουσιν, ὅσοι περ τιμωροῦνται καὶ ἰδίᾳ καὶ δημοσίᾳ. Compare Plato, Legg. xi. p. 933, where the same doctrine is announced: Seneca, De Irâ, i. 16. "Nam, ut Plato ait, nemo prudens punit, quia peccatum est, sed ne peccetur. Revocari enim præterita non possunt: futura prohibentur." Steinhart (Einleit. zum Protag. p. 423) pronounces a just encomium upon this theory of punishment, which, as he truly observes, combines together the purposes declared in the two modern theories—Reforming and Deterring. He says further, however, that the same theory of punishment reappears in the Gorgias, which I do not think exact. The purpose of punishment, as given in the Gorgias, is simply to cure a distempered patient of a terrible distemper, and thus to confer great benefit on him—but without any allusion to tutelary results as regards society.

I come now to your remaining argument, Sokrates. You urge that citizens of eminent civil virtue cannot communicate that virtue to their own sons, to whom nevertheless they secure all the accomplishments which masters can teach. Now I have already shown you that civil virtue is the one accomplishment needful,[1] which every man without exception must possess, on pain of punishment or final expulsion, if he be without it. I have shown you, moreover that every one believes it to be communicable by teaching and attention. How can you believe then that these excellent fathers teach their sons other things, but do not teach them this, the want of which entails such terrible penalties?

Why eminent men cannot make their sons eminent.

The fact is, they *do* teach it: and that too with great pains.[2] They begin to admonish and lecture their children, from the earliest years. Father, mother, tutor, nurse, all vie with each other to make the child as good as possible: by constantly telling him on every occasion which arises, This is right—That is wrong—This is honourable—That is mean—This is holy—That is unholy—Do these things, abstain from those.[3] If the child obeys them, it is well: if he do not, they straighten or rectify him, like a crooked piece of wood, by reproof and flogging. Next, they send him to a schoolmaster, who teaches him letters and the harp; but who is enjoined to take still greater pains in watching over his orderly behaviour. Here the youth is put to read, learn by heart, and recite, the compositions of able poets; full of exhortations to excellence and of stirring examples from the good men of past times.[4] On the harp also, he learns the best songs, his conduct is strictly watched, and his emotions are disciplined by the influence of rhythmical and regular measure. While his mind is thus trained to good, he is sent besides to the gymnastic trainer, to render his body a suitable instrument for it,[5] and to guard against

Teaching by parents, schoolmaster, harpist, laws, dikastery, &c.

---

[1] Plato, Protag. p. 324 E. Πότερον ἔστι τι ἕν, ἢ οὐκ ἔστιν, οὗ ἀναγκαῖον πάντας τοὺς πολίτας μετέχειν, εἴπερ μέλλει πόλις εἶναι; ἐν τούτῳ γὰρ αὕτη λύεται ἡ ἀπορία ἣν σὺ ἀπορεῖς.

[2] Plato, Protag. p. 325 B.

[3] Plato, Protag. p. 325 D. παρ' ἕκαστον καὶ ἔργον καὶ λόγον διδάσκοντες καὶ ἐνδεικνύμενοι ὅτι τὸ μὲν δίκαιον, τὸ δὲ ἄδικον, καὶ τόδε μὲν καλόν, τόδε δὲ αἰσχρόν, &c.

[4] Plato, Protag. p. 325 E—326 A. παρατιθέασιν αὐτοῖς ἐπὶ τῶν βάθρων ἀναγινώσκειν ποιητῶν ἀγαθῶν ποιήματα καὶ ἐκμανθάνειν ἀναγκάζουσιν, ἐν οἷς πολλαὶ μὲν νουθετήσεις ἔνεισι, πολλαὶ δὲ διέξοδοι καὶ ἔπαινοι καὶ ἐγκώμια παλαιῶν ἀνδρῶν ἀγαθῶν, ἵνα ὁ παῖς ζηλῶν μιμῆται καὶ ὀρέγηται τοιοῦτος γενέσθαι.

[5] Plato, Protag. p. 326 B. ἵνα τὰ σώματα βελτίω ἔχοντες ὑπηρετῶσι τῇ διανοίᾳ χρηστῇ οὔσῃ, &c.

failure of energy under the obligations of military service. If he be the son of a wealthy man, he is sent to such training sooner, and remains in it longer. As soon as he is released from his masters, the city publicly takes him in hand, compelling him to learn the laws prescribed by old and good lawgivers,[1] to live according to their prescriptions, and to learn both command and obedience, on pain of being punished. Such then being the care bestowed, both publicly and privately, to foster virtue, can you really doubt, Sokrates, whether it be teachable? You might much rather wonder if it were not so.[2]

All learn virtue from the same teaching by all. Whether a learner shall acquire more or less of it, depends upon his own individual aptitude.

How does it happen, then, you ask, that excellent men so frequently have worthless sons, to whom, even with all these precautions, they cannot teach their own virtue? This is not surprising, when you recollect what I have just said—That in regard to social virtue, every man must be a craftsman and producer; there must be no non-professional consumers.[3] All of us are interested in rendering our neighbours just and virtuous, as well as in keeping them so. Accordingly, every one, instead of being jealous, like a professional artist, of seeing his own accomplishments diffused, stands forward zealously in teaching justice and virtue to every one else, and in reproving all short-comers.[4] Every man is a teacher of virtue to others: every man learns his virtue from such general teaching, public and private. The sons of the best men learn it in this way, as well as others. The instruction of their fathers counts for comparatively little, amidst such universal and paramount extraneous influence; so that it depends upon the aptitude and predispositions of the sons themselves, whether they turn out better or worse than others. The son of a superior man will often turn out ill; while the son of a worthless man will

---

[1] Plato, Protag. p. 326 D. νόμους ὑπογράψασα, ἀγαθῶν καὶ παλαιῶν νομοθετῶν εὑρήματα, &c.
[2] Plato, Protag. p. 326 E.
[3] Plato, Protag. p. 326 E. ὅτι τούτου τοῦ πράγματος, τῆς ἀρετῆς, εἰ μέλλει πόλις εἶναι, οὐδένα δεῖ ἰδιωτεύειν.
It is to be regretted that there is no precise word to translate exactly the useful antithesis between ἰδιώτης and τεχνίτης or δημιουργός.
[4] Plato, Protag. p. 327 A. εἰ καὶ τοῦτο καὶ ἰδίᾳ καὶ δημοσίᾳ πᾶς πάντα καὶ ἐδίδασκε καὶ ἐπέπληττε τὸν μὴ καλῶς αὐλοῦντα, καὶ μὴ ἐφθόνει τούτου, ὥσπερ νῦν τῶν δικαίων καὶ τῶν νομίμων οὐδεὶς φθονεῖ οὐδ᾽ ἀποκρύπτεται, ὥσπερ τῶν ἄλλων τεχνημάτων—λυσιτελεῖ γὰρ, οἶμαι, ἡμῖν ἡ ἀλλήλων δικαιοσύνη καὶ ἀρετή· διὰ ταῦτα πᾶς παντὶ προθύμως λέγει καὶ διδάσκει καὶ τὰ δίκαια καὶ τὰ νόμιμα.

prove meritorious. So the case would be, if playing on the flute were the one thing needful for all citizens; if every one taught and enforced flute-playing upon all others, and every one learnt it from the teaching of all others.[1] You would find that the sons of good or bad flute-players would turn out good or bad, not in proportion to the skill of their fathers, but according to their own natural aptitudes. You would find however also, that all of them, even the most unskilful, would be accomplished flute-players, if compared with men absolutely untaught, who had gone through no such social training. So too, in regard to justice and virtue.[2] The very worst man brought up in your society and its public and private training, would appear to you a craftsman in these endowments, if you compared him with men who had been brought up without education, without laws, without dikasteries, without any general social pressure bearing on them, to enforce virtue: such men as the savages exhibited last year in the comedy of Pherekrates at the Lenæan festival. If you were thrown among such men, you, like the chorus of misanthropes in that play, would look back with regret even upon the worst criminals of the society which you had left, such as Eurybatus and Phrynondas.[3]

But now, Sokrates, you are over-nice, because all of us are teachers of virtue, to the best of every man's power; while no particular individual appears to teach it specially and *ex professo*.[4] By the same analogy, if you asked who was the teacher for speaking our vernacular Greek, no one special person could be pointed out:[5] nor would you find out who was the finishing teacher for those sons of craftsmen who learnt the rudiments of their art from their own fathers—while if the son of any non-professional person learns a craft, it is easy to assign the person by whom he was taught.[6]

Analogy of learning vernacular Greek. No special teacher thereof. Protagoras teaches virtue somewhat better than others.

---

[1] Plato, Protag. p. 327 C.
[2] Plato, Protag. p. 327 C-D. ὅστις σοι ἀδικώτατος φαίνεται ἄνθρωπος τῶν ἐν νόμοις καὶ ἀνθρώποις τεθραμμένων, δίκαιον αὐτὸν εἶναι καὶ δημιουργὸν τούτου τοῦ πράγματος, εἰ δέοι αὐτὸν κρίνεσθαι πρὸς ἀνθρώπους, οἷς μήτε παιδεία ἐστὶ μήτε δικαστήρια μήτε νόμοι μήτε ἀνάγκη μηδεμία διὰ παντὸς ἀναγκάζουσα ἀρετῆς ἐπιμελεῖσθαι.

[3] Plato, Protag. p. 327 D.
[4] Plato, Protag. p. 327 E. νῦν δὲ τρυφᾷς, ὦ Σώκρατες, διότι πάντες διδάσκαλοί εἰσιν ἀρετῆς, καθ' ὅσον δύναται ἕκαστος, καὶ οὐδείς σοι φαίνεται.
[5] Plato, Protag. p. 327 E. εἶθ' ὥς περ ἂν εἰ ζητοῖς τίς διδάσκαλος τοῦ ἑλληνίζειν, οὐδ' ἂν εἷς φανείη.
[6] Plato, Protag. p. 328 A.

So it is in respect to virtue. All of us teach and enforce virtue to the best of our power; and we ought to be satisfied if there be any one of us ever so little superior to the rest, in the power of teaching it. Of such men I believe myself to be one.[1] I can train a man into an excellent citizen, better than others, and in a manner worthy not only of the fee which I ask, but even of a still greater remuneration, in the judgment of the pupil himself. This is the stipulation which I make with him: when he has completed his course, he is either to pay me the fee which I shall demand—or if he prefers, he may go into a temple, make oath as to his own estimate of the instruction imparted to him, and pay me according to that estimate.[2]

I have thus proved to you, Sokrates—That virtue is teachable —That the Athenians account it to be teachable—

The sons of great artists do not themselves become great artists.

That there is nothing wonderful in finding the sons of good men worthless, and the sons of worthless men good. Indeed this is true no less about the special professions, than about the common accomplishment, virtue. The sons of Polyklêtus the statuary, and of many other artists, are nothing as compared with their fathers.[3]

Remarks upon the mythe and discourse. They explain the manner in which the established sentiment of a community propagates and perpetuates itself.

Such is the discourse composed by Plato and attributed to the Platonic Protagoras—showing that virtue is teachable, and intended to remove the difficulties proposed by Sokrates. It is an exposition of some length: and because it is put into the mouth of a Sophist, many commentators presume, as a matter of course, that it must be a manifestation of some worthless quality:[4] that it is either empty verbiage, or ostentatious self-praise, or low-minded immorality. I am unable to perceive in the discourse any of these demerits. I think it one of the best parts of the Platonic writings,

---

[1] Plato, Protag. p. 328 B. Ἀλλὰ κἂν εἰ ὀλίγον ἔστι τις ὅστις διαφέρει ἡμῶν προβιβάσαι εἰς ἀρετήν, ἀγαπητόν. Ὃν δὴ ἐγὼ οἶμαι εἷς εἶναι, &c.
[2] Plato, Protag. p. 328 B.
[3] Plato, Protag. p. 328 C.
[4] So Serranus (ad 326 E), who has been followed by many later critics. "Quæstio est, Virtusne doceri possit? Quod instituit demonstrare Sophista, sed ineptissimis argumentis et quæ contra seipsum faciant."

To me this appears the reverse of the truth. But even if it were true,

as an exposition of the growth and propagation of common sense —the common, established, ethical and social sentiment, among a community : sentiment neither dictated in the beginning, by any scientific or artistic lawgiver, nor personified in any special guild of craftsmen apart from the remaining community—nor inculcated by any formal professional teachers—nor tested by analysis—nor verified by comparison with any objective standard : but self-sown and self-asserting, stamped, multiplied, and kept in circulation, by the unpremeditated conspiracy of the general [1] public—the omnipresent agency of King Nomos and his numerous volunteers.

In many of the Platonic dialogues, Sokrates is made to dwell upon the fact that there are no recognised professional teachers of virtue ; and to ground upon this fact a doubt, whether virtue be really teachable. But the present dialogue is the only one in which the fact is accounted for, and the doubt formally answered. There are neither special teachers, nor professed pupils, nor determinate periods of study, nor definite lessons or stadia, for the acquirement of virtue, as there are for a particular art or craft : the reason being, that in that department every man must of necessity be a practitioner, more or less perfectly : every man has an interest in communicating it to his neighbour : hence every man is constantly both teacher and learner. Herein consists one main and real distinction between virtue and the

Antithesis of Protagoras and Sokrates. Whether virtue is to be assimilated to a special art.

no blame could fall on Protagoras. We should only be warranted in concluding that it suited the scheme of Plato here to make him talk nonsense.

[1] This is what the Platonic Sokrates alludes to in the Phædon and elsewhere. οἱ τὴν δημοτικήν τε καὶ πολιτικὴν ἀρετὴν ἐπιτετηδευκότες, ἣν δὴ καλοῦσι σωφροσύνην τε καὶ δικαιοσύνην, ἐξ ἔθους τε καὶ μελέτης γεγονυῖαν, ἄνευ φιλοσοφίας τε καὶ νοῦ. Phædon, p. 82 B ; compare the same dialogue, p. 68 C ; also Republic, x. p. 619 C—ἔθει ἄνευ φιλοσοφίας ἀρετῆς μετειληφότα.

The account given by Mr. James Mill (Fragment on Mackintosh, p. 259-260) of the manner in which the established morality of a society is transmitted and perpetuated, coincides completely with the discourse of the Platonic Protagoras. The passage is too long to be cited : I give here only the concluding words, which describe the δημοτικὴ ἀρετὴ ἄνευ φιλοσοφίας—

"In this manner it is that men, in the social state, acquire the habits of moral acting, and certain affections connected with it, before they are capable of reflecting upon the grounds which recommend the acts either to praise or blame. Nearly at this point the greater part of them remain : continuing to perform moral acts and to abstain from the contrary, chiefly from the habits which they have acquired, and the authority upon which they originally acted : though it is not possible that any man should come to the years and blessing of reason, without perceiving at least in an indistinct and general way, the advantage which mankind derive from their acting towards one another in one way rather than another."

special arts; an answer to the view most frequently espoused by the Platonic Sokrates, assimilating virtue to a professional craft, which ought to have special teachers, and a special season of apprenticeship, if it is to be acquired at all.

The speech is censured by some critics as prolix. But to me it seems full of matter and argument, exceedingly free from superfluous rhetoric. The fable with which it opens presents of course the poetical ornament which belongs to that manner of handling. It is however fully equal, in point of perspicuity as well as charm —in my judgment, it is even superior—to any other fable in Plato.

When the harangue, lecture, or sermon, of Protagoras is concluded, Sokrates both expresses his profound admiration of it, and admits the conclusion—That virtue is teachable—to be made out, as well as it can be made out by any continuous exposition.[1] In fact, the speaker has done all that could be done by Perikles or the best orator of the assembly. He has given a long series of reasonings in support of his own case, without stopping to hear the doubts of opponents. He has sailed along triumphantly upon the stream of public sentiment, accepting all the established beliefs —appealing to his hearers with all those familiar phrases, round which the most powerful associations are grouped—and taking for granted that justice, virtue, good, evil, &c., are known, indis-

Procedure of Sokrates in regard to the discourse of Protagoras —he compliments it as an exposition, and analyses some of the fundamental assumptions.

---

[1] Plato, Protag. pp. 328-329.
Very different indeed is the sentiment of the principal Platonic commentators. Schleiermacher will not allow the mythus of Protagoras to be counted among the Platonic mythes: he says that it is composed in the style of Protagoras, and perhaps copied from some real composition of that Sophist. He finds in it nothing but a "grobmaterialistiche Denkungsart, die über die sinnliche Erfahrung nicht hinaus philosophirt" (Einleitung zum Protagoras, vol. i. pp. 233-234).
To the like purpose Ast (Plat. Leb. p. 71)—who tells us that what is expressed in the mythus is, "the vulgar and mean sentiment and manner of thought of the Sophist: for it deduces every thing, both arts and the social union itself, from human wants and necessity". Apparently these critics, when they treat this as a proof of meanness and vulgarity, have forgotten that the Platonic Sokrates himself does exactly the same thing in the Republic—deriving the entire social union from human necessities (Republ. ii. 369 C).
K. F. Hermann is hardly less severe upon the Protagorean discourse (Gesch. und Syst. der Plat. Phil. p. 460).
For my part, I take a view altogether opposed to these learned persons. I think the discourse one of the most striking and instructive portions of the Platonic writings: and if I could believe that it was the composition of Protagoras himself, my estimation of him would be considerably raised.
Steinhart pronounces a much more rational and equitable judgment than Ast and Schleiermacher, upon the discourse of Protagoras (Einleitung zum Prot. pp. 422-423).

putable, determinate data, fully understood, and unanimously interpreted. He has shown that the community take great pains, both publicly and privately, to inculcate and enforce virtue: that is, what *they* believe in and esteem as virtue. But is their belief well founded? Is that which they esteem, really virtue? Do they and their elegant spokesman Protagoras, know what virtue is? If so, *how* do they know it, and can they explain it?

This is the point upon which Sokrates now brings his Elenchus to bear: his method of short question and answer. We have seen what long continuous speaking can do: we have now to see what short cross-questioning can do. The antithesis between the two is at least one main purpose of Plato—if it be not even *the* purpose (as Schleiermacher supposes it to be)—in this memorable dialogue. *One purpose of the dialogue. To contrast continuous discourse with short cross-examining question and answer.*

After your copious exposition, Protagoras (says Sokrates), I have only one little doubt remaining, which you will easily explain.[1] You have several times spoken of justice, moderation, holiness, &c., as if they all, taken collectively, made up virtue. Do you mean that virtue is a Whole, and that these three names denote distinct parts of it? Or, are the three names all equivalent to virtue, different names for one and the same thing? *Prot.*—They are names signifying distinct parts of virtue. *Sokr.*—Are these parts like the parts of the face,—eyes, nose, mouth, ears—each part not only distinct from the rest, but having its own peculiar properties? Or are they like the parts of gold, homogeneous with each other and with the whole, differing only in magnitude? *Prot.*— The former. *Sokr.*—Then some men may possess one part, some another. Or is it necessary that he who possesses one part, should possess all? *Prot.*—By no means necessary. Some men are courageous, but unjust: others are just, but not intelligent. *Sokr.*—Wisdom and courage then, both of them, are parts of virtue? *Prot.*—They are so. Wisdom is the greatest of the parts: but no one of the parts is the exact likeness of another: each of them has its own peculiar property.[2] *Questions by Sokrates —Whether virtue is one and indivisible, or composed of different parts? Whether the parts are homogeneous or heterogeneous.*

[1] Plato, Protag. pp. 328 E—329 B. σμικροῦ τινος ἐνδεής εἰμι πάντ' ἔχειν, πλὴν σμικρόν τί μοι ἐμποδών, ὃ δῆλον &c.
ὅτι Πρωταγόρας ῥᾳδίως ἐπεκδιδάξει. . . . [2] Plato, Protag. pp. 329-330.

Sokr.—Now let us examine what sort of thing each of these parts is. Tell me—is justice some thing, or no thing? I think it is some thing: are you of the same opinion?[1] *Prot.*—Yes. *Sokr.*—Now this thing which you call *justice*: is it itself just or unjust? I should say that it was just: what do you say?[2] *Prot.*—I think so too. *Sokr.*—Holiness also is some thing   is the thing called *holiness*, itself holy or unholy? As for me, if any one were to ask me the question, I should reply—Of course it is: nothing else can well be holy, if holiness itself be not holy. Would you say the same? *Prot.*—Unquestionably. *Sokr.*—Justice being admitted to be just, and holiness to be holy—do not you think that justice also is holy, and that holiness is just? If so, how can you reconcile that with your former declaration, that no one of the parts of virtue is like any other part? *Prot.*—I do not altogether admit that justice is holy, and that holiness is just. But the matter is of little moment: if you please, let both of them stand as admitted. *Sokr.*—Not so:[3] I do not want the debate to turn upon an "If you please": You and I are the debaters, and we shall determine the debate best without "Ifs". *Prot.*—I say then that justice and holiness are indeed, in a certain way, like each other; so also there is a point of analogy between white and black,[4] hard and soft, and between many other things which no one would pronounce to be like generally. *Sokr.*—Do you think then that justice and holiness have only a small point of analogy between them? *Prot.*—Not exactly so: but I do not concur with you when you declare that one is like the other.

---

[1] Plato, Protag. p. 330 B. κοινῇ σκεψώμεθα ποῖόν τι αὐτῶν ἐστιν ἕκαστον. πρῶτον μὲν τὸ τοιόνδε· ἡ δικαιοσύνη πρᾶγμά τί ἐστιν; ἢ οὐδὲν πρᾶγμα; ἐμοὶ μὲν γὰρ δοκεῖ· τί δὲ σοί;

[2] Plato, Protag. p. 330 C. τοῦτο τὸ πρᾶγμα ὃ ὠνομάσατε ἄρτι, ἡ δικαιοσύνη, αὐτὸ τοῦτο δίκαιόν ἐστιν ἢ ἄδικον;

[3] Plato, Protag. p. 331 C. εἰ γὰρ βούλει, ἔστω ἡμῖν καὶ δικαιοσύνη ὅσιον καὶ ὁσιότης δίκαιον. Μή μοι, ἦν δ' ἐγώ· οὐδὲν γὰρ δέομαι τὸ "εἰ βούλει" τοῦτο καὶ "εἴ σοι δοκεῖ" ἐλέγχεσθαι, ἀλλ' ἐμέ τε καὶ σέ.

This passage seems intended to illustrate the indifference of Protagoras for dialectic forms and strict accuracy of discussion. The ἀκριβολογία of Sokrates and Plato was not merely unfamiliar but even distasteful to rhetorical and practical men. Protagoras is made to exhibit himself as thinking the distinctions drawn by Sokrates too nice, not worth attending to. Many of the contemporaries of both shared this opinion. One purpose of our dialogue is to bring such antitheses into view.

[4] Plat. Prot. p. 331 D.

Sokr.—Well then! since you seem to follow with some repugnance this line of argument, let us enter upon another.[1]

Sokrates then attempts to show that intelligence and moderation are identical with each other (σοφία and σωφροσύνη). The proof which he produces, elicited by several questions, is—that both the one and the other are contrary to folly (ἀφροσύνη), and, that as a general rule, nothing can have more than one single contrary.[2]

Intelligence and moderation are identical because they have the same contrary.

Sokrates thus seems to himself to have made much progress in proving all the names of different virtues to be names of one and the same thing. Moderation and intelligence are shown to be the same: justice and holiness had before been shown to be nearly the same:[3] though we must recollect that this last point had not been admitted by Protagoras. It must be confessed however that neither the one nor the other is proved by any conclusive reasons. In laying down the maxim—that nothing can have more than one single contrary— Plato seems to have forgotten that the same term may be used in two different senses. Because the term folly (ἀφροσύνη), is used sometimes to denote the opposite of moderation (σωφροσύνη), sometimes the opposite of intelligence (σοφία), it does not follow that moderation and intelligence are the same thing.[4] Nor does he furnish more satisfactory proof of the other point, *viz.:* That holiness and justice are the same, or as much alike as possible. The intermediate position which is assumed to form the proof, *viz.:* That holiness is holy, and that justice is just—is either tautological, or unmeaning; and cannot serve as a real proof of any thing. It is indeed so futile, that if it were found in the

Insufficient reasons given by Sokrates. He seldom cares to distinguish different meanings of the same term.

---

[1] Plat. Prot. p. 332 A.
[2] Plat. Protag. p. 332.
[3] Plato, Protag. p. 333 B. σχεδόν τι ταὐτὸν ὄν.
[4] Aristotle would probably have avoided such a mistake as this. One important point (as I have already remarked, vol. ii. p. 170) in which he is superior to Plato is, in being far more careful to distinguish the different meanings of the same word—τὰ πολλαχῶς λεγόμενα. Plato rarely troubles himself to notice such distinction, and seems indeed generally unaware of it. He constantly ridicules Prodikus, who tried to distinguish words apparently synonymous.

mouth of Protagoras and not in that of Sokrates, commentators would probably have cited it as an illustration of the futilities of the Sophists. As yet therefore little has been done to elucidate the important question to which Sokrates addresses himself— What is the extent of analogy between the different virtues? Are they at bottom one and the same thing under different names? In what does the analogy or the sameness consist?

But though little progress has been made in determining the question mooted by Sokrates, enough has been done to discompose and mortify Protagoras. The general tenor of the dialogue is, to depict this man, so eloquent in popular and continuous exposition, as destitute of the analytical acumen requisite to meet cross-examination, and of promptitude for dealing with new aspects of the case, on the very subjects which form the theme of his eloquence. He finds himself brought round, by a series of short questions, to a conclusion which—whether conclusively proved or not—is proved in a manner binding upon him, since he has admitted all the antecedent premisses. He becomes dissatisfied with himself, answers with increasing reluctance,[1] and is at last so provoked as to break out of the limits imposed upon a respondent.

Protagoras is puzzled, and becomes irritated.

Meanwhile Sokrates pursues his examination, with intent to prove that justice (δικαιοσύνη) and moderation (σωφροσύνη) are identical. Does a man who acts unjustly conduct himself with moderation? I should be ashamed (replies Protagoras) to answer in the affirmative, though many people say so. *Sokr.*—It is indifferent to me whether you yourself think so or not, provided only you consent to make answer. What I principally examine is the opinion itself: though it follows perhaps as a consequence, that I the questioner, and the respondent along with me, undergo examination at the same time.[2] You answer then (though without

Sokrates presses Protagoras farther. His purpose is, to test opinions and not persons. Protagoras answers with angry prolixity.

---

[1] Plato, Protag. pp. 333 B, 335 A.
[2] Plato, Protag. p. 333 C. τὸν γὰρ λόγον ἔγωγε μάλιστα ἐξετάζω, συμβαίνει μέντοι ἴσως καὶ ἐμὲ τὸν ἐρωτῶντα καὶ τὸν ἐρωτώμενον ἐξετάζεσθαι.

Here again we find Plato drawing special attention to the conditions of dialectic debate.

adopting the opinion) that men who act unjustly sometimes behave with moderation, or with intelligence: that is, that they follow a wise policy in committing injustice. *Prot.*—Be it so. *Sokr.*—You admit too that there exist certain things called good things. Are those things good, which are profitable to mankind? *Prot.*—By Zeus, I call some things good, even though they be not profitable to *men* (replies Protagoras, with increasing acrimony).[1] *Sokr.*—Do you mean those things which are not profitable to any *man*, or those which are not profitable to any creature whatever? Do you call these latter *good* also? *Prot.*—Not at all: but there are many things profitable to men, yet unprofitable or hurtful to different animals. Good is of a character exceedingly diversified and heterogeneous.[2]

Protagoras is represented as giving this answer at considerable length, and in a rhetorical manner, so as to elicit applause from the hearers.[3] Upon this Sokrates replies, "I am a man of short memory, and if any one speaks at length, I forget what he has said. If you wish me to follow you, I must entreat you to make shorter answers." *Prot.*—What do you mean by asking me to make shorter answers? Do you mean shorter than the case requires? *Sokr.*—No, certainly not. *Prot.*—But who is to be judge of the brevity necessary, you or I? *Sokr.*—I have understood that you profess to be master and teacher both of long speech and of short speech: what I beg is, that you will employ only short speech, if you expect me to follow you. *Prot.* —Why, Sokrates, I have carried on many debates in my time; and if, as you ask me now, I had always talked just as my opponent wished, I should never have acquired any reputation at all. *Sokr.*—Be it so: in that case I must retire; for as to long speaking, I am incompetent: I can neither make long speeches, nor follow them.[4]

Remonstrance of Sokrates against long answers, as inconsistent with the laws of dialogue. Protagoras persists. Sokrates rises to depart.

---

[1] Plato, Protag. p. 333 E.
[2] Plato, Protag. p. 334 B. Οὕτω δὲ ποικίλον τί ἐστι τὸ ἀγαθὸν καὶ παντοδαπόν, &c.
The explanation here given by Protagoras of *good* is the same as that which is given by the historical Sokrates himself in the Xenophontic Memorabilia (iii. 8). Things called good are diverse in the highest degree; but they are all called *good* because they all contribute in some way to human security, relief, comfort, or prosperity. To one or other of these ends *good*, in all its multifarious forms, is relative.
[3] Plato, Protag. p. 334 D.
[4] Plato, Prot. pp. 334 E, 335 A-C.

Here Sokrates rises to depart; but Kallias, the master of the house, detains him, and expresses an earnest wish that the debate may be continued. A promiscuous conversation ensues, in which most persons present take part. Alkibiades, as the champion of Sokrates, gives, what seems really to be the key of the dialogue, when he says—"Sokrates admits that he has no capacity for long speaking, and that he is no match therein for Protagoras. But as to dialectic debate, or administering and resisting cross-examination, I should be surprised if any one were a match for him. If Protagoras admits that on this point he is inferior, Sokrates requires no more: if he does not, let him continue the debate: but he must not lengthen his answers so that hearers lose the thread of the subject."

Interference of Kallias to get the debate continued. Promiscuous conversation. Alkibiades declares that Protagoras ought to acknowledge superiority of Sokrates in dialogue.

This remark of Alkibiades, speaking altogether as a vehement partisan of Sokrates, brings to view at least one purpose—if not the main purpose—of Plato in the dialogue. "Sokrates acknowledges the superiority of Protagoras in rhetoric: if Protagoras acknowledges the superiority of Sokrates in dialectic, Sokrates is satisfied." An express *locus standi* is here claimed for dialectic, and a recognised superiority for its professors on their own ground. Protagoras professes to be master both of long speech and of short speech: but in the last he must recognise a superior.

Claim of a special locus standi and professorship for Dialectic, apart from Rhetoric.

Kritias, Prodikus, and Hippias all speak (each in a manner of his own) deprecating marked partisanship on either side, exhorting both parties to moderation, and insisting that the conversation shall be continued. At length Sokrates consents to remain, yet on condition that Protagoras shall confine himself within the limits of the dialectic procedure. Protagoras (he says) shall first question me as long as he pleases: when he has finished, I will question him. The Sophist, though at first reluctant, is constrained, by the instance of those around, to accede to this proposition.[2]

Sokrates is prevailed upon to continue, and invites Protagoras to question him.

[1] Plat. Prot. p. 336 C-D.   [2] Plat. Prot. pp. 337-338.

For the purpose of questioning, Protagoras selects a song of Simonides: prefacing it with a remark, that the most important accomplishment of a cultivated man consists in being thorough master of the works of the poets, so as to understand and appreciate them correctly, and answer all questions respecting them.[1] Sokrates intimates that he knows and admires the song: upon which Protagoras proceeds to point out two passages in it which contradict each other, and asks how Sokrates can explain or justify such contradiction.[2] The latter is at first embarrassed, and invokes the aid of Prodikus; who interferes to uphold the consistency of his fellow-citizen Simonides, but is made to speak (as elsewhere by Plato) in a stupid and ridiculous manner. After a desultory string of remarks,[3] with disputed interpretation of particular phrases and passages of the song, but without promise of any result—Sokrates offers to give an exposition of the general purpose of the whole song, in order that the company may see how far he has advanced in that accomplishment which Protagoras had so emphatically extolled—complete mastery of the works of the poets.[4]

Protagoras extols the importance of knowing the works of the poets, and questions about parts of a song of Simonides Dissenting opinions about the interpretation of the song.

He then proceeds to deliver a long harangue, the commencement of which appears to be a sort of counter-part and parody of the first speech delivered by Protagoras in this dialogue. That Sophist had represented that the sophistical art was ancient:[5] and that the poets, from Homer downward, were Sophists, but dreaded the odium of the name, and professed a different avocation with another title. Sokrates here tells us that philosophy was more ancient still in Krete and Sparta, and that there were more Sophists (he does not distinguish between the Sophist and the philosopher), female as well as male, in those regions, than anywhere else: but that they concealed their name and profession, for fear that others should copy them and acquire the like

Long speech of Sokrates, expounding the purpose of the song, and laying down an ironical theory about the numerous concealed sophists at Krete and Sparta, masters of short speech.

---

[1] Plat. Prot. p. 339 A. ἡγοῦμαι ἐγὼ ἀνδρὶ παιδείας μέγιστον μέρος εἶναι, περὶ ἐπῶν δεινὸν εἶναι.
[2] Plat. Prot. p. 339 C-D.
[3] Plat. Prot. pp. 340-341.

[4] Plat. Prot. p. 342 A. εἰ βούλει λαβεῖν μου πεῖραν ὅπως ἔχω, ὃ σὺ λέγεις τοῦτο, περὶ ἐπῶν.
[5] Plat. Prot. pp. 316-317

eminence :[1] that they pretended to devote themselves altogether to arms and gymnastic—a pretence whereby (he says) all the other Greeks were really deluded. The special characteristic of these philosophers or Sophists was, short and emphatic speech— epigram shot in at the seasonable moment, and thoroughly prostrating an opponent.[2] The Seven Wise Men, among whom Pittakus was one, were philosophers on this type, of supreme excellence : which they showed by inscribing their memorable brief aphorisms at Delphi. So great was the celebrity which Pittakus acquired by his aphorism, that Simonides the poet became jealous, and composed this song altogether for the purpose of discrediting him. Having stated this general view, Sokrates illustrates it by going through the song, with exposition and criticism of several different passages.[3] As soon as Sokrates has concluded, Hippias[4] compliments him, and says that he too has a lecture ready prepared on the same song : which he would willingly deliver : but Alkibiades and the rest beg him to postpone it.

Character of this speech —its connection with the dialogue, and its general purpose. Sokrates inferior to Protagoras in continuous speech.

No remark is made by any one present, either upon the circumstance that Sokrates, after protesting against long speeches, has here delivered one longer by far than the first speech of Protagoras, and more than half as long as the second, which contains a large theory— nor upon the sort of interpretation that he bestows upon the Simonidean song. That interpretation is so strange and forced—so violent in distorting the meaning of the poet—so evidently predetermined by the resolution to find Platonic metaphysics in a lyric effusion addressed to a Thessalian prince [5]—that if such an expo-

---

[1] Plat. Prot. p. 342.
[2] Plat. Prot. p. 342 E, 343 B-C. Ὅτι οὗτος ὁ τρόπος ἦν τῶν παλαιῶν τῆς φιλοσοφίας, βραχυλογία τις Λακωνική.
[3] Plat. Prot. pp. 344-347.
[4] Plat. Prot. p. 347.
[5] Especially his explanation of ἑκὼν ἐρδῇ (p. 345 D.). Heyne (Opuscula, i. p. 160) remarks upon the strange interpretation given by Sokrates of the Simonidean song. Compare Plato in Lysis, p. 212 E, and in Alkib. ii. p. 147 D. In both these cases, Sokrates cites passages of poetry, assigning to them a sense which their authors plainly did not intend them to bear. Heindorf in his note on the Lysis (l. c.) observes—" Videlicet, ut exeat sententia, quam Solon ne somniavit quidem, versuum horum structuram, neglecto plané sermonis usu, hanc statuit.— Cujusmodi interpretationis aliud est luculentum exemplum in Alcib. ii. p. 147 D."

See also Heindorf's notes on the Charmidês, p. 163 B ; Lachês, p. 191 B ; and Lysis, p. 214 D.

M. Boeckh observes (ad Pindar. Isthm. v. p. 528) respecting an allusion made by Pindar to Hesiod—

sition had been found under the name of Protagoras, critics would have dwelt upon it as an additional proof of dishonest perversions by the Sophists.[1] It appears as if Plato, intending in this dialogue to set out the contrast between long or continuous speech (sophistical, rhetorical, poetical) represented by Protagoras, and short, interrogatory speech (dialectical) represented by Sokrates—having moreover composed for Protagoras in the earlier part of the dialogue, an harangue claiming venerable antiquity for his own accomplishment—has thought it right to compose for Sokrates a pleading with like purpose, to put the two accomplishments on a par. And if that pleading includes both pointless irony and misplaced comparisons (especially what is said about the Spartans)—we must remember that Sokrates has expressly renounced all competition with Protagoras in continuous speech, and that he is here handling the weapon in which he is confessedly inferior. Plato secures a decisive triumph to dialectic, and to Sokrates as representing it: but he seems content here to leave Sokrates on the lower ground as a rhetorician.

Moreover, when Sokrates intends to show himself off as a master of poetical lore ($\pi\epsilon\rho\grave{\iota}$ $\dot{\epsilon}\pi\hat{\omega}\nu$ $\delta\epsilon\iota\nu\grave{o}s$), he at the same time claims a right of interpreting the poets in his own way. He considers the poets either as persons divinely inspired, who speak fine things without rational understanding (we have seen this in the Apology and the Ion)—or as men of superior wisdom, who deliver valuable truth lying beneath the surface, and not discernible by vulgar eyes. Both these views differ from that of literal interpretation, which is here represented by Protagoras and Prodikus. And these two Sophists are here contrasted with Sokrates as interpreters of the poets. Protagoras and Prodikus look upon poetical compositions as sources of instruc-

Sokrates depreciates the value of debates on the poets. Their meaning is always disputed, and you can never ask from themselves what it is. Protagoras consents reluctantly to resume the task of answering.

"Num malé intellexit poeta intelligentissimus perspicua verba Hesiodi? Non credo: sed bene sciens, consulto alium sensum intulit, suo consilio accommodatum! Simile exemplum offert gravissimus auctor Plato Theætet. p. 155 D." Stallbaum in his note on the Theætêtus adopts this remark of Boeckh. Groen van Prinsterer gives a similar opinion. (Prosopographia Platonica, p. 17.)

[1] K. F. Hermann observes (Gesch. der Plat. Philos. p. 460) that Sokrates, in his interpretation of the Simonidean song, shows that he can play the Sophist as well as other people can.

tion: and seek to interpret them literally, as an intelligent hearer would have understood them when they were sung or recited for the first time. Towards that end, discrimination of the usual or grammatical meaning of words was indispensable. Sokrates, on the contrary, disregards the literal interpretation, derides verbal distinctions as useless, or twists them into harmony with his own purpose: Simonides and other poets are considered as superior men, and even as inspired men—in whose verses wisdom and virtue *must* be embodied and discoverable [1]— only that they are given in an obscure and enigmatical manner: requiring to be extracted by the divination of the philosopher, who alone knows what wisdom and virtue are. It is for the philosopher to show his ingenuity by detecting the traces of them. This is what Sokrates does with the song of Simonides. He discovers in it supposed underlying thoughts (ὑπονοίας) : [2] distinctions of Platonic Metaphysics (between εἶναι and γενέσθαι), and principles of Platonic Ethics (οὐδεὶς ἕκων κακός)—he proceeds to point out passages in which they are to be found, and explains the song conformably to them, in spite of much violence to the obvious meaning and verbal structure.[3] But though Sokrates accepts, when required, the task of discussing what is said by the poets, and deals with them according to his own point of view— yet he presently lets us see that they are witnesses called into

---

[1] See Plato, Phædrus, p. 245 A-B; Apol. p. 22 B-C; Ion, pp. 533-534.
Compare the distinction drawn in Timæus, p. 72 A-B, between the μάντις and the προφήτης.

[2] About the ὑπόνοιαι ascribed to the poets, see Repub. ii. p. 378 D.; Xen. Sympos. iii. 6; and F. A. Wolf, Prolegom. Homer. p. clxii.-clxiv.
F. A. Wolf remarks, respecting the various allegorical interpretations of Homer and other Greek poets—
"Sed nec prioribus illis, sive allegorica et anagogica somnia sua ipsi crediderunt, sive ab aliis duntaxat credi voluerunt, idonea deest excusatio. Ita enim ratio comparata est, ut libris, quos a teneris statim annis cognoscimus, omnes propé nostras nostræque ætatis opiniones subjiciamus: ac si illi jampridem populari usu consecrati sunt, ipsa obstat veneratio, quominus in iis absurda et ridicula inesse credamus. Lenimus ergo atque adeo ornamus interpretando, quicquid proprio sensu non ferendum videtur. Atque ita factum est omni tempore in libris iis, qui pro sacris habiti sunt."
The distinction was similar in character, and even more marked in respect of earnest reciprocal antipathy, between the different schools of the Jews in Alexandria and Palestine about the interpretation of the Pentateuch. 1. Those who interpreted literally, κατὰ τὴν ῥητὴν διάνοιαν. 2. Those who set aside the literal interpretation, and explained the text upon a philosophy of their own, above the reach of the vulgar (Eusebius, Præp. Ev. viii. 10). Some admitted both the two interpretations, side by side.
Respecting these allegorising schools of the Hellenistic Jews, from Aristobulus (150 B.C.) down to Philo, see the learned and valuable work of Gfrörer—*Philo und die Jüdisch.-Alexandr. Theosophie*, vol. i. pp. 84-86, ii. p. 356 seq.

[3] Plat. Prot. p. 345.

CHAP. XXIII. POETS DELIVER WISDOM WITHOUT KNOWING IT. 287

court by his opponent and not by himself. Alkibiades urges that the debate which had been interrupted shall be resumed and Sokrates himself requests Protagoras to consent. "To debate about the compositions of poets" (says Sokrates), "is to proceed as silly and common-place men do at their banquets: where they cannot pass the time without hiring musical or dancing girls. Noble and well-educated guests, on the contrary, can find enough to interest them in their own conversation, even if they drink ever so much wine.[1] Men such as we are, do not require to be amused by singers—nor to talk about the poets, whom no one can ask what they mean; and who, when cited by different speakers, are affirmed by one to mean one thing, and by another to mean something else, without any decisive authority to appeal to. Such men as you and I ought to lay aside the poets, and test each other by colloquy of our own. If you wish to persist in questioning, I am ready to answer: if not, consent to answer me, and let us bring the interrupted debate to a close."[2]

In spite of this appeal, Protagoras is still unwilling to resume, and is only forced to do so by a stinging taunt from Alkibiades, enforced by requests from Kallias and others. He is depicted as afraid of Sokrates, who, as soon as consent is given, recommences the discussion by saying—"Do not think, Protagoras, that I have any other purpose in debating, except to sift through and through, in conjunction with you, difficulties which puzzle my own mind. Two of us together can do more in this way than any one singly.[3]

Purpose of Sokrates to sift difficulties which he really feels in his own mind. Importance of a colloquial companion for this purpose.

[1] Plato, Prot. p. 347 D. κἂν πάνυ πολὺν οἶνον πίωσιν—a phrase which will be found suitably illustrated by the persistent dialectic of Sokrates, even at the close of the Platonic Symposion, after he has swallowed an incredible quantity of wine.
[2] Plat. Prot. pp. 347-348. This remark—that the poet may be interpreted in many different ways, and that you cannot produce him in court to declare or defend his own meaning—is highly significant, in regard to the value set by Sokrates on living conversation and dialectic.
[3] Plat. Prot. p. 348 C. μὴ οἴου διαλέγεσθαι μέ σοι ἄλλο τι βουλόμενον ἢ ἃ αὐτὸς ἀπορῶ, ἑκάστοτε ταῦτα διασκέψασθαι.

The remark here given should be carefully noted in appreciating the Sokratic frame of mind. The cross-examination which he bestows, is not that of one who himself knows—and who only gets up artificial difficulties to ascertain whether others know as much as he does. On the contrary, it proceeds from one who is himself puzzled; and that which puzzles him he states to others, and debates with others, as affording the best chance of clearing up his own ideas and obtaining a solution.

The grand purpose with Sokrates is

"We are all more fertile and suggestive, with regard to thought, word, and deed, when we act in couples. If a man strikes out anything new by himself, he immediately goes about looking for a companion to whom he can communicate it, and with whom he can jointly review it. Moreover, you are the best man that I know for this purpose, especially on the subject of virtue: for you are not only virtuous yourself, but you can make others so likewise, and you proclaim yourself a teacher of virtue more publicly than any one has ever done before. Whom can I find so competent as you, for questioning and communication on these very subjects?"[1]

After this eulogy on dialectic conversation (illustrating still farther the main purpose of the dialogue), Sokrates resumes the argument as it stood when interrupted. *Sokr.*—You, Protagoras, said that intelligence, moderation, justice, holiness, courage, were all parts of virtue; but each different from the others, and each having a separate essence and properties of its own. Do you still adhere to that opinion? *Prot.*—I now think that the first four are tolerably like and akin to each other, but that courage is very greatly different from all the four. The proof is, that you will find many men pre-eminent for courage, but thoroughly unjust, unholy, intemperate, and stupid.[2] *Sokr.*—Do you consider that all virtue, and each separate part of it, is fine and honourable? *Prot.*—I consider it in the highest degree fine and honourable: I must be mad to think otherwise.[3]

The interrupted debate is resumed. Protagoras says that courage differs materially from the other branches of virtue.

Sokrates then shows that the courageous men are confident men, forward in dashing at dangers, which people in general will not affront: that men who dive with confidence into the water, are those who know how to swim; men who go into battle with confidence as

Sokrates argues to prove that courage consists in knowledge

---

to bring into clear daylight the difficulties which impede the construction of philosophy or "reasoned truth," and to sift them thoroughly, instead of slurring them over or hiding them.
[1] Plato, Protag. pp. 348-349.
[2] Plato, Protag. p. 349 D. τὰ μὲν τέτταρα αὐτῶν ἐπιεικῶς παραπλήσια ἀλλήλοις ἐστίν, ἡ δὲ ἀνδρεία πάνυ πολὺ διαφέρον πάντων τούτων.
[3] Plato, Protag. p. 349 E. κάλλιστον μὲν οὖν, εἰ μὴ μαίνομαί γε. ὅλον που καλὸν ὡς οἷόν τε μάλιστα.
It is not unimportant to notice such declarations as this, put by Plato into the mouth of Protagoras. They tend to show that Plato did not seek (as many of his commentators do) to depict Protagoras as a corruptor of the public mind.

CHAP. XXIII. DEBATE ABOUT PLEASURE AND GOOD. 289

horse-soldiers or light infantry, are those who under- *or intelli-*
stand their profession as such. If any men embark *gence. Protagoras*
in these dangers, without such preliminary know- *does not admit this.*
ledge, do you consider them men of courage? Not at *Sokrates*
all (says Protagoras), they are madmen: courage *changes his attack.*
would be a dishonourable thing, if *they* were reckoned courageous.[1]
Then (replies Sokrates) upon this reasoning, those who face
dangers confidently, with preliminary knowledge, are courageous:
those who do so without it, are madmen. Courage therefore
must consist in knowledge or intelligence?[2] Protagoras declines
to admit this, drawing a distinction somewhat confused:[3] upon
which Sokrates approaches the same argument from a different
point.

Sokr.—You say that some men live well, others badly. Do you
think that a man lives well if he lives in pain and *Identity of*
distress? *Prot.*—No. *Sokr.*—But if he passes his *the plea-*
life pleasurably until its close, does he not then *surable with the good—*
appear to you to have lived well? *Prot.*—I think so. *of the pain-*
Sokr.—To live pleasurably therefore is good: to live *ful with the evil.*
disagreeably is evil. *Prot.*—Yes: at least provided *Sokrates maintains*
he lives taking pleasure in fine or honourable things.[4] *it. Protago-*
Sokr.—What! do you concur with the generality of *Debate.*
people in calling some pleasurable things evil, and some painful
things good? *Prot.*—That is my opinion. *Sokr.*—But are not
all pleasurable things, so far forth as pleasurable, to that extent
good, unless some consequences of a different sort result from
them? And again, subject to the like limitation, are not all
painful things evil, so far forth as they are painful? *Prot.*—To
that question, absolutely as you put it, I do not know whether I
can reply affirmatively—that all pleasurable things are good,
and all painful things evil. I think it safer—with reference not
merely to the present answer, but to my manner of life generally
—to say, that there are some pleasurable things which are good,
others which are not good—some painful things which are evil,
others which are not evil: again, some which are neither, neither

---

[1] Plato, Protag. p. 350 B. Αἰσχρὸν μέντ' ἄν, ἔφη, εἴη, ἡ ἀνδρεία· ἐπεὶ οὗτοί γε μαινόμενοί εἰσιν.
[2] Plato, Protag. p. 350 C.
[3] Plato, Protag. pp. 350-351.
[4] Plat. Prot. p. 351 C. Τὸ μὲν ἄρα ἡδέως ζῆν, ἀγαθόν, τὸ δ' ἀηδῶς, κακόν; Εἴπερ τοῖς καλοῖς γ', ἔφη, ζῴη ἡδόμενος.

good nor evil.[1] *Sokr.*—You call those things pleasurable, which either partake of the nature of pleasure, or cause pleasure? *Prot.* —Unquestionably. *Sokr.*—When I ask whether pleasurable things are not good, in so far forth as pleasurable—I ask in other words, whether pleasure itself be not good? *Prot.*—As you observed before, Sokrates,[2] let us examine the question on each side, to see whether the pleasurable and the good be really the same.

Sokr.—Let us penetrate from the surface to the interior of the question.[3] What is your opinion about knowledge? Do you share the opinion of mankind generally about it, as you do about pleasure and pain? Mankind regard knowledge as something neither strong nor directive nor dominant. Often (they say), when knowledge is in a man, it is not knowledge which governs him, but something else—passion, pleasure, pain, love, fear—all or any of which overpower knowledge, and drag it round about in their train like a slave. Are you of the common opinion on this point also?[4] Or do you believe that knowledge is

Enquiry about knowledge. Is it the dominant agency in the mind? Or is it overcome frequently by other agencies, pleasure or pain? Both agree that knowledge is dominant.

---

[1] Plato, Protag. p. 351 D. ἀλλά μοι δοκεῖ οὐ μόνον πρὸς τὴν νῦν ἀπόκρισιν ἐμοὶ ἀσφαλέστερον εἶναι ἀποκρίνασθαι, ἀλλὰ καὶ πρὸς πάντα τὸν ἄλλον βίον τὸν ἐμόν, ὅτι ἔστι μὲν ἃ τῶν ἡδέων οὐκ ἔστιν ἀγαθά, ἔστι δ' αὖ καὶ ἃ τῶν ἀνιαρῶν οὐκ ἔστι κακά, ἔστι δ' ἃ ἔστι, καὶ τρίτον ἃ οὐδέτερα, οὔτε κακὰ οὔτ' ἀγαθά.

These words strengthen farther what I remarked in a recent note, about the character which Plato wished to depict in Protagoras, so different from what is imputed to that Sophist by the Platonic commentators.

[2] Plato, Protag. p. 351 E. ὥσπερ σὺ λέγεις, ἑκάστοτε, ὦ Σώκρατες, σκοπώμεθα αὐτό.

This is an allusion to the words used by Sokrates not long before,—ἃ αὐτὸς ἀπορῶ ἑκάστοτε ταῦτα διασκέψασθαι, p. 348 C.

[3] Plato, Protag. p. 352 A.

[4] Plato, Protag. p. 352 B-C. πότερον καὶ τοῦτό σοι δοκεῖ ὥσπερ τοῖς πολλοῖς ἀνθρώποις ἢ ἄλλως; . . . διανοούμενοι περὶ τῆς ἐπιστήμης ὥσπερ περὶ ἀνδραπόδου, περιελκομένης ὑπὸ τῶν ἄλλων ἁπάντων. Aristotle in the Nikomachean Ethics cites and criticises the opinion of Sokrates, wherein the latter affirmed the irresistible supremacy of knowledge, when really possessed, over all passions and desires. Aristotle cites it with the express phraseology and illustration contained in this passage of the Protagoras. Ἐπιστάμενον μὲν οὖν οὔ φασί τινες οἷόν τε εἶναι [ἀκρατεύεσθαι]. δεινὸν γάρ, ἐπιστήμης ἐνούσης, ὡς ᾤετο Σωκράτης, ἄλλο τι κρατεῖν, καὶ περιέλκειν αὐτὴν ὥσπερ ἀνδράποδον. Σωκράτης μὲν γὰρ ὅλως ἐμάχετο πρὸς τὸν λόγον, ὡς οὐκ οὔσης ἀκρασίας· οὐθένα γὰρ ὑπολαμβάνοντα, πράττειν παρὰ τὸ βέλτιστον, ἀλλὰ δι' ἄγνοιαν (Ethic. N. vii. 2, vii. 3, p. 1145, b. 24). The same metaphor περιέλκεται ἐπιστήμη is again ascribed to Sokrates by Aristotle, a little farther on in the same treatise, p. 1147, b. 15.

We see from hence that when Aristotle comments upon *the doctrine of Sokrates*, what he here means is, the doctrine of the Platonic Sokrates in the Protagoras; the citation of this particular metaphor establishes the identity.

In another passage of the Nikom. Eth., Aristotle also cites a fact respecting the Sophist Protagoras, which fact

an honourable thing, and made to govern man: and that when once a man knows what good and evil things are, he will not be over-ruled by any other motive whatever, so as to do other things than what are enjoined by such knowledge—his own intelligence being a sufficient defence to him?[1] *Prot.*—The last opinion is what I hold. To me, above all others, it would be disgraceful not to proclaim that knowledge or intelligence was the governing element of human affairs.

Sokr.—You speak well and truly. But you are aware that most men are of a different opinion. They affirm that many who know what is best, act against their own knowledge, overcome by pleasure or by pain. *Prot.*—Most men think so: incorrectly, in my judgment, as they say many other things besides.[2] *Sokr.*—When they say that a man, being overcome by food or drink or other temptations, will do things which he knows to be evil, we must ask them, On what ground do you call these things evil? Is it because they impart pleasure at the moment, or because they prepare disease, poverty, and other such things, for the future?[3] Most men would reply, I think, that they called these things evil not on account of the present pleasure which the things produced, but on account of their ulterior consequences—poverty and disease being both of them distressing? *Prot.*—Most men would say this. *Sokr.*—It would be admitted then that these things were evil for no other reason, than because they ended in pain and in privation of pleasure.[4] *Prot.*—Certainly. *Sokr.*—Again, when it is said that some good things are painful, such things are meant as gymnastic exercises, military expeditions, medical treatment. Now no one will say that these things are good because of the immediate suffering which they occasion, but because of the ulterior results of health,

Mistake of supposing that men act contrary to knowledge. We never call pleasures evils, except when they entail a preponderance of pain, or a disappointment of greater pleasures.

---

is mentioned in the Platonic dialogue Protagoras—respecting the manner in which that Sophist allowed his pupils to assess their own fee for his teaching (Ethic. Nik. ix. 1, 1164, a. 25).

[1] Plato, Protag. p. 352 C. ἀλλ' ἱκανὴν εἶναι τὴν φρόνησιν βοηθεῖν τῷ ἀνθρώπῳ.
[2] Plato, Protag. pp. 352-353.
[3] Plato, Protag. p. 353 D. πονηρὰ δὲ

αὐτὰ πῇ φατε εἶναι; πότερον ὅτι τὴν ἡδονὴν ταύτην ἐν τῷ παραχρῆμα παρέχει καὶ ἡδύ ἐστιν ἕκαστον αὐτῶν, ἢ ὅτι εἰς τὸν ὕστερον χρόνον νόσους τε ποιεῖ καὶ πενίας καὶ ἄλλα τοιαῦτα πολλὰ παρασκευάζει;

[4] Plato, Protag. p. 353 E. Οὐκοῦν φαίνεται.... δι' οὐδὲν ἄλλο ταῦτα κακὰ ὄντα, ἢ διότι εἰς ἀνίας τε ἀποτελευτᾷ καὶ ἄλλων ἡδονῶν ἀποστερεῖ;

wealth, and security, which we obtain by them. Thus, these also are good for no other reason, than because they end in pleasures, or in relief or prevention of pain.[1] Or can you indicate any other end, to which men look when they call these matters evil? *Prot.*—No other end can be indicated.

Sokr.—It thus appears that you pursue pleasure as good, and avoid pain as evil. Pleasure is what you think good: pain is what you think evil: for even pleasure itself appears to you evil, when it either deprives you of pleasures greater than itself, or entails upon you pains outweighing itself. Is there any other reason, or any other ulterior end, to which you look when you pronounce pleasure to be evil? If there be any other reason, or any other end, tell us what it is.[2] *Prot.*—There is none whatever. *Sokr.*—The case is similar about pains: you call pain good, when it preserves you from greater pains, or procures for you a future balance of pleasure. If there be any other end to which you look when you call pain good, tell us what it is. *Prot.*—You speak truly. *Sokr.*—If I am asked why I insist so much on the topic now before us, I shall reply, that it is no easy matter to explain what is meant by being overcome by pleasure; and that the whole proof hinges upon this point—whether there is any other good than pleasure, or any other evil than pain; and whether it be not sufficient, that we should go through life pleasurably and without pains.[3] If this be sufficient, and if no other good or evil can be pointed out, which does not end in pleasures and pains, mark the consequences. Good and evil being identical with pleasurable and painful, it is ridiculous to say that a man does evil voluntarily, knowing it to be evil, under the overpowering influence of pleasure: that is, under the

Pleasure is the only good—pain the only evil. No man does evil voluntarily, knowing it to be evil. Difference between pleasures present and future—resolves itself into pleasure and pain.

---

[1] Plato, Protag. p. 354 B-C. Ταῦτα δὲ ἀγαθά ἐστι δι' ἄλλο τι ἢ ὅτι εἰς ἡδονὰς ἀποτελευτᾷ καὶ λυπῶν ἀπαλλαγὰς καὶ ἀποτροπάς; ἢ ἔχετέ τι ἄλλο τέλος λέγειν, εἰς ὃ ἀποβλέψαντες αὐτὰ ἀγαθὰ καλεῖτε, ἀλλ' ἢ ἡδονάς τε καὶ λύπας; οὐκ ἂν φαῖεν, ὡς ἐγᾦμαι. . . . Οὐκοῦν τὴν μὲν ἡδονὴν διώκετε ὡς ἀγαθὸν ὄν, τὴν δὲ λύπην φεύγετε ὡς κακόν;

[2] Plato, Protag. p. 354 D. ἐπεὶ εἰ κατ' ἄλλο τι αὐτὸ τὸ χαίρειν κακὸν καλεῖτε καὶ εἰς ἄλλο τι τέλος ἀποβλέψαντες, ἔχοιτε ἂν καὶ ἡμῖν εἰπεῖν· ἀλλ' οὐχ ἕξετε. Οὐδ' ἐμοὶ δοκοῦσιν, ἔφη ὁ Πρωταγόρας.

[3] Plato, Protag. p. 354 E. ἔπειτα ἐν τούτῳ εἰσὶ πᾶσαι αἱ ἀποδείξεις· ἀλλ' ἔτι καὶ νῦν ἀναθέσθαι ἔξεστιν, εἴ πῃ ἔχετε ἄλλο τι φάναι εἶναι τὸ ἀγαθὸν ἢ τὴν ἡδονήν, ἢ τὸ κακὸν ἄλλο τι ἢ τὴν ἀνίαν, ἢ ἀρκεῖ ὑμῖν τὸ ἡδέως καταβιῶναι τὸν βίον ἄνευ λυπῶν;

CHAP. XXIII.   PLEASURE THE GOOD, PAIN THE EVIL.   293

overpowering influence of good.[1] How can it be wrong, that a man should yield to the influence of good? It never can be wrong, except in this case—when the good obtained is of smaller amount than the consequent good forfeited or the consequent evil entailed. What other exchangeable value can there be between pleasures and pains, except in the ratio of quantity—greater or less, more or fewer?[2] If an objector tells me that there is a material difference between pleasures and pains of the moment, and pleasures and pains postponed to a future time, I ask him in reply, Is there any other difference, except in pleasure and pain? An intelligent man ought to put them both in the scale, the pleasures and the pains, the present and the future, so as to determine the balance. Weighing pleasures against pleasures, he ought to prefer the more and the greater: weighing pains against pains, the fewer and the less. If pleasures against pains, then when the latter outweigh the former, reckoning distant as well as near, he ought to abstain from the act: when the pleasures outweigh, he ought to do it. *Prot.*—The objectors could have nothing to say against this.[3]

Sokr.—Well then—I shall tell them farther—you know that the same magnitude, and the same voice, appears to you greater when near than when distant. Now, if all our well-doing depended upon our choosing the magnitudes really greater and avoiding those really less, where would the security of our life be found? In the art of mensuration, or in the apparent impression?[4] Would not the latter lead us astray, causing us to vacillate and judge badly in our choice between great and little, with frequent repentance afterwards? Would not the art of mensuration set aside these false appearances, and by revealing to us the truth, impart tranquillity to our minds and security to our lives? Would not the objectors themselves

Necessary resort to the measuring art for choosing pleasures rightly—all the security of our lives depends upon it.

---

[1] Plato, Protag. p. 355 C.
[2] Plato, Protag. p. 356 A.   καὶ τίς ἄλλη ἀξία ἡδονῇ πρὸς λύπην ἐστὶν ἀλλ' ἢ ὑπερβολὴ ἀλλήλων καὶ ἔλλειψις; ταῦτα δ' ἐστὶ μείζω τε καὶ σμικρότερα γιγνόμενα ἀλλήλων, καὶ πλείω καὶ ἐλάττω, καὶ μᾶλλον καὶ ἧττον.
[3] Plato, Protag. p. 356 C.
[4] Plato, Protag. p. 356 D.   εἰ οὖν

ἐν τούτῳ ἡμῖν ἦν τὸ εὖ πράττειν, ἐν τῷ τὰ μὲν μεγάλα μήκη καὶ πράττειν καὶ λαμβάνειν, τὰ δὲ σμικρὰ καὶ φεύγειν καὶ μὴ πράττειν, τίς ἂν ἡμῖν σωτηρία ἐφάνη τοῦ βίου; ἆρα ἡ μετρητικὴ τέχνη, ἢ ἡ τοῦ φαινομένου δύναμις; . . . Ἆρ' ἂν ὁμολογοῖεν οἱ ἄνθρωποι πρὸς ταῦτα ἡμᾶς τὴν μετρητικὴν σώζειν ἂν τέχνην, ἢ ἄλλην;

acknowledge that there was no other safety, except in the art of mensuration? *Prot.*—They would acknowledge it. *Sokr.*—Again, If the good conduct of our lives depended on the choice of odd and even, and in distinguishing rightly the greater from the less, whether far or near, would not our safety reside in knowledge, and in a certain knowledge of mensuration too, in Arithmetic? *Prot.*—They would concede to you that also. *Sokr.*—Well then, my friends, since the security of our lives has been found to depend on the right choice of pleasure and pain—between the more and fewer, greater and less, nearer and farther—does it not come to a simple estimate of excess, deficiency, and equality between them? in other words, to mensuration, art, or science?[1] What kind of art or science it is, we will enquire another time: for the purpose of our argument, enough has been done when we have shown that it *is* science.

For when *we* (Protagoras and Sokrates) affirmed, that nothing was more powerful than science or knowledge, and that this, in whatsoever minds it existed, prevailed over pleasure and every thing else—*you* (the supposed objectors) maintained, on the contrary, that pleasure often prevailed over knowledge even in the instructed man: and you called upon us to explain, upon our principles, what that mental affection was, which people called, being overcome by the seduction of pleasure. We have now shown you that this mental affection is nothing else but ignorance, and the gravest ignorance. You have admitted that those who go wrong in the choice of pleasures and pains—that is, in the choice of good and evil things—go wrong from want of knowledge, of the knowledge or science of mensuration. The wrong deed done from want of knowledge, is done through ignorance. What you call being overcome by pleasure is thus, the gravest ignorance; which these Sophists, Protagoras, Prodikus, and Hippias, engage to cure: but you (the objectors whom we now address) not believing it to be ignorance, or

To do wrong, overcome by pleasure, is only a bad phrase for describing what is really a case of grave ignorance.

---

[1] Plato, Protag. p. 357 A-B. ἐπειδὴ δὲ ἡδονῆς τε καὶ λύπης ἐν ὀρθῇ τῇ αἱρέσει ἐφάνη ἡμῖν ἡ σωτηρία τοῦ βίου οὖσα, τοῦ τε πλέονος καὶ ἐλάττονος καὶ μείζονος καὶ σμικροτέρου καὶ πορρωτέρω καὶ ἐγγυτέρω, ἆρα πρῶτον μὲν οὐ μετρητικὴ φαίνεται, ὑπερβολῆς τε καὶ ἐνδείας οὖσα καὶ ἰσότητος πρὸς ἀλλήλας σκέψις; 'Αλλ' ἀνάγκη. Ἐπεὶ δὲ μετρητική, ἀνάγκη δήπου τέχνη καὶ ἐπιστήμη.

CHAP. XXIII.   RIGHT CHOICE OF PLEASURE AND PAIN.   295

perhaps unwilling to pay them their fees, refuse to visit them, and therefore go on doing ill, both privately and publicly.[1]

Now then, Protagoras, Prodikus, and Hippias (continues Sokrates), I turn to you, and ask, whether you account my reasoning true or false? (All of them pronounced it to be surpassingly true.) *Sokr.*—You agree, then, all three, that the pleasurable is good, and that the painful is evil:[2] for I take no account at present of the verbal distinctions of Prodikus, discriminating between the *pleasurable*, the *delightful*, and the *enjoyable*. If this be so, are not all those actions, which conduct to a life of pleasure or to a life free from pain, honourable? and is not the honourable deed, good and profitable?[3] (In this, all persons present concurred.) If then the pleasurable is good, no one ever does anything, when he either knows or believes other things in his power to be better. To be inferior to yourself is nothing else than ignorance: to be superior to yourself, is nothing else than wisdom. Ignorance consists in holding false opinions, and in being deceived respecting matters of high importance. (Agreed by all.) Accordingly, no one willingly enters upon courses which are evil, or which he believes to be evil: nor is it in the nature of man to enter upon what he thinks evil courses, in preference to good. When a man is compelled to make choice between two evils, no one will take the greater when he might take the less.[4] (Agreed to by all three.) Farther, no one will affront things of which he is afraid, when other things are open to him, of which he is not afraid: for fear is an expectation of evil, so that what a man fears, he of course thinks to be an evil,—and will not approach it willingly. (Agreed.)[5]

Reasoning of Sokrates assented to by all. Actions which conduct to pleasure or freedom from pain, are honourable.

Sokr.—Let us now revert to the explanation of courage, given by Protagoras. He said that four out of the five parts of virtue were tolerably similar; but that courage

Explanation of courage.

---

[1] Plato, Protag. p. 357 E.
[2] Plato, Protag. p. 358 A. ὑπερφυῶς ἐδόκει ἅπασιν ἀληθῆ εἶναι τὰ εἰρημένα. Ὁμολογεῖτε ἄρα, ἦν δ' ἐγώ, τὸ μὲν ἡδὺ ἀγαθὸν εἶναι, τὸ δὲ ἀνιαρὸν κακόν.
[3] Plato, Protag. p. 358 B. αἱ ἐπὶ τούτου πράξεις ἅπασαι ἐπὶ τοῦ ἀλύπως ζῆν καὶ ἡδέως, ἆρ' οὐ καλαί; καὶ τὸ καλὸν ἔργον, ἀγαθόν τε καὶ ὠφέλιμον;

[4] Plato, Protag. p. 358 C-D. ἐπί γε τὰ κακὰ οὐδεὶς ἑκὼν ἔρχεται, οὐδὲ ἐπὶ ἃ οἴεται κακὰ εἶναι, οὐδ' ἐστὶ τοῦτο, ὡς ἔοικεν, ἐν ἀνθρώπου φύσει, ἐπὶ ἃ οἴεται κακὰ εἶναι ἐθέλειν ἰέναι ἀντὶ τῶν ἀγαθῶν· ὅταν τε ἀναγκασθῇ δυοῖν κακοῖν τὸ ἕτερον αἱρεῖσθαι, οὐδεὶς τὸ μεῖζον αἱρήσεται, ἐξὸν τὸ ἔλαττον.
[5] Plato, Protag. p. 358 E.

It consists in a wise estimate of things terrible and not terrible.

differed greatly from all of them. And he affirmed that there were men distinguished for courage; yet at the same time eminently unjust, immoderate, unholy, and stupid. He said, too, that the courageous men were men to attempt things which timid men would not approach. Now, Protagoras, what are these things which the courageous men alone are prepared to attempt? Will they attempt terrible things, believing them to be terrible? *Prot.*—That is impossible, as you have shown just now. *Sokr.*—No one will enter upon that which he believes to be terrible,—or, in other words, will go into evil knowing it to be evil: a man who does so is inferior to himself—and this, as we have agreed, is ignorance, or the contrary of knowledge. All men, both timid and brave, attempt things upon which they have a good heart: in this respect, the things which the timid and the brave go at, are the same.[1] *Prot.*—How can this be? The things which the timid and the brave go at or affront, are quite contrary: for example, the latter are willing to go to war, which the former are not. *Sokr.*—Is it honourable to go to war, or dishonourable? *Prot.*—Honourable. *Sokr.*—If it be honourable, it must also be good:[2] for we have agreed, in the preceding debate, that all honourable things were good. *Prot.*—You speak truly.[3] I at least always persist in thinking so. *Sokr.*—Which of the two is it, who (you say) are unwilling to go into war; it being an honourable and good thing? *Prot.*—The cowards. *Sokr.*—But if going to war be an honourable and good thing, it is also pleasurable? *Prot.*—Certainly that has been admitted.[4] *Sokr.*—Is it then knowingly that cowards refuse to go into war, which is both more honourable, better, and more pleasurable? *Prot.*—We cannot say so, without contradicting our preceding admissions. *Sokr.*—What about the courageous man? does not he affront or

---

[1] Plato, Protag. p. 359 D. ἐπὶ μὲν ἃ δεινὰ ἡγεῖται εἶναι οὐδεὶς ἔρχεται, ἐπειδὴ τὸ ἥττω εἶναι ἑαυτοῦ εὑρέθη ἀμαθία οὖσα. Ὁμολόγει. Ἀλλὰ μὴν ἐπὶ ἅ γε θαρροῦσι πάντες αὖ ἔρχονται, καὶ δειλοὶ καὶ ἀνδρεῖοι, καὶ ταύτῃ γε ἐπὶ τὰ αὐτὰ ἔρχονται οἱ δειλοί τε καὶ οἱ ἀνδρεῖοι.

[2] Plato, Protag. p. 359 E. πότερον καλὸν ὂν ἰέναι (εἰς τὸν πόλεμον) ἢ αἰσχρόν; Καλόν, ἔφη. Οὐκοῦν, εἴπερ καλόν, καὶ ἀγαθὸν ὡμολογήσαμεν ἐν τοῖς ἔμ-

προσθεν· τὰς γὰρ καλὰς πράξεις ἁπάσας ἀγαθὰς ὡμολογήσαμεν;

[3] Plato, Protag. p. 359 E. Ἀληθῆ λέγεις, καὶ ἀεὶ ἔμοιγε δοκεῖ οὕτως.

This answer, put into the mouth of Protagoras, affords another proof that Plato did not intend to impute to him the character which many commentators impute.

[4] Plato, Protag. p. 360 A. Οὐκοῦν, ἦν δ' ἐγώ, εἴπερ καλὸν καὶ ἀγαθόν, καὶ ἡδύ; Ὁμολόγηται γοῦν, ἔφη.

go at what is more honourable, better, and more pleasurable? *Prot.*—It cannot be denied. *Sokr.*—Courageous men then, generally, are those whose fears, when they are afraid, are honourable and good—not dishonourable or bad: and whose confidence, when they feel confident, is also honourable and good?[1] On the contrary, cowards, impudent men, and madmen, both fear, and feel confidence, on dishonourable occasions? *Prot.*—Agreed. *Sokr.*—When they thus view with confidence things dishonourable and evil, is it from any other reason than from ignorance and stupidity? Are they not cowards from stupidity, or a stupid estimate of things terrible? And is it not in this ignorance, or stupid estimate of things terrible, and things not terrible—that cowardice consists? Lastly,[2]—courage being the opposite of cowardice—is it not in the knowledge, or wise estimate, of things terrible and things not terrible, that courage consists?

Protagoras is described as answering the last few questions with increasing reluctance. But at this final question, he declines altogether to answer, or even to imply assent by a gesture.[3] *Sokr.*—Why will you not answer my question, either affirmatively or negatively? *Prot.*—Finish the exposition by yourself. *Sokr.*—I will only ask you one more question. Do you still think, as you said before, that there are some men extremely stupid, but extremely courageous? *Prot.*—You seem to be obstinately bent on making me answer: I will therefore comply with your wish: I say that according to our previous admissions, it appears to me impossible. *Sokr.*—I have no other motive for questioning you thus, except the wish to investigate how the truth stands respecting virtue and what virtue is in itself.[4] To determine this, is the way to elucidate

Reluctance of Protagoras to continue answering. Close of the discussion. Sokrates declares that the subject is still in confusion, and that he wishes to debate it again with Protagoras. Amicable reply of Protagoras.

---

[1] Plato, Protag. p. 360 B. Οὐκοῦν ὅλως οἱ ἀνδρεῖοι οὐκ αἰσχροὺς φόβους φοβοῦνται, ὅταν φοβῶνται, οὐδὲ αἰσχρὰ θάρρη θαρροῦσιν; . . . Εἰ δὲ μὴ αἰσχρά, ἆρ᾽ οὐ καλά; . . . Εἰ δὲ καλά, καὶ ἀγαθά;

[2] Plato, Protag. p. 360 D. Οὐκοῦν ἡ τῶν δεινῶν καὶ μὴ δεινῶν ἀμαθία δειλία ἂν εἴη; . . . Ἡ σοφία ἄρα τῶν δεινῶν καὶ μὴ δεινῶν, ἀνδρεία ἐστίν, ἐναντία οὖσα τῇ τούτων ἀμαθίᾳ;

[3] Plato, Protag. p. 360 D. οὐκέτι ἐνταῦθα οὔτ᾽ ἐπινεῦσαι ἠθέλησεν, ἐσίγα τε.

[4] Plato, Protag. pp. 360-361. Οὗτοι ἄλλου ἕνεκα ἐρωτῶ πάντα ταῦτα, ἢ σκέψασθαι βουλόμενος πῶς ποτ᾽ ἔχει τὰ περὶ τῆς ἀρετῆς, καὶ τί ποτ᾽ ἐστὶν αὐτὸ ἡ ἀρετή. Οἶδα γὰρ ὅτι τούτου φανεροῦ γενομένου μάλιστ᾽ ἂν κατάδηλον γένοιτο ἐκεῖνο, περὶ οὗ ἐγώ τε καὶ σὺ

the question which you and I first debated at length :—I, affirming that virtue was not teachable—you, that it was teachable. The issue of our conversation renders both of us ridiculous. For I, who denied virtue to be teachable, have shown that it consists altogether in knowledge, which is the most teachable of all things : while Protagoras, who affirmed that it was teachable, has tried to show that it consisted in every thing rather than knowledge :—on which supposition it would be hardly teachable at all. I therefore, seeing all these questions sadly confused and turned upside down, am beyond measure anxious to clear them up ;[1] and should be glad, conjointly with you, to go through the whole investigation—First, what Virtue is,—Next, whether it is teachable or not. It is with a provident anxiety for the conduct of my own life that I undertake this research, and I should be delighted to have you as a coadjutor.[2] *Prot.*—I commend your earnestness, Sokrates, and your manner of conducting discussion. I think myself not a bad man in other respects : and as to jealousy, I have as little of it as any one. For I have always said of you, that I admire you much more than any man of my acquaintance—decidedly more than any man of your own age. It would not surprise me, if you became one day illustrious for wisdom.

Remarks on the dialogue. It closes without the least allusion to Hippokrates.

Such is the end of this long and interesting dialogue.[3] We remark with some surprise that it closes without any mention of Hippokrates, and without a word addressed to him respecting his anxious request for admission to the society of Protagoras : though such request had been presented at the beginning, with much emphasis, as the sole motive for the interven-

---

μακρὸν λόγον ἑκάτερος ἀπετείναμεν, ἐγὼ μὲν λέγων, ὡς οὐ διδακτὸν ἀρετή, σὺ δ᾽, ὡς διδακτόν.
[1] Plato, Protag. p. 361 C. ἐγὼ οὖν πάντα ταῦτα καθορῶν ἄνω κάτω ταραττόμενα δεινῶς, πᾶσαν προθυμίαν ἔχω καταφανῆ αὐτὰ γενέσθαι, καὶ βουλοίμην ἂν ταῦτα διεξελθόντας ἡμᾶς ἐξελθεῖν καὶ ἐπὶ τὴν ἀρετὴν ὅ τι ἔστιν.

[2] Plato, Protag. p. 361 D. προμηθούμενος ὑπὲρ τοῦ βίου τοῦ ἐμαυτοῦ παντός.
[3] Most critics treat the Protagoras as a composition of Plato's younger years—what they call his *first period*— before the death of Sokrates. They fix different years, from 407 B.C. (Ast) down to 402 B.C. I do not agree with this view. I can admit no dialogue

tion of Sokrates. Upon this point [1] the dialogue is open to the same criticism as that which Plato (in the Phædrus) bestows on the discourse of Lysias: requiring that every discourse shall be like a living organism, neither headless nor footless, but having extremities and a middle piece adapted to each other.

In our review of this dialogue, we have found first, towards the beginning, an expository discourse from Protagoras, describing the maintenance and propagation of virtue in an established community: next, towards the close, an expository string of interrogatories by Sokrates, destined to establish the identity of Good with Pleasurable, Evil with Painful; and the indispensable supremacy of the calculating or measuring science, as the tutelary guide of human life. Of the first, I speak (like other critics) as the discourse of Protagoras: of the second, as the theory of Sokrates. But I must again remind the reader, that both the one and the other are compositions of Plato; both alike are offspring of his ingenious and productive imagination. Protagoras is not the author of that which appears here under his name: and when we read the disparaging epithets which many critics affix to his discourse, we must recollect that these epithets, if they were well-founded, would have no real application to the historical Protagoras, but only to Plato himself. He has set forth two aspects, distinct and in part opposing, of ethics and politics: and he has provided a worthy champion for each. Philosophy, or "reasoned truth," if it be attainable at all, cannot most certainly be attained without such many-sided handling: still less can that which Plato calls knowledge be attained—or such command of philosophy as will enable a man to stand a Sokratic cross-examination in it.

Two distinct aspects of ethics and politics exhibited: one under the name of Protagoras; the other, under that of Sokrates.

In the last speech of Sokrates in the dialogue,[2] we find him proclaiming, that the first of all problems to be solved was, What virtue really is? upon which there prevails serious confusion of opinions. It was a second question—important, yet still second and presupposing the solution of the first—Whether virtue is teachable? We

Order of ethical problems as conceived by Sokrates.

---

earlier than 399 B.C.: and I consider the Protagoras to belong to Plato's full maturity.
[1] Plato, Phædrus, p. 264 C. δεῖν

πάντα λόγον ὥσπερ ζῶον συνεστάναι, σῶμά τι ἔχοντα αὐτὸν αὑτοῦ, ὥστε μήτε ἀκέφαλον εἶναι μήτε ἄπουν, &c.
[2] Plato, Protag. p. 361 C.

300   PROTAGORAS.   CHAP. XXIII.

noticed the same judgment as to the order of the two questions delivered by Sokrates in the Menon.[1]

Difference of method between him and Protagoras flows from this difference of order. Protagoras assumes what virtue is, without enquiry.

Now the conception of ethical questions in this order—the reluctance to deal with the second until the first has been fully debated and settled—is one fundamental characteristic of Sokrates. The difference of method, between him and Protagoras, flows from this prior difference between them in fundamental conception. What virtue is, Protagoras neither defines nor analyses, nor submits to debate. He manifests no consciousness of the necessity of analysis: he accepts the ground already prepared for him by King Nomos: he thus proceeds as if the first step had been made sure, and takes his departure from hypotheses of which he renders no account— as the Platonic Sokrates complains of the geometers for doing.[2] To Protagoras, social or political virtue is a known and familiar datum, about which no one can mistake: which must be possessed, in greater or less measure, by every man, as a condition of the existence of society: which every individual has an interest in promoting in all his neighbours: and which every one therefore teaches and enforces upon every one else. It is a matter of common sense or common sentiment, and thus stands in contrast with the special professional accomplishments; which are confined only to a few—and the possessors, teachers, and learners of which are each an assignable section of the society. The parts or branches of virtue are, in like manner, assumed by him as known, in their relations to each other and to the whole. This persuasion of knowledge, without preliminary investigation, he adopts from the general public, with whom he is in communion of sentiment. What they accept and enforce as virtue, he accepts and enforces also.

---

[1] See the last preceding chapter of this volume, p. 240.

Upon this order, necessarily required, of the two questions, Schleiermacher has a pertinent remark in his general Einleitung to the works of Plato, p. 26. Eberhard (he says) affirms that the end proposed by Plato in his dialogues was to form the minds of the noble Athenian youth, so as to make them virtuous citizens. Schleiermacher controverts the position of Eberhard; maintaining "that this is far too subordinate a standing-point for philosophy,—besides that it is reasoning in a circle, since philosophy has first to determine what the virtue of a citizen is".

[2] See suprà, vol. i. ch. viii. p. 358 and ch. xviii. p. 136, respecting these remarks of Plato on the geometers.

Again, the method pursued by Protagoras, is one suitable to a teacher who has jumped over this first step; who assumes virtue, as something fixed in the public sentiments—and addresses himself to those sentiments, ready-made as he finds them. He expands and illustrates them in continuous lectures of some length, which fill both the ears and minds of the listener— "Spartam nactus es, hanc exorna": he describes their growth, propagation, and working in the community: he gives interesting comments on the poets, eulogising the admired heroes who form the theme of their verses, and enlarging on their admonitions. Moreover, while resting altogether upon the authority of King Nomos, he points out the best jewel in the crown of that potentate; the great social fact of punishment prospective, rationally apportioned, and employed altogether for preventing and deterring—instead of being a mere retrospective impulse, vindictive or retributive for the past. He describes instructively the machinery operative in the community for ensuring obedience to what they think right: he teaches, in his eloquent expositions and interpretations, the same morality, public and private, that every one else teaches: while he can perform the work of teaching, somewhat more effectively than they. Lastly, his method is essentially showy and popular; intended for numerous assemblies, reproducing the established creeds and sentiments of those assemblies, to their satisfaction and admiration. He is prepared to be met and answered in his own way, by opposing speakers; and he conceives himself more than a match for such rivals. He professes also to possess the art of short conversation or discussion. But in the exercise of this art, he runs almost involuntarily into his more characteristic endowment of continuous speech: besides that the points which he raises for discussion assume all the fundamental principles, and turn only upon such applications of those principles as are admitted by most persons to be open questions, not foreclosed by a peremptory orthodoxy.

Method of Protagoras. Continuous lectures addressed to established public sentiments with which he is in harmony.

Upon all these points, Sokrates is the formal antithesis of Protagoras. He disclaims altogether the capacities to which that Sophist lays claim. Not only he cannot teach virtue, but he professes not to know what it is,

Method of Sokrates. Dwells upon that part of

the problem which Protagoras had left out. nor whether it be teachable at all. He starts from a different point of view not considering virtue as a known datum, or as an universal postulate, but assimilating it to a special craft or accomplishment, in which a few practitioners suffice for the entire public : requiring that in this capacity it shall be defined, and its practitioners and teachers pointed out. He has no common ground with Protagoras; for the difficulties which he moots are just such as the common consciousness (and Protagoras along with it) overleaps or supposes to be settled. His first requirement, advanced under the modest guise of a small doubt [1] which Protagoras must certainly be competent to remove, is, to know—What virtue is? What are the separate parts of virtue — justice, moderation, holiness, &c.? What is the relation which they bear to each other and to the whole—virtue? Are they homogeneous, differing only in quantity—or has each of them its own specific essence and peculiarity?[2] Respecting virtue as a whole, we must recollect, Protagoras had discoursed eloquently and confidently, as of a matter perfectly known. He is now called back as it were to meet an attack in the rear : to answer questions which he had never considered, and which had never even presented themselves to him as questions. At first he replies as if the questions offered no difficulty ;[3] sometimes he does not feel their importance, so that it seems to him a matter of indifference whether he replies in the affirmative or negative.[4] But he finds himself brought round, by a series of questions, to assent to conclusions which he nevertheless thinks untrue, and which are certainly unwelcome. Accordingly, he becomes more and more disgusted with the process of analytical interrogation : and at length answers with such impatience and prolixity, that the interrogation can no longer be prosecuted. Here comes in the break—the remonstrance of Sokrates—and the mediation of the by-standers.

---

[1] Plato, Protag. p. 328 E. πλὴν σμικρόν τί μοι ἐμποδών, ὃ δῆλον ὅτι Πρωταγόρας ῥᾳδίως ἐπεκδιδάξει, &c.

[2] Respecting Ariston of Chios, Diogenes Laertius tells us—'Ἀρετὰς δ' οὔτε πολλὰς εἰσῆγεν, ὡς ὁ Ζήνων, οὔτε μίαν πολλοῖς ὀνόμασιν καλουμένην— ἀλλὰ καὶ τὸ πρὸς τί πως ἔχειν (Diog. Laert. vii. 161).

[3] Plato, Protag. p. 329 D. Ἀλλὰ ῥᾴδιον τοῦτό γ', ἔφη, ἀποκρίνασθαι, &c.

[4] Plato, Protag. p. 331 D. εἰ γὰρ βούλει, ἔστω ἡμῖν καὶ δικαιοσύνη ὅσιον καὶ ὁσιότης δίκαιον. Μή μοι, ἦν δ' ἐγώ· οὐδὲν γὰρ δέομαι τὸ "εἰ βούλει" τοῦτο καὶ "εἰ σοι δοκεῖ" ἐλέγχεσθαι, ἀλλ' ἐμέ τε καὶ σέ.

CHAP. XXIII. THE RHETOR UNDER CROSS-EXAMINATION. 303

It is this antithesis between the eloquent popular lecturer, and the analytical enquirer and cross-examiner, which the dialogue seems mainly intended to set forth. Protagoras professes to know that which he neither knows, nor has ever tried to probe to the bottom. Upon this false persuasion of knowledge, the Sokratic Elenchus is brought to bear. We are made to see how strange, repugnant, and perplexing, is the process of analysis to this eloquent expositor: how incompetent he is to go through it without confusion: how little he can define his own terms, or determine the limits of those notions on which he is perpetually descanting. *Antithesis between the eloquent lecturer and the analytical cross-examiner.*

It is not that Protagoras is proved to be wrong (I speak now of this early part of the conversation, between chapters 51-62—pp. 329-335) in the substantive ground which he takes. I do not at all believe (as many critics either affirm or imply) that Plato intended all which he composed under the name of Protagoras to be vile perversion of truth, with nothing but empty words and exorbitant pretensions. I do not even believe that Plato intended all those observations, to which the name of Protagoras is prefixed, to be accounted silly—while all that is assigned to Sokrates,[1] is admirable sense and acuteness. It is by no means certain that Plato intended to be understood as himself endorsing the opinions which he ascribes everywhere to Sokrates: and it is quite certain that he does not always make the Sokrates of one dialogue consistent with the Sokrates of another. For the purpose of showing the incapacity of the respondent to satisfy the exigencies of analysis, we need not necessarily suppose that the conclusion to which the questions conduct should be a true one. If the respondent be brought, through his own admissions, to a contradiction, this is enough to prove that he did not know the subject deeply enough to make the proper answers and distinctions. *Protagoras not intended to be always in the wrong, though he is described as brought to a contradiction.*

But whatever may have been the intention of Plato, if we look at the fact, we shall find that what he has assigned to Sokrates is not always true, nor what he has given to *Affirmation of Protagoras about*

[1] Schöne, in his Commentary on the Protagoras, is of opinion that a good part of Plato's own doctrine is given under the name of Protagoras (Ueber den Protag. von Platon, p. 180 seq.).

304 PROTAGORAS. CHAP. XXIII.

courage is affirmed by Plato himself elsewhere. Protagoras, always false. The positions laid down by the latter — That many men are courageous, but unjust: that various persons are just, without being wise and intelligent: that he who possesses one virtue, does not of necessity possess all:[1]—are not only in conformity with the common opinion, but are quite true, though Sokrates is made to dispute them. Moreover, the arguments employed by Sokrates (including in those arguments the strange propositions that justice is just, and that holiness is holy) are certainly noway conclusive.[2] Though Protagoras, becoming entangled in difficulties, and incapable of maintaining his consistency against an embarrassing cross-examination, is of course exhibited as ignorant of that which he professes to know—the doctrine which he maintains is neither untrue in itself, nor even shown to be apparently untrue.

The harsh epithets applied by critics to Protagoras are not borne out by the dialogue. He stands on the same ground as the common consciousness. As to the arrogant and exorbitant pretensions which the Platonic commentators ascribe to Protagoras, more is said than the reality justifies. He pretends to know what virtue, justice, moderation, courage, &c., are, and he is proved not to know. But this is what every one else pretends to know also, and what every body else teaches as well as he—"*Hæc Janus summus ab imo Perdocet: hæc recinunt juvenes dictata senesque*". What he pretends to do, beyond the general public, he really can do. He can discourse, learnedly and eloquently, upon these received doctrines and sentiments: he can enlist the feelings and sympathies of the public in favour of that which he, in common with the public, believes to be good—and against that which he and they believe to be bad:

---

[1] Plato, Protag. p. 329 E. Protagoras is here made to affirm that many men are courageous who are neither just, nor temperate, nor virtuous in other respects. Sokrates contradicts the position. But in the Treatise De Legibus (i. p. 630 B), Plato himself says the same thing as Protagoras is here made to say: at least assuming that the Athenian speaker in De Legg. represents the sentiment of Plato himself at the time when he composed that treatise.

[2] Plato, Protag. p. 330 C, p. 333 B.

To say "Justice is just," or "Holiness is holy," is indeed either mere tautology, or else an impropriety of speech. Dr. Hutcheson observes on an analogous case:—"None can apply moral attributes to the very faculty of perceiving moral qualities: or call his moral Sense morally Good or Evil, any more than he calls the power of tasting, sweet or bitter—or the power of seeing, straight or crooked, white or black" (Hutcheson on the Passions, sect. i. p. 234).

CHAP. XXIII. HATRED OF THE PUBLIC FOR DIALECTIC. 305

he can thus teach virtue more effectively than others. But whether that which is received as virtue, be really such—he has never analysed or verified : nor does he willingly submit to the process of analysis. Here again he is in harmony with the general public : for they hate, as much as he does, to be dragged back to fundamentals, and forced to explain, defend, revise, or modify, their established sentiments and maxims : which they apply as *principia* for deduction to particular cases, and which they recognise as axioms whereby other things are to be tried, not as liable to be tried themselves. Protagoras is one of the general public, in dislike of, and inaptitude for, analysis and dialectic discussion : while he stands above them in his eloquence and his power of combining, illustrating, and adorning, received doctrines. These are points of superiority, not pretended, but real.

The aversion of Protagoras for dialectic discussion — after causing an interruption of the ethical argument, and an interlude of comment on the poet Simonides—is at length with difficulty overcome, and the argument is then resumed. The question still continues, What is virtue ? What are the five different parts of virtue ? Yet it is so far altered that Protagoras now admits that the four parts of virtue which Sokrates professed to have shown to be nearly identical, really are tolerably alike : but he nevertheless contends that courage is very different from all of them, repeating his declaration that many men are courageous, but unjust and stupid at the same time. This position Sokrates undertakes to refute. In doing so, he lays out one of the largest, most distinct, and most positive theories of virtue, which can be found in the Platonic writings.

Aversion of Protagoras for dialectic. Interlude about the song of Simonides.

Virtue, according to this theory, consists in a right measurement and choice of pleasures and pains : in deciding correctly, wherever we have an alternative, on which side lies the largest pleasure or the least pain—and choosing the side which presents this balance. To live pleasurably, is pronounced to be good : to live without pleasure or in pain, is evil. Moreover, nothing but pleasure, or comparative mitigation of

Ethical view given by Sokrates —worked out at length clearly. Good and evil consist in right or wrong calcu-

lation of pain, is good: nothing but pain is evil.[1] Good, is identical with the greatest pleasure or least pain: evil, with the greatest pain: meaning thereby each pleasure and each pain when looked at along with its consequences and concomitants. The grand determining cause and condition of virtue is knowledge: the knowledge, science, or art, of correctly measuring the comparative value of different pleasures and pains. Such knowledge (the theory affirms), wherever it is possessed, will be sure to command the whole man, to dictate all his conduct, and to prevail over every temptation of special appetite or aversion. To say that a man who knows on which side the greatest pleasure or the least pain lies, will act against his knowledge—is a mistake. If he acts in this way, it is plain that he does not possess the knowledge, and that he sins through ignorance.

lation of pleasures and pains of the agent.

Protagoras agrees with Sokrates in the encomiums bestowed on the paramount importance and ascendancy of knowledge: but does not at first agree with him in identifying good with pleasure, and evil with pain.

Protagoras is at first opposed to this theory.

---

[1] The substantial identity of Good with Pleasure, of Evil with Pain, was the doctrine of the historical Sokrates as declared in Xenophon's Memorabilia. See, among other passages, i. 6, 8. Τοῦ δὲ μὴ δουλεύειν γαστρὶ μηδὲ ὕπνῳ καὶ λαγνείᾳ, οἴει τι ἄλλο αἰτιώτερον εἶναι, ἢ τὸ ἕτερα ἔχειν τούτων ἡδίω, ἃ οὐ μόνον ἐν χρείᾳ ὄντα εὐφραίνει, ἀλλὰ καὶ ἐλπίδας παρέχοντα ὠφελήσειν ἀεί; Καὶ μὴν τοῦτό γε οἶσθα, ὅτι οἱ μὲν οἰόμενοι μηδὲν εὖ πράττειν οὐκ εὐφραίνονται, οἱ δὲ ἡγούμενοι καλῶς προχωρεῖν ἑαυτοῖς, ἢ γεωργίαν ἢ ναυκληρίαν ἢ ἀλλ' ὅ, τι ἂν τυγχάνωσιν ἐργαζόμενοι, ὡς εὖ πράττοντες εὐφραίνονται. Οἴει οὖν ἀπὸ πάντων τούτων τοσαύτην ἡδονὴν εἶναι, ὅσην ἀπὸ τοῦ ἑαυτόν τε ἡγεῖσθαι βελτίω γίγνεσθαι καὶ φίλους ἀμείνους κτᾶσθαι; Ἐγὼ τοίνυν διατελῶ ταῦτα νομίζων.

Locke says, 'Essay on Human Understanding,' Book ii. ch. 28, "Good or Evil is nothing but pleasure or pain to us—or that which procures pleasure or pain to us. Moral good or evil then is only the conformity or disagreement of our voluntary actions to some law, whereby good or evil is drawn on us by the will and power of the lawmaker; which good or evil, pleasure or pain, attending our observance or breach of the law, is that we call reward or punishment."

The formal distinction here taken by Locke between pleasure and that which procures pleasure—both the one and the other being called Good—(the like in regard to pain and evil) is not distinctly stated by Sokrates in the Protagoras, though he says nothing inconsistent with it: but it is distinctly stated in the Republic, ii. p. 357, where Good is distributed under three heads. 1. That which we desire immediately and for itself—such as Enjoyment, Innocuous pleasure. 2. That which we desire both for itself and for its consequences — health, intelligence, good sight or hearing, &c 3. That which we do not desire (perhaps even shun) for itself, but which we accept by reason of its consequences in averting greater pains or procuring greater pleasures.

This discrimination of the varieties of Good, given in the Republic, is quite consistent with what is stated by Sokrates in the Protagoras, though it is more full and precise. But it is not consistent with what Sokrates says in the Gorgias, where he asserts a radical dissimilarity of nature between ἡδὺ and ἀγαθόν

Upon this point, too, he is represented as agreeing in opinion with the Many. He does not admit that to live pleasurably is good, unless where a man takes his pleasure in honourable things. He thinks it safer, and more consistent with his own whole life, to maintain—That pleasurable things, or painful things, may be either good, or evil, or indifferent, according to the particular case.

This doctrine Sokrates takes much pains to refute. He contends that pleasurable things, so far forth as pleasurable, are always good—and painful things, so far forth as painful, always evil. When some pleasures are called evil, that is not on account of any thing belonging to the pleasure itself, but because of its ulterior consequences and concomitants, which are painful or distressing in a degree more than countervailing the pleasure. So too, when some pains are pronounced to be good, this is not from any peculiarity in the pain itself, but because of its consequences and concomitants : such pain being required as a condition to the attainment of health, security, wealth, and other pleasures or satisfactions more than counterbalancing. Sokrates challenges opponents to name any other end, with reference to which things are called *good*, except their tendency to prevent or relieve pains and to ensure a balance of pleasure : he challenges them to name any other end, with reference to which things are called *evil*, except their tendency to produce pains and to intercept or destroy pleasures. In measuring pleasures and pains against each other, there is no other difference to be reckoned except that of greater or less, more or fewer. The difference between near and distant, does indeed obtrude itself upon us as a misleading element. But it is the special task of the "measuring science" to correct this illusion—and to compare pleasures or pains, whether near or distant, according to their real worth : just as we learn to rectify the illusions of the sight in regard to near and distant objects.

Reasoning of Sokrates.

Sokrates proceeds to apply this general principle in correcting the explanation of courage given by Protagoras. He shows, or tries to show, that courage, like all the other branches of virtue, consists in acting on a just estimate of comparative pleasures and pains. No man affronts evil, or the alternative of greater pain, knowing it

Application of that reasoning to the case of courage.

to be such: no man therefore adventures himself in any terrible enterprise, knowing it to be so: neither the brave nor the timid do this. Both the brave and the timid affront that which they think not terrible, or the least terrible of two alternatives: but they estimate differently what is such. The former go readily to war when required, the latter evade it. Now to go into war when required, is honourable: being honourable, it is good: being honourable and good, it is pleasurable. The brave know this, and enter upon it willingly: the timid not only do not know it, but entertain the contrary opinion, looking upon war as painful and terrible, and therefore keeping aloof. The brave men fear what it is honourable to fear, the cowards what it is dishonourable to fear: the former act upon the knowledge of what is really terrible, the latter are misled by their ignorance of it. Courage is thus, like the other virtues, a case of accurate knowledge of comparative pleasures and pains, or of good and evil.[1]

The theory which Plato here lays down is Such is the ethical theory which the Platonic Sokrates enunciates in this dialogue, and which Protagoras and the others accept. It is positive and distinct, to a degree very unusual with Plato. We shall find that

---

[1] Compare, respecting Courage, a passage in the Republic, iv. pp. 429 C, 430 B, which is better stated there (though substantially the same opinion) than here in the Protagoras.

The opinion of the Platonic Sokrates may be illustrated by a sentence from the funeral oration delivered by Periklês, Thucyd. ii. 43, fin. 'Αλγεινοτέρα γαρ ἀνδρί γε φρόνημα ἔχοντι ἡ ἐν τῷ μετὰ τοῦ μαλακισθῆναι κάκωσις, ἢ ὁ μετὰ ῥώμης καὶ κοινῆς ἐλπίδος ἅμα γιγνόμενος ἀναίσθητος θάνατος—which Dr. Arnold thus translates in his note: "For more grievous to a man of noble mind is the misery which comes together with cowardice, than the unfelt death which befalls him in the midst of his strength and hopes for the common welfare."

So again in the Phædon (p. 68) Sokrates describes the courage of the ordinary unphilosophical citizen to consist in braving death from fear of greater evils (which is the same view as that of Sokrates in the Protagoras), while the philosopher is courageous on a different principle; aspiring only to reason and intelligence, with the pleasures attending it, he welcomes death as releasing his mind from the obstructive companionship of the body.

The fear of disgrace and dishonour, in his own eyes and in those of others, is more intolerable to the brave man than the fear of wounds and death in the service of his country. See Plato, Leg. i. pp. 646-647. He is φοβερὸς μετὰ νόμου, μετὰ δίκης, p. 647 E. Such is the way in which both Plato and Thucydides conceive the character of the brave citizen as compared with the coward.

It is plain that this resolves itself ultimately into a different estimate of prospective pains; the case being one in which pleasure is not concerned. That the pains of self-reproach and infamy in the eyes of others are among the most agonising in the human bosom, need hardly be remarked. At the same time the sentiments here conceived embrace a wide field of sympathy, comprising the interests, honour, and security, of others as well as of the individual agent.

he theorises differently in other dialogues; whether *more distinct and specific than any theory laid down in other dialogues.* for the better or the worse, will be hereafter seen. He declares here explicitly that pleasure, or happiness, is the end to be pursued; and pain, or misery, the end to be avoided: and that there is no other end, in reference to which things can be called good or evil, except as they tend to promote pleasure or mitigate suffering, on the one side—to entail pain or suffering on the other. He challenges objectors to assign any other end. And thus much is certain— that in those other dialogues where he himself departs from the present doctrine, he has not complied with his own challenge. Nowhere has he specified a different end. In other dialogues, as well as in the Protagoras, Plato has insisted on the necessity of a science or art of calculation: but in no other dialogue has he told us distinctly what are the items to be calculated.

I perfectly agree with the doctrine laid down by Sokrates in the Protagoras, that pain or suffering is the End to be avoided or lessened as far as possible—and pleasure or happiness the End to be pursued as far as attainable—by intelligent forethought and comparison: that there is no other intelligible standard of reference, for application of the terms Good and Evil, except the tendency to produce happiness or misery: and that if this standard be rejected, ethical debate loses all standard for rational discussion, and becomes only an enunciation of the different sentiments, authoritative and self-justifying, prevalent in each community. *Remarks on the theory here laid down by Sokrates. It is too narrow, and exclusively prudential.* But the End just mentioned is highly complex, and care must be taken to conceive it in its full comprehension. Herein I conceive the argument of Sokrates (in the Protagoras) to be incomplete. It carries attention only to a part of the truth, keeping out of sight, though not excluding, the remainder. It considers each man as an individual, determining good or evil for himself by calculating his own pleasures and pains: as a prudent, temperate, and courageous agent, but neither as just nor beneficent. It omits to take account of him as a member of a society, composed of many others akin or co-ordinate with himself. Now it is the purpose of an ethical or political reasoner (such as Plato both professes to be and really is) to study the means of happiness, not simply for the agent himself, but for that agent together with others around him—for the members of the community generally.[1] The Platonic Sokrates says this himself in the Republic: and accordingly, he there treats of other points which are not touched upon by Sokrates in the Protagoras. He proclaims that the happiness of each citizen must be sought only by means consistent with the security, and to a certain extent with the happiness, of others: he provides as far as practicable that all shall derive their pleasures and pains from the same causes: common pleasures, and common pains, to all.[2] The doctrine of Sokrates in the Protagoras requires to be enlarged so as to comprehend these other important elements. Since the conduct of every agent affects the happiness of others, he must be called upon to take account of its consequences under both aspects, especially where it goes to inflict hurt or privation upon others. Good and evil depend upon that scientific computation and comparison of pleasures and pains which Sokrates in the Protagoras prescribes: but the computation must include, to a certain extent, the pleasures and pains (security and rightful expectations) of others besides the agent himself, implicated in the consequences of his acts.[3]

As to this point, we shall find the Platonic Sokrates not always correct, nor even consistent with himself. This will appear especially when we come to see the account which he gives of Justice in the Republic. In that branch of the Ethical End, a direct regard to the security of others comes into the foreground. For in an act of injustice, the prominent characteristic is that of harm done to others—though that is not the whole, since the security of the agent himself is implicated with that of others in the general fulfilment of these obligations. It is this primary regard to others, and secondary regard to self, implicated in one complex

Comparison with the Republic.

---

[1] Plato, Republ. iv. pp. 420-421, v. p. 466 A.

[2] Plato, Republ. v. pp. 462 A-B-D, 464 A-D.

Throughout the first of these passages we see ἀγαθὸν used as the equivalent of ἡδονή, κακὸν as the equivalent of λύπη.

[3] See, especially on this point, the brief but valuable Tract on Utilitarianism by Mr. John Stuart Mill. In page 16 of that work attention is called to the fact, that in Utilitarianism the standard is not the greatest happiness of the agent himself alone, but the greatest amount of happiness altogether. So that we cannot with exactness call the doctrine of Sokrates, in his conversation with Protagoras, "the theory of Utilitarianism," as Mr. Mill calls it in page 1.

feeling—which distinguishes justice from prudence. The Platonic Sokrates in the Republic (though his language is not always clear) does not admit this; but considers justice as a branch of prudence, necessary to ensure the happiness of the individual agent himself.

Now in the Protagoras, what the Platonic Sokrates dwells upon (in the argument which I have been considering) is prudence, temperance, courage: little or nothing is said about justice: there was therefore the less necessity for insisting on that prominent reference to the security of others (besides the agent himself) which justice involves. If, however, we turn back to the earlier part of the dialogue, to the speech delivered by Protagoras, we see justice brought into the foreground. *The discourse of Protagoras brings out an important part of the whole case, which is omitted in the analysis by Sokrates.* It is not indeed handled analytically (which is not the manner of that Sophist), nor is it resolved into regard to pleasure and pain, happiness and misery: but it is announced as a social sentiment indispensably and reciprocally necessary from every man towards every other ($\delta \acute{\iota} \kappa \eta$—$a \grave{\iota} \delta \grave{\omega} s$), distinguishable from those endowments which supply the wants and multiply the comforts of the individual himself. The very existence of the social union requires, that each man should feel a sentiment of duties on his part towards others, and duties on their parts towards him: or (in other words) of rights on his part to have his interests considered by others, and rights on their parts to have their interests considered by him. Unless this sentiment of reciprocity—reciprocal duty and right—exist in the bosom of each individual citizen, or at least in the large majority —no social union could subsist. There are doubtless different degrees of the sentiment: moreover the rights and duties may be apportioned better or worse, more or less fairly, among the individuals of a society; thus rendering the society more or less estimable and comfortable. But without a certain minimum of the sentiment in each individual bosom, even the worst constituted society could not hold together. And it is this sentiment of reciprocity which Protagoras (in the dialogue before us) is introduced as postulating in his declaration, that justice and the sense of shame (unlike to professional aptitudes) must be distributed universally and without exception among all the members of a community. Each man must feel them, in his conduct towards others: each man must also be able to reckon that others will feel the like, in their behaviour towards him.[1]

If we thus compare the Ethical End, as implied, though not explicitly laid down, by Protagoras in the earlier part of the dialogue,—and as laid down by Sokrates in the later part—we shall see that while Sokrates restricts it to a true comparative estimate of the pains and pleasures of the agent himself, Protagoras enlarges it so as to include a direct reference to those of others also, coupled with an expectation of the like

The Ethical End, as implied in the discourse of Protagoras, involves a direct regard to the pleasures and pains of other

---

[1] Professor Bain (in his work on the Emotions and the Will, ch. xv On the Ethical Emotions, pp. 271-3) has given remarks extremely pertinent to the illustration of that doctrine which Plato has here placed under the name of Protagoras.

"The supposed uniformity of moral distinctions resolves itself into the two following particulars. First, the common end of *public security*, which is also individual preservation, demands certain precautions that are everywhere very much alike, and can in no case be dispensed with. Some sort of constituted authority to control the individual impulses and to protect each man's person and property, must exist wherever a number of human beings live together. The duties springing out of this necessary arrangement are essentially the same in all societies. . . They have a pretty uniform character all over the globe. If the sense of the common safety were not sufficiently strong to constitute the social tie of obedience to some common regulations, society could not exist. . . . It is no proof of the universal spread of a special innate faculty of moral distinctions, but of a certain rational appreciation of what is necessary for the very existence of every human being living in the company of others: Doubtless, if the sad history of the human race had been preserved in all its details, we *should have many examples of tribes that perished from being unequal to the conception of a social system, or to the restraints imposed by it.* We know enough of the records of anarchy, to see how difficult it is for human nature to comply in full with the social conditions of security; but if this were not complied with at all, the result would be mutual and swift destruction. . . . In the second place, mankind have been singularly unanimous in the practice of imposing upon individual members of societies some observances or restraints of purely *sentimental* origin, having no reference, direct or indirect, to the maintenance of the social tie, with all the safeguards implied in it. Certain maxims founded in taste, liking, aversion, or fancy, have, in every community known to us, been raised to the dignity of authoritative morality; being rendered (so to speak) 'terms of communion,' and have been enforced by punishment. . . . In the rules, founded on men's sentiments, likings, aversions, and antipathies, there is nothing common but the fact that some one or other of these are carried to the length of public requirement, and mixed up in one code with the imperative duties that hold society together."

The postulate of the Platonic Protagoras—that δίκη and αἰδώς must be felt to a certain extent in each man's bosom, as a condition to the very existence of society—agrees with the first of the two elements here distinguished by Mr. Bain, and does not necessarily go beyond it. But the unsystematic teaching and universal propagandism, which Protagoras describes as the agency whereby virtue is communicated, applies alike to both the two elements distinguished by Mr. Bain: to the factitious exigencies of King Nomos, as well as to his tutelary control. It is this mixed mass that the Sokratic analysis is brought to examine.

CHAP. XXIII.   RECIPROCITY OF REGARD INDISPENSABLE.   313

reference on the part of others.[1] Sokrates is satisfied with requiring from each person calculating prudence for his own pleasures and pains: while Protagoras proclaims that after this attribute had been obtained by man, and individual wants supplied, still there was a farther element necessary in the calculation—the social sentiment or reciprocity of regard implanted in every one's bosom : without this the human race would have perished. Prudence and skill will suffice for an isolated existence ; but if men are to live and act in social communion, the services as well as the requirements of each man must be shaped, in a certain measure, with a direct view to the security of others as well as to his own. *persons besides the agent himself.*

In my judgment, the Ethical End, exclusively self-regarding, here laid down by Sokrates, is too narrow. And if we turn to other Platonic dialogues, we shall find Sokrates still represented as proclaiming a self-regarding Ethical End, though not the same as what we read in the Protagoras. In the Gorgias, Republic, Phædon, &c., we shall find him discountenancing the calculation (recommended in the Protagoras) of pleasures and pains against each other, as greater, more certain, durable, &c., and insisting that all shall be estimated according as they bear on the general condition or health of the mind, which he assimilates to the general condition or health of the body. The health of the body, considered as an End to be pursued, is essentially self-regarding : so also is the health of the mind. I shall touch upon this farther when I consider the above-mentioned dialogues : at present, I only remark that they agree with the Sokrates of the Protagoras in assuming a self-regarding Ethical End, though they do not agree with him in describing what that End should be.

The application which Sokrates makes (in the Protagoras) of his own assumed Ethical End to the explanation of courage, is certainly confused and unsatisfactory. And indeed, we may farther remark that the general result at which Plato seems to be aiming in this dialogue, viz. : That all the different virtues are at the bottom one and the same, and that he who pos- *Plato's reasoning in the dialogue is not clear or satisfactory, especially about courage.*

[1] Plato, Protag. pp. 321-322.

sesses one of them must also possess the remainder—cannot be made out even upon his own assumptions. Though it be true that all the virtues depend upon correct calculation, yet as each of them applies to a different set of circumstances and different disturbing and misleading causes, the same man who calculates well under one set of circumstances, may calculate badly under others. The position laid down by Protagoras, that men are often courageous but unjust—just, but not wise—is noway refuted by Plato. Nor is it even inconsistent with Plato's own theory, though he seems to think it so.

Doctrine of Stallbaum and other critics is not correct: That the analysis here ascribed to Sokrates is not intended by Plato as serious, but as a mockery of the sophists.

Some of the Platonic commentators maintain,[1] that the doctrine here explicitly laid down and illustrated by Sokrates, *viz.*: the essential identity of the pleasurable with the good, of the painful with the evil—is to be regarded as not serious, but as taken up in jest for the purpose of mocking and humiliating Protagoras. Such an hypothesis appears to me untenable; contradicted by the whole tenor of the dialogue. Throughout all the Platonic compositions, there is nowhere to be found any train of argument more direct, more serious, and more elaborate, than that by which Sokrates here proves the identity of good with pleasure, of pain with evil (p. 351 to end). Protagoras begins by denying it, and is only compelled to accept the conclusion against his own will, by the series of questions which he cannot otherwise answer.[2] Sokrates admits that the bulk of mankind are also opposed to it: but he establishes it with an ingenuity which is pronounced to be triumphant by all the

---

[1] See Brandis, Gesch. d. Griech.-Röm., Phil. Part ii. sect. 114, note [3] p. 458; Stallbaum, Prolegom. ad Protag. pp. 15-33-34.

So too Ficinus says in his Argumentum to the Protagoras: (p. 765) "Tum vero de bono et malo multa tractantur. Siquidem prudentia est scientia eligendi boni, malique vitandi. Ambigitur autem utrum bonumque idem sit penitus quod et voluptas et dolor. Neque *affirmatur id quidem omnino, neque manifesté omnino negatur.* De hoc enim in Gorgiâ Philêboque et alibi," &c.

When a critic composes an Argument to the Protagoras, he is surely under obligation to report faithfully and exactly what is declared by Sokrates *in the Protagoras,* whether it be consistent or not with the Gorgias and Philêbus. Yet here we find Ficinus misrepresenting the Protagoras, in order to force it into harmony with the other two.

[2] This is so directly stated that I am surprised to find Zeller (among many other critics) announcing that Plato here accepts for the occasion the *Standpunkt* of his enemies (Philos. der Griech. vol. ii. p. 380, ed. 2nd).

hearers around.[1] The commentators are at liberty to impeach the reasoning as unsound; but to set it aside as mere banter and mockery, is preposterous. Assume it even to be intended as mockery—assume that Sokrates is mystifying the hearers, by a string of delusive queries, to make out a thesis which he knows to be untrue and silly—how can the mockery fall upon Protagoras, who denies the thesis from the beginning?[2] The irony, if it were irony, would be misplaced and absurd.

The commentators resort to this hypothesis, partly because the

[1] Plato, Protag. p. 358 A. ὑπερφυῶς ἐδόκει ἅπασιν ἀληθῆ εἶναι τὰ εἰρημένα.

[2] When Stallbaum asserts that the thesis is taken up by Sokrates as one which was maintained by Protagoras and the other Sophis s (Proleg. p. 33), he says what is distinctly at variance with the dialogue, p. 351.

Schleiermacher maintains that this same thesis (the fundamental identity of good with pleasure, evil with pain) is altogether "unsokratic and unplatonic"; that it is handled here by Sokrates in a manner visibly ironical (sichtbar ironisch); that the purpose of the argument is to show the stupidity of Protagoras, who is puzzled and imposed upon by such obvious fallacies (Einleitung zum Protag. p 230, bottom of p. 232), and who is made to exhibit (so Schleiermacher says, Einl. zum Gorgias, p 14) a string of ludicrous absurdities.

Upon this I have to remark first, that if the stupidity of Protagoras is intended to be shown up, that of all the other persons present must be equally manifested; for all of them assent emphatically, at the close, to the thesis as having been proved (Prot. p. 358 A): next, that I am unable to see either the absurdities of Protagoras or the irony of Sokrates, which Schleiermacher asserts to be so visible. The argument of Sokrates is as serious and elaborate as any thing which we read in Plato. Schleiermacher seems to me to misconceive altogether (not only here but also in his Einleitung zum Gorgias, p. 10) the concluding argument of Sokrates in the Protagoras. To describe the identity between ἡδὺ and ἀγαθὸν as a "scheinbare Voraussetzung" is to depart from the plain meaning of words.

Again, Steinhart contends that Sokrates assumes this doctrine (identity of pleasure with good, pain with evil),

"not as his own opinion, but only hypothetically, with a sarcastic side-glance at the absurd consequences which many deduced from it—only as the received world-morality, as the opinion of the majority" (Einleit. zum Protag. p. 419). How Steinhart can find proof of this in the dialogue, I am at a loss to understand. The dialogue presents to us Sokrates introducing the opinion as his own, against that of Protagoras and against that of the multitude (p. 351 C). On hearing this opposition from Protagoras, Sokrates invites him to an investigation, whether the opinion be just; Sokrates then conducts the investigation himself, along with Protagoras, at considerable length, and ultimately brings out the doctrine as proved, with the assent of all present.

These forced interpretations are resorted to, because the critics cannot bear to see the Platonic Sokrates maintaining a thesis substantially the same as that of Eudoxus and Epikurus. Upon this point, K. F. Hermann is more moderate than the others; he admits the thesis to be seriously maintained in the dialogue—states that it was really the opinion of the historical Sokrates—and adds that it was also the opinion of Plato himself during his early Sokratic stadium, when the Protagoras (as he thinks) was composed (Gesch. und Syst. der Plat. Phil. pp. 462-463).

Most of the critics agree in considering the Protagoras to be one of Plato's earlier dialogues, about 403 B.C. Ast even refers it to 407 B.C. when Plato was about twenty-one years of age. I have already given my reasons for believing that none of the Platonic dialogues were composed before 399 B.C. The Protagoras belongs, in my opinion, to Plato's most perfect and mature period.

Grounds of that doctrine. Their insufficiency.
doctrine in question is one which they disapprove —partly because doctrines inconsistent with it are maintained in other Platonic dialogues. These are the same two reasons upon which, in other cases, various dialogues have been rejected as not genuine works of Plato. The first of the two reasons is plainly irrelevant: we must accept what Plato gives us, whether we assent to it or not. The second reason also, I think, proves little. The dialogues are distinct compositions, written each with its own circumstances and purpose: we have no right to require that they shall be all consistent with each other in doctrine, especially when we look to the long philosophical career of Plato. To suppose that the elaborate reasoning of Sokrates in the latter portion of the Protagoras is mere irony, intended to mystify both Protagoras himself and all the by-standers, who accept it as earnest and convincing —appears to me far less reasonable than the admission, that the dialectic pleading ascribed to Sokrates in one dialogue is inconsistent with that assigned to him in another.

Subject is professedly still left unsettled at the close of the dialogue.
Though there is every mark of seriousness, and no mark of irony, in this reasoning of Sokrates, yet we must remember that he does not profess to leave the subject settled at the close of the dialogue. On the contrary, he declares himself to be in a state of puzzle and perplexity. The question, proposed at the outset, Whether virtue is teachable? remains undecided.

CHAPTER XXIV.

GORGIAS.

ARISTOTLE, in one of his lost dialogues, made honourable mention of a Corinthian cultivator, who, on reading the Platonic Gorgias, was smitten with such vehement admiration, that he abandoned his fields and his vines, came to Athens forthwith, and committed himself to the tuition of Plato.[1] How much of reality there may be in this anecdote, we cannot say: but the Gorgias itself is well calculated to justify such warm admiration. It opens with a discussion on the nature and purpose of Rhetoric, but is gradually enlarged so as to include a comparison of the various schemes of life, and an outline of positive ethical theory. It is carried on by Sokrates with three distinct interlocutors— Gorgias, Polus, and Kalliklês; but I must again remind the reader that all the four are only spokesmen prompted by Plato himself.[2] It may indeed be considered almost as three distinct dialogues, connected by a loose thread. The historical Gorgias, a native of Leontini in Sicily, was the most celebrated of the Grecian rhetors; an elderly man during Plato's youth. He paid visits to different cities in all parts of Greece, and gave lessons in rhetoric to numerous pupils, chiefly young men of ambitious aspirations.[3]

Persons who debate in the Gorgias. Celebrity of the historical Gorgias.

---

[1] Themistius, Or. xxiii. p. 356, Dindorf. Ὁ δὲ γεωργὸς ὁ Κορίνθιος τῷ Γοργίᾳ ξυγγενόμενος — οὐκ αὐτῷ ἐκείνῳ Γοργίᾳ, ἀλλὰ τῷ λόγῳ ὃν Πλάτων ἔγραψεν ἐπ' ἐλέγχῳ τοῦ σοφιστοῦ —αὐτίκα ἀφεὶς τὸν ἀγρὸν καὶ τοὺς ἀμπέλους, Πλάτωνι ὑπέθηκε τὴν ψυχὴν καὶ τὰ ἐκείνου ἐσπείρετο καὶ ἐφυτεύετο· καὶ οὗτός ἐστιν ὃν τιμᾷ Ἀριστοτέλης ἐν τῷ διαλόγῳ τῷ Κορινθίῳ.

[2] Aristeides, Orat. xlvi. p. 387, Dindorf. Τίς γὰρ οὐκ οἶδεν, ὅτι καὶ ὁ Σωκράτης καὶ ὁ Καλλικλῆς καὶ ὁ Γοργίας καὶ ὁ Πῶλος, πάντα ταῦτ' ἐστὶ Πλάτων, πρὸς τὸ δοκοῦν αὐτῷ τρέπων τοὺς λόγους; Though Aristeides asks reasonably enough, Who is ignorant of this?—the remarks of Stallbaum and others often imply forgetfulness of it.

[3] Schleiermacher (Einleitung zum Gorgias, vol. iii. p. 22) is of opinion

Sokrates and Chærephon are described as intending to come to a rhetorical lecture of Gorgias, but as having been accidentally detained so as not to arrive until just after it has been finished, with brilliant success. Kalliklês, however, the host and friend of Gorgias, promises that the rhetor will readily answer any questions put by Sokrates; which Gorgias himself confirms, observing at the same time that no one had asked him any new question for many years past.[1] Sokrates accordingly asks Gorgias what his profession is? what it is that he teaches? what is the definition of rhetoric? Not receiving a satisfactory answer, Sokrates furnishes a definition of his own: out of which grow two arguments of wide ethical bearing: carried on by Sokrates, the first against Polus, the second against Kalliklês. Both these two are represented as voluble speakers, of confident temper, regarding the acquisition of political power and oratorical celebrity as the grand objects of life. Polus had even composed a work on Rhetoric, of which we know nothing: but the tone of this dialogue would seem to indicate (as far as we can judge from such evidence) that the style of the work was affected, and the temper of the author flippant.

Introductory circumstances of the dialogue. Polus and Kalliklês.

Here, as in the other dialogues above noticed, the avowed aim of Sokrates is—first, to exclude long speaking—next, to get the question accurately conceived, and answered in an appropriate manner. Specimens are given of unsuitable and inaccurate answers, which Sokrates corrects. The conditions of a good definition are made plain by contrast with bad ones; which either include much more than the thing defined, or set forth what is accessory and occasional in place of what is essential and constant. These tentatives and gropings to find a definition are always instructive,

Purpose of Sokrates in questioning. Conditions of a good definition.

---

that Plato composed the Gorgias shortly after returning from his first voyage to Sicily, 387 B.C.

I shall not contradict this: but I see nothing to prove it. At the same time, Schleiermacher assumes as certain that Aristophanes in the Ekklesiazusæ alludes to the doctrines published by Plato in his Republic (Einleitung zum Gorgias, p. 20). Putting these two statements together, the Gorgias would be later in date of composition than the Republic, which I hardly think probable. However, I do not at all believe that Aristophanes in the Ekklesiazusæ makes any allusion to the Republic of Plato. Nor shall I believe, until some evidence is produced, that the Republic was composed at so early a date as 390 B.C.

[1] Plato, Gorg. pp. 447-448 A. The dialogue is supposed to be carried on in the presence of many persons, seemingly belonging to the auditory of the lecture which Gorgias has just finished, p. 455 C.

CHAP. XXIV.   DEFINITION OF RHETORIC.   319

and must have been especially so in the Platonic age, when logical distinctions had never yet been made a subject of separate attention or analysis.

About what is Rhetoric as a cognition concerned, Gorgias? *Gorg.*—About words or discourses. *Sokr.*—About what discourses? such as inform sick men how they are to get well? *Gorg.*—No. *Sokr.*—It is not then about all discourses? *Gorg.*—It makes men competent to speak: of course therefore also to think, upon the matters on which they speak.[1] *Sokr.*—But the medical and gymnastic arts do this likewise, each with reference to its respective subject: what then is the difference between them and Rhetoric? *Gorg.*—The difference is, that each of these other arts tends mainly towards some actual work or performance, to which the discourses, when required at all, are subsidiary: but Rhetoric accomplishes every thing by discourses alone.[2] *Sokr.*— But the same may be said about arithmetic, geometry, and other sciences. How are they distinguished from Rhetoric? You must tell me upon what matters the discourses with which Rhetoric is conversant turn; just as you would tell me, if I asked the like question about arithmetic or astronomy. *Gorg.*— The discourses, with which Rhetoric is conversant, turn upon the greatest of all human affairs. *Sokr.*—But this too, Gorgias, is indistinct and equivocal. Every man, the physician, the gymnast, the money-maker, thinks his own object and his own affairs the greatest of all.[3] *Gorg.*—The function of Rhetoric, is to persuade assembled multitudes, and thus to secure what are in truth the greatest benefits: freedom to the city, political command to the speaker.[4] *Sokr.*—Rhetoric is then the artisan of persuasion. Its single purpose is to produce persuasion in the minds of hearers? *Gorg.*—It is so.

Sokr.—But are there not other persons besides the Rhetor, who produce persuasion? Does not the arithmetical teacher, and every other teacher, produce persuasion?

<small>Questions about the definition of Rhetoric. It is the artisan of persuasion.</small>

<small>The Rhetor produces belief without</small>

---

[1] Plato, Gorgias, p. 449 E. Οὐκοῦν περὶ ὧνπερ λέγειν, καὶ φρονεῖν; Πῶς γὰρ οὔ;
[2] Plato, Gorgias, p. 450 B-C. τῆς ῥητορικῆς. . . . πᾶσα ἡ πρᾶξις καὶ ἡ κύρωσις διὰ λόγων ἐστίν. .
[3] Plato, Gorgias, pp. 451-452.
[4] Plato, Gorgias, p. 452 D. Ὅπερ ἔστι τῇ ἀληθείᾳ μέγιστον ἀγαθόν, καὶ αἴτιον, ἅμα μὲν ἐλευθερίας αὐτοῖς τοῖς ἀνθρώποις, ἅμα δὲ τοῦ ἄλλων ἄρχειν ἐν τῇ αὑτοῦ πόλει ἑκάστῳ.

knowledge. Upon what matters is he competent to advise?

How does the Rhetor differ from them? What mode of persuasion does he bring about? Persuasion about what? *Gorg.*—I reply—it is that persuasion which is brought about in Dikasteries, and other assembled multitudes—and which relates to just and unjust.[1] *Sokr.*—You recognise that to have learnt and to know any matter, is one thing—to believe it, is another: that knowledge and belief are different—knowledge being always true, belief sometimes false? *Gorg.*—Yes. *Sokr.*—We must then distinguish two sorts of persuasion: one carrying with it knowledge—the other belief without knowledge. Which of the two does the Rhetor bring about? *Gorg.*—That which produces belief without knowledge. He can teach nothing. *Sokr.*—Well, then, Gorgias, on what matters will the Rhetor be competent to advise? When the people are deliberating about the choice of generals or physicians, about the construction of docks, about practical questions of any kind—there will be in each case a special man informed and competent to teach or give counsel, while the Rhetor is not competent. Upon what then can the Rhetor advise—upon just and unjust—nothing else?[2]

The Rhetor can persuade the people upon any matter, even against the opinion of the special expert. He appears to know, among the ignorant.

The Rhetor (says Gorgias) or accomplished public speaker, will give advice about all the matters that you name, and others besides. He will persuade the people and carry them along with him, even against the opinion of the special *Expert*. He will talk more persuasively than the craftsman about matters of the craftsman's own business. The power of the Rhetor is thus very great: but he ought to use it, like all other powers, for just and honest purposes; not to abuse it for wrong and oppression. If he does the latter, the misdeed is his own, and not the fault of his teacher, who gave his lessons with a view that they should be turned to proper use. If a man, who has learnt the use of arms, employs them to commit murder, this abuse ought not to be imputed to his master of arms.[3]

You mean (replies Sokrates) that he, who has learnt Rhetoric from you, will become competent not to teach, but to persuade

---

[1] Plato. Gorgias, p. 454 B.   [2] Plato, Gorgias, p. 455 D.
[3] Plato, Gorgias, pp. 456-457.

the multitude :—that is, competent among the ignorant. He has acquired an engine of persuasion ; so that he will appear, when addressing the ignorant, to know more than those who really do know.[1]

Thus far, the conversation is carried on between Sokrates and Gorgias. But the latter is now made to contradict himself—apparently rather than really—for the argument whereby Sokrates reduces him to a contradiction, is not tenable, unless we admit the Platonic doctrine that the man who has learnt just and unjust, may be relied on to act as a just man ;[2] in other words, that virtue consists in knowledge.

Gorgias is now made to contradict himself. Polus takes up the debate with Sokrates.

Polus now interferes and takes up the conversation : challenging Sokrates to furnish what *he* thinks the proper definition of Rhetoric. Sokrates obeys, in a tone of pungent polemic. Rhetoric (he says) is no art at all, but an empirical knack of catering for the pleasure and favour of hearers ; analogous to cookery.[3] It is a talent falling under the general aptitude called Flattery ; possessed by some bold spirits, who are forward in divining and adapting themselves to the temper of the public.[4] It is not honourable, but a mean pursuit, like cookery. It is the shadow or false imitation of a branch of the political art.[5] In reference both to the body and the mind, there are two different conditions: one, a condition really and truly

Polemical tone of Sokrates. At the instance of Polus he gives his own definition of rhetoric. It is no art, but an empirical knack of catering for the immediate pleasure of hearers, analogous to cookery. It is a branch under the

---

[1] Plato, Gorgias, p. 459 B. Οὐκοῦν καὶ περὶ τὰς ἄλλας ἁπάσας τέχνας ὡσαύτως ἔχει ὁ ῥήτωρ καὶ ἡ ῥητορική· αὐτὰ μὲν τὰ πράγματα οὐδὲν δεῖ αὐτὴν εἰδέναι ὅπως ἔχει, μηχανὴν δέ τινα πειθοῦς εὑρηκέναι, ὥστε φαίνεσθαι τοῖς οὐκ εἰδόσι μᾶλλον εἰδέναι τῶν εἰδότων.

[2] Plato, Gorgias, p. 460 B. ὁ τὰ δίκαια μεμαθηκώς, δίκαιος. Aristotle notices this confusion of Sokrates, who falls into it also in the conversation with Euthydemus, Xenoph. Memorab. iv. 2, 20, iii. 9, 5.

[3] Plato, Gorgias, p. 462 C. ἐμπειρία . . . . χάριτός τινος καὶ ἡδονῆς ἀπεργασίας. In the Philêbus (pp. 55-56) Sokrates treats ἰατρικὴ differently, as falling short of the idea of τέχνη, and coming much nearer to what is here called ἐμπειρία or στοχαστική. Asklepiades was displeased with the Thracian Dionysius for calling γραμματικὴ by the name of ἐμπειρία instead of τέχνη : see Sextus Empiric. adv. Grammat. s. 57-72, p. 615, Bekk.

[4] Plato, Gorgias, p. 463 A. δοκεῖ μοι εἶναί τι ἐπιτήδευμα, τεχνικὸν μὲν οὔ, ψυχῆς δὲ στοχαστικῆς καὶ ἀνδρείας καὶ φύσει δεινῆς προσομιλεῖν τοῖς ἀνθρώποις· καλῶ δὲ αὐτοῦ ἐγὼ τὸ κεφάλαιον κολακείαν.

[5] Plato, Gorgias, p. 463 D. πολιτικῆς μορίου εἴδωλον.

general head good—the other, good only in fallacious appearance, flattery. and not so in reality. To produce, and to verify, the really good condition of the body, there are two specially qualified professions, the gymnast or trainer and the physician: in regard to the mind, the function of the trainer is performed by the law-giving power, that of the physician by the judicial power. Law-making, and adjudicating, are both branches of the political art, and when put together make up the whole of it. Gymnastic and medicine train and doctor the body towards its really best condition: law-making and adjudicating do the same in regard to the mind. To each of the four, there corresponds a sham counterpart or mimic, a branch under the general head *flattery* — taking no account of what is really best, but only of that which is most agreeable for the moment, and by this trick recommending itself to a fallacious esteem.[1] Thus Cosmetic, or Ornamental Trickery, is the counterfeit of Gymnastic; and Cookery the counterfeit of Medicine. Cookery studies only what is immediately agreeable to the body, without considering whether it be good or wholesome: and does this moreover, without any truly scientific process of observation or inference, but simply by an empirical process of memory or analogy. But Medicine examines, and that too by scientific method, only what is good and wholesome for the body, whether agreeable or not. Amidst ignorant men, Cookery slips in as the counterfeit of medicine; pretending to know what food is *good* for the body, while it really knows only what food is *agreeable*. In like manner, the artifices of ornament dress up the body to a false appearance of that vigour and symmetry, which Gymnastics impart to it really and intrinsically.

The same analogies hold in regard to the mind. Sophistic is Distinction between the true arts which aim at the good of the body the shadow or counterfeit of law-giving: Rhetoric, of judging or adjudicating. The lawgiver and the judge aim at what is good for the mind: the Sophist and the Rhetor aim at what is agreeable to it. This dis-

---

[1] Plato, Gorgias, p. 464 C. τεττάρων δὴ τούτων οὐσῶν, καὶ ἀεὶ πρὸς τὸ βέλτιστον θεραπευουσῶν, τῶν μὲν τὸ σῶμα, τῶν δὲ τὴν ψυχήν, ἡ κολακευτικὴ αἰσθομένη, οὐ γνοῦσα λέγω ἀλλὰ στοχασαμένη, τέτραχα ἑαυτὴν διανείμασα, ὑποδῦσα ὑπὸ ἕκαστον τῶν μορίων, προσ ποιεῖται εἶναι τοῦτο ὅπερ ὑπέδυ· καὶ τοῦ μὲν βελτίστου οὐδὲν φροντίζει, τῷ δὲ ἀεὶ ἡδίστῳ θηρεύεται τὴν ἄνοιαν καὶ ἐξαπατᾷ, ὥστε δοκεῖ πλείστου ἀξία εἶναι.

tinction between them (continues Sokrates) is true and real: though it often happens that the Sophist is, both by himself and by others, confounded with and mistaken for the lawgiver, because he deals with the same topics and occurrences: and the Rhetor, in the same manner, is confounded with the judge.[1] The Sophist and the Rhetor, addressing themselves to the present relish of an undiscerning public, are enabled to usurp the functions and the credit of their more severe and far-sighted rivals.

and mind— and the counterfeit arts, which pretend to the same, but in reality aim at immediate pleasure.

This is the definition given by Sokrates of Rhetoric and of the Rhetor. Polus then asks him: You say that Rhetoric is a branch of Flattery: Do you think that good Rhetors are considered as flatterers in their respective cities? *Sokr.*—I do not think that[2] they are considered at all. *Polus.*—How! not considered? Do not good Rhetors possess great power in their respective cities? *Sokr.*—No: if you understand the possession of power as a good thing for the possessor. *Polus.*—I do understand it so. *Sokr.*—Then I say that the Rhetors possess nothing beyond the very minimum of power. *Polus.*—How can that be? Do not they, like despots, kill, impoverish, and expel any one whom they please? *Sokr.*—I admit that both Rhetors and Despots can do what seems good to themselves, and can bring penalties of death, poverty, or exile upon

Questions of Polus. Sokrates denies that the Rhetor have any real power, because they do nothing which they really wish.

---

[1] Plato, Gorgias, p. 465 C. διέστηκε μὲν οὕτω φύσει· ἅτε δὲ ἐγγὺς ὄντων, φύρονται ἐν τῷ αὐτῷ καὶ περὶ ταὐτὰ σοφισταὶ καὶ ῥήτορες, καὶ οὐκ ἔχουσιν ὅ, τι χρήσωνται οὔτε αὐτοὶ ἑαυτοῖς οὔτε οἱ ἄλλοι ἄνθρωποι τούτοις.

It seems to me that the persons whom Plato here designates as being confounded together are, the Sophist with the lawgiver, the Rhetor with the judge or dikast; which is shown by the allusion, three lines farther on, to the confusion between the cook and the physician. Heindorf supposes that the persons designated as being confounded are, the Sophist with the Rhetor; which I cannot think to be the meaning of Plato.

[2] Plat. Gorg. p. 466 B. *Polus.* Ἆρ᾽ οὖν δοκοῦσί σοι ὡς κόλακες ἐν ταῖς πόλεσι φαῦλοι νομίζεσθαι οἱ ἀγαθοὶ ῥήτορες; . . . . *Sokr.* Οὐδὲ νομίζεσθαι ἔμοιγε δοκοῦσιν.

The play on words here—for I see nothing else in it—can be expressed in English as well as in Greek. It has very little pertinence; because, as a matter of fact, the Rhetors certainly had considerable importance, whether they deserved it or not. How little Plato cared to make his comparisons harmonise with the fact, may be seen by what immediately follows— where he compares the Rhetors to Despots? and puts in the mouth of Polus the assertion that they kill or banish any one whom they choose.

others: but I say that nevertheless they have no power, because they can do nothing which they really wish.[1]

All men wish for what is good for them. Despots and rhetors, when they kill any one, do so because they think it good for them. If it be really not good, they do not do what they will, and therefore have no real power.

That which men wish (Sokrates lays down as a general proposition) is to obtain good, and to escape evil. Each separate act which they perform, is performed not with a view to its own special result, but with a view to these constant and paramount ends. Good things, or profitable things (for Sokrates alternates the phrases as equivalent), are wisdom, health, wealth, and other such things. Evil things are the contraries of these.[2] Many things are in themselves neither good nor evil, but may become one or the other, according to circumstances—such as stones, wood, the acts of sitting still or moving, &c. When we do any of these indifferent acts, it is with a view to the pursuit of good, or to the avoidance of evil: we do not wish for the act, we wish for its good or profitable results. We do every thing for the sake of good: and if the results are really good or profitable, we accomplish what we wish: if the contrary, not. Now, Despots and Rhetors, when they kill or banish or impoverish any one, do so because they think it will be better for them, or profitable.[3] If it be good for them, they do what they wish: if evil for them, they do the contrary of what they wish—and therefore have no power.

To do evil (continues Sokrates), is the worst thing that can happen to any one; the evil-doer is the most miserable and pitiable of men. The person who suffers evil is unfortunate, and is to be pitied; but much less unfortunate and less to be pitied than the evil-doer. If I have a concealed dagger in the public market-place, I can kill any one whom I choose: but this is no good to me, nor is it a proof of great power, because I shall be forthwith taken up and punished. The result is not profitable,

---

[1] Plato, Gorgias, p. 466 E. οὐδὲν γὰρ ποιεῖν ὧν βούλονται, ὡς ἔπος εἰπεῖν· ποιεῖν μέντοι ὅ, τι ἂν αὐτοῖς δόξῃ βέλτιστον εἶναι.

[2] Plato, Gorgias, p. 467 E. Οὐκοῦν λέγεις εἶναι ἀγαθὸν μὲν σοφίαν τε καὶ ὑγίειαν καὶ πλοῦτον καὶ τἄλλα τὰ τοιαῦτα, κακὰ δὲ τἀναντία τούτων; Ἔγωγε.

[3] Plato, Gorgias, p. 468 B-C. οὐκοῦν καὶ ἀποκτίννυμεν, εἴ τιν' ἀποκτίννυμεν, ... οἰόμενοι ἄμεινον εἶναι ἡμῖν ταῦτα ἢ μή; . . . ἕνεκ' ἄρα τοῦ ἀγαθοῦ ἅπαντα ταῦτα ποιοῦσιν οἱ ποιοῦντες . . . . ἐὰν μὲν ὠφέλιμα ᾖ ταῦτα, βουλόμεθα πράττειν αὐτά· βλαβερὰ δὲ ὄντα, οὐ βουλόμεθα. . . . . τὰ γὰρ ἀγαθὰ βουλόμεθα, ὡς φῂς σύ, &c.

CHAP. XXIV. THE EVIL-DOER IS MOST MISERABLE.

but hurtful: therefore the act is not good, nor is the power to do it either good or desirable.[1] It is sometimes good to kill, banish, or impoverish—sometimes bad. It is good when you do it justly: bad, when you do it unjustly.[2]

Polus.—A child can refute such doctrine. You have heard of Archelaus King of Macedonia. Is he, in your opinion, happy or miserable? *Sokr.*—I do not know: I have never been in his society. *Polus.*—Cannot you tell without that, whether he is happy or not? *Sokr.* —No, certainly not. *Polus.*—Then you will not call even the Great King happy? *Sokr.*—No: I do not know how he stands in respect to education and justice. *Polus.*—What! does all happiness consist in that? *Sokr.*—I say that it does. I maintain that the good and honourable man or woman is happy: the unjust and wicked, miserable.[3] *Polus.*—Then Archelaus is miserable, according to your doctrine? *Sokr.* —Assuredly, if he is wicked. *Polus.*—Wicked, of course; since he has committed enormous crimes: but he has obtained complete kingly power in Macedonia. Is there any Athenian, yourself included, who would not rather be Archelaus than any other man in Macedonia?[4] *Sokr.*—All the public, with Nikias, Perikles, and the most eminent men among them, will agree with you in declaring Archelaus to be happy. I alone do not agree with you. You, like a Rhetor, intend to overwhelm me and gain your cause, by calling a multitude of witnesses: I shall prove my case without calling any other witness than yourself.[5] Do you think that Archelaus would have been a happy man, if he had been defeated in his conspiracy and punished? *Polus.*— Certainly not: he would then have been very miserable. *Sokr.* —Here again I differ from you: I think that Archelaus, or any other wicked man, is under all circumstances miserable; but he is less miserable, if afterwards punished, than he would be if

Comparison of Archelaus, usurping despot of Macedonia— Polus affirms that Archelaus is happy, and that every one thinks so —Sokrates admits that every one thinks so, but nevertheless denies it.

---

[1] Plato, Gorgias, p. 469-470.
[2] Plato, Gorgias, p. 470 C.
[3] Plato, Gorgias, p. 470 E.
[4] Plato, Gorgias, p. 471 B-C.
[5] Plato, Gorgias, p. 472 B. 'Αλλ' ἐγώ σοι εἷς ὢν οὐχ ὁμολογῶ. . . . ἐγὼ δὲ

ἂν μὴ σὲ αὐτὸν ἕνα ὄντα μάρτυρα παράσχωμαι ὁμολογοῦντα περὶ ὧν λέγω, οὐδὲν οἶμαι ἄξιον λόγου πεπεράνθαι περὶ ὧν ἂν ἡμῖν ὁ λόγος ᾖ· οἶμαι δὲ οὐδὲ σοί, ἐὰν μὴ ἐγώ σοι μαρτυρῶ εἷς ὢν μόνος, τοὺς δ' ἄλλους πάντας τούτους χαίρειν ἐᾷς.

unpunished and successful.[1] *Polus.*—How say you? If a man, unjustly conspiring to become despot, be captured, subjected to torture, mutilated, with his eyes burnt out and with many other outrages inflicted, not only upon himself but upon his wife and children—do you say that he will be more happy than if he succeeded in his enterprise, and passed his life in possession of undisputed authority over his city—envied and extolled as happy, by citizens and strangers alike?[2] *Sokr.*—More happy, I shall not say: for in both cases he will be miserable; but he will be less miserable on the former supposition.

Sokr.—Which of the two is worst: to do wrong, or to suffer wrong? *Polus.*—To suffer wrong. *Sokr.*—Which of the two is the most ugly and disgraceful? *Polus.*— To do wrong. *Sokr.*—If more ugly and disgraceful, is it not then worse? *Polus.*—By no means. *Sokr.* —You do not think then that the good—and the fine or honourable—are one and the same; nor the bad— and the ugly or disgraceful? *Polus.*—No: certainly not. *Sokr.*—How is this? Are not all fine or honourable things, such as bodies, colours, figures, voices, pursuits, &c., so denominated from some common property? Are not fine bodies said to be fine, either from rendering some useful service, or from affording some pleasure to the spectator who contemplates them?[3] And are not figures, colours, voices, laws, sciences, &c., called fine or honourable for the same reason, either for their agreeableness or their usefulness, or both? *Polus.*—Certainly: your definition of the fine or honourable, by reference to pleasure, or to good, is satisfactory. *Sokr.*—Of course therefore the ugly or disgraceful must be defined by the contrary, by reference to pain or to evil? *Polus.*—Doubtless.[4] *Sokr.*—If therefore one thing be finer or

<small>Sokrates maintains —1. That it is a greater evil to do wrong than to suffer wrong. 2. That if a man has done wrong, it is better for him to be punished than to remain unpunished.</small>

---

[1] Plato, Gorgias, p. 473 C.
[2] Plato, Gorgias, p. 473 D.
[3] Plat. Gorg. p. 474 D. ἐὰν ἐν τῷ θεωρεῖσθαι χαίρειν ποιῇ τοὺς θεωροῦντας;
[4] Plato, Gorgias, p. 474 E. *Sokr.* Καὶ μὴν τά γε κατὰ τοὺς νόμους καὶ τὰ ἐπιτηδεύματα, οὐ δήπου ἐκτὸς τούτων ἐστὶ τὰ καλά, τοῦ ἢ ὠφέλιμα εἶναι ἢ ἡδέα ἢ ἀμφότερα. *Pol.* Οὐκ ἔμοιγε δοκεῖ. *Sokr.* Οὐκοῦν καὶ τῶν μαθημάτων κάλλος ὡσαύτως; *Pol.* Πάνυ γε· καὶ καλῶς γε νῦν ὁρίζει, ἡδονῇ τε καὶ ἀγαθῷ ὁριζόμενος τὸ καλόν. *Sokr.* Οὐκοῦν τὸ αἰσχρὸν τῷ ἐναντίῳ, λύπῃ τε καὶ κακῷ; *Pol.* Ἀνάγκη.
A little farther on βλαβὴ is used as equivalent to κακόν. These words— καλόν, αἰσχρόν—(very difficult to translate properly) introduce a reference to the feeling or judgment of spectators, or of an undefined public, not concerned either as agents or sufferers.

more honourable than another, this is because it surpasses the other either in pleasure, or in profit: if one thing be more ugly or disgraceful than another, it must surpass that other either in pain, or in evil? *Polus.*—Yes.

Sokr.—Well, then! what did you say about doing wrong and suffering wrong? You said that to suffer wrong was the worst of the two, but to do wrong was the most ugly or disgraceful. Now, if to do wrong be more disgraceful than to suffer wrong, this must be because it has a preponderance either of pain or of evil? *Polus.*—Undoubtedly. *Sokr.*—Has it a preponderance of pain? Does the doer of wrong endure more pain than the sufferer? *Polus.*—Certainly not. *Sokr.*—Then it must have a preponderance of evil? *Polus.*—Yes. *Sokr.*—To do wrong therefore is worse than to suffer wrong, as well as more disgraceful? *Polus.*—It appears so. *Sokr.*—Since therefore it is both worse and more disgraceful, I was right in affirming that neither you, nor I, nor any one else, would choose to do wrong in preference to suffering wrong. *Polus.*—So it seems.[1]

<small>Sokrates offers proof —Definition of Pulchrum and Turpe— Proof of the first point.</small>

Sokr.—Now let us take the second point—Whether it be the greatest evil for the wrong-doer to be punished, or whether it be not a still greater evil for him to remain unpunished. If punished, the wrong-doer is of course punished justly; and are not all just things fine or honourable, in so far as they are just? *Polus.*—I think so. *Sokr.*—When a man does anything, must there not be some correlate which suffers; and must it not suffer in a way corresponding to what the doer does? Thus if any one strikes, there must also be something stricken: and if he strikes quickly or violently, there must be something which is stricken quickly or violently. And so, if any one burns or cuts, there must be something burnt or cut. As the agent acts, so the patient suffers. *Polus.*—Yes. *Sokr.*—Now if a man be punished for wrong doing, he suffers what is just, and the punisher does what is just? *Polus.*—He does. *Sokr.*—You admitted that all just things were honourable: therefore the agent does what is honourable, the patient suffers what is honourable.[2] But if honourable, it must be either agreeable—

<small>Proof of the second point.</small>

---

[1] Plato, Gorgias, p. 475 C-D.
[2] See Aristotle, Rhet. i. 9, p. 1366, b. 30, where the contrary of this opinion is maintained, and maintained with truth.

or good and profitable. In this case, it is certainly not agreeable: it must therefore be good and profitable. The wrong-doer therefore, when punished, suffers what is good and is profited. *Polus.*—Yes.[1] *Sokr.*—In what manner is he profited? It is, as I presume, by becoming better in his mind—by being relieved from badness of mind. *Polus.*—Probably. *Sokr.*—Is not this badness of mind the greatest evil? In regard to wealth, the special badness is poverty: in regard to the body, it is weakness, sickness, deformity, &c.: in regard to the mind, it is ignorance, injustice, cowardice, &c. Is not injustice, and other badness of mind, the most disgraceful of the three? *Polus.*—Decidedly. *Sokr.*—If it be most disgraceful, it must therefore be the worst. *Polus.*—How? *Sokr.*—It must (as we before agreed) have the greatest preponderance either of pain, or of hurt and evil. But the preponderance is not in pain: for no one will say that the being unjust and intemperate and ignorant, is more painful than being poor and sick. The preponderance must therefore be great in hurt and evil. Mental badness is therefore a greater evil than either poverty, or disease and bodily deformity. It is the greatest of human evils. *Polus.*—It appears so.[2]

Sokr.—The money-making art is, that which relieves us from poverty: the medical art, from sickness and weakness: the judicial or punitory, from injustice and wickedness of mind. Of these three relieving forces, which is the most honourable? *Polus.*—The last, by far. *Sokr.*—If most honourable, it confers either most pleasure or most profit? *Polus.*—Yes. *Sokr.*—Now, to go through medical treatment is not agreeable; but it answers to a man to undergo the pain, in order to get rid of a great evil, and to become well. He would be a happier man, if he were never sick:

The criminal labours under a mental distemper, which, though not painful, is a capital evil. Punishment is the only cure for him. To be punished is best for him.

he is less miserable by undergoing the painful treatment and becoming well, than if he underwent no treatment and remained sick. Just so the man who is mentally bad: the happiest man is he who never becomes so; but if a man has become so, the next best course for him is, to undergo punishment and to get rid of the evil. The worst lot of all is, that of

---

[1] Plato, Gorgias, p. 476 D-E.   [2] Plato, Gorgias, p. 477 E.

him who remains mentally bad, without ever getting rid of badness.[1]

This last, Polus (continues Sokrates), is the condition of Archelaus, and of despots and Rhetors generally. They possess power which enables them, after they have committed injustice, to guard themselves against being punished: which is just as if a sick man were to pride himself upon having taken precautions against being cured. They see the pain of the cure, but they are blind to the profit of it; they are ignorant how much more miserable it is to have an unhealthy and unjust mind than an unhealthy body.[2] There is therefore little use in Rhetoric: for our first object ought to be, to avoid doing wrong: our next object, if we have done wrong, not to resist or elude punishment by skilful defence, but to present ourselves voluntarily and invite it: and if our friends or relatives have done wrong, far from helping to defend them, we ought ourselves to accuse them, and to invoke punishment upon them also.[3] On the other hand, as to our enemy, we ought undoubtedly to take precautions against suffering any wrong from him ourselves: but if he has done wrong to others, we ought to do all we can, by word or deed, not to bring him to punishment, but to prevent him from suffering punishment or making compensation: so that he may live as long as possible in impunity.[4] These are the purposes towards which rhetoric is serviceable. For one who intends to do no wrong, it seems of no great use.[5]

Misery of the Despot, who is never punished. If our friend has done wrong, we ought to get him punished: if our enemy, we ought to keep him unpunished.

This dialogue between Sokrates and Polus exhibits a represen-

[1] Plato, Gorgias, p. 478 D-E.

[2] Plato, Gorgias, p. 479 B. τὸ ἀλγεινὸν αὐτοῦ καθορᾷν, πρὸς δὲ τὸ ὠφέλιμον τυφλῶς ἔχειν, καὶ ἀγνοεῖν ὅσῳ ἀθλιώτερόν ἐστι μὴ ὑγιοῦς σώματος μὴ ὑγιεῖ ψυχῇ συνοικεῖν, ἀλλὰ σαθρᾷ καὶ ἀδίκῳ καὶ ἀνοσίῳ.

[3] Plato, Gorgias, pp. 480 C, 508 B. κατηγορητέον εἴη καὶ αὑτοῦ καὶ υἱέος καὶ ἑταίρου, ἐάν τι ἀδικῇ, &c.

Plato might have put this argument into the mouth of Euthyphron as a reason for indicting his own father on the charge of murder: as I have already observed in reviewing the Euthyphron, which see above, vol. i. ch. xi. p. 442.

[4] Plato, Gorgias, p. 481 A. ἐὰν δὲ ἄλλον ἀδικῇ ὁ ἐχθρός, παντὶ τρόπῳ παρασκευαστέον καὶ πράττοντα καὶ λέγοντα, ὅπως μὴ δῷ δίκην. . . . ἐάν τε χρυσίον ἡρπακὼς ᾖ πολύ, μὴ ἀποδιδῷ τοῦτο, ἀλλ' ἔχων ἀναλίσκηται . . . ἀδίκως καὶ ἀθέως, &c.

[5] Plato, Gorgias, p. 481.

tation of Platonic Ethics longer and more continuous than is usual in the dialogues. I have therefore given a tolerably copious abridgment of it, and shall now proceed to comment upon its reasoning.

<small>Argument of Sokrates paradoxical —Doubt expressed by Kallikles whether he means it seriously.</small> The whole tenor of its assumptions, as well as the conclusions in which it ends, are so repugnant to received opinions, that Polus, even while compelled to assent, treats it as a paradox: while Kallikles, who now takes up the argument, begins by asking from Chærephon—"Is Sokrates really in earnest, or is he only jesting?"[1] Sokrates himself admits that he stands almost alone. He has nothing to rely upon, except the consistency of his dialectics—and the verdict of philosophy.[2] This however is a matter of little moment, in discussing the truth and value of the reasoning, except in so far as it involves an appeal to the judgment of the public as a matter of fact. Plato follows out the train of reasoning—which at the time presents itself to his mind as conclusive, or at least as plausible—whether he may agree or disagree with others.

<small>Principle laid down by Sokrates —That every one acts with a view to the attainment of happiness and avoidance of misery.</small> Plato has ranked the Rhetor in the same category as the Despot: a classification upon which I shall say something presently. But throughout the part of the dialogue just extracted, he treats the original question about Rhetoric as part of a much larger ethical question.[3] Every one (argues Sokrates) wishes for the attainment of good and for the avoidance of evil. Every one performs each separate act with a view not to its own immediate end, but to one or other of these permanent ends. In so far as he attains them, he is happy: in so far as he either fails in attaining the good, or incurs the evil, he is unhappy or miserable. The good and honourable man or woman is happy, the unjust and wicked is miserable. Power acquired or employed unjustly, is no boon to the possessor: for he does not thereby obtain what he really wishes, good or happiness; but incurs the contrary, evil

<small>[1] Plato, Gorgias, p. 481.
[2] Plato, Gorgias, p. 482.
[3] I may be told that this comparison is first made by Polus (p. 466 C), and that Sokrates only takes it up from him to comment upon. True, but the speech of Polus is just as much the composition of Plato as that of Sokrates. Many readers of Plato are apt to forget this.</small>

and misery. The man who does wrong is more miserable than he who suffers wrong: but the most miserable of all is he who does wrong and then remains unpunished for it.[1]

Polus, on the other hand, contends, that Archelaus, who has "waded through slaughter" to the throne of Macedonia, is a happy man both in his own feelings and in those of every one else, envied and admired by the world generally: That to say—Archelaus would have been more happy, or less miserable, if he had failed in his enterprise and had been put to death under cruel torture—is an untenable paradox.

The issue here turns, and the force of Plato's argument rests (assuming Sokrates to speak the real sentiments of Plato), upon the peculiar sense which he gives to the words Good—Evil—Happiness:—different from the sense in which they are conceived by mankind generally, and which is here followed by Polus. It is possible that to minds like Sokrates and Plato, the idea of themselves committing enormous crimes for ambitious purposes might be the most intolerable of all ideas, worse to contemplate than any amount of suffering: moreover, that if they could conceive themselves as having been thus guilty, the sequel the least intolerable for them to imagine would be one of expiatory pain. This, taken as the personal sentiment of Plato, admits of no reply. But when he attempts to convert this subjective judgment into an objective conclusion binding on all, he fails of success, and misleads himself by equivocal language.

Peculiar view taken by Plato of Good—Evil—Happiness.

Plato distinguishes two general objects of human desire, and two of human aversion. 1. The immediate, and generally transient, object—Pleasure or the Pleasurable—Pain or the Painful. 2. The distant, ulterior, and more permanent object—Good or the profitable—Evil or the hurtful.—In the attainment of Good and avoidance of Evil consists happiness. But now comes the important question—In what sense are we to understand the

Contrast of the usual meaning of these words with the Platonic meaning.

---

[1] Isokrates, in his Panathenaic Oration (Or. xii. sect. 126, pp. 257-347), alludes to the same thesis as this here advanced by Plato, treating it as one which all men of sense would reject, and which none but a few men pretending to be wise would proclaim —ἅπερ ἅπαντες μὲν ἂν οἱ νοῦν ἔχοντες ἕλοιντο καὶ βουληθεῖεν, ὀλίγοι δέ τινες τῶν προσποιουμένων εἶναι σοφῶν, ἐρωτηθέντες οὐκ ἂν φήσαιεν.

In this last phrase Isokrates probably has Plato in his mind, though without pronouncing the name.

words Good and Evil? What did Plato mean by them? Did he mean the same as mankind generally? Have mankind generally one uniform meaning? In answer to this question, we must say, that neither Plato, nor mankind generally, are consistent or unanimous in their use of the words: and that Plato sometimes approximates to, sometimes diverges from, the more usual meaning. Plato does not here tell us clearly what he himself means by Good and Evil: he specifies no objective or external mark by which we may know it: we learn only, that Good is a mental perfection—Evil a mental taint—answering to indescribable but characteristic sentiments in Plato's own mind, and only negatively determined by this circumstance—That they have no reference either to pleasure or pain. In the vulgar sense, Good stands distinguished from pleasure (or relief from pain), and Evil from pain (or loss of pleasure), as the remote, the causal, the lasting from the present, the product, the transient. Good and Evil are explained by enumerating all the things so called, of which enumeration Plato gives a partial specimen in this dialogue: elsewhere he dwells upon what he calls the Idea of Good, of which I shall speak more fully hereafter. Having said that all men aim at good, he gives, as examples of good things—Wisdom, Health, Wealth, and other such things: while the contrary of these, Stupidity, Sickness, Poverty, are evil things: the list of course might be much enlarged. Taking Good and Evil generally to denote the common property of each of these lists, it is true that men perform a large portion of their acts with a view to attain the former and avoid the latter:—that the approach which they make to happiness depends, speaking generally, upon the success which attends their exertions for the attainment of and avoidance of these permanent ends: and moreover that these ends have their ultimate reference to each man's own feelings.

But this meaning of Good is no longer preserved, when Sokrates proceeds to prove that the triumphant usurper Archelaus is the most miserable of men, and that to do wrong with impunity is the greatest of all evils.

Sokrates provides a basis for his intended proof by asking Polus,[1] which of the two is most disgraceful—To do wrong—or to suffer wrong? Polus answers—To do

Examina-.
tion of the
proof given

[1] Plat. Gorg. p. 474 C.

wrong: and this answer is inconsistent with what he had previously said about Archelaus. That prince, though a wrong-doer on the largest scale, has been declared by Polus to be an object of his supreme envy and admiration: while Sokrates also admits that this is the sentiment of almost all mankind, except himself. To be consistent with such an assertion, Polus ought to have answered the contrary of what he does answer, when the general question is afterwards put to him: or at least he ought to have said—"Sometimes the one, sometimes the other". But this he is ashamed to do, as we shall find Kallikles intimating at a subsequent stage of the dialogue:[1] because of King Nomos, or the established habit of the community—who feel that society rests upon a sentiment of reciprocal right and obligation animating every one, and require that violations of that sentiment shall be marked with censure in general words, however widely the critical feeling may depart from such censure in particular cases.[2] Polus is forced to make profession of a

by Sokrates —Inconsistency between the general answer of Polus and his previous declarations —Law and Nature.

---

[1] Plat. Gorg. p. 482 C. To maintain that τὸ ἀδικεῖν βέλτιον τοῦ ἀδικεῖσθαι was an ἄδοξος ὑπόθεσις—one which it was χείρονος ἤθους ἐλέσθαι: which therefore Aristotle advises the dialectician not to defend (Aristot. Topic. viii. 156, 6-15).

[2] This portion of the Gorgias may receive illustration from the third chapter (pp. 99-101) of Adam Smith's Theory of Moral Sentiments, entitled, "Of the corruption of our moral sentiments, which is occasioned by the disposition to admire the rich and great, and to neglect or despise persons of poor and mean condition". He says— "The disposition to admire and almost to worship the rich and the powerful, and to despise, or at least to neglect, persons of poor and mean condition, though necessary both to establish and maintain the distinction of ranks and the order of society, is, at the same time, the great and most universal cause of the corruption of our moral sentiments.... They are the wise and the virtuous chiefly—a select, though I am afraid, a small party— who are the real and steady admirers of wisdom and virtue. The great mob of mankind are the admirers and worshippers—and what may seem more extraordinary, most frequently the disinterested admirers and worshippers— of wealth and greatness..... It is scarce *agreeable to good morals*, or even to good language, perhaps, to say that mere wealth and greatness, abstracted from merit and virtue, deserve our respect. We must acknowledge, however, that they *almost constantly obtain it*: and *that they may therefore in a certain sense be considered as the natural objects of it*."

Now Archelaus is a most conspicuous example of this disposition of the mass of mankind to worship and admire, disinterestedly, power and greatness: and the language used by Adam Smith in the last sentence illustrates the conversation of Sokrates, Polus, and Kalliklês. Adam Smith admits that energetic proceedings, ending in great power, such as those of Archelaus, obtain honour and worship from the vast majority of disinterested spectators: and that therefore they are in a certain sense the *natural objects* of such a sentiment (κατὰ φύσιν). But if the question be put to him, Whether such proceedings, with such a position, are *worthy of honour*, he is constrained by good morals (κατὰ νόμον) to reply in the negative. It is true that Adam Smith numbers himself with the small minority, while Polus shares the opinion

faith, which neither he nor others (except Sokrates with a few companions) universally or consistently apply. To bring such a force to bear upon the opponent, was one of the known artifices of dialecticians:[1] and Sokrates makes it his point of departure, to prove the unparalleled misery of Archelaus.

He proceeds to define Pulchrum and Turpe ($\kappa\alpha\lambda\grave{o}\nu$-$\alpha\grave{\iota}\sigma\chi\rho\acute{o}\nu$).

<small>The definition of Pulchrum and Turpe, given by Sokrates, will not hold.</small> When we recollect the Hippias Major, in which dialogue many definitions of Pulchrum were canvassed and all rejected, so that the search ended in total disappointment—we are surprised to see that Sokrates hits off at once a definition satisfactory both to himself and Polus: and we are the more surprised, because the definition here admitted without a remark, is in substance one of those shown to be untenable in the Hippias Major.[2] It depends upon the actual argumentative purpose which Plato has in hand, whether he chooses to multiply objections and give them effect—or to ignore them altogether. But the definition which he here proposes, even if assumed as incontestable, fails altogether to sustain the conclusion that he draws from it. He defines Pulchrum to be that which either confers pleasure upon the spectator when he contemplates it, or produces ulterior profit or good—we must presume profit to the spectator, or to him along with others—at any rate it is not said *to whom*. He next defines the ugly and disgraceful ($\tau\grave{o}$ $\alpha\grave{\iota}\sigma\chi\rho\grave{o}\nu$) as comprehending both the painful and the hurtful or evil. If then (he argues) to do wrong is more ugly and disgraceful than to suffer wrong, this must be either because it is more painful—or because it is more hurtful, more evil (worse). It certainly is not more painful: therefore it must be worse.

But worse, for whom? For the spectators, who declare the <small>Worse or better for whom? The argument of Sokrates does not</small> proceedings of Archelaus to be disgraceful? For the persons who suffer by his proceedings? Or for Archelaus himself? It is the last of the three which Sokrates undertakes to prove: but his definition does

<small>of the large majority. But what is required by King Nomos must be professed even by dissentients, unless they possess the unbending resolution of Sokrates.
[1] Aristot. De Soph. Elench. pp. 172-173, where he contrasts the opinions which men must make a show of holding, with those which they really do hold—$\alpha\grave{\iota}$ $\phi\alpha\nu\epsilon\rho\alpha\grave{\iota}$ $\delta\acute{o}\xi\alpha\iota$—$\alpha\grave{\iota}$ $\grave{\alpha}\phi\alpha\nu\epsilon\hat{\iota}\varsigma$, $\grave{\alpha}\pi o\kappa\epsilon\kappa\rho\upsilon\mu\mu\acute{\epsilon}\nu\alpha\iota$, $\delta\acute{o}\xi\alpha\iota$.
[2] Plat. Hipp. Maj. pp. 45-46. See above, vol. ii. ch. xiii.</small>

not help him to the proof. Turpe is defined to be either what causes immediate pain to the spectator, or ulterior hurt—to whom? If we say—to the spectator—the definition will not serve as a ground of inference to the condition of the agent contemplated. If on the other hand, we say—to the agent—the definition so understood becomes inadmissible: as well for other reasons, as because there are a great many Turpia which are not agents at all, and which the definition therefore would not include. Either therefore the definition given by Sokrates is a bad one—or it will not sustain his conclusion. And thus, on this very important argument, where Sokrates admits that he stands alone, and where therefore the proof would need to be doubly cogent—an argument too where the great cause (so Adam Smith terms it) of the corruption of men's moral sentiments has to be combated—Sokrates has nothing to produce except premisses alike far-fetched and irrelevant. What increases our regret is, that the real arguments establishing the turpitude of Archelaus and his acts are obvious enough, if you look for them in the right direction. You discover nothing while your eye is fixed on Archelaus himself: far from presenting any indications of misery, which Sokrates professes to discover, he has gained much of what men admire as good wherever they see it. But when you turn to the persons whom he has killed, banished, or ruined —to the mass of suffering which he has inflicted—and to the widespread insecurity which such acts of successful iniquity spread through all societies where they become known—there is no lack of argument to justify that sentiment which prompts a reflecting spectator to brand him as a disgraceful man. This argument however is here altogether neglected by Plato. Here, as elsewhere, he looks only at the self-regarding side of Ethics.

specify. If understood in the sense necessary for his inference, the definition would be inadmissible.

Sokrates proceeds next to prove—That the wrong-doer who remains unpunished is more miserable than if he were punished. The wrong-doer (he argues) when punished suffers what is just: but all just things are honourable: therefore he suffers what is honourable. But all honourable things are so called because they are either agreeable, or profitable, or both together. Punishment is certainly not agreeable: it must

Plato applies to every one a standard of happiness and misery peculiar to himself. His view about the conduct of Arche-

laus is just, but he does not give the true reasons for it.

therefore be profitable or good. Accordingly the wrong-doer when justly punished suffers what is profitable or good. He is benefited, by being relieved of mental evil or wickedness, which is a worse evil than either bodily sickness or poverty. In proportion to the magnitude of this evil, is the value of the relief which removes it, and the superior misery of the unpunished wrong-doer who continues to live under it.[1]

Upon this argument, I make the same remark as upon that immediately preceding. We are not expressly told, whether good, evil, happiness, misery, &c., refer to the agent alone or to others also : but the general tenor implies that the agent alone is meant. And in this sense, Plato does not make out his case. He establishes an arbitrary standard of his own, recognised only by a few followers, and altogether differing from the ordinary standard, to test and compare happiness and misery. The successful criminal, Archelaus himself, far from feeling any such intense misery as Plato describes, is satisfied and proud of his position, which most others also account an object of envy. This is not disputed by Plato himself. And in the face of this fact, it is fruitless as well as illogical to attempt to prove, by an elaborate process of deductive reasoning, that Archelaus *must* be miserable. That step of Plato's reasoning, in which he asserts, that the wrong-doer when justly punished suffers what is profitable or good—is only true if you take in (what Plato omits to mention) the interests of society as well as those of the agent. His punishment is certainly profitable to (conducive to the security and well being of) society : it may possibly be also profitable to himself, but very frequently it is not so. The conclusion brought out by Plato, therefore, while contradicted by the fact, involves also a fallacy in the reasoning process.

Throughout the whole of this dialogue, Plato intimates decidedly how great a paradox the doctrine maintained by Sokrates must appear : how diametrically it was opposed to the opinion not merely of the less informed multitude, but of the wiser and more reflecting citizen —even such a man as Nikias. Indeed it is literally

If the reasoning of Plato were true, the point of view in which punish-

---

[1] Plato, Gorgias, pp. 477-478.

exact—what Plato here puts into the mouth of Kallikles—that if the doctrine here advocated by Sokrates were true, the whole of social life would be turned upside down.[1] If, for example, it were true, as Plato contends, —That every man who commits a crime, takes upon him thereby a terrible and lasting distemper, incurable except by the application of punishment, which is the specific remedy in the case— every theory of punishment would, literally speaking, be turned upside down. The great discouragement from crime would then consist in the fear of that formidable distemper with which the criminal was sure to inoculate himself: and punishment, instead of being (as it is now considered, and as Plato himself represents it in the Protagoras) the great discouragement to the commission of crime, would operate in the contrary direction. It would be the means of removing or impairing the great real discouragement to crime: and a wise legislator would hesitate to inflict it. This would be nothing less than a reversal of the most universally accepted political or social precepts (as Kallikles is made to express himself).

Kallikles's argument is considered would be reversed.

It will indeed be at once seen, that the taint or distemper with which Archelaus is supposed to inoculate himself, when he commits signal crime—is a pure fancy or poetical metaphor on the part of Plato himself.[2] A distemper must imply something painful, enfeebling, disabling, to the individual who feels it: there is no other meaning: we cannot recognise a distemper, which does not make itself felt in any way by the distempered person. Plato is misled by his ever-repeated analogy between bodily health and mental health: real, on some points—not real on others. When a man is in bad bodily health, his sensations warn him of it at once. He suffers pain, discomfort,

Plato pushes too far the analogy between mental distemper and bodily distemper— Material difference between the two— Distemper must be felt by the distempered person.

---

[1] Plato, Gorg. p. 481 C. *Kall.*—εἰ μὲν γὰρ σπουδάζεις τε καὶ τυγχάνει ταῦτα ἀληθῆ ὄντα ἃ λέγεις, ἄλλο τι ἢ ἡμῶν ὁ βίος ἀνατετραμμένος ἂν εἴη τῶν ἀνθρώπων, καὶ πάντα τὰ ἐναντία πράττομεν, ἢ ἃ δεῖ;

[2] The disposition of Plato to build argument on a metaphor is often shown. Aristotle remarks it of him in respect to his theory of Ideas; and Aristotle in his Topica gives several precepts in regard to the general tendency—precepts enjoining disputants to be on their guard against it in dialectic discussion (Topica, iv. 123, a. 33, vi. 139-140)—πᾶν γὰρ ἀσαφὲς τὸ κατὰ μεταφορὰν λεγόμενον, &c.

or disabilities, which leave no doubt as to the fact: though he may not know either the precise cause, or the appropriate remedy. Conversely, in the absence of any such warnings, and in the presence of certain positive sensations, he knows himself to be in tolerable or good health. If Sokrates and Archelaus were both in good bodily health, or both in bad bodily health, each would be made aware of the fact by analogous evidences. But by what measure are we to determine *when* a man is in a good or bad mental state? By his own feelings? In that case, Archelaus and Sokrates are in a mental state equally good: each is satisfied with his own. By the judgment of by-standers? Archelaus will then be the better of the two: at least his admirers and enviers will outnumber those of Sokrates. By my judgment? If my opinion is asked, I agree with Sokrates: though not on the grounds which he here urges, but on other grounds. Who is to be the ultimate referee—the interests or security of other persons, who have suffered or are likely to suffer by Archelaus, being by the supposition left out of view?

Polus is now dismissed as vanquished, after having been forced, against his will, to concede—That the doer of wrong is more miserable than the sufferer: That he is more miserable, if unpunished,—less so, if punished: That a triumphant criminal on a great scale, like Archelaus, is the most miserable of men.

Here, then, we commence with Kallikles: who interposes, to take up the debate with Sokrates. Polus (says Kallikles), from deference to the opinions of mankind, has erroneously conceded the point—That it is more disgraceful to do wrong, than to suffer wrong. This is indeed true (continues Kallikles), according to what is just by law or convention, that is, according to the general sentiment of mankind: but it is not true, according to justice by nature, or natural justice. Nature and Law are here opposed.[1] The justice of Nature is, that among men (as among other animals) the strong individual should govern and strip the weak, taking and keeping as much as he can

Kallikles begins to argue against Sokrates—he takes a distinction between Just by law and Just by nature—Reply of Sokrates, that there is no variance between the two, properly understood.

---

[1] Plato, Gorgias, p. 482 E. ὡς τὰ πολλὰ δὲ ταῦτα ἐναντία ἀλλήλοις ἐστίν, ἥ τε φύσις καὶ ὁ νόμος.

JUSTICE ACCORDING TO LAW.

grasp. But this justice will not suit the weak, who are the many, and who defeat it by establishing a different justice—justice according to law—to curb the strong man, and prevent him from having more than his fair share.[1] The many, feeling their own weakness, and thankful if they can only secure a fair and equal division, make laws and turn the current of praise and blame for their own protection, in order to deter the strong man from that encroachment and oppression to which he is disposed. *The just according to law* is thus a tutelary institution, established by the weak to defend themselves against *the just according to nature*. Nature measures right by might, and by nothing else: so that according to the right of nature, suffering wrong is more disgraceful than doing wrong. Hêraklês takes from Geryon his cattle, by the right of nature or of the strongest, without either sale or gift.[2]

But (rejoins Sokrates) the many are by nature stronger than the one; since, as you yourself say, they make and enforce laws to restrain him and defeat his projects. Therefore, since the many are the strongest, the right which they establish is the right of (or by) nature. And the many, as you admit, declare themselves in favour of the answer given by Polus—That to do wrong is more disgraceful than to suffer wrong.[3] Right by nature, and right by institution, sanction it alike.

Several commentators have contended, that the doctrine which Plato here puts into the mouth of Kalliklês was taught by the Sophists at Athens: who are said to have inculcated on their hearers that true wisdom and morality consisted in acting upon the right of the strongest and taking whatever they could get, without any regard to law or justice. I have already *What Kalliklês says is not to be taken as a sample of the teachings of Athenian sophists.*

[1] Plato, Gorgias, p. 483 B. ἀλλ, οἶμαι, οἱ τιθέμενοι τοὺς νόμους οἱ ἀσθενεῖς ἄνθρωποί εἰσι καὶ οἱ πολλοί. Πρὸς αὑτοὺς οὖν καὶ τὸ αὑτοῖς συμφέρον τούς τε νόμους τίθενται καὶ τοὺς ἐπαίνους ἐπαινοῦσι καὶ τοὺς ψόγους ψέγουσιν, ἐκφοβοῦντές τε τοὺς ἐρρωμενεστέρους τῶν ἀνθρώπων καὶ δυνατοὺς ὄντας πλέον ἔχειν, ἵνα μὴ αὐτῶν πλέον ἔχωσιν, λέγουσιν ὡς αἰσχρὸν καὶ ἄδικον τὸ πλεονεκτεῖν, καὶ τοῦτό ἐστι τὸ ἀδικεῖν, τὸ ζητεῖν τῶν ἄλλων πλέον ἔχειν· ἀγαπῶσι γάρ, οἶμαι, αὐτοὶ ἂν τὸ ἴσον ἔχωσι φαυλότεροι ὄντες.

[2] Plato, Gorgias, pp. 484-488.
[3] Plato, Gorgias, p. 488 D-E.

Kalliklês—rhetor and politician. endeavoured to show, in my History of Greece, that the Sophists cannot be shown to have taught either this doctrine, or any other common doctrine: that one at least among them (Prodikus) taught a doctrine inconsistent with it: and that while all of them agreed in trying to impart rhetorical accomplishments, or the power of handling political, ethical, judicial, matters in a manner suitable for the Athenian public— each had his own way of doing this. Kalliklês is not presented by Plato as a Sophist, but as a Rhetor aspiring to active political influence; and taking a small dose of philosophy, among the preparations for that end.[1] He depreciates the Sophists as much as the philosophers, and in fact rather more.[2] Moreover Plato represents him as adapting himself, with accommodating subservience, to the Athenian public assembly, and saying or unsaying exactly as they manifested their opinion.[3] Now the Athenian public assembly would repudiate indignantly all this pretended right of the strongest, if any orator thought fit to put it forward as over-ruling established right and law. Any aspiring or subservient orator, such as Kalliklês is described, would know better than to address them in this strain. The language which Plato puts into the mouth of Kalliklês is noway consistent with the attribute which he also ascribes to him—slavish deference to the judgments of the Athenian Dêmos.

Kalliklês is made to speak like one who sympathises with the right of the strongest, and who decorates such iniquity with the name and authority of that which he calls Nature. But this only shows the uncertainty of referring to Nature as an authority.[4] It may be pleaded in favour of different and opposite theories. Nature prompts the strong man to take from weaker men what will gratify his desires: Nature also prompts these weaker men to defeat him and protect themselves by the best means in their power. The

Uncertainty of referring to Nature as an authority. It may be pleaded in favour of opposite theories. The theory of Kalliklês is made to appear repulsive by

---

[1] Plato, Gorgias, p. 487 C, 485.
[2] Plato, Gorgias, p. 520 A.
[3] Plato, Gorgias, p. 481-482.
[4] Aristotle (Sophist. Elench. 12, p. 173, a. 10) makes allusion to this argument of Kalliklês in the Gorgias, and notices it as a frequent point made by disputants in Dialectics—to insist on the contradiction between the Just according to Nature and the Just according to Law: which contradiction (Aristotle says) all the ancients recognised as a real one (οἱ ἀρχαῖοι πάντες ᾤοντο συμβαίνειν). It was doubtless a point on which the Dialectician might find much to say on either side.

CHAP. XXIV.   AUTHORITY OF NATURE, EQUIVOCAL.   341

many are weaker, taken individually—stronger taken collectively : hence they resort to defensive combination, established rules, and collective authority.[1] The right created on one side, and the opposite right created on the other, flow alike from Nature : that is, from propensities and principles natural, and deeply seated, in the human mind. The authority of Nature, considered as an enunciation of actual and wide-spread facts, may be pleaded for both alike. But a man's sympathy and approbation may go either with the one or the other ; and he may choose to stamp that which he approves, with the name of Nature as a personified law-maker. This is what is here done by Kalliklês as Plato exhibits him.[2] He

the language in which he expresses it.

---

[1] In the conversation between Sokrates and Kritobulus, one of the best in Xenophon's Memorabilia (ii. 6, 21), respecting the conditions on which friendship depends, we find Sokrates clearly stating that the causes of friendship and the causes of enmity, though different and opposite, nevertheless both exist *by nature*. Ἀλλ' ἔχει μέν, ἔφη ὁ Σωκράτης, ποικίλως πως ταῦτα: Φύσει γὰρ ἔχουσιν οἱ ἄνθρωποι τὰ μὲν φιλικά—δέονταί τε γὰρ ἀλλήλων, καὶ ἐλεοῦσι, καὶ συνεργοῦντες ὠφελοῦνται, καὶ τοῦτο συνιέντες χάριν ἔχουσιν ἀλλήλοις—τὰ δὲ πολεμικά—τά τε γὰρ αὐτὰ καλὰ καὶ ἡδέα νομίζοντες ὑπὲρ τούτων μάχονται καὶ διχογνωμονοῦντες ἐναντιοῦνται· πολεμικὸν δὲ καὶ ἔρις καὶ ὀργή, καὶ δυσμενὲς μὲν ὁ τοῦ πλεονεκτεῖν ἔρως, μισητὸν δὲ ὁ φθόνος. Ἀλλ' ὅμως διὰ τούτων πάντων ἡ φιλία διαδυομένη συνάπτει τοὺς καλούς τε κἀγαθούς, &c.

We read in the speech of Hermokrates the Syracusan, at the congress of Gela in Sicily, when exhorting the Sicilians to unite for the purpose of repelling the ambitious schemes of Athens, Thucyd. iv. 61 : καὶ τοὺς μὲν Ἀθηναίους ταῦτα πλεονεκτεῖν τε καὶ προνοεῖσθαι πολλὴ ξυγγνώμη, καὶ οὐ τοῖς ἄρχειν βουλομένοις μέμφομαι ἀλλὰ τοῖς ὑπακούειν ἑτοιμοτέροις οὖσι· πέφυκε γὰρ τὸ ἀνθρώπειον διὰ παντὸς ἄρχειν μὲν τοῦ εἴκοντος, φυλάσσεσθαι δὲ τὸ ἐπιόν. ὅσοι δὲ γιγνώσκοντες αὐτὰ μὴ ὀρθῶς προσκοποῦμεν, μηδὲ τοῦτό τις πρεσβύτατον ἥκει κρίνας, τὸ κοινῶς φοβερὸν ἅπαντας εὖ θέσθαι, ἁμαρτάνομεν. A like sentiment is pronounced by the Athenian envoys in their debate with the Melians, Thuc. v. 105 : ἡγούμεθα γὰρ τό τε θεῖον δόξῃ, τὸ ἀνθρώπειόν τε σαφῶς διὰ παντός, ὑπὸ φύσεως ἀναγκαίας, οὗ ἂν κρατῇ, ἄρχειν. Some of the Platonic critics would have us believe that this last-cited sentiment emanates from the corrupt teaching of Athenian Sophists : but Hermokrates the Syracusan had nothing to do with Athenian Sophists.

[2] Respecting the vague and indeterminate phrases—Natural Justice. Natural Right, Law of Nature—see Mr. Austin's Province of Jurisprudence Determined, p. 160, ed. 2nd. [Jurisp., 4th ed. pp. 179, 591-2], and Sir H. S. Maine's Ancient Law, chapters iii. and iv.

Among the assertions made about the Athenian Sophists, it is said by some commentators that they denied altogether any Just or Unjust by *nature*—that they recognised no Just or Unjust, except by *law or convention*.

To say that the *Sophists* (speaking of them collectively) either affirmed or denied anything, is, in my judgment, incorrect. Certain persons are alluded to by Plato (Theætêt. 172 B) as adopting partially the doctrine of Protagoras (*Homo Mensura*) and as denying altogether the Just by *nature*.

In another Platonic passage (Protagor. 337) which is also cited as contributing to prove that the Sophists denied τὸ δίκαιον φύσει—nothing at all is said about τὸ δίκαιον. Hippias the Sophist is there introduced as endeavouring to appease the angry feeling between Protagoras and Sokrates by reminding them, "I am of opinion that we all (*i.e.* men of literature and study) are kinsmen, friends, and fellow-citizens by *nature* though not by *law*: for law, the despot of mankind, carries

sympathises with, and approves, the powerful individual. Now the greater portion of mankind are, and always have been, governed upon this despotic principle, and brought up to respect it: while many, even of those who dislike Kalliklês because many things by force, contrary to nature". The remark is very appropriate from one who is trying to restore good feeling between literary disputants: and the cosmopolitan character of literature is now so familiar a theme, that I am surprised to find Heindorf (in his note) making it an occasion for throwing the usual censure upon the Sophist, because some of them distinguished Nature from the Laws, and despised the latter in comparison with the former.

Kalliklês here, in the Gorgias, maintains an opinion not only different from, but inconsistent with, the opinion alluded to above in the Theætêtus, 172 B. The persons noticed in the Theætêtus said—There is no Natural Justice: no Justice, except Justice by Law. Kalliklês says—There is a Natural Justice quite distinct from (and which he esteems more than) Justice by Law: he then explains what he believes Natural Justice to be—That the strong man should take what he pleases from the weak.

Though these two opinions are really inconsistent with each other, yet we see Plato in the Leges (x. 889 E, 890 A) alluding to them both as the same creed, held and defended by the same men; whom he denounces with extreme acrimony. Who they were, he does not name; he does not mention σοφισταί, but calls them ἀνδρῶν σοφῶν, ἰδιωτῶν τε καὶ ποιητῶν.

We see, in the third chapter of Sir H. S. Maine's excellent work on Ancient Law, the meaning of these phrases— Natural Justice, Law of Nature. It designated or included "a set of legal principles entitled to supersede the existing laws, on the ground of intrinsic superiority". It denoted an ideal condition of society, supposed to be much better than what actually prevailed. This at least seems to have been the meaning which began to attach to it in the time of Plato and Aristotle. What this ideal perfection of human society was, varied in the minds of different speakers. In each speaker's mind the word and sentiment was much the same, though the objects to which it attached were often different. Empedokles proclaims in solemn and emphatic language that the Law of Nature peremptorily forbids us to kill any animal. (Aristot. Rhetor. i. 13, 1373 b. 15.) Plato makes out to his own satisfaction, that his Republic is thoroughly in harmony with the Law of Nature: and he insists especially on this harmony, in the very point which even the Platonic critics admit to be wrong—that is, in regard to the training of women and the relations of the sexes (Republic, v. 456 C, 466 D). We learn from Plato himself that the propositions of the Republic were thoroughly adverse to what other persons reverenced as the Law of Nature.

In the notes of Beck and Heindorf on Protagor. p. 337 we read, "Hippias præ cæteris Sophistis contempsit leges, iisque opposuit Naturam. Naturam legibus plures certé Sophistarum opposuisse, easque præ illâ contempsisse, multis veterum locis constat." Now this allegation is more applicable to Plato than to the Sophists. Plato speaks with the most unmeasured contempt of existing communities and their laws: the scheme of his Republic, radically departing from them as it does, shows what he considered as required by the exigencies of human nature. Both the Stoics and the Epikureans extolled what they called the Law of Nature above any laws actually existing.

The other charge made against the Sophists (quite opposite, yet sometimes advanced by the same critics) is, that they recognised no Just by Nature, but only Just by Law: *i.e.* all the actual laws and customs considered as binding in each different community. This is what Plato ascribes to some persons (Sophists or not) in the Theætêtus, p. 172. But in this sense it is not exact to call Kalliklês (as Heindorf does, Protagor. p. 337) "germanus ille Sophistarum alumnus in Gorgiâ Callicles," nor to affirm (with Schleiermacher, Einleit. zum Theætêt. p. 183) that Plato meant to refute Aristippus under the name of Kallikles, Aristippus maintaining that there was no Just by Nature, but only Just by Law or Convention.

they regard him as the representative of Athenian democracy (to which however his proclaimed sentiments stand pointedly opposed), when they come across a great man or so-called hero, such as Alexander or Napoleon, applaud the most exorbitant ambition if successful, and if accompanied by military genius and energy—regarding communities as made for little else except to serve as his instruments, subjects, and worshippers. Such are represented as the sympathies of Kalliklês: but those of the Athenians went with the second of the two rights—and mine go with it also. And though the language which Plato puts into the mouth of Kalliklês, in describing this second right, abounds in contemptuous rhetoric, proclaiming offensively the individual weakness of the multitude[1]—yet this very fact is at once the most solid and most respectable foundation on which rights and obligations can be based. The establishment of them is indispensable, and is felt as indispensable, to procure security for the community: whereby the strong man whom Kalliklês extols as the favourite of Nature, may be tamed by discipline and censure, so as to accommodate his own behaviour to this equitable arrangement.[2] Plato himself, in his Republic,[3] traces the generation of a city to the fact that each man individually taken is not self-sufficing, but stands in need of many things: it is no less true, that each man stands also in fear of many things, especially of depredations from animals, and depredations from powerful individuals of his own species. In the mythe of Protagoras,[4] we have fears from hostile animals—in the speech here ascribed to Kalliklês, we have fears from hostile strong men—assigned as the generating cause, both of political communion and of established rights and obligations to protect it.

Kalliklês now explains, that by *stronger* men, he means better, wiser, braver men. It is they (he says) who ought, according to right by nature, to rule over others and to have larger shares than others. *Sokr.*—Ought

Sokrates maintains that self-command

[1] Plato, Gorgias, p. 483 B, p. 492 A. οἱ πολλοί, ἀποκρυπτόμενοι τὴν ἑαυτῶν ἀδυναμίαν, &c.
[2] Plato, Gorgias, p. 483 E.
[3] Plato, Republic, ii. p. 369 B. ὅτι τυγχάνει ἡμῶν ἕκαστος οὐκ αὐτάρκης ὤν, ἀλλὰ πολλῶν ἐνδεής.
[4] Plato, Protag. p. 322 B.

and moderation is requisite for the strong man as well as for others. Kalliklês defends the negative.

they not to rule themselves as well as others:[1] to control their own pleasures and desires: to be sober and temperate? *Kall.*—No: they would be foolish if they did. The weak multitude must do so; and there grows up accordingly among *them* a sentiment which requires such self-restraint from all. But it is the privilege of the superior few to be exempt from this necessity. The right of nature authorises them to have the largest desires, since their courage and ability furnish means to satisfy the desires. It would be silly if a king's son or a despot were to limit himself to the same measure of enjoyment with which a poor citizen must be content; and worse than silly if he did not enrich his friends in preference to his enemies. He need not care for that public law and censure which must reign paramount over each man among the many. A full swing of enjoyment, if a man has power to procure and maintain it, is virtue as well as happiness.[2]

Sokr.—I think on the contrary that a sober and moderate life,

Whether the largest measure of desires is good for a man, provided he has the means of satisfying them? Whether all varieties of desire are good? Whether the pleasurable and the good are identical?

regulated according to present means and circumstances, is better than a life of immoderate indulgence.[3] *Kall.*—The man who has no desires will have no pleasure, and will live like a stone. The more the desires, provided they can all be satisfied, the happier a man will be. *Sokr.*—You mean that a man shall be continually hungry, and continually satisfying his hunger: continually thirsty, and satisfying his thirst; and so forth. *Kall.*—By having and by satisfying those and all other desires, a man will enjoy happiness. *Sokr.*—Do you mean to include all varieties of desire and satisfaction of desire: such for example as itching and scratching yourself:[4] and other bodily appetites which might be named? *Kall.* —Such things are not fit for discussion. *Sokr.*—It is you who drive me to mention them, by laying down the principle, that men who enjoy, be the enjoyment of what sort it may, are

---

[1] Plato, Gorgias, p. 491 D.
[2] Plato, Gorgias, p. 492 A-C.
[3] Plato, Gorgias, p. 493 C. ἐάν πως οἷός τ' ὦ πεῖσαι μεταθέσθαι καὶ ἀντὶ τοῦ ἀπλήστως καὶ ἀκολάστως ἔχοντος βίου τὸν κοσμίως καὶ τοῖς ἀεὶ παροῦσιν ἱκανῶς καὶ ἐξαρκούντως ἔχοντα βίον ἑλέσθαι.
[4] Plato, Gorg. p. 494 E.

CHAP. XXIV.   PLEASURE AND GOOD—DISPARATES.   345

happy; and by not distinguishing what pleasures are good and what are evil. Tell me again, do you think that the pleasurable and the good are identical? Or are there any pleasurable things which are not good?[1] *Kall.*—I think that the pleasurable and the good are the same.

Upon this question the discussion now turns: whether pleasure and good are the same, or whether there are not some pleasures good, others bad. By a string of questions much protracted, but subtle rather than conclusive, Sokrates proves that pleasure is not the same as good—that there are such things as bad pleasures and good pains. And Kalliklês admits that some pleasures are better, others worse.[2] Profitable pleasures are good: hurtful pleasures are bad. Thus the pleasures of eating and drinking are good, if they impart to us health and strength—bad, if they produce sickness and weakness. We ought to choose the good pleasures and pains, and avoid the bad ones. It is not every man who is competent to distinguish what pleasures are good, and what are bad. A scientific and skilful adviser, judging upon general principles, is required to make this distinction.[3]

Kalliklês maintains that pleasurable and good are identical. Sokrates refutes him. Some pleasures are good, others bad. A scientific adviser is required to discriminate them.

This debate between Sokrates and Kalliklês, respecting the "Quomodo vivendum est,"[4] deserves attention on more than one account. In the first place, the relation which Sokrates is here made to declare between the two pairs of general terms, Pleasurable—Good: Painful—Evil: is the direct reverse of that which he both declares and demonstrates in the Protagoras. In that dialogue, the Sophist Protagoras is represented as holding an opinion very like that which is maintained

Contradiction between Sokrates in the Gorgias, and Sokrates in the Protagoras.

---

[1] Plato, Gorg. pp. 494-495. ἢ γὰρ ἐγὼ ἄγω ἐνταῦθα, ἢ ἐκεῖνος ὃς ἂν φῇ ἀνέδην οὕτω τοὺς χαίροντας, ὅπως ἂν χαιρωσιν, εὐδαίμονας εἶναι, καὶ μὴ διορίζηται τῶν ἡδονῶν ὁποῖαι ἀγαθαὶ καὶ κακαί; ἀλλ' ἔτι καὶ νῦν λέγε, πότερον φῂς εἶναι τὸ αὐτὸ ἡδὺ καὶ ἀγαθόν, ἢ εἶναί τι τῶν ἡδέων ὃ οὐκ ἔστιν ἀγαθόν;

[2] Plato, Gorgias, pp. 496-499.
[3] Plato, Gorgias, pp. 499-500. Ἀρ' οὖν παντὸς ἀνδρός ἐστιν ἐκλέξασθαι ποῖα ἀγαθὰ τῶν ἡδέων ἐστὶ καὶ ὁποῖα κακά, ἢ τεχνικοῦ δεῖ εἰς ἕκαστον; Τεχνικοῦ.
[4] Plato, Gorgias, p. 492 D. ἵνα τῷ ὄντι κατάδηλον γένηται, πῶς βιωτέον, &c. 500 C : ὅντινα χρὴ τρόπον ζῆν.

by Sokrates in the Gorgias. But Sokrates (in the Protagoras) refutes him by an elaborate argument; and demonstrates that pleasure and good (also pain and evil) are names for the same fundamental ideas under different circumstances: pleasurable and painful referring only to the sensation of the present moment—while good and evil include, besides, an estimate of its future consequences and accompaniments, both pleasurable and painful, and represent the result of such calculation. In the Gorgias, Sokrates demonstrates the contrary, by an argument equally elaborate but not equally convincing. He impugns a doctrine advocated by Kalliklês, and in impugning it, proclaims a marked antithesis and even repugnance between the pleasurable and the good, the painful and the evil: rejecting the fundamental identity of the two, which he advocates in the Protagoras, as if it were a disgraceful heresy.

The subject evidently presented itself to Plato in two different ways at different times. Which of the two is earliest, we have no means of deciding. The commentators, who favour generally the view taken in the Gorgias, treat the Protagoras as a juvenile and erroneous production: sometimes, with still less reason, they represent Sokrates as arguing in that dialogue, from the principles of his opponents, not from his own. For my part, without knowing whether the Protagoras or the Gorgias is the earliest, I think the Protagoras an equally finished composition, and I consider that the views which Sokrates is made to propound in it, respecting pleasure and good, are decidedly nearer to the truth.

View of critics about this contradiction.

That in the list of pleasures there are some which it is proper to avoid,—and in the list of pains, some which it is proper to accept or invite—is a doctrine maintained by Sokrates alike in both the dialogues. Why? Because some pleasures are good, others bad: some pains bad, others good—says Sokrates in the Gorgias. The same too is said by Sokrates in the Protagoras; but then, he there explains what he means by the appellation. All pleasure (he there says), so far as it goes, is good—all pain is bad. But there are some pleasures which cannot be enjoyed without debarring us from greater pleasures or entailing upon us greater pains: on that ground therefore, such pleasures are bad.

Comparison and appreciation of the reasoning of Sokrates in both dialogues.

So again, there are some pains, the suffering of which is a condition indispensable to our escaping greater pains, or to our enjoying greater pleasures: such pains therefore are good. Thus this apparent exception does not really contradict, but confirms, the general doctrine—That there is no good but the pleasurable, and the elimination of pain—and no evil except the painful, or the privation of pleasure. Good and evil have no reference except to pleasures and pains; but the terms imply, in each particular case, an estimate and comparison of future pleasurable and painful consequences, and express the result of such comparison. "You call enjoyment itself evil" (says Sokrates in the Protagoras),[1] "when it deprives us of greater pleasures or entails upon us greater pains. If you have any other ground, or look to any other end, in calling it evil, you may tell us what that end is; but you will not be able to tell us. So too, you say that pain is a good, when it relieves us from greater pains, or when it is necessary as the antecedent cause of greater pleasures. If you have any other end in view, when you call pain good, you may tell us what that end is; but you will not be able to tell us."[2]

In the Gorgias, too, Sokrates declares that some pleasures are good, others bad—some pains bad, others good. But here he stops. He does not fulfil the reasonable demand urged by Sokrates in the Protagoras—"If you make such a distinction, explain the ground on which you make it, and the end to which you look". The distinction in the Gorgias stands without any assigned ground or end to rest upon. And this want *Distinct statement in the Protagoras. What are good and evil, and upon what principles the scientific adviser is to*

---

[1] Plato, Pratagoras, p. 354 D. ἐπεί, εἰ κατ' ἄλλο τι αὐτὸ τὸ χαίρειν κακὸν καλεῖτε καὶ εἰς ἄλλο τι τέλος ἀποβλέψαντες, ἔχοιτε ἂν καὶ ἡμῖν εἰπεῖν· ἀλλ' οὐχ ἕξετε. . . . ἐπεὶ εἰ πρὸς ἄλλο τι τέλος ἀποβλέπετε, ὅταν καλῆτε αὐτὸ τὸ λυπεῖσθαι ἀγαθόν, ἢ πρὸς ὃ ἐγὼ λέγω, ἔχετε ἡμῖν εἰπεῖν· ἀλλ' οὐχ ἕξετε.

[2] In a remarkable passage of the De Legibus, Plato denies all essential distinction between Good and Pleasure, and all reality of Good apart from Pleasure (Legg. ii. pp. 662-663). εἰ δ' αὖ τὸν δικαιότατον εὐδαιμονέστατον ἀποφαίνοιτο βίον εἶναι, ζητοῖ πού πᾶς ἂν ὁ ἀκούων, οἶμαι, τί ποτ' ἐν αὐτῷ τὸ τῆς ἡδονῆς κρεῖττον ἀγαθόν τε καὶ καλὸν ὁ νόμος ἐνὸν ἐπαινεῖ; τί γὰρ δὴ δικαίῳ χωριζόμενον ἡδονῆς ἀγαθὸν ἂν γένοιτο;

Plato goes on to argue as follows: Even though it were not true, as I affirm it to be, that the life of justice is a life of pleasure, and the life of injustice a life of pain—still the law giver must proclaim this proposition as a useful falsehood, and compel every one to chime in with it. Otherwise the youth will have no motive to just conduct. For no one will willingly consent to obey any recommendation from which he does not expect more pleasure than pain ; οὐδεὶς γὰρ ἂν ἑκὼν ἐθέλοι πείθεσθαι πράττειν τοῦτο ὅ, τῷ μὴ τὸ χαίρειν τοῦ λυπεῖσθαι πλέον ἔπεται (663 B).

348　　　　　　　　　GORGIAS.　　　　　　CHAP. XXIV.

proceed in discriminating them. No such distinct statement in the Gorgias.

is the more sensibly felt, when we read in the same dialogue, that—"It is not every man who can distinguish the good pleasures from the bad : a scientific man, proceeding on principle, is needed for the purpose".[1] But upon what criterion is the scientific man to proceed? Of what properties is he to take account, in pronouncing one pleasure to be bad, another good—or one pain to be bad and another good—the estimate of consequences, measured in future pleasures and pains, being by the supposition excluded? No information is given. The problem set to the scientific man is one of which all the quantities are unknown. Now Sokrates in the Protagoras[2] also lays it down, that a scientific or rational calculation must be had, and a mind competent to such calculation must be postulated, to decide which pleasures are bad or fit to be rejected—which pains are good, or proper to be endured. But then he clearly specifies the elements which alone are to be taken into the calculation—*viz.*, the future pleasures and pains accompanying or dependent upon each with the estimate of their comparative magnitude and durability. The theory of this calculation is clear and intelligible : though in many particular cases, the data necessary for making it, and the means of comparing them, may be very imperfectly accessible.

Modern ethical theories. Intuition. Moral sense—not recognised by Plato in either of the dialogues.

According to various ethical theories, which have chiefly obtained currency in modern times, the distinction—between pleasures good or fit to be enjoyed, and pleasures bad or unfit to be enjoyed—is determined for us by a moral sense or intuition : by a simple, peculiar, sentiment of right and wrong, or a conscience, which springs up within us ready-made, and decides on such matters without appeal ; so that a man has only to look into his own heart for a solution. We need not take account of this hypothesis, in reviewing Plato's philosophy : for he evidently does not proceed upon it. He expressly affirms, in the Gorgias as well as in the Protagoras, that the question is one requiring science or knowledge to determine it, and upon

---

[1] Plato, Gorgias, p. 500 A. *Ἆρ' τεχνικοῦ δεῖ εἰς ἕκαστον; Τεχνικοῦ.
οὖν παντὸς ἀνρός ἐστιν ἐκλέξασθαι ποῖα* [2] Plato, Protagoras, pp. 357 B, 356
ἀγαθὰ τῶν ἡδέων ἐστὶ καὶ ὁποῖα κακά; ἢ E.

SCIENTIFIC CHOICE REQUIRED.

which none but the man of science or *expert* (τεχνικὸς) is a competent judge.

Moreover, there is another point common to both the two dialogues, deserving of notice. I have already remarked when reviewing the doctrine of Sokrates in the Protagoras, that it appears to me seriously defective, inasmuch as it takes into account the pleasures and pains of the agent only, and omits the pleasures and pains of other persons affected by his conduct. But this is not less true respecting the doctrine of Sokrates in the Gorgias: for whatever criterion he may there have in his mind to determine which among our pleasures are bad, it is certainly not this— that the agent in procuring them is obliged to hurt others. For the example which Sokrates cites as specially illustrating the class of bad pleasures—*viz*., the pleasure of scratching an itching part of the body[1]—is one in which no others besides the agent are concerned. As in the Protagoras, so in the Gorgias—Plato in laying down his rule of life, admits into the theory only what concerns the agent himself, and makes no direct reference to the happiness of others as affected by the agent's behaviour.

In both dialogues the doctrine of Sokrates is self-regarding as respects the agent: not considering the pleasures and pains of other persons, so far as affected by the agent.

There are however various points of analogy between the Protagoras and the Gorgias, which will enable us, after tracing them out, to measure the amount of substantial difference between them; I speak of the reasoning of Sokrates in each. Thus, in the Protagoras,[2] Sokrates ranks health, strength, preservation of the community, wealth, command, &c., under the general head of Good things, but expressly on the ground that they are the producing causes and conditions of pleasures and of exemption from pains: he also ranks sickness and poverty under the head of Evil things, as productive causes of pain and suffering. In the Gorgias also, he numbers wisdom, health, strength, perfection of body, riches, &c., among Good things or profitable things[3]—(which two words he treats as

Points wherein the doctrine of the two dialogues is in substance the same, but differing in classification.

---

[1] The Sokrates of the Protagoras would have reckoned this among the bad pleasures, because the discomfort and distress of body out of which it arises more than countervail the pleasure.
[2] Plato, Protagor. pp. 353 D, 354 A.
[3] Plato, Gorgias, pp. 467-468-499.

equivalent)—and their contraries as Evil things. Now he does not expressly say here (as in the Protagoras) that these things are *good*, because they are productive causes of pleasure or exemption from pain: but such assumption must evidently be supplied in order to make the reasoning valid. For upon what pretence can any one pronounce strength, health, riches, to be *good*—and helplessness, sickness, poverty, to be *evil*—if no reference be admitted to pleasures and pains? Sokrates in the Gorgias[1] declares that the pleasures of eating and drinking are good, in so far as they impart health and strength to the body—evil, in so far as they produce a contrary effect. Sokrates in the Protagoras reasons in the same way—but with this difference—that he would count the pleasure of the repast itself as one item of good: enhancing the amount of good where the future consequences are beneficial, diminishing the amount of evil where the future consequences are unfavourable: while Sokrates in the Gorgias excludes immediate pleasure from the list of good things, and immediate pain from the list of evil things.

This last exclusion renders the theory in the Gorgias untenable and inconsistent. If present pleasure be not admitted as an item of good so far as it goes—then neither can the future and consequent aggregates of pleasure, nor the causes of them, be admitted as good. So likewise, if present pain be no evil, future pain cannot be allowed to rank as an evil.[2]

Kalliklês, whom Sokrates refutes in

Each of the two dialogues, which I am now comparing, is in truth an independent composition: in each, Sokrates has a distinct argument to combat; and in the latest of the two (whichever that was), no heed is taken of

---

[1] Plato, Gorgias, p. 499 D.

[2] Compare a passage in the Republic (ii. p. 357) where Sokrates gives (or accepts, as given by Glaukon) a description of Good much more coincident with the Protagoras than with the Gorgias. The common property of all Good is to be desired or loved; and there are three varieties of it—1. That which we desire for itself, and for its own sake, apart from all ulterior consequences, such as innocuous pleasures or enjoyments. 2. That which we desire both for itself and for its ulterior consequences, such as good health, good vision, good sense, &c. 3. That which we do not desire—nay, which we perhaps hate or shun, *per se*: but which we nevertheless desire and invite, in connection with and for the sake of ulterior consequences: such as gymnastic training, medical treatment when we are sick, labour in our trade or profession.

Here Plato admits the immediately pleasurable *per se* as one variety of good, always assuming that it is not countervailed by consequences or accompaniments of a painful character. This is the doctrine of the Protagoras, as distinguished from the Gorgias, where Sokrates sets pleasure in marked opposition to good

the argumentation in the earlier. In the Protagoras, he exalts the dignity and paramount force of knowledge or prudence: if a man knows how to calculate pleasures and pains, he will be sure to choose the result which involves the greater pleasure or the less pain, on the whole: to say that he is overpowered by immediate pleasure or pain into making a bad choice, is a wrong description—the real fact being, that he is deficient in the proper knowledge how to choose. In the Gorgias, the doctrine assigned to Kalliklês and impugned by Sokrates is something very different. That justice, temperance, self-restraint, are indeed indispensable to the happiness of ordinary men; but if there be any one individual, so immensely superior in force as to trample down and make slaves of the rest, this one man would be a fool if he restrained himself: having the means of gratifying all his appetites, the more appetites he has, the more enjoyments will he have and the greater happiness.[1] Observe — that Kalliklês applies this doctrine only to the one omnipotent despot: to all other members of society, he maintains that self-restraint is essential. This is the doctrine which Sokrates in the Gorgias undertakes to refute, by denying community of nature between the pleasurable and the good—between the painful and the evil.

the Gorgias, maintains a different argument from that which Sokrates combats in the Protagoras.

To me his refutation appears altogether unsuccessful, and the position upon which he rests it incorrect. The only parts of the refutation really forcible, are those in which he unconsciously relinquishes this position, and slides into the doctrine of the Protagoras. Upon this latter doctrine, a refutation might be grounded: you may show that even an omnipotent despot (regard for the comfort of others being excluded by the hypothesis) will gain by limiting the gratification of his appetites to-day so as not to spoil his appetites of to-morrow. Even in his case, prudential restraint is required, though his motives for it would be much less than in the case of ordinary social men. But Good, as laid down by Plato in the Gorgias, entirely disconnected from plea-

The refutation of Kalliklês by Sokrates in the Gorgias, is unsuccessful—it is only so far successful as he adopts unintentionally the doctrine of Sokrates in the Protagoras.

[1] Plato, Gorgias, p. 492 B.

sure—and Evil, entirely disconnected from pain—have no application to this supposed despot. He has no desire for such Platonic Good—no aversion for such Platonic Evil. His happiness is not diminished by missing the former or incurring the latter. In fact, one of the cardinal principles of Plato's ethical philosophy, which he frequently asserts both in this dialogue and elsewhere,[1]—That every man desires Good, and acts for the sake of obtaining Good, and avoiding Evil—becomes untrue, if you conceive Good and Evil according to the Gorgias, as having no reference to pleasure or the avoidance of pain: untrue, not merely in regard to a despot under these exceptional conditions, but in regard to the large majority of social men. They desire to obtain Good and avoid Evil, in the sense of the Protagoras: but not in the sense of the Gorgias.[2] Sokrates himself proclaims in this dialogue : " I and philosophy stand opposed to Kalliklês and the Athenian public. What I desire is, to reason consistently with myself." That is, to speak the language of Sokrates in the Protagoras—"To me, Sokrates, the consciousness of inconsistency with myself and of an unworthy character, the loss of my own self-esteem and the pungency of my own self-reproach, are the greatest of all pains: greater than those which you, Kalliklês, and the Athenians generally, seek to avoid at all price and urge me also to avoid at all price—poverty, political nullity, exposure

---

[1] Plato, Gorgias, pp. 467 C, 499 E.
[2] The reasoning of Plato in the Gorgias, respecting this matter, rests upon an equivocal phrase. The Greek phrase εὖ πράττειν has two meanings; it means *recté agere*, to act rightly; and it also means *felicem esse*, to be happy. There is a corresponding double sense in κακῶς πράττειν. Heindorf has well noticed the fallacious reasoning founded by Plato on this double sense. We read in the Gorgias, p. 507 C: ἀνάγκη τὸν σώφρονα, δίκαιον ὄντα καὶ ἀνδρεῖον καὶ ὅσιον, ἀγαθὸν ἄνδρα εἶναι τελέως, τὸν δὲ ἀγαθὸν εὖ τε καὶ καλῶς πράττειν ἃ ἂν πράττῃ, τὸν δ' εὖ πράττοντα μακάριόν τε καὶ εὐδαίμονα εἶναι, τὸν δὲ πονηρὸν καὶ κακῶς πράττοντα ἄθλιον. Upon which Heindorf remarks, citing a note of Routh, who says, "Vix enim potest credi, Platonem duplici sensu verborum εὖ πράττειν ad argumentum probandum abuti voluisse, quæ fallacia esset amphiboliæ". "Non me minerat" (says Heindorf) "vir doctus ceteros in Platone locos, ubi eodem modo ex duplici illâ potestate argumentatio ducitur, cujusmodi plura attulimus ad Charmidem, 42, p. 172 A." Heindorf observes, on the Charmidês l. c. : "Argumenti hujus vim positam apparet in duplici dictionis εὖ πράττειν significatu : quum vulgo sit *felicem esse*, non *recté facere*. Hoc aliaque ejusdem generis sæpius sic ansam præbuerunt sophismatis magis quam justi syllogismi." Heindorf then refers to analogous passages in Plato, Repub. i. p. 354 A: Alkib. i. p. 116 B, p. 134 A. A similar fallacy is found in Aristotle, Politic. vii. i. p. 1323, a. 17, b. 32—ἄριστα γὰρ πράττειν προσήκει τοὺς ἄριστα πολιτευομένους—ἀδύνατον δὲ καλῶς πράττειν τοῖς μὴ τὰ καλὰ πράττουσιν. This fallacy is recognised and properly commented on as a "logisches Wortspiel," by Bernays, in his instructive volume, Die *Dialoge des Aristoteles*, pp. 80-81 (Berlin, 1863).

to false accusation, &c."[1] The noble scheme of life, here recommended by Sokrates, may be correctly described according to the theory of the Protagoras: without any resort to the paradox of the Gorgias, that Good has no kindred or reference to Pleasure, nor Evil to Pain.

Lastly—I will compare the Protagoras and the Gorgias (meaning always, the reasoning of Sokrates in each of them) under one more point of view. How does each of them describe and distinguish the permanent elements, and the transient elements, involved in human agency? What function does each of them assign to the permanent element? The distinction of these two is important in its ethical bearing. The whole life both of the individual and of society consists of successive moments of action or feeling. But each individual (and the society as an aggregate of individuals) has within him embodied and realised an element more or less permanent—an established character, habits, dispositions, intellectual acquirements, &c.—a sort of capital accumulated from the past. This permanent element is of extreme importance. It stands to the transient element in the same relation as the fixed capital of a trader or manufacturer to his annual produce. The whole use and value of the fixed capital, of which the skill and energy of the trader himself make an important part, consists in the amount of produce which it will yield: but at the same time the trader must keep it up in its condition of fixed capital, in order to obtain such amount: he must set apart, and abstain from devoting to immediate enjoyment, as much of the annual produce as will suffice to maintain the fixed capital unimpaired—and more, if he desires to improve his condition. The capital cannot be commuted into interest; yet nevertheless its whole value depends upon, and is measured by, the interest which it yields. Doubtless the mere idea of possessing the capital is pleasurable to the possessor, because he knows that it can and will be profitably employed, so long as he chooses.

Permanent elements—and transient elements—of human agency—how each of them is appreciated in the two dialogues.

Now in the Protagoras, the permanent element is very pointedly distinguished from the transient, and is called Knowledge—the Science or Art of Calculation. *In the Protagoras.*

[1] Plato, Gorgias, pp. 481 D, 482 B.

Its function also is clearly announced—to take comparative estimate and measurement of the transient elements; which are stated to consist of pleasures and pains, present and future—near and distant—certain and uncertain—faint and strong. To these elements, manifold yet commensurable, the calculation is to apply. "The safety of life" (says Sokrates[1]) " resides in our keeping up this science or art of calculation." No present enjoyment must be admitted, which would impair it; no present pain must be shunned, which is essential to uphold it. Yet the whole of its value resides in its application to the comparison of the pleasures and pains.

In the Gorgias the same two elements are differently described, and less clearly explained. The permanent is termed, Order, arrangement, discipline, a lawful, just, and temperate, cast of mind (opposed to the doctrine ascribed to Kallikles, which negatived this element altogether, in the mind of the despot), parallel to health and strength of body: the unordered mind is again the parallel of the corrupt, distempered, helpless, body; life is not worth having until this is cured.[2] This corresponds to the knowledge or Calculating Science in the Protagoras; but we cannot understand what its function is, in the Gorgias, because the calculable elements are incompletely enumerated.

In the Gorgias.

In the Protagoras, these calculable elements are two-fold—immediate pleasures and pains—and future or distant pleasures and pains. Between these two there is intercommunity of nature, so that they are quite commensurable; and the function of the calculating reason is, to make a right estimate of the one against the other.[3] But in the Gorgias, no mention is made of future or distant pleasures and pains: the calculable element is represented only by immediate pleasure or pain—and from thence we pass at once to the permanent calculator—the mind, sound or corrupt. You must abstain from a particular enjoyment, because it will

---

[1] Plato, Protag. p. 357 A. ἐπειδὴ δὲ ἡδονῆς τε καὶ λύπης ἐν ὀρθῇ τῇ αἱρέσει ἐφάνη ἡμῖν ἡ σωτηρία τοῦ βίου οὖσα, τοῦ τε πλέονος καὶ ἐλάττονος καὶ μείζονος καὶ σμικροτέρου καὶ ποῤῥωτέρω καὶ ἐγγυτέρω, &c.
[2] Plato, Gorgias, pp. 504 B-C, 506 D-E. Τάξις — κόσμος — ψυχὴ κοσμία ἀμείνων τοῦ ἀκοσμήτου.
[3] There would be also the like intercommunity of nature, if along with the pains and pleasures of the agent himself (which alone are regarded in the calculation of Sokrates in the Protagoras) you admit into the calculation the pleasures and pains of others concerned, and the rules established with a view to both the two together—with a view to the joint interest both of the agent and of others.

taint the soundness of your mind: this is a pertinent reason (and would be admitted as such by Sokrates in the Protagoras, who instead of sound mind would say, calculating intelligence), but it is neither the ultimate reason (since this soundness of mind is itself valuable with a view to future calculations), nor the only reason: for you must also abstain, if it will bring upon yourself (or upon others) preponderating pains in the particular case—if the future pains would preponderate over the present pleasure. Of this last calculation no notice is taken in the Gorgias: which exhibits only the antithesis (not merely marked but even overdone[1]) between the immediate pleasure or pain and the calculating efficacy of mind, but leaves out the true function which gives value to the sound mind as distinguished from the unsound and corrupt. That function consists in its application to particular cases: in right dealing with actual life, as regards the agent himself and others: in ἐνέργεια, as distinguished from ἕξις, to use Aristotelian language.[2] I am far from supposing that this part of the case was absent from Plato's mind. But the theory laid out in the Gorgias (as compared with that in the Protagoras) leaves no room for it; giving exclusive prominence to the other elements, and acknowledging only the present pleasure or pain, to be set against the permanent condition of mind, bad or good as it may be.

Indeed there is nothing more remarkable in the Gorgias, than the manner in which Sokrates not only condemns the unmeasured, exorbitant, maleficent desires, but also depreciates and degrades all the actualities of life—all the recreative and elegant arts, including music and poetry, tragic as well as dithyrambic—all provision for the most essential wants, all protection against particular

<small>Character of the Gorgias generally—s discrediting all the actualities of life.</small>

---

[1] Epikurus and his followers assigned the greatest value, in their ethical theory, to the permanent element, or established character of the agent, intellectual and emotional. But great as they reckoned this value to be, they resolved it all into the diminution or mitigation of pains, and, in a certain though inferior degree, the multiplication of pleasures. They did not put it in a separate category of its own, altogether disparate and foreign to pleasures and pains.

See the letter of Epikurus to Menœkeus, Diog. L. x. 128-132; Lucretius, v. 18-45, vi. 12-25; Horat. Epist. i. 2, 48-60.

[2] Aristot. Ethic. Nikom. i. 7. The remark of Aristotle in the same treatise, i. 5—δοκεῖ γὰρ ἐνδέχεσθαι καὶ καθεύδειν ἔχοντα τὴν ἀρετήν, ἢ ἀπρακτεῖν διὰ βίου—might be applied to the theory of the Gorgias. Compare also Ethic. Nik. vii. 3 (vii. 4, p. 1146, b. 31, p. 1147, a. 12).

sufferings and dangers, even all service rendered to another person in the way of relief or of rescue[1]—all the effective maintenance of public organised force, such as ships, docks, walls, arms, &c. Immediate satisfaction or relief, and those who confer it, are treated with contempt, and presented as in hostility to the perfection of the mental structure. And it is in this point of view that various Platonic commentators extol in an especial manner the Gorgias : as recognising an Idea of Good superhuman and supernatural, radically disparate from pleasures and pains of any human being, and incommensurable with them : an Universal Idea, which, though it is supposed to cast a distant light

---

[1] Plato, Gorgias, pp. 501-502-511-512-517-519. ἄνευ γὰρ δικαιοσύνης καὶ σωφροσύνης λιμένων καὶ νεωρίων καὶ τειχῶν καὶ φόρων καὶ τοιούτων φλυαριῶν ἐμπεπλήκασι τὴν πόλιν.

This is applied to the provision of food, drink, clothing, bedding, for the hunger, thirst, &c., of the community (p. 517 D), to the saving of life (p. 511 D). The boatman between Ægina and Peiræus (says Plato) brings over his passengers in safety, together with their families and property, preserving them from all the dangers of the sea. The engineer, who constructs good fortifications, preserves from danger and destruction all the citizens with their families and their property (p. 512 B). But neither of these persons takes credit for this service : because both of them know that it is doubtful whether they have done any real service to the persons preserved, since they have not rendered them any better ; and that it is even doubtful whether they may not have done them an actual mischief. Perhaps these persons may be wicked and corrupt ; in that case it is a misfortune to them that their lives should be prolonged ; it would be better for them to die. It is under this conviction (says Plato) that the boatman and the engineer, though they do preserve our lives, take to themselves no credit for it.

We shall hardly find any greater rhetorical exaggeration than this, among all the compositions of the rhetors against whom Plato declares war in the Gorgias. Moreover, it is a specimen of the way in which Plato colours and misinterprets the facts of social life, in order to serve the purpose of the argument of the moment. He says truly that when the passage boat from Ægina to Peiræus has reached its destination, the steersman receives his fare and walks about on the shore, without taking any great credit to himself, as if he had performed a brilliant deed or conferred an important service. But how does Plato explain this? By supposing in the steersman's mind feelings which never enter into the mind of a real agent ; feelings which are put into words only when a moralist or a satirist is anxious to enforce a sentiment. The service which the steersman performs is not only adequately remunerated, but is, on most days, 'a regular and easy one, such as every man who has gone through a decent apprenticeship can perform. But suppose an exceptional day—suppose a sudden and terrible storm to supervene on the passage — suppose the boat full of passengers, with every prospect of all on board being drowned—suppose she is only saved by the extraordinary skill, vigilance, and efforts of the steersman. In that case he will, on reaching the land, walk about full of elate self-congratulation and pride : the passengers will encourage this sentiment by expressions of the deepest gratitude ; while friends as well as competitors will praise his successful exploit. How many of the passengers there are for whom the preservation of life may be a curse rather than a blessing—is a question which neither they themselves, nor the steersman, nor the public, will ever dream of asking.

upon its particulars, is separated from them by an incalculable space, and is discernible only by the Platonic telescope.

We have now established (continues Sokrates) that pleasure is essentially different from good, and pain from evil: also, that to obtain good and avoid evil, a scientific choice is required—while to obtain pleasure and avoid pain, is nothing more than blind imitation or irrational knack. There are some arts and pursuits which aim only at procuring immediate pleasure—others which aim at attaining good or the best;[1] some arts, for a single person,—others for a multitude. Arts and pursuits which aim only at immediate pleasure, either of one or of a multitude, belong to the general head of Flattery. Among them are all the musical, choric, and dithyrambic representations at the festivals—tragedy as well as comedy—also political and judicial rhetoric. None of these arts aim at any thing except to gratify the public to whom they are addressed : none of them aim at the permanent good : none seek to better the character of the public. They adapt themselves to the prevalent desires: but whether those desires are such as, if realised, will make the public worse or better, they never enquire.[2]

Sokr.—Do you know any public speakers who aim at anything more than gratifying the public, or who care to make the public better? *Kall.*—There are some who do, and others who do not. *Sokr.*—Which are those who do? and which of them has ever made the public

Argument of Sokrates resumed— multifarious arts of flattery, aiming at immediate pleasure.

The Rhetors aim only at flattering the public— even the best past

---

[1] The Sokrates of the Protagoras would have admitted a twofold distinction of aims, but would have stated the distinction otherwise. Two things (he would say) may be looked at in regard to any course of conduct: first, the immediate pleasure or pain which it yields; secondly, this item, not alone, but combined with all the other pleasures and pains which can be foreseen as its conditions, consequences, or concomitants. To obey the desire of immediate pleasure, or the fear of immediate pain, requires no science; to foresee, estimate, and compare the consequences, requires a scientific calculation often very difficult and complicated—a τέχνη or ἐπιστήμη μετρητική.

Thus we are told not only in what cases the calculation is required, but what are the elements to be taken into the calculation. In the Gorgias, we are not told on what elements the calculation of good and evil is to be based : we are told that there *must be science*, but we learn nothing more.

[2] Plato, Gorgias, pp. 502-503.

Rhetors have done nothing else —citation of the four great Rhetors by Kallikles.
better?[1] *Kall.*—At any rate, former statesmen did so; such as Miltiades, Themistokles, Kimon, Perikles. *Sokr.*—None of them. If they had, you would have seen them devoting themselves systematically and obviously to their one end. As a builder labours to construct a ship or a house, by putting together its various parts with order and symmetry—so these statesmen would have laboured to implant order and symmetry in the minds and bodies of the citizens: that is, justice and temperance in their minds, health and strength in their bodies.[2] Unless the statesman can do this, it is fruitless to supply the wants, to fulfil the desires and requirements, to uphold or enlarge the power, of the citizens. This is like supplying ample nourishment to a distempered body: the more such a body takes in, the worse it becomes. The citizens must be treated with refusal of their wishes and with punishment, until their vices are healed, and they become good.[3]

Necessity for temperance, regulation, order. This is the condition of virtue and happiness.
We ought to do (continues Sokrates) what is pleasing for the sake of what is good: not *vice versâ*. But every thing becomes good by possessing its appropriate virtue or regulation. The regulation appropriate to the mind is, to be temperate. The temperate man will do what is just—his duty towards men: and what is holy—his duty towards the Gods. He will be just and holy. He will therefore also be courageous: for he will seek only such pleasures as duty permits, and he will endure all such pains as duty requires. Being thus temperate, just, brave, holy, he will be a perfectly good man, doing well and honourably throughout. The man who does well, will be happy: the man who does ill and is wicked, will be miserable.[4] It ought to be our principal aim, both for ourselves individually and for the city, to attain temperance and to keep clear of intemperance: not to let our desires run immoderately (as you, Kallikles, advise), and then seek repletion for them: which is an endless mischief, the life of a pirate. He who pursues this plan can neither be the friend of any other man, nor of the Gods: for he is incapable of communion, and therefore of friendship.[5]

[1] Plato, Gorgias, p. 503 C.
[2] Plato, Gorgias, p. 504 D.
[3] Plato, Gorgias, p. 505 B.
[4] Plato, Gorgias, p. 507 D (with Routh and Heindorf's notes).
[5] Plato, Gorgias, p. 507 E. κοινωνεῖν γὰρ ἀδύνατος· ὅτῳ δὲ μὴ ἔνι κοινωνία, φιλία οὐκ ἂν εἴη.

CONDITIONS OF POLITICAL SUCCESS.

Now, Kallikles (pursues Sokrates), you have reproached me with standing aloof from public life in order to pursue philosophy. You tell me that by not cultivating public speaking and public action, I am at the mercy of any one who chooses to accuse me unjustly and to bring upon me severe penalties. But I tell you, that it is a greater evil to do wrong than to suffer wrong; and that my first business is, to provide for myself such power and such skill as shall guard me against doing wrong.[1] Next, as to suffering wrong, there is only one way of taking precautions against it. You must yourself rule in the city: or you must be a friend of the ruling power. Like is the friend of like:[2] a cruel despot on the throne will hate and destroy any one who is better than himself, and will despise any one worse than himself. The only person who will have influence is, one of the same dispositions as the despot: not only submitting to him with good will, but praising and blaming the same things as he does—accustomed from youth upwards to share in his preferences and aversions, and assimilated to him as much as possible.[3] Now if the despot be a wrong-doer, he who likens himself to the despot will become a wrong-doer also. And thus, in taking precautions against suffering wrong, he will incur the still greater mischief and corruption of doing wrong, and will be worse off instead of better.

Kall.—But if he does not liken himself to the despot, the despot may put him to death, if he chooses? *Sokr.*— Perhaps he may: but it will be death inflicted by a bad man upon a good man.[4] To prolong life is not the foremost consideration, but to decide by rational thought what is the best way of passing that length of life which the Fates allot.[5] Is it my best plan to do as you

Impossible to succeed in public life, unless a man be thoroughly akin to and in harmony with the ruling force.

Danger of one who dissents from the public, either for better or for worse.

---

[1] Plato, Gorgias, p. 509 C. Compare Leges, viii. 829 A, where τὸ μὴ ἀδικεῖν is described as easy of attainment; τὸ μὴ ἀδικεῖσθαι, as being παγχάλεπον: and both equally necessary πρὸς τὸ εὐδαιμόνως ζῆν.

[2] Plat. Gorg. 510 B. φίλος—ὁ ὅμοιος τῷ ὁμοίῳ. We have already seen this principle discussed and rejected in the Lysis, p. 214. See above, ch. xx., p. 179.

[3] Plato, Gorgias, p. 510 C. λείπεται δὴ ἐκεῖνος μόνος ἄξιος λόγου φίλος τῷ τοιούτῳ, ὃς ἂν, ὁμοήθης ὤν, ταὐτὰ ψέγων καὶ ἐπαινῶν, ἐθέλῃ ἄρχεσθαι καὶ ὑποκεῖσθαι τῷ ἄρχοντι. Οὗτος μέγα ἐν ταύτῃ τῇ πόλει δυνήσεται, τοῦτον οὐδεὶς χαίρων ἀδικήσει. . . . Αὕτη ὁδός ἐστιν, εὐθὺς ἐκ νέου ἐθίζειν αὐτὸν τοῖς αὐτοῖς χαίρειν καὶ ἄχθεσθαι τῷ δεσπότῃ, καὶ παρασκευάζειν ὅπως ὅ τι μάλιστα ὅμοιος ἔσται ἐκείνῳ.

[4] Plato, Gorgias, p. 511 B.

[5] Plato, Gorgias, pp. 511 B, 512 E.

recommend, and to liken myself as much as possible to the Athenian people—in order that I may become popular and may acquire power in the city? For it will be impossible for you to acquire power in the city, if you dissent from the prevalent political character and practice, be it for the better or for the worse. Even imitation will not be sufficient: you must be, by natural disposition, homogeneous with the Athenians, if you intend to acquire much favour with them. Whoever makes you most like to them, will help you forward most towards becoming an effective statesman and speaker: for every assembly delight in speeches suited to their own dispositions, and reject speeches of an opposite tenor.[1]

Such are the essential conditions of political success and popularity. But I, Kalliklês, have already distinguished two schemes of life; one aiming at pleasure, the other aiming at good: one, that of the statesman who studies the felt wants, wishes, and impulses of the people, displaying his genius in providing for them effective satisfaction—the other, the statesman who makes it his chief or sole object to amend the character and disposition of the people.

Sokrates resolves upon a scheme of life for himself—to study permanent good, and not immediate satisfaction.

The last scheme is the only one which I approve: and if it be that to which you invite me, we must examine whether either you, Kallikles, or I, have ever yet succeeded in amending or improving the character of any individuals privately, before we undertake the task of amending the citizens collectively.[2] None of the past statesmen whom you extol, Miltiades, Kimon, Themistokles, Perikles, has produced any such amendment.[3] Considered as ministers, indeed, they were skilful and effective; better than the present statesmen. They were successful in furnishing satisfaction to the prevalent wants and desires of the citizens: they provided docks, walls, ships, tribute, and other such follies, abundantly:[4]

---

[1] Plato, Gorgias, p. 513 A. καὶ νῦν δὲ ἄρα δεῖ σε ὡς ὁμοιότατον γίγνεσθαι τῷ δήμῳ τῷ Ἀθηναίων, εἰ μέλλεις τούτῳ προσφιλὴς εἶναι καὶ μέγα δύνασθαι ἐν τῇ πόλει. . . . εἰ δέ σοι οἴει ὁντινοῦν ἀνθρώπων παραδώσειν τέχνην τινὰ τοιαύτην, ἥ τίς σε ποιήσει μέγα δύνασθαι ἐν τῇ πόλει τῇδε, ἀνόμοιον ὄντα τῇ πολιτείᾳ εἴτ' ἐπὶ τὸ βέλτιον εἴτ' ἐπὶ τὸ χεῖρον, οὐκ ὀρθῶς βουλεύει· οὐ γὰρ μιμητὴν δεῖ εἶναι, ἀλλ' αὐτοφυῶς ὅμοιον τούτοις, εἰ μέλλεις τι γνήσιον ἀπεργάζεσθαι εἰς φιλίαν τῷ Ἀθηναίων δήμῳ.

[2] Plato, Gorgias, p. 515 A.

[3] Plato, Gorgias, pp. 516, 517.

[4] Plato, Gorgias, pp. 517, 519. ἄνευ γὰρ σωφροσύνης καὶ δικαιοσύνης λιμένων καὶ νεωρίων καὶ τειχῶν καὶ φόρων καὶ τοιούτων φλυαριῶν ἐμπεπλήκασι τὴν πόλιν.

but they did nothing to amend the character of the people—to transfer the desires of the people from worse things to better things—or to create in them justice and temperance. They thus did no real good by feeding the desires of the people: no more good than would be done by a skilful cook for a sick man, in cooking for him a sumptuous meal before the physician had cured him.

I believe myself (continues Sokrates) to be the only man in Athens,—or certainly one among a very few,—who am a true statesman, following out the genuine purposes of the political art.[1] I aim at what is best for the people, not at what is most agreeable. I do not value those captivating accomplishments which tell in the Dikastery. If I am tried, I shall be like a physician arraigned by the confectioner before a jury of children. I shall not be able to refer to any pleasures provided for them by me: pleasures which *they* call benefits, but which I regard as worthless. If any one accuses me of corrupting the youth by making them sceptical, or of libelling the older men in my private and public talk—it will be in vain for me to justify myself by saying the real truth.—Dikasts, I do and say all these things justly, for your real benefit. I shall not be believed when I say this, and I have nothing else to say: so that I do not know what sentence may be passed on me.[2] My only refuge and defence will be, the innocence of my life. As for death, no one except a fool or a coward fears *that:* the real evil, and the greatest of all evils, is to pass into Hades with a corrupt and polluted mind.[3]

Sokrates announces himself as almost the only man at Athens, who follows out the true political art. Danger of doing this.

Sokrates then winds up the dialogue, by reciting a Νέκυια, a mythe or hypothesis about judgment in Hades after death, and rewards and punishments to be apportioned to deceased men, according to their merits during life, by Rhadamanthus and Minos. The greatest sufferers by these judgments (he says) will be the kings, despots, and men politically powerful, who have during their lives committed the greatest in-

Mythe respecting Hades, and the treatment of deceased persons therein, according to their merits during life—

---

[1] Plato, Gorgias, p. 521 D.
[2] Plato, Gorgias, pp. 521-522.
[3] Plato, Gorgias, p. 522 E. αὐτὸ μὲν γὰρ τὸ ἀποθνήσκειν οὐδεὶς φοβεῖται, ὅστις μὴ παντάπασιν ἀλόγιστός τε καὶ ἄνανδρός ἐστι, τὸ δὲ ἀδικεῖν φοβεῖται, &c.

362   GORGIAS.   CHAP. XXIV.

the philosopher, who stood aloof from public affairs, will then be rewarded. justices,—which indeed few of them avoid.[1] The man most likely to fare well and to be rewarded, will be the philosopher, "who has passed through life minding his own business, and not meddling with the affairs of others".[2]

"Dicuntur ista magnifice,"[3]—we may exclaim, in Ciceronian words, on reaching the close of the Gorgias. It is pre-eminently solemn and impressive; all the more so, from the emphasis of Sokrates, when proclaiming the isolation in which he stands at Athens, and the contradiction between his ethico-political views and those of his fellow-citizens. In this respect it harmonises with the Apology, the Kriton, Republic, and Leges: in all which, the peculiarity of his ethical points of view stands proclaimed—especially in the Kriton, where he declares that his difference with his opponents is fundamental, and that there can be between them no common ground for debate—nothing but reciprocal contempt.[4]

Peculiar ethical views of Sokrates— Rhetorical or dogmatical character of the Gorgias.

The argument of Sokrates in the Gorgias is interesting, not merely as extolling the value of ethical self-restraint, but also as considering political phenomena under this point of view: that is, merging politics in ethics. The proper and paramount function of statesmen (we find it eloquently proclaimed) is to serve as spiritual teachers in the community: for the purpose of amending the lives and characters of the citizens, and of converting them from bad dispositions to good. We are admonished that until this is effected, more is lost than gained by realising the actual wants and wishes of the community, which are disorderly and distempered: like the state of a sick man,

He merges politics in Ethics—he conceives the rulers as spiritual teachers and trainers of the community.

---

[1] Plato, Gorgias, pp. 525-526.
[2] Plato, Gorgias, p. 526 C. φιλοσόφου τὰ αὑτοῦ πράξαντος, καὶ οὐ πολυπραγμονήσαντος ἐν τῷ βίῳ.
It must be confessed that these terms do not correspond to the life of Sokrates, as he himself describes it in the Platonic Apology. He seems to have fancied that no one was πολυπράγμων, except those who spoke habitually in the Ekklesia and the Dikastery.

[3] Cicero, De Finib. iii. 3, 11.
[4] Plato, Kriton, p. 49 D.

who would receive harm and not benefit from a sumptuous banquet.

This is the conception of Plato in the Gorgias, speaking through the person of Sokrates, respecting the ends for which the political magistrate ought to employ his power. The magistrate, as administering law and justice, is to the minds of the community what the trainer and the physician are to their bodies: he produces goodness of mind, as the two latter produce health and strength of body. The Platonic *idéal* is that of a despotic law-giver and man-trainer, wielding the compulsory force of the secular arm for what he believes to be spiritual improvement. However instructive it is to study the manner in which a mind like that of Plato works out such a purpose in theory, there is no reason for regret that he never had an opportunity of carrying it into practice. The manner in which he always keeps in view the standing mental character, as an object of capital importance to be attended to, and as the analogon of health in the body—deserves all esteem. But when he assumes the sceptre of King Nomos (as in Republic and Leges) to fix by unchangeable authority what shall be the orthodox type of character, and to suppress all the varieties of emotion and intellect, except such as will run into a few predetermined moulds—he oversteps all the reasonable aims and boundaries of the political office.

Idéal of Plato—a despotic law-giver or man-trainer, on scientific principles, fashioning all characters pursuant to certain types of his own.

Plato forgets two important points of difference, in that favourite and very instructive analogy which he perpetually reproduces, between mental goodness and bodily health. First, good health and strength of the body (as I have observed already) are states which every man knows when he has got them. Though there is much doubt and dispute about causes, preservative, destructive, and restorative, there is none about the present fact. Every sick man derives from his own sensations an anxiety to get well. But virtue is not a point thus fixed, undisputed, indubitable: it is differently conceived by different persons, and must first be discovered and settled by a process of enquiry; the Platonic Sokrates himself, in many of the dialogues—after declaring that neither he nor any

Platonic analogy between mental goodness and bodily health— incomplete analogy— circumstances of difference.

one else within his knowledge, knows what it is—tries to find it out without success. Next, the physician, who is the person actively concerned in imparting health and strength, exercises no coercive power over any one : those who consult him have the option whether they will follow the advice given, or not. To put himself upon the same footing with the physician, the political magistrate ought to confine himself to the function of advice ; a function highly useful, but in which he will be called upon to meet argumentative opposition, and frequent failure, together with the mortification of leaving those whom he cannot convince, to follow their own mode of life. Here are two material differences, modifying the applicability of that very analogy on which Plato so frequently rests his proof.

Sokrates in the Gorgias speaks like a dissenter among a community of fixed opinions and habits. Impossible that a dissenter, on important points, should acquire any public influence.

In Plato's two imaginary commonwealths, where he is himself despotic law-giver, there would have been no tolerable existence possible for any one not shaped upon the Platonic spiritual model. But in the Gorgias, Plato (speaking in the person of Sokrates) is called upon to define his plan of life in a free state, where he was merely a private citizen. Sokrates receives from Kallikles the advice, to forego philosophy and to aspire to the influence and celebrity of an active public speaker. His reply is instructive, as revealing the interior workings of every political society. No man (he says) can find favour as an adviser—either of a despot, where there is one, or of a people where there is free government—unless he be in harmony with the sentiments and ideas prevalent, either with the ruling Many or the ruling One. He must be moulded, from youth upwards, on the same spiritual pattern as they are :[1] his love and hate, his praise and blame, must turn towards the same things : he must have the same tastes, the same morality, the same *idéal*, as theirs : he must be no imitator, but a chip of the same block. If he be either better than they or worse than they,[2] he will fail in acquiring popularity, and his efforts as a competitor for public

---

[1] Plato, Gorgias, p. 510 C-D. ὁμοήθης ὤν, ταὐτὰ ψέγων καὶ ἐπαινῶν τῷ ἄρχοντι. . . . εὐθὺς ἐκ νέου ἐθίζειν αὐτὸν τοῖς αὐτοῖς χαίρειν καὶ ἄχθεσθαι τῷ δεσπότῃ, καὶ παρασκευάζειν ὅπως ὅ τι μάλιστα ὅμοιος ἔσται ἐκείνῳ. 513 B : οὐ μιμητὴν δεῖ εἶναι ἀλλ' αὐτοφυῶς ὅμοιον τούτοις.

[2] Plato, Gorgias, p. 513 A. εἴτ' ἐπὶ τὸ βέλτιον εἴτ' ἐπὶ τὸ χεῖρον.

influence will be not only abortive, but perhaps dangerous to himself.

The reasons which Sokrates gives here (as well as in the Apology, and partly also in the Republic) for not embarking in the competition of political aspirants, are of very general application. He is an innovator in religion; and a dissenter from the received ethics, politics, social sentiment, and estimate of life and conduct.[1] Whoever dissents upon these matters from the governing force (in whatever hands that may happen to reside) has no chance of being listened to as a political counsellor, and may think himself fortunate if he escapes without personal hurt or loss. Whether his dissent be for the better or for the worse, is a matter of little moment: the ruling body always think it worse, and the consequences to the dissenter are the same.

Sokrates feels his own isolation from his countrymen. He is thrown upon individual speculation and dialectic.

Herein consists the real antithesis between Sokrates, Plato, and philosophy, on the one side—Perikles, Nikias, Kleon, Demosthenes, and rhetoric, on the other. "You," (says Sokrates to Kalliklês),[2] "are in love with the Athenian people, and take up or renounce such opinions as they approve or discountenance : I am in love with philosophy, and follow her guidance. You and other active politicians do not wish to have more than a smattering of philosophy; you are afraid of becoming unconsciously corrupted, if you carry it beyond such elementary stage."[3] Each of these

Antithesis between philosophy and rhetoric.

---

[1] Plato, Gorgias, p. 522 B; Theætêtus, p. 179; Menon, p. 79.

[2] Plato, Gorgias, p. 481 E.

[3] Plato, Gorgias, p. 487 C. ἐνίκα ἐς ὑμῖν τοιάδε τις δόξα, μὴ προθυμεῖσθαι εἰς τὴν ἀκριβείαν φιλοσοφεῖν, ἀλλὰ εὐλαβεῖσθαι. . . . ὅπως μὴ πέρα τοῦ δέοντος σοφώτεροι γενόμενοι λήσετε διαφθαρέντες.

The view here advocated by Kalliklês:—That philosophy is good and useful, to be studied up to a certain point in the earlier years of life, in order to qualify persons for effective discharge of the duties of active citizenship, but that it ought not to be made the main occupation of mature life, nor be prosecuted up to the pitch of accurate theorising: this view, since Plato here assigns it to Kalliklês, is denounced by most of the Platonic critics as if it were low and worthless. Yet it was held by many of the most respectable citizens of antiquity; and the question is, in point of fact, that which has always been in debate between the life of theoretical speculation and the life of action.

Isokrates urges the same view both in Orat. xv. De Permutatione, sect. 282-287, pp. 485-486, Bekker; and Orat. xii. Panathenaic. sect. 29-32, p. 321, Bekker. διατρίψαι μὲν οὖν περὶ τὰς παιδείας ταύτας χρόνον τινὰ συμβουλεύσαιμ' ἂν τοῖς νεωτέροις, μὴ μέντοι περιιδεῖν τὴν φύσιν τὴν αὐτῶν κατασκελετευθεῖσαν ἐπὶ τούτοις, &c. Cicero quotes a similar opinion put by Ennius the poet into the mouth of Neoptolemus, Tusc. D. ii. 1, 1; Aulus

orators, discussing political measures before the public assembly, appealed to general maxims borrowed from the received creed of morality, religion, taste, politics, &c. His success depended mainly on the emphasis which his eloquence could lend to such maxims, and on the skill with which he could apply them to the case in hand. But Sokrates could not follow such an example. Anxious in his research after truth, he applied the test of analysis to the prevalent opinions—found them, in his judgment, neither consistent nor rational—constrained many persons to feel this, by an humiliating cross-examination—but became disqualified from addressing, with any chance of assent, the assembled public.

That in order to succeed politically, a man must be a genuine believer in the creed of King Nomos or the ruling force—cast in the same spiritual mould—(I here take the word *creed* not as confined to religion, but as embracing the whole of a man's critical *idéal*, on moral or social practice, politics, or taste—the ends which he deems worthy of being aspired to, or proper to be shunned, by himself or others) is laid down by Sokrates as a general position: and with perfect truth. In disposing of the force or influence of government, whoever possesses that force will use it conformably to his own maxims. A man who dissents from these maxims will find no favour in the public assembly; nor, probably, if his dissent be grave and wide, will he ever be able to speak out his convictions aloud in it, without incurring dangerous antipathy. But what is to become of such a dissenter[1]—the man who frequents the same porticos with the people, but does not hold the same creed,

Position of one who dissents, upon material points, from the fixed opinions and creed of his countrymen.

Gell. v. 16—"degustandum ex philosophiâ censet, non in eam ingurgitandum".

Tacitus, in describing the education of Agricola, who was taken by his mother in his earlier years to study at Massilia, says, c. 4 :—"Memoriâ teneo, solitum ipsum narrare, se in primâ juventâ studium philosophiæ, *ultra quam concessum Romano et senatori*, hausisse; ni prudentia matris incensum ac flagrantem animum coercuisset".

I have already cited this last passage, and commented upon the same point, in my notes at the end of the chapter on the Euthydêmus, p. 230.

[1] Horat. Epist. i. 1, 70—
"Quod si me populus Romanus forté roget, cur
Non ut porticibus, sic judiciis fruar iisdem,
Nec sequar aut fugiam quæ diligit ipse vel odit:
Olim quod vulpes ægroto cauta leoni
Respondit, referam: Quia me vestigia terrent
Omnia te adversum spectantia, nulla retrorsum."

nor share their judgments respecting social *expetenda* and *fugienda*? How is he to be treated by the government, or by the orthodox majority of society in their individual capacity? Debarred, by the necessity of the case, from influence over the public councils —what latitude of pursuit, profession, or conduct, is to be left to him as a citizen? How far is he to question, or expose, or require to be proved, that which the majority believe without proof? Shall he be required to profess, or to obey, or to refrain from contradicting, religious or ethical doctrines which he has examined and rejected? Shall such requirement be enforced by threat of legal penalties, or of ill-treatment from individuals, which is not less intolerable than legal penalties? What is likely to be his character, if compelled to suppress all declaration of his own creed, and to act and speak as if he were believer in another?

The questions here suggested must have impressed themselves forcibly on the mind of Plato when he recollected the fate of Sokrates. In spite of a blameless life, Sokrates had been judicially condemned and executed for publicly questioning received opinions, innovating upon the established religion, and instilling into young persons habits of doubt. To dissent only for the better, afforded no assurance of safety: and Plato knew well that his own dissent from the Athenian public was even wider and more systematic than that of his master. The position and plan of life for an active-minded reasoner, dissenting from the established opinions of the public, could not but be an object of interesting reflection to him.[1] The Gorgias (written, in my judgment, long after the death of Sokrates, probably after the Platonic. school was established) announces the vocation of the philosopher, and claims an open field for speculation, apart from the actualities of politics — for the self-acting reason of the individual doubter and investigator, against the authority of

Probable feelings of Plato on this subject. Claim put forward in the Gorgias of an independent locus standi for philosophy, but without the indiscriminate cross-examination pursued by Sokrates.

---

[1] I have already referred to the treatise of Mr. John Stuart Mill "On Liberty," where this important topic is discussed in a manner equally profound and enlightened. The co-existence of individual reasoners enquiring and philosophising for themselves, with the fixed opinions of the majority, is one of the main conditions which distinguish a progressive from a stationary community.

numbers and the pressure of inherited tradition. A formal assertion to this effect was worthy of the founder of the Academy —the earliest philosophical school at Athens. Yet we may observe that while the Platonic Sokrates in the Gorgias adopts the life of philosophy, he does not renew that farther demand with which the historical Sokrates had coupled it in his Apology —the liberty of oral and aggressive cross-examination, addressed to individuals personally and indiscriminately [1]—to the *primores populi* as well as to the *populum tributim*. The fate of Sokrates rendered Plato more cautious, and induced him to utter his ethical interrogations and novelties of opinion in no other way except that of lectures to chosen hearers and written dialogue: borrowing the name of Sokrates or some other speaker, and refraining upon system (as his letters[2] tell us that he did) from publishing any doctrines in his own name.

As a man dissenting from received opinions, Sokrates had his path marked out in the field of philosophy or individual speculation. To such a mind as his, the fullest liberty ought to be left, of professing and defending his own opinions, as well as of combating other opinions, accredited or not, which he may consider false or uncertified.[3] The public guidance of the state thus falls to one class of minds, the activity of speculative discussion to another: though accident

Importance of maintaining the utmost liberty of discussion. Tendency of all ruling orthodoxy towards intolerance.

---

[1] Plat. Apol. Sokr. pp. 21-22-23-28 E. τοῦ δὲ θεοῦ τάττοντος, ὡς ἐγὼ ᾠήθην τε καὶ ὑπέλαβον, φιλοσοφοῦντά με δεῖν ζῆν καὶ ἐξετάζοντα ἐμαυτόν τε καὶ τοὺς ἄλλους, &c.

[2] Plat. Epist. ii. 314 B. K. F. Hermann(Ueber Platon's Schriftstellerische Motive, p. 290) treats any such prudential discretion, in respect to the form and mode of putting forward unpopular opinions, as unworthy of Plato, and worthy only of Protagoras and other Sophists. I dissent from this opinion altogether. We know that Protagoras was very circumspect as to form (Timon ap. Sext. Emp. adv. Mathemat. ix. s. 57); but the passage of Plato cited by Hermann does not prove it.

[3] So Sokrates also says in the Platonic Apology, pp. 31-32. Οὐ γὰρ ἔστιν ὅστις ἀνθρώπων σωθήσεται οὔτε ὑμῖν οὔτε ἄλλῳ πλήθει οὐδενὶ γνησίως ἐναντιούμενος, καὶ διακωλύων πολλὰ ἄδικα καὶ παράνομα ἐν τῇ πόλει γίγνεσθαι· ἀλλ' ἀναγκαιόν ἐστι τὸν τῷ ὄντι μαχούμενον ὑπὲρ τοῦ δικαίου, καὶ εἰ μέλλει ὀλίγον χρόνον σωθήσεσθαι, ἰδιωτεύειν ἀλλὰ μὴ δημοσιεύειν.

The reader will find the speculative individuality of Sokrates illustrated in the sixty-eighth chapter of my History of Greece.

The antithesis of the philosophising or speculative life, against the rhetorical, political, forensic life—which is put so much to the advantage of the former by Plato in the Gorgias, Theætêtus (p. 173, seq.), and elsewhere—was the theme of Cicero's lost dialogue called Hortensius: wherein Hortensius was introduced pleading the cause against philosophy, (see Orelli, Fragm. Ciceron. pp. 479-480), while the other speakers were provided by Cicero with arguments mainly in defence of philosophy, partly also against

may produce, here and there, a superior individual, comprehensive or dexterous enough to suffice for both. But the main desideratum is that this freedom of discussion should exist: that room shall be made, and encouragement held out, to the claims of individual reason, and to the full publication of all doubts or opinions, be they what they may: that the natural tendency of all ruling force, whether in few or in many hands, to perpetuate their own dogmas by proscribing or silencing all heretics and questioners, may be neutralised as far as possible. The great expansive vigour of the Greek mind—the sympathy felt among the best varieties of Greeks for intellectual superiority in all its forms—and the privilege of free speech ($\pi\alpha\rho\rho\eta\sigma\iota\alpha$), on which the democratical citizens of Athens prided themselves—did in fact neutralise very considerably these tendencies in Athens. A greater and more durable liberty of philosophising was procured for Athens, and through Athens for Greece generally, than had ever been known before in the history of mankind.

This antithesis of the philosophical life to the rhetorical or political, constitutes one of the most interesting features of the Platonic Gorgias. But when we follow the pleadings upon which Plato rests this grand issue, and the line which he draws between the two functions, we find much that is unsatisfactory. Since Plato himself pleads both sides of the case, he is bound in fairness to set forth the case which he attacks (that of rhetoric), as it would be put by com-

Issue between philosophy and rhetoric not satisfactorily handled by Plato. Injustice done to rhetoric. Ignoble manner in

---

rhetoric. The competition between the teachers of rhetoric and the teachers of philosophy continued to be not merely animated but bitter, from Plato downward throughout the Ciceronian age. (Cicero, De Orat. i. 45-46-47-75, &c.)

We read in the treatise of Plutarch against the Epikurean Kolôtes, an acrimonious invective against Epikurus and his followers, for recommending a scheme of life such as to withdraw men from active political functions (Plutarch, adv. Kolôt. pp. 1125 C, 1127-1128); the like also in his other treatise, Non Posse Suaviter Vivi secundum Epicurum. But Plutarch at the same time speaks as if Epikurus were the only philosopher who had recommended this, and as if all the other philosophers had recommended an active life; nay, he talks of Plato among the philosophers actively engaged in practical reformatory legislation, through Dion and the pupils of the Academy (p. 1126, B, C). Here Plutarch mistakes: the Platonic tendencies were quite different from what he supposes. The Gorgias and Theætêtus enforce upon the philosopher a life quite apart from politics, pursuing his own course, and not meddling with others—$\phi\iota\lambda o\sigma \acute{o}\phi o \upsilon$ $\tau \grave{a}$ $a\vec{\upsilon}\tau o\vec{\upsilon}$ $\pi\rho \acute{a}\xi a\nu\tau o\varsigma$ $\kappa a\grave{\iota}$ $o\vec{\upsilon}$ $\pi o\lambda \upsilon\pi\rho a\gamma\mu o\nu\acute{\eta}$-$\sigma a\nu\tau o\varsigma$ $\grave{\epsilon}\nu$ $\tau\hat{\omega}$ $\beta\acute{\iota}\omega$ (Gorg. 526 C); which is the same advice as Epikurus gave. It is set forth eloquently in the poetry of Lucretius, but it had been set forth previously, not less eloquently, in the rhetoric of Plato.

petent and honourable advocates—by Perikles, for example, or Demosthenes, or Isokrates, or Quintilian. He does this, to a certain extent, in the first part of the dialogue, carried on by Sokrates with Gorgias. But in the succeeding portions—carried on with Pôlus and Kalliklês, and occupying three-fourths of the whole—he alters the character of the defence, and merges it in ethical theories which Perikles, had he been the defender, would not only have put aside as misplaced, but disavowed as untrue. Perikles would have listened with mixed surprise and anger, if he had heard any one utter the monstrous assertion which Plato puts into the mouth of Polus—That rhetors, like despots, kill, impoverish, or expel any citizen at their pleasure. Though Perikles was the most powerful of all Athenian rhetors, yet he had to contend all his life against fierce opposition from others, and was even fined during his last years. He would hardly have understood how an Athenian citizen could have made any assertion so completely falsified by all the history of Athens, respecting the omnipotence of the rhetors. Again, if he had heard Kalliklês proclaiming that the strong giant had a natural right to satiate all his desires at the cost of the weaker Many—and that these latter sinned against Nature when they took precautions to prevent him— Perikles would have protested against the proclamation as emphatically as Plato.[1]

If we suppose Perikles to have undertaken the defence of the rhetorical element at Athens, against the dialectic element represented by Sokrates, he would have accepted it, though not a position of his own choosing, on the footing on which Plato places it in the mouth of Gorgias : "Rhetoric is an engine of persuasion addressed to numerous assembled auditors : it ensures freedom to the city (through the free exercise of such a gift by many competing orators) and political ascendency or command to the ablest rhetor. It thus confers great power on him who possesses it in the highest measure : but he ought by no means to employ that power for unjust purposes." It is very probable that Perikles might have recommended rhetorical study to So-

[1] Perikles might indeed have referred to his own panegyrical oration in Thucydides, ii. 37.

krates, as a means of defending himself against unjust accusations, and of acquiring a certain measure of influence on public affairs.[1] But he would have distinguished carefully (as Horace does) between defending yourself against unjust attacks, and making unjust attacks upon others: though the same weapon may suit for both.

Farther, neither Perikles, nor any defender of free speech, would assent to the definition of rhetoric—That it is a branch of the art of flattery, studying the immediately pleasurable, and disregarding the good.[2] This distinction indeed represents Plato's own sentiment, and was true in the sense which the Platonic Sokrates assigns (in the Gorgias, though not in the Protagoras) to the words *good* and *evil*. But it is not true in the sense which the Athenian people and the Athenian public conceived.

<small>The Athenian people recognised a distinction between the pleasurable and the good: but not the same as that which Plato conceived.</small>

---

[1] Horat. Satir. ii. 1, 39—

"Hic stilus haud petet ultro
Quemquam animantem; et me veluti custodiet ensis
Vaginâ tectus; quem cur destringere coner,
Tutus ab infestis latronibus? Oh pater et rex
Jupiter! ut pereat positum rubigine telum,
Nec quisquam noceat cupido mihi pacis! At ille
Qui me commôrit (melius non tangere! clamo)
Flebit, et insignis totâ cantabitur urbe."

We need only read the Memorabilia of Xenophon (ii. 9), to see that the historical Sokrates judged of these matters differently from the Platonic Sokrates of the Gorgias. Kriton complained to Sokrates that life was difficult at Athens for a quiet man who wished only to mind his own business (τὰ ἑαυτοῦ πράττειν); because there were persons who brought unjust actions at law against him, for the purpose of extorting money to buy them off. The Platonic Sokrates of the Gorgias would have replied to him: "Never mind: you are just, and these assailants are unjust: they are by their own conduct entailing upon themselves a terrible distemper, from which, if you leave them unpunished, they will suffer all their lives: they injure themselves more than they injure you". But the historical Sokrates in Xenophon replies in quite another spirit. He advises Kriton to look out for a clever and active friend, to attach this person to his interest by attention and favours, and to trust to him for keeping off the assailants. Accordingly, a poor but energetic man named Archedemus is found, who takes Kriton's part against the assailants, and even brings counter-attacks against them, which force them to leave Kriton alone, and to give money to Archedemus himself. The advice given by the Xenophontic Sokrates to Kriton is the same in principle as the advice given by Kallikles to the Platonic Sokrates.

[2] The reply composed by the rhetor Aristeides to the Gorgias of Plato is well deserving of perusal, though (like all his compositions) it is very prolix and wordy. See Aristeides, Orationes xlv. and xlvi.—Περὶ 'Ρητορικῆς, and Ὑπὲρ τῶν Τεττάρων. In the last of the two orations he defends the four eminent Athenians (Miltiades, Themistoklês, Periklês, Kimon) whom Plato disparages in the Gorgias.

Aristeides insists forcibly on the partial and narrow view here taken by Plato of persuasion, as a working force both for establishing laws and carrying on government. He remarks truly that there are only two forces between which the choice must be made, intimidation and persuasion: that the substitution of persuasion in place of force is the great improvement which

men assigned to those words. Both the one and the other used the words *pleasurable* and *good* as familiarly as Plato, and had sentiments corresponding to both of them. The pleasurable and painful referred to present and temporary causes : the Good and Evil to prospective causes and permanent situations, involving security against indefinite future suffering, combined with love of national dignity and repugnance to degradation, as well as with a strong sense of common interests and common obligations to each other. To provide satisfaction for these common patriotic feelings—to sustain the dignity of the city by effective and even imposing public establishments, against foreign enemies—to protect the individual rights of citizens by an equitable administration of justice—counted in the view of the Athenians as objects *good* and *honourable* : while the efforts and sacrifices necessary for these permanent ends, were, so far as they went, a renuncia-

has made public and private life worth having (μόνη βιωτὸν ἡμῖν πεποίηκε τὸν βίον, Orat. xlv. p. 64, Dindorf); that neither laws could be discussed and passed, nor judicial trial held under them, without ῥητορική as the engine of persuasion (pp. 66-67-136) ; that Plato in attacking Rhetoric had no right to single out despots and violent conspirators as illustrations of it—εἶτ' ἐλέγχειν μὲν βούλεται τὴν ῥητορικήν, κατηγορεῖ δὲ τῶν τυράννων καὶ δυναστῶν, τὰ ἄμικτα μιγνύς—τίς γὰρ οὐκ οἶδεν, ὅτι ῥητορικὴ καὶ τυραννὶς τοσοῦτον ἀλλήλων κεχωρίσται, ὅσον τὸ πείθειν τοῦ βιάζεσθαι (p. 99). He impugns the distinction which Plato has drawn between ἰατρική, γυμναστική, κυβερνητική, νομοθετική, &c., on the one side, which Plato calls τέχναι, arts or sciences, and affirms to rest on scientific principles—and ῥητορική, μαγειρική, &c., on the other side, which Plato affirms to be only guess-work or groping, resting on empirical analogies. Aristeides says that ἰατρικὴ and ῥητορικὴ are in this respect both on a par ; that both are partly reducible to rule, but partly also driven by necessity to conjectures and analogies, and the physician not less than the rhetor (pp. 45-48-49) ; which the Platonic Sokrates himself affirms in another dialogue, Philêbus, p. 56 A.

The most curious part of the argument of Aristeides is where he disputes the prerogative which Plato had claimed for ἰατρική, γυμναστική, &c., on the ground of their being arts or reducible to rules. The effects of human art (says Aristeides) are much inferior to those of θεία μοῖρα or divine inspiration. Many patients are cured of disease by human art ; but many more are cured by the responses and directions of the Delphian oracle, by the suggestion of dreams, and by other varieties of the divine prompting, delivered through the Pythian priestess, a woman altogether ignorant (p. 11). καίτοι μικρὰ μὲν ἡ πάντας εἰδυῖα λόγους ἰατρικὴ πρὸς τὰς ἐκ Δελφῶν δύναται λύσεις, ὅσαι καὶ ἰδίᾳ καὶ κοινῇ καὶ νόσων καὶ παθημάτων ἁπάντων ἀνθρωπίνων ἐφάνθησαν. Patients who are cured in this way by the Gods without medical art, acquire a natural impulse which leads them to the appropriate remedy —ἐπιθυμία αὐτοὺς ἄγει ἐπὶ τὸ ὄνησον (p. 20). Aristeides says that he can himself depose—from his own personal experience as a sick man seeking cure, and from personal knowledge of many other such—how much more efficacious in healing is aid from the Gods, given in dreams and other ways, than advice from physicians ; who might well shudder when they heard the stories which he could tell (pp. 21-22). To undervalue science and art (he says) is the principle from which men start, when they flee to the Gods for help— τοῦ καταφυγεῖν ἐπὶ τοὺς θεοὺς σχεδὸν ἀρχή, τὸ τῆς τέχνης ὑπεριδεῖν ἐστιν.

tion of what they would call the *pleasurable*. When, at the beginning of the Peloponnesian war, the Athenians, acting on the advice of Perikles, allowed all Attica to be ravaged, and submitted to the distress of cooping the whole population within the long walls, rather than purchase peace by abnegating their Hellenic dignity, independence, and security—they not only renounced much that was pleasurable, but endured great immediate distress, for the sake of what they regarded as a permanent good.[1] Eighty years afterwards, when Demosthenes pointed out to them the growing power and encroachments of the Macedonian Philip, and exhorted them to the efforts requisite for keeping back that formidable enemy, while there was yet time—they could not be wound up to the pitch requisite for affronting so serious an amount of danger and suffering. They had lost that sense of Hellenic dignity, and that association of self-respect with active personal soldiership and sailorship, which rendered submission to an enemy the most intolerable of all pains, at the time when Perikles had addressed them. They shut their eyes to an impending danger, which ultimately proved their ruin. On both these occasions, we have the *pleasurable* and the *good* brought into contrast in the Athenian mind ; in both we have the two most eminent orators of Grecian antiquity enforcing the *good* in opposition to the *pleasurable* : the first successfully, the last vainly, in opposition to other orators.

Lastly, it is not merely the political power of the Athenians that Perikles employs his eloquence to uphold. He dwells also with emphasis on the elegance of taste, on the intellectual force and activity, which warranted him in decorating the city with the title of Preceptress of Hellas.[2] All this belongs, not to the pleasurable as distinguished from the good, but to

Rhetoric was employed at Athens in appealing to all the various established sentiments

---

[1] Nothing can be more at variance with the doctrine which Plato assigns to Kalliklês in the Gorgias, than the three memorable speeches of Perikles in Thucydides, i. 144, ii. 35, ii. 60, seq. All these speeches are penetrated with the deepest sense of that κοινωνία and φιλία which the Platonic Sokrates extols : not one of them countenances πλεονεξίαν, which the Platonic Sokrates forbids (Gorg. 508 E). Τὸ προστα- λαιπωρεῖν τῷ δόξαντι καλῷ (to use the expressive phrase of Thucydides, ii. 53) was a remarkable feature in the character of the Athenians of that day : it was subdued for the moment by the overwhelming misery of pestilence and war combined.

[2] Thucyd. ii. 41-42. ξυνελών τε λέγω τήν τε πᾶσαν πόλιν τῆς Ἑλλάδος παίδευσιν εἶναι, &c.

and opinions. Erroneous inferences raised by the Kallikles of Plato.

good (whether immediately pleasurable or not) in its most comprehensive sense, embracing the improvement and refinement of the collective mind. If Perikles, in this remarkable funeral harangue, flattered the sentiments of the people—as he doubtless did— he flattered them by kindling their aspirations towards good. And Plato himself does the same (though less nobly and powerfully), adopting the received framework of Athenian sentiment, in his dialogue called Menexenus, which we shall come to in a future chapter.

The Platonic Idéal exacts, as good, some order, system, discipline. But order may be directed to bad ends as well as to good. Divergent ideas about virtue.

The issue, therefore, which Plato here takes against Rhetoric, must stand or fall with the Platonic Idéal of Good and Evil. But when he thus denounces both the general public and the most patriotic rhetors, to ensure exclusive worship for his own Idéal of Good— we may at least require that he shall explain, wherein consists that Good—by what mark it is distinguishable—and on what authority pre-eminence is claimed for it. So far, indeed, we advance by the help of Plato's similes[1]—order, discipline, health and strength of body—that we are called upon to recognise, apart from all particular moments of enjoyment or suffering, of action or quiescence, a certain permanent mental condition and habit— a certain order, regulation, discipline—as an object of high importance to be attained. This (as I have before remarked) is a valuable idea which pervades, in one form or another, all the Hellenic social views, from Sokrates downward, and even before Sokrates; an idea, moreover, which was common to Peripatetics, Stoics, Epikureans. But mental order and discipline is not in itself an end: it may be differently cast, and may subserve many different purposes. The Pythagorean brotherhood was intensely restrictive in its canons. The Spartan system exhibited the strictest order and discipline—an assemblage of principles and habits predetermined by authority and enforced upon all—yet neither Plato nor Aristotle approve of its results. Order and discipline attained full perfection in the armies of Julius Cæsar and the French Emperor Napoleon; in the middle ages, also,

[1] Plat. Gorg. p. 504.

several of the monastic orders stood high in respect to finished discipline pervading the whole character : and the Jesuits stood higher than any. Each of these systems has included terms equivalent to justice, temperance, virtue, vice, &c., with sentiments associated therewith, yet very different from what Plato would have approved. The question—What is Virtue?—*Vir bonus est quis?*—will be answered differently in each. The Spartans — when they entrapped (by a delusive pretence of liberation and military decoration) two thousand of their bravest Helot warriors, and took them off by private assassinations,[1]—did not offend against their own idea of virtue, or against the Platonic exigency of Order—Measure—System.

It is therefore altogether unsatisfactory, when Plato—professing to teach us how to determine scientifically, which pleasures are bad, and which pains are good— refers to a durable mental order and discipline. Of such order there existed historically many varieties ; and many more are conceivable, as Plato himself has shown in the Republic and Leges. By what tests is the right order to be distinguished from the wrong ? If by its results, by *what* results ?—calculations for minimising pains, and maximising pleasures, being excluded by the supposition ? Here the Sokrates of the Gorgias is at fault. He has not told us by what scientific test the intelligent Expert proceeds in determining what pleasures are bad, and what pains are good. He leaves such determination to the unscientific sentiment of each society and each individual. He has not, in fact, responded to the clear and pertinent challenge thrown out by the Sokrates of the Protagoras.

How to discriminate the right order from the wrong. Plato does not advise us.

I think, for these reasons, that the logic of the Gorgias is not at all on a par with its eloquence. But there is one peculiar feature which distinguishes it among all the Platonic dialogues. Nowhere in ancient literature is the title, position, and dignity of individual dissenting opinion, ethical and political—against established ethical and political orthodoxy—so clearly marked out and so boldly asserted. "The Athenians will judge as they

The Gorgias upholds the independence and dignity of the dissenting philosopher.

[1] Thucydid. iv. 80.

think right: none but those speakers who are in harmony with them, have any chance of addressing their public assemblies with effect, and acquiring political influence. I, Sokrates, dissent from them, and have no chance of political influence: but I claim the right of following out, proclaiming, and defending, the conclusions of my own individual reason, until debate satisfies me that I am wrong."

CHAPTER XXV.

PHÆDON.

THE Phædon is characterised by Proklus as a dialogue wherein Sokrates unfolds fully his own mental history, and communicates to his admirers the complete range of philosophical cognition.[1] This criticism is partly well founded. The dialogue generally is among the most affirmative and expository in the Platonic list. Sokrates undertakes to prove the immortality of the soul, delivers the various reasons which establish the doctrine to his satisfaction, and confutes some dissentient opinions entertained by others. In regard to the exposition, however, we must consider ourselves as listening to Plato under the name of Sokrates: and we find it so conducted as to specify both certain stages through which the mind of Plato had passed, and the logical process which (at that time) appeared to him to carry conviction.

The Phædon is affirmative and expository.

The interest felt by most readers in the Phædon, however, depends, not so much on the argumentative exposition (which Wyttenbach[2] justly pronounces to be

Situation and circumstances

---

[1] Proklus, in Platon. Republ. p. 392. ἐν Φαίδωνι μὲν γὰρ ὅπου διαφερόντως ὁ Σωκράτης τὴν ἑαυτοῦ ζωὴν ἀναπλοῖ, καὶ πᾶν τὸ τῆς ἐπιστήμης πλῆθος ἀνοίγει τοῖς ἑαυτοῦ ζηλωταῖς, &c. Wyttenbach thinks (note, ad p. 108 E) that Plato was young when he composed the Phædon. But no sufficient grounds are given for this: and the concluding sentence of the dialogue affords good presumption that it was composed many years after the death of Sokrates —ἥδε ἡ τελευτή, ὦ Ἐχέκρατες, τοῦ ἑταίρου ἡμῖν ἐγένετο, ἀνδρός, ὡς ἡμεῖς φαῖμεν ἄν, τῶν τότε ὧν ἐπειράθημεν ἀρίστου, καὶ ἄλλως φρονιμωτάτου καὶ δικαιοτάτου. The phrase τῶν τότε, which may probably have slipped unconsciously from Plato, implies that Sokrates belonged to the past generation. The beginning of the dialogue undoubtedly shows that Plato intended to place it shortly after the death of Sokrates; but the word τότε at the end is inconsistent with this supposition, and comes out unconsciously as a mark of the real time.

[2] See the Prolegomena prefixed to Wyttenbach's edition of the Phædon, p. xxi. p. 10.

<small>assumed in the Phædon. Pathetic interest which they inspire.</small> obscure and difficult as well as unsatisfactory) as on the personality of the expounding speaker, and the irresistible pathos of the situation. Sokrates had been condemned to death by the Dikastery on the day after the sacred ship, memorable in connection with the legendary voyage of Theseus to Krete, had been dispatched on her annual mission of religious sacrifice at the island of Delos. The Athenian magistrates considered themselves as precluded from putting any one to death by public authority, during the absence of the ship on this mission. Thirty days elapsed between her departure and her return: during all which interval, Sokrates remained in the prison, yet with full permission to his friends to visit him. They passed most of every day in the enjoyment of his conversation.[1] In the Phædon, we read the last of these conversations, after the sacred vessel had returned, and after the Eleven magistrates had announced to Sokrates that the draught of hemlock would be administered to him before sunset. On communicating this intelligence, the magistrates released Sokrates from the fetters with which he had hitherto been bound. It is shortly after such release that the friends enter the prison to see him for the last time. One of the number, Phædon, recounts to Echekratês not only the conduct and discourse of Sokrates during the closing hours of his life, but also the swallowing of the poison, and the manner of his death.

More than fifteen friends of the philosopher are noted as <small>Simmias and Kebês, the two collocutors with Sokrates. Their feelings and those of Sokrates.</small> present at this last scene: but the only two who take an active part in the debate, are, two young Thebans named Kebês and Simmias.[2] These friends, though deeply attached to Sokrates, and full of sorrow at the irreparable loss impending over them, are represented as overawed and fascinated by his perfect fearlessness, serenity, and dignity.[3] They are ashamed to give vent to their grief, when their master is seen to maintain his

---

[1] Plato, Phædon, pp. 58-59.
It appears that Kriton became bail before the Dikasts, in a certain sum of money, that Sokrates should remain in prison and not escape (Plat. Phædon, p. 115 D; Kriton, 45 B). Kriton would have been obliged to pay this money if Sokrates had accepted his proposition to escape, noticed already in chap. x.

[2] Plato, Phædon, pp. 59 B, 89 A. τῶν νεανίσκων τὸν λόγον, &c. (p. 89 A).

[3] Plato, Phædon, pp. 58-59.

ordinary frame of mind, neither disquieted nor dissatisfied. The fundamental conception of the dialogue is, to represent Sokrates as the same man that he was before his trial; unmoved by the situation—not feeling that any misfortune is about to happen to him—equally delighting in intellectual debate—equally fertile in dialectic invention. So much does he care for debate, and so little for the impending catastrophe, that he persists in a great argumentative effort, notwithstanding the intimation conveyed by Kriton from the gaoler, that if he heated himself with talking, the poison might perhaps be languid in its operation, so that two or three draughts of it would be necessary instead of one.[1] Sokrates even advances the position that death appears to him as a benefit rather than a misfortune, and that every true philosopher ought to prefer death to life, assuming it to supervene without his own act—suicide being forbidden by the Gods. He is represented as "placidus ore, intrepidus verbis; intempestivas suorum lacrimas coercens"—to borrow a phrase from Tacitus's striking picture of the last hours of the Emperor Otho.[2] To see him thus undisturbed, and even welcoming his approaching end, somewhat hurts the feelings of his assembled friends, who are in the deepest affliction at the certainty of so soon losing him. Sokrates undertakes to defend himself before them as he had done before the Dikasts; and to show good grounds for his belief, that death is not a misfortune, but a benefit, to the philosopher.[3] Simmias and Kebês, though at first not satisfied with the reasonings, are nevertheless reluctant to produce their doubts, from fear of mortifying him in his last moments: but Sokrates protests against such reluctance as founded on a misconception of his existing frame of mind.[4] He is now the same man as he was before, and he calls upon them to keep up the freedom of debate unimpaired.

Indeed this freedom of debate and fulness of search—the paramount value of "reasoned truth"—the necessity of keeping up the force of individual reason by constant argumentative exercise—and the right of independent

Emphasis of Sokrates in insisting on freedom of

[1] Plato, Phædon, p. 63 D.
[2] Tacitus, Hist. ii. 48.
[3] Plato, Phædon, p. 63.
[4] Plato, Phædon, p. 84 D-E.

debate, active exercise of reason, and independent judgment for each reasoner.

judgment for hearer as well as speaker—stand emphatically proclaimed in these last words of the dying philosopher. He does not announce the immortality of the soul as a dogma of imperative orthodoxy; which men, whether satisfied with the proofs or not, must believe, or must make profession of believing, on pain of being shunned as a moral pestilence, and disqualified from giving testimony in a court of justice. He sets forth his own conviction, with the grounds on which he adopts it. But he expressly recognises the existence of dissentient opinions: he invites his companions to bring forward every objection: he disclaims all special purpose of impressing his own conclusions upon their minds: nay, he expressly warns them not to be biassed by their personal sympathies, then wound up to the highest pitch, towards himself. He entreats them to preserve themselves from becoming tinged with *misology*, or the hatred of free argumentative discussion: and he ascribes this mental vice to the early habit of easy, uninquiring, implicit, belief: since a man thus ready of faith, embracing opinions without any discriminative test, presently finds himself driven to abandon one opinion after another, until at last he mistrusts all opinions, and hates the process of discussing them, laying the blame upon philosophy instead of upon his own intellect.[1]

Anxiety of Sokrates that his friends shall be on their guard against being influenced by his authority—that they shall follow only the convic-

"For myself" (says Sokrates) "I fear that in these my last hours I depart from the true spirit of philosophy— like unschooled men, who, when in debate, think scarcely at all how the real question stands, but care only to make their own views triumphant in the minds of the auditors. Between them and me there is only thus much of difference. I regard it as a matter of secondary consequence, whether my conclusions appear true to my hearers; but I shall do my best to make them appear as much as possible

---

[1] Plato, Phædon, pp. 89 C-D, 90. Πρῶτον εὐλαβηθῶμέν τι πάθος μὴ πάθωμεν. Τὸ ποῖον, ἦν δ' ἐγώ; Μὴ γενώμεθα, ἦ δ' ὅς, μισόλογοι, ὥσπερ οἱ μισάνθρωποι γιγνόμενοι· ὡς οὐκ ἔστιν, ἔφη, ὅ, τι ἄν τις μεῖζον τούτου κακὸν πάθοι ἢ λόγους μισήσα;. p. 90 B. ἐπειδάν τις πιστεύσῃ λόγῳ τινὶ ἀληθεῖ εἶναι, ἄνευ τῆς περὶ τοὺς λόγους τέχνης, κἄπειτα ὀλίγον ὕστερον αὐτῷ δόξῃ ψευδὴς εἶναι, ἐνίοτε μὲν ὤν, ἐνίοτε δ' οὐκ ὤν, καὶ αὖθις ἕτερος καὶ ἕτερος, &c.

true to myself.[1] My calculation is as follows : mark how selfish it is. If my conclusion as to the immortality of the soul is true, I am better off by believing it : if I am in error, and death be the end of me, even then I shall avoid importuning my friends with grief, during these few remaining hours : moreover my error will not continue with me—which would have been a real misfortune—but will be extinguished very shortly. Such is the frame of mind, Simmias and Kebês, with which I approach the debate. Do you follow my advice : take little thought of Sokrates, but take much more thought of the truth. If I appear to you to affirm any thing truly, assent to me : but if not, oppose me with all your powers of reasoning: Be on your guard lest, through earnest zeal, I should deceive alike myself and you, and should leave the sting in you, like a bee, at this hour of departure." *tions of their own reason.*

This is a remarkable passage, as illustrating the spirit and purpose of Platonic dialogues. In my preceding Chapters, I have already shown, that it is no part of the aim of Sokrates to thrust dogmas of his own into other men's minds as articles of faith. But then, most of these Chapters have dwelt upon Dialogues of Search, in which Sokrates has appeared as an interrogator, or enquirer jointly with others : scrutinising their opinions, but disclaiming knowledge or opinions of his own. Here, however, in the Phædon, the case is altogether different. Sokrates is depicted as having not only an affirmative opinion, but even strong conviction, on a subject of great moment : which conviction, moreover, he is especially desirous of preserving unimpaired, during his few remaining hours of life. Yet even here, he manifests no anxiety to get that conviction into the *Remarkable manifestation of earnest interest for reasoned truth and the liberty of individual dissent.*

---

[1] Plato, Phædon, p. 91 A-C. Οὐ γὰρ ὅπως τοῖς παροῦσιν ἃ ἐγὼ λέγω δόξει ἀληθῆ εἶναι, προθυμήσομαι, εἰ μὴ εἴη πάρεργον, ἀλλ' ὅπως αὐτῷ ἐμοὶ ὅ τι μάλιστα δόξει οὕτως ἔχειν. λογίζομαι γάρ, ὦ φίλε ἑταῖρε—καὶ θέασαι ὡς πλεονεκτικῶς—εἰ μὲν τυγχάνει ἀληθῆ ὄντα ἃ λέγω, καλῶς δὴ ἔχει τὸ πεισθῆναι· εἰ δὲ μηδέν ἐστι τελευτήσαντι, ἀλλ' οὖν τοῦτόν γε τὸν χρόνον αὐτὸν τὸν πρὸ τοῦ θανάτου ἧττον τοῖς παροῦσιν ἀηδὴς ἔσομαι ὀδυρόμενος . . . ὑμεῖς μέντοι, ἂν ἐμοὶ πείθησθε, σμικρὸν φροντίσαντες Σωκράτους, τῆς δὲ ἀληθείας πολὺ μᾶλλον, ἐὰν μέν τι ὑμῖν δοκῶ ἀληθὲς λέγειν, ξυνομολογήσατε· εἰ δὲ μή, παντὶ λόγῳ ἀντιτείνετε, εὐλαβούμενοι ὅπως μὴ ἐγὼ ὑπὸ προθυμίας ἅμα ἐμαυτόν τε καὶ ὑμᾶς ἐξαπατήσας, ὥσπερ μέλιττα τὸ κέντρον ἐγκαταλιπὼν οἰχήσομαι.

minds of his friends, except as a result of their own independent scrutiny and self-working reason. Not only he does not attempt to terrify them into believing, by menace of evil consequences if they do not—but he repudiates pointedly even the gentler machinery of conversion, which might work upon their minds through attachment to himself and reverence for his authority. His devotion is to "reasoned truth": he challenges his friends to the fullest scrutiny by their own independent reason: he recognises the sentence which they pronounce afterwards as valid *for them*, whether concurrent with himself or adverse. Their reason is for them, what his reason is for him: requiring, both alike (as Sokrates here proclaims), to be stimulated as well as controlled by all-searching debate—but postulating equal liberty of final decision for each one of the debaters. The stress laid by Plato upon the full liberty of dissenting reason, essential to philosophical debate—is one of the most memorable characteristics of the Phædon. When we come to the treatise De Legibus (where Sokrates does not appear), we shall find a totally opposite view of sentiment. In the tenth book of that treatise Plato enforces the rigid censorship of an orthodox persecutor, who makes his own reason binding and compulsory on all.

Phædon and Symposion —points of analogy and contrast. The natural counterpart and antithesis to the Phædon, is found in the Symposion.[1] In both, the personality of Sokrates stands out with peculiar force: in the one, he is in the fulness of life and enjoyment, along with festive comrades—in the other, he is on the verge of approaching death, surrounded by companions in deep affliction. The point common to both, is, the perfect self-command of Sokrates under a diversity of trying circumstances. In the Symposion, we read of him as triumphing over heat, cold, fatigue, danger, amorous temptation, unmeasured potations of wine, &c.:[2]

---

[1] Thus far I agree with Schleiermacher (Einleitung zum Phædon, p. 9, &c.); though I do not think that he has shown sufficient ground for his theory regarding the Symposion and the Phædon, as jointly intended to depict the character of the philosopher, promised by Plato as a sequel to the Sophist and the Statesman. (Plato, Sophist. p. 217; Politic. p. 257.)

[2] Plato, Symposion, pp. 214 A, 219 D, 220-221-223 D: compare Phædon, p. 116, c. 117. Marcus Antoninus (i. 16) compares on this point his father Antoninus Pius to Sokrates: both were capable of enjoyment as well as of abstinence, without ever losing their self-command. Ἐφαρμόσειε δ᾽ ἂν αὐτῷ (Antoninus P.) τὸ περὶ τοῦ Σωκράτους μνημονευόμενον, ὅτι καὶ ἀπέχεσθαι καὶ

in the Phædon, we discover him rising superior to the fear of death, and to the contagion of an afflicted company around him. Still, his resolute volition is occasionally overpowered by fits of absorbing meditation, which seize him at moments sudden and unaccountable, and chain him to the spot for a long time. There is moreover, in both dialogues, a streak of eccentricity in his character, which belongs to what Plato calls the philosophical inspiration and madness, rising above the measure of human temperance and prudence.[1] The Phædon depicts in Sokrates the same intense love of philosophy and dialectic debate, as the Symposion and Phædrus : but it makes no allusion to that personal attachment, and passionate admiration of youthful beauty, with which, according to those two dialogues, the mental fermentation of the philosophical aspirant is asserted to begin.[2] Sokrates in the Phædon describes the initial steps whereby he had been led to philosophical study :[3] but the process is one purely intellectual, without reference to personal converse with beloved companions, as a necessity of the case. His discourse is that of a man on the point of death—"abruptis vitæ blandimentis"[4]—and he already looks upon his body, not as furnishing the means of action and as requiring only to be trained by gymnastic discipline (as it appears in the Republic), but as an importunate and depraving companion, of which he is glad to get rid : so that the ethereal substance of the soul may be left to its free expansion and fellowship with the intelligible world, apart from sense and its solicitations.

We have here one peculiarity of the Phædon, whereby it stands distinguished both from the Republic and the Timæus. The antithesis on which it dwells is that of Phædon— compared

ἀπολαύειν ἐδύνατο τούτων, ὧν πολλοὶ πρός τε τὰς ἀποχὰς ἀσθενῶς, καὶ πρὸς τὰς ἀπολαύσεις ἐνδοτικῶς, ἔχουσιν. Τὸ δὲ ἰσχύειν, καὶ ἔτι καρτερεῖν καὶ ἐννήφειν ἑκατέρῳ, ἀνδρὸς ἐστὶν ἄρτιον καὶ ἀήττητον ψυχὴν ἔχοντος.
[1] Plato, Symposion, pp. 174-175-220 C-D. Compare Phædon, pp. 84 C, 95 E.
[2] Plato, Sympos. p. 215 A, p. 221 D. οἶος δὲ οὑτοσὶ γέγονε τὴν ἀτοπίαν ἄνθρωπος, καὶ αὐτὸς καὶ οἱ λόγοι αὐτοῦ, οὐδ᾽ ἐγγὺς ἂν εὕροι τις ζητῶν, &c. p. 218 B : πάντες γὰρ κεκοινωνήκατε τῆς φιλοσόφου μανίας τε καὶ βακχείας,
&c. About the φιλόσοφος μανία, compare Plato, Phædrus, pp. 245-250. Plato, Phædrus, pp. 251-253. Symposion, pp. 210-211. ὅταν τις ἀπὸ τῶνδε διὰ τὸ ὀρθῶς παιδεραστεῖν ἐπανιὼν ἐκεῖνο τὸ καλὸν ἄρχηται καθορᾶν, &c. (211 B).
[3] Plato, Phædon, p. 96 A. ἐγὼ οὖν σοὶ δίειμι περὶ αὐτῶν τά γ᾽ ἐμὰ πάθη, &c.
[4] Tacitus, Hist. ii. 53. " Othonis libertus, habere se suprema ejus mandata respondit : ipsum viventem quidem relictum, sed solâ posteritatis curâ, et abruptis vitæ blandimentis."

with Republic and Timæus. No recognition of the triple or lower souls. Antithesis between soul and body. the soul or mind, on one hand—the body on the other. The soul or mind is spoken of as one and indivisible: as if it were an inmate unworthily lodged or imprisoned in the body. It is not distributed into distinct parts, kinds, or varieties: no mention is made of that tripartite distribution which is so much insisted on in the Republic and Timæus:— the rational or intellectual (encephalic) soul, located in the head —the courageous or passionate (thoracic), between the neck and the diaphragm—the appetitive (abdominal), between the diaphragm and the navel. In the Phædon, the soul is noted as the seat of reason, intellect, the love of wisdom or knowledge, exclusively: all that belongs to passion and appetite, is put to account of the body :[1] this is distinctly contrary to the Philêbus, in which dialogue Sokrates affirms that desire or appetite cannot belong to the body, but belongs only to the soul. In Phædon, nothing is said about the location of the rational soul, in the head,—nor about the analogy between its rotations in the cranium and the celestial rotations (a doctrine which we read both in the Timæus and in the Republic): on the contrary, the soul is affirmed to have lost, through its conjunction with the body, that wisdom or knowledge which it possessed during its state of pre-existence, while completely apart from the body, and while in commerce with those invisible Ideas to which its own separate nature was cognate.[2] That controul which in the Republic is exercised by the rational soul over the passionate and appetitive souls, is in the Phædon exercised (though imperfectly) by the one and only soul over the body.[3] In the Republic and Timæus, the soul is a tripartite aggregate, a community of parts, a compound: in the Phædon, Sokrates asserts it to be uncompounded, making this fact a point in his argument.[4] Again, in the Phædon, the soul is pronounced to be essentially uniform and incapable of change: as such, it is placed in antithesis with the

---

[1] Plato, Phædon, p. 66. Compare Plato, Philêbus, p. 35, C-D.
[2] Plato, Phædon, p. 76.
[3] Compare Phædon, p. 94 C-E, with Republic, iv. pp. 439 C, 440 A, 441 E, 442 C.
[4] Plato, Phædon, p. 78. ἀξύνθετον, μονοειδὲς (p. 80 B), contrasted with the

τρία εἴδη τῆς ψυχῆς (Republic, p. 439). In the abstract given by Alkinous of the Platonic doctrine, we read in cap. 24 ὅτι τριμερής ἐστιν ἡ ψυχὴ κατὰ τὰς δυνάμεις, καὶ κατὰ λόγον τὰ μέρη αὐτῆς τόποις ἰδίοις διανενέμηται: in cap. 25 that the ψυχὴ is ἀσύνθετος, ἀδιάλυτος, ἀσκέδαστος.

CHAP. XXV. DIFFERENT VIEWS ABOUT THE SOUL. 385

body, which is perpetually changing: while we read, on the contrary, in the Symposion, that soul and body alike are in a constant and unremitting variation, neither one nor the other ever continuing in the same condition.[1]

The difference which I have here noted shows how Plato modified his doctrine to suit the purpose of each dialogue. The tripartite soul would have been found inconvenient in the Phædon. where the argument required that soul and body should be as sharply distinguished as possible. Assuming passion and appetite to be attributes belonging to the soul, as well as reason—Sokrates will not shake them off when he becomes divorced from the body. He believes and expects that the post-existence of the soul will be, as its pre-existence has been, a rational existence—a life of intellectual contemplation and commerce with the eternal Ideas: in this there is no place for passion and appetite, which grow out of its conjunction with the body. The soul here represents Reason and Intellect, in commerce with their correlates, the objective Entia Rationis: the body represents passion and appetite as well as sense, in implication with their correlates, the objects of sensible perception.[2] Such is the doctrine of the Phædon; but Plato is not always consistent with himself on the point. His ancient as well as his modern commentators are not agreed, whether, when he vindicated the immortality of the soul, he meant to speak of the rational soul only, or of the aggregate soul with its three parts as above described. There are passages which countenance both suppositions.[3] Plato seems to have leaned sometimes to the

Different doctrines of Plato about the soul. Whether all the three souls are immortal, or the rational soul alone.

---

[1] Plato, Phædon, pp. 79-80; Symposion, pp. 207-208.

[2] This is the same antithesis as we read in Xenophon, ascribed to Cyrus in his dying address to his sons—ὁ ἄκρατος καὶ καθαρὸς νοῦς—τὸ ἄφρον σῶμα, Cyropæd. viii. 7, 20.

[3] Alkinous, Introduct. c. 25. ὅτι μὲν οὖν αἱ λογικαὶ ψυχαὶ ἀθάνατοι ὑπάρχουσι κατὰ τὸν ἄνδρα τοῦτον, βεβαιώσαιτ' ἄν τις· εἰ δὲ καὶ αἱ ἄλογοι, τοῦτο τῶν ἀμφισβητουμένων ὑπάρχει. Galen considers Plato as affirming that the two inferior souls are mortal—Περὶ τῶν τῆς ψυχῆς ἠθῶν, T. iv. p. 773, Kühn.

This subject is handled in an instructive Dissertation of K. F. Hermann—De Partibus Animæ Immortalibus secundum Platonem—delivered at Göttingen in the winter Session, 1850-1851. He inclines to the belief that Plato intended to represent only the rational soul as immortal, and the other two souls as mortal (p. 9). But the passages which he produces are quite sufficient to show, that Plato sometimes held one language, sometimes the other; and that Galen, who wrote an express treatise (now lost) to prove that Plato was inconsistent with himself in respect to the soul, might have produced good reasons for his

one view, sometimes to the other : besides which, the view taken in the Phædon is a third, different from both—*viz.* : That the two non-rational souls, the passionate and appetitive, are not recognised as existing.

The life and character of a philosopher is a constant struggle to emancipate his soul from his body. Death alone enables him to do this completely.

The philosopher (contends Sokrates) ought to rejoice when death comes to sever his soul altogether from his body: because he is, throughout all his life, struggling to sever himself from the passions, appetites, impulses and aspirations, which grow out of the body : and to withdraw himself from the perceptions of the corporeal senses, which teach no truth, and lead only to deceit or confusion : He is constantly attempting to do what the body hinders him from doing completely —to prosecute pure mental contemplation, as the only way of arriving at truth : to look at essences or things in themselves, by means of his mind or soul in itself apart from the body.[1] Until his mind be purified from all association with the

opinion. The "inconstantia Platonis" (Cicero, Nat. Deor. i. 12) must be admitted here as on other matters. We must take the different arguments and doctrines of Plato as we find them in their respective places. Hermann (p. 4) says about the commentators—"De irrationali animâ alii ancipites hæserunt, alii claris verbis mortalem prædicarunt: quumque Neoplatonicæ sectæ principes, Numenius et Plotinus, non modo brutorum, sed ne plantarum quidem, animas immortalitate privare ausi sunt,—mox insequentes in alia omnia digressi aut plane perire irrationales partes affirmarunt, aut mediâ quâdam viâ ingressi, quamvis corporum fato exemptis, mortalitatem tamen et ipsi tribuerunt." It appears that the divergence of opinion on this subject began as early as Xenokrates and Speusippus—see Olympiodorus, Scholia in Phædonem, § 175. The large construction adopted by Numenius and Plotinus is completely borne out by a passage in the Phædon, p. 70 E.

I must here remark that Hermann does not note the full extent of discrepancy between the Phædon and Plato's other dialogues, consisting in this— That in the Phædon, Plato suppresses all mention of the two non-rational souls, the passionate and appetitive : insomuch that if we had only the Phædon remaining, we should not have known that he had ever affirmed the triple partition of the soul, or the co-existence of the three souls.

I transcribe an interesting passage from M. Degérando, respecting the belief in different varieties of soul, and partial immortality.

Degérando—Histoire Comparée des Systèmes de Philosophie, vol. i. p. 213.

"Les habitans du Thibet, du Gröenland, du nord de l'Amérique admettent deux âmes : les Caraïbes en admettent trois, dont une, disent-ils, celle qui habite dans la tête, remonte seule au pays des âmes. Les habitans du Gröenland croient d'ailleurs les âmes des hommes semblables au principe de la vie des animaux : ils supposent que les divers individus peuvent changer d'âmes entre eux pendant la vie, et qu' après la vie ces âmes exécutent de grands voyages, avec toutes sortes de fatigues et de périls. Les peuples du Canada se représentent les âmes sous la forme d'ombres errantes : les Patagons, les habitans du Sud de l'Asie, croient entendre leurs voix dans l'écho : et les anciens Romains eux-mêmes n'étaient pas étrangers à cette opinion. Les Négres s'imaginent que la destinée de l'âme après la vie est encore liée à celle du corps, et fondent sur cette idée une foule de pratiques."

[1] Plato, Phædon, p. 66 E. εἰ μέλλομέν ποτε καθαρῶς τι εἴσεσθαι, ἀπαλ-

CHAP. XXV. LIFE A STRUGGLE BETWEEN SOUL AND BODY. 387

body, it cannot be brought into contact with pure essence, nor can his aspirations for knowledge be satisfied.[1] Hence his whole life is really a training or approximative practice for death, which alone will enable him to realise such aspirations.[2] Knowledge or wisdom is the only money in which he computes, and which he seeks to receive in payment.[3] He is not courageous or temperate in the ordinary sense: for the courageous man, while holding death to be a great evil, braves it from fear of greater evils—and the temperate man abstains from various pleasures, because they either shut him out from greater pleasures, or entail upon him disease and poverty. The philosopher is courageous and temperate, but from a different motive: his philosophy purifies him from all these sensibilities, and makes him indifferent to all the pleasures and pains arising from the body: each of which, in proportion to its intensity, corrupts his perception of truth and falsehood, and misguides him in the search for wisdom or knowledge.[4] While in the body, he feels imprisoned, unable to look for knowledge except through a narrow grating and by the deceptive media of sense. From this durance philosophy partially liberates him,—purifying his mind, like the Orphic or Dionysiac religious mysteries, from the contagion of body[5] and sense: disengaging it, as far as may be during life, from sympathy with the body: and translating it out of the world of sense, uncertainty, and mere opinion, into the invisible region of truth and knowledge. If such purification has been fully achieved, the mind of the philosopher is at the moment of death thoroughly severed from the body, and passes clean away by itself, into commerce with the intelligible Entities or realities.

On the contrary, the soul or mind of the ordinary man, which has undergone no purification and remains in close implication with the body, cannot get completely separated even at the moment of death, but remains

Souls of the ordinary or unphilosophical

λακτέον αὐτοῦ (τοῦ σώματος) καὶ αὐτῇ τῇ ψυχῇ θεατέον αὐτὰ τὰ πράγματα.
[1] Plato, Phædon, p. 67 B. μὴ καθαρῷ γὰρ καθαροῦ ἐφάπτεσθαι μὴ οὐ θεμιτὸν ᾖ.
[2] Plato, Phædon, p. 64 A. κινδυνεύουσι γὰρ ὅσοι τυγχάνουσιν ὀρθῶς ἁπτόμενοι φιλοσοφίας λεληθέναι τοὺς ἄλλους ὅτι οὐδὲν ἄλλο αὐτοὶ ἐπιτηδεύουσιν ἢ ἀποθνήσκειν τε καὶ τεθνάναι. P. 67 E. οἱ ὀρθῶς φιλοσοφοῦντες ἀποθνήσκειν μελετῶσιν.
[3] Plato, Phædon, p. 69 A. ἀλλ' ἦ ἐκεῖνο μόνον τὸ νόμισμα ὀρθόν, ἀνθ' οὗ δεῖ ἅπαντα ταῦτα καταλλάττεσθαι, φρόνησις.
[4] Plato, Phædon, pp. 69-83-84.
[5] Plato, Phædon, p. 82 E.

men pass after death into the bodies of different animals. The philosopher alone is relieved from all communion with body. encrusted and weighed down by bodily accompaniments, so as to be unfit for those regions to which mind itself naturally belongs. Such impure minds or souls are the ghosts or shadows which haunt tombs; and which become visible, because they cling to the visible world, and hate the invisible.[1] Not being fit for separate existence, they return in process of time into conjunction with fresh bodies, of different species of men or animals, according to the particular temperament which they carry away with them.[2] The souls of despots, or of violent and rapacious men, will pass into the bodies of wolves or kites: those of the gluttonous and drunkards, into asses and such-like animals. A better fate will be reserved for the just and temperate men, who have been socially and politically virtuous, but simply by habit and disposition, without any philosophy or pure intellect: for their souls will pass into the bodies of other gentle and social animals, such as bees, ants, wasps,[3] &c., or perhaps they may again return into the human form, and may become moderate men. It is the privilege only of him who has undergone the purifying influence of philosophy, and who has spent his life in trying to detach himself as much as possible from communion with the body—to be relieved after death from the obligation of fresh embodiment, that his soul may dwell by itself in a region akin to its own separate nature: passing out of the world of sense, of transient phenomena, and of mere opinion, into a distinct world where it will be in full presence of the eternal Ideas, essences, and truth; in companionship with the Gods, and far away from the miseries of humanity.[4]

Such is the creed which Sokrates announces to his friends in

[1] Plato, Phædon, p. 81 C-D. ὃ δὴ καὶ ἔχουσα ἡ τοιαύτη ψυχὴ βαρύνεταί τε καὶ ἕλκεται πάλιν εἰς τὸν ὁρατὸν τόπον, φόβῳ τοῦ ἀειδοῦς τε καὶ Ἅιδου, ὥσπερ λέγεται, περὶ τὰ μνήματά τε καὶ τοὺς τάφους κυλινδουμένη, περὶ ἃ δὴ καὶ ὤφθη ἄττα ψυχῶν σκοτοειδῆ φάσματα [al. σκιοειδῆ φαντάσματα], οἷα παρέχονται αἱ τοιαῦται ψυχαὶ εἴδωλα, αἱ μὴ καθαρῶς ἀπολυθεῖσαι ἀλλὰ τοῦ ὁρατοῦ μετέχουσαι, διὸ καὶ ὁρῶνται.
[2] Plato, Phædon, pp. 82-84.
[3] Plato, Phædon, p. 82 A. Οὐκοῦν εὐδαιμονέστατοι καὶ τούτων εἰσὶ καὶ εἰς βέλτιστον τόπον ἰόντες οἱ τὴν δημοτικὴν τε καὶ πολιτικὴν ἀρετὴν ἐπιτετηδευκότες, ἣν δὴ καλοῦσι σωφροσύνην τε καὶ δικαιοσύνην, ἐξ ἔθους τε καὶ μελέτης γεγονυῖαν ἄνευ φιλοσοφίας τε καὶ νοῦ; . . . Ὅτι τούτους εἰκός ἐστιν εἰς τοιοῦτον πάλιν ἀφικνεῖσθαι πολιτικόν τε καὶ ἥμερον γένος, ἤπου μελιττῶν ἢ σφηκῶν ἢ μυρμήκων, &c.
[4] Plato, Phædon, pp. 82 B, 83 B, 84 B. Compare p. 114 C: τούτων δὲ αὐτῶν οἱ φιλοσοφίᾳ ἱκανῶς καθηράμενοι ἄνευ τε σωμάτων ζῶσι τὸ παράπαν εἰς τὸν ἔπειτα χρόνον, &c. Also p. 115 D.

the Phædon, as supplying good reason for the readiness and satisfaction with which he welcomes death. It is upon the antithesis between soul (or mind) and body, that the main stress is laid. The partnership between the two is represented as the radical cause of mischief: and the only true relief to the soul consists in breaking up the partnership altogether, so as to attain a distinct, disembodied, existence. Conformably to this doctrine, the line is chiefly drawn between the philosopher, and the multitude who are not philosophers—not between good and bad agents, when the good agents are not philosophers. This last distinction is indeed noticed, but is kept subordinate. The unphilosophical man of social goodness is allowed to pass after death into the body of a bee, or an ant, instead of that of a kite or ass;[1] but he does not attain the privilege of dissolving connection altogether with body. Moreover the distinction is one not easily traceable: since Sokrates[2] expressly remarks that the large majority of mankind are middling persons, neither good nor bad in any marked degree. Philosophers stand in a category by themselves: apart from the virtuous citizens, as well as from the middling and the vicious. Their appetites and ambition are indeed deadened, so that they agree with the virtuous in abstaining from injustice: but this is not their characteristic feature. Philosophy is asserted to impart to them a special purification, like that of the Orphic mysteries to the initiated: detaching the soul from both the body and the world of sense, except in so far as is indispensable for purposes of life: replunging the soul, as much as possible, in the other world of intelligible essences, real forms or Ideas, which are its own natural kindred and antecedent companions. The process whereby this is accomplished is intellectual rather than ethical. It is the process of learning, or (in the sense of Sokrates) the revival in the mind of those essences or Ideas with which it had been familiar during its anterior and separate life: accompanied by the total abstinence from all other pleasures and temptations.[3] Only by such love of learning,

Special privilege claimed for philosophers in the Phædon apart from the virtuous men who are not philosophers.

---

[1] Plato, Phædon, pp. 81-82.
[2] Plato, Phædon, p. 90 A.
[3] Plato, Phædon, pp. 82-115.—τὰς δὲ (ἡδονὰς) περὶ τὸ μανθάνειν ἐσπούδασε, &c. (p. 114 E).

These doctrines, laid down by Plato in the Phædon, bear great analogy to the Sanskrit philosophy called *Sankhyá*, founded by Kapila, as expounded and criticised in the treatise of M. Barthé-

which is identical with philosophy (φιλόσοφον, φιλομαθές), is the mind rescued from the ignorance and illusions unavoidable in the world of sense.

In thus explaining his own creed, Sokrates announces a full conviction that the soul or mind is immortal, but he has not yet offered any proof of it: and Simmias as well as Kebês declare themselves to stand in need of proof. Both of them however are reluctant to obtrude upon him any doubts. An opportunity is thus provided, that Sokrates may exhibit his undisturbed equanimity—his unimpaired argumentative readiness —his keen anxiety not to relax the grasp of a subject until he has brought it to a satisfactory close — without the least reference to his speedily approaching death. This last-mentioned anxiety is made manifest in a turn of the dialogue, remarkable both for dramatic pathos and for originality.[1] We are thus brought to the more explicit statement of those reasons upon which Sokrates relies.

Simmias and Kebês do not admit readily the immortality of the soul, but are unwilling to trouble Sokrates by asking for proof. Unabated interest of Sokrates in rational debate.

If the arguments whereby Sokrates proves the immortality of the soul are neither forcible nor conclusive, not fully satisfying even Simmias[2] to whom they are addressed —the adverse arguments, upon the faith of which the doctrine was denied (as we know it to have been by many philosophers of antiquity), cannot be said to be produced at all. Simmias and Kebês are represented as Sokratic companions, partly Pythagoreans; desirous to find the doctrine true, yet ignorant of the proofs. Both of them are earnest believers in the pre-existence of the soul, and in the objective reality of Ideas or intelligible essences. Simmias however adopts in part the opinion, not very clearly explained, "That the soul is a

Simmias and Kebês believe fully in the pre-existence of the soul, but not in its post-existence. Doctrine— That the soul is a sort of harmony— refuted by Sokrates.

---

[1] Plato, Phædon, p. 89 B-C,—the remark made by Sokrates, when stroking down the head and handling the abundant hair of Phædon, in allusion to the cutting off of all this hair, which would be among the acts of mourning performed by Phædon on the morrow, after the death of Sokrates: and the impressive turn given to this remark, in reference to the solution of the problem then in debate.

lemy St. Hilaire (Mémoire sur le Sankhyâ, Paris, 1852, pp. 273-278)—and the other work, Du Bouddhisme, by the same author (Paris, 1855), pp. 116-137, 187-194, &c.

[2] Plato, Phædon, p. 107 B.

CHAP. XXV.   HISTORY OF A PHILOSOPHISING MIND.   391

harmony or mixture": which opinion Sokrates refutes, partly by some other arguments, partly by pointing out that it is inconsistent with the supposition of the soul as pre-existent to the body, and that Simmias must make his election between the two. Simmias elects without hesitation, in favour of the pre-existence: which he affirms to be demonstrable upon premisses or assumptions perfectly worthy of trust: while the alleged harmony is at best only a probable analogy, not certified by conclusive reasons.[1] Kebês again, while admitting that the soul existed before its conjunction with the present body, and that it is sufficiently durable to last through conjunction with many different bodies—still expresses his apprehension that though durable, it is not eternal. Accordingly, no man can be sure that his present body is not the last with which his soul is destined to be linked; so that immediately on his death, it will pass away into nothing. The opinion of Kebês is remarkable, inasmuch as it shows how constantly the metempsychosis, or transition of the soul from one body to another, was included in all the varieties of ancient speculation on this subject.[2]

Before replying to Simmias and Kebês, Sokrates is described as hesitating and reflecting for a long time. He then enters into a sketch of[3] his own intellectual history. How far the sketch as it stands depicts the real Sokrates, or Plato himself, or a supposed mind not exactly coincident with either—we cannot be certain: the final stage however must belong to Plato himself.

Sokrates unfolds the intellectual changes or wanderings through which his mind had passed.

"You compel me (says Sokrates) to discuss thoroughly the cause of generation and destruction.[4] I will tell you, if you like, my own successive impressions on these

First doctrine of Sokrates as

---

[1] Plato, Phædon, p. 92.
[2] Plato, Phædon, pp. 86-95. κρᾶσιν καὶ ἁρμονίαν, &c.
"Animam esse harmoniam complures quidem statuerant, sed aliam alii, et diversâ ratione," says Wyttenbach ad Phædon. p. 86. Lucretius as well as Plato impugns the doctrine, iii. 97.
Galen, a great admirer of Plato, though not pretending to determine positively wherein the essence of the soul consists, maintains a doctrine substantially the same as what is here impugned—that it depends upon a certain κρᾶσις of the elements and properties in the bodily organism—Περὶ τῶν τῆς ψυχῆς ἠθῶν, vol. iv. pp. 774-775, 779-782, ed. Kühn. He complains much of the unsatisfactory explanations of Plato on this point.
[3] Plato, Phædon, pp. 96-102.
The following abstract is intended only to exhibit the train of thought and argument pursued by Sokrates; not adhering to the exact words, nor even preserving the interlocutory form. I could not have provided room for a literal translation.
[4] Plato, Phædon, pp. 95 E—96. Οὐ φαῦλον πρᾶγμα ζητεῖς · ὅλως γὰρ δεῖ περὶ

to cause. Reasons why he rejected it.

subjects. When young, I was amazingly eager for that kind of knowledge which people call the investigation of Nature. I thought it matter of pride to know the causes of every thing—through what every thing is either generated, or destroyed, or continues to exist. I puzzled myself much to discover first of all such matters as these—Is it a certain putrefaction of the Hot and the Cold in the system (as some say), which brings about the nourishment of animals? Is it the blood through which we think—or air, or fire? Or is it neither one nor the other, but the brain, which affords to us sensations of sight, hearing, and smell, out of which memory and opinion are generated: then, by a like process, knowledge is generated out of opinion and memory when permanently fixed?[1] I tried to understand destructions as well as generations, celestial as well as terrestrial phenomena. But I accomplished nothing, and ended by fancying myself utterly unfit for the enquiry. Nay—I even lost all the knowledge of that which I had before believed myself to understand. For example—From what cause does a man grow? At first, I had looked upon this as evident—that it was through eating and drinking: flesh being thereby added to his flesh, bone to his bone, &c. So too, when a tall and a short man were standing together, it appeared to me that the former was taller than the latter by the head—that ten were more than eight because two were added to them[2]—that a rod of two cubits was greater than a rod of one cubit, because it projected beyond it by a half. Now—I am satisfied that I do not know the cause of any of these matters. I cannot explain why, when one is added to one, such addition makes them two; since in their separated state each was one. In this case, it is approximation or conjunction which is said to make the two: in another case, the opposite cause, *disjunction,* is said also to make two—when one body is bisected.[3] How two opposite causes can pro-

---

[1] Plato, Phædon, p. 96 B. ἐκ δὲ μνήμης καὶ δόξης, λαβούσης τὸ ἠρεμεῖν, κατὰ ταῦτα γίγνεσθαι ἐπιστήμην.
γενέσεως καὶ φθορᾶς τὴν αἰτίαν διαπραγματεύσασθαι. ἐγὼ οὖν σοὶ δίειμι, ἐὰν βούλῃ, τά γ' ἐμὰ πάθη, &c.
This is the same distinction between δόξα and ἐπιστήμη, as that which Sokrates gives in the Menon, though not with full confidence (Menon, pp. 97-98). See suprà, chap. xxii. p. 241.

[2] Plato, Phædon, p. 96 E. καὶ ἔτι γε τούτων ἐναργέστερα, τὰ δέκα μοι ἐδόκει τῶν ὀκτὼ πλείονα εἶναι, διὰ τὸ δύο αὐτοῖς προσεῖναι, καὶ τὸ δίπηχυ τοῦ πηχυαίου μεῖζον εἶναι διὰ τὸ ἡμίσει αὐτοῦ ὑπερέχειν.

[3] Plato, Phædon, p. 97 B.

duce the same effect—and how either conjunction or disjunction can produce two, where there were not two before—I do not understand. In fact, I could not explain to myself, by this method of research, the generation, or destruction, or existence, of any thing; and I looked out for some other method.

"It was at this time that I heard a man reading out of a book, which he told me was the work of Anaxagoras, the affirmation that Nous (Reason, Intelligence) was the regulator and cause of all things. I felt great satisfaction in this cause; and I was convinced, that if such were the fact, Reason would ordain every thing for the best: so that if I wanted to find out the cause of any generation, or destruction, or existence, I had only to enquire in what manner it was best that such generation or destruction should take place. Thus a man was only required to know, both respecting himself and respecting other things, what was the best: which knowledge, however, implied that he must also know what was worse—the knowledge of the one and of the other going together.[1] I thought I had thus found a master quite to my taste, who would tell me, first whether the earth was a disk or a sphere, and would proceed to explain the cause and the necessity why it must be so, by showing me how such arrangement was the best: next, if he said that the earth was in the centre, would proceed to show that it was best that the earth should be in the centre. Respecting the Sun, Moon, and Stars, I expected to hear the like explanation of their movements, rotations, and other phenomena: that is, how it was better that each should do and suffer exactly what the facts show. I never imagined that Anaxagoras, while affirming that they were regulated by Reason, would put upon them any other cause than this—that it was best for them to be exactly as they are. I presumed that, when giving account of the cause, both of each severally and all collectively, he would do it by setting forth what was best for each severally and for all in common. Such

Second doctrine. Hopes raised by the treatise of Anaxagoras.

---

[1] Plato, Phædon, p. 97 C-D. εἰ οὖν τις βούλοιτο τὴν αἰτίαν εὑρεῖν περὶ ἑκάστου, ὅπῃ γίγνεται ἢ ἀπόλλυται ἢ ἔστι, τοῦτο δεῖν περὶ αὐτοῦ εὑρεῖν, ὅπῃ βέλτιστον αὐτῷ ἐστιν ἢ εἶναι ἢ ἄλλο ὁτιοῦν πάσχειν ἢ ποιεῖν· ἐκ δὲ δὴ τοῦ λόγου τούτου οὐδὲν ἄλλο σκοπεῖν προσήκειν ἀνθρώπῳ καὶ περὶ αὐτοῦ καὶ περὶ τῶν ἄλλων, ἀλλ' ἢ τὸ ἄριστον καὶ τὸ βέλτιστον· ἀναγκαῖον δὲ εἶναι τὸν αὐτὸν τοῦτον καὶ τὸ χεῖρον εἰδέναι· τὴν αὐτὴν γὰρ εἶναι ἐπιστήμην περὶ αὐτῶν.

was my hope, and I would not have sold it for a large price.[1] I took up eagerly the book of Anaxagoras, and read it as quickly as I could, that I might at once come to the knowledge of the better and worse.

"Great indeed was my disappointment when, as I proceeded with the perusal, I discovered that the author never employed Reason at all, nor assigned any causes calculated to regulate things generally : that the causes which he indicated were, air, æther, water, and many other strange agencies. The case seemed to me the same as if any one, while announcing that Sokrates acts in all circumstances by reason, should next attempt to assign the causes of each of my proceedings severally :[2] As if he affirmed, for example, that the cause why I am now sitting here is, that my body is composed of bones and ligaments—that my bones are hard, and are held apart by commissures, and my ligaments such as to contract and relax, clothing the bones along with the flesh and the skin which keeps them together—that when the bones are lifted up at their points of junction, the contraction and relaxation of the ligaments makes me able to bend my limbs— and that this is the reason why I am now seated here in my present crumpled attitude : or again—as if, concerning the fact of my present conversation with you, he were to point to other causes of a like character—varieties of speech, air, and hearing, with numerous other similar facts—omitting all the while to notice the true causes, *viz.*,[3]—That inasmuch as the Athenians have deemed it best to condemn me, for that reason I too have deemed it best and most righteous to remain sitting here and to undergo the sentence which they impose. For, by the Dog, these bones and ligaments would have been long ago carried

Disappointment because Anaxagoras did not follow out the optimistic principle into detail. Distinction between causes efficient and causes co-efficient.

---

[1] Plato, Phædon, p. 98 B. καὶ οὐκ ἂν ἀπεδόμην πολλοῦ τὰς ἐλπίδας, ἀλλὰ πάνυ σπουδῇ λαβὼν τὰς βίβλους ὡς τάχιστα οἷός τ' ἦν ἀνεγίγνωσκον, ἵν' ὡς τάχιστα εἰδείην τὸ βέλτιστον καὶ τὸ χεῖρον.

[2] Plato, Phædon, p. 98 C. καί μοι ἔδοξεν ὁμοιότατον πεπονθέναι ὥσπερ ἂν εἴ τις λέγων ὅτι Σωκράτης πάντα ὅσα πράττει νῷ πράττει, κἄπειτα ἐπιχειρήσας λέγειν τὰς αἰτίας ἑκάστων ὧν πράττω, λέγοι πρῶτον μὲν ὅτι διὰ ταῦτα νῦν ἐνθάδε κάθημαι, ὅτι ξύγκειταί μου τὸ σῶμα ἐξ ὀστῶν καὶ νεύρων, καὶ τὰ μὲν ὀστᾶ ἐστι στερεὰ καὶ διαφυὰς ἔχει χωρὶς ἀπ' ἀλλήλων, &c.

[3] Plato, Phædon, p. 98 E. ἀμελήσας τὰς ὡς ἀληθῶς αἰτίας λέγειν, ὅτι ἐπειδὴ Ἀθηναίοις ἔδοξε βέλτιον εἶναι ἐμοῦ καταψηφίσασθαι, διὰ ταῦτα δὴ καὶ ἐμοὶ βέλτιον αὖ δέδοκται ἐνθάδε καθῆσθαι, &c.

CHAP. XXV. DISAPPOINTMENT WITH ANAXAGORAS. 395

away to Thebes or Megara, by my judgment of what is best—if I had not deemed it more righteous and honourable to stay and affront my imposed sentence, rather than to run away. It is altogether absurd to call such agencies by the name of *causes*. Certainly, if a man affirms that unless I possessed such joints and ligaments and other members as now belong to me, I should not be able to execute what I have determined on, he will state no more than the truth. But to say that these are the causes why I, a rational agent, do what I am now doing, instead of saying that I do it from my choice of what is best—this would be great carelessness of speech : implying that a man cannot see the distinction between that which is the cause in reality, and that without which the cause can never be a cause.[1] It is this last which most men, groping as it were in the dark, call by a wrong name, as if it were itself the cause. Thus one man affirms that the earth is kept stationary in its place by the rotation of the heaven around it : another contends that the air underneath supports the earth, like a pedestal sustaining a broad kneading-trough : but none of them ever look out for a force such as this —That all these things now occupy that position which it is best that they should occupy. These enquirers set no great value upon this last-mentioned force, believing that they can find some other Atlas stronger, more everlasting, and more capable of holding all things together : they think that the Good and the Becoming have no power of binding or holding together any thing.

"Now, it is this sort of cause which I would gladly put myself under any one's teaching to learn. But I could neither find any teacher, nor make any way by myself. Having failed in this quarter, I took the second best course, and struck into a new path in search of causes.[2] Fatigued with studying objects through my eyes and perceptions of sense, I looked out for images

Sokrates could neither trace out the optimistic principle for himself, nor find any

[1] Plato, Phædon, p. 99 A. ἀλλ' αἴτια μὲν τὰ τοιαῦτα καλεῖν λίαν ἄτοπον· εἰ δέ τις λέγοι, ὅτι ἄνευ τοῦ τὰ τοιαῦτα ἔχειν καὶ ὀστᾶ καὶ νεῦρα καὶ ὅσα ἄλλα ἔχω, οὐκ ἂν οἷός τ' ἦν ποιεῖν τὰ δόξαντά μοι, ἀληθῆ ἂν λέγοι· ὡς μέντοι διὰ ταῦτα ποιῶ ἃ ποιῶ, καὶ ταύτῃ νῷ πράττω, ἀλλ' οὐ τῇ τοῦ βελτίστου αἱρέσει, πολλὴ ἂν καὶ μακρὰ ῥᾳθυμία εἴη τοῦ λόγου. Τὸ γὰρ μὴ διελέσθαι οἷόν τ' εἶναι, ὅτι ἄλλο μέν τί ἐστι τὸ αἴτιον τῷ ὄντι, ἄλλο δ' ἐκεῖνο ἄνευ οὗ τὸ αἴτιον οὐκ ἄν ποτ' εἴη αἴτιον, &c.

[2] Plato, Phædon, p. 99 C-D. ἐπειδὴ δὲ ταύτης ἐστερήθην, καὶ οὔτ' αὐτὸς εὑρεῖν οὔτε παρ' ἄλλου μαθεῖν οἷός τε

teacher thereof. He renounced it, and embraced a third doctrine about cause.

or reflections of them, and turned my attention to words or discourses.[1] This comparison is indeed not altogether suitable : for I do not admit that he who investigates things through general words, has recourse to images, more than he who investigates sensible facts : but such, at all events, was the turn which my mind took. Laying down such general assumption or hypothesis as I considered to be the strongest, I accepted as truth whatever squared with it, respecting cause as well as all other matters. In this way I came upon the investigation of another sort of cause.[2]

He now assumes the separate existence of ideas. These ideas are the causes why particular objects manifest certain attributes.

"I now assumed the separate and real existence of Ideas by themselves—The Good in itself or the Self-Good, Self-Beautiful, Great, and all such others. Look what follows next upon this assumption. If any thing else be beautiful, besides the Self-Beautiful, that other thing can only be beautiful because it partakes of the Self-Beautiful : and the same with regard to other similar Ideas. This is the only cause that I can accept : I do not understand those other ingenious causes which I hear mentioned.[3] When any one tells me that a thing is beautiful because it has a showy colour or figure, I pay no attention to him, but adhere simply to my own affirmation, that nothing else causes it to be beautiful, except the presence or participation of the Self-Beautiful. In what way such participation may take place, I cannot positively determine. But I feel confident in affirming that it does take place : that things which are beautiful, become so by partaking in the Self-Beautiful ; things which are great or little, by partaking in Greatness or Littleness. If I am told that one man is taller than another by the head, and that this other is shorter than the first by the very same (by the head), I should not admit the proposition, but should repeat emphatically my own creed,— That whatever is greater than another is greater by nothing else

ἐγενόμην, τὸν δεύτερον πλοῦν ἐπὶ τὴν τῆς αἰτίας ζήτησιν ᾗ πεπραγμάτευμαι, βούλει σοι ἐπίδειξιν ποιήσωμαι;
[1] Plato, Phædon, p. 99 E. ἴσως μὲν οὖν ᾧ εἰκάζω, τρόπον τινὰ οὐκ ἔοικεν· οὐ γὰρ πάνυ ξυγχωρῶ τὸν ἐν τοῖς λόγοις σκοπούμενον τὰ ὄντα ἐν εἰκόσι μᾶλλον

σκοπεῖν ἢ τὸν ἐν τοῖς ἔργοις.
[2] Plato, Phædon, p. 100 B. ἔρχομαι γὰρ δὴ ἐπιχειρῶν σοι ἐπιδείξασθαι τῆς αἰτίας τὸ εἶδος ὃ πεπραγμάτευμαι, &c.
[3] Plato, Phædon, p. 100 C. οὐ τοίνυν ἔτι μανθάνω, οὐδὲ δύναμαι τὰς ἄλλας αἰτίας τὰς σοφὰς ταύτας γιγνώσκειν.

IDEAS ARE THE ONLY CAUSES.

except by Greatness and through Greatness—whatever is less than another is less only by Littleness and through Littleness. For I should fear to be entangled in a contradiction, if I affirmed that the greater man was greater and the lesser man less by the head—First, in saying that the greater was greater and that the lesser was less, by the very same—Next, in saying that the greater man was greater by the head, which is itself small : it being absurd to maintain that a man is great by something small.[1] Again, I should not say that ten is more than eight by two, and that this was the cause of its excess ;[2] my doctrine is, that ten is more than eight by Multitude and through Multitude: so the rod of two cubits is greater than that of one, not by half, but by Greatness. Again, when One is placed alongside of One, —or when one is bisected—I should take care not to affirm, that in the first case the juxtaposition, in the last case the bisection, was the cause why it became two.[3] I proclaim loudly that I know no other cause for its becoming two except participation in the essence of the Dyad. What is to become two, must partake of the Dyad : what is to become one, of the Monad. I leave to wiser men than me these juxtapositions and bisections and other such refinements : I remain entrenched within the safe ground of my own assumption or hypothesis (the reality of these intellegible and eternal Ideas).

"Suppose however that any one impugned this hypothesis itself ? I should make no reply to him until I had followed out fully the consequences of it : in order to ascertain whether they were consistent with, or contradictory to, each other. I should, when the proper time came, defend the hypothesis by itself, assuming some other hypothesis yet more universal, *Procedure of Sokrates if his hypothesis were impugned. He insists upon keeping apart the discus-*

---

[1] Plato, Phædon, p. 101 A. φοβούμενος μή τίς σοι ἐναντίος λόγος ἀπαντήσῃ, ἐὰν τῇ κεφαλῇ μείζονά τινα φῇς εἶναι καὶ ἐλάττω, πρῶτον μὲν τῷ αὐτῷ τὸ μεῖζον μεῖζον εἶναι καὶ τὸ ἔλαττον ἔλαττον, ἔπειτα τῇ κεφαλῇ σμικρᾷ οὔσῃ τὸν μείζω μείζω εἶναι, καὶ τοῦτο δὴ τέρας εἶναι, τὸ σμικρῷ τινὶ μέγαν τινὰ εἶναι.

[2] Plato, Phædon, p. 101 B. Οὔκουν τὰ δέκα τῶν ὀκτὼ δυοῖν πλείω εἶναι, καὶ διὰ ταύτην τὴν αἰτίαν ὑπερβάλλειν, φοβοῖο ἂν λέγειν, ἀλλὰ μὴ πλήθει καὶ διὰ τὸ πλῆθος ; καὶ τὸ δίπηχυ τοῦ πηχυαίου ἡμίσει μεῖζον εἶναι, ἀλλ᾽ οὐ μεγέθει ;

[3] Plato, Phædon, p. 101 B-C. τί δέ ; ἑνὶ ἑνὸς προστεθέντος, τὴν πρόσθεσιν αἰτίαν εἶναι τοῦ δύο γενέσθαι, ἢ διασχισθέντος τὴν σχίσιν, οὐκ εὐλαβοῖο ἂν λέγειν, καὶ μέγα ἂν βοῴης ὅτι οὐκ οἶσθα ἄλλως πως ἕκαστον γιγνόμενον ἢ μετασχὸν τῆς ἰδίας οὐσίας ἑκάστου οὗ ἂν μετάσχῃ · καὶ ἐν τούτοις οὐκ ἔχεις ἄλλην τινὰ αἰτίαν τοῦ δύο γενέσθαι ἀλλ᾽ ἢ τὴν τῆς δυάδος μετάσχεσιν, &c.

sion of the hypothesis and the discussion of its consequences. such as appeared to me best, until I came to some thing fully sufficient. But I would not permit myself to confound together the discussion of the hypothesis itself, and the discussion of its consequences.[1] This is a method which cannot lead to truth : though it is much practised by litigious disputants, who care little about truth, and pride themselves upon their ingenuity when they throw all things into confusion."—

Exposition of Sokrates welcomed by the hearers. Remarks upon it. The exposition here given by Sokrates of successive intellectual tentatives (whether of Sokrates or Plato, or partly one, partly the other), and the reasoning embodied therein, is represented as welcomed with emphatic assent and approbation by all his fellow-dialogists.[2] It deserves attention on many grounds. It illustrates instructively some of the speculative points of view, and speculative transitions, suggesting themselves to an inquisitive intellect of that day.

The philosophical changes in Sokrates all turned upon different views as to a true cause. If we are to take that which precedes as a description of the philosophical changes of Plato himself, it differs materially from Aristotle : for no allusion is here made to the intercourse of Plato with Kratylus and other advocates of the doctrines of Herakleitus : which intercourse is mentioned by Aristotle[3] as having greatly influenced the early speculations of Plato. Sokrates describes three different phases of his (or Plato's) speculative point of view : all turning upon different conceptions of what constituted a true Cause. His first belief on the subject was, that which he entertained before he entered on physical and physiological investigations. It seemed natural to him that eating and drinking should be the cause why a young man grew taller : new bone and new flesh was added out of the food. So again, when a tall man appeared standing near to a short man, the former was tall by the head, or because of the head : ten were more than eight, because two were added on :

---

[1] Plato, Phædon, p. 101 E. ἐπειδὴ δὲ ἐκείνης αὐτῆς (τῆς ὑποθέσεως) δέοι σε διδόναι λόγον, ὡσαύτως ἂν διδοίης, ἄλλην αὖ ὑπόθεσιν ὑποθέμενος, ἥτις τῶν ἄνωθεν βελτίστη φαίνοιτο . . . . ἅμα δὲ οὐκ ἂν φύροιο, ὥσπερ οἱ ἀντιλογικοί, περί τε τῆς ἀρχῆς διαλεγόμενος καὶ τῶν ἐξ ἐκείνης ὡρμημένων, εἴπερ βούλοιό τι τῶν ὄντων εὑρεῖν.

[2] Plato, Phædon, p. 102 A. Such approbation is peculiarly signified by the intervention of Echekrates.

[3] Aristotel. Metaphys. A. 987, a. 32.

the measure of two cubits was greater than that of one cubit, because it stretched beyond by one half. When one object was added on to another, the addition was the cause why they became two: when one object was bisected, this bisection was the cause why the one became two.

This was his first conception of a true Cause, which for the time thoroughly satisfied him. But when he came to investigate physiology, he could not follow out the same conception of Cause, so as to apply it to more novel and complicated problems; and he became dissatisfied with it altogether, even in regard to questions on which he had before been convinced. New difficulties suggested themselves to him. How can the two objects, which when separate were each one, be made *two*, by the fact that they are brought together? What alteration has happened in their nature? Then again, how can the very same fact, the change from one to two, be produced by two causes perfectly contrary to each other—in the first case, by juxtaposition—in the last case, by bisection?[1]

That which is interesting here to note, is the sort of Cause which first gave satisfaction to the speculative mind of Sokrates. In the instance of the growing youth, he notes two distinct facts, the earliest of which is (assuming certain other facts as accompanying conditions) the cause of the latest. But in most of the other instances, the fact is one which does not admit of explanation. Comparisons of eight men with ten men, of a yard with half a yard, of a tall man with a short man, are mental appreciations, beliefs, affirmations, not capable of being farther explained or accounted for: if any one disputes your affirmation, you prove it to him, by placing him in a situation to make the comparison for himself, or to go through the computation which establishes the truth of what you affirm. It is not the juxtaposition of eight men which makes them to be eight (they were so just as much when separated by ever so wide an interval): though it may dispose or enable the spectator to count them as eight. We may count the yard measure (whether actually bisected or not), either as one yard, or as two half yards, or as three feet, or thirty-

Problems and difficulties of which Sokrates first sought solution.

---

[1] Sextus Empiricus embodies this argument of Plato among the difficulties which he starts against the Dogmatists, adv. Mathematicos, x. s. 302-308.

six inches. Whether it be one, or two, or three, depends upon the substantive which we choose to attach to the numeral, or upon the comparison which we make (the unit which we select) on the particular occasion.

With this description of Cause Sokrates grew dissatisfied when he extended his enquiries into physical and physiological problems. Is it the blood, or air, or fire, whereby we think? and such like questions. Such enquiries —into the physical conditions of mental phenomena —did really admit of some answer, affirmative, or negative. But Sokrates does not tell us how he proceeded in seeking for an answer: he only says that he failed so completely, as even to be disabused of his supposed antecedent knowledge. He was in this perplexity when he first heard of the doctrine of Anaxagoras. "*Nous* or Reason is the regulator and the cause of all things." Sokrates interpreted this to mean (what it does not appear that Anaxagoras intended to assert)[1] that the Kosmos was an animal or person[2] having mind or Reason analogous to his own: that this Reason was an agent invested with full power and perpetually operative, so as to regulate in the best manner all the phenomena of the Kosmos; and that the general cause to be assigned for every thing was one and the same—"It is best thus"; requiring that in each particular case you should show *how* it was for the best. Sokrates took the type of Reason from his own volition and movements; supposing that all the agencies in the Kosmos were stimulated or checked by cosmical Reason for her purposes, as he himself put in motion his own bodily members. This conception of Cause, borrowed from the analogy of his own rational volition, appeared to Sokrates very captivating, though it had not been his own first conception. But he found that Anaxagoras, though proclaiming the doctrine as a principium or initiatory influence, did not make applications of it in detail; but assigned as causes, in most of the particular cases, those agencies which Sokrates considered to be subordinate and instrumental, as his own muscles were to his own volition.

Expectations entertained by Sokrates from the treatise of Anaxagoras. His disappointment. His distinction between causes and co-efficients.

---

[1] I have given (in chap. i. p. 48 seq.) an abridgment and explanation of what seems to have been the doctrine of Anaxagoras.

[2] Plato, Timæus, p. 30 D. τόνδε τὸν κόσμον, ζῷον ἔμψυχον ἔννουν τε, &c.

CHAP. XXV.   PHYSICAL EXPLANATIONS ODIOUS.   401

Sokrates will not allow such agencies to be called Causes: he says that they are only co-efficients indispensable to the efficacy of the single and exclusive Cause—Reason. But he tells us himself that most enquirers considered them as Causes; and that Anaxagoras himself produced them as such. Moreover we shall see Plato himself in the Timæus, while he repeats this same distinction between Causes Efficient and Causes Co-efficient—yet treats these latter as Causes also, though inferior in regularity and precision to the Demiurgic Nous.[1]

In truth, the complaint which Sokrates here raises against Anaxagoras—that he assigned celestial Rotation as the cause of phenomena, in place of a quasi-human Reason—is just the same as that which Aristophanes in the Clouds advances against Sokrates himself.[2] The comic poet accuses Sokrates of displacing Zeus to make room for Dinos or Rotation. According to the popular religious belief, all or most of the agencies in Nature were personified, or supposed to be carried on by persons—Gods, Goddesses, Dæmons, Nymphs, &c., which army of independent agents were conceived, by some thinkers, as more or less systematised and *Sokrates imputes to Anaxagoras the mistake of substituting physical agencies in place of mental. This is the same which Aristophanes and others imputed to Sokrates.*

---

[1] Plato, Timæus, p. 46 C-D. αἴτια—ξυναίτια—ξυμμεταίτια. He says that most persons considered the ξυναίτια as αἴτια. And he himself registers them as such (Timæus, p. 68 E). He there distinguishes the αἴτια and ξυναίτια as two different sorts of αἴτια, the *divine* and the *necessary*, in a remarkable passage: where he tells us that we ought to study the divine causes, with a view to the happiness of life, as far as our nature permits—and the necessary causes for the sake of the divine: for that we cannot in any way apprehend, or understand, or get sight of the divine causes alone, without the necessary causes along with them (69 A).

In Timæus, pp. 47-48, we find again νοῦς and ἀνάγκη noted as two distinct sorts of causes co-operating to produce the four elements. It is farther remarkable that Necessity is described as "the wandering or irregular description of Cause"—τὸ τῆς πλανωμένης εἶδος αἰτίας. Eros and 'Ανάγκη are joined as co-operating—in Symposion, pp. 195 C, 197 B.

[2] Aristophan. Nubes, 379 - 815.

Δῖνος βασιλεύει, τὸν Δί' ἐξεληλακώς. We find Proklus making this same complaint against Aristotle, "that he deserted theological *principia*, and indulged too much in physical reasonings"—τῶν μὲν θεολογικῶν ἀρχῶν ἀφιστάμενος, τοῖς δὲ φυσικοῖς λόγοις πέρα τοῦ δέοντος ἐνδιατρίβων (Proklus ad Timæum, ii. 90 E, p. 212, Schneider). Pascal also expresses the like displeasure against the Cartesian theory of the vortices. Descartes recognised God as having originally established rotatory motion among the atoms, together with an equal, unvarying quantity of motion: these two points being granted, Descartes considered that all cosmical facts and phenomena might be deduced from them.

"Sur la philosophie de Descartes, Pascal était de son sentiment sur l'automate; et n'en était point sur la matière subtile, dont il se moquait fort. Mais il ne pouvait souffrir sa manière d'expliquer la formation de toutes choses; et il disait très souvent,—Je ne puis pardonner à Descartes: il voudrait bien, dans toute sa philosophie, pouvoir

consolidated under the central authority of the Kosmos itself. The causes of natural phenomena, especially of the grand and terrible phenomena, were supposed agents, conceived after the model of man, and assumed to be endowed with volition, force, affections, antipathies, &c. : some of them visible, such as Helios, Selênê, the Stars ; others generally invisible, though showing themselves whenever it specially pleased them.[1] Sokrates, as we see by the Platonic Apology, was believed by his countrymen to deny these animated agencies, and to substitute instead of them inanimate forces, not put in motion by the quasi-human attributes of reason, feeling and volition. The Sokrates in the Platonic Phædon, taken at this second stage of his speculative wanderings, not only disclaims such a doctrine, but protests against it. He recognises no cause except a Nous or Reason borrowed by analogy from that of which he was conscious within himself, choosing what was best for himself in every special situation.[2] He tells

se passer de Dieu : mais il n'a pu s'empêcher de lui accorder une chiquenaude pour mettre le monde en mouvement : après cela, il n'a que faire de Dieu." (Pascal, Pensées, ch. xi. p. 237, edition de Louandre, citation from Mademoiselle Périer, Paris, 1854.)

Again, Lord Monboddo, in his Ancient Metaphysics (bk. ii. ch. 19, p. 276), cites these remarks of Plato and Aristotle on the deficiencies of Anaxagoras, and expresses the like censure himself against the cosmical theories of Newton :— "Sir Isaac puts me in mind of an ancient philosopher Anaxagoras, who maintained, as Sir Isaac does, that mind was the cause of all things ; but when he came to explain the particular phænomena of nature, instead of having recourse to mind, employed airs and æthers, subtle spirits and fluids, and I know not what—in short, any thing rather than mind : a cause which he admitted to exist in the universe ; but rather than employ it, had recourse to imaginary causes, of the existence of which he could give no proof. The Tragic poets of old, when they could not otherwise untie the knot of their fable, brought down a god in a machine, who solved all difficulties : but such philosophers as Anaxagoras will not, even when they cannot do better, employ *mind* or divinity. Our philosophers, since Sir Isaac's time, have gone on in the same track, and still, I think, farther."

Lord Monboddo speaks with still greater asperity about the Cartesian theory, making a remark on it similar to what has been above cited from Pascal. (See his Dissertation on the Newtonian Philosophy, Appendix to Ancient Metaphysics, pp. 498-499.) ,

[1] Plato, Timæus, p. 41 A. πάντες ὅσοι τε περιπολοῦσι φανερῶς καὶ ὅσοι φαίνονται καθ' ὅσον ἂν ἐθέλωσι θεοὶ, &c.

[2] What Sokrates understands by the theory of Anaxagoras, is evident from his language—Phædon, pp. 98-99. He understands an indwelling cosmical Reason or Intelligence, deliberating and choosing, in each particular conjuncture, what was best for the Kosmos ; just as his own (Sokrates) Reason deliberated and chose what was best for him (τῇ τοῦ βελτίστου αἱρέσει), in consequence of the previous determination of he Athenians to condemn and punish him.

This point deserves attention, because it is altogether different from Aristotle's conception of Nous or Reason in the Kosmos : in which he recognises no consciousness, no deliberation, no choice, no reference to any special situation : but a constant, instinctive, undeliberating, movement towards Good as a determining End—*i.e.* towards the reproduction and perpetuation of regular Forms.

us however that most of the contemporary philosophers dissented from this point of view. To them, such inanimate agencies were the sole and real causes, in one or other of which they found what they thought a satisfactory explanation.

It is however singular, that Sokrates, after he has extolled Anaxagoras for enunciating a grand general cause, and has blamed him only for not making application of it in detail, proceeds to state that neither he himself, nor any one else within his knowledge, could find the way of applying it, any more than Anaxagoras had done. If Anaxagoras had failed, no one else could do better. The facts before Sokrates could not be reconciled, by any way that he could devise, with his assumed principle of rational directing force, or constant optimistic purpose, inherent in the Kosmos. Accordingly he abandoned this track, and entered upon another: seeking a different sort of cause (τῆς

The supposed theory of Anaxagoras cannot be carried out, either by Sokrates himself, or any one else. Sokrates turns to general words, and adopts the theory of ideas.

Hegel, in his Geschichte der Philosophie (Part i. pp. 355, 368-369, 2nd edit.), has given very instructive remarks, in the spirit of the Aristotelian Realism, both upon the principle announced by Anaxagoras, and upon the manner in which Anaxagoras is criticised by Sokrates in the Platonic Phædon. Hegel observes:—

"Along with this principle (that of Anaxagoras) there comes in the recognition of an Intelligence, or of a self-determining agency—which was wanting before. Herein we are not to imagine thought, subjectively considered: when thought is spoken of, we are apt to revert to thought as it passes in our consciousness: but here, on the contrary, what is meant is, the Idea, considered altogether objectively, or Intelligence as an effective agent: (N.B. *Intellectum*, or *Cogitatum*—not *Intellectio*, or *Cogitatio*, which would mean the conscious process—see this distinction illustrated by Trendelenburg ad Aristot. De Animâ, i. 2, 5, p. 219: also Marbach, Gesch. der Phil. s. 54, 99 not. 2): as we say, that there is reason in the world,—or as we speak of Genera in nature, which are the Universal. The Genus Animal is the Essential of the Dog—it is the Dog himself: the laws of nature are her immanent Essence. Nature is not formed from without, as men construct a table: the table is indeed constructed intelligently, but by an Intelligence extraneous to this wooden material. It is this extraneous form which we are apt to think of as representing Intelligence, when we hear it talked of: but what is really meant is, the Universal—the immanent nature of the object itself. The Νοῦς is not a thinking Being without, which has arranged the world: by such an interpretation the Idea of Anaxagoras would be quite perverted and deprived of all philosophical value. For to suppose an individual, particular, Something without, is to descend into the region of phantasms and its dualism: what is called, a thinking Being, is not an Idea, but a Subject. Nevertheless, what is really and truly Universal is not for that reason Abstract: its characteristic property, quâ Universal, is to determine in itself, by itself, and for itself, the particular accompaniments. While it carries on this process of change, it maintains itself at the same time as the Universal, always the same; this is a portion of its self-determining efficiency."—What Hegel here adverts to seems identical with that which Dr. Henry More calls an Emanative Cause (Immortality of the Soul, ch. vi. p. 18), "the notion of a thing possible. An Emanative Effect is co-existent with the very substance of that which is

αἰτίας τὸ εἶδος), not by contemplation of things, but by propositions and ratiocinative discourse. He now assumed as a principle an universal axiom or proposition, from which he proceeds to deduce consequences. The principle thus laid down is, That there exist substantial Ideas—universal Entia. Each of these Ideas communicates or imparts its own nature to the particulars which bear the same name: and such communion or participation is the cause why they are what they are. The cause why various objects are beautiful or great, is, because they partake of the Self-Beautiful or the Self-Great: the cause why they are two or three is, because they partake of the Dyad or the Triad.

Here then we have a third stage or variety of belief, in the speculative mind of Sokrates, respecting Causes. The self-existent Ideas ("propria Platonis supellex," to use the words of Seneca [1]) are postulated as Causes: and in this belief Sokrates at last finds satisfaction. But these Causative Ideas, or Ideal Causes, though satisfactory to Plato, were accepted by scarcely any one else. They were transformed—seemingly even by Plato himself before his death, into Ideal Numbers, products of the One implicated with Great and Little or the undefined Dyad—and still farther transformed by

Vague and dissentient meanings attached to the word Cause. That is a cause, to each man, which gives satisfaction to his inquisitive feelings.

said to be the Cause thereof. That which *emanes*, if I may so speak, is the same in reality with its Emanative Cause."

Respecting the criticism of Sokrates upon Anaxagoras, Hegel has further acute remarks which are too long to cite (p. 368 seq.)

[1] Seneca, Epistol.

About this disposition, manifested by many philosophers, and in a particular manner by Plato, to "embrace logical phantoms as real causes," I transcribe a good passage from Malebranche.

"Je me sens encore extrêmement porté à dire que cette colonne est dure *par sa nature;* ou bien que les petits liens dont sont composés les corps durs, sont des atômes, dont les parties ne se peuvent diviser, comme étant les parties *essentieles* et dernières des corps —et qui sont *essentiellement* crochues ou branchues.

"Mais je reconnois franchement, que ce n'est point expliquer la difficulté; et que, quittant les préoccupations et les illusions de mes sens, j'aurais tort de recourir à une forme abstraite, et d' *embrasser un fantôme de logique* pour la cause que je cherche. Je veux dire, que j'aurois tort de concevoir, comme quelque chose de réel et de distinct, l'idée vague de *nature* et d' *essence*, qui n'exprime que ce que l'on sait : et de prendre ainsi une forme abstraite et universelle, comme une cause physique d'un effet très réel. Car il y a deux choses dont je ne saurais trop défier. La première est, l'impression de mes sens : et l'autre est, la facilité que j'ai de prendre les natures abstraites et les idées générales de logique, pour celles qui sont réelles et particulières : et je me souviens d'avoir été plusieurs fois séduit par ces deux principes d'erreur." (Malebranche — Recherche de la Vérité, vol. iii., liv. vi., ch. 8, p. 245, ed. 1772.)

his successors Speusippus and Xenokrates: they were impugned in every way, and emphatically rejected, by Aristotle.

The foregoing picture given by Sokrates of the wanderings of his mind (τὰς ἐμὰς πλάνας) in search of Causes, is interesting, not only in reference to the Platonic age, but also to the process of speculation generally. Almost every one talks of a Cause as a word of the clearest meaning, familiar and understood by all hearers. There are many who represent the Idea of Cause as simple, intuitive, self-originated, universal; one and the same in all minds. These philosophers consider the maxim—that every phenomenon must have a Cause—as self-evident, known *à priori* apart from experience: as something which no one can help believing as soon as it is stated to him.[1] The gropings of Sokrates are among the numerous facts which go to refute such a theory: or at least to show in what sense alone it can be partially admitted. There is no fixed, positive, universal Idea, corresponding to the word Cause. There is a wide divergence, as to the question what a Cause really is, between different ages of the same man (exemplified in the case of Sokrates): much more between different philosophers at one time and another. Plato complains of Anaxagoras and other philosophers for assigning as Causes that which did not truly deserve the name: Aristotle also blames the defective conceptions of his predecessors (Plato included) on the same subject. If there be an intuitive idea corresponding to the word Cause, it must be a different intuition in

---

[1] Dugald Stewart, Elem. Philos. Hum. Mind, vol. i. ch. 1, sect. 2, pp. 98-99, ed. Hamilton, also note c same volume.

"Several modern philosophers (especially Dr. Reid, On the Intell. Powers) have been at pains to illustrate that law of our nature which leads us to refer every change we perceive in the universe to the operation of an efficient cause. This reference is not the result of reasoning, but necessarily accompanies the perception, so as to render it impossible for us to see the change, without feeling a conviction of the operation of some cause by which it is produced; much in the same manner in which we find it impossible to conceive a sensation, without being impressed with a belief of the existence of a sentient being. Hence I conceive it is that when we see two events constantly conjoined, we are led to associate the idea of causation or efficiency with the former, and to refer to it that power or energy by which the change is produced; in consequence of which association we come to consider philosophy as the knowledge of efficient causes, and lose sight of the operation of mind in producing the phenomena of nature. It is by an association somewhat similar that we connect our sensations of colour with the primary qualities of body. A moment's reflection must satisfy any one that the sensation of colour can only reside in a mind.... In the same way we are led to associate with inanimate matter the ideas of power, force, energy, causation, which are all attributes of mind, and can exist in a mind only."

Plato and Aristotle—in Plato himself at one age and at another age : in other philosophers, different from both and from each other. The word is equivocal—πολλαχῶς λεγόμενον, in Aristotelian phrase—men use it familiarly, but vary much in the thing signified. *That* is a Cause, to each man, which gives satisfaction to the inquisitive feelings—curiosity, anxious perplexity, speculative embarrassment of his own mind. Now doubtless these inquisitive feelings are natural and widespread : they are emotions of our nature, which men seek (in some cases) to appease by some satisfactory hypothesis. That answer which affords satisfaction, looked at in one of its aspects, is called Cause ; Beginning or Principle—Element—represent other aspects of the same Quæsitum :—

"Felix, qui potuit rerum cognoscere causas,
Atque metus omnes et inexorabile Fatum
Subjecit pedibus strepitumque Acherontis avari,"

is the exclamation of that sentiment of wonder and uneasiness out of which, according to Plato and Aristotle, philosophy springs.[1] But though the appetite or craving is common, in greater or less degree, to most persons—the nourishment calculated to allay it is by no means the same to all. Good (says Aristotle) is that which all men desire :[2] but all men do not agree in their judgment, what Good is. The point of communion between mankind is here emotional rather than intellectual : in the painful feeling of difficulty to be solved, not in the manner of conceiving what the difficulty is, nor in the direction where solution is to be sought, nor in the solution itself when suggested.[3]

[1] Virgil, Georg. ii. 490-92. Compare Lucretius, vi. 50-65, and the letter of Epikurus to Herodotus, p. 25, ed. Orelli. Plato, Theætêt. p. 155 D. μάλα γὰρ φιλοσόφου τοῦτο τὸ πάθος, τὸ θαυμάζειν· οὐ γὰρ ἀρχὴ ἄλλη φιλοσοφίας, ἢ αὕτη :—Aristotel. Metaphys. A. p. 982, b. 10-20. διὰ γὰρ τὸ θαυμάζειν οἱ ἄνθρωποι καὶ νῦν καὶ τὸ πρῶτον ἤρξαντο φιλοσοφεῖν, ὁ δὲ ἀπορῶν καὶ θαυμάζων οἴεται ἀγνοεῖν.

[2] Aristotel. Ethic. Nikom. i. 1. διὸ καλῶς ἀπεφήναντο τἀγαθόν, οὗ πάντες ἐφίενται. Plato, Republ. vi. p. 505 E. Ὁ δὴ διώκει μὲν ἅπασα ψυχὴ καὶ τούτου ἕνεκα πάντα πράττει, ἀπομαντευομένη τι εἶναι, ἀποροῦσα δὲ καὶ οὐκ ἔχουσα

λαβεῖν ἱκανῶς τί ποτ' ἐστίν, &c.
Seneca, Epistol. 118. "Bonum est, quod ad se impetum animi secundum naturam movet."

[3] Aristotle recognises the different nature of the difficulties and problems which present themselves to the speculative mind : he looks back upon the embarrassments of his predecessors as antiquated and even silly, Metaphysic. N. 1089, a. 2. Πολλὰ μὲν οὖν τὰ αἴτια τῆς ἐπὶ ταύτας τὰς αἰτίας ἐκτροπῆς, μάλιστα δὲ τὸ ἀπορῆσαι ἀρχαϊκῶς, which Alexander of Aphrodisias paraphrases by ἀρχαϊκῶς καὶ εὐηθῶς. Compare A 993, a. 15.

In another passage of the same book,

CHAP. XXV.   MEN AGREE IN SEARCHING ONLY.   407

When Sokrates here tells us that as a young man he felt anxious curiosity to know what the cause of every phenomenon was, it is plain that at this time he did not know what he was looking for: that he proceeded only by successive steps of trial, doubt, discovered error, rejection: and that each trial was adapted to the then existing state of his own mind. The views of Anaxagoras he affirms to have presented themselves to him as a new revelation: he then came to believe that the only true Cause was, a cosmical reason and volition like to that of which he was conscious in himself. Yet he farther tells us, that others did not admit this Cause, but found other causes to satisfy them: that even Anaxagoras did not follow out his own general conception, but recognised Causes quite unconnected with it: lastly, that neither could he (Sokrates) trace out the conception for himself.[1] He was driven to renounce it, and to turn to another sort of Cause— the hypothesis of self-existent Ideas, in which he then acquiesced. And this last hypothesis, again, was ultimately much modified in the mind of Plato himself, as we know from Aristotle. All this shows that the Idea of Cause—far from being one and the same to all, like the feeling of uneasiness which prompts the search for it—is complicated, diverse, relative, and modifiable.

Dissension and perplexity on the question,— What is a cause? revealed by the picture of Sokrates —no intuition to guide him.

The last among the various revolutions which Sokrates represents himself to have undergone—the transition from designing and volitional agency of the Kosmos conceived as an animated system, to the sovereignty of universal Ideas—is analogous to that transition which Auguste Comte considers to be the natural

Different notions of Plato and Aristotle about causation, causes

---

Aristotle notes and characterises the emotion experienced by the mind in possessing what is regarded as truth— the mental satisfaction obtained when a difficulty is solved, 1090, a. 38. Οἱ δὲ χωριστὸν ποιοῦντες (τὸν ἀριθμόν), ὅτι ἐπὶ τῶν αἰσθητῶν οὐκ ἔσται τὰ ἀξιώματα, ἀληθῆ δὲ τὰ λεγόμενα καὶ σαίνει τὴν ψυχήν, εἶναί τε ὑπολαμβάνουσι καὶ χωριστὰ εἶναι· ὁμοίως δὲ τὰ μεγέθη τὰ μαθηματικά.

The subjective origin of philosophy —the feelings which prompt to the theorising process, striking out different hypotheses and analogies—are well stated by Adam Smith, 'History of Astronomy,' sect. ii. and iii.

[1] The view of Cause, which Sokrates here declares himself to renounce from inability to pursue it, is substantially the same as what he lays down in the Philêbus, pp. 23 D, 27 A, 30 E.

In the Timæus Plato assigns to Timæus the task (to which Sokrates in the Phædon had confessed himself incompetent) of following into detail the schemes and proceedings of the Demiurgic or optimising Νοῦς. But he also assumes the εἴδη or Ideas as co-ordinate and essential conditions.

regular and irregular. Inductive theory of causation, elaborated in modern times.

progress of the human mind: to explain phenomena at first by reference to some personal agency, and to pass from this mode of explanation to that by metaphysical abstractions. It is true that these are two distinct modes of conceiving Causation; and that in each of them the human mind, under different states of social and individual instruction, finds satisfaction. But each of the two theories admits of much diversity in the mode of conception. Plato seems to have first given prominence to these metaphysical causes; and Aristotle in this respect follows his example: though he greatly censures the incomplete and erroneous theories of Plato. It is remarkable that both these two philosophers recognised Causes irregular and unpredictable, as well as Causes regular and predictable. Neither of them included even the idea of regularity, as an essential part of the meaning of Cause.[1] Lastly, there has been elaborated in modern times, owing to the great extension of inductive science, another theory of Causation, in which unconditional regularity is the essential constituent: recognising no true Causes except the phenomenal causes certified by experience, as interpreted inductively and deductively—the assemblage of phenomenal antecedents, uniform and unconditional, so far as they can be discovered and verified.

---

[1] Monboddo, Ancient Metaphysics, B. 1. ch. iv. p. 32. "Plato appears to have been the first of the Ionic School that introduced *formal causes* into natural philosophy. These he called *Ideas*, and made the principles of all things. And the reason why he insists so much upon this kind of cause, and so little upon the other three, is given us by Aristotle in the end of his first book of Metaphysics, *viz.*, that he studied mathematics too much, and instead of using them as the handmaid of philosophy, made them philosophy itself.... Plato, however, in the Phædon says a good deal about final causes; but in the system of natural philosophy which is in the Timæus, he says very little of it."

I have already observed that Plato in the Timæus (48 A) recognises erratic or irregular Causation—ἡ πλανωμένη αἰτία. Aristotle recognises Αἰτία among the equivocal words πολλαχῶς λεγόμενα; and he enumerates Τύχη and Αὐτόματον—irregular causes or causes by accident—among them (Physic. ii. 195-198; Metaphys. K. 1065, a.) Schwegler, ad Aristot. Metaphys. vi. 4, 3, "Das Zufällige ist ein nothwendiges Element alles Geschehens". Alexander of Aphrodisias, the best of the Aristotelian commentators, is at pains to defend this view of Τύχη— Causation by accident, or irregular.

Proklus, in his Commentary on the Timæus (ii. 80-81, p. 188, Schneider), notices the labour and prolixity with which the commentators before him set out the different varieties of Cause; distinguishing sixty-four according to Plato, and forty-eight according to Aristotle. Proklus adverts also (ad Timæum, iii. p. 176) to an animated controversy raised by Theophrastus against Plato, about Causes and the speculations thereupon.

An enumeration, though very incomplete, of the different meanings assigned to the word Cause, may be seen in Professor Fleming's Vocabulary of Philosophy.

Certain it is that these are the only causes obtainable by induction and experience: though many persons are not satisfied without looking elsewhere for transcendental or ontological causes of a totally different nature. All these theories imply—what Sokrates announces in the passage just cited—the deepseated influence of speculative curiosity, or the thirst for finding the Why of things and events, as a feeling of the human mind: but all of them indicate the discrepant answers with which, in different enquirers, this feeling is satisfied, though under the same equivocal name *Cause*. And it would have been a proceeding worthy of Plato's dialectic, if he had applied to the word Cause the same cross-examining analysis which we have seen him applying to the equally familiar words—Virtue—Courage—Temperance—Friendship, &c. "First, let us settle what a Cause really is: then, and not till then, can we succeed in ulterior enquiries respecting it."[1]

[1] See Sir William Hamilton, Discussions on Philosophy, Appendix, p. 585. The debates about what was meant in philosophy by the word Cause are certainly older than Plato. We read that it was discussed among the philosophers who frequented the house of Perikles ; and that that eminent statesman was ridiculed by his dissolute son Xanthippus for taking part in such useless refinements (Plutarch, Perikles, c. 36). But the Platonic dialogues are the oldest compositions in which any attempts to analyse the meaning of the word are preserved to us.

Αἰτίαι, Ἀρχαί, Στοιχεῖα (Aristot. Metaph. Δ.), were the main objects of search with the ancient speculative philosophers. While all of them set to themselves the same problem, each of them hit upon a different solution. That which gave mental satisfaction to one, appeared unsatisfactory and even inadmissible to the rest. The first book of Aristotle's Metaphysica gives an instructive view of this discrepancy. His own analysis of Cause will come before us hereafter. Compare the long discussions on the subject in Sextus Empiricus, Pyrrhon. Hypo. iii. 13-30 ; and adv. Mathemat. ix. 195-250. The discrepancy was so great among the dogmatical philosophers, that he pronounces the reality of the causal sequence to be indeterminable—ὅσον μὲν οὖν ἐπὶ τοῖς λεγομένοις ὑπὸ τῶν δογματικῶν, οὐδ' ἂν ἐννοῆσαί τις τὸ αἴτιον δύναιτο, εἴ γε πρὸς τῷ διαφώνους καὶ ἀλλοκότους (ἀποδιδόναι) ἐννοίας τοῦ αἰτίου ἔτι καὶ τὴν ὑπόστασιν αὐτοῦ πεποιήκασιν ἀνεύρετον διὰ τὴν περὶ αὐτὸ διαφωνίαν. Seneca (Epist. 65) blends together the Platonic and the Aristotelian views, when he ascribes to Plato a quintuple variety of Causa.

The quadruple variety of Causation established by Aristotle governed the speculations of philosophers during the middle ages. But since the decline of the Aristotelian philosophy, there are few subjects which have been more keenly discussed among metaphysicians than the Idea of Cause. It is one of the principal points of divergence among the different schools of philosophy now existing. A volume, and a very instructive volume, might be filled with the enumeration and contrast of the different theories on the subject. Upon the view which a man takes on this point will depend mainly the scope or purpose which he sets before him in philosophy. Many seek the solution of their problem in transcendental, ontological, extra-phenomenal causes, lying apart from and above the world of fact and experience ; Reid and Stewart, while acknowledging the existence of such causes as the true efficient causes, consider them as being

There is yet another point which deserves attention in this history given by Sokrates of the transitions of his own mind. His last transition is represented as one from things to words, that is, to general propositions:[1] to the assumption in each case of an universal proposition or hypothesis calculated to fit that case. He does not seem to consider the optimistic doctrine, which he had before vainly endeavoured to follow out, as having been an hypothesis, or universal proposition assumed as true and as a principle from which to deduce consequences. Even if it were so, however, it was one and the same assumption intended to suit all cases: whereas the new doctrine to which he passed included many distinct assumptions, each adapted to a certain number of cases and not to the rest.[2] He assumed an untold multitude of self-existent Ideas—The Self-Beautiful, Self-Just, Self-Great, Self-Equal, Self-Unequal, &c.—each of them adapted to a certain number of particular cases: the Self-Beautiful was assumed as the cause why all particular things were beautiful—as that, of which all and each of them partakes —and so of the rest.[3] Plato then explains his procedure. He

Last transition of the mind of Sokrates from things to words—to the adoption of the theory of ideas. Great multitude of ideas assumed, each fitting a certain number of particulars.

out of the reach of human knowledge; others recognise no true cause except personal, quasi - human, voluntary, agency, grounded on the type of human volition. Others, again, with whom my own opinion coincides, following out the analysis of Hume and Brown, understand by causes nothing more than phenomenal antecedents constant and unconditional, ascertainable by experience and induction. See the copious and elaborate chapter on this subject in Mr. John Stuart Mill's 'System of Logic,' Book iii. ch. 5, especially as enlarged in the fourth, fifth, and sixth editions of that work, including the criticism on the opposite or volitional theory of Causation; also the work of Professor Bain, 'The Emotions and the Will,' pp. 472-584. The opposite view, in which Causes are treated as something essentially distinct from Laws, and as ultra-phenomenal, is set forth by Dr. Whewell, 'Novum Organon Renovatum,' ch. vii. p. 118 seq.

[1] Aristotle (Metaphysic. A. 987, b. 31, Θ. 1050, b. 35) calls the Platonici

οἱ ἐν τοῖς λόγοις: see the note of Bonitz.
[2] Plato, Phædon, p. 100 A. ἀλλ' οὖν δὴ ταύτῃ γε ὥρμησα, καὶ ὑποθέμενος ἑκάστοτε λόγον ὃν ἂν κρίνω ἐρρωμενέστατον εἶναι, ἃ μὲν ἄν μοι δοκῇ τούτῳ ξυμφωνεῖν, τίθημι ὡς ἀληθῆ ὄντα, καὶ περὶ αἰτίας καὶ περὶ τῶν ἄλλων ἁπάντων· ἃ δ' ἂν μή, ὡς οὐκ ἀληθῆ.
[3] Aristotle controverts this doctrine of Plato in a pointed manner, De Gen. et Corrupt. ii. 9, p. 335, b. 10, also Metaphys. A. 991, b. 3. The former passage is the most animated in point of expression, where Aristotle says— ὥσπερ ὁ ἐν τῷ Φαίδωνι Σωκράτης· καὶ γὰρ ἐκεῖνος, ἐπιτιμήσας τοῖς ἄλλοις ὡς οὐδὲν εἰρηκόσιν, ὑποτίθεται—which is very true about the Platonic dialogue *Phædon*, &c. But in both the two passages, Aristotle distinctly maintains that the Ideas cannot be *Causes* of any thing.

This is another illustration of what I have observed above, that the meaning of the word *Cause* has been always fluctuating and undetermined.
We see that, while Aristotle affirmed

CHAP. XXV.   TRUTH RESIDES IN UNIVERSALS.   411

first deduced various consequences from this assumed hypothesis, and examined whether all of them were consistent or inconsistent with each other. If he detected inconsistencies (as *e.g.* in the last half of the Parmenidês), we must suppose (though Plato does not expressly say so) that he would reject or modify his fundamental assumption : if he found none, he would retain it. The point would have to be tried by dialectic debate with an opponent : the logical process of inference and counter-inference is here assumed to be trustworthy. But during this debate Plato would require his opponent to admit the truth of the fundamental hypothesis provisionally. If the opponent chose to impugn the latter, he must open a distinct debate on that express subject. Plato insists that the discussion of the consequences flowing from the hypothesis, shall be kept quite apart from the discussion on the credibility of the hypothesis itself. From the language employed, he seems to have had in view certain disputants known to him, by whom the two were so blended together as to produce much confusion in the reasoning.

But if your opponent impugns the hypothesis itself, how are you to defend it ? Plato here tells us : by means of some other hypothesis or assumption, yet more universal than itself. You must ascend upwards in the scale of generality, until you find an assumption suitable and sufficient.[1]

Ultimate appeal to hypothesis of extreme generality.

We here see where it was that Plato looked for full, indisputable, self-recommending and self-assuring, certainty and truth. Among the most universal propositions. He states the matter here as if we were to provide defence for an hypothesis less universal by ascending to another hypothesis more universal. This is illustrated by what he says in the Timæus—Propositions are cognate with the matter which they affirm : those whose affirmation is purely intellectual, comprising only matter of the intelligible world, or of genuine Essence, are solid and inexpugnable : those which take in more or less of the sensible world, which is a mere copy of the intelligible exemplar, become less and less trustworthy—mere probabilities. Here we have the Platonic worship of the most universal propositions, as the only primary

that the Ideas could not be Causes of anything, Plato here maintains that they are the only true Causes.
[1] Plato, Phædon, p. 101 E.

and evident truths.[1] But in the sixth and seventh books of the Republic, he delivers a precept somewhat different, requiring the philosopher not to rest in any hypothesis as an ultimatum, but to consider them all as stepping-stones for enabling him to ascend into a higher region, above all hypothesis—to the first principle of every thing : and he considers geometrical reasoning as defective because it takes its departure from hypothesis or assumptions of which no account is rendered.[2] In the Republic he thus contemplates an intuition by the mind of some primary, clear, self-evident truth, above all hypotheses or assumptions even the most universal, and transmitting its own certainty to every thing which could be logically deduced from it : while in the Phædon, he does not recognise any thing higher or more certain than the most universal hypothesis—and he even presents the theory of self-existent Ideas as nothing more than an hypothesis, though a very satisfactory one. In the Republic, Plato has come to imagine the Idea of Good as distinguished from and illuminating all the other Ideas : in the Timæus, it seems personified in the Demiurgus ; in the Phædon, that Idea of Good appears to be represented by the Nous or Reason of Anaxagoras. But Sokrates is unable to follow it out, so that it becomes included, without any pre-eminence, among the Ideas generally : all of them transcendental, co-ordinate, and primary sources of truth to the intelligent mind—yet each of them exercising a causative influence in its own department, and bestowing its own special character on various particulars.

It is from the assumption of these Ideas as eternal Essences, that Plato undertakes to demonstrate the immortality of the soul. One Idea or Form will not admit, but peremptorily excludes, the approach of that other

Plato's demonstration of the immortality of the soul.

[1] Plato, Timæus, p. 29 B. ὧδε οὖν περί τε εἰκόνος καὶ τοῦ παραδείγματος διοριστέον, ὡς ἄρα τοὺς λόγους, ὧνπέρ εἰσιν ἐξηγηταί, τούτων αὐτῶν καὶ ξυγγενεῖς ὄντας. Τοῦ μὲν οὖν μονίμου καὶ βεβαίου καὶ μετὰ νοῦ καταφανοῦς, μονίμους καὶ ἀμεταπτώτους . . . τοὺς δὲ τοῦ πρὸς μὲν ἐκεῖνο ἀπεικασθέντος, ὄντος δὲ εἰκόνος, εἰκότας ἀνὰ λόγον τε ἐκείνων ὄντας· ὅ,τιπερ πρὸς γένεσιν οὐσία, τοῦτο πρὸς πίστιν ἀληθεία.

[2] Plato, Republic, vi. p. 511. τῶν ὑποθέσεων ἀνωτέρω ἐκβαίνειν

. . . . τὸ ἕτερον τμῆμα τοῦ νοητοῦ, οὗ αὐτὸς ὁ λόγος ἅπτεται τῇ τοῦ διαλέγεσθαι δυνάμει, τὰς ὑποθέσεις ποιούμενος οὐκ ἀρχὰς ἀλλὰ τῷ ὄντι ὑποθέσεις, οἷον ἐπιβάσεις τε καὶ ὁρμάς, ἵνα μέχρι τοῦ ἀνυποθέτου ἐπὶ τὴν τοῦ παντὸς ἀρχὴν ἰών, ἁψάμενος αὐτῆς, πάλιν αὖ ἐχόμενος τῶν ἐκείνης ἐχομένων, οὕτως ἐπὶ τελευτὴν καταβαίνῃ, αἰσθητῷ παντάπασιν οὐδενὶ προσχρώμενος, ἀλλ' εἴδεσιν αὐτοῖς δι' αὐτῶν εἰς αὐτά, καὶ τελευτᾷ εἰς εἴδη. Compare vii. p. 533.

CHAP. XXV.   PROOF OF IMMORTALITY OF THE SOUL.   413

Form which is opposite to it. Greatness will not receive the form of littleness: nor will the greatness which is in any particular subject receive the form of littleness. If the form of littleness be brought to bear, greatness will not stay to receive it, but will either retire or be destroyed. The same is true likewise respecting that which essentially has the form: thus fire has essentially the form of heat, and snow has essentially the form of cold. Accordingly fire, as it will not receive the form of cold, so neither will it receive snow: and snow, as it will not receive the form of heat, so neither will it receive fire. If fire comes, snow will either retire or will be destroyed. The Triad has always the Form of Oddness, and will never receive that of Evenness: the Dyad has always the Form of Evenness, and will never receive that of Oddness—upon the approach of this latter it will either disappear or will be destroyed: moreover the Dyad, while refusing to receive the Form of Oddness, will refuse also to receive that of the Triad, which always embodies that Form—although three is not in direct contrariety with two. If then we are asked, What is that, the presence of which makes a body hot? we need not confine ourselves to the answer—It is the Form of Heat —which, though correct, gives no new information: but we may farther say—It is Fire, which involves the Form of Heat. If we are asked, What is that, the presence of which makes a number odd, we shall not say—It is Oddness: but we shall say —It is the Triad or the Pentad—both of which involve Oddness.

the soul rests upon the assumption of the Platonic ideas. Reasoning to prove this.

In like manner, the question being asked, What is that, which, being in the body, will give it life? we must answer— It is the soul. The soul, when it lays hold of any body, always arrives bringing with it life. Now death is the contrary of life. Accordingly the soul, which always brings with it life, will never receive the contrary of life. In other words, it is deathless or immortal.[1]

The soul always brings life, and is essentially living. It cannot receive death; in other words, it is immortal.

[1] Plato, Phædon, p. 105 C-E. Ἀποκρίνου δή, ᾧ ἂν τί ἐγγένηται σώματι, ζῶν ἔσται; 'Ωι ἂν ψυχή, ἔφη. Οὐκοῦν ἀεὶ τοῦτο οὕτως ἔχει; Πῶς γὰρ οὐχί; ἦ δ' ὅς. Ἡ ψυχὴ ἄρα ὅ, τι ἂν αὐτὴ κατάσχῃ, ἀεὶ ἥκει ἐπ' ἐκεῖνο φέρουσα ζωήν; Ἥκει μέντοι, ἔφη. Πότερον δ' ἔστι τι ζωῇ ἐναντίον, ἢ οὐδέν; Ἔστιν, ἔφη. Τί; Θάνατος. Οὐκοῦν ἡ ψυχὴ τὸ ἐναντίον ᾧ αὐτὴ ἐπιφέρει ἀεὶ οὐ μή ποτε δέξηται, ὡς ἐκ τῶν πρόσθεν ὡμολόγηται; Καὶ μάλα σφόδρα, ἔφη ὁ Κέβης. . . . Ὁ δ'

Such is the ground upon which Sokrates rests his belief in the immortality of the soul. The doctrine reposes, in Plato's view, upon the assumption of eternal, self-existent, unchangeable, Ideas or Forms :[1] upon the congeniality of nature, and inherent correlation, between these Ideas and the Soul : upon the fact, that the soul knows these Ideas, which knowledge must have been acquired in a prior state of existence : and upon the essential participation of the soul in the Idea of life, so that it cannot be conceived as without life, or as dead.[2] The immortality of the soul is conceived as necessary and entire, including not merely post-existence, but also pre-existence. In fact the reference to an anterior time is more essential to Plato's theory than that to a posterior time ; because it is employed to explain the cognitions of the mind, and the identity of learning with reminiscence : while Simmias, who even at the close is not without

The proof of immortality includes pre-existence as well as post-existence—animals as well as man—also the metempsychosis, or translation of the soul from one body to another.

ἂν θάνατον μὴ δέχηται, τί καλοῦμεν; 'Αθάνατον, ἔφη. 'Αθάνατον ἄρα ἡ ψυχή; 'Αθάνατον.

Nemesius, the Christian bishop of Emesa, declares that the proofs given by Plato of the immortality of the soul are knotty and difficult to understand, such as even adepts in philosophical study can hardly follow. His own belief in it he rests upon the inspiration of the Christian Scriptures (Nemesius de Nat. Homin. c. 2, p. 55, ed. 1565).

[1] Plato, Phædon, pp. 76 D-E, 100 B-C. It is remarkable that in the Republic also, Sokrates undertakes to demonstrate the immortality of the soul : and that in doing so he does not make any reference or allusion to the arguments used in the Phædon, but produces another argument totally distinct and novel : an argument which Meiners remarks truly to be quite peculiar to Plato, Republic, x. pp. 609 E, 611 C ; Meiners, Geschichte der Wissenschaften, vol. ii. p. 780.

[2] Zeller, Philosophie der Griech. Part ii. p. 267.

" Die Seele ist ihrem Begriffe nach dasjenige, zu dessen Wesen es gehört zu leben—sie kann also in keinem Augenblicke als nicht lebend gedacht werden : In diesem ontologischen Beweis für die Unsterblichkeit, laufen nicht bloss alle die einzelnen Beweise des Phædon zusammen, sondern derselbe wird auch schon im Phaedrus vorgetragen," &c. Compare Phædrus, p. 245.

Hegel, in his Geschichte der Philosophie (Part ii. pp. 186-187-189, ed. 2), maintains that Plato did not conceive the soul as a separate thing or reality —that he did not mean to affirm, in the literal sense of the words, its separate existence either before or after the present life—that he did not descend to so crude a conception (zu dieser Rohheit herabzusinken) as to represent to himself the soul as a thing, or to enquire into its duration or continuance after the manner of a thing— that Plato understood the soul to exist essentially as the Universal Notion or Idea, the comprehensive aggregate of all other Ideas, in which sense he affirmed it to be immortal—that the descriptions which Plato gives of its condition, either before life or after death, are to be treated only as poetical metaphors. There is ingenuity in this view of Hegel, and many separate expressions of Plato receive light from it : but it appears to me to refine away too much. Plato had in his own mind and belief both the soul as a particular thing—and the soul as an universal. His language implies sometimes the one sometimes the other.

CHAP. XXV   BELIEF IN PRE-EXISTENCE.   415

reserve on the subject of the post-existence, proclaims an emphatic adhesion on that of the pre-existence.[1] The proof, moreover, being founded in great part on the Idea of Life, embraces every thing living, and is common to animals[2] (if not to plants) as well as to men : and the metempsychosis—or transition of souls not merely from one human body to another, but also from the human to the animal body, and *vice versâ*—is a portion of the Platonic creed.

Having completed his demonstration of the immortality of the soul, Sokrates proceeds to give a sketch of the condition and treatment which it experiences after death. The Νεκυία here following is analogous, in general doctrinal scope, to those others which we read in the Republic and in the Gorgias : but all of them are different in particular incidents, illustrative circumstances, and scenery. The sentiment of belief in Plato's mind attaches itself to general doctrines, which appear to him to possess an evidence independent of particulars. When he applies these doctrines to particulars, he makes little distinction between such as are true, or problematical, or fictitious : he varies his mythes at pleasure, provided that they serve the purpose of illustrating his general view. The mythe which we read in the Phædon includes a description of the Earth which to us appears altogether imaginative and poetical : yet it is hardly more so than several other current theories, proposed by various philosophers antecedent and contemporary, respecting Earth and Sea. Aristotle criticises the views expressed in the Phædon, as he criticises those of Demokritus and Empedokles.[3] Each soul of a deceased person is conducted by his Genius to the proper place, and there receives sentence of condemnation to suffering, greater or less according

After finishing his proof that the soul is immortal, Sokrates enters into a description, what will become of it after the death of the body. He describes a Νεκυία.

---

[1] Plato, Phædon, pp. 92 D, 107 B.
[2] See what Sokrates says about the swans, Phædon, p. 85 A-B.
[3] Plato, Phædon, pp. 107-111. Olympiodorus pronounces the mythe to be a good imitation of the truth, Republ. x. 620 seq. ; Gorgias, p. 520 ; Aristotle, Meteorol. ii. pp. 355-356. Compare also 356, b. 10, 357, a. 25, where he states and canvasses the doctrines of Demokritus and Empedokles ; also 352, a. 35, about the ἀρχαῖοι θεόλογοι. He is rather more severe upon these others than upon Plato. He too considers, like Plato, that the amount of evidence which you ought to require for your belief depends upon the nature of the subject ; and that there are various subjects on which you ought to believe on slighter evidence : see Metaphysic. A. 995, a. 2-16 ; Ethic. Nikom. i. 1, 1094, b. 12-14.

to his conduct in life, in the deep chasm called Tartarus, and in the rivers of mud and fire, Styx, Kokytus, Pyriphlegethon.[1] To those who have passed their lives in learning, and who have detached themselves as much as they possibly could from all pleasures and all pursuits connected with the body—in order to pursue wisdom and virtue—a full reward is given. They are emancipated from the obligation of entering another body, and are allowed to live ever afterwards disembodied in the pure regions of Ideas.[2]

Such, or something like it, Sokrates confidently expects will be the fate awaiting himself.[3] When asked by Kriton, among other questions, how he desired to be buried, he replies with a smile—"You may bury me as you choose, if you can only catch me. But you will not understand me when I tell you, that I, Sokrates, who am now speaking, shall not remain with you after having drunk the poison, but shall depart to some of the enjoyments of the blest. You must not talk about burying or burning Sokrates, as if I were suffering some terrible operation. Such language is inauspicious and depressing to our minds. Keep up your courage, and talk only of burying the body of Sokrates: conduct the burial as you think best and most decent."[4]

Sokrates expects that his soul is going to the islands of the blest. Reply to Kriton about burying his body.

Sokrates then retires with Kriton into an interior chamber to bathe, desiring that the women may be spared the task of washing his body after his decease. Having taken final leave of his wife and children, he returns to his friends as sunset is approaching. We are here made to see the contrast between him and other prisoners under like circumstances. The attendant of the Eleven Magistrates comes to warn him that the

Preparations for administering the hemlock. Sympathy of the gaoler. Equanimity of Sokrates.

---

[1] Plato, Phædon, pp. 111-112. Compare Eusebius, Præp. Ev. xiii. 13, and Arnobius adv. Gentes, ii. 14. Arnobius blames Plato for inconsistency in saying that the soul is immortal in its own nature, and yet that it suffers pain after death—"Rem inenodabilem suscipit (Plato) ut cum animas dicat immortales, pérpetuas, et ex corporali soliditate privatas, puniri eas dicat tamen et doloris afficiat sensu. Quis autem hominum non videt quod sit immortale, quod simplex, nullum posse dolorem admittere; quod autem sentiat dolorem, immortalitatem habere non posse?"

[2] Plato, Phædon, p. 114 C-E. τούτων δὲ αὐτῶν οἱ φιλοσοφίᾳ ἱκανῶς καθηράμενοι ἄνευ τε σωμάτων ζῶσι τὸ παράπαν εἰς τὸν ἔπειτα χρόνον, &c.

[3] Plato, Phædon, p. 115 A.

[4] Plato, Phædon, p. 115 D. ὡς ἐπειδὰν πίω τὸ φάρμακον οὐκέτι ὑμῖν παραμενῶ, ἀλλ' οἰχήσομαι ἀπιὼν εἰς μακάρων δή τινας εὐδαιμονίας.

hour has come for swallowing the poison : expressing sympathy and regret for the necessity of delivering so painful a message, together with admiration for the equanimity and rational judgment of Sokrates, which he contrasts forcibly with the discontent and wrath of other prisoners under similar circumstances. As he turned away with tears in his eyes, Sokrates exclaimed—"How courteous the man is to me—and has been from the beginning! how generously he now weeps for me! Let us obey him, and let the poison be brought forthwith, if it be prepared: if not, let him prepare it." "Do not hurry" (interposed Kriton): "there is still time, for the sun is not quite set. I have known others who, even after receiving the order, deferred drinking the poison until they had had a good supper and other enjoyments." "It is natural that they should do so" (replied Sokrates). "They think that they are gainers by it: for me, it is natural that I should not do so—for I shall gain nothing but contempt in my own eyes, by thus clinging to life, and saving up when there is nothing left."[1]

Kriton accordingly gave orders, and the poison, after a certain interval, was brought in. Sokrates, on asking for directions, was informed, that after having swallowed it, he must walk about until his legs felt heavy : he must then lie down and cover himself up : the poison would do its work. He took the cup without any symptom of alarm or change of countenance: then looking at the attendant with his usual full and fixed gaze, he asked whether there was enough to allow of a libation. "We prepare as much as is sufficient" (was the answer), "but no more." "I understand" (said Sokrates): "but at least I may pray, and I must pray, to the Gods, that my change of abode from here to there may be fortunate." He then put the cup to his lips, and drank it off with perfect ease and tranquillity.[2]

Sokrates swallows the poison. Conversation with the gaoler.

His friends, who had hitherto maintained their self-control, were overpowered by emotion on seeing the cup swallowed, and broke out into violent tears and lamentation. No one was unmoved, except Sokrates him-

Ungovernable sorrow of the friends

---

[1] Plato, Phædon, p. 117 A. γλιχόμενος τοῦ ζῆν, καὶ φειδόμενος οὐδενὸς ἔτι ἐνόντος.
Hesiod. Opp. et Dies, 367. δειλὴ δ' ἐνὶ πυθμένι φειδώ.
[2] Plato, Phædon, p. 117 C.

418   PHÆDON.   CHAP. XXV.

present. Self-command of Sokrates. Last words to Kriton, and death. self: who gently remonstrated with them, and exhorted them to tranquil resignation: reminding them that nothing but good words was admissible at the hour of death. The friends, ashamed of themselves, found means to repress their tears. Sokrates walked about until he felt heavy in the legs, and then lay down in bed. After some interval, the attendant of the prison came to examine his feet and legs, pinched his foot with force, and enquired whether he felt it. Sokrates replied in the negative. Presently the man pinched his legs with similar result, and showed to the friends in that way that his body was gradually becoming chill and benumbed: adding that as soon as this should get to the heart, he would die.[1] The chill had already reached his belly, when Sokrates uncovered his face, which had been hitherto concealed by the bed-clothes, and spoke his last words:[2] " Kriton,

Plato, Phædon, p. 118. These details receive interesting confirmation from the remarkable scene described by Valerius Maximus, as witnessed by himself at Julis in the island of Keos, when he accompanied Sextus Pompeius into Asia (Val. M. ii. 6, 8). A Keian lady of rank, ninety years of age, well in health, comfortable, and in full possession of her intelligence, but deeming it prudent (according to the custom in Keos, Strabo, x. p. 486) to retire from life while she had as yet nothing to complain of—took poison, by her own deliberate act, in the presence of her relatives and of Sextus Pompeius, who vainly endeavoured to dissuade her. "Cupido haustu mortiferam traxit potionem, ac sermone significans quasnam subindè partes corporis suis rigor occupâret, cum jam visceribus eum et cordi imminere esset elocuta, filiarum manus ad supremum opprimendorum oculorum officium advocavit. Nostros autem, tametsi novo spectaculo obstupefacti erant, suffusos tamen lacrimis dimisit."

[2] Plato, Phædon, p. 118. ἤδη οὖν σχεδόν τι αὐτοῦ ἦν τὰ περὶ τὸ ἦτρον ψυχόμενα, καὶ ἐκκαλυψάμενος (ἐνεκεκάλυπτο γὰρ) εἶπεν, ὃ δὴ τελευταῖον ἐφθέγξατο, *Ὦ Κρίτων, ἔφη, τῷ Ἀσκληπιῷ ὀφείλομεν ἀλεκτρυόνα· ἀλλ' ἀπόδοτε καὶ μὴ ἀμελήσητε.*

Cicero, after recovering from a bilious attack, writes to his wife Terentia (Epist. Famil. xiv. 7): "Omnes molestias et solicitudines deposui et ejeci.

Quid causæ autem fuerit, postridié intellexi quam à vobis discessi. Χολὴν ἄκρατον noctu ejeci: statim ita sum levatus, ut mihi Deus aliquis medicinam fecisse videatur. Cui quidem Deo, quemadmodum tu soles, pié et casté satisfacies: id est, Apollini et Æsculapio." Compare the rhetor Aristeides, Orat. xlv. pp. 22-23-155, ed. Dindorf. About the habit of sacrificing a cock to Æsculapius, see also a passage in the Ἱερῶν Λόγοι of the rhetor Aristeides (Orat. xxvii. p. 545, ed. Dindorf, at the top of the page). I will add that the five Ἱερῶν Λόγοι of that Rhetor (Oratt. xxiii.-xxvii.) are curious as testifying the multitude of dreams and revelations vouchsafed to him by Æsculapius : also the implicit faith with which he acted upon them in his maladies, and the success which attended the curative prescriptions thus made known to him. Aristeides declares himself to place more confidence in these revelations than in the advice of physicians, and to have often acted on them in preference to such advice (Orat. xlv. pp. 20-22, Dind.).

The direction here given by Sokrates to Kriton (though some critics, even the most recent, see Krische, Lehren der Griechischen Denker, p. 227, interpret it in a mystical sense) is to be understood simply and literally, in my judgment. On what occasion, or for what, he had made the vow of the cock, we are not told. Sokrates was a very religious man, much influenced

we owe a cock to Æsculapius : pay the debt without fail." "It shall be done" (answered Kriton) ; "have you any other injunctions?" Sokrates made no reply, but again covered himself up.[1] After a short interval, he made some movement : the attendant presently uncovered him, and found him dead, with his eyes stiff and fixed. Kriton performed the last duty of closing both his eyes and his mouth.

The pathetic details of this scene—arranged with so much dramatic beauty, and lending imperishable interest to the Phædon of Plato—may be regarded as real facts, described from the recollection of an eye-witness, though many years after their occurrence. They present to us the personality of Sokrates in full harmony with that which we read in the Platonic Apology. The tranquil ascendancy of resolute and rational conviction, satisfied with the past, and welcoming instead of fearing the close of life—is exhibited as triumphing in the one case over adverse accusers and judges, in the other case over the unnerving manifestations of afflicted friends.

Extreme pathos, and probable trustworthiness of these personal details.

But though the personal incidents of this dialogue are truly Sokratic—the dogmatic emphasis, and the apparatus of argument and hypothesis, are essentially Platonic. In these respects, the dialogue contrasts remarkably with the Apology. When addressing the Dikasts, Sokrates not only makes no profession of dogmatic certainty, but expressly disclaims it. Nay more—he considers that the false persuasion of such dogmatic certainty, universally prevalent among his countrymen, is as pernicious as it is illusory : and that his own superiority over others consists merely in consciousness of his own ignorance, while they are unconscious of theirs.[2] To dissipate such false persuasion of knowledge, by perpetual cross-examination of every one around, is the special mission imposed upon him by the Gods : in which mission, indeed, he has the firmest belief—but it is a belief, like

Contrast between the Platonic Apology and the Phædon.

---

by prophecies, oracles, dreams, and special revelations (Plato, Apol. Sokr. pp. 21-29-33 ; also Phædon, p. 60).

[1] Euripid. Hippol. 1455.

Κεκαρτέρηται τἀμ'· ὄλωλα γάρ, πάτερ.

Κρῦψον δέ μου πρόσωπον ὡς τάχος πέπλοις.

[2] Plato, Apol. Sokr. pp. 21-29. καὶ τοῦτο πῶς οὐκ ἀμαθία ἐστὶν αὕτη ἡ ἐπονείδιστος, ἡ τοῦ οἴεσθαι εἰδέναι ἃ οὐκ οἶδεν; (29 A-B).

that in his Dæmon or divine sign, depending upon oracles, dreams, and other revelations peculiar to himself, which he does not expect that the Dikasts will admit as genuine evidence.[1] One peculiar example, whereby Sokrates exemplifies the false persuasion of knowledge where men have no real knowledge, is borrowed from the fear of death. No man knows (he says) what death is, not even whether it may not be a signal benefit: yet every man fears it as if he well knew that it was the greatest evil.[2] Death must be one of two things: either a final extinction—a perpetual and dreamless sleep—or else a transference of the soul to some other place. Sokrates is persuaded that it will be in either case a benefit to him, and that the Gods will take care that he, a good man, shall suffer no evil, either living or dead: the proof of which is, to him, that the divine sign has

[1] Plato, Apol. Sokr. pp. 21-23, 31 D; 33 C: ἐμοὶ δὲ τοῦτο, ὡς ἐγώ φημι, προστέτακται ὑπὸ τοῦ θεοῦ πράττειν καὶ ἐκ μαντειῶν καὶ ἐξ ἐνυπνίων καὶ παντὶ τρόπῳ, ᾧπέρ τίς ποτε καὶ ἄλλη θεία μοῖρα ἀνθρώπῳ καὶ ὁτιοῦν προσέταξε πράττειν. p. 37 E: ἐάν τε γὰρ λέγω ὅτι τῷ θεῷ ἀπειθεῖν τοῦτ' ἐστὶ καὶ διὰ τοῦτ' ἀδύνατον ἡσυχίαν ἄγειν, οὐ πείσεσθέ μοι ὡς εἰρωνευομένῳ.

[2] Plato, Apol. S. p. 29 B.

In the Xenophontic Apology of Sokrates, no allusion is made to the immortality of the soul. Sokrates is there described as having shaped his defence under a belief that he had arrived at a term when it was better for him to die than to live, and that prolonged life would only expose him to the unavoidable weaknesses and disabilities of senility. It is a proof of the benevolence of the Gods that he is withdrawn from life at so opportune a moment. This is the explanation which Xenophon gives of the haughty tone of the defence (sects. 6-15-23-27). In the Xenophontic Cyropædia, Cyrus, on his death-bed, addresses earnest exhortations to his two sons: and to give greater force to such exhortations, reminds them that his own soul will still survive and will still exercise a certain authority after his death. He expresses his own belief not only that the soul survives the body, but also that it becomes more rational when disembodied; because—1. Murderers are disturbed by the souls of murdered men. 2. Honours are paid to deceased persons, which practice would not continue, unless the souls of the deceased had efficacy to enforce it. 3. The souls of living men are more rational during sleep than when awake, and sleep affords the nearest analogy to death (viii. 7, 17-21). (Much the same arguments were urged in the dialogues of Aristotle. Bernays, Dialog. Aristot. pp. 23-105.) He however adds, that even if he be mistaken in this point, and if his soul perish with his body, still he conjures his sons, in the name of the Gods, to obey his dying injunctions (s. 22). Again, he says (s. 27), "Invite all the Persians to my tomb, to join with me in satisfaction that I shall now be in safety, so as to suffer no farther harm, whether I am united to the divine element, or perish altogether" (συνησθησομένους ἐμοί, ὅτι ἐν τῷ ἀσφαλεῖ ἤδη ἔσομαι, ὡς μηδὲν ἂν ἔτι κακὸν παθεῖν, μήτε ἢν μετὰ τοῦ θείου γένωμαι, μήτε ἢν μηδὲν ἔτι ᾦ). The view taken here by Cyrus, of death in its analogy with sleep (ὕπνῳ καὶ θανάτῳ διδυμάοσιν, Iliad, xvi. 672) as a refuge against impending evil for the future, is much the same as that taken by Sokrates in his Apology. Sokrates is not less proud of his past life, spent in dialectic debate, than Cyrus of his glorious exploits. Ὁ θάνατος, λιμὴν κακῶν τοῖς δυσδαιμονεῦσιν, Longinus, de Subl. c. 9, p. 23. Compare also the Oration of Julius Cæsar in Sallust, Bell. Catilin. c. 51—"in luctu atque miseriis, mortem ærumnarum requiem, non cruciatum esse: illam cuncta mortalium mala dissolvere: ultra neque curæ neque gaudio locum esse".

CHAP. XXV.   OPINION OF SOKRATES ON DEATH.   421

never interposed any obstruction in regard to his trial and sentence. If (says he) I am transferred to some other abode, among those who have died before me, how delightful will it be to see Homer and Hesiod, Orpheus and Musæus, Agamemnon, Ajax or Palamêdes—and to pass my time in cross-examining each as to his true or false knowledge![1] Lastly, so far as he professes to aim at any positive end, it is the diffusion of political, social, human virtue, as distinguished from acquisitions above the measure of humanity. He tells men that it is not wealth which produces virtue, but virtue which produces wealth and other advantages, both public and private.[2]

If from the Apology we turn to the Phædon, we seem to pass, not merely to the same speaker after the interval of one month (the ostensible interval indicated) but to a different speaker and over a long period. We have Plato speaking through the mouth of Sokrates, and Plato too at a much later time.[3] Though the moral character (ἦθος) of Sokrates is fully maintained and even strikingly dramatised—the intellectual personality is altogether transformed. Instead of a speaker *Abundant dogmatic and poetical invention of the Phædon compared with the profession of ignorance which we read in the Apology.* who avows his own ignorance, and blames others only for believing themselves to know when they are equally ignorant—we have one who indulges in the widest range of theory and the boldest employment of hypothesis. Plato introduces his own dogmatical and mystical views, leaning in part on the Orphic and Pythagorean creeds.[4] He declares the distinctness of nature, the incompatibility, the forced temporary union and active conflict, between the soul and the body. He includes this in the still wider and more general declaration, which recognises antithesis between the two worlds : the world of Ideas, Forms, Essences, not perceivable but only cogitable, eternal, and unchangeable, with which the soul or mind was in kindred and communion—the world of sense, or of transient and ever-

---

[1] Plato, Apol. S. pp. 40-41.
[2] Plato, Apol. S. pp. 20 C, 29-30. λέγων ὅτι οὐκ ἐκ χρημάτων ἀρετὴ γίγνεται, ἀλλ' ἐξ ἀρετῆς χρήματα, καὶ τἆλλα ἀγαθὰ τοῖς ἀνθρώποις ἅπαντα, καὶ ἰδίᾳ καὶ δημοσίᾳ (30 B). Compare Xenophon, Memorab. i. 2, 8-9.
[3] In reviewing the Apology (supra,

vol. i. ch. ix. p. 410) I have already noticed this very material discrepancy, which is insisted upon by Ast as an argument for disallowing the genuineness of the Apology.

[4] Plato, Phædon, pp. 69 C, 70 C, 81 C, 62 B.

changing appearances or phenomena, never arriving at permanent existence, but always coming and going, with which the body was in commerce and harmony. The philosopher, who thirsts only after knowledge and desires to look at things[1] as they are in themselves, with his mind by itself—is represented as desiring, throughout all his life, to loosen as much as possible the implication of his soul with his body, and as rejoicing when the hour of death arrives to divorce them altogether.

Such total renunciation of the body is put, with dramatic propriety, into the mouth of Sokrates during the last hour of his life. But it would not have been in harmony with the character of Sokrates as other Platonic dialogues present him—in the plenitude of life— manifesting distinguished bodily strength and soldierly efficiency, proclaiming gymnastic training for the body to be co-ordinate with musical training for the mind, and impressed with the most intense admiration for the personal beauty of youth. The human body, which in the Phædon is discredited as a morbid incumbrance corrupting the purity of the soul, is presented to us by Sokrates in the Phædrus as the only sensible object which serves as a mirror and reflection of the beauty of the ideal world :[2] while the Platonic Timæus proclaims (in language not unsuitable to Locke) that sight, hearing, and speech are the sources of our abstract Ideas, and the generating causes of speculative intellect and philosophy.[3] Of these, and of the world of sense generally, an opposite view was appropriate in the Phædon ; where the purpose of Sokrates is to console his distressed friends by showing

Totalrenunciation and discredit of the body in the Phædon. Different feeling about the body in other Platonic dialogues.

---

[1] Plato, Phædon, p. 66 E. ἀπαλλακτέον αὐτοῦ (τοῦ σώματος) καὶ αὐτῇ τῇ ψυχῇ θεατέον αὐτὰ τὰ πράγματα.
[2] Plato, Charmidês, p. 155 D. Protagoras, init. Phædrus, p. 250 D. Symposion, pp. 177 C, 210 A.
Æschines, one of the Socratici viri or fellow disciples of Sokrates along with Plato, composed dialogues (of the same general nature as those of Plato) wherein Sokrates was introduced conversing or arguing. Æschines placed in the mouth of Sokrates the most intense expressions of passionate admiration towards the person of Alkibiades. See the Fragments cited by the Rhetor Aristeides, Orat. xlv. pp. 20-23, ed. Dindorf. Aristeides mentions (p. 24) that various persons in his time mistook these expressions ascribed to Sokrates for the real talk of Sokrates himself. Compare also the Symposion of Xenophon, iv. 27.

[3] Plato, Timæus, p. 47, A-D. Consult also the same dialogue, pp. 87-88, where Plato insists on the necessity of co-ordinate attention both to mind and to body, and on the mischiefs of highly developed force in the mind unless it be accompanied by a corresponding development of force in the body.

that death was no misfortune, but relief from a burthen. And Plato has availed himself of this impressive situation,[1] to recommend, with every charm of poetical expression, various characteristic dogmas respecting the essential distinction between Ideas and the intelligible world on one side—Perceptions and the sensible world on the other : respecting the soul, its nature akin to the intelligible world, its pre-existence anterior to its present body, and its continued existence after the death of the latter: respecting the condition of the soul before birth and after death, its transition, in the case of most men, into other bodies, either human or animal, with the condition of suffering penalties commensurate to the wrongs committed in this life : finally, respecting the privilege accorded to the souls of such as have passed their lives in intellectual and philosophical occupation, that they shall after death remain for ever disembodied, in direct communion with the world of Ideas.

The main part of Plato's argumentation, drawn from the general assumptions of his philosophy, is directed to prove the separate and perpetual existence of the soul, before as well as after the body. These arguments, interesting as specimens of the reasoning which satisfied Plato, do not prove his conclusion.[2] But even if

Plato's argument does not prove the immortality of the soul. Even if it

---

[1] Compare the description of the last discourse of Pætus Thrasea. Tacitus, Annal. xvi. 34.

[2] Wyttenbach has annexed to his edition of the Phædon an instructive review of the argumentation contained in it respecting the Immortality of the soul. He observes justly—" Videamus jam de Phædone, qui ab omni antiquitate is habitus est liber, in quo rationes immortalitatis animarum gravissimé luculentissiméque exposita essent. Quæ quidem libro laus et auctoritas conciliata est, non tam firmitate argumentorum, quam eloquentiâ Platonis," &c. (Disputat. De Placit. Immort. Anim. p. 10). The same feeling, substantially, is expressed by one of the disputants in Cicero's Tusculan Disputations, who states that he assented to the reasoning while he was reading the dialogue, but that as soon as he had laid down the book, his assent all slipped away from him. I have already mentioned that Panætius, an extreme admirer of Plato on most points, dissented from him about the immortality of the soul (Cicero, Tusc. Disp. i. 11, 24 —i. 32, 79), and declared the Phædon to be spurious. Galen also mentions (De Format. Fœtûs, vol. iv. pp. 700-702. Kühn) that he had written a special treatise (now lost) to prove that the reasonings in the Phædon were self contradictory, and that he could not satisfy himself, either about the essence of the soul, or whether it was mortal or immortal. Compare his treatise Περὶ Οὐσίας τῶν φυσικῶν δυνάμεων— iv. pp. 762-763—and Περὶ τῶν τῆς Ψυχῆς ἠθῶν, iv. 773. In this last passage, he represents the opinion of Plato to be—That the two inferior souls, the courageous and the appetitive, are mortal, in which he (Galen) agrees, and that the rational soul alone is immortal, of which he (Galen) is not persuaded. Now this view of Plato's opinion is derived from the Republic and Timæus, not from the Phædon, in which last the triple soul is not acknowledged. We may thus partly

did prove that, yet the mode of pre-existence, and the mode of post-existence, of the soul, would be quite undetermined.

that conclusion were admitted to be proved, the condition of the soul, during such anterior and posterior existence, would be altogether undetermined, and would be left to the free play of sentiment and imagination. There is no subject upon which the poetical genius of Plato has been more abundantly exercised.[1] He has given us two different descriptions of the state of the soul before its junction with the body (Timæus, and Phædrus), and three different descriptions of its destiny after separation from the body (Republic, Gorgias, Phædon). In all the three, he supposes an adjudication and classification of the departed souls, and a better or worse fate allotted to each according to the estimate which he forms of their merits or demerits during life : but in each of the three, this general idea is carried out by a different machinery. The Hades of Plato is not announced even by himself as anything more than approximation to the truth : but it embodies his own ethical and judicial sentence on the classes of men around him—as the Divina Commedia embodies that of Dante on antecedent individual persons. Plato distributes rewards and penalties in the measure which he conceives to be deserved : he erects his own approbation and disapprobation, his own sympathy and antipathy, into laws of the unknown future state : the Gods, whom he postulates, are imaginary agents introduced to execute the sentences which he dictates. While others, in their conceptions of posthumous existence, assured the happiest fate, sometimes even divinity itself, to great warriors and law-givers—to devoted friends and patriots like Harmodius and Aristogeiton—to the exquisite beauty of Helen—or to favourites of the Gods like Ganymêdes or Pelops [2]—Plato claims that supreme distinction for the departed philosopher.

---

understand the inconsistencies, which Galen pointed out in his lost Treatise, in the argumentation of the Phædon : wherein one of the proofs presented to establish the immortality of the soul is—That the soul is inseparably and essentially identified with life, and cannot admit death (p. 105 D). This argument, if good at all, is just as good to prove the immortality of the two inferior souls, as of the superior and rational soul. Galen might therefore remark that it did not consist with the conclusion which he drew from the Timæus and the Republic.

[1] Wyttenbach, l. c. p. 19. "Vidimus de philosophâ hujus loci parte, quâ demonstratur, Animos esse immortales. Altera pars, quâ ostenditur, qualis sit ille post hanc vitam status, fabulosé et poeticé à Platone tractata est," &c.

[2] Skolion of Kallistratus, Antholog. Græc. p. 155. Isokrates, Encomium

THE PHILOSOPHER AFTER DEATH.

The Philosopher, as a recompense for having detached himself during life as much as possible from the body and all its functions, will be admitted after death to existence as a soul pure and simple, unattached to any body. The souls of all other persons, dying with more or less of the taint of the body attached to each of them,[1] and for that reason haunting the tombs in which the bodies are buried, so as to become visible there as ghosts—are made subject, in the Platonic Hades, to penalty and purification suitable to the respective condition of each; after which they become attached to new bodies, sometimes of men, sometimes of other animals. Of this distributive scheme it is not possible to frame any clear idea, nor is Plato consistent with himself except in a few material features. But one feature there is in it which stands conspicuous —the belief in the metempsychosis, or transfer of the same soul from one animal body to another: a belief very widely diffused throughout the ancient world, associated with the immortality of the soul, pervading the Orphic and Pythagorean creeds, and having its root in the Egyptian and Oriental religions.[2]

The philosopher will enjoy an existence of pure soul, unattached to any body.

Helenæ, Or. x. s. 70-72. Compare the Νέκυια of the Odyssey and that of the Æneid, respecting the heroes—
  "Quæ gratia currûm
Armorumque fuit vivis, quæ cura nitentes
Pascere equos, eadem sequitur tellure repostos." (Æn. vi. 653-5.)

[1] Plato, Phædon, p. 81 C-D. ὁ δὴ καὶ ἔχουσα ἡ τοιαύτη ψυχὴ βαρύνεται τε καὶ ἕλκεται πάλιν εἰς τὸν ὁρατὸν τόπον, φόβῳ τοῦ ἀειδοῦς τε καὶ Ἅιδου, ὥσπερ λέγεται, περὶ τὰ μνήματά τε καὶ τοὺς τάφους καλινδουμένη· περὶ ἃ δὴ καὶ ὤφθη ἄττα ψυχῶν σκιοειδῆ φαντάσματα οἷα παρέχονται αἱ τοιαῦται ψυχαὶ εἴδωλα, αἱ μὴ καθαρῶς ἀπολυθεῖσαι, ἀλλὰ τοῦ ὁρατοῦ μετέχουσαι, διὸ καὶ ὁρῶνται.

Lactantius—in replying to the arguments of Demokritus, Epikurus, and Dikæarchus against the immortality of the soul—reminded them that any *Magus* would produce visible evidence to refute them; by calling up before them the soul of any deceased person to give information and predict the future—" qui profecto non auderent de animarum interitu mago præsente disserere, qui sciret certis carminibus cieri ab infernis animas et adesse et præbere se videndas et loqui et futura prædicere: et si auderent, re ipsâ et documentis præsentibus vincerentur" (Lactant. Inst. vii. 13). See Cicero, Tusc. Disp. i. 31.

[2] Compare the closing paragraph of the Platonic Timæus: Virgil, Æneid vi. 713, Herodot. ii. 123, Pausanias, iv. 32, 4, Sextus Empiric. adv. Math. ix. 127, with the citation from Empedokles:—
"Tum pater Anchises: 'Animæ quibus altera fato
Corpora debentur, Lethæi ad fluminis undam
Securos latices et longa oblivia potant'."

The general doctrine, upon which the Metempsychosis rests, is set forth by Virgil in the fine lines which follow, 723-751; compare Georgic iv. 218. The souls of men, beasts, birds, and fishes, are all of them detached fragments or portions from the universal soul, mind, or life, ætherial or igneous, which pervades the whole Kosmos. The soul of each individual thus detached to be conjoined with a distinct body, be-

We are told that one vehement admirer of Plato — the Ambrakiot Kleombrotus — was so profoundly affected and convinced by reading the Phædon, that he immediately terminated his existence by leaping from a high wall; though in other respects well satisfied with life. But the number of persons who derived from it such settled conviction, was certainly not considerable. Neither the doctrine nor the reasonings of Plato were adopted even by the immediate successors in his school: still less by Aristotle and the Peripatetics — or by the Stoics — or by the Epikureans. The Epikureans denied altogether the survivorship of soul over body: Aristotle gives a definition of the soul which involves this same negation, though he admits as credible the separate existence of the rational soul, without individuality or personality. The Stoics, while affirming the soul to

Plato's demonstration of the immortality of the soul did not appear satisfactory to subsequent philosophers. The question remained debated and problematical.

comes tainted by such communion; after death it is purified by penalties, measured according to the greater or less taint, and becomes then fit to be attached to a new body, yet not until it has drunk the water of Lêthê (Plato, Philêbus, p. 30 A; Timæus, p. 30 B).

The statement of Nemesius is remarkable, that all Greeks who believed the immortality of the soul, believed also in the metempsychosis — Κοινῇ μὲν οὖν πάντες Ἕλληνες, οἱ τὴν ψυχὴν ἀθάνατον ἀποφηνάμενοι, τὴν μετενσωμάτωσιν δογματίζουσιν (De Naturâ Hominis, cap. ii. p. 50, ed. 1565). Plato accepted the Egyptian and Pythagorean doctrine, continued in the Orphic mysteries (Arnob. adv. Gentes, ii. 16), making no essential distinction between the souls of men and those of animals, and recognising reciprocal interchange from the one to the other. The Platonists adhered to this doctrine fully, down to the third century A.D., including Plotinus, Numenius, and others. But Porphyry, followed by Jamblichus, introduced a modification of this creed, denying the possibility of transition of a human soul into the body of another animal, or of the soul of any other animal into the body of a man, — yet still recognising the transition from one human body to another, and from one animal body to another. (See Alkinous, Introd. in Platon. c. 25.) This subject is well handled in a learned work published in 1712 by a Jesuit of Toulouse, Michel Mourgues. He shows in opposition to Dacier and others, who interpreted the doctrine in a sense merely spiritual and figurative) that the metempsychosis was a literal belief of the Platonists down to the time of Proklus. "Les quatre Platoniciens qui ont tenu la Transmigration bornée" (*i.e.* from one human body into another human body) "n'ont pas laissé d'admettre la pluralité d'animations ou de vies d'une même âme: et cela sans figure et sans métaphore. Cet article, qui est l'essentiel, n'a jamais trouvé un seul contradicteur dans les sectes qui ont cru l'âme immortelle: ni Porphyre, ni Hiérocle, ni Procle, ni Salluste, n'ont jamais touché à ce point que pour l'approuver. D'où il suit que la réalité de la Métempsychose est indubitable; c'est à dire, qu'il est indubitable que tous les sectateurs de Pythagore et de Platon l'ont soutenue dans un sens très réel quant à la pluralité des vies et d'animations" (Tom. i. p. 525: also Tom. ii. p. 432). M. Cousin and M. Barthélemy St. Hilaire are of the same opinion.

M. Barthélemy St. Hilaire observes, in his Premier Mémoire sur le Sankhyâ, p. 416, Paris, 1852.

"Voilà donc la transmigration dans les plus grands dialogues de Platon — le Timée, la République, le Phèdre, le Phédon. On peut en retrouver la

be material as well as the body, considered it as a detached fragment of the all-pervading cosmical or mundane soul, which was re-absorbed after the death of the individual into the great whole to which it belonged. None of these philosophers were persuaded by the arguments of Plato. The popular orthodoxy, which he often censures harshly, recognised some sort of posthumous existence as a part of its creed; and the uninquiring multitude continued in the teaching and traditions of their youth. But literary and philosophical men, who sought to form some opinion for themselves without altogether rejecting (as the Epikureans rejected) the basis of the current traditions—were in no better condition for deciding the question with the assistance of Plato, than they would have been without him. While the knowledge of the bodily organism, and of mind or soul as embodied therein, received important additions, from Aristotle down to Galen—no new facts either were known or could become known, respecting soul *per se*, considered as pre-existent or post-existent to body. Galen expressly records his dissatisfaction with Plato on this point, though generally among his warmest admirers. Questions of this kind remained always problematical, standing themes for rhetoric or dialectic.[1] Every man could do,

trace manifeste dans d'autres dialogues moins considérables, le Menon et le Politique, par exemple. La transmigration est même positivement indiquée dans le dixième Livre des Lois, où Platon traite avec tant de force et de solennité de la providence et de la justice divines.

"En présence de témoignages si serieux, et de tant de persistance à revenir sur des opinions qui ne varient pas, je crois que tout esprit sensé ne peut que partager l'avis de M. Cousin. Il est impossible que Platon ne se fasse de l'exposition de ces opinions qu'un pur badinage. Il les a répetées, sans les modifier en rien, au milieu des discussions les plus graves et les plus étendues. Ajoutez que ces doctrines tiennent intimément à toutes celles qui sont le fond même du platonisme, et qu'elles s'y entrelacent si étroitement, que les en détacher, c'est le mutiler et l'amoindrir. Le système des Idées ne se comprend pas tout entier sans la réminiscence : et la réminiscence elle même implique nécessairement l'existence antérieure de l'âme."

Dr. Henry More, in his 'Treatise on the Immortality of the Soul,' argues at considerable length in defence of the pre-existence of each soul, as a part of the doctrine. He considers himself to have clearly proved—"That the pre-existence of the soul is an opinion both in itself the most rational that can be maintained, and has had the suffrage of the most renowned philosophers in all ages of the world". Of these last-mentioned philosophers he gives a list, as follows—Moses, on the authority of the Jewish Cabbala—Zoroaster, Pythagoras, Epicharmus, Empedocles, Cebês, Euripides, Plato, Euclid, Philo, Virgil, Marcus Cicero, Plotinus, Jamblichus, Proclus, Boethius, Psellus, Synesius, Origen, Marsilius Ficinus, &c. See chapters xii. and xiii. pages 116, 117, 121 of his Treatise. Compare also what he says in Sect. 18 of his Preface General, page xx.-xxiv.

[1] Seneca says, Epist. 88. "Innumerabiles sunt quæstiones de animo: unde sit, qualis sit, quando esse incipiat, quamdiu sit; an aliunde aliò transeat, et domicilium mutet, ad alias animalium formas aliasque conjectus, an

though not with the same exuberant eloquence, what Plato had done—and no man could do more. Every man could coin his own hopes and fears, his own æsthetical preferences and repugnances, his own ethical aspiration to distribute rewards and punishments among the characters around him—into affirmative prophecies respecting an unknowable future, where neither verification nor Elenchus were accessible. The state of this discussion throughout the Pagan world bears out the following remark of Lord Macaulay, with which I conclude the present chapter :—

"There are branches of knowledge with respect to which the law of the human mind is progress. . . . But with theology, the case is very different. As respects natural religion—revelation being for the present altogether left out of the question—it is not easy to see that a philosopher of the present day is more favourably situated than Thales or Simonides. . . . As to the other great question—the question, what becomes of man after death—we do not see that a highly educated European, left to his unassisted reason, is more likely to be in the right than a Blackfoot Indian. Not a single one of the many sciences in which we surpass the Blackfoot Indians, throws the smallest light on the state of the soul after the animal life is extinct. In truth, all the philosophers, ancient and modern, who have attempted, without the help of revelation, to prove the immortality of man—from Plato down to Franklin—appear to us to have failed deplorably. Then again, all the great enigmas which perplex the natural theologian are the same in all ages. The ingenuity of a people just emerging from barbarism, is quite sufficient to propound them. The genius of Locke or Clarke is quite unable to solve them. . . . Natural Theology, then, is not a progressive science."[1]

non amplius quam semel serviat, et emissus evagetur in toto; utrum corpus sit, an non sit: quid sit facturus, quum per nos aliquid facere desierit : quomodo libertate usurus, cum ex hâc exierit caveâ : an obliviscatur priorum et illic nosse incipiat, postquam de corpore abductus in sublime secessit." Compare Lucretius, i. 113.

[1] Macaulay, Ranke's History of the Popes (Crit. and Hist. Essays, vol. iii. p. 210). Sir Wm. Hamilton observes (Lectures on Logic, Lect. 26, p. 55): "Thus Plato, in the Phædon, demonstrates the immortality of the soul from its simplicity: in the Republic, he demonstrates its simplicity from its immortality"

END OF VOL. II.